P9-CAL-313

# THE CIVILWAR
## A VISUAL HISTORY

# SMITHSONIAN

# THE CIVIL WAR

## A VISUAL HISTORY

**DORLING KINDERSLEY**
**Senior Editors** Jemima Dunne, Paula Regan
**Senior Art Editor** Gadi Farfour
**Picture Research** Jo Walton
**dkimages** Romaine Werblow
**Senior Cartographic Editor** Simon Mumford
**US Editors** Beth Landis, Margaret Parrish, Rebecca Warren
**Production Editors** Ben Marcus, Jamie McNeill
**Production Controller** Erika Pepe
**Managing Art Editor** Karen Self
**Managing Editor** Camilla Hallinan
**Art Director** Philip Ormerod
**Associate Publisher** Liz Wheeler
**Publisher** Jonathan Metcalf

**DK INDIA**
**Managing Art Editor** Arunesh Talapatra
**Project Art Editor** Mitun Banerjee
**Art Editors** Shriya Parameswaran, Pallavi Narain
**Assistant Art Editors** Niyati Gosain, Shreya Anand,
Payal Rosalind Malik, Arushi Nayar
**Production Manager** Pankaj Sharma
**DTP Manager/CTS** Balwant Singh
**DTP Designers** Tanveer Zaidi, Mohammad Usman
**DTP Operator** Neeraj Bhatia

**TOUCAN BOOKS**
**Managing Editor** Ellen Dupont
**Senior Editor** Alice Peebles
**Senior Art Editor** Thomas Keenes
**Editors** Helen Douglas-Cooper, Natasha Kahn, Andrew Kerr-Jarrett,
Ferdie McDonald, Donald Sommerville, Anna Southgate
**Editorial Assistant** David Hatt
**Designers** Nick Avery, Ralph Pitchford, Mark Scribbins
**Proofreader** Marion Dent
**Indexer** Marie Lorimer

**Editorial Consultants** James G. Barber (National Portrait Gallery)
Jennifer Jones, Barton Hacker, Lisa Kathleen Graddy,
Harry Rubenstein (National Museum of American History)

**Contributors** Tony Allan, Mark Collins Jenkins, R. G. Grant, Dr. Wayne Hsieh,
Dr. Christian Keller, Dr. Katherine Pierce, Dr. Robert Sandow

**Additional Text** Laura Davis, Angela Elder, Donald Sommerville

First American Edition, 2011
This revised edition, 2015
Published in the United States by DK Publishing
345 Hudson Street
New York, New York 10014
A Penguin Random House Company

17 18 19   10 9 8 7 6 5 4 3
008–180017–Jan/15

Copyright © 2011, 2015 Dorling Kindersley Limited
Foreword copyright © 2011 Smithsonian Institution

All rights reserved under International and Pan-American Copyright Conventions.
No part of this publication may be reproduced, stored in a retrieval system, or
transmitted in any form or by any means, electronic, mechanical, photocopying,
recording, or otherwise, without the prior written permission of the copyright owner.
Published in Great Britain by Dorling Kindersley Limited.

A catalog record for this book is available from the Library of Congress.
978-1-4654-2957-5

Printed and bound in China by Leo Paper Products Ltd.

A WORLD OF IDEAS:
SEE ALL THERE IS TO KNOW

www.dk.com

# CONTENTS

## AN IMPERFECT UNION
## 1815–1860

## SECESSION TRIGGERS WAR
## 1861

JEFFERSON DAVIS AND HIS GENERALS (BELOW)

# 3

# CLASH OF ARMIES
## 1862

FIRST BATTLE OF BULL RUN

BATTLE OF HAMPTON ROADS

# 4

# THE UNION
# TIGHTENS
# ITS GRIP
# 1863

# 5

# GRANT,
# SHERMAN, AND
# TOTAL WAR
# 1864

UNION GENERALS                                        ASSAULT ON FORT WAGNER

WINFIELD SCOTT HANCOCK AT GETTYSBURG

UNION TROOPS IN THE TRENCHES

*The Sick Soldier*
The Smithsonian holds many Civil War-era photographs by noted cameramen Timothy O'Sullivan, George Barnard, George Cook, Alexander Gardner, and Mathew Brady, whose studio in the field recorded this image *c.* 1863.

# Foreword

A unifying thread woven indelibly throughout the fabric of America is our compelling need to remember the Civil War. In the summer of 1961, as a boy of nine, I witnessed an event that some people were calling Third Bull Run. The Civil War Centennial was beginning in earnest with this much-hyped battlefield reenactment. The day of "battle" dawned hot, and when it turned sultry, heat exhaustion began taking a toll on spectators and reenactors alike. To my surprise, the event as choreographed proved to be largely underwhelming; too few soldiers charged with fixed bayonets and too few cannons spewed plumes of white smoke that billowed over the rolling fields broad enough to dwarf the entire spectacle. It was never clear in my mind which side was winning or losing the war.

Try as we might it is nearly impossible to recreate history, even well documented history like the Civil War, America's first national experience to be recorded visually on a grand scale. Understanding fully the nuances of that era of discord is in itself a challenge. Robert E. Lee would have freed "every slave in the South" to avoid going to war—words Abraham Lincoln could have endorsed heartily. Both men prayed to the same God, and each followed his own conscience. Ultimately, their exemplary humility and charity—and that of a third party, Ulysses S. Grant—prevailed at Appomattox, changing the nation forever.

The sacrifices Americans made long ago are truly gifts for Americans now. So too are the effects they left behind. This visual survey draws from collections throughout the country, and most especially from the Smithsonian Institution. Founded in 1846, the Smithsonian has been collecting and preserving Civil War memorabilia of every description since the war itself. Within these covers you will experience a rare look into the museum's rich and unique coffers. Many of the daguerreotypes and painted portraits herein are much more than mere book illustrations, but in reality are family heirlooms which have been generously handed down to the American people. Such is the case with dozens of personal items like Jeb Stuart's English-made Tranter revolver, William T. Sherman's campaign hat and sword, and George B. McClellan's chess set. Two Lincoln relics are national treasures: the black top hat he last wore to Ford's Theatre and the presentation Henry repeating rifle—gold mounted and engraved with the president's name—which is a prize of the Smithsonian's smallarms collection.

In the genre of Civil War art, battlefield sketches and "photographs by Brady" are as close as we can be visually to experiencing the conflict firsthand. Yet selected postwar illustrations have been added to examine the sectional sentiments which influenced how Americans, Northerners and Southerners, wanted to remember their war. Included are illustrated timelines, colorful maps, eyewitness narratives, and gallery spreads filled with vintage military trappings. Every page offers a virtual tour worth revisiting again and again.

*James G. Barber*

JAMES G. BARBER
EDITORIAL CONSULTANT

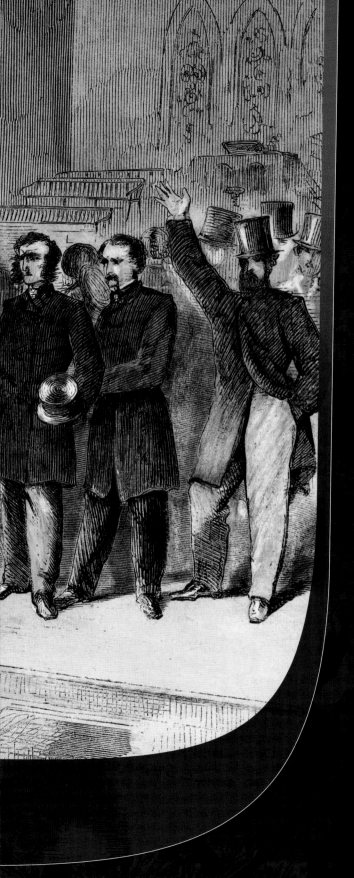

# 1

# AN IMPERFECT UNION

## 1815–1860

As America expanded across the West, the future of slavery split churches, political parties, and eventually the nation itself. It took a Civil War and more than 625,000 dead to decide the fundamental proposition that all men are created equal.

≪ **Mob attack**
A contemporary engraving shows protestors and the police breaking up an abolitionist meeting at Boston's Tremont Temple Baptist Church on December 3, 1860—a year after the execution of abolitionist John Brown. Although Northerners were widely opposed to the extension of slavery, many regarded those in favor of outright abolition as troublemakers fomenting

# AN IMPERFECT UNION

**The Mason-Dixon Line**
The line is the symbolic divide between North and South. It dates back to the 1760s, when surveyors Charles Mason and Jeremiah Dixon resolved disputes between Pennsylvania, Maryland, and Delaware and established their borders.

**The 1850 Compromise**
In Washington, Senator Henry Clay of Kentucky helps persuade Congress to accept a political compromise. It prevents an open split between North and South, but hardliners in both sections are unhappy with its measures. The Fugitive Slave Law will soon prove especially contentious.

## VIRGINIA AND SURROUNDING AREA

PENNSYLVANIA

Philadelphia

Mason-Dixon Line

Potomac River

Harpers Ferry · Baltimore

Winchester

NEW JERSEY

Appalachian Mountains

Shenandoah River

WASHINGTON, D.C.
DISTRICT OF COLUMBIA

Centreville

Delaware Bay

DELAWARE

MARYLAND

Harrisonburg

Fredericksburg

Rappahannock River

Mattaponi River

Chesapeake Bay

Charlottesville

VIRGINIA

James River · Richmond

York River

ATLANTIC OCEAN

Roanoke · Lynchburg · Petersburg · James River

Cape Charles

Hampton

Cape Henry

Portsmouth

NORTH CAROLINA

CANADA

WASHINGTON TERRITORY

Portland

OREGON

R O C K Y

NEBRASKA TERRITORY

Snake River

M o u n t a i n s

Sacramento · Virginia City

Salt Lake City

San Francisco

UTAH TERRITORY

CALIFORNIA

PACIFIC OCEAN

Colorado River

Santa Fe

NEW MEXICO TERRITORY

MEXICO

**John Brown on the way to the scaffold**
In the hope of acquiring arms for a slave uprising, abolitionist John Brown raids the Federal arsenal at Harpers Ferry in 1859. The raid is a failure, but Brown is tried and executed. His death divides North and South even further.

**California gold rush**
The 1849 gold rush causes a vast increase in the territory's population. California adopts an anti-slavery constitution and seeks admission to the Union, bringing to the fore the issue of the free or slave status of territories gained from Mexico. California is granted statehood in 1850.

**VOTING IN U.S. PRESIDENTIAL ELECTION 1860**
- Republican
- Southern Democratic
- Constitutional Union
- Northern Democratic
- U.S. Territories
- Slave state

W hen the South Carolina state convention voted unanimously on December 20, 1860, to secede from the Union, it was the culmination of a long process by which, in Abraham Lincoln's words, the nation had become a "house divided." Though victory in the Revolutionary War and the ratification of the U.S. Constitution had created a common sense of nationhood, many political differences had never been resolved. In particular, a growing number of Americans disagreed over the place of slavery in the nation's future and the Federal government's role in upholding it.

The period up to 1860 had seen great material changes for the nation and its people. The extent of the national territory multiplied with the Louisiana Purchase in 1803 and victory over Mexico in 1848. While most Americans still farmed or lived in small towns, technological developments and mass immigration were increasing

**Bleeding Kansas**
Violence between pro and anti-slavery factions dominates Kansas in the mid-1850s. This cartoon ridicules President Pierce's pro-slavery stance.

**The voice of abolition**
*The Liberator* newspaper, founded in Boston in 1831 by William Lloyd Garrison, is published weekly until the last issue on December 29, 1865. It is uncompromising in its call for the complete and immediate abolition of slavery.

**A county election**
In this 1852 painting of a Missouri county election by George Caleb Bingham, the voters, all of them white and male, cast their votes orally. Bingham, himself a member of the Missouri legislature, illustrated many aspects of American politics in his work.

the population and the national wealth. Southern cotton planters and Northern merchants prospered from sales of cotton, from the growth of Northern factories, and from financial institutions that linked the interests of North and South.

Yet despite these links, by 1860, tensions ran high between North and South. Most white Americans remained indifferent or hostile to the aspirations of blacks, but many in the North feared that Southern domination of the Federal government could lead to the spread of slavery as new states entered the Union. Southerners saw critiques of slavery as deeply threatening and a denial of the nation's historic acceptance of slaves as property.

Since the 1820 Missouri Compromise, a series of political deals had kept disunion at bay, but the election in 1860 of a president seen as hostile by many in the South brought matters to a head.

# TIMELINE 1776–1860

The Declaration of Independence ▪ **The Constitution** ▪ Invention of the Cotton Gin ▪ **Missouri Compromise** ▪ Rise of Abolitionism ▪ **War with Mexico** ▪ Compromise of 1850 ▪ *Uncle Tom's Cabin* ▪ Kansas-Nebraska Act ▪ **Raid on Harpers Ferry** ▪ Election of Lincoln ▪ **Secession of South Carolina**

| BEFORE 1800 | 1800–15 | 1816–30 | 1831–40 | 1841–45 | 1846–50 |
|---|---|---|---|---|---|

**JULY 1776**
Declaration of Independence proclaims the "self-evident" truth that "all men are created equal." But its principal author, Thomas Jefferson, and many other signatories are slave-owners.

**APRIL 1803**
American negotiators agree to the Louisiana Purchase, a treaty to buy the vast Louisiana territory from France. Its slave or free status becomes controversial when it is settled by white Americans.

**MARCH 1820**
Missouri Compromise. Maine is admitted to the Union as a free state, Missouri will follow as a slave state in 1821. Slavery is forbidden in northern part of the Louisiana Purchase—land bought from Napoleon.

**AUGUST 1831**
Nat Turner leads a slave revolt in Virginia. Some 60 whites are killed before the rebellion is suppressed. Turner is later caught and executed.

**JULY 1787**
Congress passes the Northwest Ordinance forbidding slavery in the Northwest Territory—the future states of Ohio, Illinois, Michigan, and Wisconsin.

**NOVEMBER 1832**
A long-running quarrel between Congress and the states comes to a head when a South Carolina convention adopts a law nullifying Federal tariffs and asserting the state's right to secede from the Union—the Nullification Crisis.

**JANUARY 1842**
Supreme Court rules it unconstitutional to block Fugitive Slave Act.

**NOVEMBER 1844**
James K. Polk narrowly beats Henry Clay in presidential election. Polk favors annexation of Texas and Western expansion.

⌃ Battle of Buena Vista, 1847, during the War with Mexico

**MAY 1846**
Following clashes in Mexican territory between American and Mexican troops, the United States declares war on Mexico.

**SEPTEMBER 1787**
The new Constitution permits slavery.

**SEPTEMBER 1789**
In an amendment to the Constitution, a slave counts as three-fifths of a white person in calculations for Congressional representation.

⌃ Erie Canal in Utica City

**OCTOBER 1825**
Opening of Erie Canal, which links the Hudson River to the Great Lakes. It is one of many transportation developments that will underpin the North's economic and industrial growth.

**MARCH 1833**
A political compromise ends the Nullification Crisis, but South Carolina still claims the right to nullify other measures or to secede from the Union.

HENRY CLAY, **AND** A PROTECTIVE TARIFF.

NO ANNEXATION OF TEXAS!

No Extension of Slavery!!

With Henry Clay
We'll win the day,
And Home Industry defend;
With Polk and Dallas
We'll to the gallows
Free Trade and Texas send.

**AUGUST 1846**
Wilmot Proviso proposes to ban slavery in territories acquired from Mexico. It is passed by the House, but not approved by the Senate. Divisions on slavery deepen.

**FEBRUARY 1793**
Fugitive Slave Act makes it easier for owners to recover escaped slaves. It results in free blacks being sold into slavery.

**APRIL 1793**
Introduction of cotton gin revolutionizes the cotton industry.

**JANUARY 1808**
Under the terms of the Constitution, the importation of slaves into the United States becomes illegal; the internal slave trade continues.

AM I NOT A MAN AND A BROTHER

« Abolitionist medallion

**DECEMBER 1833**
The American Anti-Slavery Society is founded.

**FEBRUARY 1848**
Treaty of Guadalupe Hidalgo ends the War with Mexico. The vast new lands added to the United States will be subjects of dispute between pro- and anti-slavery forces.

⌃ Cotton gin

**JUNE 1812**
The United States declares war on Britain, beginning the War of 1812. Fighting continues into 1815.

**APRIL 1836**
After defeating Mexican forces at the Battle of San Jacinto, Texas confirms its independence and seeks admission to the Union. If it suceeds it will be as a slave state.

⌃ Henry Clay presidential campaign ribbon

**JULY 1845**
A Texas convention accepts annexation to the United States, despite opposition. Texas is formally admitted to the Union in December.

**SEPTEMBER 1850**
Congress passes series of measures known as the Compromise of 1850. On the one hand California is admitted as a free state, but on the other a stricter Fugitive Slave Act is passed.

> **"I believe this government cannot endure permanently, half slave and half free.** I do not expect the Union to be dissolved ... but I do expect it will cease to be divided."
> ABRAHAM LINCOLN, JUNE 16, 1858

| 1851–52 | 1853–54 | 1855–56 | 1857–58 | 1859 | 1860 |
|---|---|---|---|---|---|
| Newspaper advertises a reward for a fugitive slave | **APRIL 1854** The Emigrant Aid Society is formed in Massachusetts to help antislavery settlers move to Kansas to ensure it remains a free territory under the doctrine of "popular sovereignty." | **MARCH 1855** Thousands of Missourians vote fraudulently in elections for the Kansas territorial legislature, ensuring a pro-slavery majority. The result is recognized by the Federal governor of the territory. | **MARCH 1857** In the Dred Scott case, the Supreme Court rules that Congress cannot deprive citizens of their property, including slaves, anywhere in the United States, and that blacks are not citizens. | **MARCH 1859** The Supreme Court confirms that the Fugitive Slave Act is constitutional by overturning a Wisconsin court decision. | ⌃ Frederick Douglass |
| PRIL 1851 scaped slave Thomas ms is arrested in oston, Massachusetts, nder the Fugitive Slave ct and sent back to eorgia. This, and imilar cases, cause utrage in the North. | **MAY 1854** The Kansas-Nebraska Act divides the former Kansas territory into two. The slave or free status of Kansas is uncertain, though it lies north of the line established by the 1820 Missouri Compromise. | **JULY 1855** The pro-slavery Kansas legislature begins to enact measures to protect slavery in the territory. | ⌃ .52 caliber Sharps carbine, known as the "Beecher's Bible" | | **MAY 1860** The Republican Party selects Abraham Lincoln as presidential candidate. Supporters include the abolitionist Frederick Douglass. |
| ≪ Harriet Beecher Stowe | | **OCTOBER 1855** Free-Soilers in Kansas set up their own legislature and adopt a constitution outlawing slavery. Anti-slavery settlers are sent guns hidden in boxes marked "Bibles." These become known as "Beecher's Bibles." | **DECEMBER 1857** The Lecompton legislature adopts a constitution for Kansas. The status of slaves already in the territory remains unchanged. A vote will decide whether or not to allow new slaves. | **OCTOBER 1859** John Brown leads an attack on the Union arsenal at Harpers Ferry, Virginia, hoping to inspire a slave rebellion. He is quickly arrested, tried, and executed. | **JUNE 1860** The Democratic Party splits into Northern and Southern factions, nominating Stephen Douglas and John Breckinridge as their respective presidential candidates. Constitutional Union Party nominates fourth candidate, John Bell. |
| UNE 1851 he novel *Uncle Tom's Cabin* by Harriet eecher Stowe is first erialized. By the end f 1853, 1.5 million opies of the book will ave been sold. It ermanently changes lorthern attitudes o slavery. | **JULY 1854** The new Republican Party holds its first convention in Michigan. It opposes the Kansas-Nebraska Act and supports slavery in the territories. | **MAY 21 1856** In ongoing violence between pro- and anti-slavery factions in Kansas, pro-slavery men "sack" the town of Lawrence. A few days later, abolitionist John Brown carries out a retaliatory attack at Pottawatomie Creek. | **APRIL 1858** Although Kansan voters reject the Lecompton Constitution, President Buchanan asks Congress to admit Kansas as a state under its terms. Congress calls for a further vote in Kansas. | ≪ Abraham Lincoln | **NOVEMBER– DECEMBER 1860** Lincoln is elected President. In reaction to this, South Carolina holds a state convention that votes for secession on December 20. |
| | | **MAY 22 1856** Charles Sumner is beaten on the floor of the Senate after delivering an anti-slavery speech. ≪ The attack on Sumner | **AUGUST–NOVEMBER 1858** Abraham Lincoln challenges Stephen Douglas for election as U.S. senator for Illinois. Their debates bring Lincoln to national prominence, but Douglas wins the election. | | |

« BEFORE

Victory in the American Revolution did not finally settle the new republic's borders. It remained surrounded by the colonial territories of Britain, France, and Spain.

#### THE LOUISIANA PURCHASE

In 1803, in order to ensure access to the mouth of the Mississippi River, **Thomas Jefferson** sent a delegation to the French Emperor Napoleon I to negotiate the **purchase of New Orleans**. To the surprise of the U.S. representatives, Napoleon offered to sell the **entire Louisiana Territory** for $15 million to finance his European wars. Overnight, the nation nearly **doubled in size**.

#### EXPANSION TO THE WEST

Jefferson announced the purchase on July 4, 1803, and the very next day the 28-year-old

Army Captain **Meriwether Lewis**, a personal friend and aide to the president, set out from Washington to begin his and **William Clark's exploration of the West**. Their epic journey, which lasted until September 1806, revealed a vast expanse of territory inhabited by indigenous peoples, and ripe for **settlement by future generations of Americans**.

A COMPASS FROM THE LEWIS AND CLARK EXPEDITION

TECHNOLOGY

#### THE COTTON GIN

In 1793, Eli Whitney traveled south to take up a tutoring post on a plantation. Intrigued by the time-consuming manual labor of separating the sticky seeds from the fibers of short-staple cotton, he designed a simple hand-cranked machine. His cotton engine, or "gin," used rollers to comb the seeds from the fiber, enabling one slave to clean 50lb (23kg) of cotton fiber per day instead of just 1lb (0.5kg) processed by hand. The gin opened the interior of the South to cotton production, giving a financial incentive for expanding the hold of slavery on Southern society.

COTTON GIN

# The **State** of the **Nation**

**In the four decades after the War of 1812, the United States experienced profound changes in its population, economy, boundaries, and social relations. New states joined the union at a rate of almost one every three years. By 1855, the country had more cities with at least 150,000 residents than any other nation on Earth.**

In 1800, most Americans still farmed, and lived in small communities poorly connected by rough roads. When Thomas Jefferson entered the White House in March 1801, the nation had around 5.3 million people living between the Atlantic seaboard and the Mississippi River—most within 50 miles (80km) of the eastern coastline. If more western territory could be added, Jefferson envisaged a nation mighty enough to compete economically with and to defend itself against the great European powers. Skeptics pointed to transportation difficulties, the presence of Native Americans, and foreign claims to North American territory as barriers to expansion.

In the early 19th century, a letter mailed in Maine took 20 days to arrive in Charleston, South Carolina, because of the scarcity and roughness of the roads. The War of 1812—which lasted until 1815—encouraged people to build better roads and connections among the various states for the purpose of defense. After the war, growing markets, westward migration,

and military concerns continued to drive communities and private investors to construct roads, bridges, and canals, which speeded up the exchange of goods and tied people together. One of the most ambitious of these projects, the Erie Canal, eventually connected New York City to Lake Erie and the Upper Midwest states and territories. New York state and private investors funded the canal, which was started in 1817 and completed in 1825. It would pay for itself in seven years.

In the 1830s, railroads began to supplant canals as a faster, cheaper mode of carrying passengers and freight. Popular demand and congressional policy encouraged the creation of post offices along the frontiers, and soon the nation had more postal clerks than soldiers. The telegraph appeared in the 1840s following alongside the railroads, as

cities, hoping to exchange business and political intelligence, clamored to join the network. Advances in paper and printing technology made newspapers cheaper, and the advent of the Associated Press in 1846 created rapid standardized reporting from around the nation.

#### Northern transformations

Most Northern farming families focused on self-reliance and subsistence, raising their own food and bartering locally to maintain their independence. As transportation improved, people farming near cities planted more specialized crops for sale in regional markets. Farmers in New England and the states of the Mid-Atlantic seaboard used cash from these market sales to buy improved equipment, which reduced their labor costs and increased their yields. Steel cutting blades, threshers, iron plows,

**31,443,321** The U.S. population in 1860. This represented an increase of over 35 percent in the 10 years since 1850, and over 270 percent since 1815, when the population stood at 8.4 million.

> "The **greatness of America** lies not in being **more enlightened** than any other nation, but rather in her ability to **repair her faults**."
>
> ALEXIS DE TOCQUEVILLE, FRENCH HISTORIAN, IN *DEMOCRACY IN AMERICA*, 1835

**Voting in a rural community**
George Bingham's painting *The County Election 1852* shows the democratic system in operation, as residents from many walks of life come together to cast their vote. In the 1800s, voting was still very much a white, male domain.

and horse-drawn rakes enabled one farmer to do the work that formerly needed six men. In the Northeast, the growing populations in mill towns and urban centers required increasing quantities of meat, corn, wheat, wool, fruit, vegetables, and dairy produce.

There was a steady drift of people to the expanding cities. Seven out of eight immigrants who arrived in the United States before 1860 settled in cities such as New York, Boston, Philadelphia, Pittsburgh, Rochester, and Chicago—all north of the Mason-Dixon Line. This historic geographic line was surveyed in the 1760s by the astronomer Charles Mason and the surveyor Jeremiah Dixon to resolve a border dispute between Pennsylvania and Maryland.

### Industry takes off
Between 1815 and 1860, the people of the United States transformed the country's economy. Following his development of the cotton gin, Eli Whitney devised a system of interchangeable parts for weapons

manufacture that was soon used to produce other goods, such as clocks, sewing machines, and farm equipment. This simplification of the manufacturing process, known as the "American system," greatly reduced the costs of production and finished goods. New Englanders pioneered the first large, water-powered factories, employing local women to produce cotton textiles.

By the 1830s, U.S. industry had gained unstoppable momentum. In 1807, there were fewer than 20 cotton mills with around 8,000 spindles for making thread; by 1831, a greater number of mills had nearly 1.2 million spindles. Steam engines transformed mining and iron production, powered mills and workshops, and moved goods by rail and water. Factories replaced craftsmen and household production of daily items. A "market revolution" stimulated far-reaching changes in American society and the economy.

### North and South diverge
In 1808, a ban on the importation of slaves—which had been prohibited by the Constitution until that date—became the law. Many Americans hoped slavery would gradually decline. North of the Mason-Dixon Line, individual states had already passed laws banning or slowly abolishing slavery. The free African-American population grew rapidly in the North, particularly in urban areas, where African Americans founded their own churches and schools. Many also sheltered runaways from enslavement. Although free, Northern

**4 MILLION** The number of bales of cotton produced annually in the United States by 1860. Each bale weighed 450lb (204kg).

#### Boom town
With the Erie Canal providing vital transportation links, Utica grew from a small settlement into a thriving city. Its population exploded during the 1820s, with many workers staying on after the canal's completion.

**A slave economy**
While the North grew rich through industrial processes developed in Europe, the sources of wealth in the South were raw materials—chiefly cotton—grown and picked by slaves.

African Americans faced racism and legal barriers, preventing full participation in society.

Life in the South was a very different matter. Between 1800 and 1861, the southern United States became the world's largest and richest slave society. Plantations in the South generated vast wealth, while the numbers of those enslaved rose, as did their monetary value. New states such as Texas, as well as new lands that had been seized from Native Americans drew thousands of white men seeking to make quick profits on virgin soil. Tens of thousands of slaves were separated from their families in the older seaboard states and sold to the new ones in the Southwest. The slave population grew from 700,000 in 1790 to four million in 1860.

### Cotton-based economy
On the Southern plantations, slaves cultivated sugar, rice, and tobacco and many acquired the skills necessary to keep a plantation operating. It was cotton, however, that dominated, and as production soared, slaves worked ever longer hours in the cotton fields. Cotton was the key American export, accounting for more than half of all goods exported through 1850. In 1860, Britain took the

bulk of American cotton exports—nearly 75 percent of the cotton Britain used came from the United States. But the labor of slaves and production of cotton were not merely matters for the South. The entire domestic economy was bound up in them. Western food fed the slave population, which grew and tended the cotton, while early Northeastern textile and shoe factories sold their output to the South for masters to provide for their slaves. Firms in New York City and New England benefited by providing financial backing and insurance for the burgeoning cotton and slave trades.

---

At the start of the Civil War, about a quarter of U.S. factory workers were women. Five years later, the proportion had risen to a third.

#### MODEL WORKING CONDITIONS
By 1860, the **United States' largest industrial complex was Lowell**, Massachusetts, whose textile mills were famous for their "Mill Girls."

The Lowell mills had been **set up as a social experiment to avoid the harsh conditions** of British mill towns. Young, single women from farms and small towns as far away as Maine made up the bulk of the workers. **Employers promised parents that each girl would be provided with room and board** in a supervised dormitory and that church attendance on the one day off was mandatory. The women published their own periodical, *The Lowell Offering*, and had **access to circulating libraries, musical instruments, and traveling lecturers**.

After the war, the Lowell mills became more dependent on French Canadian and European immigrants, until by 1900 nearly half the city's population was foreign-born.

#### WOMEN TAKING CHARGE
In the South, there were fewer factories, but outside the wealthy planter class, **most white women were accustomed to hard work** on smaller farms, which had few if any slaves. The chief difference the war made was that many women had to **take on the running of farms** or plantations in the absence of their menfolk.

**PIONEERS GAZE IN AWE AT THE NEW WORLD**
In his iconic painting, *Westward the Course of Empire Takes its Way* (1861), Emanuel Leutze promoted the idea of Manifest Destiny— a 19th-century notion that encouraged westward expansion to the Pacific Ocean. Occupying the New World was perceived by many European Americans to be a democratic right and people journeyed west in search of a better life, urged by the journalist John L. O'Sullivan to "overspread the continent allotted by Providence."

# A Question of Union

**As America's population grew and people moved west, the driving forces in politics were domestic issues and personal rivalry, complicated by conflicts between federal power and the rights of individual states. The War with Mexico increased political divisions along sectional lines.**

The nature and practice of American politics changed fundamentally in the decades following 1820. The Federal Constitution and state laws originally restricted voting and office-holding to those who met property and residency requirements. By the 1830s, however, most states had rewritten their laws to expand suffrage and office-holding to nearly all white male citizens. Fewer people shared the Founders' ideals of political service by the best educated and wealthy. Politics became a profession, as men sought office, wealth, and status by service to a political party. The Democratic Party, in particular, pioneered a system of party discipline that dispensed jobs at the local, state, and national level.

> Andrew Jackson's supporters came from every state for his inaugural celebration in 1829, horrifying many by surging into the White House and climbing onto tables until bowls of punch were carried onto the lawn.

## The Jacksonian age

One man who mastered the new politics of personality and orchestrated campaigns was Andrew Jackson of Tennessee. Voters admired his record as the victor of New Orleans—the last major battle of the War of 1812—and as an Indian fighter. Jackson's rise to wealth and influence from rural poverty made him a symbol of the "age of the common man." As a contestant in a bitterly contested presidential election in 1824, he narrowly lost to John Quincy Adams. But his turn for the White House came after the 1828 election, which he won on the Democratic ticket.

Like many frontier men, Jackson resented the dominance of the East. He was the first president to translate his national appeal into a vision of a strong executive that defended the people against abuse by both local and state governments and private interests. In this he was opposed by the Whig Party, dominated by a redoubtable trio, the "Great Triumvirate," comprising Senators John C. Calhoun of South Carolina, Henry Clay of Kentucky, and Daniel Webster of Massachusetts. The Whigs firmly asserted the supremacy of Congress over the president. Jackson easily won a second term in 1832, growing in his conviction that the president represented the popular will. His belief was displayed in a series of crises, triggered by the inconsistent ways that the sections of the

<< **BEFORE**

When slave-owning Missouri petitioned for statehood in 1819, the more populous North dominated the House of Representatives. In the Senate, 11 free states to 11 slave states kept the balance.

### THE MISSOURI COMPROMISE
Missouri's petition provoked mixed responses. A **debate in the Senate about the future of slavery** saw the first attempt to block admission of a new slave state. To restore calm, Henry Clay of Kentucky arranged a series of measures known as the **Missouri Compromise**. In 1820, Missouri entered the Union as a slave state and Maine as a free one. Slavery was barred from the Louisiana Purchase north of Missouri's southern border.

### END OF AN ERA
The departure of James Monroe from the White House in 1825 marked **the passing of the Revolutionary generation**. Virginians and slaveholders had held the presidency for 32 of the United States' first 36 years, due to the 3/5 clause that overrepresented Southern whites.

**John C. Calhoun**
One of the "Great Triumvirate," Calhoun was a brilliant defender of Southern slaveholding interests. Unusually, he served as vice president under two presidents: John Quincy Adams and Andrew Jackson.

NEWSPAPER EDITOR AND REFORMER 1811–72

## HORACE GREELEY

In 1831, Horace Greeley moved from New Hampshire to New York City where he founded the news and literary journal, the *New Yorker*. He went on to edit the Whig Party's campaign paper, *The Log Cabin*, before setting up the New York *Tribune* in 1841. For the next 30 years he advocated an eclectic array of political and social causes and used his paper to oppose the "slave power" that ruled the nation. An early convert to the Republican Party, he offered his printing presses to the party to mass-produce campaign material. After the Civil War, Greeley tried to challenge President Ulysses S. Grant in the 1872 campaign. Ridiculed and soundly defeated, he died soon after the election.

**Henry Clay Campaign ribbon**
A social lion with great charisma, Senator Henry Clay received the Whig Party's presidential nomination in 1832 and 1844, but was unsuccessful both times. He advocated protective tariffs to aid Western development.

HENRY CLAY,
AND
A PROTECTIVE TARIFF.

NO ANNEXATION OF TEXAS!

COMMERCE.
MECHANIC ARTS
PROTECTIVE
AGRICULTURE
MANUFACTURES
POLICY
INTERNAL IMPROVEMENTS

No Extension of Slavery!!

With Henry Clay
We'll win the day,
And Home Industry defend;
With Polk and Dallas
We'll to the gallows
Free Trade and Texas send.

nation responded to the rival claims of federal power and states' rights. Southern states had long coveted Indian lands east of the Mississippi. Although federal treaties and the U.S. Supreme Court denied these states the right to steal Indian territory, Jackson chose to support the state of Georgia's right to seize Indian land. He sent in the army to ensure the removal of Cherokee and other tribes that resisted. Thousands died on this "Trail of Tears" as the refugees trekked west.

## Nullification Crisis

Disputes also arose over federal tariffs, or taxes, intended to protect industry in the North. The South resented the tariff because it made European imports into the region more costly. In 1830, South Carolina considered refusing to enforce a tariff passed by Congress in 1828. When another tariff was passed in 1832, South Carolina declared that this and the 1828 tariff were null and void within the borders of the state. Congress denied South Carolina's right to opt out and authorized Jackson to do whatever was necessary to enforce federal law. The Nullification Crisis came to an end in 1833 when South Carolina, finding itself isolated and its claims rejected by other Southern states, backed down.

## War with Mexico

As Jackson's term ended, his approach to another crisis was more cautious. In the 1820s, many Americans had emigrated to the territory of Texas, and by 1835 were seeking its independence. After trying to negotiate with Mexican leader Antonio López de Santa Anna, the Texans took to arms. In the ensuing hostilities, they rallied from defeat at the Alamo in March 1836 to capture Santa Anna at San Jacinto a few months later. They then established their own republic and inquired about joining the Union. Jackson and his successor, Martin Van Buren, demurred for fear of precipitating war with Mexico.

### The Battle of Buena Vista

At Buena Vista in February 1847, General Zachary Taylor used his artillery to such good effect that he defeated a larger force under the Mexican leader, Santa Anna. The victory helped propel him into the presidency in 1849.

> **TARIFFS** Customs duties that are levied on certain imported goods. These taxes are usually designed to protect domestic producers of similar goods.

Later presidents were more supportive, however, and in 1845 Texas joined the United States. Mexico rejected the annexation, and hostilities began when American dragoons engaged Mexican cavalry along the disputed Rio Grande border. On May 10, 1846, President James K. Polk declared, "American blood has been shed on American soil." Despite the opposition of influential figures such as New York *Tribune* editor Horace Greeley, Congress declared war three days later.

In September, an army under General Zachary Taylor captured the Mexican city of Monterey. Santa Anna, whose career had taken several twists since his capture in 1836, returned to Mexico from exile and declared himself president once more. In February 1847, Taylor defeated him at the Battle of Buena Vista. In March, General Winfield Scott launched the largest amphibious landing ever, when his 12,000 troops disembarked near Veracruz. Scott's army finally entered Mexico City on September 14.

# "Our federal Union—it must and **shall be preserved**."
ANDREW JACKSON, 1830

**AFTER** »

The War with Mexico 1846–48 was generally popular in the South, but split the North and reopened discussions on slavery. The philosopher and writer Henry David Thoreau went to jail rather than pay taxes during the war. Others saw it as part of the nation's Manifest Destiny to occupy the entire continent.

## SCHOOL OF WAR

This war served as the training ground for **future Civil War commanders**, including Winfield Scott, Ulysses S. Grant, and Robert E. Lee **64–65** ».

**SCOTT'S MEDAL**

They learned to wage war far from supply lines, command and train soldiers, and participate in operations with the Navy. **Scott was rewarded with a gold medal** from Congress, after his troops occupied Mexico City in September 1847.

## NEW BORDERS

In the Treaty of **Guadalupe Hidalgo**, which ended the war on February 2, 1848, the **Americans gained land** including the modern states of Arizona, New Mexico, California, and parts of Colorado, Utah, and Nevada. Apart from some minor issues, **the treaty finalized the borders** of the United States.

# Slavery Divides the Country

**In the 30 years prior to the Civil War, churches, political parties, and families split on the nature of the American republic and the status of slavery. Victory over Mexico fixed the national boundaries, but the question of how new lands would be organized—free or slave—fractured national institutions.**

Even before the War with Mexico ended, the debate about the future of slavery in the newly conquered territories divided Congress. In 1846, Pennsylvania Democratic Congressman David Wilmot introduced a proviso, or amendment, to an Army finance bill that would ban slavery from all territories acquired from Mexico. In the House, 52 out of 56 Northern Democrats and all Northern Whigs voted for the Wilmot Proviso—a unity across party lines that foreshadowed future Northern opposition to the extension of slavery to the West. In the Senate, however, the proviso met defeat. Southerners condemned it as an attempt to block their right to take their property to the territories.

### Slave ownership

The South by this time was a socially and economically diverse region. In the mountainous areas of northern Alabama, eastern Kentucky, Tennessee, and western Virginia, there were few plantations. Most whites farmed to support their families and traded locally. The majority of these yeomen farmers owned no slaves, although they still supported the institution.

**350,000** The number of Southerners who owned slaves in 1850—less than 25 percent of the white population. Half of slaveowners had five slaves or fewer; only one percent owned a hundred or more.

It was on the cotton and tobacco plantations where most slaves toiled. Other slaves were house servants, and a growing number worked as skilled artisans or were hired out in urban areas. The price of a slave quadrupled between 1800 and 1860, indicating a growing demand for black labor even as the number of slaves increased.

**Congressman David Wilmot**
Wilmot himself proposed his proviso on essentially racist grounds. He intended to preserve Western lands for white men free of "the disgrace" of mixing slavery and free labor.

During this same period, more than 800,000 slaves from the Eastern states were sold or moved to work on the new cotton lands of the Southwest, breaking the ties of slave families in the process.

Southerners started to see their society as distinctive and threatened. Politicians and intellectuals began to defend slavery as a "positive good." Paternalism on the plantation was compared with the situation of Northern workers desperately seeking employment, which created class tension.

### Splits emerge

Church ministers and congregations were divided. Well before the rise of sectional political parties, the three largest Protestant groups—Baptists, Presbyterians, and Methodists—formally split their national denominations into sectional factions. The Presbyterians were first to split in 1837, followed by the Baptists in 1844. In the Methodist Church, the largest denomination, a lengthy debate over the right of a slaveholder to serve as a presiding bishop triggered the formation of the breakaway Methodist Episcopal Church South in 1846. For the vast majority of Southerners, slavery was not a sin—slaveowners provided their slaves with Christian instruction and "rescued" them from barbarism and heathenism.

Northerners, meanwhile, were fearful of this new militant defense of slavery. As West and East grew closer through railroads, telegraph, and print, the South was aggressively seeking to send slavery into new territories and states where it had been outlawed for decades. One response to this trend was the Free-Soil Party, established in 1848 under the slogan, "Free Soil, Free Speech, Free Labor, and Free Men." Free-Soilers contended that a society where free men worked free soil was

not only morally superior to a slave society, but also more efficient economically. By 1849, they had won 14 seats in the U.S. House of Representatives and two in the Senate.

At the same time, Northern workers feared economic competition from black labor. As tens of thousands of European immigrants arrived in the North, urban crowding and a scarcity of work increased pressures on the free black community there, with riots and mob actions from New England through the Midwest.

It was against this background that the federal government had to decide the future of the territory acquired after the War with Mexico. The solution, the Compromise of 1850,

## BEFORE

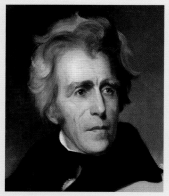
**ANDREW JACKSON**

**In the 1820s and 1830s, sectional divisions over slavery were always an issue, but never dominated politics in the way they would after the War with Mexico.**

#### THE NULLIFICATION CRISIS
Men like **President Andrew Jackson** **« 20–21** were passionate supporters of the Union and strongly resisted the demands of individual states whenever they threatened national unity. One such moment was the **Nullification Crisis** of 1832 **« 21** when, in an assertion of states' rights, South Carolina refused to implement the **import tariffs** imposed by the federal government.

#### SLAVERY AND THE WEST
As cotton production spread into the new lands of Alabama, Mississippi, Missouri, Arkansas, and Texas, the **soil of the Eastern states' plantations was becoming exhausted**. The expansion of cotton production meant the **spread of slavery to the West**.

**Sutter's gold**
In 1848, John Sutter found gold on his land in California, sparking off the Gold Rush. The free-or-slave status of the new territory proved controversial. Pro-slavery advocates pointed out that slaves could work in gold mining.

consisted of five bills designed to balance the interests of North and South. These bills admitted California to the Union as a free state, thus ending the balance in the Senate between slave states and free states that had lasted since the Missouri Compromise of 1820—senators from the free states would now outnumber those from the slave ones. As a concession to the South, the territories of Utah and New Mexico were to choose slavery or freedom according to the principle of "popular sovereignty." The Fugitive Slave Act, which had been federal law since 1793, was given new teeth. It became an offense, punishable by a large fine, for any citizen to resist or refuse to assist in the recapture of suspected runaways, even in states that opposed slavery.

## Compromise and growth

In the decade following the Compromise, Southern economic development surged. Railroad mileage quadrupled, with much of the track laid by slaves. By 1860, an independent South would have been the fourth wealthiest nation on Earth. The number of slaveholders decreased; by 1860, the percentage of whites with slaves had fallen to less than a quarter. But slavery was not dying or unprofitable.

"Our slaves are black, of **another and an inferior race.** The status in which we have placed them is **an elevation …**"

SOUTH CAROLINA U.S. SENATOR JAMES HENRY HAMMOND, MARCH 4, 1858

**Writers on both sides of the argument grew steadily more impassioned in their defense or condemnation of slavery.**

### LEGITIMIZING SLAVERY

Religious leaders across the South marshaled arguments such as **the existence of slavery in the Bible** and St. Paul's injunction to slaves to obey their masters as justification.

Most presidents, Supreme Court justices, and Congressional leaders had been slaveholders. The Constitution **sanctioned slavery** and promised to **protect private property**. A man's property—his slaves—should be protected wherever he went in the United States.

### THE CASE FOR ABOLITION

In the face of these biblical and historical justifications of slavery, **abolitionists in the North** also appealed to **Christian doctrine** and preached ever more vociferously against

FIGURINE OF UNCLE TOM

the **inhumanity of the system 26–27 ⟫**. One surprisingly powerful ally in their cause was the novel *Uncle Tom's Cabin*, by **Harriet Beecher Stowe 26 ⟫**, published in 1852. The book was serialized in newspapers and tens of thousands of copies sold across the nation, reaching a far larger sympathetic audience than earlier abolitionist appeals.

### VIOLENCE ERUPTS

The Compromise of 1850 averted conflict for the time being. But in 1854, the act that established the **territories of Kansas and Nebraska 30–31 ⟫** provoked violent clashes between opponents and supporters of slavery. One prominent abolitionist involved in the fighting in Kansas was **John Brown**, who was subsequently hanged after gaining lasting notoriety for leading the **Raid at Harpers Ferry 34–35 ⟫**.

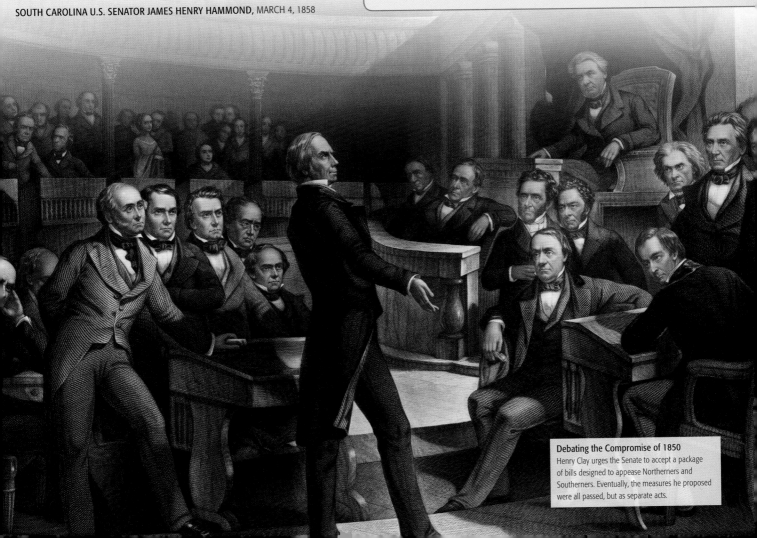

**Debating the Compromise of 1850**
Henry Clay urges the Senate to accept a package of bills designed to appease Northerners and Southerners. Eventually, the measures he proposed were all passed, but as separate acts.

ANTI-SLAVERY CAMPAIGNER Born 1818 Died 1895

# Frederick Douglass

> "It **rekindled** the few expiring **embers of freedom**, and revived within me a **sense of my own manhood.**"

FREDERICK DOUGLASS, ON FIGHTING BACK AGAINST FARMER EDWARD COVEY, 1834

The son of a slave woman and an unknown white man, Douglass was born Frederick Augustus Washington Bailey in Maryland. He rarely saw his mother and lived in slave quarters until he was eight. In 1826, he was sent by his owner to serve Hugh Auld in Baltimore. Auld's wife taught him to read but her husband halted the lessons, claiming that education gave slaves dangerous ideas. Frederick, however, continued to read in secret.

At 15, he was sent to the country to work for Edward Covey. Frequently beaten by this infamous "slave-breaker," he fought back, risking death. In January 1836 he made his first escape attempt, but ended up in jail. Two years later, while working in a Baltimore shipyard, he succeeded. With money loaned from his fiancée Anna Murray, a free black woman from the city, he traveled northward to New Bedford, Massachusetts. There he settled, marrying Murray and changing his name to Douglass.

While Douglass was impressed with New Bedford, he was aware of the segregation in the churches. White employers refused to hire him and he was forced to take menial jobs. He became a preacher at the local Zion Methodist Church and a subscriber to the abolitionist newspaper, *The Liberator*, published by William Lloyd Garrison, founder of the American Anti-Slavery Society. "The paper became my meat and drink. My soul was set all on fire." Joining the local chapter of the Anti-Slavery Society, Douglass published his first writings denouncing colonization, a campaign encouraging blacks to move to Liberia. He argued that the United States, and not Africa, was the rightful home of black Americans. He also gave a speech at the society's convention and was hired as a traveling lecturer by Garrison.

**An imposing character**
This portrait of the young Douglass by an unknown artist was probably based on the image in his 1845 *Narrative* (opposite), and captures his unswerving sense of purpose.

### A career is launched

From 1841 to 1851, Douglass worked with the abolitionists allied with Garrison. These men sought to end slavery by peaceful means, through the education and moral persuasion of slaveholders. Douglass rejected violence and, like Garrison, thought the existing political parties corrupt and the Constitution a pro-slavery document. In 1843, he toured the West giving speeches, and his skill as an orator improved rapidly. He became so eloquent, one white abolitionist advised him to keep "a little of the plantation manner" in his speech. Douglass, however, refused to conform to the public's expectations.

**Abolitionist assembly**
In 1850, Douglass attended the Fugitive Slave Law Convention in Upstate New York to protest against proposals to tighten the Fugitive Slave Act. Douglass called upon the town's men and women to "awake, arise, and do their duty."

During the winter of 1844–45, Douglass wrote the first of three autobiographies. Friends advised him to destroy the manuscript for fear of it leading to his re-enslavement but Douglass was determined. The book was published in 1845, the first 5,000 copies selling out. It was a powerful indictment of the brutality and corruption that slavery inflicted on slaves, owners, and society. As sales increased, so did the danger, and Douglass fled to England, where he remained for two years, until two Englishmen "purchased" his freedom by paying his former master. Aged 28, he was now free to travel without fear. Douglass moved his family west to Rochester, New York, and set up a weekly anti-slavery newspaper, the *North Star*. Its slogan read, "Right is of no sex—Truth is of no color—God is the Father of us all, and we are all Brethren." The paper advocated women's rights as well as abolition.

**Fighting for freedom**
In 1847, Douglass met the radical abolitionist John Brown, who convinced him that liberty should come at any price, whatever the consequences. Douglass began sheltering runaway slaves, and his home became a "station" on the Underground Railroad, a system of safe houses and hidden routes for fugitives. During this time, Douglass questioned Garrison's argument that the Constitution was a pro-slavery document. By 1851, the *North Star* (soon to merge with the *Liberty Party Paper*) was urging readers to fight through politics. Douglass's Fourth of July speech in

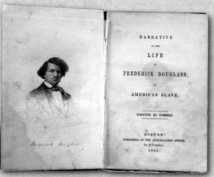

**Slavery unmasked**
Douglass's first autobiography was one of many that exposed the horrors of a life enslaved. It silenced his critics and helped to pave the way for abolition.

Rochester in 1852 attacked the hypocrisy of a nation half free, and called slavery "the great sin and shame of America."
In 1859, John Brown asked Douglass to join the slave revolt he was planning in Virginia. Believing the plan would fail, Douglass declined. After Brown and his men were executed for the Harpers Ferry raid, letters implicating Douglass were found at a nearby farm. On learning this, Douglass escaped to Canada; he was not charged.
In the 1860 presidential election Douglass backed Abraham Lincoln, but was disheartened by the Republican Party's attempts to appease the South. The new president promised to uphold the fugitive slave laws and not to interfere with slavery in the slave states. Then, in the spring of 1861, the first shots of the Civil War rang out at Fort Sumter.
Douglass had always hoped that a "liberating army" of black men would march south and "raise the banner of emancipation." In the wake of the Battle of Antietam, when Union armies forced a Confederate retreat, Lincoln issued the Emancipation Proclamation on New Year's Day, 1863. This declared that all slaves in the Confederate states were free—the end of slavery was now the war's objective.
Congress authorized black enlistments in the Union Army, and Douglass helped with the recruitment, writing a call to arms for the Massachusetts 54th Regiment, the first black unit. Overall, more than 180,000 blacks enlisted in the Union army and navy. In March, Douglass attended Lincoln's second inaugural address. Yet prejudice was never far away; he was barred, along with others, from the reception in the White House. Douglass sent word of this to Lincoln, who ordered that he be admitted, then warmly greeted him with, "Here comes my friend Douglass."

**A changing land**
War's end brought the passage of the Thirteenth Amendment, ending slavery forever. As a backlash in the South unfolded, Douglass began to focus on black rights. During the 1868 presidential contest, he campaigned for Ulysses S. Grant, who was the Republican candidate. With Grant in office, Congress passed the Fifteenth Amendment guaranteeing all men the right to vote, regardless of race. In 1870, Douglass and his family moved to Washington, D.C., where he continued to lecture and write. The Equal Rights Party nominated him for vice president in the 1872 election but he declined. In 1889, he became U.S. minister resident to Haiti, and died of a heart attack six years later.

> "This Fourth of July is yours, not mine. **You may rejoice, I must mourn** ...What, to the slave, is your Fourth of July? **A sham.**"
> FREDERICK DOUGLASS SPEAKING AT ROCHESTER, NEW YORK, JULY 5, 1852

**TIMELINE**

- **February 1818** Born Frederick Bailey, a slave, in Tuckahoe, Maryland. His mother is a slave and his father a white man, rumored to be his master, Aaron Anthony.
- **1826–27** Sent to Baltimore to Hugh and Sophia Auld. Sophia Auld teaches Frederick to read.
- **January 1834** Auld sends Frederick to work for "slave-breaker" Edward Covey.
- **1836** Makes first failed escape attempt. Frederick is returned to Baltimore where he is hired out to a shipyard. Plans another breakout.
- **September 1838** Escapes from slavery and changes his last name to Douglass. Moves to New Bedford and marries Anna Murray.
- **August 1841** Speaks at an American Anti-Slavery Society meeting. Begins lecturing for the Massachusetts Anti-Slavery Society.
- **May 1845** His first autobiography, *Narrative of the Life of Frederick Douglass*, is published. He flees to England, where English supporters "purchase" his freedom for $711.66.
- **1847** Buys a printing press and begins publishing the *North Star* in Rochester, New York.
- **1848** Attends first women's rights convention. Meets John Brown. Begins sheltering slaves fleeing north on the Underground Railroad.
- **1851** Merges *North Star* with Gerrit Smith's *Liberty Party Paper* to form *Frederick Douglass' Paper*.
- **1855** Publishes his second autobiography, *My Bondage and My Freedom*.
- **1861** Urges recruitment of black soldiers and a proclamation of freedom for the slaves to undermine the Confederate war effort.
- **1863** Becomes a recruiter for the 54th Massachusetts Infantry, the first regiment of African-American soldiers; his sons enlist.
- **1864** Meets with President Abraham Lincoln to formulate plans to lead African Americans out of the South in case of a Union defeat.
- **1872** The Equal Rights Party nominates him for the vice-presidential candidacy. Douglass declines.
- **1877** Buys Cedar Hill, a mansion in southeast Washington, D.C., which becomes his home.
- **1881** Publishes his final autobiography, *The Life and Times of Frederick Douglass*.
- **1889–91** Accepts post of U.S. minister resident and consul general to Haiti.
- **February 20, 1895** Dies in Washington after giving a speech to the National Council of Women.

**DOUGLASS'S WRITING DESK, CEDAR HILL**

# The Fury of Abolition

**The great majority of prominent abolitionists were white, many of them pastors who were loath to preach a doctrine of violent insurrection. With their personal experience and hatred of slavery, black abolitionists challenged these white abolitionists who preached pacifism and patience.**

## BEFORE

Opposition to slavery began in the colonial era, but in the 30 years prior to the Civil War, abolitionist organizations formed to promote freedom at the local and national level.

### RELIGIOUS INSPIRATION

Few white Americans actively opposed slavery before 1830, but the **abolition of slavery** in many **Northern states**, by the **British Empire**, and in most of the **new nations of Latin America** marked its **continuation in the American South** as an **anomaly**.

Numerous **religious revivalist movements**, particularly across the North, stimulated newly energized evangelicals to seek the perfection of American society by **eliminating shameful social and political evils**, such as slavery.

### DIFFERING APPROACHES

**White abolitionists** attacked slavery as a **moral and political evil** even as they disagreed among themselves. One faction demanded **immediate emancipation** and complete political equality for blacks. They would tolerate **no compromises with slaveholders** and offered no compensation. **Gradualists** hoped to **minimize social and economic upheaval** by emancipating slaves slowly and providing owners with some kind of compensation.

David Walker, a free black, wrote his *Appeal to the Colored Citizens of the World* in 1829, demanding the immediate abolition of slavery. Echoing the Declaration of Independence, he asserted that blacks were Americans and entitled to the rights of citizens. He denounced moderate anti-slavery leaders who advocated sending free blacks to the struggling colony of Liberia, and accused the United States of hypocrisy as a Christian nation.

Shortly after its publication, copies of Walker's *Appeal* were discovered in South Carolina, Georgia, Virginia, and Louisiana, carried South by free black sailors. White Southerners feared that free blacks and sympathetic Northerners were inciting slaves to rebellion. To prevent such insurrections, most Southern states banned teaching all blacks—slave or free—to read.

### Rebellion in Virginia

In 1831, Southerners' worst fears were realized when the slave Nat Turner led an insurrection in Southampton County, Virginia. Turner and his allies swiftly moved between isolated farms, killing all the whites they encountered, some 70 people in all. Terrified Virginians killed anyone believed associated with the revolt and finally captured Turner two months later and executed him. The revolt underscored the lie of contented slaves who harbored no ambitions for freedom or vengeance. After the revolt,

**Am I not a Man and a Brother?**
London abolitionists campaigning for the end of slavery in the British Empire produced this copper medallion, designed by the firm of Josiah Wedgwood, in the 1790s. U.S. abolitionists adopted its motif of the kneeling slave.

the Virginia legislature debated the future of slavery in the state. Some recognized the evils of slavery; others feared that it slowed economic development and discouraged immigration. Yet others defended slavery as a financial necessity and as a part of God's plan to Christianize and civilize Africans. The possibility of gradual emancipation was discussed, but in the end, by a close vote, it was decided to end public discussion of the issue and to regulate the slave community more tightly.

**1,350** The number of chapters in the American Anti-Slavery Society in 1838—a more than threefold increase in three years. With 150,000 members, the society was a small but vociferous proportion of the population.

### William Lloyd Garrison

That same year, 1831, William Lloyd Garrison printed the first copy of his abolitionist newspaper, *The Liberator*. He saw slavery as a grave national sin and demanded its immediate abolition. Two years later, he helped form the American Anti-Slavery Society (AAS) with many members drawn from evangelical churches in New England and western New York. Many of these religiously inspired activists saw blacks and whites as one family created by God, although many remained paternalistic toward blacks and were reluctant to accept the notion of full social equality. Garrison and his followers also alienated more traditional abolitionists by supporting women's rights. Some Southerners saw a link between *The Liberator* and Nat Turner's insurrection and demanded that Garrison's paper be shut down.

### The postal campaign of 1835

The abolitionists were a tiny minority, but they used newspapers and the postal system to spread their message—even to the South. In 1835, members of the AAS gathered the names and addresses of politicians, clergymen, businessmen, and prominent citizens to create a national mailing list. They then mailed abolitionist papers, pamphlets, tracts, children's books, and sheet music across the nation, including the South.

Southerners were outraged. Many Southern states had already banned the circulation of abolitionist literature, and President Andrew Jackson authorized postmasters in each community to censor the mails as they saw fit. Mail bags were opened and literature deemed inflammatory or dangerous was seized and frequently burned. Even Northerners opposed to these tactics by abolitionists were troubled by this restriction on the free speech of fellow white citizens.

Southern politicians demanded that public "agitation" about slavery cease as a matter of safety and sectional peace. Southern Democrats and Whigs agreed that the right of citizens to petition Congress on the subject of slavery must also stop. A "gag rule" was devised that blocked presentation of citizen petitions in Congress between 1836 and 1844.

### Violence against abolitionists

In a nation where slavery was legal and its products the core of the export economy, abolitionists often met a

### ABOLITIONIST AND AUTHOR 1811–96
## HARRIET BEECHER STOWE

Harriet Beecher Stowe wrote *Uncle Tom's Cabin* at the peak of Northern resentment against the Fugitive Slave Act of 1850. First appearing in 40 installments in the anti-slavery newspaper, the *National Era*, it was published as a book by a Boston company in 1852. It would outsell all others, except the Bible, throughout the 19th century. Southerners resented its portrayal of slavery and the audacity of a Northern woman who dared condemn it. Among Northerners, many responded with tears and pity for the fictional slaves—a sympathy that many had rarely felt for those actually enslaved. The book created an emotional climate that made more Northerners receptive to anti-slavery appeals and sectional claims of the moral superiority of the free states.

> **"Strike** for your **lives and liberties** ... Rather **die freemen** than **live to be slaves**."
>
> HENRY HIGHLAND GARNET, IN A SPEECH DELIVERED IN BUFFALO, AUGUST 21, 1843

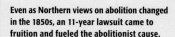

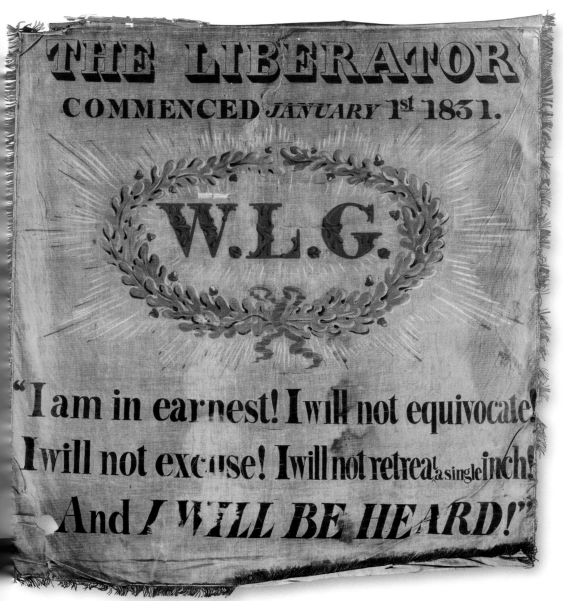

# THE LIBERATOR

## COMMENCED JANUARY 1st 1831.

### W.L.G.

"I am in earnest! I will not equivocate! I will not excuse! I will not retreat a single inch! And *I WILL BE HEARD!*"

**A cover for *The Liberator* newspaper**
William Lloyd Garrison's weekly newspaper campaigned for the abolition of slavery from 1831 right through the Civil War. The last issue appeared in 1865.

**AFTER**

Even as Northern views on abolition changed in the 1850s, an 11-year lawsuit came to fruition and fueled the abolitionist cause.

### THE DRED SCOTT CASE

Since the mid-1840s a lawsuit brought by a slave, **Dred Scott**, had slowly worked its way from the courts of Missouri to the **U.S. Supreme Court**. Scott claimed that when his owner had moved to the free territories in the upper Midwest, he and his family were **entitled to their freedom**.

In January 1857, **Chief Justice Roger Taney**, a Democrat, delivered a decision that shocked the North. He ruled that Scott's case had no legal standing, since **blacks could never become citizens** and were "unfit to associate with the white race." He declared that **Congress had no right to restrict slavery in the territories**. As Southerners celebrated, Republicans seized on the decision as more evidence of a Slave Power conspiracy and warned that it would lead to the legalizing of slavery across the nation.

The decision in fact **aided the anti-slavery cause** and swelled the new Republican party, leading to its election victory in 1860 **36–37 ≫**.

**DRED SCOTT**

---

hostile response. Many people resented their attacks on the political system and critiques of America, while an even larger number rejected the idea of political and civic equality for blacks.

Occasionally, Northerners showed their hostility toward abolitionists by attacking them physically. Between 1834 and 1838, approximately 30 such attacks occurred. Buildings were torched, newspaper presses destroyed, and abolitionist speakers were shouted down and roughed up. Many of the attacks were organized by political and business leaders trying to prove to Southerners that abolitionists were just a deluded minority. However, in Alton,

Illinois, one attack proved fatal. Elijah Lovejoy moved to St. Louis in 1834 to serve as a Presbyterian minister and publisher of a religious newspaper in whose pages he advocated abolition. After witnessing a slave burned alive at the stake, Lovejoy condemned slavery, the legal system, and the thousands who had joined the mob. His press was destroyed in 1836 and he moved across the river to Alton where he set up the *Alton Observer*. His anti-slavery editorials angered many of Alton's citizens, who attacked his office three times and destroyed his presses. In November, 1837, Lovejoy and about 20 men were gathered to hide and protect a new press from a mob when shots were exchanged and Lovejoy was killed.

Yet mob violence, Southern condemnation, and Federal acceptance of censorship of the mail and right of

petition failed to halt the growing spread of anti-slavery and abolition societies. Attacks and attempts to limit freedom of speech troubled a Northern public that had so far been indifferent or opposed to abolitionists' goals. Issues about the expansion of slavery and a growing sectional rift over the place of slavery in the West and in the nation made hostile Northerners listen again to abolitionist critiques of the South.

## Political anti-slavery

Throughout the 1840s and 1850s, many Northerners grew increasingly opposed to the spread of slavery. These anti-slavery supporters did not necessarily advocate emancipation. Often hostile to Southern interests, many were simply opposed to the existence of more slave states. Some used anti-slavery as a way of playing the political system, running candidates, and seeking office. Garrison and his followers rejected any political activity as corrupt, while others such as Frederick Douglass were suspicious of the absence of concern for black rights.

Events of the 1850s would move radical ideas about slavery into the political mainstream in the North, a gradual shift observed by Southerners with anger and alarm.

## Mob rule in Illinois

A contemporary engraving shows the attack on the warehouse in Alton where abolitionist Elijah Lovejoy had hidden his printing press. In the riot, Lovejoy was fatally wounded by five bullets and the press destroyed.

# Slave Auction

**Throughout the South, slave auctions supplied the demand for slave labor, especially among plantation owners. African-Americans were questioned, examined, and bid for in large auctions. Buyers often bought slaves without regard to family ties, dividing husbands, wives, mothers, and children. Usually, separations were permanent and slaves would never see their loved ones again.**

"The buyers were generally of a rough breed, slangy, profane, and bearish, being for the most part, from the back river and swamp plantations, where the elegancies of polite life are not perhaps developed to the fullest extent ... how many aching hearts have been divorced by this summary proceeding, no man can ever know ... the negroes were examined with as little consideration as if they had been brutes indeed; the buyers pulling their mouths open to see their teeth, pinching their limbs to find how muscular they were, walking them up and down to detect any signs of lameness ... all of these humiliations were submitted to without a murmur ... the expression on the faces of all who stepped on the block was always the same, and told of more anguish than it is in the power of words to express. Blighted homes, crushed hopes and broken hearts was the sad story to be read in all the anxious faces. Some of them regarded the sale with perfect indifference, never making a motion save to turn from one side to the other at the word of the dapper Mr. Bryan, that all the crowd might have a fair view of their proportions, and then, when the sale was accomplished, stepping down from the block without caring to case a look at the buyer, who now held all their happiness in his hands. Others, again, strained their eyes with eager glances from one buyer to another as the bidding went on, trying with earnest to follow the rapid voice of the auctioneer. Sometimes, two persons only would be bidding for the same chattel, all the other having resigned the contest, and then the poor creature on the block, conceiving an instantaneous preference for one of the buyers over the other, would regard the rivalry with the intensest interest ... settling down into a look of hopeless despair if the other won the victory."

FROM AN ARTICLE DESCRIBING A LARGE SALE OF SLAVES IN SAVANNAH, GEORGIA, *NEW YORK TRIBUNE*, MARCH 9, 1859

**Slaves going South**
English artist Eyre Crowe based his painting *After the Sale* on sketches he made in Richmond, Virginia, in 1853. Superficially picturesque, it captures the anguish of slaves being sold to new masters and parted from their families.

# Bleeding Kansas

**By 1854, land to the west and northwest of Missouri had been settled. This land had to be organized as a U.S. territory, but would it be slave or free? Pro-slavery forces were determined to spread slavery westward, abolitionists were determined to stop them. Two years later, the result was near civil war in Kansas.**

**Democratic divide**
In order to get the votes he needed, Douglas had to please the South. But bowing to their wishes would cause rifts within his own Democratic party.

## BEFORE

**In August 1846, Congressman David Wilmot introduced an amendment, or proviso, to an army appropriations bill that would have banned slavery forever in territories acquired from Mexico.**

### WILMOT PROVISO
Although the Wilmot Proviso passed the U.S. House of Representatives, it **failed in the Senate**. As a result, the **future of slavery was still not settled** in the West.

### VARYING VIEWS
The political parties offered different solutions during the 1848 presidential election campaign. John C. Calhoun **<< 20–21** argued that the **Constitution protected property**, and so slave-owners had the right to take slaves into the territories. Democratic nominee Lewis Cass argued that settlers should vote on the issue, while the **Whig Party tried to avoid** it and nominated Zachary Taylor, a Virginia slaveholder and hero of the War with Mexico.

### ANTI-SLAVERY PARTY
The **Liberty Party** joined with anti-slavery Whigs and the **Free-Soil Party** to nominate former president Martin Van Buren for president. The Free-soil Party pledged itself to **no new slave states** and called slavery a "barbarism."

The first steps to decide if the new territory should be slave or free were legislative. Illinois senator Stephen A. Douglas worked to balance the demands of the militant pro-slavery faction, led by Missouri senator David Atchison, with those Northern Democrats who were fearful of conceding too much to Southern interests. Douglas suggested that it be left to a vote in the territory. Atchison thought Douglas's plan of "popular sovereignty" was not enough and demanded the repeal of 1820's Missouri Compromise. Douglas agreed to argue for the repeal, thus opening up the West for the potential expansion of slavery.

The proposed Kansas-Nebraska Act triggered a passionate response. Since the Compromise of 1850 and the publication of Harriet Beecher Stowe's *Uncle Tom's Cabin*, Northern aversion to appeasing Southern "Slave Power" had grown.

Abraham Lincoln strongly believed slavery to be "an unqualified evil" and that no man had the right to hold another as property. He denounced both the act and Douglas in public. A former Whig, Lincoln now joined with others in the North who opposed slavery's expansion but as yet had no formal political party. This so-called "anti-Nebraska" group included Free-Soilers, abolitionists, and Northern Whigs. Yet, despite an outcry across the North, Douglas was able to convince and coerce enough Senate Democrats to approve the Kansas-Nebraska Act—15 of the 20 Northern Democrats supported it. In the House, where Southern influence was weaker, it just barely passed. In the elections that followed, half of the incumbent Northern Democrats lost their seats.

The way was now open to let the settlers vote. Neighboring Missouri, a slave state, encouraged a first wave of pro-slavery migrants, but as 1854 went on, anti-slavery settlers from across the North and Midwest entered the territory. Missouri politicians helped organize militia and citizens' groups prepared to ride into the state's border regions to scare Northern or free-state advocates. The Missourians also voted illegally, hoping to elect delegates who would support slavery.

Atchison personally led a large group of "Border Ruffians"—as the Missouri citizens were called by abolitionists—across the Kansas state line to vote. He boasted that 1,100 people were on the way and he could gather another 5,000 if needed. The count for the first territorial legislature included those 5,000 fraudulent tallies and resulted in a pro-slavery body. The territorial governor begged President Franklin Pierce to invalidate the election, but Pierce, a political ally of Atchison, fired the governor instead.

### Rival state governments
The new pro-slavery legislature legalized slavery and banned anti-slavery speeches and texts. Those who aided runaway slaves were to be punished with death.

**"Beecher's Bible"**
The .52 caliber Sharps carbine was shipped to anti-slavery settlers in Kansas in boxes labeled "Bibles." The weapon's nickname came from abolitionist preacher Henry Ward Beecher, who believed that there was "more moral power in one [carbine] … than in a hundred Bibles."

This intimidation enraged the larger free-state faction of Kansas residents. Rejecting the official territorial government as invalid, in the fall of 1855 they gathered in Topeka where they formed their own legislature, elected a governor, and wrote the Topeka Constitution. By January 1856, two rival governments competed for control of Kansas and dominated national politics. Pierce recognized the pro-slavery government in the city of Lecompton, while the new Republican Party, founded in 1854, backed the free-state legislature and attacked Democrats as tools of Southern Slave Power. The Massachusetts abolitionist, Senator Charles Sumner, was incensed. In May, he delivered a two-day speech entitled "The Crime Against Kansas," in which he accused pro-slavery men of carrying on with the "harlot, Slavery." Popular sovereignty had failed.

On May 21, 1856, pro-slavery men rode into Lawrence, a free-state town, and destroyed its newspaper's press and burned its Free State Hotel. Republican newspapers and campaign speeches

**1,000** The approximate number of Sharps rifles that were smuggled to anti-slavery fighters in Kansas during the period of bitter conflict between 1854 and 1858.

---

**KEY MOMENT**

## THE KANSAS-NEBRASKA ACT

In January 1854, in an attempt to defuse the controversy over whether or not slavery should be permitted in the Nebraska Territory, Senator Douglas devised a plan to split the Nebraska Territory into two separate future states: Kansas to the west of Missouri, a slave state; and Nebraska to the west of Iowa and Minnesota, a free state.

If passed, the Kansas-Nebraska Act would repeal the Missouri Compromise of 1820, which had outlawed slavery from all land north of Missouri's southern border. Douglas called for "popular sovereignty," which would make the decision about slavery in each new territory subject to the will of the voters. This would, he hoped, remove the issue from the national stage and make it a local issue.

Abolitionists argued that slavery would have been banned in both states under the terms of the Missouri Compromise. The Democratic Party was split, but Douglas was stubborn, and the act was passed by Congress on May 30, 1854. Far from ending the controversy, the Kansas-Nebraska Act threw Kansas into turmoil, earning it the name Bleeding Kansas.

---

**JAYHAWKER An anti-slavery guerrilla from Kansas. Named after a make-believe bird, the Jayhawkers clashed with Missouri's Border Ruffians. Both sides terrorized the residents of Missouri and Kansas.**

# "A noisome, squat, and nameless animal … **not a proper model** for an American senator."

SENATOR CHARLES SUMNER ON SENATOR STEPHEN DOUGLAS IN HIS "CRIME AGAINST KANSAS SPEECH," MAY 19–20, 1856

described it as the "sack" of Lawrence, regarding the event as further proof of Southern intent to create a society dominated by powerful slaveholders.

In January 1857, the U.S. Supreme Court reached the notorious Dred Scott decision. The court's ruling said that prohibiting slavery in a federal territory was unconstitutional, and that African-Americans, free or slave, were not citizens of the United States. This emboldened pro-slavery leaders in Kansas, who met in Lecompton and proposed a new state constitution.

## The Lecompton Constitution

Their idea was to give voters in Kansas a referendum between their own Lecompton Constitution "with slavery" or a "future" free state "without slavery." In the latter case, the 200 slaves in Kansas would remain in bondage as would any children they bore, but there would be no extension of slavery beyond that.

While Republicans and free-state supporters denounced the plan, it put severe strains on the Democratic Party. Across the North, Democrats faced a dilemma. They knew that backing the Lecompton Constitution would be seen as a betrayal of the ideal of popular sovereignty and too sympathetic to Southern interests. On the other hand, opposing the constitution would alienate the Southern Democrats, who made up the party's largest and most powerful group in Congress.

Four years earlier, Stephen Douglas had promised the voters of Kansas the right to decide about slavery in a free and fair election. In 1858, he rose in the Senate to denounce the Lecompton Constitution, even as a new president, Democrat James Buchanan, urged its acceptance. Southern senators ostracized Douglas and made it clear he would never have their support for a future presidential run. In Kansas, meanwhile, federal troops monitored the vote as citizens overwhelmingly rejected slavery. In Congressional elections, Northern voters swept most pro-Southern Democrats from office.

### Lincoln's ally
Senator Charles Sumner had much in common with Lincoln. Both were opponents of slavery, and though Sumner sometimes clashed with Lincoln over matters of policy, he never lost confidence in him.

During the era of turmoil in Kansas, politics in the North was chaotic as new parties rose to replace the fading Whigs. In 1854, a new party would pose a challenge to the increasingly divided Democratic Party.

#### THE KNOW-NOTHINGS
From the mid-1840s, many Americans fixated on the threats Catholics and large numbers of immigrants presented to their image of a white, Anglo-Saxon, Protestant nation. **Secret societies** emerged and pledged **to oppose the influence of Catholics and new arrivals.** When questioned, they answered, "I know nothing." Opponents used the phrase to label the movement.

**Know-Nothings** shocked party leaders by **sending their members,** as many as 500,000, to the polls. By 1855, they dominated much of the East, replacing the Whigs as the opponents of the Democrats in the Mid-Atlantic states, California, and large areas of the South. **The party split in 1856** following a convention vote on slavery, and most Northern Know-Nothings would eventually support the Republican Party.

### Liberty assailed
An 1856 cartoon shows Liberty, the "fair maid of Kansas," being tormented by Democratic politicians, including President Pierce in the buckskins of a "Border Ruffian" (third from left) and Stephen Douglas (far right).

# The **Rise** of the **Republican Party**

**Founded to oppose the extension of slavery, the Republican Party in 1855 had organized members in fewer than half the Northern states, most of which often ran third to the Democrats in elections. Less than a year later, the Republicans had transformed themselves from a disorganized coalition into a powerful sectional party.**

In May 1856, three violent events—two in Washington, D.C., and one in Kansas—convinced many white Northerners that the South really did constitute a threat to their rights and liberties. The unconnected events inspired Northern enthusiasm for the Republican Party—founded just two years earlier by a coalition that included abolitionists, former anti-slavery Whigs, and former Free-Soilers—and led to a sudden surge in support for the party.

On May 8, Alabama-born Congressman Philemon Herbert, furious when he was refused service at the Willard Hotel in Washington, D.C.,

**BEFORE**

**In the 1850s, anti-Catholicism and concerns about both slavery and immigration drew Americans to new political parties.**

**NEW POLITICAL PARTIES**
As the Whig party faded, local nativist groups organized into the anti-immigration **"Know Nothing" Party ‹‹ 30–31**. At the same time, many Northerners who advocated **"Free Soil"** in the West joined anti-Southern and anti-slavery coalitions that became the **Republican Party**.

**SLAVE POWER**
Many Northerners feared the expansion of slavery into the West. Southern political power was frequently characterized as a conspiracy or **"Slave Power."** These perceived threats to white liberties in the North mobilized popular support for the Republicans more than any moral commitment to the **abolition of slavery and justice for African Americans ‹‹ 26–27**.

attacked waiter Thomas Keating, triggering a dining room melee that ended with Herbert shooting the waiter dead. The Republicans printed handbills, speeches, and pamphlets stressing slaveholders' disdain for "menials" and portraying the attack as a blow against white workers and farmers. Party editors quoted inflammatory items from the Southern press as proof of the tyrannical nature of slaveholders.

Two weeks later, on May 22, Senator Charles Sumner of Massachusetts was brutally beaten on the floor of the Senate by a Southern congressman, Preston Brooks. Republicans, joined by a number of former Democrats, organized "indignation meetings" that drew thousands of Northern men and women into public condemnation of the assault.

**A climate of fear**
That same evening, reports arrived that Lawrence, Kansas, the center of free-state settlers, had been sacked and burned by pro-slavery militia from Missouri. Stories circulated of murder, pillage, and rape, but in fact the only casualty was a Missouri raider, killed by a brick falling from a burning hotel. Confrontations over slavery in Kansas suddenly became part of a larger pattern of violence. Previously skeptical opponents of the Republicans now accepted that "The Slave Power is the same in Missouri as it is in Washington." These violent acts seemed

**1,342,345** The number of popular **votes for the Republican candidate John C. Frémont in the presidential election of 1856: 33.1 percent of the votes cast.**

**MURDER!!! help.. neighbors help, O my poor Wife and Children.**

**Forcing slavery down the throat of a Free-Soiler**
The Free-Soil Party opposed the spread of slavery in the West. This cartoon refers to the divisive Kansas-Nebraska Act of 1854, after which many Free-Soilers chose to join the emerging Republican Party.

to prove Republican assertions of Southern "Slave Power" and its threat to white men, whether they were laborers, settlers, or senators.

The failure of the president, the Congress, and the courts to render justice as demanded by an enraged Northern public added indignity to a sense of imminent danger. The Republican Party took advantage of this and used an extensive network of editors, ministers, and party workers to print and distribute a vast amount of political propaganda. The Southern press retaliated. In May 1856, the *Enquirer* in Richmond, Virginia, urged that "vulgar abolitionists ... must be lashed into submission." Later that year, an Alabama editor fumed, "Free society, we sicken at the name ... a conglomeration of greasy mechanics,

filthy operatives, small-fisted farmers, and moonstruck theorists ... hardly fit for association with a Southern gentleman's body servant." Such provocative statements only served to remind Northerners that Republicans stood ready to defend their interests against the South.

**Rapidly growing support**
Heated debates and political violence erupted over what party was fit to rule. The rapid spread of anger at Southern attitudes about slavery enabled the Republican Party to attract both abolitionists and moderates willing to vote against Southern institutions and culture.

The aim of stopping the expansion of slavery unified the Republican Party. Slave holders cringed at this political dogma, given the increase of populations in the North and West. Southerners feared losing the political balance in Congress, which protected their interests. They knew that slavery ultimately would be subjected to the will of the majority.

For a party that had been founded as recently as 1854, the Republicans achieved a remarkable result in their first presidential election. Their candidate John C. Frémont carried 11 states to Democratic candidate James Buchanan's 19. The 1856 election was seen by them as a "victorious defeat."

**KEY MOMENT**
## THE CANING OF MASSACHUSETTS SENATOR CHARLES SUMNER

On May 19–20, 1856, Charles Sumner delivered a two-day speech in the Senate attacking slavery and its sexual abuses. Two days later Congressman Preston Brooks of South Carolina, having read the text of the speech, was so enraged that he marched into the Senate and attacked Sumner at his

**THE SUMNER CANING, A PROVOCATIVE EXAMPLE OF SOUTHERN CHIVALRY**

desk, beating him unconscious with his cane, which shattered as a result of the violent blows. Brooks believed that Sumner's speech had slandered his uncle, Senator Andrew Butler.

This unprecedented attack on the Senate floor shocked Northerners, who considered it an assault on free speech. Republicans used the attack to create effective campaign rhetoric "proving" the threat to Northern liberties posed by Southern slaveholders.

" The **question** to be decided is **who shall rule this nation**—the **Slave States** or the **Free States**."

*THE FREMONTER*, AUGUST 22, 1856

**Republican running mates in the 1856 election**
The presidential candidate was John C. Frémont, senator for California in 1850–51. His vice presidential candidate, William L. Dayton, won the nomination over Abraham Lincoln. They campaigned under the slogan "Free soil, free labor, free speech, free men."

**AFTER** »»

The Republican Party exercised increasing power in Congress, but it prepared for the election of 1860 by seeking candidates who could carry the more moderately anti-slavery states it lost in 1856.

**A NORTH IS BORN**
Republicans tapped into the resentment of Northerners who knew, based on the 1850 census, that they had the majority of the nation's population, wealth, and industry. They used **corruption in Kansas ‹‹ 30–31** and the **Dred Scott decision by the U.S. Supreme Court ‹‹ 26–27** to raise fears of the spread of slavery throughout the Union.

**THE 1860 ELECTION**
**Four groups competed in the election**: the Republican Party, the Constitutional Union Party (which also advocated Union), and the Northern and Southern factions of a now split Democratic Party. The Republicans selected a moderate candidate in **Abraham Lincoln 38–39 ››**, who won without a single electoral vote from the South and without a popular majority **36–37 ››**.

**REPUBLICAN RIBBON**

JOHN C. FREMONT. REPUBLICANS CHOICE FOR PRESIDENT

WM. L. DAYTON. VICE PRESIDENT FROM 1857 TO 1861

AND

**Inside the engine house**
This engraving in a contemporary newspaper imagines the scene inside the engine house just before the Marines broke down the door. The hostages taken by Brown are standing on the left.

« **BEFORE**

# The **Raid** at Harpers Ferry

**On October 16, 1859, abolitionist John Brown and 21 men, including five free blacks and three of Brown's sons, crossed the Potomac River and marched to Harpers Ferry, Virginia, in the rain. They cut telegraph lines, rounded up hostages, and seized parts of the federal arsenal.**

In 1858, the year the ruling Democratic Party lost control of Congress, many Republicans made powerful speeches on how the issue of slavery divided the nation.

**HALF SLAVE AND HALF FREE**
Most famous of these speeches was **Abraham Lincoln's "House Divided" speech** delivered in Springfield, Illinois, in May 1858, in which he declared, "I believe this government cannot endure, permanently **half slave and half free**." The speech went on to refer to the situation in **Kansas << 30–31** and the upholding of the **Dred Scott decision << 26–27**.

**IRREPRESSIBLE CONFLICT**
Even more inflammatory was a speech delivered by New York **Senator William Seward** in October 1858 in Rochester. He argued that an "**irrepressible conflict**" existed within the country. The nation "must and will … become **either entirely a slave-holding nation or a free-labor nation**." Democrats condemned the speech as dangerous agitation and when, a year later, John Brown led the attack on Harpers Ferry, **Northern Democratic and Southern newspapers blamed Seward's theory** of an "irrepressible conflict" for Brown's actions.

Within 12 hours of Brown's raid, militia and locals trapped him and his men in the federal armory's fire engine house. By midnight the next day, Colonel Robert E. Lee arrived with 87 Marines to rescue the hostages and subdue the raiders. Brown refused to surrender and the Marines rushed the engine house, battering down the door, killing or wounding many of the remaining raiders, and collecting the hostages unharmed.

### Abolitionist roots
Born in Connecticut in 1800, Brown as a youth and adult moved regularly, usually after one of his many business

**Robert E. Lee**
By a curious quirk of fate, the man who would subsequently command the armies of the Confederacy led the Federal troops that foiled the Harpers Ferry raid.

failures. His deeply religious parents instilled in him a hatred of slavery that led to an early involvement in abolition. He served as a member of the "Underground Railroad" and lived for two years in a freedman's community. By the age of 50, Brown saw himself as ordained by God to avenge the evils of slavery.

In August 1855, he joined five of his sons in Kansas to fight against the pro-slavery faction there. Following the reports of the "sack" of Lawrence, Kansas, Brown sought vengeance. He led six men, including four of his sons, to the homes of pro-slavery families living near Pottawatomie Creek and hacked the men and

older boys to death with broadswords. In another incident at Osawatomie, he and his men killed a large number of pro-slavery raiders from Missouri. These exploits gained Brown an infamous reputation and the nickname "Old Osawatomie Brown."

### Funding the raid
Brown now seized upon the idea of inciting slave insurrection. He believed that if slaves rose up in great numbers, the economy of the South would collapse. In spite of his actions in Kansas, he traveled openly in New England, routinely appearing at abolitionist meetings and private parties. His exploits and appearance—simple clothing and an intensity of expression—attracted those tired of simply talking about slavery. One by one, Brown gathered a small group of radical abolitionists, six in all, who would support and fund his fight

**Confiscated pike**
This pike was confiscated at the time of John Brown's capture at Harpers Ferry. Brown commissioned 1,000 such weapons with a view to arming insurgent slaves.

## "I, **John Brown**, am now quite certain that the **crimes of this guilty land** will never be **purged** away, but **with blood**."

A NOTE FROM BROWN TO HIS JAILER BEFORE HIS EXECUTION, DECEMBER 2, 1859

against slavery. The "Secret Six" were Thomas Wentworth Higginson, a minister and future Civil War officer; Dr. Samuel Gridley Howe, a Boston physician; Reverend Theodore Parker, a renowned speaker and Unitarian minister; Franklin Sanborn, a friend of Thoreau and Emerson; Gerrit Smith, a wealthy reformer and philanthropist who had previously given Brown land in the Adirondacks; and George Luther Stearns, a key financier of the Emigrant Aid Company, which funded settlement of Kansas by anti-slavery homesteaders.

### Planning the raid
By the summer of 1859, Brown had switched his focus to Virginia. His target was the federal armory at Harpers Ferry, which would provide arms for some 18,000 slaves living in the surrounding counties. He already had a large quantity of weapons. The Massachusetts-Kansas Committee provided him with 200 Sharps rifles in 1857 and he paid a Connecticut blacksmith to craft 1,000 pikes with 10-in (25-cm) blades. He

> Brown's raid and death inspired an unknown writer or writers to compose the marching song, "John Brown's Body." By the outbreak of the Civil War, it was already a favorite with Union troops.

shipped 198 rifles and 950 of the pikes to the Maryland farm near Harpers Ferry, where his men were to gather. At a secret meeting in Chambersburg, Pennsylvania, Brown tried to persuade prominent abolitionist Frederick Douglass to participate in the raid. He refused, warning Brown that the enterprise seemed doomed.

### Sentenced to death
Douglass's misgivings proved correct. The attackers failed to remove any of the arsenal's weapons and only five escaped capture and death. Brown's own trial was swift. He had been wounded in the raid, but was declared fit to stand to trial at Charles Town, Virginia, on October 27. Found guilty of treason against Virginia, he was sentenced to hang on December 2.

Americans generally condemned Brown's violence, but a clear division characterized views on his goals and personal courage. Abolitionist Lydia Maria Child wrote to Virginia Governor Henry Wise and offered to nurse Brown as he awaited execution. Republican newspapers noted Brown's extremism, but reminded readers that it resulted from the presence of slavery—a moral and political evil. Southern editors pointed out that no slaves had joined Brown's attack. On October 26, 1859, a North Carolina paper, the Wilmington *Daily Herald*, wrote that this proved that "slaves love, honor, and obey their masters." Those who wanted an independent Southern government warned that only independence could protect Southern slavery from future attacks by emboldened abolitionists.

### Reactions to the execution
Public sentiment was polarized between those who celebrated Brown's execution and those who publicly mourned him. Southerners deeply resented Northern expressions of support for Brown. Especially galling was that national figures, such as Ralph Waldo Emerson, compared Brown to Christ and his gallows to the cross. A Richmond editor remarked that the raid and public responses to it "advanced the cause of disunion more than any event … since the formation of the government."

**John Brown's last moments**
As his legend grew, Brown's "martyrdom" was wildly romanticized by writers and artists. This apocryphal scene of Brown kissing a black baby on his way to the scaffold was painted in 1882–84 by Thomas Hovenden.

**John Brown**
This daguerreotype was taken in 1846–47 by African-American photographer Augustus Washington in Hartford, Connecticut. The pose recalls Brown's oath to dedicate his life to the destruction of slavery.

### AFTER

While many labeled Brown a fanatic or a lunatic, others—both in the North and the South—cherished his memory, albeit for widely differing motives.

**FREE BLACKS PREPARE**
After decades of ineffectual talk, a white abolitionist had finally joined hands with black men to **attack slavery on its home soil**. In the North, free blacks organized military companies in cities such as Philadelphia, Boston, New York, and Pittsburgh. **Brown was lionized**, becoming a potent symbol and subject of a popular song on the lips of **black soldiers** when they **joined the Union army** in 1863 **168–69 ≫**.

**BOOST TO THE CAUSE OF SECESSION**
**Fears of slave revolts** wracked the South throughout 1860. Those intent on secession used Brown's raid as a warning of the horrors of insurrection. One such advocate, Edmund Ruffin of Virginia, went to great lengths to keep the memory of the raid alive. He asked officials at Harpers Ferry to send him the pikes seized after the raid, labeled them **"Samples of the favors designed for us by our Northern Brethren,"** and sent one to each Southern governor.

# The Election of 1860

**The passions and conflicts of the preceding decade over states' rights and slavery were embodied in the presidential contest of November 1860. Americans participated in the election campaign with great enthusiasm but little or no sense that the outcome would be disunion and war.**

A number of outspoken Southern advocates of secession were opposed not only to any compromise with the North, but also to the Union itself. Known by their opponents as "fire-eaters," they were hostile to the growing power of the North, and any open discussion of abolition fueled their commitment to an independent South. They included men like Virginian Edmund Ruffin,

who had long spoken out in defense of slavery. He actually hoped that the Republicans would win the election, since this would force Southerners to "choose between secession and submission to abolition domination."

### The Democrats divided

In late April 1860, the Democrats gathered in Charleston, South Carolina, to nominate their candidate. They could not have chosen to meet in a more polarized city. Street orators called for disunion, while fire-eaters among the Southern delegates openly scorned Senator Stephen A. Douglas and his Northern supporters. At a certain point, the Northern majority reaffirmed its support for popular sovereignty, which allowed the local voters to determine the legality of slavery in the territories. In reaction to this, Southern delegates stormed from the hall.

After 57 failed ballots and a hasty compromise, the convention was rescheduled for June in Baltimore,

Maryland, but radical Southerners again disrupted the proceedings and marched out. While the remaining Democrats nominated Stephen A. Douglas, the Democrats of the Deep South and their allies reconvened in Richmond, where they chose Vice President John Breckinridge as their candidate for president.

### Lincoln, Bell, and Douglas

In mid-May, the Republicans gathered in Chicago in a newly built convention center—dubbed the Wigwam—that could hold 12,000. Promising not to threaten slavery in the South, the Republican candidates repeated their opposition to its spread into the West. They also pledged free homesteads for westward-bound settlers and tariffs to protect Northern industry.

Recognizing the need for a moderate candidate who would be able to carry Pennsylvania and the Midwestern states, Republican delegates selected Abraham Lincoln on the third ballot.

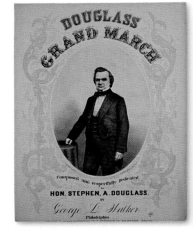

**Music for victory**
In order to win the public's vote, political parties had portraits of their candidates printed on the covers of sheet music, like this one for the Douglas campaign.

Lincoln was not an abolitionist, but he articulated the sentiment of a growing number of Northerners who saw slavery as the gravest threat to the Union and the future greatness of the nation.

Following the division of the Democrats, a new coalition and rival faction came together in Baltimore. The Constitutional Union Party was made up of conservative ex-Whigs

« **BEFORE**

**Two of the four major candidates for the presidency in 1860—Lincoln and Douglas—had been opponents in the senatorial campaign in Illinois two years before.**

**LINCOLN AT THE PODIUM**

**THE LINCOLN–DOUGLAS DEBATES**
In 1858, **Abraham Lincoln 38-39 »** accepted the challenge to unseat the powerful Democrat Senator from Illinois, Stephen A. Douglas **« 30–31**. Their **seven public debates** were transcribed by reporters and published across the nation. Although his calm, logical arguments frequently discomfited Douglas, **Lincoln lost by 4,000 votes**. Yet he gained a reputation as a **restrained anti-slavery moderate.**

**A four-way contest**
Lincoln, the watchman, foils the efforts of the three other candidates trying to break into the White House—Breckinridge is hauled up to a window by President James Buchanan; Bell is lookout as Douglas unlocks a door.

and men from the Border States who opposed disunion. By ignoring the issue of slavery they appealed to the Southern residents of Tennessee, Virginia, and Kentucky who threw their support behind them. The party's presidential nominee, John Bell of Tennessee, promised to abide by the Constitution and preserve the Union.

A vicious campaign ensued. In traditional election spirit, public speakers and political newspapers attacked and defamed their opponents using sectional language and personal insults.

Douglas traveled the country warning against disunion, despite facing hostile crowds and accusations of drunkenness. Racial epithets were flung at the Republicans, who were called advocates of African-American equality and mixing of the races. Lincoln's running mate, the swarthy senator from Maine, Hannibal Hamlin, was often described as a mulatto. John Breckinridge faced shouts of "traitor" and "destroyer of the Union," while Bell was characterized as the leader of an elderly and irrelevant faction.

## Lincoln elected

Although Lincoln won a majority of the electoral votes with 180, he carried less than 40 percent of the national popular vote and 54 percent of the Northern popular vote. Douglas won only New Jersey and Missouri, while Kentucky, Tennessee, and Virginia selected John

> "The Democratic Party **Gone to Smash**. The Work is done. The irrepressible conflict has **rent the Democratic Party asunder**."
>
> *CHICAGO DEMOCRAT,* MAY 1, 1860

### Lincoln campaign torch
The election set the scene for vast rallies and parades. About 10,000 Lincoln supporters marched through Chicago carrying torches in what was "the longest and most imposing thing of its kind ever witnessed."

### Political advertisement
The Carolina Clothing Depot used a single notice to advertise the store's clothes and take a political stance, declaring the intention of South Carolina to secede from the Union in the event of a Lincoln victory.

Bell. Breckinridge carried the remaining Southern states, most of which barred Lincoln's name from appearing on the ballot. Lincoln won, but he faced a nation in which one region had given him almost no support. He would be vulnerable in four years and many believed he would be forced to form a cautious, conservative government.

Although the states of Virginia, Kentucky, and Tennessee rejected the Democratic and Republican candidates, they recognized the risk they faced as states of the Upper South bordering free states. Living along the northern boundary of a slave republic, their slaves would be tempted by the freedom that lay across the border. Also, if it came to war, it was the Upper South that would become the likely battlefield.

In the majority of these slave states, many wealthy slaveholders hoped to preserve the Union. They believed slavery was safer protected by federal law than within an independent slave state bordering free territory. Many of these states had also developed more mixed economies and were less dependent on cotton exports. They had broad connections to their Northern neighbors, but feared they would face hostility from the Deep South.

### A chance for compromise?

No candidate captured a majority of the popular vote, and neither Lincoln nor Breckinridge received much more than a bare majority in his region. Lincoln's opponents together outpolled him by nearly a million votes. In the South, Breckinridge lost the popular vote in the slave states to a combined opposition, which received 55 percent of the total Southern vote. The upper South wanted compromise, not conflict.

**1,865,908** Votes cast for Lincoln.

**2,819,121** Votes for his opponents.

### THE QUESTION

**IF LINCOLN** will be elected or not, is one which interests all parties, North and South. Whether he **IS ELECTED** or not, the people of **SOUTH CAROLINA** (whose rights have been for a number of years trampled upon) have the advantage of supplying themselves with CLOTHING, at the well-known CAROLINA CLOTHING DEPOT, 261 King-street, at such prices as **WILL LEAD** them to be satisfied that the reputation of this Establishment has been **BOLDLY** and fearlessly maintained **FOR A** number of years, supplying its **SOUTHERN** Customers with all the Latest Styles, and at as low prices as any Clothing House in the present **CONFEDERACY** of all the States.

Thankful for the liberal patronage extended, the Proprietors desire merely to inform their customers and the public generally, that their present STOCK OF CLOTHING IS COMPLETE in all its departments, and are now prepared to offer Goods on the most reasonable and satisfactory terms. A call is therefore solicited by OTTOLENGUIS, WILLIS & BARRETT, 261 King-street.
November 5

## AFTER

The nation was divided. Northerners disagreed among themselves, but a majority opposed the expansion of slavery. Most white Southerners owned no slaves, but were connected to slave society by ties of exchange and kinship.

### SECESSION AND WAR

Within days of Lincoln's election, **South Carolina** passed a bill scheduling **a secession convention.** On December 20, it **severed its union with the United States 46–47** »

In the months between his election and his inauguration on March 4, 1861, Lincoln hoped disunion could be averted. But the day after his inauguration he found **a desperate dispatch** on his desk **from Fort Sumter 50–53** »

**LINCOLN'S INAUGURATION IN WASHINGTON**

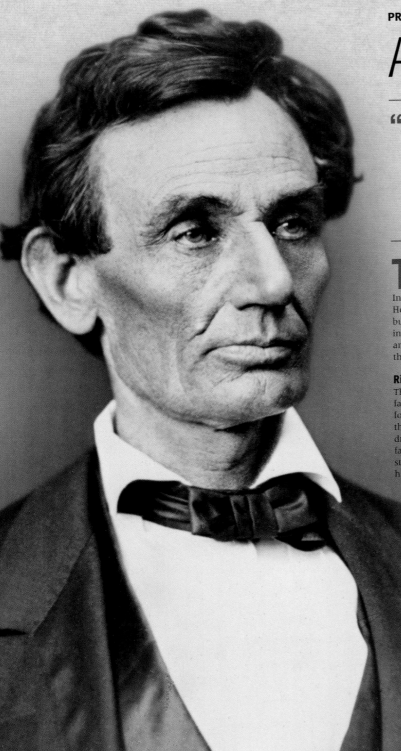

PRESIDENT OF THE UNITED STATES  Born 1809  Died 1865

# Abraham Lincoln

## "In giving **freedom to the slave**, we assure **freedom to the free** ..."

ABRAHAM LINCOLN, MESSAGE TO CONGRESS, DECEMBER 1, 1862

Tireless ambition was the driving force in Abraham Lincoln's journey to the White House. In the words of William H. Herndon, with whom he built a successful law practice in Springfield, Illinois, "his ambition was a little engine that knew no rest."

### Rise to fame

The son of a poor Kentucky farmer, the young Lincoln struggled for an education while earning a living through manual labor and working in a dry goods store. When he was 21, his family moved to Illinois, where he studied with a local attorney and began his political career as a Whig. From 1834 to 1840, he served in the Illinois legislature. In 1842, aged 33, he married

### The rail candidate

An 1860 cartoon shows Lincoln borne along on a fence rail, held aloft by the slavery issue and the Republican party, represented by newspaper editor Horace Greeley. Much was made of Lincoln's frontier, "rail-splitting" youth.

Mary Todd, the daughter of a wealthy Kentucky slaveholder. Later that decade, he served briefly in the U.S. House of Representatives.

In the 1850s, Lincoln abandoned the decaying Whig Party to join the newly formed Republican Party, which opposed the extension of slavery to the West, and in 1858 he ran for the U.S. Senate against the Democrat Stephen A. Douglas. In seven debates with Douglas, Lincoln declared slavery immoral, although he denied the right to interfere with it in the South, where it was protected by the Constitution. He believed only that it should not be allowed to expand westward.

Lincoln lost the Senate race, but his debates with Douglas had garnered him a national reputation. At the Republican Convention in Chicago in May 1860, he won the presidential nomination on the third ballot. In the campaign, the Republicans rallied supporters with

### Lincoln in 1860

Standing 6ft 4in (1.93m) tall, Lincoln was a lanky but imposing figure. He grew a beard only after his election in 1860—reportedly in response to a girl named Grace Bedell who wrote to him saying that "whiskers" would improve his appearance.

### In memory of Lincoln's home

A log cabin commemorates the home on Knob Creek Farm, Kentucky, where Lincoln lived with his family from 1811 to 1816. The Lincolns' cabin was demolished; this one was the home of their friends, the Gollahers.

torchlight parades, barbecues, and picnics. In November, Lincoln carried all the Northern states except New Jersey in the popular vote and was elected president.

The effect of the election was dramatic. Lincoln's rejection of the expansion of slavery was unacceptable to radical Southern politicians, and in December South Carolina seceded from the Union. Lincoln denied the right of secession: to destroy the Union without a just cause was "simply a wicked exercise of physical power." He carefully prepared his inaugural address with the hope of keeping the upper South from joining the secessionists.

### Attempt to conciliate

Lincoln's speech, delivered on March 4, 1861, was clear but conciliatory: "In your hands, my dissatisfied fellow countrymen, and not in mine, is the momentous issue of civil war. The government will not assail you … You have no oath registered in Heaven to destroy the government, while I shall have the most solemn one to preserve, protect and defend it."

His words were to no avail. The next day, he read a dispatch from Major Robert Anderson warning of a crisis at Fort Sumter in Charleston. The threat of hostilities was escalating and would lead to war just over six weeks later.

### Balancing act

From the start of his administration, Lincoln had to balance military and political demands. Abolitionists wanted immediate emancipation, but he knew he had to hold the loyalty of the border states of Maryland, Kentucky, and Missouri. Only in the fall of 1862, after

### At the front

On October 3, 1862, Lincoln visits the headquarters of General George B. McClellan at Antietam, Maryland, after McClellan's victory there the previous month.

> "Let us have faith that **right makes might**; and in that faith let us to the end, **dare to do our duty** as we understand it."
>
> ABRAHAM LINCOLN, SPEECH AT COOPER UNION, NEW YORK, FEBRUARY 27, 1860

victory at Antietam, did he feel ready to shift the purpose of the war from restoring the Union to ending slavery. On January 1, 1863, he issued the Emancipation Proclamation, freeing all slaves in areas that were in rebellion against the United States.

In 1864, Lincoln chose General Ulysses S. Grant as overall army commander. In Grant, Lincoln found a man who would lead the Union to victory, although the horrific casualties from the campaign against the Confederacy's General Robert E. Lee threatened his reelection. General William T. Sherman's capture of Atlanta in September helped save the

president, who won the election decisively. Lincoln, however, never lived to see the nation reunited. On Good Friday, April 14, 1865, he was fatally shot at Ford's Theatre in Washington by a Confederate sympathizer.

It fell to Lincoln's successors to lead America through the years of Reconstruction. His second inaugural address stated Lincoln's vision for reconciliation—"with malice toward none; with charity for all; with firmness in the right, as God gives us to see the right … to bind up the nation's wounds …"

### TIMELINE

**February 12, 1809** Born in a one-room log cabin in Kentucky, second child of Thomas and Nancy Lincoln.

**1830** Lincoln's family moves to Illinois.

**1834** Elected to the Illinois General Assembly as a Whig. Begins his study of law.

**1842** Marries Mary Todd in Springfield, Illinois.

**1846** Elected to the U.S. House of Representatives as a Whig.

**1856** Organizes the Republican Party in Illinois.

**1858** Nominated as the Republican U.S. Senate candidate from Illinois, opposing Democrat Stephen A. Douglas. Takes on Douglas in seven debates across the state, drawing large crowds. In a close vote he loses to Douglas for Senate.

**May 18, 1860** Nominated as the Republican candidate for president.

**November 6, 1860** Elected as 16th president of the United States, receiving almost 40 percent of the popular vote and 180 of 303 possible electoral college votes.

**December 20, 1860** South Carolina secedes from the Union, followed within two months by Mississippi, Florida, Alabama, Georgia, Louisiana, and Texas.

**March 4, 1861** Lincoln delivers his first inaugural address in Washington, D.C.

**April 12, 1861** Confederate artillery fires on Fort Sumter in Charleston. Civil War begins.

**April 15, 1861** Lincoln calls for 75,000 volunteers to restore the Union.

**April 17, 1861** Virginia secedes, followed by North Carolina, Tennessee, and Arkansas.

**February 20, 1862** Lincoln's third son, Willie, dies at age 11. His wife is emotionally devastated and never fully recovers.

**January 1, 1863** Issues the Emancipation Proclamation.

**November 19, 1863** Delivers a carefully drafted speech at the dedication of the Soldiers' National Cemetery— the Gettysburg Address.

**November 8, 1864** Re-elected as president, receiving 55 percent of the popular vote and 212 out of 233 electoral votes.

**April 9, 1865** General Robert E. Lee surrenders his army at Appomattox Court House in Virginia.

**April 14, 1865** John Wilkes Booth shoots the president at Ford's Theatre. Lincoln is buried in Oak Ridge Cemetery near Springfield, Illinois.

MARY TODD LINCOLN

CAMPAIGN BUTTON

# 2

# SECESSION TRIGGERS WAR

## 1861

When Republicans won the 1860 presidential election, many white Southerners envisaged a threat to slavery, and some Southern states seceded from the Union. Most Northerners saw secession as treason and refused to accept peaceful disunion—a rift that ended in civil war.

**《 Opening shots of the Civil War**
The garrison at Fort Sumter replies to Confederate shelling on April 12, 1861. Located in Charleston harbor, South Carolina, the Union fort was seen as an insult to the new Confederacy. The commander of the fort, Major Robert Anderson (far left), agreed to withdraw the garrison the next day.

# SECESSION TRIGGERS WAR

**Union troops attacked in Baltimore**
Pro-secession feeling in Baltimore, Maryland, leads to clashes with troops passing through from New York to Washington on April 19. In Maryland and Delaware, slavery is permitted. Lincoln's firm response to the event persuades the two states to remain within the Union.

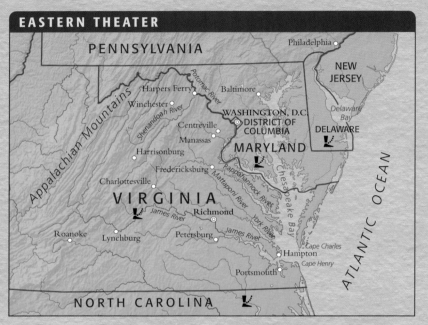

## EASTERN THEATER

**First major battle**
Manassas, near Washington D.C., is the scene of the first major land battle, known to the Union as Bull Run. Here, a wrecked wagon blocks the road of the retreating Union army, panic sets in, and defeat becomes a rout.

**Call to arms in the South**
This Confederate poster of May 1861 calls for local volunteers in Tennessee to fight in the "Yankee War." It proposes to raise "an infantry company to be offered to the Government as part of the defense of the state and of the Confederate States."

FREEMEN!
of
TENNESSEE!

TO ARMS!

J. B. Murray.
H. C. Witt.

THE UNION AND THE CONFEDERACY, 1861
- States remaining in the Union
- States seceding to form the Confederacy
- U.S. Territories
- Slave state

D espite last-ditch attempts to work out a political compromise, the first months of 1861 saw a steady disintegration of relations between North and South and between the political leaders of the two sections. By early February, seven states had seceded from the Union and taken steps toward establishing the Confederacy. President Abraham Lincoln continued to maintain that conflict was unnecessary, but the reality was that positions were hardening every day. Across the South, the seceded states started taking over Federal outposts. Not surprisingly, one of these confrontations between Southern forces and troops loyal to the Union erupted in violence—at Fort Sumter in Charleston Harbor, on April 12.

With the nation's small prewar armed forces divided between the two sections, neither at first had the means to fight the other on any significant scale. Both sides began assembling volunteer armies

**Confederate victory in Missouri**
The Battle of Wilson's Creek, fought in Missouri on August 10, gives the South a victory in the Western Theater. Although the Union army is heavily outnumbered and forced to retreat, casualties in the fighting are roughly equal.

**Volunteers in New York**
The streets of New York City are lined with large, enthusiastic crowds on April 19 as the 7th New York Infantry Regiment parades through the metropolis. On April 25, the regiment arrives in Washington, D.C., where its men bolster the capital's defenses.

**The war starts**
Fort Sumter, Charleston, comes under Confederate attack on April 12. Earlier Major Robert Anderson, the commander of the Union garrison, transferred men from Fort Moultrie to the more easily defensible Fort Sumter.

**Union Strategy**
Command of the coast and the Mississippi are key to the strategy outlined in May by General Winfield Scott, Union general-in-chief. Intended to throttle the life out of the Confederacy, it is dubbed the Anaconda Plan.

and based their recruitment on calls that emphasized principled outrage over the perceived iniquity of their opponents, a process that could only deepen the divide.

From the start, it was an asymmetrical struggle. In one respect, the South had the advantage. To win, the North needed to defeat its enemies and bring secession to an end; the South needed only to survive. In other respects, the North's superiority was massive—a much larger population accompanied by an overwhelming advantage in industrial power and financial resources. These strategic realities meant that the war was unlikely to be decided quickly, whatever the results of the early battles. At the start, the South was better served by its generals than the North, and the Confederacy was made safe for the moment on land. On the Confederacy's coast and its rivers, however, the Union's superior resources promised greater success.

# TIMELINE 1861

Secession of the Lower South ▪ **Southern seizure of Federal property** ▪ Congress of the Confederacy
▪ **Inauguration of Lincoln** ▪ Surrender of Fort Sumter ▪ **Lincoln's call for volunteers** ▪ Blockade of
the South ▪ **Secession of Virginia** ▪ Union success in Kentucky ▪ **First Battle of Bull Run** ▪ *Trent* Affair

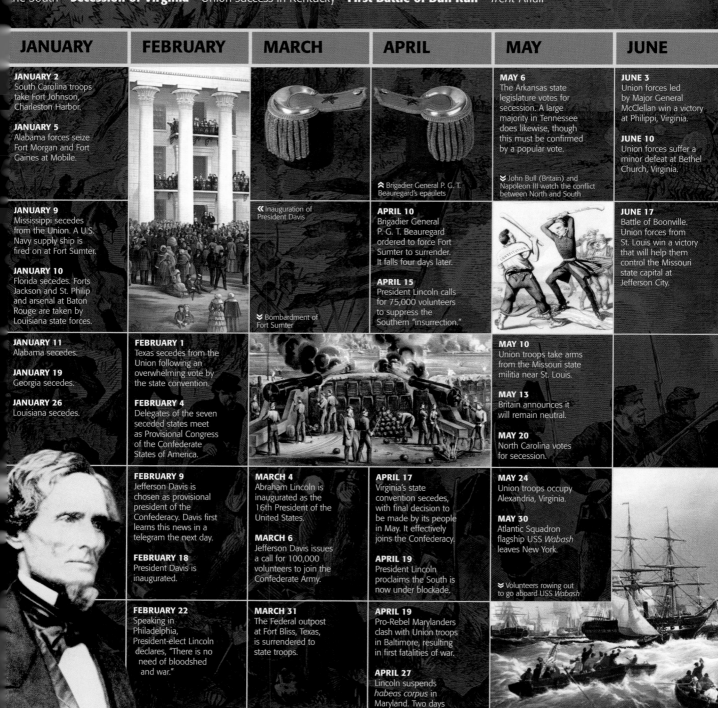

| JANUARY | FEBRUARY | MARCH | APRIL | MAY | JUNE |
|---|---|---|---|---|---|
| **JANUARY 2** South Carolina troops take Fort Johnson, Charleston Harbor.<br><br>**JANUARY 5** Alabama forces seize Fort Morgan and Fort Gaines at Mobile. | | | ☆ Brigadier General P. G. T. Beauregard's epaulets | **MAY 6** The Arkansas state legislature votes for secession. A large majority in Tennessee does likewise, though this must be confirmed by a popular vote.<br><br>≫ John Bull (Britain) and Napoleon III watch the conflict between North and South | **JUNE 3** Union forces led by Major General McClellan win a victory at Philippi, Virginia.<br><br>**JUNE 10** Union forces suffer a minor defeat at Bethel Church, Virginia. |
| **JANUARY 9** Mississippi secedes from the Union. A U.S. Navy supply ship is fired on at Fort Sumter.<br><br>**JANUARY 10** Florida secedes. Forts Jackson and St. Philip and arsenal at Baton Rouge are taken by Louisiana state forces. | ≪ Inauguration of President Davis<br><br>≫ Bombardment of Fort Sumter | | **APRIL 10** Brigadier General P. G. T. Beauregard ordered to force Fort Sumter to surrender. It falls four days later.<br><br>**APRIL 15** President Lincoln calls for 75,000 volunteers to suppress the Southern "insurrection." | | **JUNE 17** Battle of Boonville. Union forces from St. Louis win a victory that will help them control the Missouri state capital at Jefferson City. |
| **JANUARY 11** Alabama secedes.<br><br>**JANUARY 19** Georgia secedes.<br><br>**JANUARY 26** Louisiana secedes. | **FEBRUARY 1** Texas secedes from the Union following an overwhelming vote by the state convention.<br><br>**FEBRUARY 4** Delegates of the seven seceded states meet as Provisional Congress of the Confederate States of America. | | | **MAY 10** Union troops take arms from the Missouri state militia near St. Louis.<br><br>**MAY 13** Britain announces it will remain neutral.<br><br>**MAY 20** North Carolina votes for secession. | |
| | **FEBRUARY 9** Jefferson Davis is chosen as provisional president of the Confederacy. Davis first learns this news in a telegram the next day.<br><br>**FEBRUARY 18** President Davis is inaugurated. | **MARCH 4** Abraham Lincoln is inaugurated as the 16th President of the United States.<br><br>**MARCH 6** Jefferson Davis issues a call for 100,000 volunteers to join the Confederate Army. | **APRIL 17** Virginia's state convention secedes, with final decision to be made by its people in May. It effectively joins the Confederacy.<br><br>**APRIL 19** President Lincoln proclaims the South is now under blockade. | **MAY 24** Union troops occupy Alexandria, Virginia.<br><br>**MAY 30** Atlantic Squadron flagship USS *Wabash* leaves New York.<br><br>≫ Volunteers rowing out to go aboard USS *Wabash* | |
| | **FEBRUARY 22** Speaking in Philadelphia, President-elect Lincoln declares, "There is no need of bloodshed and war."<br><br>≪ Jefferson Davis | **MARCH 31** The Federal outpost at Fort Bliss, Texas, is surrendered to state troops. | **APRIL 19** Pro-Rebel Marylanders clash with Union troops in Baltimore, resulting in first fatalities of war.<br><br>**APRIL 27** Lincoln suspends *habeas corpus* in Maryland. Two days later the state votes against secession. | | |

> "My countrymen, one and all, **think calmly** and well … In **your hands**, my **dissatisfied fellow countrymen**, and not in **mine**, is the **momentous issue of civil war.**"

ABRAHAM LINCOLN, INAUGURAL ADDRESS, MARCH 4, 1861

| JULY | AUGUST | SEPTEMBER | OCTOBER | NOVEMBER | DECEMBER |
|------|--------|-----------|---------|----------|----------|

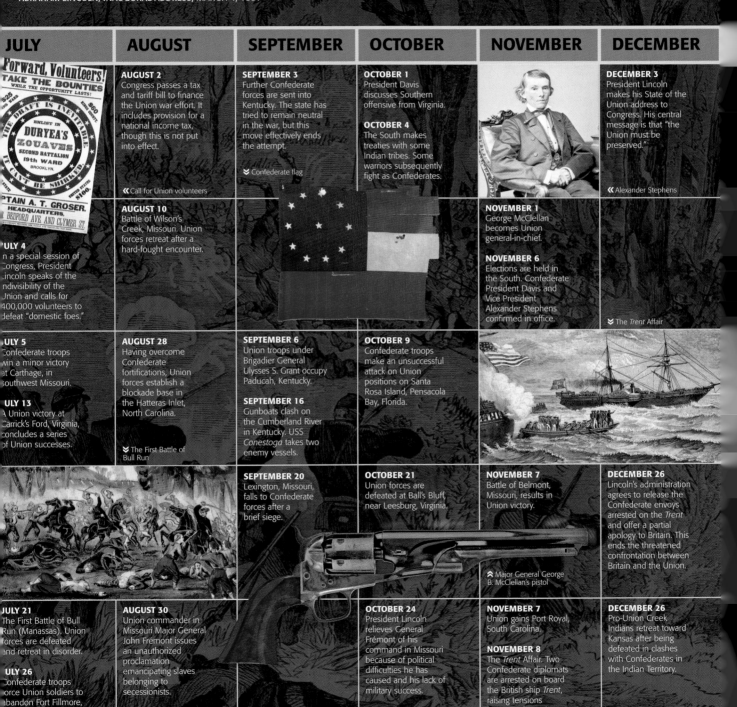

**Forward, Volunteers!**
TAKE THE BOUNTIES
WHILE THE OPPORTUNITY LASTS!
THE DRAFT IS INEVITABLE
ENLIST IN
DURYEA'S
ZOUAVES
SECOND BATTALION
19th WARD
BROOKLYN.
U CAN'T BE SHIRKED
TAIN A. T. GROSER,
HEADQUARTERS.
BEDFORD AVE. AND CLYMER ST.

**AUGUST 2**
Congress passes a tax and tariff bill to finance the Union war effort. It includes provision for a national income tax, though this is not put into effect.

« Call for Union volunteers

**SEPTEMBER 3**
Further Confederate forces are sent into Kentucky. The state has tried to remain neutral in the war, but this move effectively ends the attempt.

⌄ Confederate flag

**OCTOBER 1**
President Davis discusses Southern offensive from Virginia.

**OCTOBER 4**
The South makes treaties with some Indian tribes. Some warriors subsequently fight as Confederates.

**DECEMBER 3**
President Lincoln makes his State of the Union address to Congress. His central message is that "the Union must be preserved."

« Alexander Stephens

**ULY 4**
n a special session of Congress, President incoln speaks of the ndivisibility of the Union and calls for 400,000 volunteers to defeat "domestic foes."

**AUGUST 10**
Battle of Wilson's Creek, Missouri. Union forces retreat after a hard-fought encounter.

**NOVEMBER 1**
George McClellan becomes Union general-in-chief.

**NOVEMBER 6**
Elections are held in the South. Confederate President Davis and Vice President Alexander Stephens confirmed in office.

⌄ The *Trent* Affair

**ULY 5**
Confederate troops win a minor victory at Carthage, in southwest Missouri.

**ULY 13**
A Union victory at Carrick's Ford, Virginia, concludes a series of Union successes.

**AUGUST 28**
Having overcome Confederate fortifications, Union forces establish a blockade base in the Hatteras Inlet, North Carolina.

⌄ The First Battle of Bull Run

**SEPTEMBER 6**
Union troops under Brigadier General Ulysses S. Grant occupy Paducah, Kentucky.

**SEPTEMBER 16**
Gunboats clash on the Cumberland River in Kentucky. USS *Conestoga* takes two enemy vessels.

**OCTOBER 9**
Confederate troops make an unsuccessful attack on Union positions on Santa Rosa Island, Pensacola Bay, Florida.

**SEPTEMBER 20**
Lexington, Missouri, falls to Confederate forces after a brief siege.

**OCTOBER 21**
Union forces are defeated at Ball's Bluff, near Leesburg, Virginia.

**NOVEMBER 7**
Battle of Belmont, Missouri, results in Union victory.

**DECEMBER 26**
Lincoln's administration agrees to release the Confederate envoys arrested on the *Trent* and offer a partial apology to Britain. This ends the threatened confrontation between Britain and the Union.

**JULY 21**
The First Battle of Bull Run (Manassas). Union forces are defeated and retreat in disorder.

**ULY 26**
Confederate troops orce Union soldiers to abandon Fort Fillmore, New Mexico.

**AUGUST 30**
Union commander in Missouri Major General John Frémont issues an unauthorized proclamation emancipating slaves belonging to secessionists.

**OCTOBER 24**
President Lincoln relieves General Frémont of his command in Missouri because of political difficulties he has caused and his lack of military success.

⌃ Major General George B. McClellan's pistol

**NOVEMBER 7**
Union gains Port Royal, South Carolina.

**NOVEMBER 8**
The *Trent* Affair. Two Confederate diplomats are arrested on board the British ship *Trent*, raising tensions between the Union and Britain.

**DECEMBER 26**
Pro-Union Creek Indians retreat toward Kansas after being defeated in clashes with Confederates in the Indian Territory.

# The **Union** is **Dissolved**

**After the lower South seceded to form the Confederacy, Lincoln acted to preserve the Union, while adhering to the Free-Soil principles of the Republican Party. Union sentiment remained strong in the upper South, including Virginia. Confusion, regret, and conflict divided the U.S. Army's officer corps.**

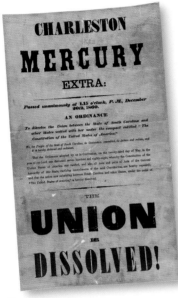

**First broadside**
A broadside from the *Charleston Mercury* was the first Secession publication, going to press 15 minutes after the secession ordinance was passed. Crowds cheered as it was distributed, and they saw the dramatic headline.

« **BEFORE**

**Lincoln was the first president to be elected on a purely sectional basis with almost exclusively Northern votes.**

**FREE-SOIL PLATFORM**
Not only did Lincoln win without any Southern electoral college votes « **38–39**, but he also ran on an **explicitly anti-slavery platform**, pledging to prevent further territorial expansion of slavery. Republicans **recognized the constitutional protection of slavery** in states where it already existed, and focused on **preventing the expansion of slavery** in territories that had not yet attained statehood.

**PREVIOUS ATTEMPTS AT SECESSION**
South Carolina had seriously contemplated secession during the **Nullification Crisis of 1833** « **20–21**, but retreated due to a lack of support from other Southern states. Sectional tensions flared again in relation to slavery in **the territories captured in the War with Mexico** « **20–21**, but calmed after the passage of the **Compromise of 1850** « **22–23**.

Shortly after Abraham Lincoln's election as president, the entire lower South (South Carolina, Mississippi, Florida, Alabama, Georgia, Louisiana, and Texas) seceded from the Union through the device of state conventions. On the principle that each state was a sovereign entity in and of itself, they voted to form a new nation called the "Confederate States of America." Furthermore, Alexander Stephens, vice president of the new nation, declared of its government that "its foundations are laid, its cornerstone rests, upon the great truth that the negro is not equal to the white man; that slavery, subordination to the superior race, is his natural and moral condition."

### The upper South's dilemma

The new Confederacy began its preparations for war, but the fate of the states of the upper South remained ambiguous. Virginia, Arkansas, and Missouri elected conventions with Unionists in the majority, while North Carolina and Tennessee chose not to have conventions at all. The border states of Maryland, Kentucky, and Delaware, where slavery existed in a limited form, also hung in the balance. While these states refused to join the Confederacy, they also made it clear that they would oppose any Federal attempt to coerce the states of the lower South back into the Union.

In this confused situation, the sitting President James Buchanan did next to nothing. With the chief executive acting as a lame duck, President-elect Lincoln sought to support Unionist sentiment in the South, while remaining committed to the Free-Soil principles of the Republican Party's platform.

When Lincoln assumed the powers and office of the presidency on March 4, 1861, he faced the thorny political dilemma of how to respond to the

**Calling for secession**
With the news of Lincoln's election, huge crowds gathered in Savannah's Johnson Square, calling for a state secession convention. South Carolina, the first to secede, left the Union on December 20, 1860.

newly formed Confederacy's seizure of Federal property in the lower South, which Buchanan had not opposed. By this time, only two important military installations—Fort Sumter in Charleston, South Carolina, and Fort Pickens in Florida—remained in Federal hands. Lincoln wished to sustain the claims of the Federal government to sovereign authority in the seceded states, but he also did not want to trigger a shooting war that might drive the upper South into the Confederacy.

As Lincoln confronted the question of how to enforce the Federal government's claims to the two endangered Federal forts, the upper

> In February 1861, Republicans in Congress helped pass a 13th amendment to the Constitution protecting slavery in the states where it already existed as a conciliatory gesture. It never received state approval.

South continued to wrestle with secession. The state of Virginia, in particular, played a critical role in this debate, because of its large population, substantial economic resources, and its symbolic importance to the history of the republic. Upper South and border state legislators led last-ditch attempts at crafting another intersectional compromise to preserve the Union, as had been done in the past, but moderates faced the dual challenges of a president elected on a platform that would prohibit any extension of slavery and the physical fact of the lower South's secession and the divisions that it created. Meanwhile, as the politicians schemed and quarreled, the Federal military establishment found itself divided.

Most U.S. Army officers came from West Point Military Academy, which ensured sectional balance, because appointments were allotted on the basis of congressional districts. Most, but not all, lower South officers immediately

**Inauguration of President Davis**
Jefferson Davis was inaugurated as President of the Confederate States of America on February 18, 1861. The event was held in Montgomery, Alabama, at the Alabama Capitol.

**CONFEDERATE VICE PRESIDENT (1812–83)**

## ALEXANDER HAMILTON STEPHENS

Alexander Stephens was a long-serving Georgia Representative in the U.S. Congress with Unionist instincts and a Whig background, who found himself elected as Confederate vice president. He had supported the Compromise of 1850, and he argued that Lincoln's election was not an immediate threat to slavery.

Nevertheless, he seemed fatalistic in private about the inevitability of secession, and he helped write the Confederate constitution. On March 21, 1861, Stephens gave his famous "cornerstone" speech, declaring slavery the bedrock of the Confederacy. A true believer in states' rights, he quarreled with Jefferson Davis over his use of emergency powers to carry out the war and opposed conscription. Stephens served on various peace missions to the North. He returned to politics after the war, even aligned himself with Republicans for a time, and was elected governor of Georgia in 1882.

resigned their commissions to go off and fight for the Confederacy. In contrast, officers from the upper South found themselves as torn and conflicted as their states.

General in Chief of the Army, Winfield Scott—a grand old Virginian who had fought with distinction as a division commander in the War of 1812 with Britain, and had conquered

> # 11
> The number of Confederate states at the end of May 1861, while 23 stayed in the Union.

Mexico City in 1846—advocated a cautious course of conciliation that found *de facto* support in Buchanan's policy of inaction.

### The problem of Fort Sumter
When Lincoln assumed office, Scott advised the president to abandon the Federal garrison stationed at Fort Sumter in order to avoid a direct military confrontation, but Lincoln's first loyalty remained with the Federal government. Scott obeyed Lincoln's orders to resupply the fort with provisions, despite Confederate threats to respond with force. Lincoln hoped to avoid bloodshed by initially using only announced and unarmed vessels carrying nonmilitary supplies, but he would not relinquish the post.

From the Confederate perspective, the very fact that Federal troops were manning a military installation in Charleston Harbor within the cradle of secession mocked the idea of Southern independence. The two sides were on a collision course, and the most important question would be how the upper South would respond to an outbreak of violence.

## AFTER

The war began at Fort Sumter in Charleston harbor, when Confederate forces fired on the Union resupply vessel, galvanizing public opinion in both sections.

### FORT SUMTER SURRENDERED
The secession crisis finally found a violent resolution at Fort Sumter. The fort was surrendered to the Confederacy on April 13 after a day of bombardment **52–53 》**.

### CONFEDERATE CONSOLIDATION
The outbreak of war forced the states of the **upper South to make a decision**. Four of them—Arkansas, North Carolina, Tennessee, and Virginia—decided they must cast their lot in with their slaveholding brethren.

SEAL OF THE CONFEDERATE STATES OF AMERICA

### PUBLIC OUTRAGE IN THE NORTH
The powerful symbolism of a successful Confederate attack on a U.S. military installation had a **transforming effect** on Northern public opinion, with the result that even most Northern Democrats were now **prepared to commit themselves to war**. Before the attack, staunchly radical Republicans had been among those happy to consider the idea of "letting them [the Confederate states] go," to use editor Horace Greeley's words in an editorial in the *New York Tribune*. The **assault on Fort Sumter** galvanized people's patriotism and inspired a **desire to avenge** the Confederacy's insult to the flag.

**CONFEDERATE PRESIDENT** Born 1808 Died 1889

# Jefferson Davis

## "I do **not despond** and will **not shrink** from **the task imposed** upon me."

JEFFERSON DAVIS IN A LETTER TO HIS WIFE, FEBRUARY 20, 1861

Jefferson Davis had considerable talents, including a deep and thorough knowledge of military affairs. However, his personality and temperament poisoned his relations with some of his generals and helped doom the Confederate war effort.

Davis's prewar record seemed to suit him far better for the role of a wartime commander-in-chief than his Northern counterpart, Abraham Lincoln. While Lincoln mocked his own brief stint as a militia officer, Davis had commanded a regiment with distinction in the War with Mexico. Later, Davis served as an effective reformist Secretary of War. He supervised the adoption of the rifle-musket and new infantry tactics to accompany this important change. However, at the War Department, Davis also showed his difficult personality in his bitter rows with General-in-Chief Winfield Scott.

Davis's contentious personality had been apparent even at West Point, which nearly expelled him for disciplinary reasons. These traits also led to

**Senator Davis**
This portrait was taken of Davis in 1860 by the famous Northern photographer Matthew Brady, who captured his distinguished features and somewhat austere expression.

his army court martial in 1835 for insubordination. After the trial, Davis resigned his commission and embarked on a life in politics.

Before he joined President Pierce's administration as Secretary of War, Davis had served as U.S. senator

**"Jeff sees the elephant"**
Seeing the elephant was a phrase Civil War soldiers used for experiencing the reality of combat. In this cartoon Davis (the donkey), his troops armed with pitchforks, wakes up to the true military might of the Union.

for Mississippi, where he earned a reputation as a Southern radical. He opposed the Compromise of 1850, which helped lead to his defeat in the 1851 gubernatorial election in Mississippi. Davis reentered the Senate in 1857, where he charted a more moderate course. During the secession winter after Lincoln's election to the presidency, he even offered to support the last-ditch Crittenden Compromise, which unsucccessfully tried to curtail the creation of new slave states.

The newly formed Confederacy chose Davis as president, in the hope that his somewhat moderate prewar record might attract the support of the upper South.

## Davis and his generals
The depiction of Davis (center) in military uniform reflects his prior military experience and his tendency to involve himself in the details of military affairs.

Davis's considerable talents, dedication to the cause, and real military knowledge benefited the Confederacy, even if errors in judgment and failures of temperament detracted from those contributions. He established a strong relationship with his most talented general, Robert E. Lee, and recognized the need to concentrate military power in viable field armies rather than try to defend every square mile of Confederate territory. He extended central authority to mobilize the South's limited economic resources, including such controversial measures as conscription and the commandeering of supplies.

Davis realized that international aid would come only after decisive signs of Confederate success, and that the South could not rely on Britain and France to win its independence. He even proved willing to sacrifice slavery for the Southern cause, supporting Lee's proposal in 1864 to enroll slaves—with the promise of freedom—to serve in the depleted Confederate armies. While Lincoln had the political savvy to hold together a fractious domestic political environment in the North, Davis's cold, imperious manner and inability to rally public opinion hurt the South's war effort.

### Flawed leadership
More seriously, Davis had poor relationships with some of his generals. The trouble began as early as the First Battle of Bull Run (First Manassas), when the relationship between Davis and Generals Joseph E. Johnston and P. G. T. Beauregard began to fail. The egotism of both generals was the main cause, but Davis could have managed the problems better.

Davis's failings in personnel management had the most serious consequences in the important Western theater. He relied too much on the capabilities of General Albert Sidney Johnston at the start of the war. More seriously, he allowed the high command of the Army of Tennessee to become a dysfunctional nest of intrigue, as various corps commanders worked to undermine General Braxton Bragg.

Bragg had certain virtues, including organizational acumen, but mixed abilities on the battlefield —revealed in the Chaplin Hills (Perryville) campaign of 1862—and his troops and subordinates heartily disliked him. In October 1863 matters came to a head, and Davis traveled west in an attempt to resolve the issue. Unfortunately, Davis left Bragg in command, instead of replacing him with a general who had the confidence of the army and punishing those officers who had been most insubordinate. The crisis would fester until Bragg was removed.

### After the war
Davis survived the war and two years of imprisonment at Fort Monroe. He continued to defend the Southern cause in print and engaged in various unsuccessful business ventures. But he refused to seek a pardon from the Federal government, which would have allowed him to resume a political career. His death in 1889 was marked by a funeral of imposing proportions.

**Varina Davis**
This miniature of Davis's wife, Varina Howell, shows her at the age of 23 after four years of marriage. They had five children, two born during the war.

> " Let me beseech you to lay aside **all rancor** [and] bring about a consummation devoutly to be wished—a **reunited country**."
> JEFFERSON DAVIS'S LAST PUBLIC ADDRESS, MISSISSIPPI CITY, 1888

## TIMELINE
- **June 3, 1808** Born in west central Kentucky, near the Tennessee border.
- **1824–28** Trains at West Point, emerging 23rd out of a class of 33, and joins the infantry branch of service.
- **February 1835** Court-martialed on a charge of insubordination, Davis is acquitted but resigns from the U.S. Army in May.
- **June 1835** Marries Sarah Knox Taylor, daughter of future president Zachary Taylor.
- **September 1835** His young wife dies— probably of malaria—on a Louisana plantation. Davis himself is seriously ill.
- **1846** Elected colonel of 1st Mississippi Volunteer regiment.
- **February 1847** Plays an important role in the American victory against Mexico at Buena Vista.
- **August 1847** The Mississippi state legislature appoints Davis to be a U.S. Senator.
- **1851** Defeated by Unionist support for the Compromise of 1850, Davis leaves the Senate and loses the gubernatorial race in Mississippi.
- **1853–57** Becomes Secretary of War in the administration of President Franklin Pierce.
- **1857** Returns to the Senate.
- **February 9, 1861** The Montgomery secession convention chooses Davis to be the first President of the Confederate States of America.
- **March 1862** Davis asks the Confederate Congress to pass a conscription act.
- **June 1862** After General Joseph E. Johnston is badly wounded at Seven Pines, Davis chooses Robert E. Lee to take command of what later becomes the Army of Northern Virginia.
- **July 1864** Replaces Johnston at the head of the Confederate Army of Tennessee with John Bell Hood—a disastrous appointment.
- **March 1865** Signs a bill authorizing the enlistment of slaves as soldiers.
- **1865–67** Imprisoned by the Federal authorities and indicted for treason.
- **1868** President Andrew Johnson issues an amnesty on Christmas Day that includes Jefferson Davis's pending charge of treason.
- **1881** Publishes *The Rise and Fall of the Confederate Government*, a defense of secession and his own conduct.
- **1886–87** Tours the South and is warmly received at numerous Lost Cause ceremonies.
- **December 6, 1889** Dies in New Orleans.

**THREE GENERATIONS, 1885**

# VOLUNTEERS WANTED!

1776! 1861!

---

## AN ATTACK UPON WASHINGTON ANTICIPATED !!

---

# THE COUNTRY TO THE RESCUE!

---

## A REGIMENT FOR SERVICE

## UNDER THE FLAG  OF THE UNITED STATES

IS BEING FORMED IN JEFFERSON COUNTY.

---

☞ # NOW IS THE TIME TO BE ENROLLED !

Patriotism and love of Country alike demand a ready response from every man capable of bearing arms in this trying hour, to sustain not merely the existence of the Government, but to vindicate the honor of that Flag so ruthlessly torn by traitor hands from the walls of Sumter.

---

# RECRUITING RENDEZVOUS

# The **Call** to **Arms**

**As the attack on Fort Sumter unified Northern public opinion, Lincoln issued a call for volunteers. Crucial Upper South states, including Virginia, joined the Confederacy. The Union held West Virginia and Maryland; Missouri and Kentucky teetered on the brink.**

At 4:30 a.m. on April 12, 1861, Confederate batteries around the harbor at Charleston, South Carolina, opened fire on Fort Sumter, a Federal fortification built on a small island at the harbor's mouth. The fort's commander, Major Robert Anderson, began surrender negotiations the next afternoon. Anderson had staunchly maintained the Union position at Fort Sumter

### A plea to the nation
The government lured new recruits into the army with promises of bonuses and well-equipped units. Patriotic posters, such as this 1861 example, demanded "a ready response" from those men capable of bearing arms.

## BEFORE

**Lincoln's election on a sectional basis and on a party platform that aimed to limit slavery, combined with the swift secession of the Lower South, made war nearly inevitable.**

#### SOWING THE SEEDS
The Republicans did not even try to contest elections in ten Southern states, and the Lower South saw any legal restriction on slavery by the Federal government as paving the way for more serious attacks on the institution.

#### THE LIMITS OF COMPROMISE
A native of Kentucky and admirer of Henry Clay, Lincoln had conciliatory instincts, but he also remained true to the Free-Soil principles of the Republican Party **‹‹ 32–33**. This, combined with Confederate intransigence, made some kind of violent clash all but unavoidable **‹‹ 38–39**.

### CONFEDERATE GENERAL (1818–93)
## P. G. T. BEAUREGARD

Pierre Gustave Toutant Beauregard, born on a plantation in St. Bernard Parish, Louisiana, had a distinguished record in the prewar army, including combat service in Mexico. While he had significant talents, he likened himself too much to Napoleon, and his fame after the fall of Fort Sumter further inflated his ego. Beauregard's performance was mixed at the battles of First Bull Run (First Manassas) and Shiloh, but during the summer of 1864, he served the Confederacy well at Bermuda Hundred and Petersburg.

since South Carolina's secession the previous December, but the approach of a Union naval squadron with fresh supplies for the fort had provoked a definitive confrontation.

Local Confederate commander P. G. T. Beauregard had been given orders to demand the immediate evacuation of the fort. When Anderson refused, hostilities began, and were concluded without any combat fatalities on either side. While the Confederacy believed the attack to be a necessary and reasonable defense of its sovereignty, most Northerners saw it as an immoral assault on American troops.

The Republican Party had swept the North in the presidential election of 1860, but the Democrats remained a potent political force, with much weaker anti-slavery instincts. However, most Democrats remained loyal Unionists, and the Confederate attack on "Old Glory" (the national flag) at Sumter outraged their nationalist sensibilities, which led to an outpouring of public support for a military campaign to crush secession.

### Lincoln's response
On April 15, Lincoln issued a proclamation calling for 75,000 90-day volunteers. The Northern response overwhelmed the capacity of both Federal and state governments to organize, train, and equip

### Charleston cannonball
Thousands of rounds of artillery fire showered cannonballs like this on Fort Sumter before Major Anderson and his garrison surrendered.

the soldiers. This outpouring of popular support vindicated Lincoln's cautious approach during the secession winter. His attempts to placate Southern opinion by providing only nonmilitary supplies to Anderson's command had caused even Northern Democrats to view the Confederacy as the unprovoked aggressor at Fort Sumter.

> **Major Robert Anderson was a Kentuckian and former slaveowner, with a stellar record as a leading artillery reformer and in combat in the War with Mexico.**

### The Confederacy expands
In the crucial Upper South states of Arkansas, North Carolina, Tennessee, and Virginia, the calling out of a large Federal army meant war. When forced to take sides, these four states chose the Confederacy. Southern views were summed up by the *Staunton Spectator*, until now a Unionist Virginia newspaper. A day after the president's call for volunteers it declared that "After all his declarations in favor of peace, President Lincoln has taken a course calculated inevitably to provoke a collision, and to unite the whole South in armed resistance."

While strategically important Virginia seceded on April 17, along with Arkansas, North Carolina, and Tennessee in the following month, Maryland remained with the Union. Moreover, even in Virginia, the poorest and mostly nonslaveholding farmers of the state's western counties held out for the Union cause—leading eventually to the founding of the state of West Virginia.

Virginia and Tennessee made the Confederacy a viable nation, but there still remained the prize of Kentucky, with its large population and a northern border on the Ohio River that could serve as a defensive barrier against Union invasion. Slavery had a weaker status in the Bluegrass state than in the Old Dominion, and the state did not immediately secede in response to Lincoln's call for many volunteers. Instead, Kentucky acted in the tradition of Henry Clay, the great sectional compromiser, and hoped to adopt a neutral stance toward both the U.S. and Confederate governments.

The fate of Missouri, the origin of so many of the troubles in "Bleeding Kansas" also hung in the balance, although the state did not have the strategic significance of Kentucky.

### Occupying Fort Sumter
On December 26, 1860, Anderson's command at Fort Moultrie, Charleston, moved secretly to the more defensible Fort Sumter.

## AFTER

**The first fatalities of the Civil War occurred in Baltimore, Maryland, on April 19, a week after the fall of Fort Sumter.**

#### LEXINGTON OF 1861
Although Maryland stayed in the Union, sentiment in Baltimore was strongly pro-Confederate. When the Massachusetts 6th Regiment passed through on its way to Washington, D.C., a riot erupted, leaving four soldiers and 12 civilians killed in the ensuing melee. The incident is often called the "Lexington of 1861"—after the first skirmish of the American Revolution, at Lexington, Massachusetts.

**THE BALTIMORE RIOT**

# Fort Sumter

**After years of swirling debates and threats, the first shots of the Civil War echoed across South Carolina's Charleston Harbor on April 12, 1861. When Major Robert Anderson refused to surrender Fort Sumter to General P. G. T. Beauregard, Confederate batteries opened fire upon the provision-depleted fort. Fort Sumter surrendered 34 hours later, and the Civil War began.**

"By 11 a.m. the conflagration was terrible and disastrous. One-fifth of the fort was on fire, and the wind drove the smoke in dense masses into the angle where we had all taken refuge. It seemed impossible to escape suffocation. Some lay down close to the ground, with handkerchiefs over their mouths ... every one suffered severely ... the scene at this time was really terrific. The roaring and crackling of the flames, the dense masses of whirling smoke, the bursting of the enemy's shells, and our own which were exploding in the burning rooms, the crashing of the shot, and the sound of masonry falling in every direction, made the fort a pandemonium. When at last nothing was left of the building but the blackened walls and smoldering embers, it became painfully evident that an immense amount of damage had been done ... about 12:48 p.m. the end of the flag-staff was shot down, and the flag fell."

ABNER DOUBLEDAY, CAPTAIN OF COMPANY E, 1ST UNITED STATES ARTILLERY, FROM *REMINISCENCES OF FORTS SUMTER AND MOULTRIE 1860–61*. DOUBLEDAY GAVE THE ORDER TO FIRE THE FIRST GUN IN THE DEFENSE OF FORT SUMTER

"Thank God! Thank God! The day has come; the war is open, and we will conquer or perish. We have defeated their twenty millions, and we have humbled the proud flag of the Stars and Stripes that never before lowered to any nation on earth. We have lowered it in humility before the Palmetto and Confederate flags, and have compelled them to raise a white flag and ask for honorable surrender. The Stars and Stripes have triumphed for 70 years, but on this 13th of April it has been humbled by the little State of South Carolina. And I pronounce here, before the civilized world, that your independence is baptized in blood. Your independence is won upon a glorious battlefield, and you are free, now and forever, in defiance of the world in arms."

FRANCIS WILKINSON PICKENS, GOVERNOR OF SOUTH CAROLINA, IN A SPEECH FROM THE BALCONY OF THE CHARLESTON HOTEL

**Bombardment of Fort Sumter**
Congress saw Fort Sumter as a bastion of "structural durability," but its 60 cannons and 85-man garrison were not enough to save it from a barrage of 3,000 Confederate shells, and its brick walls soon crumbled.

**« BEFORE**

The Southern economy relied heavily on cotton exports, mostly to Britain. Before the war, these had earned large amounts of hard currency. However, the dominance of cotton-growing **« 22–23** suppressed the South's industrial capacity.

**RISING PRODUCTION**
Boosted by Eli Whitney's invention of the cotton gin for separating the fibers from the seeds **« 16–17**, Southern **cotton production soared** during the 19th century. From 720,000 bales in 1830, it rose to 2.85 million bales in 1850 and was still rising at the outbreak of the Civil War. By then, the slave plantations of the South were the source of **75 percent** of the world's commercially grown cotton.

**FAILED DIPLOMACY**
The Confederates hoped that **"King Cotton" diplomacy** would force Britain to intervene on their behalf because, without Southern cotton, British textile mills would be idle. They underestimated the strength of **British anti-slavery sentiment** and the ability of British industrialists to find alternative sources of cotton in India, Egypt, and Argentina. Hopes of French intervention were similarly dashed.

# The South's Challenge

**The Confederacy's vast geographic expanse made it difficult for the enemy to occupy and conquer. At the same time, the South's straightforward war goal of independence gave it greater domestic unity than the North, which wrestled internally with the question of emancipation's proper place in the war.**

The long and destructive nature of the Civil War, combined with the immense stakes involved—the fate of the old Federal Union, the existence of the Confederate nation, and the status of slavery—made it a war of mass mobilization in both sections. Both sides had to find the human, material, and technological resources for waging a war at a time of rapid industrialization, with its railroads, mass-produced weapons and equipment, and comparatively new technologies. Although the North possessed more of all of these things, the Confederate cause was by no means hopeless and doomed.

**A well-resourced enemy**
During the 19th century, the new era of rail and steam that marked the Industrial Revolution was centered in the Northern states, and a summary of economic and human resources shows their advantages. In 1860, the North possessed most of the country's manufacturing capacity, including 97 percent of firearms production. Altogether it had 110,000 manufacturing enterprises and 1.3 million industrial workers. The future Confederacy could count only 18,000 factories employing 110,000 individuals. These Southern factories, however, did include the Tredegar Iron Works in Richmond, Virginia, one of the few places capable of providing the

**General Josiah Gorgas**
At the start of hostilities, Gorgas was commander of the U.S. Army arsenal at Frankford, near Philadelphia. He resigned to join the Confederates.

Confederacy with heavy ordnance. During the war, the task of trying to make up for this industrial imbalance fell to the Confederacy's ever-resourceful ordnance chief, General Josiah Gorgas. The Union also had twice the density of railroads per square mile; the future Confederate states produced only 19 of 470 locomotives manufactured that year. In terms of population, the Union had 20.7 million people, against the Confederacy's

**Southern charm**
For many, life in the prewar South was secure and prosperous—a quality captured by German artist Edward Beyer in his view of Salem, Virginia, painted in 1855.

### Manufacturing might

Smoke belches from the chimneys of the Jones and Laughlin iron mills, on the Monongahela River south of Pittsburgh. Enterprises like this gave the North an industrial edge over the South.

population of just over 9.1 million, of whom more than 3.6 million were African Americans—most of them slaves and holding dubious loyalty to their white masters. In the financial sector, Southern banking before the war had been based not in any major Southern city, such as New Orleans or Richmond, but in New York.

### The South's advantages

Counterbalancing the North's larger pool of material resources was the Confederacy's immense size. This offered important geographical advantages. The South occupied about the same amount of territory as Western Europe, which gave it what military historians call "strategic depth." This allows an army defending its territory to retreat in the face of a stronger force, obliging the invader to disperse its strength in garrisons and outposts over an ever-increasing area in order to defend vulnerable lines of communication against guerrillas and

## "The Army … has been **compelled to yield** to **overwhelming numbers** and resources."

ROBERT E. LEE, FAREWELL ADDRESS TO THE ARMY OF NORTHERN VIRGINIA, 1865

The key Confederate strategists and commanders were well aware of the Union's material advantages.

#### PUSH FOR VICTORY

When **General Robert E. Lee** assumed command of the Army of Northern Virginia in June 1862, one of his chief goals was to win **swift battlefield victories**. These, he hoped, would shatter enemy morale before the Confederacy collapsed under the weight of Northern industrial superiority.

## 31,246 MILES

of railroad crisscrossed the North. In the South, by contrast, there were just 9,283 miles of railroad, less than 30 percent of the Northern total.

#### GUERRILLA WARFARE

The wide expanse of Confederate territory, especially in the West, made it perfect for guerrilla activity 224–25 ››. This successfully **hampered Federal operations** by tying down large numbers of Union troops in occupation and garrison duties. But the guerrillas were not above preying on Southern civilians as well as Northern soldiers, which made them a **problematic military tool**.

small detachments of organized forces. In addition, the South's rudimentary road and rail network made logistics a nightmare for any invading army.

While the Confederates could see British struggles against the sweep of American geography during the American Revolution as a heartening example for their own war of independence, they could also draw lessons from the eventual collapse of British political will at the time. During the Revolution, internal divisions in Britain allowed the Americans to exhaust their former rulers and win independence. In the Civil War, while the fall of Fort Sumter unified Northern opinion behind a struggle for Union, what Union really meant remained a point of political contention, even among Republicans. Questions of Federal authority, involving issues such as emancipation, conscription, and the draft, would be points of partisan controversy within the North. For their part, the Confederates were united behind the more straightforward goal of sovereign independence.

Even the South's enslaved population gave it certain advantages. An economy based on slavery and cotton-cultivation allowed the Confederacy to mobilize an unprecedented percentage of its white male

population. Because fewer white men of military age were needed to keep the basic domestic economy running, around three out of four of them became soldiers—and one in five would die during the war. Eventually, however, the Union turned African Americans living in the Confederacy into a potent resource for victory by arming many of them and enlisting them as U.S. soldiers.

### Underlying weakness

Despite the Confederacy's important advantages, the more advanced state of industrialization in the North, its larger supply of natural resources such as iron and coal, and its greater economic strength, enabled it to sustain war for a longer time than the South could. And, unlike Britain during the American Revolution and the War of 1812, the North did not have to cross an ocean to bring its military power to bear.

### King Cotton?

A Southern senator once declared: "No, you dare not to make war on cotton. No power on the earth dares to make war upon it. Cotton is King." He was wrong.

# Union and Confederate Flags

**Flags provided identification for military units and were symbols of pride. Today, the surviving tattered banners bearing state and other insignia confirm the importance of local volunteer organizations throughout the Civil War.**

**1** National color of the 84th Regiment U.S. Colored Troops (Union) The red stripes bear the regiment's name and number and detail a number of the unit's battles. **2** "Old Glory" (Union) This flag, made in 1824, was the first to bear the name "Old Glory." It was unfurled for the last time when Union troops occupied Nashville in 1862. **3** 69th New York Infantry flank marker (Union) This flag was captured by the Confederates at Fredericksburg on December 13, 1862. **4** Union 33-star flag The 33-star flag was the national flag before the Civil War. No stars were removed at the outbreak of war, since the Federal government believed secession was illegal. **5** Union 34-star flag, adopted on July 4, 1861, after the admission of Kansas as the 34th state earlier that year. **6** Flag of 111th Pennsylvania Regiment (Union) This regimental flag displays an image of a bald eagle, a prominent patriotic symbol among Union troops. **7** National flag of the Confederacy The Confederate Congress adopted a seven-star version of this flag, designed by Nicola Marschall and referred to as the "Stars and Bars," on March 4, 1861. Stars were added as more states seceded. **8** Flag of 1st Louisiana Special Battalion (Confederate) This version of the Confederate battle flag was carried by Wheat's Tigers of Louisiana. **9** Regimental Flag, 25th Louisiana Infantry (Confederate), embroidered with the regiment's motto "Trust and go forward." **10** Flag of Washington Artillery (Confederate) This was the flag of the 5th Company of the New Orleans Washington Artillery. **11** Guidon of 24th Louisiana Crescent Regiment (Confederate) This guidon (company standard) belonged to the regiment's A Company. **12** Flag of Cowan's Mississippi Battery (Confederate) In 1862 General Earl Van Dorn ordered units under his command to adopt this flag as the regimental color. **13** Flag of Ware's Tigers (Confederate) This national flag, used by Ware's Tigers of Corpus Christi, has 13 stars, representing the seceded states as well as Missouri and Kentucky, which possessed competing state governments. **14** Confederate battle flag Owing to possible confusion on the battlefield between the Confederate and Union national flags, this battle flag was adopted by the Army of Northern Virginia and, later, by Southern forces generally.

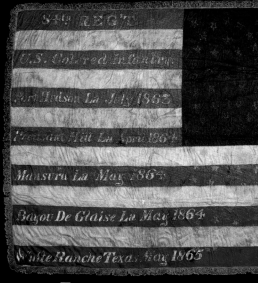

**1** 84TH REGIMENT, U.S. COLORED TROOPS

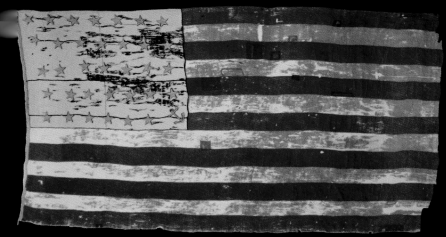

**2** "OLD GLORY"

**3** 69TH NEW YORK INFANTRY

7 CONFEDERATE "STARS AND BARS"

8 1ST LOUISIANA SPECIAL BATTALION

9 25TH LOUISIANA INFANTRY

11 A COMPANY, 24TH LOUISIANA

10 5TH COMPANY, WASHINGTON ARTILLERY

12 COWAN'S BATTERY, MISSISSIPPI

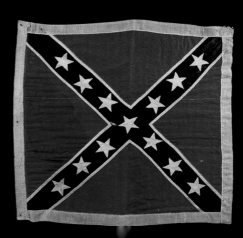

# Raising Armies

**Military enthusiasm gripped both sides and volunteers rushed to join up, all believing their camp would achieve a swift victory. They hoped their moral excellence as citizen soldiers fighting a righteous cause would crush their opponent almost by itself, making training and discipline unnecessary.**

## « BEFORE

The unavoidable disorganization and confusion in forming both the Northern and Southern armies masked the North's overwhelming material superiority.

**SOUTHERN OPPORTUNITY**
The North had vastly **greater resources than the South «« 54–55**. But its impressive industrial and economic capacity had to be organized and mobilized before it became militarily useful—and this gave the Confederacy a timely **opportunity to win independence**.

**AN IDENTICAL MILITARY MODEL**
Both sections used the prewar U.S. Army as a common administrative and tactical model for creating **new field armies**. Veterans such as Josiah Gorgas utilized their expertise to help the Confederacy **mobilize its limited resources**.

**CENTRAL AUTHORITY**
Given the South's strong **attachment to states' rights**, it was difficult for President Jefferson Davis to impose the centralized organization **essential to military efficiency «« 48–49**.

By the time of the Civil War, the American Revolution was a distant memory, and few citizens had served in the more recent War with Mexico (1846–47), in which General Winfield Scott had conquered Mexico City with an army of only 11,000 men. Attitudes to war tended to romanticize it, drawing on a variety of cultural influences: tributes to the Founding Fathers and the American Revolution; images of overseas wars in exotic settings, such as French Algeria or the Halls of Montezuma in Mexico; and the long-standing militia tradition whereby common people banded together to defeat their enemies, returning home after a short but sharp war.

**I25** The percentage of U.S. Army officers who resigned to join the Confederate army.

## A nation's differences

Sectionalism added potently to this collection of ideas. Southerners saw themselves as a martial people more familiar with horses and weapons than shopkeeping Yankees. Northerners believed they were a free people defending the Constitution. They were fighting against a society ruled by abusive slaveholders who had been corrupted by the illegitimate power they held over fellow human beings. While notions of war could be both romantic and ridiculous, a genuine undercurrent of fierce patriotism motivated many volunteers. One Union soldier explained in a letter that he enlisted because "I performed but a simple duty—a duty to my country and myself … to give up life if need be … in this battle for freedom and right, opposed to slavery and wrong." A Southern volunteer reflected many others' views when he said, "I would give all I have got just to be in the front rank of the first brigade that marches against the invading foe who now pollute the sacred soil of my native state [Virginia] with their unholy tread." This patriotism would help sustain both armies' fighting abilities through a long and difficult war, but it also tended to denigrate the importance of professional competence and discipline. Both armies

paid too little attention to the warnings of prewar professional soldiers that troops needed training and discipline to be effective, and that the coming conflict might be long and grueling.

## Romantic ideas

Many who claimed to possess military expertise had a notion of war far more romantic than realistic. Volunteer officers, such as Unionist Colonel Elmer Ellsworth, had more military knowledge than the average volunteer, and his interpretation of the tactics used by France's Zouave (North African) light infantry regiments—who were renowned as elite and disciplined fighters—reflected current and future military developments in infantry tactics. These included formations of troops trained to move quickly, spread out, and fire accurately. Nevertheless, Ellsworth did not fully understand these tactical evolutions.

## Lack of trained officers

While the small number of military-age men with formal training at either West Point or various state military academies (the most important being the Virginia Military Institute) rose to instant prominence during the

### 1st Virginia Infantry
Within weeks of secession, the 1st Virginia Infantry was raised as a volunteer unit. It fought at the Battle of Gettysburg, where more than half were killed or wounded.

### UNION VOLUNTEER OFFICER (1837–61)

### ELMER EPHRAIM ELLSWORTH

Born in Malta, New York, Ellsworth hoped to attend West Point but failed to obtain an appointment. He moved to Chicago in 1859, where he became a prominent militia officer, leading a unit attired in the flamboyant style of French Zouaves. In 1860, he entered the law office of Abraham Lincoln and campaigned for the future president in the election that year.

When war broke out, Ellsworth raised a regiment recruited from the firefighters of New York, the "Fire Zouaves." He led them into Alexandria, Virginia, in May 1861, where he was killed by an innkeeper for pulling down a Confederate flag flying from his hotel. In the North, Ellsworth's youth and his connection with Lincoln magnified the importance of his death; he came to be seen as one of the first heroes of the war.

**Departing for war—April 19, 1861**
Thomas Nast's huge painting of the 7th New York Regiment being cheered on by their fellow citizens includes the hero of Fort Sumter, Major Robert Anderson, above the entrance of Ball, Black & Co. on the left.

organization of the new armies, the sheer size of the forces and their democratic organization required most officers to come from civilian life.

In this phase of the war, before the rise of conscription, local leaders raised companies and regiments by personal influence (and sometimes even using their own money). In keeping with democratic practice, regiments also elected their officers. These volunteers thus tended to hold their roles by virtue of a whole range of factors unrelated to military competence, such as political influence, wealth, social standing, and simple popularity. As early as September 1861, one officer, Wilder Dwight of the 2nd Massachusetts,

grumbled that "Today our army is crippled by the ideas of equality and independence which have covered the whole life of our people. Men elect their officers, and then expect them to behave themselves!" Such opinions were rare among his peers during the early part of the war.

### Equipment shortages
Not only would the armies struggle with training and discipline, they also had to cope with

**Zouave recruiting poster**
Colonel Abram Duryea's Zouaves (the 5th New York Volunteers) was one of the most celebrated Zouave units, noted for its defensive role at Second Bull Run (Manassas).

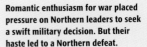

shortages of equipment and supplies. Even after factoring in militia arsenals and other small depositories of military supplies, both armies had difficulty acquiring the most basic materials. They also needed to create the logistical and administrative machinery necessary for sustaining lengthy active operations in the field.

Despite all of these challenges, both armies also had the important advantage of drawing from a patriotic and highly motivated citizenry that believed their causes to be just. With training and battlefield seasoning, this raw material could and would become the bedrock of powerful and effective forces.

**AFTER** »

Romantic enthusiasm for war placed pressure on Northern leaders to seek a swift military decision. But their haste led to a Northern defeat.

**VICTORIOUS SOUTH**
This rush to battle helped lead to **Union defeat at First Bull Run (First Manassas) 60–61** », a battle and campaign waged in part against the better judgment of General-in-Chief Winfield Scott. This first major battle of the war showed both the strengths and the weakness of the early Union and Confederate armies. The volunteers on both sides displayed **admirable fighting spirit**, but even the victorious Confederates revealed flaws in discipline, training, and organization. Their victory did, however, **enhance the South's credibility** in the eyes of foreign powers.

**Retreat at Bull Run**
After the battle, the Union Army retreated in total confusion to the fortifications around Washington. Military wagons and the carriages of fleeing spectators blocked their route, and many men were captured.

« **BEFORE**

First Bull Run dwarfed any other clashes that the U.S. Army had hitherto fought. Its use of new technology helped the Confederacy gain advantage.

**SMALL ARMIES**
Washington had fewer than 17,000 men at Yorktown, the decisive battle of the American Revolution, and General Winfield Scott had taken Mexico City in 1847 with an army of only about 11,000 men. At First Bull Run, Union general McDowell led 35,000 to his opponents' 30,000.

**DEVELOPMENT OF RAILROADS**
When the British invaded the American colonies, they could not benefit from industrialized forms of transportation, such as the railroad. This **new form of technology** could be used for defensive purposes by both sides in the Civil War.

**GEORGE B. McCLELLAN**
Shortly before First Bull Run, Union commander George B. McClellan won a few skirmishes in western Virginia, which helped secure the important Baltimore and Ohio Railroad, laying the groundwork for the formation of West Virginia. McClellan's success before the disaster of First Bull Run made him the **natural replacement for McDowell**.

# The First Battle of Bull Run

**Pre-Civil War America had seen little real military action and knew nothing of war beyond fantastic portrayals in books—the First Battle of Bull Run (known as Manassas by the Confederates) of July 21, 1861, represented a grim beginning to the Civil War and a portent of things to come.**

The First Battle of Bull Run took place at the important railroad intersection of Manassas Junction, Virginia. In the wide expanses of the Confederacy, where the primitive road network and the highly dispersed population made it difficult for an army to live off the countryside, railroads were indispensable. They carried much-needed supplies and became strategic assets. The crossing at Manassas Junction, where the Orange and Alexandria Railroad met the Manassas Gap Railroad, was a vital line of communication—leading south into the heart of Virginia, and west to the agriculturally fertile Shenandoah Valley.

The Confederacy posted two field armies to cover these possible lines of advance—General Joseph E. Johnston's force in the northern Shenandoah Valley, numbering a little less than 10,000, and 18,000 men under General P. G. T. Beauregard at Manassas. The Confederate leaders hoped that the railroad in between the two armies would allow them to move reinforcements between both positions more swiftly than the Union army, which did not have access to a direct rail connection.

## Line advantage
Military thinkers from the Civil War era and modern historians call this Confederate geographic advantage "interior lines." For example, if a straight line is drawn, connecting two points on an arc, the line is much shorter than the arc. The Confederacy, as the country defending the arc, had the advantage of "interior lines" across its territory, while the Union had to operate on "exterior lines" outside of it. First Bull Run was the first example of a larger Confederate advantage in terms of defensive positioning.

Eventually, the Union would find that the best way to overcome the Confederate advantage of interior lines was to use its superior resources to coordinate multiple and simultaneous attacks along the entire "arc" of the Confederacy's defensive perimeter. This goal would be achieved to some extent by the Union offensives of 1864, which eventually brought the war to an end. However, as early as First Bull Run, General Winfield Scott attempted such a coordinated strategy on exterior lines when he ordered Major General Robert Patterson in the Shenandoah Valley to advance and try to prevent Johnston from moving his troops eastward from the valley to reinforce

**2,000** Approximate number of Confederate casualties.

**3,000** Approximate number of Union casualties.

# "Let us **determine** to die here, and **we will conquer**. **Rally** behind the Virginians."

ATTRIBUTED TO BRIGADIER GENERAL BARNARD E. BEE, CONFEDERATE ARMY

**General's epaulets**
Beauregard shared command responsibilities with General Johnston at Bull Run. After the battle, at the recommendation of Johnston, Beauregard was promoted to full (four-star) general.

Beauregard's units. Unfortunately for the Union side, Patterson proved to be too timid a commander for even this relatively modest objective. The Confederates made good use of the railroads to concentrate their forces at Bull Run in opposition to Brigadier General Irwin McDowell's advance on Manassas Junction.

## Union plans—and weaknesses
McDowell conducted his attack on Beauregard's position partly in response to the heavy political pressure exerted by overconfident and overeager Northern politicians. The Union commander fretted that "for the most part our regiments are exceedingly raw and the best of them, with few exceptions, not over steady in line." Although the Confederate army was smaller (McDowell commanded 35,000 men), it fought on the defensive—a potent advantage when considering two ill-disciplined, indifferently trained, and inexperienced armies. Nevertheless, McDowell's battle plan also had merit, as he hoped to turn the Confederate left flank by ordering two divisions to cross Bull Run Creek at points upstream from the bulk of Confederate strength near Blackburn's Ford.

## First clashes
The battle itself was a close-run affair. McDowell's flanking movements were delayed by defective staffwork and inexperience, while an aggressive defense by Confederate units on the left flank bought the Confederates crucial time to ward off the Union commander's attempt to turn them.
Beauregard at first dreamed of a Confederate offensive, but confusing orders and poor staffwork

**Union Brigadier General McDowell**
McDowell was an able military administrator who was less suited to senior combat command. He served in more junior roles after Bull Run but was dismissed in 1862.

resulted more in bewilderment than anything else. Foreshadowing problems that would persist throughout much of the war, Union forces struggled to coordinate their assaults, and instead of amassing their strength to take a position, the individual units (in this case, single regiments) made their attacks piecemeal. Even so, the battle went well for the Union forces in the early part of the day, as they pushed past Matthews Hill down toward Henry Hill, threatening to turn the Confederate left.

In the end, however, all the delays and lack of coordination allowed the Confederates to man a powerful defensive position on Henry Hill, where the battle finally reached its climax. It was here that Brigadier General Thomas J. Jackson earned his nickname, "Stonewall," for his well-handled and vital defense of the position.

### Federal disorder
Johnston, having only recently arrived, fed Confederate troops into this crucial site, and the Union side continued to waste its strength in badly organized assaults. Two Union batteries held important positions on the hill, but one was mauled by a Confederate regiment that a senior Union officer had misidentified as friendly. This problem stemmed from the confusing variety of clothing worn by early Civil War regiments, before blue and gray became standard uniform colors. The Union infantry supports had also performed poorly.
The Confederate capture of the two Union batteries on Henry Hill became the turning point of the battle, and one last Federal attempt to turn the Confederates at Chinn Ridge, west of Henry Hill, failed.

Most regiments elected their own officers, reflecting Jacksonian America's traditional suspicion of hierarchy and technical proficiency. Nevertheless, the volunteers' enthusiasm showed the ensuing conflict to be truly a "people's contest."

When Confederate forces counter-attacked at the ridge, strengthened by two brigades newly arrived from the Shenandoah Valley, the Federals panicked and retreated in disarray. They were joined in their retreat by fleeing Union civilians from Washington—spectators who had attended the battle expecting it to be an outdoor stage where treason would be justly chastised.
While the Northern volunteers had in many ways fought well, their lack of experience and discipline showed. However, chaos also reigned among the victorious Confederates—likewise a product of their inexperience—and this would allow Union troops to return to the safety of the fortifications surrounding Washington, despite the frantic disorder accompanying their retreat.

The battle served as a fitting herald for the start of the war, and Confederate President Jefferson Davis himself traveled to the site before the combat ended. He afterward wrote the telegram reporting the victory to the Confederate War Department in Richmond. The Confederacy had survived, and the battle would ensure that the new nation would not be crushed in one demoralizing blow at the beginning of the war.

### Confederate credibility
The new nation gained instant credibility both at home and abroad. Nevertheless, the inability of the secessionists to force the Union to concede defeat after the first battle, or to mount an effective

military pursuit of the broken Union army, foretold the long and grinding nature of the larger conflict.
Both armies needed time to recover, and the Union would redouble its efforts in the wake of its crushing defeat. Meanwhile, the Confederacy would become rather complacent and too easily saw the battle as a vindication of its belief that the average white Southerner was more warriorlike than any money-grubbing Yankee.

### AFTER

Defeat chastened the North, while the Confederates anticipated that further successes would soon follow—a dangerous assumption, as it turned out.

#### NORTHERN PLANS
Northerners had expected a swift win, and they found themselves rudely disabused of the idea that their **moral superiority** would lead to an easy victory. Many recognized the necessity of **improved discipline** and organization.

#### A WASTED WINTER
While the North began to mobilize its substantial material resources, the Confederacy rested on its laurels. This nearly led to the disastrous defeats in the spring of 1862 with Johnston's early setbacks in the **Peninsula Campaign 116–17 »**, and much of Tennessee lost.

**GENERAL JOSEPH E. JOHNSTON**

## OBSERVATION BALLOONS

The Union Army's Balloon Corps was formed in the summer of 1861 at the request of Lincoln who, after a demonstration by aeronaut Thaddeus S. C. Lowe, hoped to be able to use balloons both to conduct surveillance and to communicate with the commanders on the battlefield. The technology was used by McClellan during the Peninsula Campaign for observations and mapping, where balloons were connected to a military telegraph.

# First Encounter

**Union and Confederate forces met for the first time at Bull Run. With local Washingtonians watching from a nearby hill, the untested armies fought chaotically. Toward the end of the day, the Confederates, fresh with reinforcements, gained the advantage and routed the Union lines. As they scattered, frantically retreating Northern soldiers were impeded by onlookers, adding to their sense of humiliation.**

"The political hostilities of a generation were now face to face with weapons instead of words. Defeat to either side would be a deep mortification, but defeat to the South must turn its claim of independence into an empty vaunt ...

SUNDAY, July 21st, bearing the fate of the new-born Confederacy, broke brightly over the fields and woods that held the hostile forces ... We found the commanders resolutely stemming the further flight of the routed forces, but vainly endeavoring to restore order, and our own efforts were as futile. Every segment of line we succeeded in forming was again dissolved while another was being formed; more than two thousand men were shouting ... their voices mingling with the noise of the shells hurtling through the trees overhead, and all word of command drowned in the confusion and uproar."

GENERAL P. G. T. BEAUREGARD, FROM *BATTLES AND LEADERS OF THE CIVIL WAR*, 1887

"A perfect hail storm of bullets, round shot and shell was poured upon us, tearing through our ranks and scattering death and confusion everywhere ... As I emerged from the woods I saw a bomb shell strike a man in the breast and literally tear him to pieces ... As we had nothing but infantry to fight against their batteries, the command was given to retreat ...

As we gained the cover of the woods the stampede became even more frightful, for the baggage wagons and ambulances became entangled with the artillery and rendered the scene even more dreadful than the battle, while the plunging of the horses broke the lines of our infantry, and prevented any successful formation ... As we neared the bridge the rebels opened a very destructive fire upon us, mowing down our men like grass, and caused even greater confusion than before ..."

CORPORAL SAMUEL J. ENGLISH, 2ND RHODE ISLAND VOLUNTEERS, FROM *ALL FOR THE UNION: THE CIVIL WAR DIARY AND LETTERS OF ELISHA HUNT RHODES*, 1995

**The melee at the First Battle of Bull Run**
A contemporary print shows brightly clad Zouaves clashing with rebel Black Horse cavalry. The battle was witnessed by several members of Congress who later complained about poor Union generalship.

**BEFORE**

During the War with Mexico, the American military attached civilian volunteer units to a core of permanent army professionals.

**PERMANENT FORCE**
Zachary Taylor commanded an army in northern Mexico in 1846 composed of regulars, while Winfield Scott relied on a permanent veteran core in the force he used to conquer Mexico City.

# 165

**The number of steps per minute soldiers would march at "double quick time," the swiftest pace used by American infantry tactics.**

For the North, the 16,000-man U.S. Army of 1860 could not serve as the bedrock of a new field army, because the force still needed to guard the frontier. About one-quarter of its officer strength resigned and traveled South. **The Confederacy, in contrast, had to build a new army from scratch ≪ 58–59**.

**MEXICAN TRAINING GROUND**
While Scott was now too old to take the field, many Civil War commanders (including Grant and Lee) had **earned valuable combat experience** during the War with Mexico.

# Organizing for the Fight

**After Bull Run, both the Union and the Confederacy realized that the war would not end in one single climactic battle. As they mobilized, both struggled with problems of scale and shortages of trained personnel. McClellan's talents as a trainer helped stamp his personality on the Army of the Potomac.**

After Bull Run, Union forces had to face the deficiencies of their organization. General James B. Ricketts argued that at Bull Run, "The men were of as good material as any in the world, and they fought well until they became confused on account of their officers not knowing what to do." Perceptions of officer incompetence led to officer examination boards for weeding out the worst leaders, and by March 1862 the boards had expelled 310 officers from the Army.

While the Confederate armies also used the winter after Bull Run to cull weak officers, and train and organize others, overly romantic views of warfare persisted. Shortly after the battle, the Richmond *Examiner* declared that "Ohio and Pennsylvania ought to feel ... the terrors which agitate the cowardly and guilty when retributive vengeance is at hand ... In four weeks our generals should be levying contributions in money and property from their own towns and villages."

Unfortunately for the Confederacy, overheated rhetoric could not by itself produce armies capable of offensive operations in the North. The South should have used the winter to mobilize its national resources through measures such as conscription, but instead waited until the spring, when Confederate fortunes began to slide.

In the North, meanwhile, the veteran, 75-year-old General in Chief Winfield Scott, before his retirement in November 1861, had helped formulate a war strategy, dubbed the Anaconda Plan, that included a naval blockade and the capture of the Mississippi River. This would result in signficant Federal victories during the spring of 1862, when the port of New Orleans and much of Tennessee fell to the Union.

## Training programs
In all theaters of the war and on both sides, soldiers drilled and organized, with varying degrees of effectiveness. In the primary Federal army in the Eastern Theater, General George B.

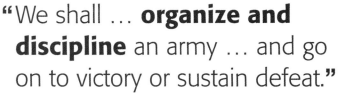

"We shall ... **organize and discipline** an army ... and go on to victory or sustain defeat."

DIARY ENTRY OF JOSIAH MARSHALL FAVILL, 71ST NEW YORK, AFTER BULL RUN

**Cannon squad during drill**
Aiming accurately, and rapidly firing and reloading artillery weapons demanded a high standard of teamwork from the crew, all the more so in difficult battle conditions under enemy fire.

# SCOTT'S GREAT SNAKE.

Winfield Scott's retirement in late 1861 helped trigger unprecedented changes in the size and scale of American warfare—and a new man eager to take his place.

## FLAWED SUCCESSOR

The **new general-in-chief was George B. McClellan**, who had been unashamedly scheming to replace his elderly but still clear-minded predecessor. McClellan would prove to be a **flawed choice for the command**, combining a deficit in moral courage with arrogance. Yet he remained a talented organizer, and his background in railroad management **66–67 ≫** matched his talent for **logistical organization**. His strategic concept for besieging the Confederate army was also fundamentally sound, even if he failed to execute it properly.

## GIANT ARMIES

Scott's retirement pointed the way forward to **armies of unparalleled size** that would now wage war across the continent. Future battles would be giant confrontations where, for example, a total of more than 113,000 men clashed at Antietam **132–33 ≫** and more than 111,000 at Gettysburg **180–83 ≫**.

**Winfield Scott's "Anaconda Plan"**
Scott advocated winning the war by a gradual strategy, likened to the crushing attack of a snake, based on blockading the South's ports and then cutting it in two with offensives up and down the Mississippi River.

McClellan put his army through a reasonably coherent training program; he also benefited from the North's relative abundance of equipment. Despite his hesitancy in committing troops in battle, McClellan had a real talent for organizing an army. He also played a major role in choosing the senior leaders of his force. The officers he selected for command would remain influential long after his departure. While the western Federal armies did not have the same spit and polish as McClellan's eastern showpiece, they had better organization and greater resources than their Confederate opponents.

The Confederate army facing McClellan did not receive the same systematic training, but it did benefit from a large number of Virginia Military Institute graduates who supplemented the cadre of regular officers. What later became the Army of Northern Virginia also had a disproportionate share of

**Union powder flask**
Older flintlock weapons primed by loose powder were still used in the early part of the Civil War.

officers from West Point Military Academy compared to the western Confederate armies.

For Civil War armies, training centered on close order drill, which provided the methods they used to move from one position to another on the battlefield. The intensely regimented system of drill evolutions allowed units to maintain their organization and coordinate the firing of their weapons. Unfortunately, officers received little formal instruction in how to use terrain or what sorts of movements were most advantageous in which circumstances. Even so, rudimentary training through parade-ground drill was better than no training at all, and McClellan's program also included some target practice, mock battles, and training marches.

### Mixed results

The Union Army of the Potomac's mixed performance on the battlefield proved that excellence on the parade ground did not necessarily translate into victory. Indeed, McClellan's

cautious temperament had a stronger influence on the Army of the Potomac's command culture than did his training program. As Lieutenant Colonel Alexander S. Webb put it after the Battle of Chancellorsville, his hesitancy helped to create an army in which most of the leaders were "cautious, stupid and without any dash." They "delay 20,000 men ... in order to skirmish with 20 or 30 cav[alr]y and one piece of art[iller]y.

They all think the enemy wiser and braver and quicker than themselves and such men should not command."

Webb would not have attributed this failing to McClellan's temperament, but the Army of the Potomac did have an overly defensive mindset, which would remain a problem even after General Ulysses S. Grant took over command during the Overland Campaign in summer 1864.

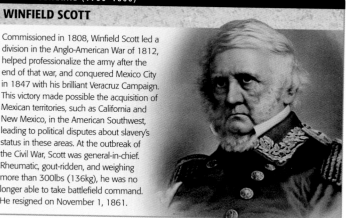

**UNION GENERAL (1786–1866)**

## WINFIELD SCOTT

Commissioned in 1808, Winfield Scott led a division in the Anglo-American War of 1812, helped professionalize the army after the end of that war, and conquered Mexico City in 1847 with his brilliant Veracruz Campaign. This victory made possible the acquisition of Mexican territories, such as California and New Mexico, in the American Southwest, leading to political disputes about slavery's status in these areas. At the outbreak of the Civil War, Scott was general-in-chief. Rheumatic, gout-ridden, and weighing more than 300lbs (136kg), he was no longer able to take battlefield command. He resigned on November 1, 1861.

**Young Napoleon**
Arrogant and ambitious, McClellan was often called the "Young Napoleon." He was also an authority on cavalry tactics, inventing a saddle adopted by the army in 1859.

**UNION GENERAL-IN-CHIEF** Born 1826 Died 1885

# George B. McClellan

> "I believe that [Lincoln] liked me personally, and … he was always **much influenced by me**."

McCLELLAN RECALLING HIS RELATIONSHIP WITH PRESIDENT LINCOLN

George Brinton McClellan served as the talented, if mercurial, father of the Army of the Potomac. He also became the political standard bearer for the significant minority of Northerners who believed in the Union, but deemed it unproductive and unconstitutional to make emancipation a war goal.

Intelligent and precocious, McClellan completed his military training at West Point in 1846 at the age of 19. He came second out of a class of 59 graduates, and his peers included Thomas "Stonewall" Jackson, George Pickett, and his successor at the head of the Army of the Potomac, Ambrose Burnside. The War with Mexico began the year he graduated, and McClellan served as an engineer officer in General Winfield Scott's Veracruz campaign. He compiled an excellent combat record, winning two brevet (acting) promotions.

After the War with Mexico ended, McClellan was sent by Secretary of War Jefferson Davis to observe the Crimean War. He left the Army in 1857 and became head of the Illinois Central Railroad, remaining a railroad man until the outbreak of the Civil War, when he returned to the Army as commander of the Ohio Volunteers. McClellan had voted for Stephen Douglas in the 1860 election, and while he had no sympathies for anti-slavery causes, like Douglas, he remained a strong Union man.

### General-in-chief

Shortly before the humiliating Union defeat at First Bull Run, McClellan's forces had won a series of notable victories in western Virginia. Following these successes, he took command of the Army of the Potomac, then became the Union Army's general-in-chief on Scott's retirement in 1861.

McClellan's organizational brilliance did much to restore confidence to the Union war effort, and most importantly, to Irvin McDowell's volunteers, who had just been disgraced at Bull Run. A chastened North, which had now seen firsthand the potential downsides of precipitate military action, was more than willing to give McClellan ample time to train and prepare his army.

### Presidential protection

McClellan did not have unlimited time, and his imperious manner toward civilian leaders, including his commander-in-chief, won him few friends. Lincoln did his best both to shield his top general from political pressures and to educate him in political realities, but McClellan's egotism made him a poor student. Republican leaders became increasingly frustrated with

**Music cover dedicated to McClellan**
This patriotic song *Hail! Glorious Banner of Our Land*, published in 1861, is dedicated to Major General George B. McClellan. In his early career McClellan was a popular figure with the public.

### McClellan's revolver

This .44 caliber Colt Dragoon was carried by McClellan during the Civil War. This popular model was first issued to troops after the War with Mexico in 1848.

the outspoken Democrat and opponent of emancipation, who, as yet, had won no significant victories on the battlefield to erase the shameful memory of Bull Run. Furthermore, McClellan slavery would make the Civil War a cruel revolutionary struggle, with reunion impossible, and the Union Army demoralized. As he would later lecture his commander-in-chief, "Military power should not be allowed to interfere with the relations of servitude ... A system of policy thus constitutional and conservative, and pervaded by the influences of Christianity and freedom, would receive the support of almost all truly loyal men, would deeply impress the rebel masses and all foreign nations,

## "I begin to feel as if he would never get ready to fight!"

PRESIDENT LINCOLN TO HIS SECRETARY, WILLIAM O. STODDARD

surrounded himself with officers of a similar political and military persuasion. These staunch Union men were, nevertheless, opposed to making emancipation a primary war goal, and were extremely cautious in their conduct of military affairs. Because of the Union Army's respect for seniority, these officers remained influential in the Army of the Potomac long after McClellan was relieved of command.

In McClellan's view, "radical" war goals that hoped to transform Southern society through the destruction of

and it might be humbly hoped that it would commend itself to the favor of the Almighty." McClellan's vision of civil and military policy was defensible, but his own failures as a battlefield general would discredit it.

### The Peninsula Campaign

In March 1862, McClellan launched a campaign against the Confederate capital of Richmond. After much delay, his army finally sailed down to the peninsula southeast of the city. His campaign plan had much merit, but he moved so cautiously that he gave the Confederates time to ready their forces. Even so, he probably would have eventually forced the Confederate commander, Joseph Johnston, into a siege of Richmond that would have spelled doom for the Confederacy, if it had not been for the wounding of Johnston at Seven Pines on May 31.

Robert E. Lee took command of what would become the Army of Northern Virginia. He launched a series of audacious attacks on

### McClellan's chess set

McClellan is said to have looked at war like a game of chess in which he maneuvered his men into strong tactical positions. He, however, lacked the aggressive instincts of a Lee or a Grant.

McClellan between June 25 and July 1, in what became known as the Seven Days Battles. McClellan's men fought well, and the Confederates suffered grievous casualties, but Lee's aggressiveness unnerved McClellan's already shaky morale. Convinced that he faced an army larger than his own, McClellan retreated to Harrison's Landing on the James River, shattering his remaining credibility.

### Lincoln's frustration

Frustrated with McClellan, Lincoln handed the primary eastern field command to General John Pope, who was promptly crushed by Lee

### Contemporary battle map of Antietam

Antietam was the first battle of the Civil War fought on Northern soil, and despite having so many advantages McClellan still failed to destroy Lee's army.

at Second Bull Run. Lincoln had no choice but to turn to McClellan to rally the Union Army against a Confederate invasion of Maryland. But despite his early capture of Lee's campaign plan and a numerical superiority of around two to one, McClellan failed to destroy Lee's army at the Battle of Antietam (Sharpsburg) on September 17, 1862. However, he did force Lee to retreat back to Virginia.

Lincoln used the "victory" at Antietam to issue the Preliminary Emancipation Proclamation and, finally losing patience with McClellan's lethargic military movements, relieved him of his post on November 5. The general then ran for president on the Democratic ticket in 1864, attempting to balance his Unionist convictions with the radical peace platform of some Northern Democrats. Lincoln won an emphatic victory, and McClellan finally departed the scene.

**McCLELLAN AND RUNNING MATE IN THE 1864 ELECTION, GEORGE H. PENDLETON**

# The Sinews of War

**Both the Union and the Confederacy had to build the bureaucratic and physical infrastructure necessary for waging a large industrial war in North America. Both proved successful, largely due to the work of two veterans of the prewar U.S. Army, Montgomery Meigs for the North and Josiah Gorgas for the South.**

**Montgomery Cunningham Meigs**
Southern-born Meigs had served in the U.S. Army since 1836. Arlington National Cemetery, established after the Civil War, was his brainchild.

## ‹‹ BEFORE

**Thanks to reforms overseen by Senator John C. Calhoun—President James Monroe's secretary of war from 1817 to 1825 ‹‹ 20–21—the prewar U.S. Army was the most sophisticated bureaucratic organization in mid-19th-century America.**

**READY FOR SMALL-SCALE WAR**
Despite a primitive transportation infrastructure and a penny-pinching Congress, the **prewar army supplied and equipped troops** across a continent-wide frontier. Arms were stockpiled in **federal and state arsenals**, such as **Harpers Ferry ‹‹ 34–35**. Shortages of weapons occurred on both sides at the start of the Civil War because stocks were never intended to supply such huge numbers of soldiers.

When the war began, the North had clear economic and industrial advantages over the South. Yet in spite—or perhaps because—of this, the Union had at first an astonishing capacity for undermining its position through self-inflicted mistakes. Alongside this, the North also faced the logistical difficulties of supplying armies of invasion in hostile territory.

### The North's faltering start
One of the North's first challenges to efficient mobilization was Lincoln's choice of secretary of war—Simon Cameron, a veteran of the seedy side of prewar politics. Appointed for political reasons, Cameron presided over a War Department rife with corruption and profiteering. In the words of a Congressional investigating committee, Cameron's poor judgment led to "a system of public policy [that] must lead inevitably to personal favoritism at the public expense, the corruption of public morals, and a ruinous profligacy in the expenditure of public treasure." Things improved after January 1862, when

Lincoln replaced Cameron with former Attorney General Edwin Stanton, who brought much needed energy, efficiency, and honesty to the War Department.

Screws for removing rounds jammed in rifle barrels

Cup to create hollow base in bullet

Brass grip

Clamp to hold mold closed

Wrench for adjusting percussion caps

Rifle-cleaning tool

**Bullet mold and rifleman's tools**
When ammunition ran out, blacksmiths or the soldiers themselves had to melt lead to make bullets on the spot, often collecting used rounds from the battlefield.

> " Upon the … performance of the duties of **Quartermaster**, an army depends for its **ability to move**."
>
> MONTGOMERY MEIGS, ANNUAL REPORT TO THE SECRETARY OF WAR, 1862

Montgomery Meigs, the other major figure in managing the North's resources, was a U.S. Army officer who became head of the Quartermaster Bureau in May 1861, after his predecessor, Joseph E. Johnston, left to join the Confederacy. Meigs's bureau supplied the armies with material, other than weapons and food, which included the infrastructure necessary to transport these supplies. During the course of the war, Meigs oversaw an expenditure of $1.5 billion, nearly half the Union's wartime appropriations.

### Supplying the South
While the Confederacy did not face the challenges associated with supplying armies of invasion across vast distances, it began the conflict with little of the industrial capacity needed for waging war. When Josiah Gorgas—another prewar U.S. Army officer and a veteran of the War with Mexico—became head of the crucial Ordnance Bureau, he could count only on the Tredegar Iron Works in Richmond, Virginia, to produce heavy ordnance. There were two small arsenals at Richmond and Fayetteville, North Carolina, for the production of small arms.

With astonishing ingenuity, Gorgas found ways around these difficulties, including blockade running, domestic scavenging, and simple improvisation. During the war's first year, while the Union blockade on the South remained

**Josiah Gorgas, a native of Pennsylvania, was not a Southerner, but he had married the daughter of a former governor of Alabama. These connections helped lead him to choose the Confederacy.**

relatively porous, he purchased much of the new nation's needs in Europe. At home, in his search for the raw materials for ordnance production, Gorgas tapped resources as diverse as limestone caves in the Appalachians, chamberpots, stills, church bells, and weapons discarded on the battlefield. The men responsible for feeding and

**Warfare by rail**
The "General Haupt" was a specially built wood-burning military locomotive. It was named after Herman Haupt, the engineer who headed the Union's bureau for constructing and running military railroads.

clothing the Southern armies had far less success. Quartermaster General Abraham Myers—eventually relieved in August 1863—and Commissary General Lucius B. Northrop never really found ways to surmount the Confederacy's basic disadvantages, which included its limited rail network.

## The gulf widens

Over the course of the war, the Union gained strength as its supply systems became more efficient and it began to incorporate technological innovations, such as the repeating rifle. In contrast, the Confederacy's supply situation worsened as it lost territory and its population became further exhausted. An increasingly effective Union naval blockade put an end to coastal shipping, which placed even more pressure on the South's overstretched ground transportation. The blockade also prevented the Confederacy from importing material from Europe. Not being able to buy equipment from

### West Point gun foundry
Artist John Ferguson Weir, son of a professor of drawing at West Point Military Academy, started work on this painting in 1864. It depicts the West Point Iron and Cannon Foundry at Cold Spring, New York.

abroad also affected the railroad network, because repairs required machinery that the Confederacy did not possess.

Yet, despite the growing industrial inequality between the two sides, in the final analysis the Confederacy lost the war because of its inability to defeat Union armies on the battlefield. Poorly equipped though the Confederate soldier was in comparison to his Union counterpart, he usually had enough arms and equipment to fight. As late as the Appomattox campaign in 1865, when Lee's troops went hungry at Amelia Court House, it was largely due to the misdirection of some of their rations. Poor Confederate staffwork, not scarcity, had caused the supply problem.

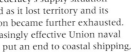

### Tredegar Iron Works
One of the largest foundries in America, Tredegar was a key asset for the Confederacy. It is believed to have produced about half of the artillery pieces manufactured for the South during the war.

**AFTER** »

As the years passed, the Union's superiority became increasingly apparent in developments such as the use of new weapons and transportation systems.

**FASTER FIREPOWER**
A key innovation was to arm Union cavalrymen with **breech-loading repeating rifles** that used metallic cartridges. The most famous of these was the **Spencer carbine 149–49 »**. Previous firearms required a complicated loading process involving a paper cartridge, ramrod, and percussion cap. With the new firearms, a soldier simply pulled a lever to get rid of the spent cartridge, allowing him to fire multiple shots.

**RAPID REPAIR**
Transportation innovations included **rapid railroad repair and protection** inside Union territory, demonstrated by Sherman's use of a railroad for resupply during the Atlanta campaign **292–93 »**. Meigs also organized seaborne resupply for Sherman after his March to the Sea **296–97 »**.

**‹‹ BEFORE**

While Missouri had helped inflame sectional tensions before the war, the state of Kentucky had been a source of moderation and compromise.

**CLAY THE COMPROMISER**

Kentucky produced the greatest prewar compromiser, **Senator Henry Clay**, while Senator John J. Crittenden from the same state tried to broker another compromise in 1861. If Clay had won the presidency in 1844 he would have rejected the annexation of Texas and **probably prevented the War with Mexico**. Without the problem over slavery in the new territories **‹‹ 22–23**, the Civil War might well have been averted.

**MISSOURI AND "BLEEDING KANSAS"**

Not only had Missouri been the **center of the controversy over slavery** that led to the Missouri Compromise of 1820, pro-slavery settlers there had caused much sectional violence in the 1850s across the border in "Bleeding Kansas" **‹‹ 30–31**, where they clashed with Free-Soilers—some of whom had emigrated from New England. During the Civil War, Free-Soil Kansans served in Missouri, and Missouri guerrillas engaged in cross-border raids.

**NEW ENGLAND EMIGRANT AID CO. UP ONE FLIGHT.**

**AID COMPANY SIGN FOR NEW ENGLANDERS**

# Missouri and Kentucky

**While Missouri remained in the Union, it was beset by the war's worst violence on both sides. The more strategically important state of Kentucky tried to maintain a neutral stance early on, but eventually fell into the Union camp due to Confederate missteps and Lincoln's political dexterity.**

Missouri was no stranger to sectional violence. The state's role in the problems of "Bleeding Kansas" across the border in the 1850s, where its pro-slavery settlers battled Free-Soilers, had become a prologue to the Civil War. Nevertheless, Union sentiment in the territory had great strength, and nearly three-quarters of the white Missourians who served as Civil War soldiers fought for the Union.

Unfortunately for Missouri, a complex tangle of personalities and politics stirred up a hornet's nest. The state's governor, Claiborne F. Jackson, was a staunch secessionist and did everything in his power to deliver the state for the Confederacy. Opposing him were Francis P. Blair, Jr., of the politically important Blair family, and Captain Nathaniel Lyon, U.S. Army, who commanded the U.S. arsenal at St. Louis. Lyon was vigorous and aggressive, warning Jackson, "Rather than concede to the State of Missouri … the right to dictate to my Government … I would see … every man, woman, and child in the State, dead and buried." Anti-immigrant

**Crittenden of Kentucky**

Senator John Crittenden expended huge efforts in trying to avert war by a compromise over the extension of slave states—but he did help to prevent his own state from seceding.

**Anger in St. Louis**

Riots broke out in St. Louis after Captain Lyon took the secessionist Fort Jackson. Southern sympathizers targeted Lyon's hurriedly recruited German militia army for their anti-slavery sentiments.

feeling among some Missourians worsened matters, as German settlers formed the bedrock of Republican and Unionist support in St. Louis.

Lyon effectively ended Jackson's schemes to support secession and chose to go on the offensive in May 1861 by capturing a secessionist militia camp called Fort Jackson near St. Louis. The militiamen surrendered peacefully, but violence broke out afterwards in the city itself, and it quickly took on ethnic overtones. Lyon's measures outraged some moderate Unionists and pushed them into the secessionist camp. While Lyon swiftly crushed Jackson and his allies in the state legislature, small groups of Confederate guerrillas, or "bushwhackers," would plague the state for the rest of the war.

Lyon, who was promoted to general in July 1861, was killed during the Confederate victory at the Battle of Wilson's Creek the

**Anti-Confederate satire**
The Union blasts away at the monster of secession in a cartoon of 1861. Demons represent secessionist states—divided Kentucky is depicted as a creature with two torsos just above the monster's head.

### AFTER

**Kentucky's Unionism was a strategic blow to the Confederacy, but its Unionists became increasingly unhappy with the Federal war effort.**

#### FORTS HENRY AND DONELSON
The Tennessee and Cumberland rivers provided convenient lines of advance for Federal forces. On February 6, 1862, Ulysses S. Grant led the **capture of Fort Henry** and received the **surrender of Fort Donelson 104–05 >>** on February 16. These captures were the **first substantial Union military successes** of the war.

#### KENTUCKY'S DISSATISFACTION
Despite their importance to the early Union war effort, many Kentuckians became ever more disenchanted with the Lincoln administration as it moved in an increasingly anti-slavery direction. In the 1864 election **236–37 >>**, McClellan received **61,000 civilian votes** from Kentucky, **compared to 26,000 for Lincoln**, the state's native son.

#### QUANTRILL'S RAIDS
William Quantrill was the **most controversial** of the guerrilla "bushwhackers" who operated in Missouri and Kansas during the war. His exploits included attacks on Independence, Missouri, and Lawrence, Kansas **224–25 >>**.

## "This means war … One of my officers will call for you and conduct you out of my lines."

CAPTAIN LYON TO GOVERNOR JACKSON, JUNE 12, 1861

following month, and meaningful Southern defiance would be crushed at Pea Ridge in March 1862. This made the resistance of Confederate guerrillas strategically insignificant, but it was cold comfort for the civilians who had to cope with the chaos of a fierce and brutal civil war, triggered in part by overly aggressive reactions by Missouri's Union leaders in 1861.

### The Kentucky divide
Kentucky was in many ways the quintessential border state. Birthplace of both Lincoln and Davis, its northern border on the Ohio River had always been a symbolic and powerful dividing line between the Free-Soil North and the slaveholding South. In Harriet Beecher Stowe's famous *Uncle Tom's Cabin*, one character makes a daring escape to freedom with her son across the Ohio River in order to save him from an unscrupulous slave-trader. Unionist sympathies were qualified, however. Only 1,364 Kentuckians voted for Lincoln in the election of 1860, while 91,000 chose the conservative Unionists, Douglas and Bell.

The Ohio River also formed a useful natural military boundary for the newly formed Confederacy. If Kentucky did not ally itself with the Confederacy, Tennessee would be vulnerable to Federal invasion, because both the

Tennessee and Cumberland rivers provided avenues of invasion into central Tennessee. Both ran north to south in the border area, and thus could serve as convenient supply routes for Federal armies attempting to penetrate the Confederate border, as Grant did in the campaign of forts Henry and Donelson in February 1862.

Kentucky's Northern location tied it economically to the Union, and many Kentuckians lived in Northern states, including 100,000 in Missouri, 60,000 in Illinois, 68,000 in Indiana, 15,000 in Ohio, and 13,000 in Iowa. While slavery played an important role in Kentucky's economy, as in Unionist

> **The ferocious guerrilla war in Missouri produced the notorious James brothers (Jesse and Frank), Confederate "bushwhackers" from Clay County.**

Maryland, the state had little enthusiasm for the "King Cotton" nationalism of the Lower South. After all, its most famous son, Senator Henry Clay, was the man who saved the Union three times with compromises in 1820, 1833, and 1850.

On an individual level, Kentuckians would remain profoundly divided until the end of the war. At least two-fifths of Kentuckian soldiers fought for the Confederacy, including four brothers of Lincoln's own Kentucky-born wife.

Four grandsons of Lincoln's old political hero, Henry Clay, fought for the South, another three for the Union. Political compromiser Senator Crittenden saw one son become a Union general and another a Confederate general.

### Strategic state
With its people so finely divided, Kentucky tried to remain neutral after the attack on Fort Sumter. But this was an inherently untenable position, and by September 1861 it had collapsed. The governor, Beriah Magoffin, sympathized with the Confederacy but was only willing to go as far as a secret agreement that permitted its recruiters to enter the territory.

Unionist and pro-Confederate Kentuckians began to arm themselves during the state's tense period of

neutrality. Lincoln, who knew this region well, bided his time, initially humoring his home state's desire to stay out of the war, and even allowing the Confederacy to purchase supplies there. In Congressional and legislative elections that summer, Unionists scored crushing victories, and Kentucky finally declared itself for the Union after Confederate forces crossed the border from Tennessee and entered Columbus, Kentucky, on September 3, 1861.

#### Death of a general
Missouri's Nathaniel Lyon was a bold and aggressive political leader, and he conducted his final battle, at Wilson's Creek in August 1861, in the same manner. He was the first Union general to be killed in combat.

# Blockading the South

**The Union government considered the naval blockade of the Southern coastline to be an important part of the strategy to defeat the Confederacy, and it became increasingly effective over the course of the war. However, while it undoubtedly weakened the South, the blockade could not by itself end the war.**

The blockade played an important part in Union general-in-chief Winfield Scott's Anaconda Plan. Scott hoped to isolate and divide the Confederacy by blockading its ports and reestablishing Federal control over the Mississippi River. He hoped this strategy would bring the South back into the Union, using gradual pressure but avoiding great bloodshed. Although this approach was superseded by events, increasing the effectiveness of the blockade remained an important Union objective for the rest of the war.

### Naval obstacles

A blockade was likely to harm the Confederate war effort by restricting the flow of imported military supplies. But it also presented two huge challenges: the sheer length of the Southern coastline, on the one hand, and the small size of the Union navy, on the other. The new nation in the South had 3,549 miles (5,712km) of coastline, including 180 inlets, and when President Lincoln ordered the blockade to begin just after the fall of Fort Sumter, the Union navy had only 14 ships available.

⟨⟨ **B E F O R E**

**The U.S. navy had greater experience in trying to elude blockades than in attempting to enforce them.**

**PREVIOUS BLOCKADES**
During the War with Mexico, the United States had **enforced a blockade** against Mexico, but the last two wars with Britain—the American Revolution and the Anglo-American War of 1812—had seen the United States on the receiving end of actions by a superior naval power trying to enforce restrictions on commerce.

**ANGLO-AMERICAN WAR OF 1812**
Most **diplomatic tensions** between America and Europe during the Napoleonic Wars involved the question of how the United States could trade with countries that were at war with one another. The issues that led to the War of 1812 were caused, in large part, by British attempts to enforce their blockade of French-controlled Europe. In 1812, despite various successes by individual U.S. navy ships, **Britain brought American trade to a standstill** and almost bankrupted the country.

**The Union navy belittled**
Two Union vessels—essentially washtubs—try to block a Confederate steamer's path in this cartoon, mocking the government's attempt to update the Union fleet.

At the start of the Civil War, while the blockade did little to stop ships engaged in blockade-running—an activity that became a major industry during the war—it did help to isolate the South diplomatically. The British government ultimately declared itself neutral, but it also respected the Union's right to enforce a blockade in wartime. This acknowledgment of the Union navy's right to inspect shipping entering

**Impact on exports**
A Union man-of-war (far right) pursues a Confederate blockade-runner (right). Built for speed, the blockade-runners could outsail the larger Union ships, but their small holds limited their carrying capacity and Southern cotton exports fell markedly.

Confederate ports and seize contraband property became significant as the Union navy increased in size, thus becoming more and more able to enforce the blockade. As the world's preeminent naval power, and one that wished to set legal precedents for its own imposition of blockades in future wars as in the past, the British government had good reason to recognize the legality of

this Union war measure, and little reason to risk a war with Lincoln's government over this issue.

In order to enforce this blockade, the Union rapidly expanded its navy. By the end of the war, the Department of the Navy under Gideon Welles's leadership had purchased some 418 additional ships and built another 208. Most were in the service of tightening

**1,149** The number of ships that were captured by the Union navy while attempting to run the North's blockade of the South.

the blockade. The Union navy also increased in numbers from about 1,500 officers and men to 58,000. Although the maritime force very much remained the junior service to the

**Union Flag Officer Samuel du Pont**
Du Pont scored an important victory in November 1861 by capturing Port Royal, South Carolina, which was the best natural harbor on the south Atlantic coast and provided an important base for Union blockaders.

capture of the South's ports could provide a foolproof way of restricting Confederate shipping. Swift steamers traveling at night often eluded Union patrol ships, and even in 1865, when the siege was at its tightest, about half of all Confederate blockade-runners completed their voyages.

**Taking the ports**
Joint army-navy operations to close down various Confederate ports became an important part of the war effort, and the first Federal military successes post-Bull Run involved the capture of ports in North Carolina and South Carolina. Not only did these amphibious operations close coastal entry points into the Confederacy, but they also

provided bases at which Union ships could fuel and draw supplies near their assigned duty stations, instead of making the long journey to their posts from their Northern bases. The Union navy would capture Wilmington, North Carolina—the last Confederate port—in January 1865.

The effectiveness of the blockade remains uncertain. Some historians have argued that it "won" the war for the Union, while others see its effects as negligible. The answer probably lies somewhere in between.

By itself, the Union blockade could not have ensured a Federal victory, but the siege played an important role in the eventual exhaustion of Southern resources. Its increasing effectiveness prevented the Confederacy from easily importing military supplies (including those related to railroads), and the closing of coastal shipping in the Southern territories put extra strain on the under-repaired railroad network.

hugely expanded Union army, this still represented an unprecedented increase in U.S. naval power.

While the increase in ships clearly tightened the blockade, only the

**UNION POLITICIAN (1802–78)**

## GIDEON WELLES

An important prewar newspaper editor and politician in Connecticut, Welles worked in the Navy Department during the War with Mexico. He developed anti-slavery views and opposed the Compromise of 1850's controversial Fugitive Slave Law. He joined the Republican Party after the passage of the Kansas-Nebraska Act in 1854.

As navy secretary during the Civil War, he and his chief deputy, Gustavus Vasa Fox, proved to be energetic and effective administrators. Not only did they supervise the rapid expansion of the Union navy, but they also exercised good judgment in selecting senior officers.

# "We propose a powerful movement down the Mississippi to the ocean."

GENERAL WINFIELD SCOTT, IN A LETTER TO GEORGE B. McCLELLAN, MAY 3, 1861

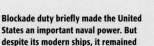

## AFTER

Blockade duty briefly made the United States an important naval power. But despite its modern ships, it remained inferior to Britain's Royal Navy.

### BRITAIN'S SUPERIOR FLEET
The Union navy's **vast expansion increased its fighting power**, but the sheer number of its ships still did not make it a match for the British Royal Navy, accustomed to patrolling the seas of the entire globe. Most Union navy ships were designed for the relatively simple purpose of enforcing the blockade near the Southern coast. They were **only lightly armed**, since their targets, the Confederate blockade-runners, carried few if any weapons.

### POSTWAR DEMOBILIZATION
Before the Civil War, the United States had looked toward its vast land frontier, as opposed to trading overseas. This put limits on how much it was willing to invest in naval power. The need to blockade the Confederacy provided a temporary **surge in the navy's resources**, but after the Civil War the **Union navy was swiftly demobilized**. The United States would not become a major naval power or fight a naval war until the **Spanish-American War** in the last decade of the 19th century.

**YOUNG RECRUITS JOIN THEIR SHIP**
*The USS* Wabash *leaving New York for the Seat of War*, painted by
Edward Moran in 1861, captures the enthusiasm of newly joined up
volunteers at the beginning of the war as they are shipped out to
the waiting *Wabash*. A screw frigate launched in 1855, the *Wabash*
had seen action before the war and was recommissioned at the
outbreak of war to serve as flagship of the Atlantic Blockading
Squadron under Rear Admiral Silas H. Stringham.

# Courting European Allies

**Many Confederates believed that Great Britain would intervene in their favor, but it proved reluctant to risk war with the Union and instead declared its neutrality. The Confederacy was able to acquire important military supplies from Europe, including the infamous ships known as "commerce raiders".**

**British and French involvement**
In this cartoon, Jefferson Davis assails a Union soldier with a club marked "Alabama"—a reference to the Confederate ships being built in England. John Bull, representing Britain, and Napoleon III look on.

According to the Confederates who believed in the power of "King Cotton," the fact that Britain's valuable textile industry depended on Southern cotton meant that Britain would inevitably side with the South. James Hammond, a South Carolinian, famously declared in 1858 that "England would topple headlong and carry the whole civilized world with her, save the South," if it was deprived of cotton supplies for three years. When war broke out in 1861, Confederates thus hoped to exert pressure on Great Britain by refusing to export cotton, believing that the resulting economic pain would force Britain to use the power of the Royal Navy to break the Union blockade.

More perceptive Confederates realized that they should not rely on foreign powers to win their independence. During the war's first year, Lee grumbled about excessive hopes for foreign aid and declared that "we must make up our minds to fight our battles ourselves."

As it turned out, the British had built up large stockpiles of cotton because of bumper crops before the war, and the Confederate self-embargo also led British mill owners to look to alternative sources in Egypt and India. Finally, and most crucially, the British government did not want to risk war and years of poor relations with the United States for the sake of the South's cause, until it could show its independence to be imminent and inevitable.

Britain declared neutrality, granting the Confederacy belligerent status in international law, on May 13, 1861, but this was more of a practical response to the situation than a strong desire to intervene on the side of the South. The South's new status gave Southern agents important benefits, such as the ability to buy arms, and it also legalized Confederate attacks on Union merchant shipping. These attacks would prove devastating to the Union fleet.

### Relations with Britain

Northerners took great offense at the British declaration, but from the European perspective, the Confederacy had obviously created a government that deserved this level of international recognition. The Union declaration of a blockade represented a tacit recognition that the Confederacy was more than just a small band of rebels. France and its emperor, Napoleon III, were more sympathetic to the Southern cause due to its ambitions in Mexico, but it would not act without the British.

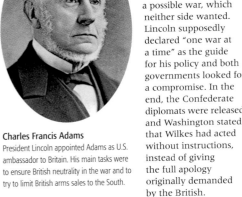

**Charles Francis Adams**
President Lincoln appointed Adams as U.S. ambassador to Britain. His main tasks were to ensure British neutrality in the war and to try to limit British arms sales to the South.

Frictions between the Union government and Britain reached their most dangerous point when Captain Charles Wilkes of the USS *San Jacinto* violated international law by detaining two Confederate diplomats traveling from Cuba on a British vessel, the *Trent*. This provoked wild talk on both sides, along with British preparations for a possible war, which neither side wanted. Lincoln supposedly declared "one war at a time" as the guide for his policy and both governments looked for a compromise. In the end, the Confederate diplomats were released, and Washington stated that Wilkes had acted without instructions, instead of giving the full apology originally demanded by the British.

The other variable inhibiting British recognition was the continued influence of anti-slavery sentiment in Great Britain. While some British aristocrats had a fondness for the Confederacy, Britain was the home of the modern anti-slavery movement, having abolished slavery in all British territories in 1833. As Northern war goals became increasingly friendly toward emancipation, it grew more difficult for the British government to support an administration whose vice president had declared slavery to be its cornerstone. While the British government remained concerned about the high loss of life caused by the war, the long-term result of Lincoln's Emancipation Proclamation was to make British intervention all but impossible, because now the war had become an explicit contest between freedom and slavery.

### Arms supplies to the South

Real tensions would persist, especially with Confederate agents buying ships in Britain, and then arming and

◀◀ **BEFORE**

White Southerners badly misjudged both the significance of cotton to the British economy, and the continuing importance of British anti-slavery.

**SOUTHERN WEALTH AND VULNERABILITY**
Historians have sometimes characterized the antebellum South as a backward slave society, in comparison to the industrializing North. This is not altogether fair. The South did, after all, have a significant role to play in the **industrialization of Great Britain** through the export of cotton to textile manufacturers in northern England. The South also generated more than half of U.S. export earnings before the war **◀◀ 16–17**. Nevertheless, many future Confederates failed to realize that relying too much on the production of a **single cash crop** made them vulnerable to the rise of alternate sources of supply.

**ABOLITIONIST MOVEMENT**
The modern anti-slavery movement had begun among Quakers based in England, and **Britain had abolished slavery** through a program of compensated emancipation in the British West Indies in the 1830s. The Royal Navy also devoted substantial resources to patrol operations off the African coast to **suppress the slave trade**. Confederates underestimated the importance of this anti-slavery legacy in Britain.

> "Davis and other leaders of the South … have **made a nation**."
> W. E. GLADSTONE, BRITISH CHANCELLOR OF THE EXCHEQUER, OCTOBER 1862

**Cotton famine**
The break in the South's cotton exports had a devastating effect on England's mill workers. With no raw fiber to process, their jobs did not exist. Unable to work, they relied on various charities for cheap food.

**When Charles Francis Adams was presented to Queen Victoria after the *Trent* Affair, he sought to defuse tensions by appearing in stockings and lace, as opposed to the customary black republican broadcloth used by most American ministers.**

**Emperor Napoleon III**
Napoleon intended to build up French influence and trade in the New World. Toward this he hoped to make a formal alliance with the Confederacy.

**KEY MOMENT**

## THE TRENT AFFAIR

On November 8, 1861, Union Captain Charles Wilkes, commanding USS *San Jacinto*, boarded the British steamer, *Trent*, traveling from Havana to England, and arrested Confederate envoys James Murray Mason and John Slidell. Many overly enthusiastic Anglophobic Americans declared Captain Wilkes a hero, while the British were outraged by the breach of neutral rights and the insult given to the British flag. The British government even dispatched 8,000 troops to Canada, though in reality the British armed forces were poorly prepared for war.

In the end, cooler heads prevailed on both sides of the Atlantic, and the Union government released the envoys, while avoiding any acknowledgment of guilt.

converting them into commerce raiders—ships that were used to disrupt or destroy the enemy's merchant shipping— in other ports. However, British leaders gradually responded to Northern complaints about this issue, and the adept American minister to London, Charles Francis Adams, ably served the administration's interests. Matters came to a head when the British government finally moved to prevent the Confederacy from acquiring the "Laird Rams," two ironclad warships being built in Liverpool, England, that could have wreaked havoc on the Union blockade patrols. The Union government went as far as to threaten war with Britain over the two ships, and the British relented, buying the ships for their own navy in the fall of 1863.

The South found that if it wished to win its independence, it would have to rely on its own efforts and exertions. It could not hope for the same sort of assistance that the United States had received from France during the American Revolution.

## AFTER

**Lincoln's Preliminary Emancipation Proclamation, issued after the Battle of Antietam, doomed Confederate hopes for international recognition.**

### CONFLICTING BRITISH CONCERNS
In the short term, the war's bloody outcome concerned the British government, which wished to **end the bloodshed in North America for humanitarian reasons**, but in the long term, it would be difficult for any British government to side with slavery against freedom.

### CSS *ALABAMA*
Some tensions between Northerners and Britain would persist until after the war, especially in relation to the destruction of Union merchant shipping by the Confederate commerce raiders that had been built in British shipyards.

Massachusetts senator Charles Sumner famously declared after the war that **Great Britain should compensate the United States** for the damages inflicted by the most famous Confederate commerce raider, CSS *Alabama*, by giving it the territory of Canada. In the end, Britain paid compensation instead.

Built in Britain and commissioned in 1862 after being armed and fitted out in Portugal's Azores Islands, **the *Alabama* never visited any Confederate ports in its two-year career**. It raided Union shipping around the world, capturing or destroying 65 Union vessels without loss of life on either side. The ship was brought to battle off Cherbourg, France, in 1864, and **sunk by USS *Kearsarge* 284–85 >>**.

# 3

# CLASH OF ARMIES

## 1862

In Virginia, the Confederates resisted a campaign against their capital, Richmond, and took the offensive themselves, briefly invading Maryland. In the Western Theater, they suffered a series of disasters, from the loss of New Orleans to a failed invasion of Kentucky.

« **Battle of Williamsburg**
One of a set of 36 Civil War prints made nearly 30 years after the war, this scene shows fighting at the Battle of Williamsburg. Here, on May 5, 1862 a large army under Union general George B. McClellan met the retreating army of General Joseph E. Johnston in a rearguard action, which the Union lost.

# CLASH OF ARMIES

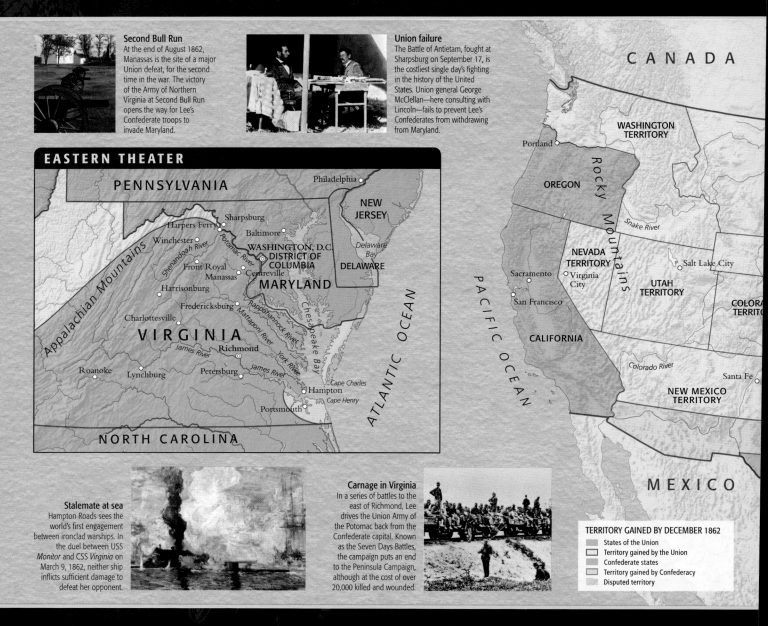

**Second Bull Run**
At the end of August 1862, Manassas is the site of a major Union defeat, for the second time in the war. The victory of the Army of Northern Virginia at Second Bull Run opens the way for Lee's Confederate troops to invade Maryland.

**Union failure**
The Battle of Antietam, fought at Sharpsburg on September 17, is the costliest single day's fighting in the history of the United States. Union general George McClellan—here consulting with Lincoln—fails to prevent Lee's Confederates from withdrawing from Maryland.

## EASTERN THEATER

CANADA

WASHINGTON TERRITORY

Portland

OREGON

Rocky Mountains

Snake River

NEVADA TERRITORY

Salt Lake City

Sacramento
Virginia City

UTAH TERRITORY

San Francisco

COLORADO TERRITO

PACIFIC OCEAN

CALIFORNIA

Colorado River

Santa Fe

NEW MEXICO TERRITORY

MEXICO

PENNSYLVANIA
Philadelphia
NEW JERSEY
Sharpsburg
Harpers Ferry
Baltimore
Winchester
Potomac River
Delaware Bay
WASHINGTON, D.C.
DISTRICT OF COLUMBIA
DELAWARE
Shenandoah River
Front Royal
Centreville
Manassas
MARYLAND
Harrisonburg
Fredericksburg
Rappahannock River
Mattaponi River
Chesapeake Bay
Charlottesville
VIRGINIA
James River
Richmond
York River
Roanoke
Lynchburg
Petersburg
James River
Cape Charles
Hampton
Appalachian Mountains
Cape Henry
Portsmouth
ATLANTIC OCEAN
NORTH CAROLINA

**Stalemate at sea**
Hampton Roads sees the world's first engagement between ironclad warships. In the duel between USS *Monitor* and CSS *Virginia* on March 9, 1862, neither ship inflicts sufficient damage to defeat her opponent.

**Carnage in Virginia**
In a series of battles to the east of Richmond, Lee drives the Union Army of the Potomac back from the Confederate capital. Known as the Seven Days Battles, the campaign puts an end to the Peninsula Campaign, although at the cost of over 20,000 killed and wounded.

**TERRITORY GAINED BY DECEMBER 1862**
- States of the Union
- Territory gained by the Union
- Confederate states
- Territory gained by Confederacy
- Disputed territory

In the early months of 1862, the Confederacy faced imminent defeat. The Union's naval blockade tightened, enabling the North to ship the Army of the Potomac to the Virginia Peninsula in March. The army's commander, General George B. McClellan, was slow and over-cautious, but his troop strength gave him a numerical advantage to take Richmond. Meanwhile, in the Western Theater, the Union at last found a fighting general in Ulysses S. Grant, whose victories at Fort Donelson and Shiloh laid open the defenses of Tennessee. To the south, New Orleans fell to a naval attack in April; by June most of the Mississippi was in Union hands.

But as spring turned to summer, the Confederates fought back. A spirited campaign by Jackson in the Shenandoah Valley drew Union forces away from the drive on Richmond. Then Lee took command of the Army of Northern Virginia and seized the initiative. He forced

# 1862

**The Union battered yet triumphant**
This panel from the Travis Panorama shows the Confederate forces under Braxton Bragg retreating to Tennessee after hard fighting at Perryville on October 8. Unable to sustain their campaign, they leave Kentucky in Union hands.

**Ironclads in action on the Tennessee River**
Union ironclads and timberclads provide the first vital step in taking Confederate-held forts Henry and Donelson in February. Fort Henry on the Tennessee River is given up after naval bombardment; Fort Donelson on the Cumberland River after a grim winter battle.

**Union win at Shiloh**
The Battle of Shiloh, fought amid woods and swamps alongside the Tennessee River, is a savage two-day encounter. The Union forces under General Ulysses S. Grant comes close to defeat on April 6, but wins the battle the following day.

**New Orleans taken**
The river defenses of New Orleans are breached by a Union naval squadron under Admiral David Farragut on April 24–25, 1862. The city reluctantly surrenders under threat of a naval bombardment. Here, Union sailors are met by a hostile crowd of locals as they try to come ashore.

McClellan to retreat in the Seven Days Battles, won a major victory at the Second Battle of Bull Run (Manassas), and invaded Maryland. At the same time, farther west, General Braxton Bragg invaded Kentucky. The war hung in the balance. In both Kentucky and Maryland, however, the Confederates failed to get the popular support they expected and had to withdraw, Lee extricating himself from potential disaster in a fight against the odds at Antietam (Sharpsburg). Lincoln felt sufficiently empowered to issue the Emancipation Proclamation, and any prospect of European support for the South faded. The Confederates, however, were still able to defy the Union armies. Another attempted advance on Richmond ended in defeat at Fredericksburg in December. On the Mississippi, Vicksburg held out against the Union. The year ended in carnage at Stones River (Murfreesboro), Tennessee, with heavy losses on both sides producing no clear victor.

81

# TIMELINE 1862

Forts Henry and Donelson ▪ Hampton Roads ▪ **New Orleans** ▪ The Mississippi River ▪ **Jackson in the Shenandoah Valley** ▪ McClellan and the Army of the Potomac ▪ The Peninsula Campaign ▪ **Lee and the Army of Northern Virginia** ▪ Seven Days Battles ▪ Second Bull Run ▪ **Antietam** ▪ Confederate invasion of Kentucky

| JANUARY | FEBRUARY | MARCH | APRIL | MAY | JUNE |
|---|---|---|---|---|---|
| **JANUARY 9** David Farragut takes command of the Union West Gulf Blockading Squadron. | **FEBRUARY 6** Union forces capture Fort Henry on the Tennessee River. | **MARCH 7–8** A victory for outnumbered Union forces at Pea Ridge (Elkhorn Tavern) in Arkansas confirms Union control of the state of Missouri. | | | |
| **JANUARY 9** Edwin Stanton is made Secretary of War by Lincoln, a post he keeps for the rest of the war. | **FEBRUARY 8** Roanoke Island off North Carolina is seized by Brigadier General Ambrose Burnside's forces. | | | | |

❯ Farragut's sword

❮ Union troops, siege of Yorktown

❯❯ General Robert E. Lee

| | **FEBRUARY 16** The Confederates surrender Fort Donelson on the Cumberland River to Brigadier General Ulysses S. Grant. | **MARCH 8–9** In the Battle of Hampton Roads, the Confederate ironclad CSS *Virginia* clashes with USS *Monitor*, the first combat between ironclad warships. | **APRIL 4** McClellan opens his Peninsula Campaign, settling down to a siege at Yorktown. | **MAY 5** The Confederate army fights a defensive battle at Williamsburg as it withdraws to Richmond. | |
| | | | **APRIL 6–7** In the Battle of Shiloh, Grant gains a hard-won victory after the Confederates launch a surprise attack. | **MAY 8** The Battle of McDowell gives Jackson the first win of his Shenandoah Valley Campaign. | |

❯❯ The Battle of Hampton Roads

| | **FEBRUARY 25** The Confederates abandon Nashville, Tennessee, which becomes the first Confederate state capital to fall to the Union. | | | **MAY 25** Jackson's successes in the Shenandoah Valley cause Lincoln to divert Union forces from the advance on Richmond. | **JUNE 2** Confederate general Robert E. Lee assumes command of the Army of Northern Virginia. |
| | | | | **MAY 31–JUNE 1** A Confederate counter-attack is repulsed at Seven Pines (Fair Oaks). | **JUNE 6** Union ironclads score a crushing victory on the Mississippi River at the Battle of Memphis. |

| **JANUARY 19** Confederate forces are defeated at the Battle of Mill Springs in Kentucky. | | **MARCH 17** McClellan begins moving the Army of the Potomac by sea to the Virginia Peninsula. | **APRIL 8** Island Number Ten, a key Confederate position on the Mississippi, is lost to Union forces. | | **JUNE 12–15** Confederate cavalry commander Jeb Stuart rides around McClellan's Army of the Potomac on a reconnaissance mission. |

❮ Confederate belt plate with bullet hole

| **JANUARY 30** USS *Monitor* is launched in New York, a revolutionary new design of ironclad warship. | | **MARCH 23** Confederate general Stonewall Jackson is checked in a battle at Kernstown in the Shenandoah Valley. | **APRIL 24–25** Farragut's West Coast Blockading Squadron fights its way through Confederate defenses on the Mississippi River to take New Orleans. | | **JUNE 26** Lee launches an offensive against the Army of the Potomac that becomes the Seven Days Battles. |
| | | **MARCH 28** A Confederate thrust through New Mexico toward Colorado and California is repulsed. | | | |

❮❮ Union troops marching in the Shenandoah Valley

> "Lee has **an army great in numbers and spirit**, and I believe he will wield it greatly. He is silent, inscrutable, strong, like a god."

LIEUTENANT JOHN H. CHAMBERLAYNE, VIRGINIA ARTILLERY, AUGUST 15, 1862, BEFORE THE SECOND BATTLE OF BULL RUN

| JULY | AUGUST | SEPTEMBER | OCTOBER | NOVEMBER | DECEMBER |
|---|---|---|---|---|---|

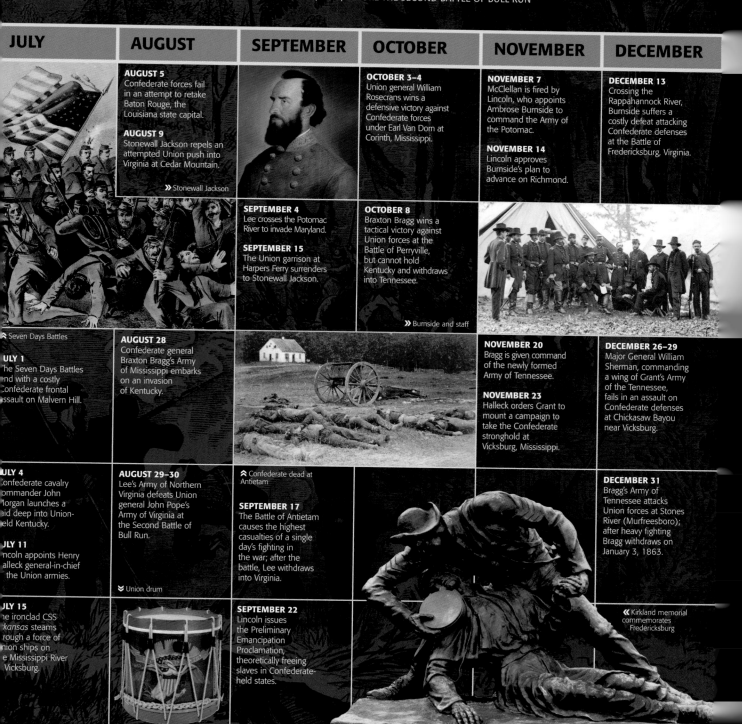

**AUGUST 5**
Confederate forces fail in an attempt to retake Baton Rouge, the Louisiana state capital.

**AUGUST 9**
Stonewall Jackson repels an attempted Union push into Virginia at Cedar Mountain.

≫ Stonewall Jackson

**OCTOBER 3–4**
Union general William Rosecrans wins a defensive victory against Confederate forces under Earl Van Dorn at Corinth, Mississippi.

**NOVEMBER 7**
McClellan is fired by Lincoln, who appoints Ambrose Burnside to command the Army of the Potomac.

**NOVEMBER 14**
Lincoln approves Burnside's plan to advance on Richmond.

**DECEMBER 13**
Crossing the Rappahannock River, Burnside suffers a costly defeat attacking Confederate defenses at the Battle of Fredericksburg, Virginia.

**SEPTEMBER 4**
Lee crosses the Potomac River to invade Maryland.

**SEPTEMBER 15**
The Union garrison at Harpers Ferry surrenders to Stonewall Jackson.

**OCTOBER 8**
Braxton Bragg wins a tactical victory against Union forces at the Battle of Perryville, but cannot hold Kentucky and withdraws into Tennessee.

≫ Burnside and staff

⌃ Seven Days Battles

JULY 1
The Seven Days Battles end with a costly Confederate frontal assault on Malvern Hill.

**AUGUST 28**
Confederate general Braxton Bragg's Army of Mississippi embarks on an invasion of Kentucky.

**NOVEMBER 20**
Bragg is given command of the newly formed Army of Tennessee.

**NOVEMBER 23**
Halleck orders Grant to mount a campaign to take the Confederate stronghold at Vicksburg, Mississippi.

**DECEMBER 26–29**
Major General William Sherman, commanding a wing of Grant's Army of the Tennessee, fails in an assault on Confederate defenses at Chickasaw Bayou near Vicksburg.

JULY 4
Confederate cavalry commander John Morgan launches a raid deep into Union-held Kentucky.

JULY 11
Lincoln appoints Henry Halleck general-in-chief of the Union armies.

JULY 15
The ironclad CSS *Arkansas* steams through a force of Union ships on the Mississippi River at Vicksburg.

**AUGUST 29–30**
Lee's Army of Northern Virginia defeats Union general John Pope's Army of Virginia at the Second Battle of Bull Run.

≫ Union drum

⌃ Confederate dead at Antietam

**SEPTEMBER 17**
The Battle of Antietam causes the highest casualties of a single day's fighting in the war; after the battle, Lee withdraws into Virginia.

**SEPTEMBER 22**
Lincoln issues the Preliminary Emancipation Proclamation, theoretically freeing slaves in Confederate-held states.

**DECEMBER 31**
Bragg's Army of Tennessee attacks Union forces at Stones River (Murfreesboro); after heavy fighting Bragg withdraws on January 3, 1863.

≪ Kirkland memorial commemorates Fredericksburg

# Soldiers in Gray

**Outnumbered and poorly supplied, the soldiers of the Confederate army nevertheless succeeded in sustaining war with the Union through four grueling years. In the words of General Robert E. Lee: "Their courage in battle entitles them to rank with the soldiers of any army and of any time."**

**Portrait of a Confederate**
A Confederate soldier poses for a photograph before leaving for the war. The average soldier was in his mid-20s, came from a rural background, and had probably not been away from home before.

## BEFORE

**At the start of the Civil War, only a few men on the Confederate side had military training. Recruits were volunteers, often led by amateur military enthusiasts.**

### FORMING AN ARMY
At first the Confederacy based its army on **state militias**, preexisting **volunteer companies**, and a rush of one-year volunteers at the **outbreak of war << 58–59**. The army's dependence on **one-year enlistment** from spring 1861 held **the prospect of a crisis** when the volunteers' term of service expired. In December 1861, the Confederate Congress **offered inducements to tempt men into reenlisting**. They were offered a 60-day furlough (or break), a cash bounty, and the right to join a new regiment and to elect new officers.

### INTRODUCTION OF CONSCRIPTION
Generals, however, feared that these measures would disrupt the war effort. On April 16, 1862, the Confederacy decided to **introduce conscription**, known as the "draft." **White males aged 18–35** were subject to **compulsory military service** and one-year service men had to stay for three years. In September, the **upper age limit was raised to 45**. Initially, planters with 20 or more slaves were exempt. In addition, the wealthy could pay someone to fight on their behalf. Many men **volunteered rather than be conscripted**: of around 200,000 enrolments in 1862, the majority were volunteers.

The majority of Confederate troops—more than 60 percent of the total—were farmers and farm laborers, a proportion that broadly reflected the social makeup of the Southern states. Some were just boys—normally serving as buglers or drummers—but most were between 18 and 29 years of age. In contrast to the Union forces, the Confederates were ethnically homogeneous, their ranks including relatively few recent immigrants and no African Americans.

The Confederate soldier was as committed to his cause as was the Northerner—perhaps more so. He saw the war as a defense of his home and home state, his freedom, and his way of life. And while only a third of Confederate soldiers owned slaves or came from slave-owning families, almost all believed that the preservation of slavery was essential to their status and security. Southerners tended to believe the myth that they were natural fighters compared to the decadent urban Yankees from the North, and cultivated a self-conscious sense of personal honor that impelled them into combat. This self-image also sustained their commitment to the war.

As the Confederate soldiers' initial enthusiasm waned, many came to feel that they were poor men fighting a rich man's war. The exemption from the draft (military service) for planters who owned 20 or more slaves—motivated

> **FURLOUGH** An enlisted man's leave was called a furlough. A soldier on leave left his weapons in camp and carried papers describing his appearance and giving his unit and his departure and return dates.

by Confederate fears that slaves would revolt or escape if unsupervised—caused great resentment. The ability of the wealthy to pay substitutes to perform their military service for them was seen as unfair and resulted in draft evasion; it was eventually abandoned. Yet the Confederates fielded a more egalitarian army than that of the North, with conscription applied more consistently across society, and the mercenary motives that drew so many of the poor into the Union Army ranks were less common.

### Army life
The concentration of thousands of newly recruited farm boys in military camps led to outbreaks of disease, initially spread by poor sanitary practices. Disease was just one of the disagreeable aspects of army life.

The profanity, drunkenness, gambling, and general immorality were a shock to those who came from orderly homes. Many men who had signed up to defend an ill-defined freedom resented finding themselves subjected to the rigors of a military discipline that denied them liberty of speech and action. But over time, most adapted successfully to the rhythms of military life. A man's regiment became his home, within which he would bond with a buddy and the men he lived and fought alongside. This male bonding was the cement that held the army together and sustained each individual soldier in hardship and combat. Drill and training, capped by the experience of battle itself, completed the transformation of a civilian into a soldier.

### Lack of necessities
Shortages of almost everything were a Confederate soldier's lot. He could expect a weapon and ammunition, plus a water canteen and tin cup, but most other items, from food to blankets and boots, were in short supply. Although officially clad in gray, Confederate troops often had to make do with homespun uniforms dyed with solutions of walnut shells and copper. Men marched barefoot, drawing a perverse pride from

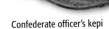

**Confederate officer's kepi**
The gray woolen kepi was standard headgear for the Confederate soldier, although it offered little protection against the elements. The broad-brimmed slouch hat was also in common use among troops.

their evident raggedness. Soldiers dug rifle pits with tin cups for lack of shovels. Much of a soldier's time was devoted to scavenging for the basics of sustenance and kit. Overcoats, blankets, and boots were plundered from captured Union stores or stolen from the Union dead and prisoners of war. Foraging

**Sewing kit**
Soldiers carried a mending kit known as a "housewife," which included needles, thread, and buttons. Men who were used to being looked after by womenfolk had to learn essential skills, such as sewing and cooking, when they entered the army.

**Identity badges**
Neither army issued identity tags, so troops inscribed their names or units onto pieces of bone, like these Confederate ones, metal, paper, or even acorns, so that their bodies could be identified if they were killed in battle.

AFTER

At the end of the war, 174,223 Confederate soldiers surrendered to the Union, but some former soldiers resisted Northern control of the South for years to come.

**RETURNING HOME**
The **surrender agreement 316–17 »** made by **Grant and Lee** at **Appomattox in 1865** allowed Southern troops to return home **without being prosecuted for treason**. They had to **surrender their weapons**, except for officers' sidearms, but were allowed to keep their own horses. Most soldiers returned home on foot, **dressed in little more than rags**, and begged for food along the way.

**KU KLUX KLAN**
Many Confederate **war veterans** were reluctant to accept **Northern domination** and the according of **civil rights to freed slaves**. Groups of loosely associated vigilantes formed the **Ku Klux Klan 342–43 »**, which resisted U.S. rule in the South and terrorized African Americans. Although the Klan was suppressed, other **armed vigilante groups**, such as **the White League**, continued the fight **against black rights and Republicanism** into the 1870s.

Confederate soldiers pillaged farms in search of food or firewood, even though the people they robbed were civilians on their own side. This quest for necessities easily slipped into straightforward crime, with the theft of money and valuables.

## Desertions and casualties

Discipline was seen by senior Confederate commanders as a serious and persistent problem. The Southern soldier was a tough fighter but had an ingrained resistance to authority. Officers below the rank of brigadier general were elected by the men, and this no doubt led to a tolerance of minor infringements. But larger issues, such as straggling on the march and shirking combat, had to be addressed. Tough commanders imposed severe punishments, including hanging and branding, for the gravest offenses. Yet desertion rates remained high: around one in seven soldiers deserted from the Army of Northern Virginia. The causes included disillusion with the rigors of army life and concern for the welfare of their families back home, who were seen as needing the man's aid and protection in the face of increasing hardship and danger. The rarity of leave led to frequent shorter episodes of absence without permission, and troops stationed near home accepted a mild punishment for taking an unauthorized break to visit loved ones.

At its height, the Confederate army numbered some 460,000 men, and more than a million soldiers served in its ranks during the course of the war. Of these, around 250,000 were killed in combat or died from disease or hardship. Many more were wounded, only one in four coming through unscathed. Later in the war, as pessimism and casualties mounted, religious revivals swept through the Confederate camps and desertion grew to epidemic proportions. Yet thousands of hardened veterans fought on to the last, with the courage of despair and pride in their regiments.

Confederates were often viewed as unkempt and undisciplined. One of their own commanders, Brigadier General Cadmus Wilcox, even described Confederate troops as "little better than an armed mob." But the feats of hard marching, general endurance, and fighting against the odds achieved by the Confederate soldiers of the Civil War have been equaled by few other armies.

"We are a **dirty, ragged set** … but **courage and heroism** find many a **true disciple** among us."
THEODORE T. FOGLE OF THE 2ND GEORGIA INFANTRY, LETTER TO HIS PARENTS, OCTOBER 13, 1862

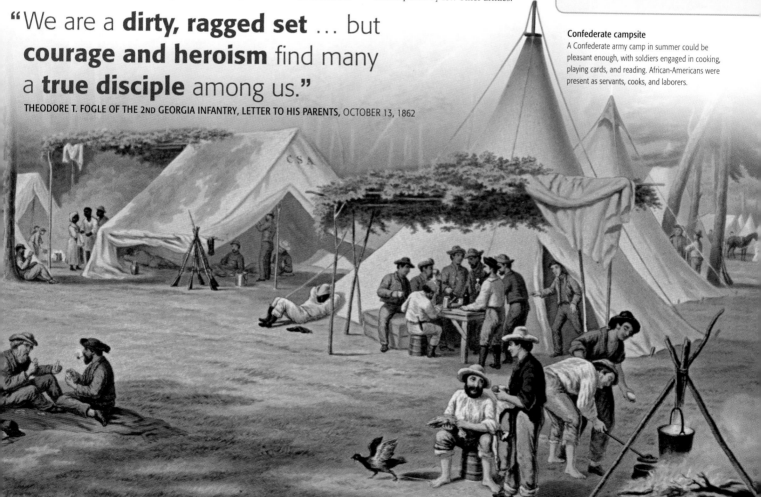

**Confederate campsite**
A Confederate army camp in summer could be pleasant enough, with soldiers engaged in cooking, playing cards, and reading. African-Americans were present as servants, cooks, and laborers.

# Confederate Uniforms

Typically dyed in colors of gray or butternut (brown), Southern uniforms were noted more for their simplicity of cut and style than for their military panache. Many a Yankee observed that the Confederate uniform was barely a uniform at all.

**1 Cartridge box** This box belonged to a member of the Washington Artillery, a New Orleans unit. **2 Haversack** Used by soldiers to carry rations. **3 Cherrywood canteen** The Confederacy was often short of metals such as tin, causing soldiers to create homemade alternatives. **4 Belt plate** A bullet pierced this Alabama belt plate. **5 General service belt buckle** Brass buckles embossed with CS and CSA were standard issue for Confederate soldiers. **6 Knapsack** Designed to carry a range of items, mainly camping equipment. **7 Tailcoat, 4th Georgia Militia Regiment** Some state units retained this traditional design, although it had generally been replaced by the frock coat or shell jacket. **8 Kepi** Copied from the hat worn by French officers, this one, worn by Captain Bardland of the Washington Artillery, was standard-issue headgear. The crown could be colored according to the branch of service of the wearer; red denoted artillery. **9 Kepi** of A. J. Charbaron. **10 and 11 Slouch hats** Throughout the war, supply shortages meant Confederate soldiers frequently had to provide their own clothing. This produced a wide variety of colors and styles of dress. **12 Shell jacket** The red piping and chevrons on this homespun jacket signify that the wearer was a sergeant in the artillery. **13 Battle shirt** Also known as an overshirt, this would have been worn as a substitute for a proper uniform. The colors and styles again varied widely. **14 Infantryman's uniform jacket** This style was cheaper and easier to make than the frock coat. **15 Butternut uniform** Confederate soldiers earned the nickname "Butternuts" due to the practice of dyeing cloth in a mixture of walnuts and copper to make uniforms a yellowish-brown color. **16 Artillery jacket and vest** The Washington Artillery changed to the regulation Confederate uniform, since their original militia blue coat was too similar to the Union uniform. **17 Officer's uniform pants, Washington Artillery** The red line running down the seam of these butternut pants identifies the wearer as an artilleryman.

**1 CARTRIDGE BOX, WASHINGTON ARTILLERY**

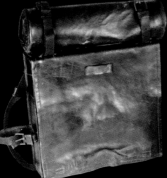

**2 HAVERSACK**

**3 WOODEN CANTEEN**

**4 BELT PLATE WITH BULLET HOLE**

**5 GENERAL SERVICE BELT BUCKLE**

**6 KNAPSACK**

**7 TAIL COAT**

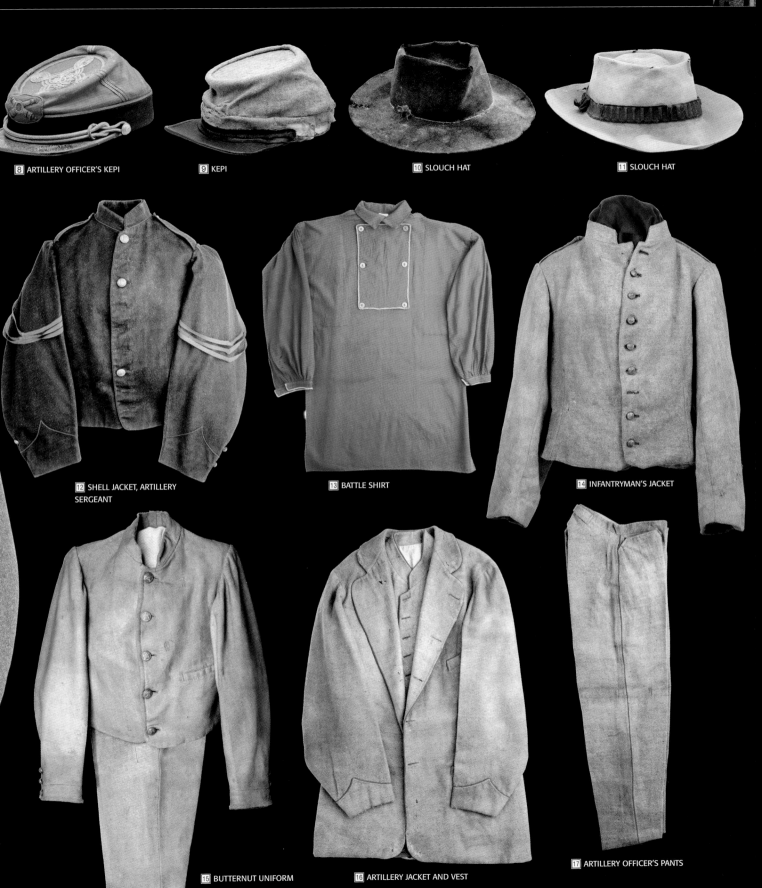

8 ARTILLERY OFFICER'S KEPI

9 KEPI

10 SLOUCH HAT

11 SLOUCH HAT

12 SHELL JACKET, ARTILLERY SERGEANT

13 BATTLE SHIRT

14 INFANTRYMAN'S JACKET

15 BUTTERNUT UNIFORM

16 ARTILLERY JACKET AND VEST

17 ARTILLERY OFFICER'S PANTS

# Soldiers in Blue

**The Union army enjoyed numerical superiority in the Civil War, but this did not make its soldiers' experiences, in and out of combat, any less harsh. Whether they fought for principle or for pay, Union troops served with an endurance and tenacity that ultimately prevailed.**

## « BEFORE

Although the Northern states had a large pool of manpower to draw on, they had difficulty in fulfilling the demand for soldiers in a long war.

### A VOLUNTEER ARMY

The Union army was initially a wholly volunteer force. A commitment to 90 days' service quickly proving inadequate, recruits were mostly required to **sign up for three years**, although some two-year volunteers were enrolled in certain states. The **attractions of army service declined** sharply as the risks and hardships of military life became more widely understood, and an **economic boom**—stimulated by the war—made **well-paid civilian work** readily available.

### CONSCRIPTION

In 1863, **conscription was introduced for men aged 20–45**. However, those selected could pay for **substitutes to take their place**. Many were also **exempted** for various reasons and large numbers disappeared to **evade conscription**. Only 51,000 conscripts served in the Union army during the war, compared with 118,000 substitutes.

To avert a crisis in 1864, when the initial three-year volunteers reached the end of their term, the government offered **bonus payments and a furlough** (leave) to men who agreed to reenlist. Some **200,000 veteran volunteers stayed in the army**. Cash bonuses were also routinely paid to attract fresh volunteers.

The Union army was as diverse as the society of the states from which the soldiers were drawn. By civilian occupation, farmers and farm laborers were the largest group, making up almost a half of the troops, while skilled workers—carpenters, blacksmiths, shoemakers, machinists, printers—constituted about a quarter of the army. Although, as the war dragged on, recruits were increasingly drawn from the poorer layers of society, only one in seven of the Union soldiers were unskilled laborers. It was a slightly younger army than that of the South, with two out of every five soldiers under 21 years of age. Although the lower age for conscription was 20, many of the substitutes, paid to take the place of unwilling conscripts, were adventurous youths of 18 or 19. Much younger boys served as drummers or buglers, although in 1864 the engagement of children under 16 was officially banned.

### Makeup of the Union army

Most striking was the ethnic diversity of the Union forces. About a quarter of those who served in the Union armies were foreign-born, reflecting the high level of immigration into the Northern states starting in the 1840s. The largest contingent were Germans, of whom some 200,000 served the Union during the war. The second-largest immigrant group in the ranks were the Irish, with around 150,000 men engaged. Both Germans and Irish often served in their own regiments—the 69th New York Infantry Regiment (dubbed "the Fighting 69th") was Irish, the 74th Pennsylvania Regiment was German. But members of these and other immigrant groups also served in regiments that were not ethnically defined. The same was not true of African Americans who

**Union officer's kepi**
The blue kepi-style cap with black visor was standard wear for Union soldiers. The horn insignia on the front was that of the infantry.

became an important component of Union fighting forces from 1863—black troops made up 10 percent of the Union army by the war's end—but who fought in segregated units.

### Reasons for fighting

The motivation of Union troops was mixed. Patriotism drove many into the ranks, outraged at the rebel threat to the integrity of the United States. An idealistic opposition to slavery was far less common. Abolitionism was supported in some Massachusetts regiments, but on the whole Union troops were indifferent to emancipation; some were even opposed to it.

The simple desire for adventure and the experience of war attracted many young men to enlist, but material considerations often predominated. The bounty money offered for volunteering and the money paid for substitutes were considerable sums to ordinary working men. Even without cheating the system—it was not too difficult to enlist several times for the bounty and evade the service—a man could feel well-off with the one-time payment. Late in the war immigrants arriving in the United States were often enlisted straight off the boat, some having embarked on the voyage specifically to sign up.

Box containing shaving brush

Razor    Shaving soap

**Shaving equipment**
Soldiers usually carried a straight razor and soap, although few would have had a shaving kit as elegant as this. Army rules, often ignored, prescribed a face wash every day and a full bath once a week.

> **"I hope and trust** that **strength** will be given to me to **stand and do my duty."**
> PRIVATE EDWARD EDES, LETTER TO HIS FATHER, APRIL 1863

## Improving morale

Loyalty to his colleagues and proud identification with his regiment, brigade, and corps were the bonds that held a man in place and, more than any other factor, made him ready to fight. Although obedience never came easily, the Union army developed into a reasonably well-drilled and disciplined force, with order enforced by harsh corporal punishments. From 1862 onward, Union troops were generally well supplied and equipped. Northern factories provided sufficient standard uniforms and footwear, even if

**281,881** The estimated number of Union soldiers wounded in the course of the Civil War. One in every four Union soldiers who served in the conflict either died or was wounded.

sometimes of poor quality, and the official food ration was quite generous in its portions of bacon, beef, bread, and beans. But men easily became ragged and hungry during hard campaigning. Even when the supply system had not broken down, the temptation to pillage farms along the line of march, usually in Confederate territory, was rarely resisted. When marching, endurance was required— the pack was heavy, feet were sore— but even in a well supplied camp the military routines could be both boring and wearing. Disease was a serious threat, especially in the early period before sanitation improved. A Union soldier had a one-in-eight chance of dying of disease, compared with a one-in-18 chance of dying in battle.

## Disillusion and desertion

The quality of Union troops was diluted in the last years of the war. The proud if war-weary volunteers who had fought since 1861 were often contemptuous of the mercenary "bounty men" and substitutes raked in from 1863 onward— Private Frank Wilkeson dismissed them as "conscienceless and cowardly scoundrels." Desertion rates were always high, men slinking away, discouraged by army life or needing to cope with difficulties at home. But those who joined up for a lump sum payment were notorious for disappearing. Grant complained in September 1864 that: "The men we have been getting in this way almost all desert." Yet Union troops always proved tough fighters when it mattered. There was no questioning the courage and fighting spirit of the soldiers in blue.

### Taking a break

This scene of soldiers playing cards was painted in 1881 by Civil War veteran Julian Scott, who had served as a musician in a Vermont regiment. It reflects the mix of uniforms worn early in the war.

### Unknown Union soldier

This young recruit of the 8th New York Heavy Artillery has the Hardee hat of his full dress uniform alongside him and carries an infantry musket. Eighteen was considered the youngest age for a combat role, although many volunteers lied about their birth date.

## AFTER

Some 2.5 million men served in the Union army in the course of the Civil War. Of these, around 360,000 died in battle or of hardship and disease.

### DEMOBILIZATION

No thought was given during the war to the problem of **returning men to civilian life**. Soldiers whose terms of service ended and who chose not to reenlist simply returned to their homes. At the war's end public opinion demanded swift demobilization. **Union soldiers were gathered in camps** for discharge, but many deserted before the slow and tedious mustering out process was complete.

### VETERANS' PENSIONS

By 1865, **a system of pensions** had been put in place **for disabled veterans and for the widows and orphans** of Union soldiers who had died in the war. In 1904, pensions were in effect extended to **all surviving Civil War veterans** in their old age. There were still individuals drawing Civil War pensions in the 1950s.

### A CONTINUING ROLE

Rapidly depleted, the U.S. Army nonetheless was burdened with important tasks after the Civil War. **The South** came under **military rule** during the **Reconstruction period 340–45 »**, while the **Plains Indian Wars** kept the army actively employed into the 1880s, many Civil War veterans seeing action against the Native Americans.

[1] MILITIA OFFICER'S KEPI

[2] INFANTRY FORAGE CAP

[3] MODEL 1858 DRESS HAT

[4] OFFICER'S SLOUCH HAT

[5] ZOUAVE FEZ

[6] OFFICER'S EPAULETS

[7] MILITIA FROCK COAT

[8] CAVALRYMAN'S CAPED GREATCOAT

# Union Uniforms

**Early in the war, volunteers proudly donned local militia uniforms of varying colors, including rebel gray, which attracted friendly fire from unwitting comrades. The dark blue frock coat and light blue trousers then became standard issue for infantrymen.**

[1] **Militia officer's kepi**, 23rd Regiment, New York State Militia. [2] **Infantry forage cap** with hunting horn insignia. [3] **Model 1858 Dress Hat** or Hardee hat—the army's regulation prewar dress hat. [4] **Officer's slouch hat**, popular in the Western Theater. [5] **Zouave fez** of the 114th Pennsylvania Volunteer Infantry. Zouave units were raised by both sides in the war and initially sported highly colorful uniforms. [6] **Officer's epaulets**. Epaulets were specified for all U.S. Army officers in 1832. They were fastened to the shoulder by a strap. [7] **Militia frock coat**. At the outset of the war, state militia units wore a large variety of uniforms in various colors. [8] **Caped greatcoat**, issued to Union cavalry for use in cold conditions. [9] **Cartridge box**, used to store ammunition for a pistol. [10] **Tin canteen**, covered with a cotton and wool cloth that would, when wet, help keep the water cool. [11] **Belt plate**. This embossed brass plate was standard issue for Union soldiers. [12] **Belt set**, issued to infantrymen. It came with a cartridge box, percussion-cap pouch, and bayonet scabbard. [13] **Belt and pouch** for percussion caps, 8th New York Infantry. [14] **Shell jacket**. This short, hip-length style of jacket was worn chiefly by the cavalry and artillery, but the white piping on this one shows it belonged to an infantryman. [15] **Cavalry pants**. The yellow piping on these blue wool pants indicates the cavalry branch of service. [16] **Frock coat**. The frock coat was piped with the branch of service color around the cuffs and collar. Light blue signified the infantry.

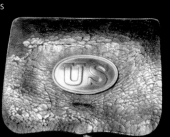

[9] CARTRIDGE BOX

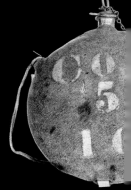

[10] CANTEEN

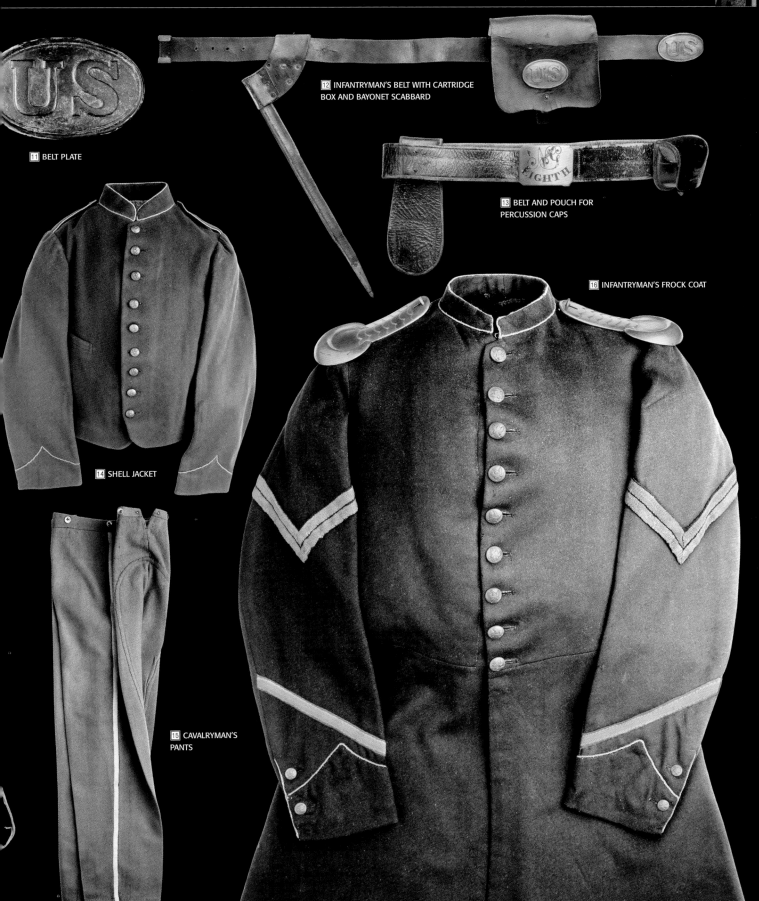

11 BELT PLATE

12 INFANTRYMAN'S BELT WITH CARTRIDGE
BOX AND BAYONET SCABBARD

13 BELT AND POUCH FOR
PERCUSSION CAPS

16 INFANTRYMAN'S FROCK COAT

14 SHELL JACKET

15 CAVALRYMAN'S
PANTS

BEFORE

Civil War commanders adopted infantry tactics based on a European tradition that had proved effective since the introduction of the flintlock musket around 1700.

**FIGHTING DRILL**
European infantry were taught to fight as **rigidly drilled automatons**. When on the defensive, they **stood in the open**, firing disciplined volleys with their muskets. For the offense, they **advanced steadily across open ground in tight formation** of column or line with bayonets fixed. For **defense against charging cavalry, the infantry formed squares**.

These basic infantry tactics, which had been used in the Napoleonic Wars, were studied as

**THE WAR WITH MEXICO**

models at American military colleges and were employed by American infantry in the **War with Mexico** in 1846–48.

Later European conflicts, such as the Crimean War of 1854–56, showed that **improved weaponry made traditional frontal infantry assaults very costly**, especially when defenders were entrenched in field fortifications. These lessons were largely ignored in the United States and had to be learned over again in the Civil War.

# Fighting on Foot

Infantry tactics in the Civil War were based on existing technology, local terrain, and the European tradition of warfare in which American officers were steeped. Heavy casualties resulted from the failure to adapt battlefield tactics to take account of the increased defensive firepower of infantry and artillery.

Infantry began the Civil War equipped with an assortment of weapons, including inaccurate, old-fashioned smoothbore flintlock muskets. By the second year of the war, however, the standard weapon on both sides had become the rifle musket—either an Enfield or a Springfield. The rapid loading and firing of this weapon in the heat of conflict was a foot soldier's essential skill. Before he could fire, he had to take out a paper cartridge containing the minié ball and powder charge; rip open the cartridge with his teeth; ram powder and ball down the barrel with his ramrod; and take a

**Rifle cartridges**
A cartridge consisted of a minié ball and its powder charge wrapped in paper. The soldier bit open the cartridge before loading, a process that left his face blackened by powder. In some new models of rifle, paper cartridges were superseded by metal cartridges during the Civil War.

percussion cap from its box and place it in the firing mechanism. Yet this apparently clumsy, muzzle-loaded weapon marked a vital evolution in warfare. An experienced man might fire his Springfield three times a minute, its rifled, or grooved, barrel offering improved accuracy and an effective range of 300–400yd (274–366m)— three times that of a smoothbore flintlock. Under pressure, men would make mistakes, leaving the ramrod in the barrel or even forgetting to load the powder and ball. But a rifle musket, correctly used, was a reliable arm. In defense, its range and rate of fire

presented a serious problem for an attacking force that had to cover open ground in a frontal assault.

**The line breaks down**
Both Northern and Southern generals had no doubt that battles could only be won by large bodies of drilled and disciplined troops automatically obeying orders. Popular manuals, such as W. J. Hardee's *Rifle and Light Infantry Tactics*, stated that infantry should attack by advancing steadily in close packed lines, kept in strict formation by their officers, with men acting as "file closers" at the rear to stop the cowardly

### Bayonet charge
This Winslow Homer illustration shows an attack on an enemy line early in the war. On the left in the background, infantrymen advance in orderly ranks; in the foreground a bayonet charge develops into hand-to-hand fighting.

of fighting was inevitable. Troops were often inadequately disciplined, especially early in the war. The more likely sequence of events in an encounter was that one side would advance and fire, the other side would rush forward from their defensive position to fire, and a general melee ensued. But above all, the traditional European method of infantry attack was in crisis because improvements in

**5** The factor by which firepower was improved when flintlock muskets were replaced by rifle muskets, increasing both the effective firing range of Civil War infantry and the rate of fire.

artillery and the adoption of the rifle musket had tipped the balance decisively against the attacker.

### Defensive superiority
Men advancing in line shoulder-to-shoulder were hopelessly vulnerable to infantry volleys and cannon firing canister and grapeshot. A straightforward method for reducing casualties was the adoption of a looser formation, with men spread out as in a skirmish line. In contrast, defenders were almost invulnerable until overrun, especially if they had dug rifle pits or found a wall or bank to shelter behind.

Soldiers found their own ways to preserve their lives, exploiting cover, firing in a kneeling or prone position,

designed to discourage them from halting to return fire. By advancing swiftly and relentlessly, the columns were expected to smash a hole in Confederate defensive positions, and on occasion they succeeded. But as field fortifications became more elaborate, protected by abbatis (barricades made from trees piled on top of each other), successful frontal infantry assaults became almost impossible.

### The value of maneuverability
The answer to the stalemate imposed by the superiority of defensive firepower was maneuver. By marching around the flank or to the rear of enemy defenses, troops could attack from an unexpected quarter or force an enemy withdrawal. Well-drilled troops, capable of swift marching maneuvers, were responsible for some striking victories. Yet even such a master of maneuver as General Robert E. Lee could find no alternative to launching "Pickett's Charge," the notorious frontal assault at Gettysburg in 1863. The trench warfare of the late Civil War made frontal assaults deadly, and deprived both sides of the freedom to maneuver. The Civil War thus drifted into a tactical stalemate decided by attrition.

AFTER

**Developments in military technology under way at the time of the Civil War would make offensive infantry tactics even more problematic over the next 50 years.**

### REPEATING RIFLES
The infantry weapons that would make the rifle musket obsolete were **breech-loading rapid-fire guns** using metal cartridges. Repeater rifles, especially the Spencer rifle, were used quite widely in the Union army by the end of the war. **The Spencer could fire 20 rounds a minute**, compared with the maximum three rounds of a muzzle-loader. The **Gatling gun**, used experimentally in the Civil War, was capable of firing 200 rounds a minute and heralded the era of automatic weapons.

### TRENCH WARFARE
In the decades after the Civil War, **artillery also became dramatically more efficient** in range, rate of fire, and the explosive power of shells. Along with the use of barbed wire to protect entrenchments, these weapons developments led to the trench warfare of World War I, where the **same fundamental infantry tactics were employed**, with even higher casualty rates for even less result.

> "I have seen pictures of battles—they would **all be in line, standing in a nice level field** fighting ... but **it isn't so.**"
> UNION PRIVATE WILLIAM BREARLEY, LETTER FROM ANTIETAM, SEPTEMBER 1862

### Standard issue rifle musket
The 1861 Springfield percussion rifle musket was the standard infantry weapon throughout the war. It had a 40-in (101.6-cm) barrel, weighed 9lb (4kg), and its range and accuracy made it popular with the troops.

from skulking away. When close enough to the enemy position, infantry would charge with bayonets fixed, either putting the defenders to flight or engaging in hand-to-hand combat, often grasping their muskets by the barrel and wielding them like clubs.

Although Civil War operations sometimes approximated this ideal of an infantry attack, mostly they did not. Terrain was against it. European tactics were designed for fighting on open ground; in the swamps and forests of the American wilderness a looser style

and reloading lying on their backs. Experienced troops learned to lie low when fire was intense, then advance in short rushes when defensive volleys faltered, with colleagues covering the move with suppressive fire. The disadvantage of this method was that once troops had "gone to ground," they were likely to stay there if the defensive fire remained hot, especially if they judged success unlikely.

In 1864, in an effort to restore the momentum of frontal assault, Union troops were driven forward in tight columns, with no percussion caps pre-placed in their guns—a measure

### Union trenches at Vicksburg
During sieges, troops dug elaborate trench systems that discouraged attack. Although earthworks were rarely as salubrious as those shown here, once in a trench a soldier was often reluctant to leave it.

**«** **BEFORE**

In 1861, when the Civil War began, ironclad warships were novelties in naval ship design. Not surprisingly, both the Union and the Confederates sought to employ this new technology.

During the Crimean War, the French and British navies **attached iron plates** to the **wooden hulls** of some of their warships as armor. The experiment was considered a success and **in 1859 France launched the *Gloire*,** an ironclad battleship. The British responded with their own armored battleship, *Warrior*, the following year.

**DEVELOPMENTS IN THE UNITED STATES**
The Confederacy saw the possibility of using an ironclad to challenge Union naval supremacy. In the first days of the war they **captured Norfolk**

**10** The guns carried by CSS *Virginia*—two 7-in rifled guns, fore and aft, six 9-in smoothbore Dahlgren guns in broadside, and two 6.4-in rifled guns.

**Navy Yard** and with it the burned-out hull of the steam-and-sail frigate **USS *Merrimack*.** The ship was salvaged and **rebuilt as the steam-driven "ironclad" CSS *Virginia*,** encased to the waterline in **4in (10cm) iron plate armor.** Meanwhile, the Union raced to produce the far **more radical all-metal USS *Monitor*** in time to confront the *Virginia* on her first sortie.

**TECHNOLOGY**

## USS *MONITOR*

The design for USS *Monitor* was submitted to the U.S. Navy's Ironclad Board by Swedish-born engineer John Ericsson. This semi-submerged metal raft had an armored deck that supported a rotating gun turret and a small pilothouse. It was armed with two 11-in (280-mm) smoothbore Dahlgren guns (below). Their swollen shape allowed the use of larger amounts of explosive propellant without the risk of the gun bursting. The steam engine drove an innovative marine screw, also designed by Ericsson. The *Monitor*'s low profile in the water made it a tough target but rendered it barely seaworthy. Built in sections at different foundries, the vessel was launched on January 30, 1862.

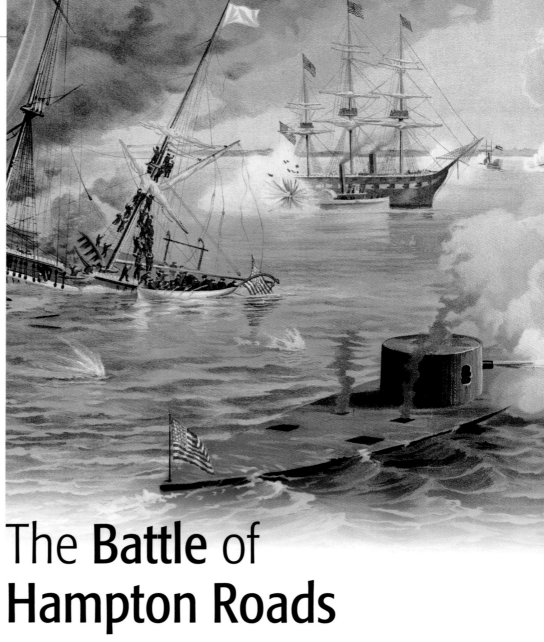

# The Battle of Hampton Roads

In March 1862, USS *Monitor* and CSS *Virginia* fought the world's first battle between steam-powered, ironclad warships. Their encounter was a stalemate that left the naval balance of power in the Civil War unchanged, but it marked an epoch-making advance in the technology of naval warfare.

The Confederacy was desperate to break the Union naval blockade that cut off Richmond's access to international trade through the James River. On March 8, 1862, the ironclad CSS *Virginia* steamed out of the Norfolk Navy Yard to challenge the Union blockade force in Hampton Roads, where the James River opens out into Chesapeake Bay. To the crews of the Union warships on blockade duty, the ungainly, slow-moving warship with her sloped ironplate armor was a sinister sight. The *Virginia*'s captain, 61-year-old Franklin Buchanan, had an array of guns at his disposal, but his intended principal weapon was an iron ram fitted

to his ship's prow. As he steamed toward the sloop USS *Cumberland*, the Union ship's shells bounced off *Virginia*'s metal plates. The ram tore into the *Cumberland*'s wooden hull and sent her to the bottom—almost taking the *Virginia* with her as the ram stayed locked in the sloop's hull. Fortunately for Buchanan and his crew, the ram snapped off and the *Virginia* was able to turn her attention to the frigate USS *Congress*. Having witnessed the

*Cumberland*'s fate, the captain of the *Congress* ran his ship aground to make it impossible for the Confederate ironclad to ram. This left the frigate a sitting target for the *Virginia*'s guns and other vessels of the Confederate squadron. Helpless under bombardment, the *Congress* "struck her colors," the time-honored gesture of surrender in naval warfare, but Union soldiers on shore were unaware of this

**Catesby ap Roger Jones**
A Virginian of Welsh ancestry, Catesby ap Roger Jones resigned from the U.S. Navy to join the Confederacy. He took over command of CSS *Virginia* at Hampton Roads.

The Confederacy failed to break the blockade. Over the next two months the *Virginia* made occasional sorties into Hampton Roads, but the epic duel was not repeated.

The *Virginia* was scuttled in May when the advance of Union land forces left it exposed to capture. Never seaworthy, **Monitor** sank on December 31, 1862, while under tow in an Atlantic gale off Cape Hatteras, North Carolina. However, the design spawned a **whole class of vessels**, designated **"monitors,"** for use in **inshore and river warfare**. Monitors were still in service up to the 1930s. **Rams and rotating gun turrets** were soon adopted as standard features of warships.

**ARMORED VESSELS IN THE WAR**
Ironclads and monitors played a major part in later naval actions, including the **struggle for control of the Mississippi 96–101, 190–93 ››** and the **Battle of Mobile Bay 286–87 ››**.

### Battle of the ironclads
USS *Monitor* (far left) and CSS *Virginia* (left) exchange fire at close range. The *Virginia* suffered much superficial damage, but neither vessel carried powerful enough armament to have a decisive effect.

visibility was limited for both crews, and the two ships went almost blindly around one another as they blasted away. The *Monitor* was smaller and faster and her flat bottom was an advantage in the shallow waters. At one point, the *Virginia* ran aground on shoals, but she was freed and the battle continued.

### Solid shot
A memento of the Battle of Hampton Roads—a solid shot flattened on striking CSS *Virginia*'s sloping ironplate armor. The *Virginia* remained known to the Union side by its original name, *Merrimack*.

## "My men and myself were perfectly black with smoke and powder."

UNION LIEUTENANT SAMUEL GREENE, ON BOARD USS *MONITOR*

### Final clashes
The *Virginia* tried to crush the *Monitor* by ramming, but the *Monitor* moved into shallow water to escape. No resolution seemed in view when by chance a Confederate shell exploded in the eyeslit of the *Monitor*'s pilothouse. Worden suffered a facial wound that blinded him. There was some confusion before command passed to his first officer, Samuel Greene. In the interim, the *Virginia*'s Catesby ap Roger Jones assumed that the *Monitor* had given up the fight and withdrew, claiming victory. Greene, ready to resume the fight, saw the *Virginia* leave, and also claimed to have won.

### Monitor's commander
John Worden was a lieutenant when he took command of USS *Monitor* in January 1861. He recovered from his wound at Hampton Roads, retiring from the navy as a rear admiral in 1886.

convention. As the surrender was being organized, they opened fire, seriously wounding Buchanan in the leg. In retaliation he ordered red-hot shot to be fired at the *Congress*, setting her ablaze—the ship finally blew up in the early hours of the following morning. Another frigate, USS *Minnesota*, had also run aground and was marked as

the next target for destruction, but with the approach of night the *Virginia* withdrew for repairs. The Union navy had lost two ships and the lives of more than 230 sailors.

### USS Monitor enters the fray
The next morning, the *Virginia* reappeared, with Lieutenant Catesby ap Roger Jones commanding in place of the wounded Buchanan. Jones was puzzled to see a strange low-lying metal object between the *Virginia* and the stranded *Minnesota*. This was the Union ironclad USS *Monitor*. Towed south from New York in great haste, it had taken up position during the night. The *Monitor* had undergone a hair-raising voyage, nearly sinking in heavy seas. Its crew of 59 officers and men, commanded by

John Worden, were exhausted and hungry. Nonetheless, Worden immediately set course to attack the *Virginia*.

The two vessels closed to point-blank range and opened fire. The *Monitor*'s armor warded off the hammer blows of the *Virginia*'s guns, but the *Monitor*'s fire had no more effect on the *Virginia*'s iron plates. In cramped, fume-ridden conditions, the *Monitor*'s gunners had problems with the innovative gun turret, which eventually had to be kept in permanent rotation, firing as the guns swept across their target. In the smoke,

# BEFORE

New Orleans had seen rapid expansion of trade and growing prosperity in the years leading up to the Civil War. It also occupied a vital strategic location on the Mississippi.

## MULTIPLE UNION THREATS
Despite its importance to the Confederacy, **New Orleans had reduced its defenses** because of the Union threat to the north in Tennessee, where General Ulysses S. **Grant was advancing on forts Henry and Donelson ‹‹ 104–105**. Both land and naval forces had been dispatched northward, including eight ships of the River Defense Fleet.

## SEABORNE LANDINGS
Union experience of amphibious warfare early in the war led it to believe that **New Orleans** could be taken by a **seaborne operation**. Both at Hatteras Inlet, North Carolina, in August 1861, and the following November at Port Royal, South Carolina, **Union warships** showed they could **subdue coastal forts** with naval gunfire. This suggested that the river forts defending access to New Orleans might be overcome with **a naval attack supported by troop landings**. Both these previous operations had strengthened the Union blockade of the South's ports ‹‹ **72–73**.

# The Fall of New Orleans

**The Confederates suffered a major setback when New Orleans fell to Union forces in April 1862. It happened after a bold nighttime naval operation in which Union warships commanded by David Farragut forced a passage past the guns of Confederate forts Jackson and St. Philip.**

Union plans for an attack on New Orleans began in the winter of 1861–62. Initial estimates called for up to 50,000 Union troops. However, by February 1862, the main role had passed to the Union navy's West Coast Blockading Squadron under Captain David Farragut.

Farragut chose to plan a purely naval operation to breach New Orleans' only serious defenses, forts Jackson and St. Philip. Sited on opposite sides of the Mississippi around 75 miles (120km) south of New Orleans, the forts held an estimated 126 guns. Conventional wisdom believed that warships trying to pass them would be blown out of the

water. The Union squadron would also have to take on assorted ironclads and "cottonclads"—ships with cotton bales attached as a form of armor. In March, Farragut moved 17 ships past the initial obstacle: the sandbars that lay at the mouth of the Mississippi. Farragut's squadron included his flagship USS *Hartford*, and some mortar schooners for land bombardments. He then took a month to complete his preparations. The Confederate forts were scouted, as was the chain of sunken hulks, stretching from bank to bank, intended to block passage up the river.

The bombardment began on April 18. Thousands of shells rained down on the forts, but the effects were minimal.

> ## 168,675
> **The population of New Orleans** according to the 1850 census. This made the city the sixth largest in the United States and by far the largest in the Confederacy.

Return fire from the forts was equally ineffectual. Farragut, who had never placed much faith in the mortars, soon determined to proceed with his favored plan of forcing a passage upriver. A raid by his gunboats succeeded in opening up a navigable passage through the chain. At around 2 a.m. on April 24, the Union ships steamed upriver to the chain under cover of darkness. They were formed in three divisions, with Farragut commanding the center. Most had passed through the gap in the chain when, at 3:40 a.m., the moon rose, revealing them to the enemy, who unleashed a storm of fire from the forts' guns. As Farragut's ships fired back and the mortar schooners joined in, the

### Before the engagement
En route to New Orleans, the crew of a Federal mortar schooner is pictured on deck with the ship's formidable 25,000lb (11,340kg) gun.

**Mayhem on the Mississippi**
The running of the forts under cover of darkness led to a chaotic moonlit river battle. Fort Jackson can be seen on the left of the picture firing on the Union ships as they round the bend in the river.

New Orleans came under the military rule of Union General Benjamin Butler. His abrasive approach to controlling a hostile city provoked international controversy.

**BRUTAL OCCUPATION**
Butler **cracked down on demonstrations of support for the Confederacy** in the occupied city. Newspapers were censored and churchmen arrested for expressing Confederate sympathies in their services. When **William Mumford was hanged** for having torn down a Union flag at the time of the city's surrender, Jefferson Davis declared Butler himself a criminal worth hanging.

Moreover, from a Union point of view, **Butler outraged international opinion**. France's government denounced the arrest of champagne merchant Charles Heidsieck as a spy. Most damaging was Butler's General Order of May 15, 1862, stating that any woman who insulted Union soldiers "shall be ... treated as a woman of the town"—in other words, as a prostitute. **Butler succeeded in keeping order** and improving public health, **but he was removed** from command of the Department of the Gulf in late 1862.

**BENJAMIN BUTLER**

night was lit up like a fireworks display. Farragut's boldness paid off, for as he had anticipated, the land batteries fired wildly in their panic and confusion. Only three of the gunboats in the Union rear division failed to pass the forts. One was disabled by gunfire and the other two turned back, rather than attempt to push through the passage as dawn broke. Confederate warships beyond the barrier responded in piecemeal fashion. Their tugs pushed rafts heaped with burning wood toward Union ships, setting fire to Farragut's flagship, which was rescued by the efforts of its crew.

**Battle rattle**
This 10½-in (26-cm) wide wooden rattle was of the type used on small warships to summon all hands to their action stations at the moment of battle.

**Cottonclad vs. gunboat**
Meanwhile, CSS *Governor Moore*, a cottonclad converted from a civilian paddle steamer, attacked boldly under the command of Lieutenant Beverly Kennon. Finding USS *Varuna* isolated, he relentlessly pursued her, despite taking heavy casualties in a fierce exchange of fire. The *Governor Moore* twice rammed into the *Varuna* with her reinforced bow before CSS *Stonewall Jackson* sank the Union gunboat. The

*Varuna* was the only Union loss of the battle. The *Governor Moore* was later shot up by several Union warships and, out of control, was sunk by her crew.

The strangest-looking vessel in the battle was CSS *Manassas*, a cigar-shaped ironclad with a ram and a single gun. Her curved armor performed excellently as she attempted a series of ramming attacks. The sidewheel steamer USS *Mississippi* and the sloop USS *Brooklyn* were both struck, and the *Brooklyn* suffered serious damage. The *Manassas* finally ran aground and was destroyed. The other Confederate ironclad, CSS *Louisiana*, was only able to fire a few shots—she was later scuttled to avoid capture. With the Southern naval force routed, Farragut had a clear path to New Orleans. He reached the city on April 25 and demanded its surrender. The garrison by then had been evacuated, leaving New Orleans defenseless, but the Confederate authorities refused to surrender, while Union officers and sailors who landed to take formal possession of the city were harassed. Farragut wisely waited, allowing feelings to cool down. After four days his marines were able to raise the Union flag over the major public buildings in New Orleans.

The forts, meanwhile, remained in Confederate hands, but shortly after the mortar bombardment was resumed on

April 29, the Fort Jackson garrison mutinied. General Johnson Duncan, commander of the forts, decided that it was time to give in. As a result, when General Benjamin Butler's Union troops marched into New Orleans on May 1, they were unopposed. They had taken the city without seeing any fighting.

> "The passing [of the forts] was one of the **most awful sights and events I ever saw.**"
>
> LETTER OF DAVID FARRAGUT TO THE ASSISTANT NAVAL SECRETARY, APRIL 27, 1862

**Unwelcome arrivals**
Sailors sent ashore to take formal possession of New Orleans after the Union victory met a hostile reception from angry crowds. The city was not occupied by Union soldiers until a week after the victory.

**UNION ADMIRAL** Born 1801 Died 1870

# David **Farragut**

## "**Admiral Farragut** has … the unassuming and the unpresuming **gentleness of a true hero**"

DIARY OF GIDEON WELLES, UNION SECRETARY OF THE NAVY, SEPTEMBER 12, 1863

**A**merica's greatest naval hero of the Civil War, David Farragut, was approaching his 60th birthday when the conflict erupted. He probably supposed that he had reached the peak of a solid naval career and could now look forward to imminent retirement. Instead, the war thrust him into action and the limelight of celebrity.

Farragut was the son of a Spanish immigrant, a merchant sailor who had fought for his new country in the

**USS** *Hartford*
Farragut's flagship through the Civil War, the *Hartford* was a screw sloop of war that had been recently built. As usual for the time, it had a mix of steam propulsion and sails. Its armament included 20 9in (23cm) Dahlgren guns.

Revolutionary War. But the most important early influence on him was American naval officer David Porter, who took the young Farragut into his household and into the Navy as a midshipman at the tender age of nine—a precocious initiation even by the standards of the day.

The boy soon saw combat in the Anglo-American War of 1812, when Porter's frigate *Essex*, with Farragut aboard, cruised the Pacific in search of British whalers. Aged 12, Farragut was given his first command, when he took a captured vessel into port. In March 1814, however, the *Essex* was trapped at

Valparaíso, Chile, by two Royal Navy vessels. Porter tried to fight but, with 24 of his crew dead and twice as many wounded, he had to surrender. Farragut was taken prisoner but released on parole, then took no further part in the war.

From 1815, peacetime service created a frustrating environment for any career sailor. Promotion was slow and chances to demonstrate ability very few and far between. Farragut seemed to miss any opportunities that arose, even failing to see significant action during the War with Mexico in 1846–48. He performed administrative roles on shore, supervising ordnance at the Navy Yard at Norfolk, Virginia, and organized the founding of the Mare Island Navy Yard in California.

### War breaks out

When Farragut offered his services to the Union in April 1861, turning his back on his Southern roots, there was no reason to believe he would become an exceptional leader. For eight months he languished without significant employment, partly because of suspicion of his Southern origins, until Secretary of the Navy Gideon Welles selected him to command the naval attack on New Orleans.

Farragut's new role placed him in charge of the West Gulf Blockading Squadron in early 1862, and he immediately showed skills that were to be repeated in other operations. Although the original plan for the

### Portrait of an admiral
This studio portrait of Farragut in dress uniform was taken during the Civil War, around 1863. He was, sequentially, the first rear admiral, vice admiral, and full admiral in the history of the U.S. Navy.

### Sword of honor

This jeweled sword was presented to Farragut by admiring New Yorkers on April 23, 1864. The blade is inscribed: "... as a token of their appreciation of his gallant services rendered in defense of his country."

Elaborately decorated blade

## "You fellows will **catch the devil** before you get **through with this business**."

**FARRAGUT ADDRESSING CONFEDERATES**

attack on New Orleans had been a land assault supported by the navy, Farragut largely ignored the army's role, preferring to do the job on his own. He was meticulous and unhurried in his preparations, but then carried out the attack on the Mississippi River defenses with resolution and aggression. When his flagship, USS *Hartford*, was set on fire, he responded with admirable calmness and inspired his crew to bring the blaze under control.

The bold manner of the capture of New Orleans earned Farragut fame, promotion, and the thanks of Congress. The United States had previously scorned the term admiral, according instead the more "democratic" rank of flag officer to its senior naval commanders, but Farragut was made a rear admiral to general acclaim.

### River and ocean setbacks

When Farragut led his ships up the Mississippi to Vicksburg in June 1862, he found that the Confederate fortress stood too high above the river for bombardment by his squadron's naval guns to have any real effect.

Returning to the sea, he worked tirelessly at the blockade of the Gulf ports, only to suffer a double blow in January 1863 when USS *Hatteras* was sunk by CSS *Alabama* off Galveston, Texas, and CSS *Florida* was allowed to escape from the port of Mobile,

Alabama. On neither of these occasions was Farragut in personal command during the action. At Port Hudson the following spring, he was very much in charge. Apart from Vicksburg farther to the north, Port Hudson was the last remaining Confederate stronghold on the Mississippi River. In mid-March, Farragut planned to run seven ships past the batteries at Port Hudson while the Union Army mounted a diversionary land attack. But coordination failed and Farragut carried out his river operation without support. The Confederate guns disabled five of Farragut's ships; only USS *Hartford* and a gunboat made it past the batteries. The losses were a serious setback, but the surviving force was still sufficient for Farragut to help the Army in the subsequent siege of Port Hudson, by preventing Confederate supplies coming down the Red River.

### Inspiring courage

After a period of well-earned rest in New York, Farragut was given the task in 1864 of attacking Mobile, Alabama. Lack of troops for a land-sea operation

to take the city of Mobile meant that Farragut settled for the capture of Mobile Bay and the ships there. This was in itself an ambitious goal, for Confederate defenses were well prepared. Farragut's squadron would have to pass under the guns of Fort Morgan along a channel sown with mines (then called torpedoes) and fight Confederate ships that included the large ironclad CSS *Tennessee*.

This was the kind of operation for which Farragut seemed to have been born, demanding what Gideon Welles called his "innate fearless moral courage." When one of Farragut's lead ships was sunk by a mine the whole venture almost foundered, but he led the squadron through the minefield, famously calling out, "Damn the torpedoes, full speed ahead!" He was also in the forefront of the subsequent naval battle in which CSS *Tennessee* was, with difficulty, overcome.

The hard-fought success at Mobile Bay carried Farragut's reputation to unparalleled heights. He played no further significant part in the Civil War, exhaustion and poor health taking their toll, but he was much celebrated afterward. He acted as a pallbearer at Lincoln's funeral, was promoted to full admiral, and was sent with a squadron across the Atlantic to be feted in European capitals.

Farragut was buried in Woodlawn Cemetery in the Bronx district of New York in 1870, after being accorded a funeral of memorable grandeur.

### The Battle of Mobile Bay

Farragut stands in the rigging of USS *Hartford* as the battle rages in Mobile Bay on August 5, 1864. He mounted the ship's rigging at the height of the combat to see above the smoke of the guns.

## TIMELINE

**July 5, 1801** Born James Glasgow Farragut near Knoxville on the Tennessee River, where his Spanish-born father, Jorgé Farragut, was a ferryboat operator.

**1808** After the death of his mother, Farragut is adopted by naval officer David Porter, in whose honor he later changes his first name from James to David.

**December 1810** Appointed a naval midshipman, sailing under Porter aboard the frigate USS *Essex*.

**March 28, 1814** During the War of 1812, Farragut is taken prisoner by the British after the capture of the *Essex* off Valparaíso harbor, Chile.

**1821** After seeing service in the Mediterranean, Farragut is promoted lieutenant; he is made first lieutenant in 1825, and commander in 1841.

**September 1823** Marries Susan C. Marchant of Norfolk, Virginia; takes up residence in Norfolk, where he works at the Navy Yard.

**December 1843** Three years after the death of his first wife, Farragut marries Virginia Loyall; they have one son.

**1854–58** Establishes the Navy Yard at Mare Island, California, as a facility for ship repair on the West Coast; promoted to captain (September 1855).

**April 18, 1861** The day after Virginia's secession, Farragut, choosing to stay loyal to the Union, leaves Norfolk for New York.

**January 9, 1862** Given command of the West Gulf Blockading Squadron with orders to capture New Orleans.

**April 24–25, 1862** Farragut's squadron defies the guns of the Mississippi forts and fights through to New Orleans; this feat wins him promotion to rear admiral, a rank not previously accorded in the U.S. Navy.

**June–July 1862** Farragut's squadron takes part in an unsuccessful attempt to reduce the Confederate fortress at Vicksburg by naval action.

**March 14, 1863** Fails to coordinate effectively with land forces at Port Hudson on the Mississippi.

**August 5, 1864** In his most famous action, Farragut leads a naval force into Mobile Bay off the Alabama coast and destroys a squadron of Confederate warships.

**December 21, 1864** Becomes the first man appointed to the rank of vice admiral in the U.S. Navy.

**July 26, 1866** Made a full admiral—the United States' first—a post created specifically for him by Congress.

**August 14, 1870** Dies of a stroke in New Hampshire; on September 30 he is given a magnificent state funeral.

**FARRAGUT IN ABOUT 1840**

# Action on the Mississippi River

**The struggle for control of the Mississippi in 1862 brought strange warships into conflict, from cottonclad rams to "Pook Turtles," in battles at Island Number Ten, Plum Point Bend, and Memphis. The campaign was a disaster for the Confederacy, but the Union side also fell short of its final objective.**

At the outset of the Civil War, the Anaconda Plan proposed by Union general-in-chief Winfield Scott gave priority to an advance down the Mississippi to cut the Confederacy in two. Whether considered desirable or not, such an offensive was not immediately possible because it required the creation of a Union river fleet that could cooperate with the army to overcome the Confederate fortresses dominating the waterway. For the construction of a flotilla of ironclad river gunboats, the Union turned to engineer and industrialist James Eads. He built seven vessels from scratch to a design by Samuel Pook, a naval architect based in Cairo, Illinois. They were shallow-draft ships driven by a paddlewheel at the stern and enclosed in sloping iron armor. Officially called City-class gunboats, they were better known by their nickname: Pook Turtles. The seven ironclads formed the core of the Western Gunboat Flotilla, initially under U.S. Army control. The Confederates, in contrast, had to make do with adapting riverboats into ships of war, usually by adding cotton bales as armor—making them "cottonclads"—then reinforcing the prow with iron to make a ram, and by arming them with one or two guns.

### Island Number Ten
The first strongpoint that Union forces needed to overcome as they pressed down the Mississippi was Island Number Ten, a fortified position at a turn in the river near the town of New Madrid. At the start of March 1862, Major General John Pope's newly formed Army of the Mississippi, advancing through Missouri, arrived outside New Madrid. Unable to resist Union siege guns, the Confederates quickly abandoned the town, but the island was a tougher obstacle. The Union

**The "Pook Turtle"**
USS *Cairo* was one of the Union City-class ironclad gunboats designed by Samuel Pook for the river war. Commissioned in January 1862, she initially had 16 guns and a crew of 250.

> " ... they **struck terror** into every guilty soul as they **floated down the river**."
>
> CREW MEMBER OF A POOK TURTLE, 1862

**The Battle of Memphis**
The Confederate cottonclad CSS *General Beauregard* is rammed by USS *Monarch* off Memphis on June 6, 1862. The revival of the ancient naval tactic of ramming was an unexpected result of the use of armored steam ships.

## BEFORE

Both sides in the Civil War recognized that control of the Mississippi River was a major strategic objective. The Union held Cairo, Illinois, at the confluence of the Mississippi and Ohio, but the Confederates hoped to prevent them from advancing farther south.

**CONFEDERATE MOVES**
In September 1861, Confederate troops under General **Leonidas Polk seized Columbus on the Mississippi** in Kentucky. He turned it into a **fortress with 143 guns** trained on the river, which was blocked by a chain. This **"Gibraltar of the West"** presented a **formidable obstacle to any Union advance** down the Mississippi.

However, after the **fall of Fort Donelson in February 1862 104–105 》》** Columbus was abandoned without a fight, rendered untenable by the threat to its supply lines. Part of the garrison and many of its guns were relocated 50 miles (80km) south at **Island Number Ten**.

**UNION STRATEGY**
On February 23, 1862, the **Union commander in the Western theater, General Henry Halleck,** ordered the creation of the **Army of the Mississippi.** With 25,000 men under Major General John Pope, the army's task was to **advance down the Mississippi River** in cooperation **with the river fleet.**

### James Buchanan Eads

An inventive civil engineer and businessman, Eads helped to think up the idea of a Union flotilla of ironclads in the Mississippi. The seven City-class ships were constructed at his shipyards.

river flotilla arrived with its seven ironclads plus a group of mortar schooners, but their guns failed to have a decisive impact on the island's defenses. Pope's solution was to work his way around the Confederate position and cut its supply line through Tennessee. He dug a canal to move troop transports downstream of the island and also had two ironclads slip past the island's batteries under cover of darkness. With this support, his troops were able to cross the river to the Tennessee shore. Surrounded and outnumbered, the island garrison surrendered on April 8.

### Confederate success

The chief remaining obstacle between the Union gunboats and their destination Memphis was Fort Pillow, which the gunboats started to bombard in May. Desperate to defend Memphis, the Confederates sent eight cottonclad rams north, leaving New Orleans seriously

short of naval defense. On May 10, the cottonclads, commanded by James Montgomery, inflicted a sharp reverse on the Union flotilla at Fort Pillow. They pressed through Union gunfire to ram the ironclads USS *Mound City* and USS *Cincinatti*, both of which sank.

### Memphis falls

This action, often known as the Battle of Plum Point Bend, boosted Confederate morale, but did not reverse the tide of the war. Fort Pillow fell regardless, abandoned by the Confederates after the Union capture of the vital railroad junction at Corinth in late May left it exposed to land attack.

By June 1862, New Orleans had fallen to Farragut's fleet and Memphis was now indefensible in the face of Union armies pushing south from Tennessee. A climactic river battle was fought in sight of the city on June 6. Impressed by the effectiveness of Confederate rams at Plum Point Bend, the Union

**1** The number of Union casualties recorded at the naval battle of Memphis. The victim was Charles Ellet, commander of the Union rams, who was fatally wounded. The Confederates lost about 180 men.

flotilla had acquired its own squadron of nine rams—converted tugs rebuilt by Pennsylania engineer Charles Ellet and crewed by civilian riverboat men. When Montgomery's cottonclad rams steamed out to meet the Union flotilla, cheered on by crowds of spectators on the Memphis bluffs, they were crushed by Ellet's rams and the gunfire of the five remaining Union Pook Turtles. Only one Confederate ship escaped.

### Vicksburg stands firm

With the fall of Memphis, only the Confederate fortress at Vicksburg stood in the way of Union control of the Mississippi. In late June, Farragut's fleet steamed upriver to join the river flotilla in a combined attack on Vicksburg, but their guns made little impression on a determined garrison. On July 15, CSS *Arkansas*, a Confederate ironclad arrived at Vicksburg and sailed through the Union fleet, disabling the ironclad USS *Carondelet* and inflicting substantial casualties before taking refuge under the fortress's guns. This act of bravado was followed by the withdrawal of the Union ships in late July, conceding that for now Vicksburg could not be overcome.

## AFTER

Confederate efforts to reverse Union gain on the Mississippi failed, but Union forces found it difficult to make further progress

### ASSAULT ON BATON ROUGE

In late July, Confederate troops under **John C. Breckinridge** were sent to retake Baton Rouge with support from the **ironclad CSS Arkansas** and a **river squadron**. Breckinridge attacked on August 5 with some success, but his **naval support never materialized**, as the *Arkansas* suffered engine failure. Exposed to fire from Union gunboats, the Confederates withdrew.

**THE BATTLE OF BATON ROUGE**

### ATTEMPTS TO TAKE VICKSBURG

Through the second half of 1862, efforts by Union **General Grant** to mount a land assault on Vicksburg were equally **unsuccessful**. The **Confederate fortress** at Vicksburg was not **conquered until July 1863 190–193 »**

# The CSS *Arkansas* Runs Through the Union Fleet

**Armed with ten guns, the CSS *Arkansas*, a largely homemade ironclad, sailed through the large Union fleet anchored above Vicksburg. The fearless Confederates let loose a firestorm of shot, crippling the ironclad USS *Carondelet* and damaging a number of other ships. The *Arkansas* then slipped boldly past the Union forces to be greeted ecstatically by the citizens of Vicksburg.**

"Aided by the current of the Mississippi, we soon approached the Federal fleet—a forest of masts and smokestacks—ships, rams, iron-clads, and other gun-boats on the left side, and ordinary river steamers and bomb-vessels along the right. To any one having a real ram at command the genius of havoc could not have offered a finer view, the panoramic effect of which was intensified by the city of men spread out with innumerable tents opposite on the right bank. We were not yet in sight of Vicksburg, but in every direction, except astern, our eyes rested on enemies. It seemed at a glance as if a whole navy had come to keep me away from the heroic city—six or seven rams, four or five iron-clads ...

As we advanced, the line of fire seemed to grow into a circle constantly closing ... The shock of missiles striking our sides was literally continuous, and as we were now surrounded without room for anything but pushing ahead, and shrapnel shot were coming on our shield deck, twelve pounds at a time, I went below to see how our Missouri backwoodsmen were handling their 100-pounder Columbiads. At this moment I had the most lively realization of having steamed into a real volcano, the Arkansas from its center firing rapidly to every point of the circumference, without the fear of hitting a friend or missing an enemy ... It was a little hot this morning all around; the enemy's shot frequently found weak places in our armor, and their shrapnel and minié-balls also came through our port-holes. Still, under a temperature of 120, our people kept to their work ...

We were now at the end of what had seemed the interminable line, and also past the outer rim of the volcano ... As the little group of heroes closed around me with their friendly words of congratulation, a heavy rifle-shot passed close over our heads: it was the parting salutation ..."

CAPTAIN ISAAC N. BROWN, COMMANDER OF THE CSS *ARKANSAS*, FROM *BATTLES AND LEADERS OF THE CIVIL WAR*, 1888

**Exchange of fire**
The daring *Arkansas* is seen carving her way between Union shipping on the Mississippi, exchanging fire at close range. The ironclad sank no enemy ships, but caused significant casualties in the Union navy.

# Grant Takes Forts Henry and Donelson

**Ulysses S. Grant first came to prominence through the capture of these two Confederate forts on the Cumberland and Tennessee rivers in February 1862. The loss of the forts was a serious setback for the Confederacy, leading directly to the fall of the Tennessee state capital, Nashville, to the Union.**

### BEFORE

Based at Cairo, Illinois, Union land and naval forces were well placed to invade Confederate territory along three rivers—the Mississippi, Tennessee, and Cumberland.

#### AMPHIBIOUS OFFENSIVE
The prelude to river operations was the **building of seven ironclads ‹‹ 100–101**, completed in January 1862, to create the **Western Gunboat Flotilla**. Union General **Henry W. Halleck** still hesitated to take action, but his subordinate **Brigadier General Ulysses S. Grant** was **more eager to fight**. Grant, who had made an **amphibious sortie** against **Belmont** on the Mississippi in November 1861, now proposed an **attack on Fort Henry** on the Tennessee.

The decision to attack Fort Henry was made at the end of January 1862. Built the previous year, the fort was poorly sited and unlikely to be able to withstand infantry assault or naval gunfire for very long. The attack was to be a joint operation by two army divisions under General Grant—some 15,000 men—and a flotilla under Commander Andrew H. Foote, comprising four of the new City-class ironclads and three timberclads (with timber, rather than iron, armor). The two commanders were contrasting characters, Grant a down-to-earth man

with a reputation for drinking, Foote a high-minded teetotaler. But they formed a harmonious team, good relations aided by Grant's acceptance that reducing the fort would be a matter for the gunboats.

#### Fall of Fort Henry
Steaming down the Tennessee on February 5, the gunboats and troop transports encountered mines, but these caused no damage. The troops landed several miles from Fort Henry and were still struggling to reach their objective across difficult terrain when, on February 6, Foote opened the naval

**Bombarding Fort Henry**
The ironclads and timberclads of Foote's Western Gunboat Flotilla overcame resistance from the shore batteries at Fort Henry on the Cumberland River by naval bombardment alone.

attack. Most of the Confederates swiftly left for Fort Donelson, 12 miles (19km) away on the Cumberland River. Artillerymen remained with their guns, but after two hours the defenders of the wrecked fort surrendered.

Confederate General Albert Sidney Johnston, commander of the Western Military Department, now had to

> "No terms except an **unconditional and immediate surrender** can be accepted."
> ULYSSES S. GRANT'S REPLY TO GENERAL BUCKNER'S REQUEST FOR TERMS AT FORT DONELSON, FEBRUARY 16, 1862

decide whether to attempt a defense of Fort Donelson and with what strength. When Fort Henry fell, he withdrew his forces from Kentucky to Nashville, but instead of concentrating all his troops there, he sent 12,000 men to reinforce Fort Donelson. Command of the fort was placed in the hands of John Floyd, a controversial secretary of war in the Buchanan government before the war.

### First attacks on Fort Donelson

General Halleck's intention after the fall of Fort Henry was to hold what had been gained. Grant had finally arrived at Fort Henry on February 14 after a

**Grant looking over the battlefield**
On horseback, Ulysses Grant surveys the scene at snowy Fort Donelson on February 15, 1862. Some 2,500 Union soldiers and around 1,500 Confederates were killed or wounded in the battle.

difficult march, but set off for Fort Donelson as soon as he could. There he was reinforced by a further 10,000 troops sent by Halleck, giving him clear numerical superiority over the fort's defenders—25,000 Union soldiers faced 16,000 Confederates. The Confederate strongpoint was not a fort in the conventional sense. It was a 15-acre (6-hectare) encampment defended on the river side by batteries of heavy guns dug into the high cliffs and on the landward side by field fortifications that exploited the rugged terrain of wooded slopes and ravines.

The first attempt on the fort was made by Foote's flotilla, but the accurate fire from the high-placed shore batteries, directed downward to crash through the ships' decks, disabled the Union vessels one by one. There followed an attack on the landward side of the fort, led by one of Grant's divisional commanders, John McClernand, but this was also repulsed. Grant faced the uncomfortable prospect of a long siege in harsh winter weather. His men settled down opposite the Confederate

**James Tuttle**
Colonel James Tuttle led the 2nd Iowa Regiment in the final assault on Fort Donelson and planted the Union flag inside the Confederate earthworks.

trenches in conditions of considerable hardship, some without overcoats or blankets, sleeping on the bare ground in freezing rain and snow.

### Attempted breakout

The Confederate commanders, however, had already decided that their position was hopeless. Floyd decided to attempt a breakout that would enable his force to rejoin General Albert S. Johnston at Nashville. The bulk of the defenders, under Brigadier General Gideon Pillow, were concentrated in front of McClernand's division on the Union right, and at dawn on February 15 they attacked with their blood-chilling rebel yell. By chance, Grant had left to consult with Foote some way down river. With no one to coordinate a Union response, McClernand's troops were driven back, taking heavy casualties. The Confederate cavalry, under Colonel Nathan Bedford Forrest, distinguished itself in a series of flanking attacks. For the Union side, Brigadier General Lew Wallace (future author of *Ben Hur*) reinforced the flank and held a vital hill line.

The opportunity was there for Pillow to complete the breakout, but, shocked by the condition of his troops, he withdrew back to the trenches. When Grant arrived at the battle, he pointed out to his badly shaken officers that if many of their own troops were demoralized, the Confederates, having fallen back, must be even more so. Grant ordered an assault on the center of the Confederate line, which he reasoned must have been weakened to provide troops for the flank breakout. Colonel James Tuttle's 2nd Iowa Regiment duly penetrated the Confederate defenses, while, on the right, Wallace regained all the ground lost earlier in the day. That night, in a rush to save their own troops, Floyd and Pillow slipped away under cover of darkness. Forrest escaped with 700 troopers by riding through the Union lines. Command devolved to Brigadier General Simon Bolivar Buckner. The next morning, Buckner's request for terms was met by Grant's demand for "immediate surrender." Buckner had no choice but to comply, passing into captivity along with more than 12,000 other Confederate soldiers.

## AFTER

**The loss of Fort Donelson undermined the Confederate strategic position in the Western theater, leading to the loss of all of Kentucky and most of Tennessee.**

### CONFEDERATE WITHDRAWALS

With Grant advancing down the Tennessee River and under pressure from Buell's Army of the Ohio, **Albert Johnston abandoned Nashville** on February 23, handing the Tennessee state capital to the Union without a fight. The Confederate stronghold at **Columbus on the Mississippi was abandoned** shortly after. The withdrawn Confederate forces **concentrated at Corinth, Mississippi**. From there a **counter-offensive was mounted** that led to the **Battle of Shiloh at Pittsburg Landing 106–107 »**.

### UNION VICTORY AT PEA RIDGE

Shortly after Fort Donelson, the Confederacy suffered another defeat in the Western theater. At the **Battle of Pea Ridge**, fought in **northern Arkansas** on March 6–8, 1862, a Confederate army under Major General Earl Van Dorn was **decisively defeated** by a **smaller Union force** commanded by Brigadier General Samuel Curtis.

**General Buckner's tunic**
A few Confederate generals wore this style of pleated tunic rather than the usual double-breasted frock coat. The wealthy Buckner had been a friend of Grant's before the war and had helped him out of financial difficulties.

# The Battle of Shiloh

The battle fought at Pittsburg Landing on April 6–7, 1862—and usually named for the nearby Shiloh Church—was by far the most bloody up to that point in the Civil War, leaving some 20,000 men dead or wounded. The Confederacy came close to a major victory, but instead suffered another crushing reverse.

## BEFORE

After taking Fort Donelson, the Union Army of West Tennessee advanced toward Corinth, Mississippi, where the Confederates were planning to strike back.

### THE ROAD TO SHILOH

On March 4, 1862, the victor at **Fort Donelson** ❮❮ **104–105**, **Ulysses S. Grant**, was relieved of his command by Henry W. Halleck for alleged neglect and inefficiency, but the decision was **reversed** under **pressure from President Lincoln**. By early April, Grant was back in command at Pittsburg Landing on the west bank of the Tennessee. Halleck ordered Don Carlos Buell to march his Army of Ohio to join Grant's six divisions.

Confederate generals **Albert S. Johnston** and **P. G. T. Beauregard** concentrated their forces at Corinth. Reinforced by 15,000 troops under Braxton Bragg, they intended to **attack and destroy Grant before Buell arrived.**

---

### CONFEDERATE GENERAL 1803–62

## ALBERT S. JOHNSTON

Born in Kentucky, Johnston fought against Mexico as a general in the Texan Army and the U.S. Army. He was commander of the Pacific Department in California when the Civil War broke out, making a hazardous crossing of the southwest to join the Confederacy. Much admired by President Davis, he was appointed a full general and commander of the Western Department. Although the loss of forts Henry and Donelson had harmed his reputation, his death at Shiloh was still a blow to the Confederate cause.

---

In the run-up to the battle, Grant was culpably complacent. The Union encampment among creeks and swamps at Pittsburg Landing was not protected by field fortifications, one Union division under Lew Wallace was positioned 5 miles (8km) away from the rest, and Grant's headquarters were even farther away, at Savannah. The march of 42,000 Confederates from Corinth was slow and ill-conducted, but Union commanders failed to detect the threat of an imminent attack. The first of Buell's troops reached Savannah on April 5, but there was no rush to move them to Pittsburg Landing.

### Dawn attack

At first light on April 6 the Confederates attacked, achieving almost total surprise. The brunt of the onslaught was borne by two previously unblooded divisions under generals William T. Sherman and Benjamin M. Prentiss. Their hastily improvised response bought the Union forces time and averted a rout. Grant arrived from Savannah by steamboat around 8:30 a.m. and found the position on the 6-mile (10-km) wide battlefield desperate. Many raw troops had fled the battle, cowering along the riverbank. Leaving Sherman in control of the Union defense on the right flank, Grant ordered Prentiss to hold the line in the center in a position that would become known as the Hornet's Nest. By early afternoon the Union left flank was collapsing, some units having sustained in excess of 50 percent casualties. Confederate losses were also high, however. General Johnston was riding forward to urge his exhausted men to press for victory when he was wounded and bled to death. Beauregard took over command.

### The Union onslaught

The defense of the Hornet's Nest ended around 5:30 p.m., when 62 Confederate field guns were trained upon the few thousand defenders. By then, Union reinforcements were arriving to help Grant hold a last-ditch line along a ridge overlooking a steep ravine. In gathering twilight, Beauregard soon abandoned an attempt to assault this strong defensive position in the face of a concentrated artillery barrage and fire from river gunboats.

The two exhausted armies endured a night of heavy rain and thunderstorms. Many shaken officers on the Union side

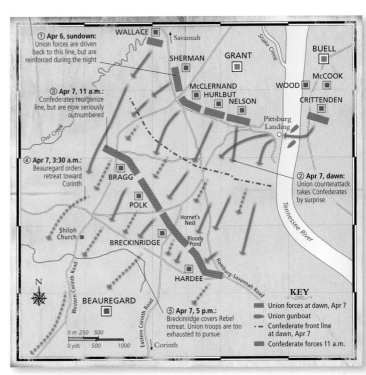

① Apr 6, sundown:
Union forces are driven back to this line, but are reinforced during the night

③ Apr 7, 11 a.m.:
Confederates reorganize line, but are now seriously outnumbered

④ Apr 7, 3:30 a.m.:
Beauregard orders retreat toward Corinth

② Apr 7, dawn:
Union counterattack takes Confederates by surprise

⑤ Apr 7, 5 p.m.:
Breckinridge covers Rebel retreat. Union troops are too exhausted to pursue

WALLACE · Savannah · SHERMAN · GRANT · BUELL · McCOOK · McCLERNAND · HURLBUT · WOOD · NELSON · CRITTENDEN · Pittsburg Landing · Owl Creek · BRAGG · POLK · Hornet's Nest · Shiloh Church · Bloody Pond · BRECKINRIDGE · Tennessee River · HARDEE · Hamburg-Savannah Road · BEAUREGARD · Western Corinth Road · Eastern Corinth Road · N · Corinth

0 m 250 500 1000
0 yds 500 1000

**KEY**

| | |
|---|---|
| ▬ | Union forces at dawn, Apr 7 |
| ▬ | Union gunboat |
| ·-· | Confederate front line at dawn, Apr 7 |
| ▬ | Confederate forces 11 a.m. |

**The second day of the battle**
After the first day, many Confederate troops moved back from the front line to sleep. The next morning, the Union onslaught caught them unawares, driving them back over the ground they had won the previous day.

felt beaten, but when Grant was asked if he intended to retreat he replied, "No! I propose to attack at daylight and whip them." Buell's and Wallace's fresh troops continued to arrive throughout the night. By the morning of April 7, the Union army had the superiority of numbers to launch a counteroffensive. This time it was Beauregard who was caught by surprise. Rebel troops fell back in disarray as Union forces advanced across the previous day's corpse-strewn battlefield. After hard fighting in the early afternoon, Beauregard, fearing a rout, ordered a general retreat.

Grant did not attempt a pursuit, but on the next day he sent Sherman on a reconnaissance mission to see whether the Confederates were regrouping for another attack. This led to a clash with Colonel Nathan Bedford Forrest's cavalry at Fallen Timbers, in which Forrest was seriously wounded. This skirmish marked the end of the fighting.

## AFTER

In the Battle of Shiloh, the Union army lost over 13,000 men—casualties and prisoners—while the Confederates had fewer than 11,000 losses. It took time for the reality of the Confederate defeat to be acknowledged.

### AFTERMATH OF THE BATTLE

**Ulysses S. Grant** came under severe **criticism in the Northern press**, with reports exaggerating the unpreparedness of Union troops. It was even **rumored that he had been drunk**. Lincoln continued to support him, however, stating, **"I can't spare this man, he fights."**

After the battle, Halleck, relegating Grant to second in command, led a cautious **advance on Corinth**. Rather than face a siege, Beauregard withdrew south to Tupelo, Mississippi, in late May. For this, **he was fired by President Davis**, who **appointed Bragg** in his place.

The Union fleet engaged in a series of actions on the Mississippi ❮❮ **100–101**. On June 6, they took Memphis, where Grant, restored four days later as **commander of the Federal Army of the Tennessee**, made his headquarters.

**Infantry clash**
Confederate troops encounter fire from a close-packed Union infantry line during the Battle of Shiloh. In the absence of prepared defenses, the only cover was provided by trees and other natural features.

EYEWITNESS April 6, 1862

# The Hornet's Nest at Shiloh

**On the first day of the Battle of Shiloh the Confederates launched a surprise attack that forced the Union army back toward the Tennessee River. In confused and ferocious fighting, General Benjamin Prentiss's men stood firm, defending a roadside position against repeated enemy charges—the noise of shrapnel and bullets buzzing through the trees gave the place its nickname of the Hornet's Nest. Although the Union troops surrendered after many hours, their resistance provided time for the Union forces to reorganize. The next day, Grant's reinforced army drove the Confederates back across the captured ground.**

"Oh! The angry tempest that rolls around here! Belching cannons, shotted to the muzzle, are now plowing deep lanes in the Union ranks. How can we describe the sound of a storm of grape and canister, cutting their hellish paths through serried ranks of human beings. It is impossible ... the mighty armies are now struggling—struggling desperately for the life or death of a nation. Fiercer and fiercer rages the battle ... but fearful odds are against us ... the harsh, fierce barking of the dogs of war made the earth tremble, as if in the midst of a convulsion ... confusion reigns; brave men are falling like rain drops. All seems dark—seems that the Union army will be crushed by this wild sweep of treason ... the old Union banner seems to be drooping in the wrathful storm, but by an almost superhuman effort the tide is checked ... night comes ... the sable curtains have now fallen, closing to our eyes the terrible scene. Soon it commences to rain. Dark, dark night for the army of the Tennessee. Many brave men are sleeping silently. They have fought their last battle. Fearful, desolating war has done a desperate work ... the Seventh, tired and almost exhausted, drops down to the ground, unmindful of the falling rain, to rest themselves ... disastrous war has wrapped its winding sheet around the cold form of many a fond mother's boy, and before many days there will be weeping in the lonely cottage homes; weeping for the loved and lost who are now sleeping beneath the tall oaks on the banks of the Tennessee. About the noble men of the Seventh who fell today, we will speak hereafter; we shall not forget them. How could we forget them, when they have played their part so well in the great tragedy?"

DANIEL AMBROSE, 7TH ILLINOIS INFANTRY, *FROM SHILOH TO SAVANNAH*, 1868;
ENLISTED AT 18 YEARS OLD, AMBROSE FOUGHT IN THE ACTION AT THE HORNET'S NEST

**Holding back the Confederates**
Swedish-born artist Thure de Thulstrup created this color lithograph depicting the fighting at the Hornet's Nest. Two Union divisions managed to hold out along this stretch of road for seven hours before they surrendered.

# Jackson in the Shenandoah Valley

**The Confederates' Shenandoah Valley Campaign was a diversionary operation that kept large bodies of Union troops occupied and unable to support McClellan's attack on Richmond. Taking enormous risks, General Jackson won victories through rapid movement, surprise, and the incompetence of his opponents.**

**BEFORE**

By spring 1862, Confederate survival was threatened by a series of military setbacks. Jackson's campaign in the Shenandoah Valley looked set to be another.

**POOR RELATIONS**
General Stonewall Jackson was placed in command of the **Confederate Department of Northern Virginia** in October 1861, with responsibility for the defense of the 150-mile (240-km) long Shenandoah Valley. The following winter his insistence on campaigning in harsh weather **brought his troops close to mutiny**. Some of his officers complained to politicians and it was with some difficulty that he was **dissuaded from resigning**.

**UNION VICTORIES**
The Confederacy's **setbacks in the Western Theater** in the first months of 1862 included the **losses of New Orleans ≪ 96–97 and of forts Henry and Donelson ≪ 104–05**. In Virginia, by May, Union General George B. McClellan's **Army of the Potomac** had landed on **the Virginia Peninsula** and had advanced to within **a few miles of Richmond 116–17 ≫**.

Union forces made the first move in the campaign in March 1862. Their aim was to eliminate any offensive threat from General Jackson's small army in the Valley, thereby allowing Union troops to be switched from the defense of Washington to the attack on Richmond. Major General Nathaniel Banks led an army across the Potomac River, forcing Jackson, who was heavily outnumbered, to withdraw south from his base at Winchester.

Pursuing the Confederates for some 50 miles (80km), a Union division under Brigadier General James Shields lost contact and assumed Jackson had withdrawn. But as Shields returned toward Winchester, Jackson pursued him and counterattacked. Wounded, Shields ceded command to Colonel Nathan Kimball, who defeated the Confederates at Kernstown on March 23. Jackson retreated, having lost around a third of his force, yet the strategic effect of the battle was everything the Confederates could have desired. Startled by Jackson's aggression, Union commanders

**35,000** The number of Union troops in the Valley in March 1862

**5,000** The number of Confederate troops in the Valley in March 1862

redoubled their efforts to crush him. As long as Jackson kept campaigning, Union troops would not be transferred from Washington to Richmond.

Jackson's success in the subsequent campaign would depend on two factors: speed of movement, achieved by driving his marching men so hard they became known as the "foot cavalry;" and superior intelligence. The latter derived both from cooperation on the part of the local population, who gave Jackson information about enemy movements, and from the work of staff cartographer Jedediah Hotchkiss, who made accurate maps of the Valley.

**Confederate numbers bolstered**
Backed by Robert E. Lee, then President Davis's military adviser, Jackson was reinforced by the dispatch of a division under Major General Richard S. Ewell. Jackson and Ewell proved effective partners, both thoroughly eccentric men but fierce fighting generals.

By mid-April, Jackson was on the move again. He utterly confused his enemy by crossing the Blue Ridge

Mountains toward Richmond, only to return by train to Staunton at the southern end of the Valley. He then struck westward, where a Union army under Major General John C. Frémont was trying to push through the mountains of western Virginia into east Tennessee. Jackson's men defeated Frémont's advanced guard at the hamlet of McDowell on May 8, which alerted Union General Nathaniel Banks to expect trouble. He took up a position

Iron heel plate

Iron nails

**Infantryman's boots**
Hobnail boots were standard issue footwear for infantrymen. Known as brogans (from the Irish brogue) or Jefferson bootees, the nails gave the leather soles a better grip in the field.

**KEY MOMENT**
## THE BATTLE OF WINCHESTER

On May 25, 1862, Jackson's 16,000 Confederates advanced on Winchester in hot pursuit of Banks's 7,000 retreating Union soldiers. Although exhausted by marches and firefights, the Confederate troops maintained their momentum, preventing Banks from consolidating a defensive line. Jackson's forces attacked the Union right, while Ewell's small force put pressure on their left. After serious fighting, in which General Richard Taylor's Louisiana Brigade played a key role, the Union troops withdrew through the town and on to the Potomac River. Jackson's weary men failed to mount a vigorous pursuit, but they had taken Winchester.

**The Shenandoah Valley**
The Valley was important to Confederate armies as it offered a strategic route to attack Washington, Maryland, and Pennsylvania. It also became an important source of food for the Confederacy.

**March to Cross Keys**
Artist Edwin Forbes accompanied Union troops advancing to Cross Keys in June 1862. This sketch shows Frémont's troops pursuing Jackson through the woods.

across the main road at Strasburg, but Jackson and Ewell marched hard and fast around his flank. They defeated a small Union force at Front Royal on May 22 and threatened to cut Banks's line of communication. As his column raced to withdraw from Strasburg to Winchester, the Confederates attacked. With an extraordinary effort, Jackson's and Ewell's exhausted troops continued the fight until Winchester was taken.

## Union forces diverted
President Lincoln was pushed into the aggressive response that Confederate strategy had desired. He diverted a corps under Brigadier General Irvin McDowell, previously bound for Richmond, into the Valley to join with Frémont and Banks in an operation to trap and destroy Jackson's army. Together they would have 60,000 men to Jackson's 17,000. Alert to the danger, Jackson drove his men by a series of forced marches from the environs of

Harpers Ferry back through Strasburg—just before a Union pincer movement would have cut the road—to the only surviving bridge across the South Fork of the Shenandoah River at Port Republic. The Confederates had marched 140 miles (225km) in a week, losing hundreds of stragglers along the way. Now Jackson and Ewell turned their forces to face their pursuers.

Two Union columns, led respectively by Frémont and Shields, advanced on Port Republic. They were separated by the river, the Confederates controlling the only bridge. Ewell's division met Frémont's troops at Cross Keys on June 8 and repelled them, despite a Union numerical advantage of almost two to one. The following day two brigades of Shields's division reached Port Royal and narrowly failed to seize the bridge—almost capturing Jackson as well. Jackson's troops fought back, forcing the Union forces to quit the field after heavy losses on both sides. As neither Frémont nor Shields chose to renew the fighting, the Shenandoah Valley Campaign came to an end.

### The Shenandoah Valley Campaign
The feats of marching achieved by Jackson's forces were prodigious. In seven weeks, they marched some 650 miles (1,050km), won several small battles, and, most importantly, kept Union troops that were needed for the Peninsula Campaign occupied in the Valley.

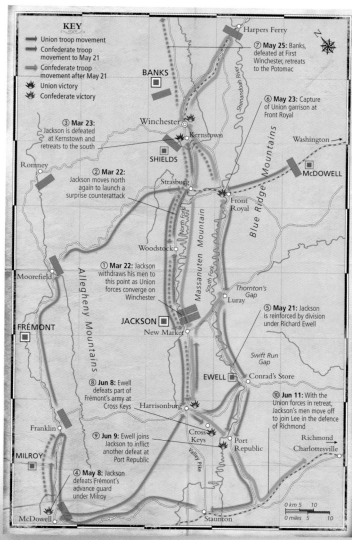

**AFTER**

Occurring against a backdrop of Confederate defeats elsewhere, Jackson's victories in the Shenandoah Valley were a major morale-booster for the Confederacy.

**JACKSON IN DEMAND**
In June 1862, under the command of Robert E. Lee, Jackson moved out of the Valley to lead **a surprise attack** on the right flank of the Union army in front of Richmond, in what would become the **Seven Days Battles 118–19 »**.

**REVERSAL OF FORTUNES**
The Shenandoah Valley was the scene of heavy fighting in **two further campaigns in 1864 268–69 »**. In the second, Union General Philip Sheridan used **scorched earth tactics** to render the Valley useless to the Confederates.

**CONFEDERATE MAJOR GENERAL** Born 1824 Died 1863

# Thomas J. Jackson

## "My men have sometimes failed to take a position, but to defend one, never!"

STATEMENT TO MAJOR HEROS VON BORCKE, DECEMBER 13, 1862

Widely regarded as the most inspired tactician of the Civil War, Thomas Jonathan Jackson lacked the showmanship frequently associated with heroic leaders of men. He was ungainly and introverted with an awkward and uncommunicative manner that often left people unimpressed. Yet he also possessed a total inner confidence that imposed itself upon subordinates.

An orphan raised by relatives in rural Virginia, Jackson had little formal education. As a result, he entered West Point at a disadvantage to most of his fellow students. Through sheer hard work he graduated with creditable grades. When the United States went to war with Mexico in 1846, he won the admiration of his superiors as an artillery officer with courage and determination, sufficiently confident in his own judgment to refuse an order he considered clearly wrong. However, when he was a professor at the Virginia Military Institute in the 1850s, his students found his manner and appearance ridiculous, his classes dull, and his punishments excessive.

### A damned stone wall

Jackson chose to serve the Confederacy in April 1861 out of loyalty to his home state. Given command of a Virginia brigade, he transformed its volunteers into a disciplined force with high morale, qualities demonstrated on the battlefield at First Bull Run. As his infantry stood firm on Henry House Hill, facing a Union onslaught, Confederate General Barnard E. Bee cried, "There stands Jackson like a stone wall!" Intended as praise of his resolve, Jackson was known as "Stonewall" ever after.

**Posthumous portrait**
This 1864 painting of Jackson was based on the last photograph of him taken before his death in 1863. It captures his reflective and driven character.

**Jackson memorabilia**
These items belonging to Jackson include a forage cap, the spurs he was wearing when mortally wounded, a cloth stained with blood from his wound, and a patriotic songsheet entitled "Stonewall Jackson's Way."

# "Captain, my **religious belief** teaches me to feel **as safe in battle as in bed.**"

JACKSON SPEAKING TO CAPTAIN JOHN D. IMBODEN, JULY 24, 1861

Through the following winter in the Shenandoah Valley, Jackson's career as a Civil War general looked uncertain. He seemed indifferent to the hardships imposed on troops by forced marches in foul weather and harsh conditions. Secretive and paranoid, he alienated his subordinate officers by ordering operations with no explanations. When they complained of his incompetence to the Confederate Congress, Jackson resigned in protest at political interference. Although persuaded to stay on, his relations with other officers remained a problem.

Jackson's religious faith gave him an absolute belief in his actions as the expression of a divine will. He was utterly unforgiving toward those whom he saw as falling short of the highest standard. The discipline he imposed was backed up by severe punishment.

## Supreme military competence

The Shenandoah Valley campaign of 1862 made Jackson the most admired general in the Confederate camp, a man with almost magical prestige that weighed upon the imagination of his enemies as it inspired his own people. The campaign revealed that Jackson had thought deeply about military tactics, and especially about how, in his words, "a small army may defeat a large one in detail." His principles were to "mystify, mislead, and surprise the enemy," and not to fight against heavy odds, instead

using maneuvers to "hurl your own force on the weakest part of the enemy." True to these principles, Jackson could drive his army to almost superhuman feats of endurance on the march, achieving a speed of movement that constantly exhausted his opponents and brought them to battle on his terms.

## A man of complexity

Jackson's performance in the Seven Days Battles, immediately after the Valley campaign, strikingly lacked the qualities of generalship for which he was renowned, instead highlighting disturbing eccentricities.

Preparation for the fight was slowed at a vital moment by one of Jackson's intermittent decisions to treat Sunday as a sacred Sabbath. His movement of troops during the offensive was slow and hesitant, missing opportunities for decisive maneuver. He had a startling tendency to sleep at crucial moments, paralyzing command. Nonetheless, he retained Lee's confidence, remaining his most favored lieutenant.

Jackson excelled in the Northern Virginia campaign of August 1862 that climaxed at Second Bull Run. His subsequent capture of Harpers Ferry through bombardment showed the skills of a former artillery officer. At Antietam and Fredericksburg he demonstrated his capacity for conducting a stubborn static defense in situations where maneuver was impossible. He always acted with an absolute disregard for personal safety, convinced that God would preserve him from harm until He chose the moment to strike him down. Jackson had no luxuries to ease the hardship of campaigning, often sleeping on the ground in all kinds of weather. He chose as his mount a plain, sturdy

horse—Little Sorrel—rather than a fine charger. To see their commander simply dressed, sharing their hardships and risks, reconciled his soldiers to their lot.

In May 1863, Jackson marched most of Lee's army across the Union front for a devastating surprise flank attack at Chancellorsville. It was a supreme exhibition of his skill. When the day's fighting subsided, he led his staff on a reconnaissance beyond his own lines. As they rode back in moonlit darkness nervous Confederate soldiers, believing them to be Union cavalry, opened fire. Jackson was hit three times. As a result, his left arm was amputated, prompting Lee's heartfelt comment, "He has lost his left arm; but I have lost my right." Initially, it seemed that Jackson would recover, but he succumbed to an attack of pneumonia and died eight days later.

### The Battle of Cedar Mountain
Artist Edwin Forbes sketched troops encamped before the battle on August 9, 1862—part of the Northern Virginia campaign—a hard-fought victory for Jackson.

### Henry House Hill
A sign marks the place where Jackson's men made their stand during First Bull Run, earning both brigade and commander the sobriquet "Stonewall."

## TIMELINE

- **January 21, 1824** Born in Clarksburg, Virginia, son of an attorney. Both parents die by the time he is seven years old. He is mostly raised by an uncle at Jackson's Mill, Lewis County.
- **1842–46** Studies at West Point, graduating 17th in his class of 59.
- **1846–48** Fights as an artillery officer in the War with Mexico, distinguishing himself at the battles of Veracruz, Contreras, Chapultepec, and Mexico City. Starting as a second lieutenant, he ends the war with the brevet rank of major.
- **1851** Resigning from the army, Jackson becomes a professor at the Virginia Military Institute in Lexington; he embraces Calvinism.

**JACKSON IN 1852**

- **1853** Marries Elinor Junkin, who dies a year later; subsequently he marries Mary Morrison in 1857.
- **April, 1861** At the start of the Civil War, Jackson opts for the Confederacy and is appointed an infantry colonel.
- **July 21, 1861** Having been promoted to brigadier general on July 3, Jackson distinguishes himself at the First Battle of Bull Run in command of the 1st Virginia Brigade, earning the nickname "Stonewall."
- **October 7, 1861** Put in command of the defense of the Shenandoah Valley with the rank of major general.
- **March 23, 1862** At the Battle of Kernstown, Jackson suffers the only tactical defeat of his military career.
- **April–June, 1862** Outfoxes superior Union forces in the Valley campaign, winning victories at McDowell (May 8), Front Royal (May 23), Winchester (May 25), Cross Keys (June 8), and Port Republic (June 9).
- **June 25–July 1, 1862** Performs poorly under Lee in the Seven Days Battles, participating nonetheless in another Confederate victory.
- **August 9, 1862** Jackson forestalls a Union offensive with a hard-fought victory at Cedar Mountain.
- **August 29–September 1, 1862** Plays an outstanding role in the major Confederate victory at the Second Battle of Bull Run.
- **September 15–17, 1862** Jackson captures Harpers Ferry, taking 12,500 prisoners; then supports Lee in the desperate defensive battle of Antietam.
- **December 13, 1862** Having been promoted major general in command of Second Corps (October 10), Jackson aids Lee in the crushing defensive victory at Fredericksburg.
- **May 2, 1863** Executes a daring flanking maneuver at Chancellorsville, but is later wounded by friendly fire; as a result, his left arm has to be amputated.
- **May 10, 1863** Dies of pneumonia contracted after surgery.

1 MODEL 1822 SPRINGFIELD MUSKET

2 MISSISSIPPI RIFLE

3 ENFIELD RIFLE MUSKET

4 HALL RIFLE

# Rifles and Muskets

**Infantry arms were in transition in the Civil War. Most were percussion-firing rifled weapons, like modern firearms, rather than smoothbore, flintlock muskets. But most were muzzle-loaded, unlike modern breechloading firearms.**

**1 Model 1822 Springfield musket (Confederate and Union)** Both sides used older firearms, such as this Model 1822, manufactured at the Springfield Armory in Massachusetts. It has been converted from a flintlock firing system to the more modern percussion system. **2 Model 841 Mississippi rifle (Confederate and Union)** An accurate .54-caliber percussion rifle, often carried by Confederate NCOs, skirmishers, and sharpshooters. **3 Pattern 1853 Enfield rifle musket (Confederate and Union)** This British weapon was highly prized by both sides. After the Model 1861, it was the second most widely used infantry weapon of the war. **4 Model 1819 Hall rifle (Confederate and Union)** The first percussion firearm to be produced for the U.S. military, patented in 1811. A number survived to see action on both sides. **5 Percussion caps** Most weapons of the Civil War used these brass caps filled with explosive fulminate of mercury to fire their charges. They enabled muzzle-loading weapons to fire reliably in any weather. **6 Fayetteville rifle musket (Confederate)** Produced in North Carolina from machinery seized at Harpers Ferry, this

model used brass fittings in place of scarce steel and iron. **7 Richmond rifle musket (Confederate)** Based on the Springfield Model 1855 rifle musket but fitted with a British Enfield barrel. More were produced than any other rifle in the Confederacy. **8 Tower rifle (Confederate and Union)** Enfield-type weapons produced in Birmingham, England, were known as Tower muskets or rifles. **9 Lorenz rifle (Confederate and Union)** A .54-caliber Austrian weapon that was widely imported by both sides. This example was used by the 2nd Virginia Infantry. **10 Barnett rifle (Confederate)** An Enfield variant made by the British makers Barnett & Sons. **11 Rifle cover** Made of cloth, this was an important piece of equipment to keep a rifle clean and dry. **12 Sword bayonet** Rarer than the spike bayonet, this was a deadly weapon when taking on the enemy in hand-to-hand combat. It could be attached to the end of a rifle or used separately. **13 Enfield Model 1853 bayonet and scabbard** A spike bayonet for attachment to the barrel of a rifle.

5 PERCUSSION CAPS

6 FAYETTEVILLE RIFLE MUSKET

7 RICHMOND RIFLE MUSKET

8 TOWER RIFLE

9 LORENZ RIFLE

10 BARNETT RIFLE

12 SWORD BAYONET

11 RIFLE COVER

13 SPIKE BAYONET AND SCABBARD

«
## BEFORE

The armies confronting one another in Virginia at the start of 1862 were both commanded by generals who were regarded as too negative-minded by their presidents.

### SOUTHERN ANTAGONISM
In March 1862, Confederate general **Joseph E. Johnston** withdrew his army from **Bull Run** « **60–61**. This retreat, together with the destruction of many supplies, was initially carried out **without informing President Davis**. Johnston's obstinacy angered Davis, and on March 13, **General Lee assumed the role as his military adviser**.

# 22
The number of pages in a letter sent by General McClellan to President Lincoln, rejecting the president's proposal for an overland offensive against Richmond in 1862.

### McCLELLAN'S DETERMINATION
Lincoln repeatedly urged an **offensive to break through** the Confederate line between Washington and Richmond. General **George B. McClellan**, commanding the Army of the Potomac, instituted his own plan to **outflank the Confederate defenses** and take Richmond.

# The Peninsula Campaign

In the hands of an aggressive Union commander, a seaborne landing on the Virginia Peninsula might have been a bold and imaginative way to attack the Confederate capital, Richmond. But a hesitant, over-cautious execution made General George B. McClellan's Peninsula Campaign slow and unsuccessful.

The Virginia Peninsula is a tongue of land stretching east from Richmond, between the York River to the north and the James River to the south. Eager to exploit Union command of the sea, General McClellan originally planned to transport his troops from Washington along the Potomac River into Chesapeake Bay for a landing at Urbanna on the Rappahannock River. Having bypassed the Confederate army at Manassas, south of Washington, he would then have a relatively clear run at the Confederate capital. Yet Southern General Joseph Johnston's retreat south of the Rappahannock in March 1862 forestalled him. Instead, the Union Army of the Potomac landed at Fort Monroe on the tip of the Virginia Peninsula. By April 4, McClellan had almost 60,000 troops with which to

### Army of the Potomac
McClellan established a vast camp for his 120,000-strong army on the banks of the Pamunkey River near Richmond in May 1862. This panoramic view by James Hope shows McClellan riding in the foreground.

begin an advance up the Peninsula to Richmond, and thousands more were arriving. In front was a Confederate line on the Warwick River at Yorktown, lightly manned by 14,000 troops. In Washington, Lincoln, afraid that McClellan's move had left the capital exposed to a surprise attack, urged the general to make haste with an immediate assault on the Warwick River defenses, but McClellan dismissed this as military naïveté. Johnston later commented: "No one but McClellan would have hesitated to attack."

### Johnston's reverse
Consistently overestimating Southern strength, McClellan was obsessed by the notion that his forces were insufficient. Lincoln's later decision to hold back troops to defend Washington and counteract Jackson's campaign in the Shenandoah Valley only fed McClellan's belief that he was being starved of resources. On the other side of the line,

### Artillery at Yorktown
The battle for Yorktown in April–May 1862 was largely an artillery duel. McClellan was confident his guns were superior to those of the enemy and was hesitant to attack Confederate fortifications without prior reconnaissance.

Confederate General Johnston was equally—but more rationally—convinced of the weakness of his army. In mid-April, Johnston took command at Yorktown, and planned to abandon the Peninsula and concentrate his forces in front of Richmond. On May 3, the Confederates abandoned Yorktown and the Warwick River defenses. Breaking contact with the enemy in a deftly executed maneuver, Johnston's troops, now numbering some 50,000, fell back toward Richmond. A part of the army was designated to fight a holding action on a defensive line at Williamsburg, and on May 5 this inflicted a reverse on pursuing Union troops. The fiercely fought encounter was almost as costly for both sides as the First Battle of Bull Run, despite the engagement of far smaller forces.

### Cautious approach
McClellan advanced up the Peninsula at a snail's pace along muddy roads. His army took two weeks to march 50 miles (80km) from Williamsburg, before setting up camp near Richmond between the Pamunkey and Chickahominy rivers. McClellan called for reinforcements. Lincoln refused to send any by sea, but he did order a 40,000-strong corps under Irvin McDowell to advance overland from Fredericksburg to join the Army of the Potomac. Much to McClellan's anger, this move was canceled in response to Jackson's victory at Winchester in the

### CONFEDERATE GENERAL 1807–91
## JOSEPH E. JOHNSTON

Virginian Joseph Eggleston Johnston was quartermaster general of the U.S. Army in April 1861 when he resigned to serve the Confederacy. Although made a full general by Davis, he developed a lasting feud with the Confederate president. When he was wounded at Seven Pines in May 1862, Davis replaced him with Robert E. Lee. After his recovery, Johnston held a series of commands in the Western Theater. His cautious attitude repeatedly enraged Davis, but his skill in conducting a retreat demanded respect. Surviving the war, he was elected for a term in Congress in 1878.

> "You may find **those who will go faster than I**, Mr. President; but it is **very doubtful** if you will find **many who will go further**."
>
> GENERAL GEORGE B. McCLELLAN, IN A LETTER TO LINCOLN AFTER HIS REMOVAL FROM COMMAND, NOVEMBER 1862

## AFTER

After the wounding of General Johnston at Seven Pines on May 31, General Lee was given command of forces that he renamed as the Army of Northern Virginia.

### LEE'S STRATEGY

Despite heavy casualties on both sides—more than 4,000 Union and 5,500 Confederate troops killed or wounded—**Seven Pines** was an **indecisive battle** that left the **Army of the Potomac** in a position **threatening Richmond**. Lee's first action on taking command was to **reinforce the earthwork fortifications** around the city—and many expected him to adopt a defensive stance. Instead, Lee ordered General **Stonewall Jackson's army** to join him from the **Shenandoah Valley** ≪ 110–11 and began planning an attack on the Union right flank, which would initiate the **Seven Days Battles 118–19 ≫**.

### McCLELLAN DISCONCERTED

Struck down by malaria, McClellan had been out of action during the battle. Despite **claiming a victory**, he was **demoralized by the heavy casualties** his army had sustained, finding many reasons to **postpone his offensive** against Richmond. He was convinced, contrary to reality, that he faced "overwhelming numbers."

Shenandoah Valley on May 25. The Confederates, meanwhile, viewed their situation with alarm, and the people of Richmond were thrown into a state of panic by the approach of a Union naval squadron, including two ironclads, up the James River on which the city stands.

### Fight for the capital

Plans were made by the Confederates to abandon Richmond, but on May 15, a combination of shore batteries and underwater obstacles blocked the passage of the Union squadron at Drewry's Bluff. Despite this reprieve, Richmond's defenses could not be expected to hold out under prolonged bombardment by Union siege guns, which were now being brought up to the front. Offensive action was required to drive back McClellan's army.

Union engineers had bridged the Chickahominy, and two corps, made up of about a third of McClellan's 100,000 troops, had crossed the river. Johnston planned to isolate and overwhelm these corps while the rest of the Union army stayed north of the river. It was not a bad plan for an army with inferior numbers taking on a stronger enemy, for in principle the Confederates would gain local superiority. Heavy rain on the eve of

the battle—known as Fair Oaks or Seven Pines—made the river a raging torrent. But the execution of the Southern attack on the morning of May 31 was chaotic. Confused and contradictory orders meant that units blocked one another in their advance. Union soldiers were driven back, but late in the afternoon reinforcements began to arrive from the other side of the swollen river across the rickety Grapevine Bridge. Going forward to watch the fighting, Johnston was seriously wounded and carried from the field, his command devolving briefly to Gustavus Smith. The next day, the battle resumed but, with Smith almost paralyzed with anxiety, the Confederates could make no further impact.

### From the Union landings to Seven Pines

McClellan was held up for a month at Yorktown, then made slow progress as Johnston withdrew toward Richmond. Johnston was wounded at Seven Pines, after which Lee took command of the Confederate forces.

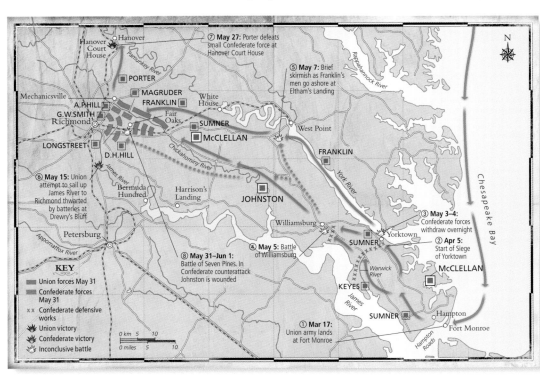

**Malvern Hill**
Frontal assaults on Malvern Hill, a position defended by powerful Union artillery, cost the Confederates dearly. General D. H. Hill later said of the battle: "It was not war—it was murder."

## BEFORE

**In the spring of 1862, the Peninsula Campaign brought the Union Army of the Potomac to within striking distance of the Confederate capital, Richmond.**

### STUART'S RIDE

Appointed commander of the Confederate Army of Northern Virginia in June, Lee suspected that the **Union right flank was open to attack** and ordered cavalry commander, **Jeb Stuart**, to carry out reconnaissance. Between June 12–16, Stuart rode with 1,200 men in a **100-mile (160-km) circuit** around the Union Army, returning with the news that the flank was indeed unprotected **north of the Chickahominy River**.

### LEE SUMMONS JACKSON

Lee ordered General "**Stonewall**" **Jackson** to move toward Richmond from the **Shenandoah Valley**, where his army was resting after a **highly successful but exhausting campaign** **<< 110–11**. Jackson arrived just in time to participate in Lee's offensive.

# The Seven Days Battles

**Between June 25 and July 1, 1862, Robert E. Lee led the Army of Northern Virginia in a seven-day offensive that drove the Army of the Potomac back from the gates of Richmond. Although costly and clumsily executed, the battles constituted a major strategic victory for the Confederacy.**

Lee's offensive began with a scare. With around 54,000 of his men committed to the attack, he had left minimal forces in the defensive lines in front of Richmond, counting on the cautious general, George McClellan, not to launch an assault. But on June 25, the day before the Confederate advance was scheduled to begin, Union forces probed the defenses at Oak Grove. To Lee's relief this turned out to be just a minor operation, although the skirmish it provoked has since been regarded as the first of the Seven Days Battles.

The Confederate offensive began on June 26, but neither on time nor as planned. Lee intended for the fighting

to start in the morning, with General Jackson attacking the exposed corps on the Union right from the rear. Generals A. P. Hill, D. H. Hill, and James Longstreet would join in after Jackson. Inexplicably, however, Jackson did nothing, and in late afternoon, tired of waiting for him to make a move, A. P. Hill mounted an assault of his own against entrenched Northern troops at Beaver Dam Creek. The Confederates were repulsed with heavy casualties.

**Private Edwin Francis Jemison**
At only 17 years of age, Confederate Private Jemison was killed by cannon fire while serving with the 2nd Louisiana Infantry in the assault on Malvern Hill. His portrait is a poignant memento of the war.

# "The **soul of the brave general** was fit to burst for the **awful and useless sacrifice**."

CAPTAIN MOXLEY SORREL OF MAJOR GENERAL RICHARD EWELL AFTER MALVERN HILL

McClellan's response to having won this tactical victory was to order his men to withdraw from the positions they had so determinedly held, to higher ground behind a swamp. Still convinced he would be assaulted by large numbers of Confederates, he also set about shifting his supply base to the James River. Lee, however, was determined to continue his offensive.

## Lee's victory at Gaines' Mill
Pursuing the retreating enemy the next day, Lee came up against the Union army's new defensive line at Gaines' Mill. Once again, coordination between Lee's subordinates failed and A. P. Hill's

**5,400** The number of Southern casualties at the Battle of Malvern Hill on July 1, 1862. In total, the Confederacy lost 20,204 soldiers in the Seven Days Battles, compared with 15,855 losses for the Union Army.

division took heavy casualties, fighting alone for much of the afternoon. Late in the day Brigadier General John Bell Hood's tough Texan brigade pierced the Union center with a charge in which every officer but Hood himself was killed or wounded. The Union forces withdrew, leaving the Confederates victorious but at a heavy cost, losing around 9,000 men. While this brutal contest took place on its right flank, the majority of the Union army remained inactive, more than 60,000 men being kept out of the fight.

## McClellan's rage
After Gaines' Mill, McClellan lost his nerve. Despite his superior forces, he retreated toward Harrison's Landing on the James River, convinced that he was saving his army from imminent destruction and firing off angry telegrams to Washington blaming the government for the debacle.

Lee pursued his adversary ruthlessly, seeking to land a decisive blow, but repeatedly failed. His ambitious orders for coordinated maneuvers to outflank and trap Union forces proved beyond the capacity of his subordinates. Jackson was unusually sluggish, singularly failing to

### Union casualties
The Battle of Gaines' Mill on June 27 saw thousands of Union casualties. Many of the wounded were transferred by flatbed rail cars to a Northern field hospital at Savage's Station. When the Confederates attacked the site on June 29 the hospital was abandoned and the patients captured.

master the speed and decisiveness he had shown in the Shenandoah Valley campaign. At Savage's Station on June 29, the Union rearguard escaped ruin because Jackson was slow crossing the Chickahominy River. Yet Lee saw a prime opportunity the next day as much of the Army of the Potomac struggled along congested roads between White Oak Swamp and Glendale. The Confederate commander was determined to bring all his forces to bear in a climactic battle, but divisions lost their way or were stuck on blocked roads. Jackson, ordered to attack from the north across White Oak Swamp, failed to join in, even when fighting broke out within earshot of his position. Only two divisions, under Longstreet and A. P. Hill, attacked the Yankees, who put up stiff resistance despite failing to form a proper defensive line. Casualties on both sides were heavy and the result indecisive.

### Bloodshed at Malvern Hill
Meanwhile, McClellan withdrew to the safety of the ironclad USS *Galena* off shore, leaving effective command

### Medal of Honor
The award of the Medal of Honor for conspicuous bravery was instituted for the Union Army in 1862. This one was awarded to Brigadier General Daniel Butterfield for his "distinguished gallantry" at Gaines' Mill.

to Brigadier General Fitz John Porter. Most of the retreating Army of the Potomac concentrated in a formidable defensive position on Malvern Hill. Flanked by ravines, it could only be assaulted from the front by troops advancing up a slope and across an open plain. The Union artillery unlimbered its cannons and waited for the enemy to show.

Lee guessed that the Union soldiers were demoralized and would crack if put under pressure. He devised a plan for his artillery to open holes in the Union line for his infantry to exploit. But everything went wrong. The Confederate guns could not be moved forward in sufficient strength and faired poorly in the artillery duel. Next, Lee's infantry assaults began piecemeal as men stormed forward singly and were shot down by shrapnel, canister, and grapeshot. Those few units that reached the Union lines were driven back by counterattacks. The following day, McClellan again ordered a Union withdrawal, but Lee did not pursue and the fighting ended.

AFTER

The Seven Days Battles drove the Union army back 20 miles (32km), lifting the threat to Richmond and ensuring that McClellan's campaign ended in failure.

**CONFEDERATE STRATEGY**
Lee had not demonstrated masterly generalship in the Seven Days Battles. He admitted: "Our success has not been as great or as complete as we should have desired." But he had set up a **moral supremacy** over the Union army, aiming to **keep up the initiative**. As soon as his own army had recovered, he marched it north of Richmond.

Lee counted on **McClellan remaining inactive**, which he did. The Army of the Potomac dug in defensively at **Harrison's**

**9 MILES** The closest McClellan's Army of the Potomac came to Richmond during the Peninsula Campaign.

**Landing** under the **protection of naval guns**. While continuing to demand reinforcements, McClellan did not **resume the offensive**. In August he reluctantly obeyed orders to **ship the Army of the Potomac back to Washington** to assist in the **fighting in northern Virginia 120–21 »**.

**HARRISON'S LANDING**

**Troops at Bull Run**
Edwin Forbes's sketch shows the right wing of the
Confederate army under Longstreet advancing through
gunpowder smoke on General McDowell's corps. Forbes
was the artist-correspondent for Frank Leslie's magazines.

**«** **BEFORE**

After the defeat of General McClellan's
Army of the Potomac in the Seven Days
Battles, President Lincoln launched a new
Union offensive in northern Virginia.

**THE UNION ARMY OF VIRGINIA**
While the **Seven Days Battles «** 118–19,
were being fought in late June 1862, a **Union
Army of Virginia** was formed. General John
Pope, a commander with a **reputation for
aggression**, was recalled from the Western
Theater to **lead the new force** southward from
Washington. In late July, McClellan was ordered
to bring his army back from the Peninsula to
**defend Washington** and reinforce Pope's army.

**CONFEDERATE ACTIVITY**
Confederate General Robert E. Lee rested and
reorganized his **Army of Northern Virginia**,
dividing it into two corps under **Stonewall
Jackson «** 112–13 and **James Longstreet
186–87 »**. Lee warily watched McClellan's
army, camped **within striking distance** of
Richmond, but dispatched Jackson to disrupt
Pope's invasion of northern Virginia. On seeing
that McClellan was to remain inactive, Lee
contemplated **an offensive of his own**.

# The Second Battle of Bull Run

**The campaigns of summer 1862 had seen the Army of Northern Virginia achieve supremacy over Union
forces that seemed incapable of finding commanders to match Lee and Jackson. If a second clash near
Manassas Junction brought the Confederates victory, they could threaten Washington again.**

The campaign opened in mid-July
1862, with General Stonewall
Jackson's advance to the railroad
junction at Gordonsville, northwest of
Richmond, which was threatened by
the advance of General John Pope's
Union Army of Virginia. Reinforced by
a division under General A. P. Hill,
Jackson set out to strike the center of
the Union army, hoping to gain the
upper hand by rapid maneuver.

## Lee's audacious offensive
On August 9, Jackson's troops
encountered Union forces under Major
General Nathaniel Banks in a strong
defensive position on a ridge near Cedar
Mountain. The battle began with much
of the Confederate column still marching
well to the rear. A Union counterattack
put some of Jackson's army to flight,
but he rallied his troops in person and,
aided by Hill's division, the Confederates

carried the day. The blow was far from
decisive, however, and the approach of
stronger Union forces saw Jackson
withdraw back to Gordonsville.

By mid-August, Lee had correctly
assessed the strategic situation. Despite
General George McClellan's reluctance
to support his rival, General Pope, the
Army of the
Potomac was being
withdrawn from
the Peninsula to
support the Union
offensive in
northern Virginia.
The Confederates had a brief
opportunity to seize the initiative
before these reinforcements arrived.
Leaving only a small force in front of
Richmond, Lee moved most of his
Army of Northern Virginia and joined
Jackson at Gordonsville. After Pope's
army fell back across the Rappahannock

**16,000** The estimated Union
casualties in five days'
fighting from August 27 to September 1,
1862—almost double the number of
casualties suffered by the Confederates.

River, the Confederates embarked
on a bold offensive. Facing a superior
enemy—the Confederates were
outnumbered by about 55,000 to
75,000—Lee divided his forces, gambling
that Pope would not attack. On August
25, Jackson led his 24,000-strong corps
on a march to the northwest and crossed
the Rappahannock,
swinging around
the right flank of
Pope's army.
He then headed
east through
Thoroughfare Gap
in the Bull Run Mountains, following
the line of the railroad toward
Manassas. His men marched 50 miles
(80km) in two days. They captured
Bristoe Station, wrecking trains and
tearing up tracks, and then descended
upon Manassas Junction, the main
supply base for the Army of Virginia.

## Jackson's defiance and Longstreet's attack

On the afternoon of August 29, Jackson held his defensive position on Stony Ridge against all the attacks the Union launched. The following day, the battle was turned by Longstreet's belated assault on the Union left.

The Confederates feasted on bacon and canned lobster, while Jackson resupplied his army with Union horses, artillery, and ammunition.

### Seizing the advantage

Pope was startled to find the Confederates behind his front line, but their position was precarious, and he saw a chance for victory. With the Army of the Potomac arriving, Pope hoped to trap and annihilate Jackson's forces.

On August 27, Jackson withdrew from Manassas Junction, taking up a defensive position on a ridge at Groveton, near the 1861 Bull Run battlefield. If discovered, he knew he could not expect to hold out for long against Pope's reinforced army. Confederate support was arriving in the form of Longstreet's corps, with Lee in attendance, but Jackson was still alone when the fighting started in earnest.

Pope's scouts failed to locate Jackson's position. In the afternoon of August 28, a Union column marched unawares along the Warrenton Turnpike into sight of the Confederate guns on the ridge. Jackson could not resist the chance of a flank attack and opened fire. Soon the opposing infantry were engaged at close quarters around Brawner's Farm. Union Brigadier General John Gibbon's Black Hat Brigade distinguished itself in a fight that cost some regiments 70 percent in casualties. After nightfall the Union troops withdrew.

The next day, August 29, Pope raced to bring the weight of his army to bear on Jackson, assuming that the Confederate general intended to slip away, which he did not. As a result, Union columns were thrown piecemeal

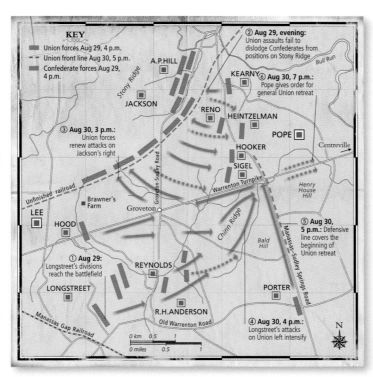

**UNION MAJOR GENERAL (1822–92)**

### JOHN POPE

Born in Kentucky, John Pope made a career in the Corps of Engineers. In the Civil War, he commanded an Illinois brigade before leading the Army of Mississippi to victory at New Madrid in spring 1862. Transferred to the Army of Virginia he offended his new troops by comparing them unfavorably to Union soldiers in the West. He was not missed when sent to fight the Sioux after defeat at Second Bull Run. Pope served with distinction in the postwar army.

## "The **men were brought down** from the field ... till **they covered acres.**"

CLARA BARTON, WHO CARED FOR THE WOUNDED AFTER SECOND BULL RUN

against Confederate defenders, who fiercely counterattacked. The most desperate fighting pitted Union Major General Philip Kearny's division against A. P. Hill, defending the railway cut on the Confederate left. Kearny came close to victory, but counterattacks drove the Union troops back.

Perhaps the day's most striking aspect, however, was the number of soldiers who did not fight. On the Union side, two corps under Pope's command failed to engage because of confused orders; and McClellan held back reserves of the Army of the Potomac. Longstreet's corps reached Jackson's right flank in the morning but, when ordered by Lee to join the battle, Longstreet demurred, and Lee did not insist.

### Repeat battlefield

Henry House Hill was the scene of fighting both at the First and Second Battles of Bull Run. It is now part of the Manassas National Battlefield Park.

On the morning of August 30, the Union assaults resumed with redoubled fury. Pope believed he was attacking nearly defeated Rebel units. But Longstreet was ready to intervene. He had placed his artillery in a commanding position on the right flank and raked advancing Union troops with deadly fire. When the momentum of the enemy attacks faltered, Longstreet unleashed his five divisions upon Pope's army.

### The final encounter

It seemed that Pope would be utterly routed, but as his men fell back in disarray, the general succeeded in organizing a defense that checked the Confederate surge and allowed an orderly withdrawal to Centreville after nightfall. The next day, Jackson was dispatched on another flanking march in an attempt to cut Pope off from Washington, but the Confederates were weary. After fighting the Union rearguard in a thunderstorm at Chantilly—an engagement in which Kearny was killed—the Confederates called off the pursuit. Pope's army was saved, although the battle had been lost.

**AFTER**

In the aftermath of his defeat at Second Bull Run, Pope retreated to the outer defenses of Washington. Recriminations began immediately as a scapegoat was sought.

**McCLELLAN'S OBSTRUCTION**
President Lincoln believed that **McClellan was the most culpable**: having wanted Pope to fail, McClellan had **intentionally delayed his troops** from coming to his rival's aid.

**POPE'S ILL FORTUNE**
Lincoln also reluctantly accepted that McClellan was the best man to take over the **defense of Washington** when morale was at its lowest. While Pope was **relegated to fighting Indians** in Minnesota, McClellan was allowed to integrate the Army of Virginia into his Army of the Potomac. His appointment was greeted with **relief and enthusiasm** by soldiers and civilians alike.

**McCLELLAN PASSING THROUGH FREDERICK CITY**

# Longstreet's Flank Attack at Second Bull Run

**On the first two days of battle, Stonewall Jackson's corps bore the brunt of the fighting. James Longstreet arrived with his corps to support Jackson's right flank, but he waited until the afternoon of the third day to launch a counterattack. This was immediately effective. Union commander John Pope had completely misread Longstreet's intentions and was forced to order a retreat.**

"A fair opportunity was offered me, and the intended diversion was changed into an attack. My whole line was rushed forward at a charge. The troops sprang to their work, and moved forward with all the steadiness and firmness that characterizes warworn veterans. The batteries, continuing their play upon the confused masses, completed the rout of this portion of the enemy's line, and my attack was therefore made against the forces in my front ... The attacking columns moved steadily forward, driving the enemy from his different positions as rapidly as he took them ... The battle continued until 10 o'clock at night, when utter darkness put a stop to our progress. The enemy made his escape across Bull Run before daylight."

LIEUTENANT GENERAL JAMES LONGSTREET, IN HIS REPORT OF OCTOBER 10, 1862, FROM *OFFICIAL RECORDS OF THE WAR OF THE REBELLION*

"We were near enough to see some wavering in the blue masses, then halt, and then a flight back to cover. But it was all up with John Pope. No rest was given his army. Longstreet started every man of us to his division to push them into attack, and soon everything was hotly engaged. The easy, rounded ridges ran at right angles to the turnpike, and over these infantry and artillery poured in pursuit. The artillery would gallop furiously to the nearest ridge, limber to the front, deliver a few rounds until the enemy were out of range, and then gallop again to the next ridge. And thus it went on until black darkness stopped operations ... Losses on both sides were heavy. Alas! the butcher's bill is always to be paid after these grand operations, and at Manassas especially there were some splendid young lives laid down for our cause and our homes ... Longstreet was seen at his best during the battle. His consummate ability in managing troops was well displayed that day and his large bodies of men were moved with great skill and without the least confusion."

G. MOXLEY SORREL, LONGSTREET'S CHIEF OF STAFF, FROM *AT THE RIGHT HAND OF LONGSTREET: RECOLLECTIONS OF A CONFEDERATE STAFF OFFICER*, 1905

**The Union Army before the final clash**
Hastily redeployed in an attempt to thwart Longstreet's flank attack, Union forces stave off disaster long enough for Pope to withdraw in good order. They are seen in the foreground of this sketch by Union artist Edwin Forbes.

CONFEDERATE GENERAL-IN-CHIEF Born 1807 Died 1870

# Robert E. Lee

## "The **feeling for him was one of love**, not of awe and dread."

GENERAL LONG'S DESCRIPTION OF LEE'S RELATIONS WITH HIS MEN, c.1864

Robert Edward Lee embodied the South's ideal image of itself—courteous and honorable, an inspired leader winning through superior fighting skill and spirit against overwhelming odds. The reality of Lee's military performance was more mixed than this suggests, but there is no doubting his exceptional abilities and the dignity of his conduct.

Lee was, first and foremost, a Virginian. Son of Henry Lee, a hero of the Revolutionary War, he grew up among the privileged First Families of Virginia. His childhood was not an easy one. He was 11 when his

**Letter of resignation**
On April 20, 1861, Lee wrote to General Winfield Scott, regretfully resigning from the U.S. Army in order to place himself at the service of his native Virginia.

father died, leaving the family in dire financial straits. Lee's marriage later connected him indirectly with the lineage of George Washington, thus securing his place in Virginia's landed aristocracy. In this milieu slavery was regarded as regrettable, even deplorable, but for the time being necessary. These were views that Lee himself shared.

### Early military career
After studying at West Point Military Academy, Lee spent his pre-Civil War career in the engineers and then the cavalry. He served as a staff officer during the War with Mexico in 1847–48, when his talent for imaginative flanking movements around prepared defenses and coolness under pressure earned the admiration of his commander, General Winfield Scott. Yet, by the time Lee entered his 50s, his military career had stalled; his overriding concerns were his wife's health and the finances of their Arlington estate.

Lee was on extended leave because of these issues when called to suppress the revolt of the abolitionist John Brown at Harpers Ferry in 1859. The

**Southern gentleman**
John Adams Elder's 1864 portrait of Lee conveys the gentlemanly manner that belied a gambler's temperament, for Lee took risks and favored aggressive tactics. His civility sometimes made him overly tolerant of ineffectual subordinates.

**Surrendered general**
Lee was photographed by Mathew Brady a week after the surrender at Appomattox, flanked by his eldest son Custis on the left and his aide Walter Taylor.

approach of Civil War in 1861 made Lee—still a lieutenant colonel at the start of the year—valuable to both sides. He chose the South once Virginia seceded, because his state allegiance outweighed his loyalty to the Union. His first experience of field command ended in defeat in western Virginia and he was hampered trying to defend the coasts of Carolina and Georgia against Union incursions.

## Adviser and general
Despite these setbacks, Lee secured the enduring respect of Confederate president Jefferson Davis, who retained him as his personal military adviser. Using his engineering background, Lee set Confederate troops to digging extensive earthworks for the defense of Richmond. But by spring 1862, he had decided that the Confederates' only hope of success against a materially superior enemy lay in taking the offensive. Given command of the Army of Northern Virginia after the wounding of Joseph Johnston, Lee attacked the inert General George McClellan in the swift campaign known as the Seven Days Battles. Lee was still an inexperienced field commander, but succeeded in driving the Union forces away from Richmond. After this, his reputation was largely unassailable and he was able to pursue his own aggressive strategy.

## Victories and fatal mistakes
Lee repeatedly took risks and, supported by his most gifted subordinate, Stonewall Jackson, his bold maneuvers secured outstanding offensive victories at Second Bull Run and Chancellorsville. Yet he came close to disaster through dividing his forces in the ill-judged invasion of Maryland in September

1862. Lee's decision not to retreat into Virginia but to stand and fight with a weary, outnumbered army at Antietam was a gamble, and would have been an opportunity for an opponent less cautious than McClellan. Antietam showed Lee's skill and resolution in a defensive battle and, with the success that followed at Fredericksburg, bolstered his belief in pursuing an

offensive-defensive strategy. But in June 1863, Lee fatefully invaded Pennsylvania. At Gettysburg, the terrain was not in his favor and he was reduced to ordering futile frontal assaults. After Gettysburg Lee tried to resign, but President Jefferson Davis could not spare him. Forced onto the defensive in the brutal campaigns against Ulysses S. Grant in 1864 and 1865, he fought with tenacity and tactical brilliance. When it became futile to continue the struggle, he surrendered with dignity at Appomattox.

After the war, Lee was excluded from the general amnesty. Arlington House had been confiscated and was not returned. Nevertheless, Lee never lost his spirit of reconciliation. After his death, his reputation continued to grow, especially among Southern admirers who idolized his memory.

> "So far from engaging in a **war** to perpetuate slavery, I am **rejoiced** that **slavery** is **abolished**."
>
> STATEMENT BY LEE TO JOHN LEYBURN, MAY 1, 1870

**Interior of Lee's field tent**
Relics of Lee are treasured objects. Here his field tent is preserved with his boots, saddle, and hat, along with his mess chest, assorted plates, cutlery, and cooking utensils.

## TIMELINE

- **January 19, 1807** Born in Westmoreland County, Virginia, son of Major General Henry Lee, governor of Virginia. He is one of six children.

- **1829** Graduating second in his class from West Point, Lee chooses to serve in the Corps of Engineers.

- **June 30, 1831** Marries his cousin Mary Custis, daughter of the step-grandson of George Washington; the couple lives at the Custis mansion, Arlington House.

- **1847–48** In the War with Mexico, Lee serves on the staff of General Winfield Scott, distinguishing himself at Cerro Gordo and Churubusco.

- **1852** Appointed superintendent of West Point.

- **1855** Transfers to the cavalry, serving as a lieutenant colonel on the western frontier.

- **October 1859** On home leave, Lee commands the successful assault on John Brown's abolitionists at the U.S. Arsenal at Harpers Ferry.

- **March 1861** Promoted to colonel with command of the U.S. First Cavalry.

- **April 1861** As the Civil War breaks out, Lee rejects an invitation to command Union forces; he resigns to offer his services to Virginia.

- **May 1861** Federal troops occupy Arlington House; Lee is appointed a brigadier general in the Confederate Army.

**ARLINGTON HOUSE OCCUPIED BY UNION TROOPS**

- **June 1–July 1, 1862** Takes command of the Army of Northern Virginia and defeats the Union Army of the Potomac in the Seven Days Battles.

- **August–September 1862** After a victory at Second Bull Run on August 29–30, Lee invades Maryland, but withdraws after his army narrowly escapes destruction at Antietam (September 17).

- **December 1862–July 1863** After victories at Fredericksburg (December 13,1862) and Chancellorsville (May 2–4, 1863), Lee again invades the North, but is decisively beaten at Gettysburg (July 1–3, 1863).

- **May–June 1864** Conducts desperate battles at the Wilderness (May 5–7), Spotsylvania (May 7–20), and Cold Harbor (3 June).

- **February 6, 1865** Appointed general-in-chief of the Confederate Army, while remaining in command of the Army of Northern Virginia.

- **April 9, 1865** Surrenders his army to Grant at Appomattox Court House, Virginia.

- **August 1865** Accepts the post of president of Washington College in Lexington, Virginia.

- **October 12, 1870** Dies, and is buried in the Lee Chapel, which he had built, at Lexington.

# Lee Invades Maryland

**The Confederate invasion of Maryland in September 1862 was a gamble based on a false estimate that the Union Army was unorganized and vulnerable. Desperate to strike an offensive blow against the North, Lee exposed his Army of Northern Virginia to potential disaster.**

**Lee astride Traveler**
General Lee was deeply attached to his gray stallion Traveler, his mount from the fall of 1861. However, for much of the campaign in Maryland, Lee could not ride because he had broken a bone in his hand.

## ‹‹ BEFORE

**Success at the Second Battle of Bull Run ‹‹ 120–23 left Confederate general Robert E. Lee facing an important decision: how to follow up his victory.**

**DRIVING FORWARD**
The Union troops defeated by Lee had retreated into the defenses of Washington, D.C. Now Lee **chose to invade the North**. On every front, the Confederates were poised for action. In Arkansas, General Thomas Hindman was preparing to retake Missouri. In Mississippi, Earl van Dorn and Sterling Price were gathering forces for a possible offensive against Ulysses S. Grant's Army of the Tennessee. On September 3, 1862, just three days after Second Bull Run, Lee wrote to President Jefferson Davis: "The present seems to be the **most propitious time . . . for the Confederate Army to enter Maryland**."

A dvanced units of General Robert E. Lee's army began fording the Potomac River on September 4. He was acutely aware that the physical state of his force was poor: "It lacks much of the material of war," he wrote to President Davis, "is feeble in transportation, the animals being much reduced, and the men are poorly provided with clothes and in thousands of instances are destitute of shoes." Lee believed that the Union forces around Washington were also "in a very demoralized and chaotic condition" after Second Bull Run, and that the cautious General George McClellan now commanding them would stay in his defensive positions for at least four weeks. Lee's presence in Maryland might tip opinion in the North against continuing the war; at the very least, it would keep the Union armies on the defensive. But if Lee thought the Union Army was dispirited, he also had concerns about his own.

### A shrinking force

Many of the Confederate troops were euphoric as a result of their victories through the summer, and advanced into Maryland with enthusiasm. But others were tired of soldiering barefoot on an empty stomach and reluctant to venture beyond the limits of the Confederacy. While Lee called for stiff disciplinary action against "stragglers," troops deserted in the thousands. Hopes that Marylanders would flock to fill the ranks quickly evaporated. Those who wanted to fight for the Confederate cause had already gone South earlier in the war. Except by slaveholders, the invading army was not welcomed as liberators. Most civilians barred their

**Union signal officers**
The Union Signal Corps played a vital role in tracking the enemy during the invasion. They collected intelligence, surveyed the battlefield, and sent messages.

doors against them. The locals observed the ragged condition of the army with shock and awe. Describing the "gaunt starvation" evident in their faces, one Maryland woman, Mary Mitchell, wrote: "That they could march or fight at all seemed incredible." Initially Lee had hoped Maryland's fertile land would provide food and fodder. The reality was that his troops ate green corn and suffered in consequence.

> **DEFEAT IN DETAIL** If a general has divided his army, in an adverse situation it can open up the possibility for his enemy to attack and crush each part separately or defeat it "in detail."

### Union stand

Lee had assumed that garrisons threatened by his advance into Maryland would be withdrawn to avoid capture. But the Union army at Harpers Ferry was ordered by the commander-in-chief, General Henry Halleck, to hold its position, despite McClellan's protests.

On September 9, General Stonewall Jackson marched the bulk of the Confederate army back across the river to seize Harpers Ferry. General James Longstreet was sent to Boonsboro to defend Jackson against a possible Union assault through the passes across South Mountain. But he was diverted to Hagerstown after a false report of a Union column marching toward him. Defense of the passes was left primarily to a division under General D. H. Hill, aided by General Jeb Stuart's cavalry. By dividing his army, Lee exposed himself to "defeat in detail," but again he gambled on McClellan's inertia. With his forces scattered, Lee was to find he had miscalculated the state of the Union army.

The merger of the Army of Virginia into McClellan's Army of the Potomac after Second Bull Run resulted in a remarkable revival of morale. Soldiers greeted McClellan as a savior.

**Battle of South Mountain**
On September 14, Confederate troops defended the mountain passes against superior Union forces, buying valuable time for Lee to concentrate his army.

> " The [soldiers] looked to me **not made of flesh** and blood **but stone and iron**."
>
> MARYLAND'S ELIZABETH K. HOWARD DESCRIBING THE SOUTHERNERS, SEPTEMBER 1862

Ordered by President Lincoln "to destroy the rebel army," McClellan led a revitalized 70,000-strong force out of Washington in pursuit of Lee.

## Union luck

On September 13, McClellan's troops entered Frederick, recently vacated by the Army of Northern Virginia. McClellan then enjoyed a stroke of luck. A copy of Lee's Special Order 191, circulated to all the Confederate commanders on September 9, was found in a field outside the town and passed to McClellan's staff. It gave full details of the location of Lee's forces.

**120,000** The number of soldiers that General McClellan estimated Lee had in his army during the Maryland campaign. The actual number of Confederate troops never exceeded around 55,000.

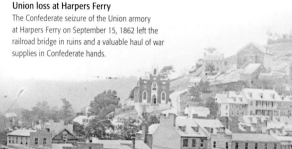

### Union loss at Harpers Ferry
The Confederate seizure of the Union armory at Harpers Ferry on September 15, 1862 left the railroad bridge in ruins and a valuable haul of war supplies in Confederate hands.

McClellan was exultant, declaring: "Here is a paper with which if I cannot whip Bobbie Lee, I will be willing to go home." On the night of September 13, Union forces moved toward South Mountain. Once through the passes they would be able to attack Lee's army before it could concentrate or escape. While Longstreet marched back from Hagerstown, the Confederate defenses at the mountain passes were lightly held. Fighting raged through September 14. Crampton's Gap fell after hours of resistance by a handful of Confederates faced with 12,000 Union troops, but

this was exploited too late. Turner's Gap and Fox's Gap were held by D. H. Hill's division throughout the day. The delay that this imposed on McClellan's army was enough to allow Lee to escape. On September 15, McClellan ordered his troops to retreat to the town of Sharpsburg, between Antietam Creek and the Potomac.

## Taking Harpers Ferry

Meanwhile, Jackson was threatening Harpers Ferry. The arsenal was guarded by 11,000 green Union troops under Colonel Dixon Miles. Holding the high ground, the Confederates sited their artillery and attacked at will. Harpers Ferry surrendered on September 15. Jackson seized military stores as well as 11,000 prisoners. Leaving Major

General A. P. Hill's men in charge, Jackson joined Lee at Sharpsburg. He arrived on September 16 to find Lee facing McClellan's army across Antietam Creek. All day the opposing artillery batteries had been dueling. Darkness brought the additional rattle of heavy skirmishing up and down the lines, a prelude to impending battle.

# AFTER

Lee's decision to fight at Sharpsburg **132–33 »**, rather than withdraw across the Potomac into Virginia, showed a confidence in his troops' superior ability.

**GEORGE BRINTON McCLELLAN**

### LEE RALLIES
Although Lee was buoyed by news of Jackson's success at Harpers Ferry, he was also unwilling to accept that his **Maryland campaign had failed**. McClellan, meanwhile, proceeded with his habitual caution. On September 15, his Army of the Potomac had begun arriving at Antietam Creek, but **left Lee undisturbed** on the opposite bank. The next day, McClellan had some 60,000 men facing 25,000 Confederates. By September 17 he was ready, but Lee had **amassed most of his men**, so the chance of a decisive Union victory was missed.

# Field Artillery

**Although modern rifled artillery made of cast or wrought iron was used during the war, the most common gun was the so-called Napoleon cannon, a brass smoothbore that fired round shot, spherical case shot, and canister. It normally took six horses to pull a gun and its limber. Ammunition was transported on a caisson, also pulled by a limber and a team of six horses. A Union artillery battery, commanded by a captain, consisted of six guns. Each cannon had a crew of a sergeant and seven men.**

**1** Canister shot was fired at short range against infantry. The tin canister was filled with lead slugs and sawdust. Upon exiting the muzzle, the container disintegrated and the deadly balls fanned out. **2** Twelve-pound solid shot contained no explosive charge. It was used against infantry and cavalry, but its destructive power was most effective when firing against enemy fortifications or batteries. The cannonball is attached by iron bands to a wooden sabot, to which the bag containing the propellant charge was attached. **3** Case shot was a hollow sphere that contained an explosive charge and was loaded with iron balls. It was normally fired to burst above the enemy lines so that balls and fragments of the case rained down on them. **4** Shells for rifled guns came in a variety of cylindrical shapes according to the rifling of the gun barrel. **5** The limber was a two-wheeled cart to which horses were hitched. The field gun itself was pulled behind the limber. There was room for three gunners to sit on top of the ammunition chest. **6** Binoculars were often used for registering the gun to the correct range. **7** This brass sight is fitted with a spirit level to check that the gun is horizontal before firing. It was set at the breech end of the barrel and lined up with the sight on the muzzle. **8** This packet of paper fuses was made at the Union's Arsenal at Frankford,

Pennsylvania. Union fuses were all made there to ensure consistency. **9** This paper fuse could be cut to the desired length. The fuse was inserted in the fuse plug when the gun was fired. **10** The wooden fuse plug was inserted into the nose of shells or into hollow case shot. **11** The quadrant and friction primer were used to aim and fire the gun. The quadrant was placed in the muzzle to determine the angle of elevation. The primer, attached to a long lanyard, was inserted in the vent hole to ignite the powder charge below. **12** The Bormann fuse, made of pewter, was screwed into the nose of a shell. The marks on the face indicate quarter seconds. The gunner would set the fuse by puncturing the face at the time desired. **13** The pendulum Hausse was a bottom-weighted brass sight hung on a bracket that allowed it to swing. In this way, the sight stayed vertical. It was lined up with the blade sight on the muzzle of the gun. **14** A thumbstall was worn when an artilleryman pressed his thumb over the cannon's vent hole to kill any sparks before the gun was reloaded. **15** The Napoleon cannon was the most common smoothbore cannon of the war, manufactured and used by both sides. Its official name was the Model 1857 gun-howitzer. This brass cannon was first made in France in 1853, and is named for Emperor Napoleon III.

**1** CANISTER WITH LEAD SLUGS

**2** TWELVE-POUND SOLID SHOT

**3** CASE SHOT WITH IRON BALLS

**4** SHELLS FOR RIFLED GUNS

**5** LIMBER AND AMMUNITION CHEST

**6** BINOCULARS AND CASE

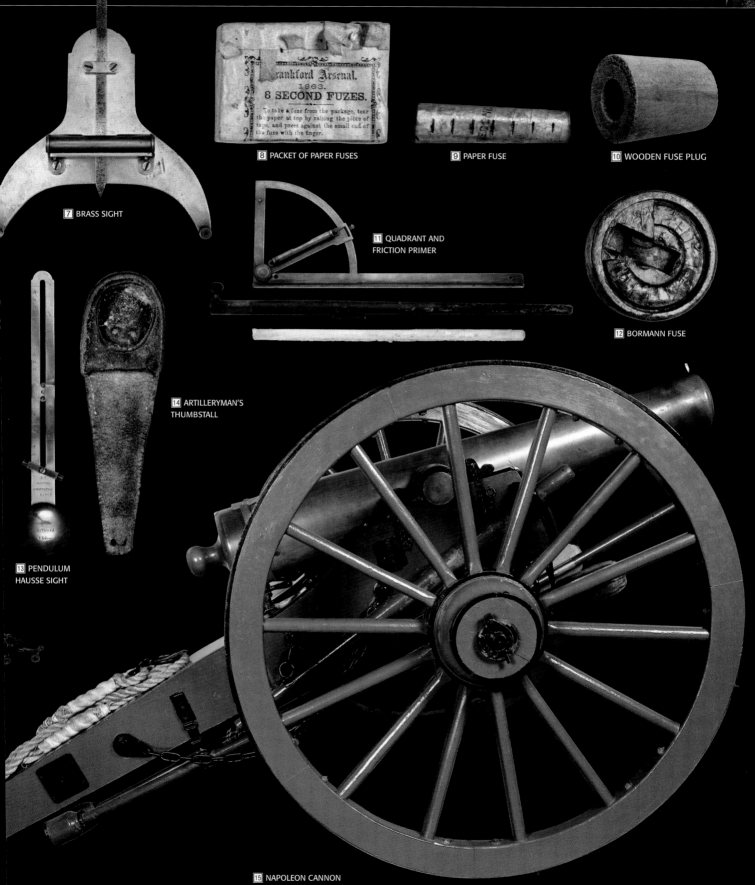

**7** BRASS SIGHT

**8** PACKET OF PAPER FUSES

**9** PAPER FUSE

**10** WOODEN FUSE PLUG

**11** QUADRANT AND FRICTION PRIMER

**12** BORMANN FUSE

**14** ARTILLERYMAN'S THUMBSTALL

**13** PENDULUM HAUSSE SIGHT

**15** NAPOLEON CANNON

« «

## BEFORE

By the mid-19th century, intelligence was recognized as a crucial element in warfare. But when the Civil War erupted, neither side had intelligence organizations.

### NAPOLEON'S INFORMATION GATHERING

Civil War generals had studied the **Napoleonic Wars** of 1803–15 and were aware of the importance the French emperor, Napoleon, had accorded to intelligence. Information gathered from varied sources—foreign newspapers, interrogation of prisoners, and secret agents—was sifted and collated by Napoleon's general staff to build **a picture of the enemy's strength, movements, and intentions**. The efforts of the enemy to gather information were countered by the use of **ciphers for written messages** and secret police to track down enemy spies.

### U.S. INTELLIGENCE

America had no such system. The Signal Corps, a U.S. Army innovation of 1860, was in its infancy. In the early days of the war, **intelligence and counterintelligence were improvised**. Private detective Allan Pinkerton was a key figure on the Union side, his agents acting as a proto-secret service. Virginia governor John Letcher set up a spy network in Washington, while **Virginians still had free access to the capital**.

# Espionage and Intelligence

**With Confederate and Union sympathizers not readily distinguishable and security lax, the Civil War created ideal conditions for espionage to flourish. Yet the availability of information from secret sources did not necessarily translate into an accurate understanding of enemy dispositions or intentions.**

Sources of intelligence in the Civil War were varied, some traditional and some innovative. For example, alongside cavalry reconnaissance came observation from balloons. Pioneered by the French in the 1790s, the idea for balloons was revived in 1861 through the initiative of an individual enthusiast, Thaddeus Lowe, who offered his services to the Union. Interception of written communications was age-old, but during the war telegraph-tapping also became common, increasing the need for ciphers to make messages secure.

Uncensored newspapers procured from the enemy lines were a prime source of information. Journalists often naively revealed details of movements and plans, although false articles were sometimes planted to confuse the enemy. Mapmaking was an important intelligence activity when fighting over uncharted terrain. The Confederates,

fighting mostly on their own soil, could expect local people to update them on Union movements. For Northerners, slaves and former slaves—known collectively as "black dispatches"—were a valuable source of information. Documents found on dead or wounded enemies, or simply left in a field—as happened during Lee's Maryland campaign—all potentially aided the opponent's cause.

### Passing on information

Secret agents and spies took their place among this panoply of intelligence sources. Security was absurdly slack on both sides: officers gave tours of their positions to interested strangers and openly discussed their plans or orders. Thus, well-connected Washington socialite Rose O'Neal Greenhow had easy access to military information that she passed on to Confederate

commanders. Her arrest in August 1861 was an early Civil War success for Allan Pinkerton's counterespionage detectives. Another Confederate spy was Belle Boyd of Martinsburg, Virginia; she supplied information to Stonewall Jackson during his Shenandoah Valley Campaign in 1862, before being reported and arrested.

For the Union, Elizabeth Van Lew ran a successful spy network in the Confederate capital, Richmond. One of her most useful contacts was Mary Bowser, a freed slave, who worked as a servant for Jefferson Davis's wife. Both the Union and Confederacy organized

### Confederate cipher reel

This cipher machine captured in Richmond was used by Confederates to encode messages. It used a matrix of 26 alphabets, shifted one letter for each row, from which a substitute letter was chosen for each letter of the message. The cipher was easily cracked by Union code-breakers.

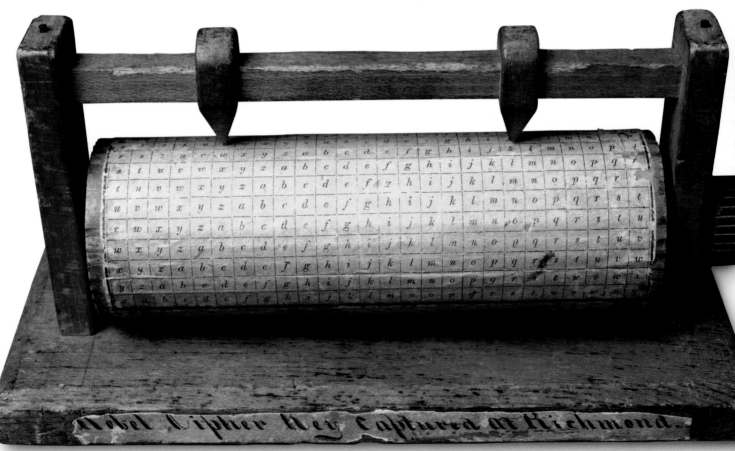

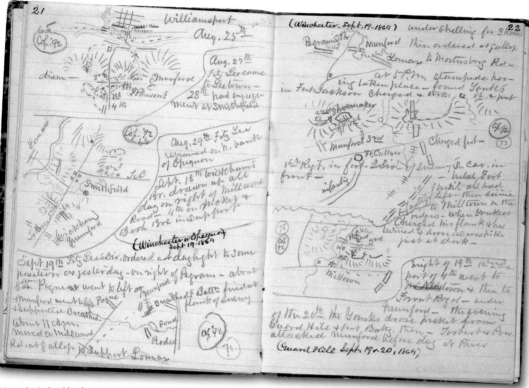

**Mapmaker's sketchbook**
This annotated sketch of terrain and military movements was made by Jedediah Hotchkiss, who worked as a mapmaker for the Confederates. He made the first detailed maps of the Shenandoah Valley.

secret rings to send messages, and move sympathizers, agents, and escaped prisoners between North and South.

When spies were caught, their gender often determined their treatment. Women were usually released after brief incarceration: Greenhow was held for nine months, Boyd for two. But male spies were dealt with more harshly. Timothy Webster, a Union agent sent

"You have sent me the **most valuable information** received from Richmond during the war."

**PRESIDENT LINCOLN SPEAKING OF ELIZABETH VAN LEW**

to the South by Pinkerton in 1861, was arrested, tried, and hanged by the Confederates the following year. Even scouts on horseback, if caught out of uniform, could face execution.

### Interpreting data
Successful intelligence hinged on the ability to analyze and interpret information. As well as running espionage and counterespionage rings, Pinkerton, who remained a civilian, was hired by General George B. McClellan as intelligence chief for the Army of the Potomac. But his naive interpretations of data meant he often gave McClellan gross overestimates of Confederate

### Rebel Rose
Photographed with her youngest daughter at the Old Capitol Prison in Washington, jailed Confederate spy Rose O'Neal Greenhow was released in summer 1862. She then traveled to Europe where she was feted as a celebrity.

army strength, which the general's overcautious disposition made him only too ready to believe.

An organized military surveillance system was not set up until January 1863, when General Joseph Hooker took command of the Army of the Potomac. He ordered Colonel George H. Sharpe to set up a unit, which became the Bureau of Military Information. Sharpe's organization marked a great step forward in professionalism and it would further flourish under Ulysses S. Grant's command in 1864.

The Confederacy never achieved this level of organization. Much of its "secret war" was conducted abroad, agents playing an important role in Europe by procuring arms and ships in defiance of neutrality laws. In 1864 the Confederacy set up a unit in Canada to undertake operations across the border into the North. Supporters carried out acts of sabotage but fell far short of their aim of detaching the northwestern states from the Union.

Records of undercover operations were destroyed at the end of the war, making it impossible for historians to glean facts from fiction.

**LINCOLN'S ASSASSINATION**
Confederate secret files were burned on the instructions of Secretary of State Judah P. Benjamin before the **fall of Richmond in 1865 314–15 »**. Speculation about what these documents may have contained has been especially intense because of possible links between Confederate covert operations and the **assassination of President Lincoln 320–21 »**. His assassin, John Wilkes Booth, had met with Confederate secret agents in Canada, and one theory is that Booth was tasked with a mission to **kidnap the president**, but instead he assassinated him.

**POSTWAR HONOR**
Individuals were honored after the war for spying for the Union. Despite the **perceived value of such work**, it took two decades for the U.S. Army's Military Intelligence Division to be created, and not until 1903 did the **Army integrate its intelligence unit** into a general staff.

**UNION MEDAL FOR SPYING**

**The spying actress**
The actress Pauline Cushman allegedly served as a Union spy, hiding the information she gathered in her shoes. After the war she gave lectures about her exploits, wearing the uniform of an honorary major.

# The Battle of Antietam

**September 17, 1862, was the costliest day of fighting in American history. A desperate Confederate defense against repeated assaults by determined Union troops resulted in 22,700 casualties. Despite superiority in numbers, however, Union general George B. McClellan failed to destroy the Rebel army.**

« **BEFORE**

After defeat at the Second Battle of Bull Run, morale in the Union ranks was low. It was partially restored by the reappointment of George McClellan as commander of the Army of the Potomac.

**THE CONFEDERATE POSITION**
Robert E. Lee's Maryland Campaign began well with the **capture of the Union arsenal at Harpers Ferry by General Stonewall Jackson** « **126–27**. But sooner or later he was going to have to face McClellan's **numerically superior Army of the Potomac**. The two forces met at Sharpsburg. Lee took up a **defensive position** overlooking Antietam Creek. With **scattered forces** still arriving, by nightfall on September 16 he had just 25,000 men. Lee gave command of the left of his line to **Jackson** and the right to **James Longstreet**, the two wings **meeting at Dunker Church**.

**UNION STRATEGY**
McClellan had some **75,000 troops** on the opposite side of Antietam Creek. On the evening of September 16, he started moving **Joseph Hooker's corps** across the creek to Lee's left. Initial skirmishes allowed the Confederates to **identify the direction of the main Union thrust** of the following morning.

At dawn on September 17, as Joseph Hooker's corps advanced up the Hagerstown Pike to slam into the left flank of General Robert E. Lee's army, the prospect for the Confederates was grim. Union troops advanced in daunting mass, well equipped and uniformed, in marked contrast to the ragged Rebels. There were no earthworks, so the soldiers fought in the open or were sheltered only by trees or terrain from the storm of artillery and infantry fire that erupted. Furious fighting raged in the Cornfield and the West Woods—locations lost and retaken time and again at an appalling cost in lives.

## Battle for the West Woods
Brigadier General John Bell Hood's Texans, reportedly angered at having their breakfast interrupted, seized the West Woods back from the Union Iron Brigade at the expense of 64 percent

**Union general**
Edwin Vose Sumner commanded a corps at Antietam. He was criticized for alleged blunders that saw a division cut to shreds at the West Woods.

casualties, with the 1st Texas Infantry Regiment sustaining losses of 82 percent. A Union division ordered forward by Major General Edwin Sumner counterattacked from the flank out of the West Woods, losing more than 2,000 men in half an hour.

### Lee holds his ground
McClellan, in the safety of the Philip Pry House on the other side of Antietam Creek, well away from the savagery of the battlefield, failed to coordinate the action of his different corps. Thus, while the Confederates weathered storm after storm on their left—at one point even losing Dunker Church only to retake it later—there was no pressure on their right or center. Even when joined by two more divisions in the course of the morning, Lee still did not have half McClellan's strength. But he was able to maneuver troops across from his

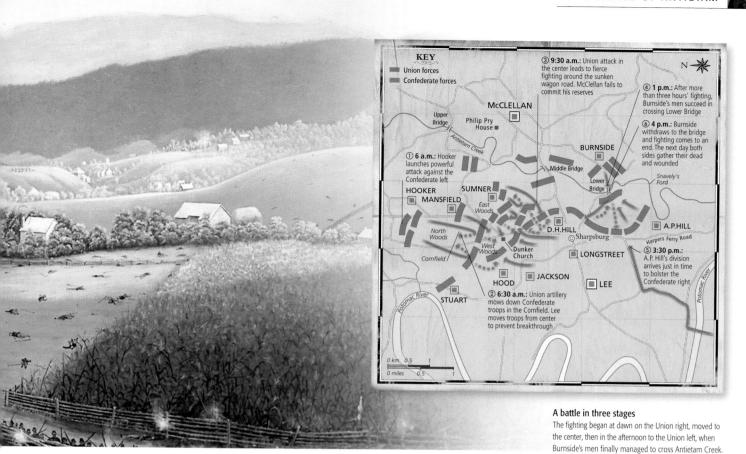

**A battle in three stages**
The fighting began at dawn on the Union right, moved to the center, then in the afternoon to the Union left, when Burnside's men finally managed to cross Antietam Creek.

Map labels:

KEY
- Union forces
- Confederate forces

③ 9:30 a.m.: Union attack in the center leads to fierce fighting around the sunken wagon road. McClellan fails to commit his reserves

④ 1 p.m.: After more than three hours' fighting, Burnside's men succeed in crossing Lower Bridge

⑥ 4 p.m.: Burnside withdraws to the bridge and fighting comes to an end. The next day both sides gather their dead and wounded

① 6 a.m.: Hooker launches powerful attack against the Confederate left

② 6:30 a.m.: Union artillery mows down Confederate troops in the Cornfield. Lee moves troops from center to prevent breakthrough

⑤ 3:30 p.m.: A.P. Hill's division arrives just in time to bolster the Confederate right

MCCLELLAN, BURNSIDE, SUMNER, HOOKER, MANSFIELD, D.H. HILL, A.P. HILL, LONGSTREET, JACKSON, HOOD, STUART, LEE, Upper Bridge, Philip Pry House, Middle Bridge, Lower Bridge, Snavely's Ford, East Woods, North Woods, West Woods, Cornfield, Dunker Church, Sharpsburg, Antietam Creek, Potomac River, Harpers Ferry Road

### The battlefield looking north
Captain James Hope of the 2nd Vermont Infantry was unfit for action at Antietam, but made sketches of the battle, from which he later painted a series of panoramas. The burning farmhouse on the left was set alight on the orders of Confederate General D. H. Hill.

center and right to reinforce his left, and by midmorning he had fought the Union troops on that flank to a standstill.

### Holding the sunken road
It was 9:30 a.m. before a Union division attacked the Confederate center, held by 2,500 men under Major General D. H. Hill. Holding a sunken wagon road that, with good reason, became known as Bloody Lane, Hill's outnumbered infantry repulsed a series of Union assaults, inflicting some 3,000 casualties

on their enemy before being forced to withdraw when their exposed flank was caught in enfilading fire—sweeping the length of their line. Even then Union forces were unable to break through; two entire corps that could have been committed to the sector were standing idle across the creek.

McClellan's original battle plan had envisaged Major General Ambrose Burnside distracting the Confederate right, while the main Union attack went in on the left. But Burnside did not move until 10 a.m. and then chose to feed his divisions across the Lower Bridge, which would later come to bear his name. On the Confederate side, Burnside's Bridge was covered by the fire of Georgian sharpshooters and artillery under the command of Brigadier General Robert

**38,000** The number of Confederate troops eventually engaged at Antietam. Lee had started his invasion of Maryland two weeks before with an army of 55,000.

### The reality of war
A photograph taken after the battle by Alexander Gardner shows Confederate dead lying near Dunker Church. Such images were a shock to a public unused to war photography.

Toombs. Union forces took three hours to fight their way across and even then could not exploit their success.

### McClellan's folly
Union luck appeared to change in the afternoon, with Lee facing potential disaster. Federal troops belatedly found a crossing to Lee's right at Snavely's Ford. They threatened not only to stave in his right flank, but to cut off his only line of retreat to the Potomac River. Had McClellan committed all his forces at this moment he would surely have won the day but, ever cautious, he insisted on retaining his reserves—20,000 men who never fired a shot.

Lee was saved by the belated arrival of A. P. Hill's division, force-marched from Harpers Ferry. Its unexpected appearance on his flank led Burnside to withdraw prudently back across the creek. In the late afternoon, fighting ceased. There seemed every reason to expect that McClellan would resume his offensive the following day, but he did not. After some skirmishing, the Confederate forces were able to withdraw unmolested to the Potomac River and cross into Virginia.

AFTER

Victory at Antietam strengthened President Lincoln's political position—he issued the Preliminary Emancipation Proclamation just a few days later, on September 22.

**LINCOLN'S TIMING**
Lincoln had intended to proclaim **the freedom of Confederate slaves 160–61 »** during the summer, but had been advised that to do so at a **time of military setbacks** might smack of desperation. Now he saw his opportunity.

**McCLELLAN'S INACTIVITY**
Visiting **McClellan's camp** in early October the president urged him to **pursue Lee** across the Potomac River. **McClellan's response** was to prove **too slow for Lincoln to tolerate.**

**LINCOLN AND McCLELLAN AFTER ANTIETAM**

# Burnside's Bridge at Antietam

**General Ambrose Burnside commanded the Ninth Corps on the Union left. He sent his troops across a narrow stone bridge over Antietam Creek, but this was overlooked by tall wooded bluffs that provided excellent cover for the Georgian sharpshooters in the Confederate line facing them. Later in the day, another crossing point was found at a nearby ford, but by then it was too late. Confederate reinforcements soon arrived and drove the Union troops back to the bridge.**

"A silence fell on every one at once, for each felt that the momentous 'now' had come. Just as we started I saw, with a little shock, a line-officer take out his watch to note the hour, as though the affair beyond the creek were a business appointment which he was going to keep.

When we reached the brow of the hill the fringe of trees along the creek screened the fighting entirely, and we were deployed as skirmishers under their cover. We sat there two hours. All that time the rest of the corps had been moving over the stone bridge and going into position on the other side of the creek. Then we were ordered over a ford which had been found below the bridge ... One man was shot in mid stream ...

At the word a rush was made for the fences. The line was so disordered by the time the second fence was passed that we hurried forward to a shallow undulation a few feet ahead, and lay down among the furrows to re-form, doing so by crawling up into line ... A moment after, I heard a man cursing a comrade for lying on him heavily. He was cursing a dying man.

As the range grew better, the firing became more rapid, the situation desperate and exasperating to the last degree. Human nature was on the rack, and there burst forth from it the most vehement, terrible swearing I have ever heard. Certainly the joy of conflict was not ours that day ... I only remember that as we rose and started all the fire that had been held back so long was loosed. In a second the air was full of the hiss of bullets and the hurtle of grape-shot ... The whole landscape for an instant turned slightly red."

PRIVATE DAVID L. THOMPSON, 9TH NEW YORK VOLUNTEERS, IN AN ARTICLE FOR *THE CENTURY MAGAZINE*, 1887. THOMPSON WAS CAPTURED AFTER THE BATTLE AND TAKEN TO PRISON CAMP IN RICHMOND, VIRGINIA, BUT WAS SOON PAROLED IN A PRISONER EXCHANGE

**Advancing across the bridge**
Here Burnside's troops have finally made it across the bridge and are ready to attack. It had taken them three hours to cross the creek in the face of accurate enemy fire. This costly delay was one of the reasons the Union army failed to defeat the much smaller Confederate force.

**Burnside with his staff**
Alexander Gardner—from Mathew Brady's studio—took this photograph of Burnside (seated, center) in November 1862, prior to Fredericksburg.

# Burnside Takes the Offensive

Given command of the Army of the Potomac, Union general Ambrose Burnside launched a swift offensive to seize Richmond that caught the Confederate forces off guard, but the operation ended in Union defeat at Fredericksburg in one of the most one-sided battles of the Civil War.

« **BEFORE**

After the Battle of Antietam, Lincoln was determined that McClellan's Army of the Potomac should pursue the Confederates into Virginia and seek to inflict defeat.

**NORTHERN ADVANCE**
General Lee's first thought after Antietam was also to **return to the offensive ‹‹ 132–133**. Only the poor condition of his Army of Northern Virginia persuaded him **to rest and refit**. Meanwhile General McClellan, goaded by Lincoln, began reluctantly moving his army across the Potomac in late October 1862.

Incensed by his delays and lack of offensive spirit, as well as his insubordinate attitude toward the government, **Lincoln fired McClellan** on November 7, **appointing Major General Ambrose Burnside** in his place.

Major General Ambrose Burnside was not eager to command the Army of the Potomac, feeling that he lacked the competence required of an army commander. Even so, within days of taking charge he responded to Lincoln's demand for offensive action with a plan to seize Richmond, the Confederate capital. He would shift his force rapidly and abruptly to cross the Rappahannock River at Fredericksburg, driving toward the town before General Robert E. Lee could react. Lincoln favored fighting Lee's army rather than sidestepping it, but approved the plan.

Burnside's maneuver was finely executed. On November 15, his army of 120,000 men, organized into three "Grand Divisions," set off on a march that caught the Confederates by surprise. Within two days, Union troops were streaming into Falmouth, on the opposite bank of the Rappahannock from Fredericksburg. Nothing stood between Burnside and Richmond except the 400-ft (122-m) wide river. Bridging this obstacle had been given high priority in the planning, with urgent orders for pontoons to be sent, but these floating bridges were delayed.

**Giving Lee time**
Burnside would not send troops across fords because he anticipated that rising water levels might render them impassable, and he did not want to find himself with part of his army cut off on the other side of the river. So he waited for the pontoons, which gave Lee the time to assemble his troops. When all the bridging equipment had arrived at the end of the month, the two halves of Lee's army—General James Longstreet's and General Stonewall Jackson's corps—were facing Burnside's soldiers

**900** The number of enemy that General Robert E. Lee reported he had taken prisoner following the Battle of Fredericksburg.

across the river. Because of the long delay, both sides had plenty of time to prepare their positions. Burnside placed his artillery above Fredericksburg on Stafford Heights to the east—such a weight of firepower that not even Lee could contemplate taking the offensive.

On the other side of the river, Longstreet took up position on Marye's Heights behind the town, amassing a formidable concentration of artillery and infantry along the base of the ridge, while Jackson spread out his forces downstream to his right. Lee had a panoramic view of the battlefield from a nearby hilltop. In all, the Confederate troops ranged across 8 miles (13km) of ridges along the western side of the valley. A frontal assault on such prepared defenses, held by more than 70,000 men, many of whom had a clear view of the plain beneath them, was unlikely to succeed. But Burnside felt committed to the operation and would not call it off. On the morning of December 11, the bridging of the river began.

Although the fire from the Union guns on Stafford Heights made it impossible for Confederate troops to advance in the open to the riverbank and contest the crossing, the buildings of Fredericksburg, now deserted by the civilians, made excellent cover for sharpshooters of the Mississippi brigade. Northern engineers struggled to complete the pontoons under their harassing fire. Union artillery reduced much of the town to rubble, but the sharpshooters were not driven out until a Union advance guard crossed by boat and flushed them out.

**11** The percentage of Union troops killed, wounded, or captured.

**7.4** The percentage of Confederates killed, wounded, or captured.

## Burnside's advance

The bulk of the Union Army began marching over the pontoon bridges on December 12, many soldiers looting the abandoned Virginian homes. The battle was fought on December 13. Burnside's best hope rested on Major General William Franklin's Grand Division, which had crossed the river south of Fredericksburg. Burnside thought that the Confederate right flank in front of Franklin was weakly held, but Jackson had amassed his forces around the peak of Prospect Hill. When a Confederate officer expressed anxiety about their situation, Jackson put him firmly in his place. He was proved right, because the Union troops' frontal assaults on his well-placed infantry and cannon were systematically repulsed. Startled early on by an unexpected flank attack from Confederate horse artillery, Franklin cautiously held many of his soldiers back in defensive positions.

The breakthrough occurred when a rush through an undefended wooded valley by Major General George Meade's troops penetrated deep into the Confederate army's lines. But Franklin failed to reinforce Meade, and his men were soon driven back by counterattacks and suffered heavy losses as a result. Nothing on Jackson's flank, however, equaled the appalling slaughter inflicted by Longstreet's corps at Marye's Heights. Union brigades were thrown forward in frontal assaults uphill across open ground swept by Longstreet's artillery. They then faced a line of 2,000 North Carolina and Georgia infantry positioned in a sunken road behind a stone wall. Under General Thomas Cobb, the Confederate infantry maintained a rapid rate of fire. The advancing Union ranks were cut down, most of the men not even coming to within 300ft (90m) of the wall before they fell or fled. By nightfall, the Union Army had suffered 12,700 casualties to Confederate losses of 5,400. On December 15, Burnside withdrew back across the river.

**TECHNOLOGY**

### PONTOONS

The military use of floating bridges dates back to ancient times, Persian ruler Xerxes famously building one to cross the Hellespont in 480 BCE. Originally, they were improvized by laying wooden planks over a line of moored boats. By the 19th century, however, army engineers had purpose-built flat-bottomed pontoons as part of their standard equipment. Mounted on wheels for ease of mobility, they were threaded together on a cable with wooden beams laid across them to form a roadway.

> "It is well that **war is so terrible**. We should grow too fond of it."
>
> ROBERT E. LEE TO JAMES LONGSTREET DURING THE BATTLE OF FREDERICKSBURG

**Defending the sunken road**
Confederate infantry take turns loading and shooting, maintaining a constant fire from behind the stone wall on Telegraph Road at the foot of Marye's Heights. Repeated Northern assaults over open ground failed to reach the sunken road.

**AFTER**

The slaughter at Fredericksburg was greeted with jubilation in the South and consternation in Washington. Lincoln came in for heavy criticism and anti-war sentiment flourished in the Union ranks.

**BURNSIDE'S HOPES DASHED**
Ambrose Burnside dreamed of redeeming his reputation with **another crossing of the Rappahannock River** that would outflank Lee. However, attempting this maneuver in January 1863 his army merely became bogged down on muddy roads. **After this "Mud March"** was called off, **Burnside was doomed**. On January 26, he was replaced by Major General "Fightin' Joe" Hooker.

**SOLDIER'S BRAVERY**
A story surfaced 17 years after the Battle of Fredericksburg, telling how Confederate soldier Richard Kirkland—**"the Angel of Marye's Heights"**—had risked his life to take water to wounded Union troops. **Kirkland's selfless act** is now commemorated by a monument in front of the stone wall at Fredericksburg.

KIRKLAND MEMORIAL AT FREDERICKSBURG

**THE BATTLE OF FREDERICKSBURG**
On December 13, 1862, Union General Burnside ordered a series of attacks on Marye's Heights, a ridge west of Fredericksburg. General Longstreet and his Confederate First Corps were positioned behind a stone wall at the base of the hill, and the Union troops advancing across open fields became easy targets. This painting by Frederic Cavada, a Union lieutenant, shows the action from behind the Federal lines, with troops beginning to fall under fire.

# The Far West

At the time of the Civil War, the U.S.'s western frontier was a wild place of isolated forts, gold prospectors, settler wagon trains, and often hostile Native Americans. The Confederates decided to extend the war westward, in the hope of wresting Colorado and California goldfields and silver mines from Union control.

## BEFORE

The U.S. extended its lands westward after victory in the War with Mexico. This confirmed the annexation of Texas and added California, New Mexico, and Utah.

### THE GOLD RUSH
California achieved statehood in 1850, while Utah and New Mexico were absorbed into the United States as territories. These thinly populated areas took on **economic importance after the discovery of their precious metals**. The **California Gold Rush** had begun in 1848. The discovery of silver and gold at the Comstock Lode in western Utah and at sites in western Kansas in the late 1850s was followed by the organization of these areas into the territories of **Nevada and Colorado** in early 1861.

**CALIFORNIA ADVERTISEMENT**

### DIVIDING UP AMERICA
The creation of **new states and territories** was a fraught political issue, affecting the balance between "slave" and "free" states **≪ 22–23**. In 1861, **Texas was among the original states that formed the Confederacy**, while California, New Mexico, Utah, Nevada, and Colorado all stayed within the Union.

The first Confederate thrust westward from Texas took place early in the war on the initiative of an aggressive battalion commander, Lieutenant Colonel John R. Baylor. A one-time politician and Indian fighter, Baylor was sent with a 250-strong detachment of mounted Texan volunteers to seize undefended forts along the state's western border with New Mexico. He interpreted his orders as license to enter New Mexico on the grounds of preempting a potential Union counterattack. Deciding that a U.S. Army garrison at Fort Fillmore constituted a threat, Baylor set out to attack it on July 23, 1861. The garrison commander, Major Isaac Lynde, left the fort with his troops to confront Baylor. On July 25 Baylor's Texans and their allies repulsed Union infantry and cavalry assaults, driving them back to Fort Fillmore. During the night the Union commander Lynde led a withdrawal from Fort Fillmore but was pursued to San Augustin Springs where he and his men all surrendered. Baylor declared the south of New Mexico the Confederate Arizona Territory.

Baylor had scant resources to fight hostile Apaches and resist a Northern counterattack. But when another Southern force was sent into Confederate Arizona in early 1862, it was dispatched with offensive rather than defensive intentions.

## The Confederate push west
Brigadier General Henry H. Sibley had devised an ambitious plan to use Confederate Arizona as a launch pad for a drive into the gold- and silver-rich states of Colorado and California. With three regiments of cavalry from Texas, he advanced up the Rio Grande River as far as Fort Craig, absorbing most of Baylor's troops along the way. The fort,

**Confederate commander**
Louisiana-born Henry Hopkins Sibley was a career officer in the U.S. Army who chose to join the Confederacy. After its failure, he never held another significant command.

a Union stronghold, was under the command of Colonel Edward Canby, whose regulars were supported by New Mexican volunteers. Sibley's force was too weak to seize the fort and tried to bypass it, but Canby marched out to block his path at a ford near Valverde. The two forces joined battle on February 21. In the end, Canby and his men had to retreat back into the fort. Sibley continued to push northward, reaching Santa Fe on March 10.

Ahead of Sibley, Union forces from Colorado under Colonel John Slough joined a Northern garrison at Fort Union. The campaign's crucial battle occurred at Glorieta Pass in the Sangre

**Hostile environment**
The Confederates underestimated the difficulty of campaigning across the wild, sparsely populated terrain of the southwestern territories, such as this mesa landscape near Santa Fe. The mountains and deserts made living off the land nearly impossible.

"**The men and teams suffered severely with the intense heat and want of water.**"
UNION MAJOR ISAAC LYNDE, REPORT ON THE SURRENDER AT SAN AUGUSTIN SPRINGS, AUGUST 7, 1861

de Cristo Mountains. On March 26, forward units of Northern soldiers pushing south from Fort Union met the foremost contingent of Confederate cavalry advancing north from Santa Fe. After an initial skirmish, both sides moved up reinforcements and were ready to fight on March 28. Both moved to attack because each assumed the other would stand on the defensive. Despite suffering as many casualties as their enemies, the Confederates held the field after a fierce engagement. But a Union detachment dispatched to carry out a flanking attack found itself behind the Confederates, surprising their almost undefended supply train. The Southern wagons and supplies were destroyed, and their horses and mules driven off.

## California retaliates

Unable to sustain an advance without supplies, Sibley pulled back first to Albuquerque and then began a grueling retreat to Texas in mid-April. By then another Union force was in play. Colonel James H. Carleton's California volunteers were marching eastward to intervene in the fighting in Arizona and New Mexico.

In March 1862, the Californians met the Confederates at Stanwix Station—a skirmish that impelled the much weaker Confederates to fall back to Tucson. The Californians then won a clash at Picacho Pass before driving the Rebels out of Tucson in May. They withdrew into Texas, and Carleton, now brigadier general, was put in charge of the Department of New Mexico. The Confederate Arizona Territory ceased to exist in all but name.

### Military rations

Soldiers in the southwest would have received the standard rations issued by both sides, including sugar, tobacco, coffee, and a sewing kit called a housewife (or "hussif").

Water can

Coffee sack

Tobacco twist

Sugar bag

Oil lamp

Soldier's "housewife" or sewing kit

## AFTER

Many Native American tribes took advantage of the war to try to reassert their freedom. In the southwest, the Apache Wars flared up once again.

**APACHE LEADER GERONIMO (THIRD FROM RIGHT)**

### RESILIENT WARRIORS

In New Mexico Union general James H. Carleton found Native Americans tougher opponents than the Confederates. At the **Battle of Adobe Wells** in 1864, a Union force led by Colonel Kit Carson **narrowly avoided defeat** at the hands of the Plains Apache, Kiowa, and Comanche tribes. The legendary **Apache leader Geronimo** managed to maintain resistance until 1886, when he and a small group of followers finally surrendered.

### INCORPORATING THE WEST

Much of the **West came under firm Union control** in the latter half of the war. Nevada **became a state** in October 1864. Later arrivals were Colorado in 1876, Utah in 1896, and Arizona and New Mexico in 1912.

# Bragg Invades Kentucky

**Throughout the second half of 1862, the Confederates tried to seize the initiative in the Western Theater, mounting a bold invasion of Kentucky. But the Confederate commander, Braxton Bragg, was first driven out of Kentucky and then forced to concede the field at the bloody Battle of Stones River (Murfreesboro).**

Its population split between Confederate and Union sympathizers, Kentucky initially opted for neutrality. Perhaps inevitably, it was soon drawn into the conflict.

**BATTLE FOR KENTUCKY**
On September 3, 1861, Confederate commander Leonidas Polk entered Kentucky, taking Columbus on the Mississippi. The Union then seized Paducah and Smithland. **The state's congress called for war** against the Southern invaders, while the pro-Confederates formed an **alternative government**, recognized by the Confederacy.

Union troops took over most of the state, with the Confederate army controlling the southwest. The two clashed at Fort Donelson **« 104–105** and Shiloh **« 106–107**. Union victories at both forced a Confederate withdrawal from most of Kentucky—their last position lost in June 1862. They were encouraged, however, when General John H. Morgan's cavalry force made a **sweep through Kentucky** in July, raiding towns and attracting recruits.

**GENERAL JOHN H. MORGAN**

In summer 1862, the Western Theater was a disaster for the Confederates. They had lost Nashville and western Tennessee, though they still held Vicksburg, which denied the Union control of the Mississippi. As a Union force under Major General Don Carlos Buell advanced slowly on Chattanooga,

**Confederate Bowie knife**
Probably designed by Rezin Bowie (brother of Jim Bowie) for cowboys to catch and skin animals, the Bowie knife was a standard Confederate weapon. This one was found on the battlefield at Perryville.

General Braxton Bragg was at Tupelo, Mississippi, trying to restore discipline and morale to his beaten men. In this grim picture, Confederate General John H. Morgan's cavalry raid on Kentucky in July shone out like a beacon of hope.

The raid prompted the idea that the Bluegrass state might be the Union's weak point, full of Southern sympathizers eager to join the Confederate ranks. In late July and early August, Bragg moved the Army of Mississippi to Chattanooga by railroad—he sent in a division at a time on a roundabout route. This

maneuver contrasted with the difficulty Buell had in moving his men, his supply lines harassed by the Confederate cavalry of Morgan and Nathan Bedford Forrest.

**Invading Kentucky**
Installed at Chattanooga, Bragg devised a plan with Major General Edmund Kirby Smith, commander of the Army of East Tennessee. Moving north from Knoxville, Smith would retake the Cumberland Gap and join with Bragg in an invasion of Kentucky. But Smith then decided that the Gap was too

Wooden handle — Brass quillon — 13-in (33-cm) steel blade — Curved blade for skinning animals

### Confederate retreat after Perryville

This section from William Travis's panorama shows the battered but triumphant Union forces in the foreground, Bragg in retreat in the distance. Travis shadowed the Army of the Cumberland, often sketching on site.

Like Lee's invasion of Maryland, the Confederate offensive had been based on the assumption that local people would greet the invaders as a liberation force. Bragg brought with him rifles to arm thousands of Kentucky volunteers. He also brought the state's Confederate governor, Richard Hawes, who was formally inaugurated in the state capital, Frankfort, on October 4. But it became obvious that the state's enthusiasm for the South had been exaggerated when the volunteers never materialized.

### The Battle of Perryville

Meanwhile, goaded by Lincoln, Buell had advanced from Louisville on October 1. Hawes's inauguration ceremony at Frankfort was ruined as the town came under attack by the Union. By this time the South should have concentrated their forces, but Bragg's army was based at Bardstown while Smith's was some 60 miles (97km) away at Lexington. The campaign's key battle was fought before the two could unite.

While away at Frankfort for the inauguration, Bragg left his army at Bardstown under the command of General Leonidas Polk. Confronted by three columns of Buell's army advancing on him on October 7, Polk fell back to Perryville on the Chaplin River. A drought had struck Kentucky and the marching Union troops were desperate for drinking water—which the Confederates controlled. A Union division under Brigadier General Philip Sheridan seized control of a creek in fierce fighting early on October 8, the men strongly motivated by thirst. Bragg was slow to realize that a major battle was beginning, but returned to assume command in the late morning.

On the afternoon of October 8, a daring Confederate assault almost routed the Union left, but the Union right pushed into the streets of Perryville. When darkness fell, Bragg prudently withdrew his forces,

### The Slaughter Pen

The site of Sheridan's stiff four-hour resistance to the Confederates was dubbed "the Slaughter Pen" for its gory appearance on the first day of the Battle of Stones River.

which would have faced superior Union numbers if combat had resumed the following day.

Bragg, at last, joined up with Smith, and the two Confederate commanders hotly debated their next move. Neither Bragg's nor Smith's forces had the strength in numbers or the logistical organization to keep a hold on the state of Kentucky once a Northern counteroffensive got underway. Controversially, Bragg decided to abandon the invasion and pull back to Tennessee. With the almost simultaneous defeat of a Confederate army under Major General Earl Van Dorn at the Second Battle of Corinth, and Lee's withdrawal from Maryland after the Battle of Antietam, the picture for the Confederacy looked bleak.

### In the Stones River Valley

Bragg faced criticism for his decision but he kept his job. Buell did not, and was replaced by Major General William S. Rosecrans as head of what would soon become known as the Army of the Cumberland. Bragg and Smith ended up at Murfreesboro, Tennessee, in the Stones River Valley, with their armies united to form the Army of Tennessee under Bragg's command.

On December 26, Rosecrans marched out of Nashville to engage Bragg, in response to Lincoln's continued pressure for offensive action. By December 30, he was facing the Confederates at Stones River. That evening, bands from both armies struck up to help raise their men's spirits. In the words of Sam Seay of the Confederates' 1st Tennessee Infantry, "The still winter night carried [the bands'] strains to great distance. At every pause on our side, far away could be heard the military bands of the other. Finally one of them struck up 'Home Sweet Home.' As if by common consent, all other airs ceased, and the bands of both armies as far as the ear could reach, joined in the refrain."

The next morning, real battle succeeded the previous night's dueling bands. The Confederates attacked at dawn, catching the Union troops still eating their breakfast. The panicked Union right wing was driven back 3 miles (4.8km) in what would have been a fatal rout, but for resistance organized by Sheridan, who held a position for four hours at great cost to his division. A Union defensive line was stabilized, hinging on woods known as the Round Forest. When nightfall

**AFTER** »

After the Battle of Stones River, General Braxton Bragg faced harsh criticism and an ugly internal dispute. The state of Kentucky became the scene of guerrilla fighting.

**SUBORDINATE INSURRECTION**
While Rosecrans was turning Murfreesboro into an **impregnable fortified base**, Bragg faced a revolt of his subordinate officers, orchestrated by Polk. President Jefferson Davis elevated General Joseph E. Johnston to theater commander, and **expected him to relieve Bragg**. But Johnston left Bragg in his command.

**KENTUCKY UNDER THE HEEL**
There was no further Confederate attempt to invade Kentucky, but it remained the **target of cavalry raids**—by John H. Morgan in December 1862 and July 1863, and by Nathan Bedford Forrest in spring 1864. **Guerrilla warfare** in the state was met in July 1864 by the **imposition of military rule** under Union **Major General Stephen Burbridge**. His harsh regime earned him the nickname "the Butcher of Kentucky."

> ## "To lose Kentucky is nearly the same as to lose the whole game."
> PRESIDENT LINCOLN, LETTER TO SENATOR ORVILLE BROWNING, SEPTEMBER 1861

strongly defended to take by assault, so without consulting Bragg, he chose to bypass it. Smith took an unopposed route to Kentucky instead, routing Union forces at Richmond on August 30. Braxton Bragg, racing to catch up, left Chattanooga on August 28 and crossed into Kentucky. Advancing toward Louisville, Bragg's progress was delayed by a Union garrison at Munfordville, which held out for three days before surrendering. This gave Buell enough time to hurry back to defend Kentucky.

**ORPHAN BRIGADE** The name given to the Confederate 1st Kentucky Brigade, possibly because of the brigade's forced exile from its home state.

brought combat to an end, Bragg felt he had won a great victory. But Union commanders resolved to fight on. Over the next two days Bragg could make no further progress, and by the afternoon of January 2, he had to order Major General John C. Breckinridge to lead his Kentucky Orphan Brigade in a near suicidal assault. Bragg resolved to withdraw the next day, conceding the field to Rosecrans. Union losses were 13,249 out of 43,400 engaged; the Confederates lost 10,266 out of 37,712.

**General William S. Rosecrans**
As commander of the Army of the Cumberland, Rosecrans showed resolute leadership in the Battle of Stones River, rejecting the option of withdrawal after a disastrous first day's combat.

CONFEDERATE GENERAL Born 1817 Died 1876

# Braxton **Bragg**

## "**Not a single soldier** in the whole army ever **loved or respected him**."

PRIVATE SAM WATKINS WRITING OF BRAGG IN HIS MEMOIRS, 1882

D uring 1862–63 Braxton Bragg was the most prominent Confederate general in the Western Theater. In some ways he resembled Stonewall Jackson—both men were harsh disciplinarians, quarrelsome, and uncommunicative, and had a poor relationship with their subordinates. The big difference was that Bragg's character failings were not offset by outstanding success in the field. From the start of his military career he showed himself

**A general's burden**
The haggard face of General Braxton Bragg during the Civil War reveals a man weighed down by responsibility and plagued with terrible migraines.

irritable and argumentative, and a harsh disciplinarian. He meticulously enforced the minutiae of military procedure, although he frequently bucked the authority of those above him in the chain of command.

Serving as an artillery officer in the War with Mexico in 1846–48 Bragg proved his courage and steadiness, yet so alienated the men serving under him that he reportedly survived two attempts on his life by his own soldiers. An enthusiastic supporter of the Confederate cause, Bragg welcomed the bombardment of Fort Sumter in 1861 by writing that you could "reach the sensibilities of such dogs only through their heads and a big stick."

### Campaign in Mississippi
Consigned to the backwater of the Gulf Coast for the first year of the Civil War, Bragg leaped at the chance to take his army to join the forces in the front line at Corinth, Mississippi, in spring 1862. His performance at Shiloh in April was impressive for the determination with which he pressed home his corps' attack on the Union defenses. But he lacked subtlety or tactical flair, and soldiers' lives were thrown away too cheaply in piecemeal frontal assaults. Bragg nonetheless emerged from the battle with his reputation intact.

One man who had admired him since they served together in the War with

Mexico was President Jefferson Davis. The president correctly judged that Bragg's disciplinarian approach would allow him to toughen up and train volunteers into an effective fighting force. But by giving him the senior command in the Western Theater, Davis failed to take into account what other qualities might be needed in such a role.

## Leadership failings
Two major faults emerged as Bragg conducted operations in the bold invasion of Kentucky and the ensuing fighting in Tennessee. One was a loss of nerve that repeatedly led him to withdraw at precisely the moment when those around him felt he should stand firm or vigorously advance. The other fault was a chronic inability to collaborate with other generals or to establish any relationship of trust or mutual respect with his subordinates.

Bragg's bad temper and readiness to blame others contributed to a near breakdown in command that occurred in 1863 after the Battle of Stones River. He argued with his corps and divisional

### Badge of status
During the Civil War swords were worn by officers as symbols of rank. Braxton Bragg's sword and scabbard is now in the Confederate Memorial Hall in New Orleans.

generals while they campaigned to have him removed. Sometimes his anger was justified—his contempt for the military abilities of Lieutenant General Leonidas Polk, for example. The politically well-connected Polk's resistance to his orders was clearly insubordinate. But Bragg cannot escape his share of the responsibility for a situation that undermined the military efficiency of the Army of Tennessee. Despite the near mutinous stance of his subordinates, Bragg remained in command through most of 1863.

### Brief reprieve
Bragg's victory at Chickamauga was won at heavy cost, but momentarily gave him sufficient prestige to have Polk and some other unruly subordinates removed. But criticism that he had

**Zachary Taylor and Braxton Bragg**
General Zachary Taylor (in the center) set up camp at Walnut Springs during the War with Mexico in 1846. Bragg, the third man standing to Taylor's left, served with him at Fort Brown, Monterrey, and Buena Vista.

moved too slowly in pursuit of the defeated Union forces after the battle cancelled out any long-term gain to his reputation. His own self-belief, never secure, had long been waning. When Union counterattacks drove his army from the heights outside Chattanooga in November, the mental and physical strain became unbearable and Bragg begged to be relieved of his command. There is no doubting his competence as a planner and administrator, or his ability in training troops, but he lacked the inner strength and decisiveness required of a fighting general.

> **"I am convinced that nothing but the hand of God can save us … as long as we have our present commander."**
> JAMES LONGSTREET, IN A LETTER OF COMPLAINT ABOUT BRAGG, 26 SEPTEMBER, 1863

**BRAGG'S TOMBSTONE IN MOBILE, ALABAMA**

# The Battle of Stones River

**With orders to strike the Confederate encampment, General William S. Rosecrans advanced toward Murfreesboro. At dawn on December 31, General Braxton Bragg launched the Rebel attack, driving back the Union line. After marking time on New Year's Day, Bragg attacked again on January 2, forcing Union troops back across the river. The Northerners retaliated with artillery fire and the Rebels retreated.**

"The battle of Stone's River, Tennessee, on the 31st of December, 1862, and the 2nd of January, 1863, was one of the most fiercely contested and bloody conflicts of the war ... I do not think that two better armies, as numerous and so nearly matched in strength, ever met in battle ...

Before this battle I had been inclined to underrate the importance of artillery ... but I never knew that arm to render such important service as at this point. The sound judgment, bravery, and skill of Major John Mendenhall, who was my chief of artillery, enabled me to open 58 guns almost simultaneously on Breckinridge's men and to turn a dashing charge into a sudden retreat and rout ... I witnessed the effect of this cannonade upon the Confederate advance ... The very forest seemed to fall before our fire, and not a Confederate reached the river."

LIEUTENANT COLONEL G. C. KNIFFIN, ON THE STAFF OF UNION GENERAL THOMAS L. CRITTENDEN AT STONES RIVER, IN *BATTLES & LEADERS OF THE CIVIL WAR*, 1887

"The Confederate brigades, now melted to three-fourths their original numbers, wavered and fell back; again and again they re-formed in the woods and advanced to the charge, only to meet with a bloody repulse. All along the line from Harker's right to Wood's left, the space gradually narrowed between the contending hosts. The weak had gone to the rear; there was no room now for any but brave men, and no time given for new dispositions; every man who had a stomach for fighting was engaged on the front line ...

The enemy had fallen back, stubbornly fighting, and made a stand on the left of Cheatham. Brave old Van Cleve, his white hair streaming in the wind, the blood flowing from a wound in his foot, rode gallantly along the line to where Harker was stiffly holding his position ..."

MAJOR GENERAL THOMAS L. CRITTENDEN, IN *BATTLES & LEADERS OF THE CIVIL WAR*, 1887

**Triumph in the making**
A drawing by Alfred E. Mathews of the 31st Ohio Volunteer Infantry shows a Union brigade from Horatio P. Van Cleve's division counterattacking the Rebel advance toward the Nashville Road on December 31, 1862.

« BEFORE

# Cavalry in the Civil War

**Initially neglected, cavalry emerged as an important element on both sides of the Civil War. Whether engaged in long-distance raids into hostile territory, carrying out reconnaissance, or fighting dismounted with rifles and carbines, cavalrymen proved their value time and again.**

In European warfare, cavalry was held in high regard, traditionally seen as a high-status arm with decisive impact. The U.S. Army, by contrast, had neglected it.

**ATTITUDES TO CAVALRY**
The first two U.S. Army regiments to bear the "cavalry" designation were not established until 1855. In 1861, these two units existed alongside three other mounted units: two of dragoons (a kind of cavalryman) and one of mounted infantry. The Union government was **prejudiced against cavalry**, considering it expensive and frivolous.

In Europe, the traditional role of the cavalry was threatened by the **increased firepower** of both **infantry and artillery**. This was clearly demonstrated in the disastrous **Charge of the Light Brigade in 1854** during the **Crimean War**.

**FRENCH SHAKO, OR CAVALRY HAT**

More used to horses as a means of transportation, the South utilized cavalry from the war's outset. Self-consciously "aristocratic" Confederates were attracted to the dashing image of cavalry, and mounted regiments were formed by volunteers enlisting with their own horses. The impressive performance of General Jeb Stuart's 1st Virginia Cavalry at Bull Run in July 1861 stimulated enthusiasm for mounted units on the Union side too. The government swiftly established the centralized supply of horses and equipment. Volunteers to the Union cause were not generally accomplished horsemen, and many troopers had to be

taught the basics of riding. The South continued to depend on men providing their own mounts—if their horse was killed, they had to go home and find another or accept transfer to the infantry. Capturing or stealing horses became crucial for Confederate cavalry as the war went on, since the Union controlled major sources of mounts in Missouri, Kentucky, Tennessee, and West Virginia.

## Practical weapons
Neither side adopted the European practice of flamboyant cavalry uniforms, although there was the occasional flourish, such as the peacock feather Jeb Stuart wore in his hat. The saber was traditionally regarded as the true

**Guidon flag**
This flag belonged to the 1st Vermont Volunteer Cavalry Regiment, formed to fight for the Union in November 1861. The regiment sustained heavy losses in an ill-considered charge at the Battle of Gettysburg.

## Union cavalry skirmishing

This contemporary sketch shows troopers of the 1st Maine Cavalry Regiment. They are fighting dismounted in a skirmish line—the most common and often most effective way for cavalry to engage in Civil War battles.

weapon of the cavalryman, but in the Civil War sabers were rarely more than decorative; Southern cavalry often did not carry them at all. Pistols, such as Colt or Remington revolvers, were the standard weapons. Union troopers were issued carbines—typically the Sharps model—and later in the war sometimes with the repeater Spencer rifle. Southern units could not match this level of weaponry, often equipping themselves with infantry rifled muskets or even shotguns.

### Roles of the cavalry

The Confederates were the first to create cavalry units that operated independently, while the Union initially tended to distribute horsemen among infantry formations, where they performed mundane duties as scouts, camp pickets, and guards for railroads. Jeb Stuart's spectacular ride around

> # "There are only two arms
> that cavalry should use … the repeating **magazine gun** … and the **revolver**."
>
> UNION CAVALRY COMMANDER JAMES H. WILSON

the Union army during the Peninsula Campaign in June 1862 pointed the way to the use of cavalry for reconnaissance and raids into enemy-held territory.

Few efforts were made to introduce the traditional European-style cavalry charge against infantry and artillery; the firepower present on the field would have made this move effectively suicidal. Cavalrymen did play a key role in battles, usually by dismounting and fighting on foot ahead of their line in the style of skirmishing infantry. On foot, Union cavalry with carbines were formidable opponents in a firefight.

### Destructive raids

It was the long-distance raid behind enemy lines where a cavalry unit came into its own. In the wide open spaces of the West, a body of horsemen could move undetected, striking suddenly to destroy railroad or telegraph links, plunder depots, and overrun isolated garrisons. The Confederates set the example. In 1862, General Nathan Bedford Forrest and General John Morgan led raids badly disrupting Union operations in the Western Theater. In effect fighting as guerrilla forces, the South's cavalry roamed across hundreds of miles in the Union rear, tying down troops ten times their number. Their impact was such that, during General

William T. Sherman's advance on Atlanta in 1864, almost 100,000 Union troops were engaged in the defense of communications and pursuit of enemy marauders. But the Union responded. General Benjamin Grierson's 400-mile (640-km) sweep through Confederate-held territory from Tennessee to Louisiana in 1863 played a major part in Grant's Vicksburg Campaign.

### Northern advantage

In the end, the Union's superior resources would give it the advantage. From 1864, General Philip Sheridan's cavalry corps was a dominant force in the Eastern Theater. His pursuit of Lee's army in the final stage of the war was an example of cavalry used in a traditional role to great effect. By the war's end, Union cavalry outnumbered Confederate horsemen by two to one. Short of decent mounts and fodder, the Confederate cavalry was reduced to a sorry condition, some of its units little better than bandits engaged in a struggle for survival.

### Sheridan at the Battle of Winchester

One of the rare saber charges of the war was conducted by two of Sheridan's divisions at Winchester in the Shenandoah Valley on September 19, 1864. Even at this battle, however, Union cavalry did the most damage with their carbines.

After the Civil War the cavalry became, for a time, the most prestigious and most numerous branch of the U.S. Army.

### PLAINS INDIAN WARS

After the war, attention turned to **subduing Native American tribes** on the Plains of the Western frontier. Congress authorized the U.S. Army to raise **ten cavalry units**, two of which were African-American regiments—nicknamed "buffalo soldiers." Despite the disaster suffered by

**80,000** The number of Union cavalry enrolled at the end of the Civil War. In contrast, Confederate cavalry numbered around 40,000.

Custer's 7th Cavalry at Little Big Horn, the U.S. cavalry finally defeated the Indians. By 1877, the **regular army contained 10,970 cavalry**, compared with fewer than 10,000 infantry.

### FINAL FLOURISH

The last major cavalry operation was in 1916 when General Pershing pursued **Pancho Villa's irregulars** into Mexico. By World War II, all cavalry divisions were abandoning horses to become **armored** or **mechanized formations**—later extended to the introduction of **airborne cavalry** relying on helicopters for mobility.

## Sergeant's boots

These leather boots belonged to Union Sergeant Charles Darling. Cavalrymen normally bought their own boots. Even well-worn boots were highly desirable plunder to be stolen from any fallen enemy.

Built-up sole

Roweled spur

Spur strap

**CLASH OF CAVALRY**
Ordered to ravage the fertile Shenandoah Valley, Union cavalry commander Philip Sheridan rode into Winchester on September 19, 1864, with an army of 39,000—more than double that of the Confederates. In the ensuing battle, Sheridan's three cavalry divisions thundered down Berryville Pike with such force that the Confederates were shattered. A witness recalled: "The enemy's line broke into a thousand fragments under the shock."

# Cavalry Equipment

**Although sabers and other traditional cavalry weapons were still issued, the Civil War saw mounted troops on both sides depend increasingly on firearms. The men often dismounted to fight, but also used new multiple-shot breechloading carbines from the saddle.**

**1 Morse carbine (Confederate)** Around 1,000 were produced by the State Military Works in Greenville, South Carolina. **2 Henry rifle (Union)** It could hold 15 .44-caliber rimfire cartridges. Much prized for its rapid rate of fire, it was purchased by Union military units. **3 Spencer carbine (Union)** First issued in the later part of 1863; the Federal government purchased more than 95,000. **4 Tarpley carbine (Confederate)** A few hundred of these breechloading .52-caliber guns were made in Greensboro, North Carolina, in 1863–64. **5 Carbine strap** A leather sling helped cavalrymen transport their weapons. **6 Model 1840 saber (Union and Confederate)** Due to its heavy, flat-backed blade, the saber was nicknamed "Old Wristbreaker." Though production ceased in 1858, it remained more readily available than the later Model 1860. **7 Saber and scabbard (Confederate)** This "Old Wristbreaker" was carried by 2nd Lieutenant P. P. Brewer. **8 Dragoon pistol** The heavy single-shot weapon was becoming obsolete by the start of the war. **9 Lance (Union)** The 6th Pennsylvania Cavalry were known for their use of 15-ft (4.6-m) lances, though these were replaced by carbines in 1863. **10 Bridle** made of

leather and brass. **11 McClellan saddle** This saddle, used by Confederate Captain E. M. Hudson, follows the prewar design of future Union general George B. McClellan. **12 Saddlebag** The leather bag had a buckle to attach it behind the saddle. **13 Western-style spur** Bronze spurs with rowels (toothed wheels) were worn by Confederate Captain E. M. Hudson. **14 Swan-neck spur** The neck of the spur rises at an angle, giving this type its name. **15 Uniform gloves, 6th Virginia Cavalry (Confederate)** Cavalrymen wore leather riding gloves.

**1 MORSE CARBINE**

**2 HENRY RIFLE**

**3 SPENCER CARBINE**

**4 TARPLEY CARBINE**

**5 CARBINE STRAP**

**6 "OLD WRISTBREAKER" SABER**

**7 SABER AND SCABBARD**

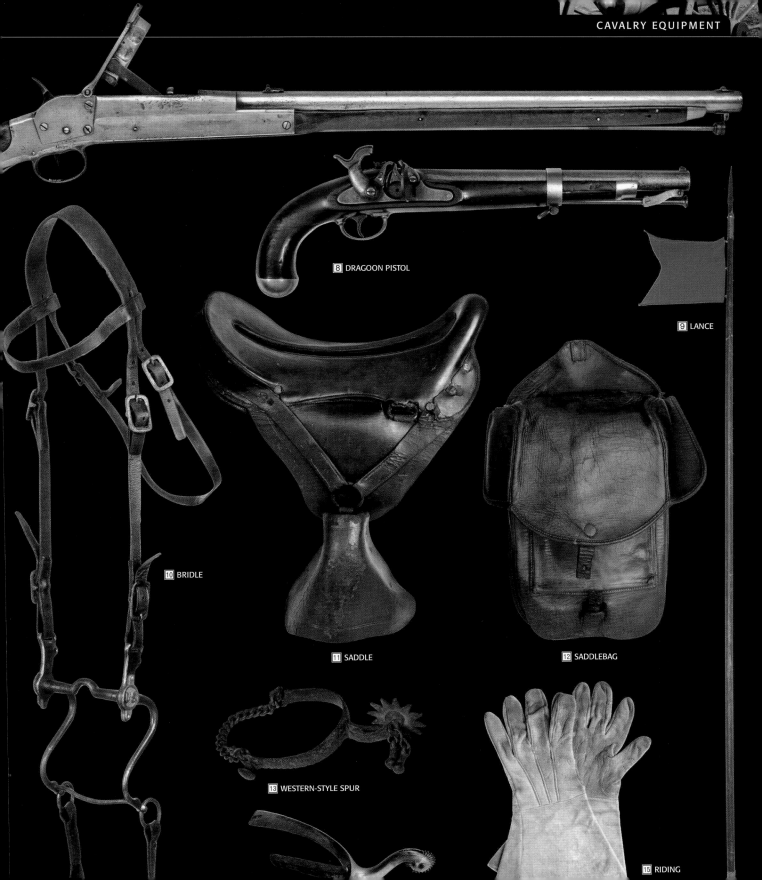

8 DRAGOON PISTOL

9 LANCE

10 BRIDLE

11 SADDLE

12 SADDLEBAG

13 WESTERN-STYLE SPUR

15 RIDING

# 4

# THE UNION TIGHTENS ITS GRIP

## 1863

Both sides wrestled with new realities that changed the nature of the war. As the Confederacy reached its military zenith, sound Northern political and military leadership won key victories on and off the battlefield, which set the stage for Union triumph.

« **Under fire on the Mississippi**
This Currier & Ives print, made shortly after the Battle of Vicksburg, shows Admiral David Porter's fleet under Confederate bombardment beneath the bluffs of Vicksburg—Porter's ship, USS *Benton*, is in the lead. Although Confederate guns fired for three hours, only one ship was lost and the fleet met Ulysses S. Grant below the city, as planned.

# THE UNION TIGHTENS ITS GRIP

**Invading the North**
Lee's army crosses the Potomac to invade the North. With a presidential election to come in the fall, Lee and President Davis feel that a Confederate victory on Northern soil may pay untold political dividends.

**Hancock at Gettysburg**
On July 1, stiff Union resistance helps General Winfield Scott Hancock create a steady Federal line at the end of the first day of fighting. Hancock appears here in a vast mural of the battle painted by F. D. Briscoe in 1885.

## EASTERN THEATER

PENNSYLVANIA
Gettysburg
Philadelphia
NEW JERSEY
WEST VIRGINIA
Harpers Ferry
Potomac River
Baltimore
Winchester
Shenandoah River
Centreville
WASHINGTON, D.C.
DISTRICT OF COLUMBIA
Delaware Bay
DELAWARE
Manassas
MARYLAND
Appalachian Mountains
Harrisonburg
Fredericksburg
Chancellorsville
Charlottesville
Rappahannock River
Mattaponi River
Chesapeake Bay
VIRGINIA
James River
Richmond
York River
ATLANTIC OCEAN
Roanoke
Lynchburg
Petersburg
James River
Cape Charles
Newport News
Hampton
Cape Henry
Portsmouth
NORTH CAROLINA

CANADA
WASHINGTON TERRITORY
Portland
IDAHO TERRITORY
OREGON
Rocky Mountains
Snake River
NEVADA TERRITORY
Salt Lake City
Sacramento
Virginia City
San Francisco
UTAH TERRITORY
COLO. TERR.
PACIFIC OCEAN
CALIFORNIA
Colorado River
Santa Fe
ARIZONA TERRITORY
NEW MEX. TERRITO.
MEXICO

**TERRITORY GAINED BY DECEMBER 1863**
- States of the Union
- Territory gained by the Union
- Confederate states
- Territory gained by the Confederacy
- Disputed territory

**Lee at Chancellorsville**
This portrait of Robert E. Lee is by French-born artist L. M. D. Guillaume, who painted portraits of a number of Confederate leaders. Chancellorsville is considered one of Lee's greatest victories.

**The death of Jackson**
At the Battle of Chancellorsville, Confederate general Stonewall Jackson is shot by accident in growing darkness by his own troops. His death soon afterward leaves Lee without his most gifted lieutenant, an event recorded in history as a crucial moment in the Civil War.

he nature of the war changed decisively with President Lincoln's Emancipation Proclamation on the first day of 1863. The extent of slavery had been one of the war's principal causes, but from now a Union victory would mean its effective abolition. The mobilization of black troops would also bring an important addition to Union strength. After all the disappointments and command changes of the previous months, 1863 saw the Union begin to deploy its strength with real effectiveness, with Lincoln at last finding the commanders with the administrative competence and ruthless aggressiveness to bring this power to bear.

The Confederacy until now had had most of its successes in the Eastern Theater, but was clearly under pressure elsewhere. The Union blockade was growing ever tighter, and Union forces were advancing steadily up and down the Mississippi. By year's end, after

**Lincoln with his cabinet**
In Washington, D.C., President Lincoln issues the Emancipation Proclamation on January 1. This document specifies the states and areas in which it will apply. Here he presents the draft proclamation to his cabinet.

**New York Draft Riots**
The riots of July 1863 begin with protests over the exemptions allowed to the wealthy in the North's conscription law. However, the rioters, many of them Irish, also target blacks and abolitionists, fearing that black advancement threatens the jobs of poor whites.

**Battle of Chickamauga**
A Union offensive from Tennessee is halted at Chickamauga, Georgia. The battle is portrayed here in a Kurz and Allison print of the late 1800s, which captures the difficult wooded terrain and ferocious fighting that marked the battle.

**Earthworks at Vicksburg**
The siege of Vicksburg sees the besiegers and defenders both taking refuge in a system of trenches and dugouts little different from those of World War I half a century later. Starvation proves the Union army's strongest weapon.

MINNESOTA

DAKOTA TERRITORY

WISCONSIN

MICHIGAN

VERMONT

MAINE

NEW HAMPSHIRE

NEW YORK

Concord

Buffalo    Boston    MASSACHUSETTS

RHODE ISLAND
CONNECTICUT

New York City

PENNSYLVANIA

NEW JERSEY

Philadelphia

DELAWARE

MARYLAND

Washington, D.C.
Manassas

Inset map area

Richmond    Norfolk
VIRGINIA

NEBRASKA TERRITORY

IOWA

Des Moines

Chicago

ILLINOIS    INDIANA    OHIO

Indianapolis    Cincinnati

WEST VIRGINIA

KANSAS

Kansas City

St. Louis

MISSOURI

Ohio River    Louisville

KENTUCKY

Cumberland River

Nashville    Knoxville

NORTH CAROLINA

Memphis    Chattanooga    Wilmington

TENNESSEE

Arkansas River

Corinth    Chickamauga    SOUTH CAROLINA

Indian Territory

ARKANSAS    ALABAMA    Atlanta

Red River

MISSISSIPPI    GEORGIA

Charleston

Vicksburg    Montgomery    Savannah

TEXAS    LOUISIANA    Meridian

Austin    Mobile    Jacksonville

Baton Rouge    Pensacola    FLORIDA

New Orleans

Galveston

Rio Grande

Missouri River

Mississippi River

Tennessee River

ATLANTIC OCEAN

GULF OF MEXICO

the succession of great and by no means one-sided battles, the Union clearly held the initiative in both of the war's main theaters. The Deep South lay open to attack, and Lee's army in Virginia could only expect to fight yet more battles against heavy odds.

The nature of the fighting was also increasingly taking on the characteristics that would dominate the wars of the industrialized 20th century—strategic maneuvers and the movement of supplies

of mass armies being made by rail, and the battles of these armies being centered around fighting for entrenchments under ferocious artillery bombardments.

The North still had weaknesses. Social and racial tensions were made plain by the Draft Riots, but the home front in the South was more vulnerable with galloping inflation and food shortages. Southern prospects for 1864 were turning bleak.

# TIMELINE 1863

**Emancipation Proclamation** ▪ River operations in Arkansas, Mississippi, and Louisiana ▪
**Battle of Chancellorsville** ▪ Siege of Vicksburg ▪ Combahee River raid ▪ **Gettysburg** ▪
Chickamauga Campaign ▪ Chattanooga Campaign ▪ **Gettysburg Address**

| JANUARY | FEBRUARY | MARCH | APRIL | MAY | JUNE |
|---------|----------|-------|-------|-----|------|

⌃ Inkwells used to draft the Emancipation Proclamation

**MARCH 3**
The U.S. Congress passes the Conscription Act, though in practice this does less to boost Union recruitment than its supporters hoped.

**APRIL 7**
Admiral Samuel F. Du Pont leads an unsuccessful Union naval assault on Charleston, South Carolina.

**MAY 1**
The Confederate Congress resolves to punish white Union officers captured while commanding black units.

**JANUARY 1**
President Lincoln issues the final version of the Emancipation Proclamation, announcing the freeing of all slaves in states that seceded.

**FEBRUARY 1**
Union troops capture Franklin, Tennessee.

**MAY 1**
Battle of Port Gibson. Grant's troops defeat Confederate forces on the east bank of the Mississippi River.

**JANUARY 3**
Battle of Stones River (Murfreesboro), Tennessee, begun on December 31, 1862, ends indecisively. General Braxton Bragg's Confederate forces withdraw.

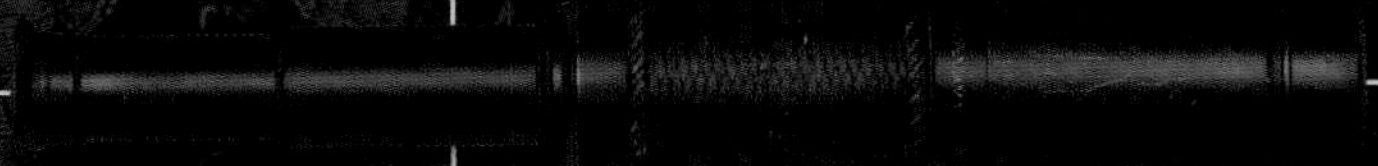

**FEBRUARY 3–20**
Operations on the Yazoo River, Arkansas. Union troops fail in attempts to close in on Vicksburg, Mississippi, using the river system to the city's north and west.

⌃ Union gunboats slip past Vicksburg

**APRIL 16–17**
Union gunboats and transports pass Vicksburg in a daring night move. General Ulysses S. Grant's army is meanwhile concentrating to the south, at Hard Times.

**MAY 1–6**
Battle of Chancellorsville. Although outnumbered, General Robert E. Lee outmaneuvers and defeats Hooker's Union army. Stonewall Jackson is mortally wounded.

⌄ The Battle of Chancellorsville

⌃ Harriet Tubman

**JUNE 1–2**
Harriet Tubman helps lead Union troops in their successful Combahee River raid in South Carolina.

⌃ Union Navy telescope

**JANUARY 11**
The CSS *Alabama* sinks the USS *Hatteras* off Galveston, Texas. Fort Hindman, Arkansas, is captured by Union forces.

**FEBRUARY 5**
Britain announces that it will not attempt to mediate between the North and South.

**MARCH 5**
Confederate forces take Franklin, Tennessee.

**JANUARY 26**
General Joseph Hooker is appointed to command the Union Army of the Potomac, succeeding General Ambrose Burnside.

**MARCH 14**
Part of Admiral David G. Farragut's Union squadron succeeds in getting past Port Hudson, Louisiana, after which it will win supremacy on the central Mississippi River.

**APRIL 17**
Colonel Benjamin Grierson leads Union cavalry from La Grange, Tennessee, on what will be a three-week raid through Mississippi and Louisiana, to Baton Rouge, distracting Confederate generals from the growing threat to Vicksburg.

**MAY 6–17**
Big Black River Campaign. Grant defeats Confederate forces under generals Joseph E. Johnston and John C. Pemberton. Pemberton retreats to Vicksburg.

**MAY 19**
Siege of Vicksburg by Grant's forces begins.

**JUNE 3**
The main body of Lee's Army of Northern Virginia begins to leave the Fredericksburg area to start what will become the Gettysburg campaign.

Joseph Hooker »

> "But this war goes **on and on**, and the **men die**, and the **price gets ever higher** ... We are adrift here in a sea of blood and ... I want this to be the **final battle**."

GENERAL ROBERT E. LEE, BATTLE OF GETTYSBURG, JULY 2, 1863

| JULY | AUGUST | SEPTEMBER | OCTOBER | NOVEMBER | DECEMBER |
|------|--------|-----------|---------|----------|----------|
| **JULY 1** Bragg's Confederate forces withdraw from Tullahoma toward Chattanooga in Tennessee. | **AUGUST 8** Lee offers President Davis his resignation, but Davis refuses to accept it. | **SEPTEMBER 2** Ambrose Burnside's Union Army of the Ohio occupies Knoxville, Tennessee. | **OCTOBER 2** The Union Army of the Cumberland under Rosencrans is short of supplies and besieged in Chattanooga. | | **DECEMBER 3** As Union reinforcements approach Knoxville, Longstreet abandons the Confederate siege. |
| | **AUGUST 16** General William S. Rosecrans's Union Army of the Cumberland begins an advance from Tullahoma to attack Bragg's Army of Tennessee around Chattanooga. | **SEPTEMBER 5** The British government detains the two "Laird rams," warships being built for the Confederate Navy. | **OCTOBER 5** The Confederate submersible *David* makes a damaging attack on the USS *New Ironsides* off Charleston, South Carolina. | **NOVEMBER 4** The Confederates weaken their forces around Chattanooga by sending troops to the Knoxville area. | |
| | | **SEPTEMBER 7** Union forces enter Chattanooga, on their advance in Tennessee. | **OCTOBER 17** Grant is appointed to command all Union armies in the Western Theater. He appoints George Thomas to replace Rosecrans. | | |
| The Battle of Gettysburg **JULY 1–3** Battle of Gettysburg. Confederate forces are soundly defeated and forced to retreat. | **AUGUST 17** Union batteries begin a major bombardment of Fort Sumter in Charleston harbor on the South Carolina coast. | **SEPTEMBER 19–20** Battle of Chickamauga. Bragg's Confederate forces defeat the Army of the Cumberland under Rosecrans, ending the Union's Chickamauga Campaign in Georgia. | | **NOVEMBER 19** President Lincoln delivers his Gettysburg Address at the dedication of a national memorial cemetery. | **DECEMBER 8** In his annual message to Congress, President Lincoln outlines plans for the postwar reconstruction of the South. Most Confederates are to receive amnesty and have all property except slaves restored. |
| **JULY 4** Confederate forces surrender Vicksburg. | | | | **NOVEMBER 28** In Dalton, Georgia, Braxton Bragg telegraphs his resignation to President Davis. | **DECEMBER 16** General Joseph E. Johnston is given command of the Confederate Army of Tennessee, and General Leonidas Polk takes charge of the Army of Mississippi. |

Climbing Lookout »
Mountain, Chattanooga

« Chickamauga Campaign

« Ulysses S. Grant

⌃ Napoleon cannon, used by both sides

**First Reading, July 22, 1862**
This depiction of Lincoln's presentation of his momentous document to his cabinet is a copy of Francis Carpenter's *First Reading of the Emancipation Proclamation of President Lincoln* in the U.S. Capitol.

« **BEFORE**

In June 1862, President Lincoln completed drafting a Preliminary Emancipation Proclamation to free slaves in the Rebel states. He presented it to his cabinet in July.

**THE WRONG MOMENT**
All members of the cabinet **approved the spirit of the document**. But **Secretary of State William H. Seward** claimed that issuing it now, in the wake of General George B. McClellan's withdrawal from the Virginia Peninsula, would appear as "our last shriek on the retreat." Lincoln decided to **postpone discussion** of the matter until the North achieved a decisive victory.

**PRELIMINARY PROCLAMATION**
The Battle of Antietam in September 1862 **offered the "victory" Lincoln needed**. Although a tactical draw, Confederate general Robert E. Lee was forced to abandon his offensive into Maryland and retreat to Virginia. On September 22, Lincoln released the **Preliminary Emancipation Proclamation**. The rebellious states were offered **100 days to return to the Union** and adopt some form of gradual or immediate emancipation; otherwise, slaves in the Confederacy would be "forever free."

# The Emancipation Proclamation

**The Emancipation Proclamation of New Year's Day, 1863, transformed the nature of the Civil War and the Union war effort. Until then, for the North, it had been a war to preserve the Union and to restore the rebellious states to their prewar status. Now it had also become a war for freedom.**

Lincoln's Preliminary Emancipation Proclamation of September 1862 offered the Confederate states a chance to return to the Union and retain slavery at least for the time being. In spite of this enticement, none of the rebellious states came back into the Federal fold. Throughout the unconquered South, the Preliminary Proclamation was ignored as an empty measure that presented no real change in how the war would be fought.

Southerners were well aware that slaves, through their labor on farms and plantations and their work on entrenchments and fortifications, were vital to the Southern cause. In November 1861, the *Montgomery Advertiser* had asserted that "the institution of slavery in the South alone enables her to place in the field a force much larger in proportion to her white population than the North … The institution is a tower of strength to the South."

## The need to act

Lincoln knew this as well, and after the Union's military setbacks in the East during the first year of the war, he was anxious to do something that would make significant and visible inroads against the Confederate effort. At this point, Northern public morale was faltering, pressure from the powerful abolitionist bloc in the Republican Party

> **ARTICLE II, SECTION 2** The clause in the U.S. Constitution, under which Lincoln issued the Emancipation Proclamation, using his authority as commander-in-chief of the U.S. Army and Navy.

was growing, while across the Atlantic Britain and France were showing disturbing signs of moving toward a quick recognition of Confederate independence. All of these factors, along with Lincoln's own predisposition

**Eckert's inkwells**
Lincoln liked to work in the telegraph office of the War Department while waiting for news. Here he started drafting his Emancipation Proclamation, using the desk—and inkwells—of Major Thomas Eckert.

against slavery, obliged the president to act decisively—he had, after all, run for the White House in 1860 on a platform devoted to restricting the institution's spread into the territories.

Federal generals had already flirted with emancipation in various different locations, which posed a threat to the political effect and long-term moral value of a presidentially issued policy. In August 1861, Union General John C. Frémont tried to emancipate all the slaves in Missouri by a simple military declaration. In May 1862, General David Hunter did the same for the slaves of Florida, Georgia, and South Carolina.

## Careful preparation
Lincoln acknowledged the good intentions behind these military efforts at emancipation, but was forced to overrule both generals' edicts. Too few people in the North were ready to consider the freeing of slaves as an additional Federal war aim, and a premature or partial emancipation might force one or more of the border states into seceding. Missouri, especially, was still close to the tipping point. The Supreme Court, headed by pro-slavery Chief Justice Roger Taney, was another potential problem. Taney had the power to declare a rash emancipation proclamation as unconstitutional, thereby creating huge obstacles for the government.

Lincoln had much to consider before acting. His delays and apparent wavering enraged some members of the Republican Party in Congress, who

claimed that if the president continued to prevaricate, they themselves would have to take action. They had already passed several Confiscation Acts that allowed Union generals to confiscate and use rebel property, including slaves.

Even as the pressure on him mounted, Lincoln remained determined to wait until the time was right to issue his formal policy. He believed that only he as president, through constitutionally sanctioned war powers, had the ability to enforce emancipation. He later explained, "I felt the measures,

**Emancipation Proclamation**
Declaring "that all persons held as slaves" within the rebel states "are, and henceforward shall be free," the Proclamation went on to "enjoin upon [the freed slaves] ... to abstain from all violence, unless in necessary self-defence; and ... labor faithfully for reasonable wages."

otherwise unconstitutional, might become lawful, by becoming indispensable to the preservation of the Constitution, through the preservation of the nation."

Carefully timing the release of the Preliminary Proclamation in September 1862 allowed Lincoln to prepare the way for the Final Emancipation Proclamation, which formally went into effect on January 1, 1863. Technically, the Final Proclamation only freed slaves in the rebellious states, leaving all those in the border states and in Union-held portions of the Confederate states still in bondage. Those deep behind Southern lines would have to await the arrival of Union armies to enforce their liberation. Indeed, in many areas of Texas and southern Georgia, slaves knew nothing about Lincoln's proclamation until well after the war was over.

Anywhere near Union lines, however, and even in locations at a considerable distance from Union forces, rumors quickly spread among slave communities that they were now free. To some degree, slaves had been taking matters into their own hands and slipping off to freedom since the war began, especially in Virginia, Tennessee, and Louisiana, where Union armies had occupied large swaths of former rebel territory. Now, in ones and twos and small groups, slaves left with a conviction, a feeling, or just an idea that the "day of Jubilo" (liberation) had come and that they were truly free to go. Many went straight to the Union armies, where they found work cooking, nursing wounded soldiers, and caring for horses.

## Freedom at last
In the free black communities of the North, the response to the Emancipation Proclamation was electric. Henry Turner, pastor of an African Methodist Church in Washington, D.C., was present as the Proclamation was printed off in a local newspaper: "Down Pennsylvania [Avenue] I ran as for my life, and when the people saw me coming with the paper in my hand they raised a shouting cheer that was almost deafening." It was from such heartfelt enthusiasm that thousands of black volunteers for the Union army were raised. This Final Emancipation Proclamation included a provision for enlisting former slaves in the army and navy, and thus the seeds for the United States Colored Troops (USCT) were sown. Various states had already begun

recruitment of free black citizens into segregated regiments, but now recently liberated slaves could join them as well.

In Democratic parts of the North, especially in districts that had voted against Lincoln in 1860, many whites frowned upon the new war measure. Activities increased among Copperheads (Northern Democrats opposed to the war), and newspaper editors blasted the administration for abandoning the preservation of the Union and embracing emancipation instead. One Union regiment drawn from an area like this deserted almost to a man upon hearing the news. But in most sections of the loyal states, public opinion was cautiously optimistic that emancipation might hasten the end of the war.

**Hiding out**
In *Fugitive Slaves in the Dismal Swamp, Virginia* (1888), artist David Cronin depicts a favorite place of refuge on the border of Virginia and North Carolina, where hundreds of slaves managed to hide out.

## AFTER

In Europe, the British Prime Minister Lord Palmerston and the French Emperor Napoleon III had been cautiously sympathetic toward the Confederates.

**EUROPE BACKS AWAY**
News of the Emancipation Proclamation, along with Southern general Robert E. Lee's retreat from Maryland, changed the minds of Lord Palmerston and the British cabinet. They **postponed plans to recognize Confederate independence** and offer mediation between the warring sections. The British Empire, which had freed its slaves in 1833, **could not morally support a slaveholding republic** against a nation that fought to make men free. France followed Britain's lead.

**BRITISH PRIME MINISTER PALMERSTON**

# African-Americans in the War

**The plight of African-Americans during the Civil War varied tremendously, depending on where they lived, their socio-economic status, and whether they were enslaved or free. Regardless, the war transformed their lives and set them on the path to equality with whites.**

## BEFORE

**From its founding in 1818, the American Colonization Society strove to send freed slaves and free Northern blacks to foreign shores, in particular Liberia.**

**JOSEPH ROBERTS, FIRST PRESIDENT OF LIBERIA**

### COLONIZATION
It was believed, not only by slaveholders, but also by some abolitionists, that blacks and whites could not ultimately coexist in the United States. The only successful colony was **Liberia** in West Africa, which became an independent state in 1847. **Lincoln** himself was a known **proponent of colonization** before issuing the **Emancipation Proclamation ‹‹ 160–61** and supported several schemes during the war, most of which ended in tragedy for the emigrants.

### RIGHTS FOR NORTHERN BLACKS
Before the war, only **Massachusetts** legally extended **full voting rights** to its **black citizens**. Some other **New England** states allowed **black male suffrage**, and in New York those with **$250 worth of property** could vote. To have a vote in Ohio, over half a citizen's ancestry had to be white. No other state allowed black people to vote.

During the war, some **gains were made in civil rights**. Blacks could ride alongside whites in Philadelphia and Washington streetcars and in 1864 they were allowed to appear as both **witnesses and lawyers in federal courts**, but further reforms would have to wait for the **14th Amendment 338–41 ››**.

Union policy toward slaves and escaped slaves in the rebellious states wavered between decisive, proactive measures and lethargic inaction or neglect. Overall, the government was slow to implement a coherent policy. The Union army, U.S. Treasury Department, various philanthropic organizations, the president, and Congress all got involved and had different, often competing proposals and procedures on how to deal with the great number of freedmen (freed slaves) or soon-to-be freedmen. Power ultimately rested with the military officers in any given area, and as early as the summer of 1861, Union commanders were confronted with large numbers of escaped slaves who had run to safety within their lines.

### Horrors of the "contraband" camps
These early refugees from slavery became known as "contraband of war," a phrase coined by Brigadier General Benjamin Butler, commander of Fortress Monroe in Virginia. It meant that the slaves did not have to be returned to their owners as fugitives under federal law. However, their fate varied considerably from one theater of war to another.

Many of the former slaves were rounded up and placed in special "contraband camps," where sanitation was poor and medical care even worse.

Death rates were as high as 25 percent, and despite the presence of well-meaning missionaries, who provided spiritual and educational guidance, life in the camps was miserable.

In 1861–63, the camps followed the advances of the Union armies, and as time wore on, conditions improved slightly as Union officers found employment for large numbers of contrabands. The men worked as dockworkers, pioneers, trench-diggers, teamsters, and personal servants, and some of the women served as cooks and laundresses for the soldiers. In such capacities they performed the same functions as slaves did for the Confederate armies, but at least they earned a "wage," even though this could simply be room, board, and clothing. The families of the employed lived in the local camp or precariously hung around the margins of the Union picket lines.

### Wage slavery under Unionists
Marginally more fortunate were former slaves on abandoned plantations that the Unionists confiscated and returned to working order. Early in the war, the Union army overran some of the South's best plantation districts: the sea islands off Charleston, southern Louisiana, and the fertile lands of the Mississippi River Valley. Owners ran to safety behind Confederate lines and simply left their land and slaves to their fate.

Realizing the potential profits to be had, Northern civilian entrepreneurs responded eagerly to the federal government's offers to manage these plantations. In theory, the government would receive the lion's share of the sale of cotton, sugar, or other staple crops, and the former slaves would be paid a fair wage. In reality, plantation managers and local Union army officers conspired to split most of the profits among themselves, and often paid the laborers just enough to keep them

**Permanently scarred**
However badly they were treated when they came North, nothing could compare with the brutality and cruelty slaves had suffered at the hands of their owners. This former slave was photographed after he escaped to the North and served in the Federal army.

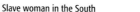

### Slave woman in the South
In this 1866 painting by Winslow Homer entitled *Near Andersonville* or *Captured Liberators,* a black woman looks on as captured Union troops, her potential liberators, are marched off to Andersonville Prison.

working. After "deductions" for food, housing, and clothing, most earned absolutely nothing, and therefore lived an existence akin to slavery. Local military laws that forbade blacks from being unemployed forced many of them back into the cotton or cane fields, or otherwise face imprisonment.

By the last 18 months of the war, under pressure from both Northern abolitionists and missionaries who were outraged at the "wage slavery" that existed in the Union-occupied South, both Congress and the Union army began to change their policies. Land was the key issue behind this new direction.

Through various pieces of legislation, or under the supervision of Yankee generals, almost 20 percent of the former Confederate territory captured by the Union was given to African-Americans. The prominent abolitionist Wendell Phillips wrote, "Let me confiscate the land of the South, and put it into the hands of Negroes and the white men who fought for it, and I have planted a Union sure to grow as an acorn to become an oak." However, the question remained whether the freedmen would be able to hold on to any land they had gained after the war was over.

**180,000** The number of African-Americans who fought for their freedom in the war. About one-third of them died.

## Black Confederates
The vast majority of blacks under Confederate control were slaves who, either by coercion or suggestion, remained on plantations or farms until liberated by invading Union forces. It is difficult to determine how many wished to stay with their masters, serving in the army as servants, teamsters, or laborers, or remain at home as fieldworkers and house servants. Few Confederate-enlisted men owned slaves and so never

**AFTER** »

As the Confederate army lost more and more fighting men, the idea of enlisting slaves into the ranks was finally accepted by the Confederate Congress in Richmond.

### FIRST PROPOSALS REJECTED
Certain Rebel generals, including **Richard Ewell**, **Patrick Cleburne**, and, ultimately, **Robert E. Lee**, proposed at different points in the war that the Richmond government grant **freedom in return for slaves' military service.** Even President Davis offered a bill in November 1864 extending emancipation to future enlisted slaves, but Congress refused to consider it.

### CONGRESS ACCEPTS BLACK TROOPS
By February 1865, facing imminent defeat, and with the **powerful backing of both Lee and Davis**, the Congress grudgingly agreed to a limited form of emancipation for slaves who fought. Some **companies of black Confederate soldiers** were actually **drilling in the streets of Richmond** right before the **city fell 314–15 »**, but it was too little, too late.

brought them along to war; a sizeable percentage of officers, especially early in the conflict, did bring a slave with them, but this declined significantly as the war dragged on. As an institution, slavery was irrevocably weakened after the Emancipation Proclamation, and by the last year of the war, many slaves—even those in unconquered areas of the South—refused to work, or had no incentive to do so, as the majority of white men had left home. White female or black overseers, increasingly common by 1864, could not maintain discipline, and as slavery began to die so, too, did the remaining economic power of the Confederacy.

### Escaping to relative freedom
Escaped slaves were placed in camps which followed the Union army and both men and women found work helping the officers and soldiers. However, for many the reality of life away from the plantations was harsh.

# Journey to Freedom

**In the early stages of the Civil War, slaves living in the Confederacy who escaped to the Union side were known as contraband. Thousands of former slaves worked for the Union cause, receiving a small wage; others took over the plantations they had previously worked on.**

"In the summer of 1862, freedmen began to flock into Washington from Maryland and Virginia. They came with a great hope in their hearts, and with all their worldly goods on their backs. Fresh from the bonds of slavery, fresh from the benighted regions of the plantation, they came to the Capital looking for liberty, and many of them not knowing it when they found it. Many good friends reached forth kind hands, but the North is not warm and impulsive. For one kind word spoken, two harsh ones were uttered; there was something repelling in the atmosphere, and the bright joyous dreams of freedom to the slave faded—were sadly altered, in the presence of that stern, practical mother, reality."

ELIZABETH HOBBS KECKLEY (1808–1907), FORMER SLAVE WHO BECAME A SUCCESSFUL SEAMSTRESS IN WASHINGTON, D.C., FROM HER MEMOIR *BEHIND THE SCENES*, 1868

"The way we can best take care of ourselves is to have land, and turn it and till it by our own labor—that is, by the labor of the women and children and old men; and we can soon maintain ourselves and have something to spare. And to assist the Government, the young men should enlist in the service of the Government, and serve in such manner as they may be wanted ... We want to be placed on land until we are able to buy it and make it our own."

REVEREND GARRISON FRAZIER AT A MEETING OF AFRICAN-AMERICAN MINISTERS AND CHURCH OFFICERS WITH EDWIN M. STANTON, SECRETARY OF WAR, AND MAJOR GENERAL WILLIAM T. SHERMAN IN SAVANNAH, GEORGIA, JANUARY 12, 1865

**Taking over the plantation**
After Union troops captured Hilton Head Island, South Carolina, in 1861, hundreds of escaped slaves gathered there. A community was built for them at Mitchelville and some began to harvest and gin cotton for their own profit.

ABOLITIONIST AND ACTIVIST  Born c.1820  Died 1913

# Harriet **Tubman**

## "**God** won't let master **Lincoln** beat the South till he **does** the right thing."

HARRIET TUBMAN ON LINCOLN'S INITIAL RELUCTANCE TO EMANCIPATE SLAVES, 1862

As with many slaves, the exact date of Tubman's birth is not known. What is certain is that she was born Araminta ("Minty") Ross on a plantation in Dorchester County, Maryland. She often found herself in the wrong place at the wrong time and was beaten by her master, Edward Brodess, who saw her as a nuisance and regularly hired her out to other abusive neighbors. Gaining a strong sense of self-reliance, she grew fearless in the face of physical punishment.

One day, while Minty was running an errand in a local dry goods store, an overseer from another plantation demanded she help restrain a runaway slave. Tubman refused and the slave broke free, running out of the store. While trying to stop the slave, the overseer threw a two-pound metal weight from the counter. The weight hit Minty's forehead, fracturing her skull, and for the rest of her life she suffered from severe headaches, seizures, and deep sleeps from which

**Tubman's iron resolution**
With grim determination and knowing no fear, Tubman escorted more than 300 slaves to freedom—including most of her own family. She would later note with pride that on all her journeys, she "never lost a passenger."

no one could wake her. During these episodes she claimed to commune with God and learn His plans for her life. Her physical bravery was thus augmented by a Christian spirituality that girded her throughout her future work.

In 1844, she married freedman John Tubman, and took her mother's name, Harriet. She escaped from slavery in 1849, and resolved to bring as many kinsmen and friends to freedom as possible.

**Passport to freedom**
Maryland's eastern shore was only 90 miles (145km) from Pennsylvania, and with her intimate knowledge of the swamps, estuaries, and woodlands of her home state, Tubman brought hundreds of slaves across them to freedom in the North along the "Underground Railroad." Traveling mainly at night, and preferably during the winter, she fast gained a reputation among abolitionists, including John Brown, who called her "General Tubman." She may also have conferred with Brown in planning his famous attack on Harpers Ferry. She often deposited her "passengers" as far north as Canada after the lower Northern states became unsafe when the Fugitive Slave Law was passed. To the many ex-slaves who owed their freedom to her in the later prewar period, she was simply "Moses."

When the Civil War broke out, Tubman was overjoyed at the prospects for the abolition of slavery, but became disappointed when

**Tubman's hymn book**
On the Underground Railroad, Tubman sang hymns to alert slaves of their imminent departure. Her well-worn hymn book bears her name inscribed in pencil.

- **c.1820** Born Araminta "Minty" Ross in Dorchester County, Maryland, to slave parents Harriet "Rit" Green and Ben Ross.
- **1834** Struck on head by an iron weight, which causes serious side effects for the rest of her life.
- **1844** Marries freedman John Tubman. Takes the first name of "Harriet."
- **1849** Runs away from slavery in the late fall after hearing rumors she might be sold.
- **1850** Fugitive Slave Act passed. Tubman conducts her niece and niece's two children to freedom in the North.
- **1851–52** Conducts other slaves, including her brother Moses, from the Eastern Shore of Maryland to freedom. Her husband John, who has remarried, refuses to relocate North.
- **1854–60** Makes many trips to the Eastern Shore, personally guiding hundreds to freedom; comes to the attention of the leading abolitionists during this time.
- **1858** Meets John Brown at her home in St. Catharines, Ontario, Canada. Confers on, but does not participate in, the Harpers Ferry raid.
- **1859** Lectures in New England about her work on the Underground Railroad.
- **1862–65** Works in an unofficial but valuable capacity for the Union forces at Hilton Head, South Carolina, as a nurse, cook, and scout.
- **1863** Along with Colonel James Montgomery, Tubman co-leads the Combahee River Raid on June 2, in which 700 slaves are liberated and critical Confederate supplies are burned.
- **1865** Nurses wounded soldiers at Fortress Monroe, Virginia.
- **1869** Marries Civil War veteran Nelson Davis.
- **1870–90** Farms her small property in Auburn, New York, and engages in numerous small enterprises, most of which do not prosper. Supports former slaves and the destitute.
- **1888** Nelson Davis dies.

President Lincoln seemed to reverse his anti-slavery stance by publicly reprimanding Union General David Hunter's "local" abolition of slavery in the district of Port Royal, South Carolina. She became acquainted with Hunter while serving with a group of Northeastern abolitionists who had accompanied the Federal armies occupying the South Carolina coastal islands. There, she became indispensable both as a nurse, and as an intermediary between the officers and fugitive slaves who ran to the safety of Hunter's lines.

Tubman likened the necessity for the abolition of slavery to treating a snake bite: "You send for a doctor to cut the bite; but the snake, he rolled up there, and while the doctor doing it, he bite you again. The doctor dug out that bite; but while the doctor doing it, the snake, he spring up and bite you again; so he keep doing it, till you kill him."

### Union adviser

After the Emancipation Proclamation, she redoubled her efforts on behalf of the Union cause in the South Carolina coastal areas, leading a group of Union scouts through the area's complex system of waterways, islands, and marshes. These forays gave Union commanders priceless local knowledge, and Secretary of War, Edwin Stanton, officially supported her efforts. In July 1863, using information she had gleaned during her scouting trips, Tubman advised and assisted Colonel James Montgomery in his raid of the Combahee River

plantations by guiding Union steamboats past Confederate torpedoes to safe landing zones. Once ashore, the Union troops burned several plantations and bridges, confiscated thousands of dollars of supplies, and liberated over 700 slaves. Confederate soldiers arrived too late to stop the destruction and the escaped slaves crowded onto the Federal steamboats. Many of them later joined the black regiments that were forming.

### Humanitarian to the last

A few weeks later, Tubman traveled with the 54th Massachusetts to its launching point at Battery Wagner, reportedly serving Colonel Robert Gould Shaw his last meal. For the rest of the war, she worked without pay for Union forces as they tightened the noose around Charleston, South Carolina, assisting with fugitive slaves, scouting deeper into Confederate territory, and advising Federal officers about the needs of the freedmen. Toward the end of the war she served as a volunteer nurse in Virginia, finally heading back to New York following Lee's surrender.

Tubman never enjoyed official status during the Civil War, even though her contributions to the Northern cause were well-known in Washington. She

### The Underground Railroad

Small groups of slaves were secretly conducted north along the Underground Railroad, stopping at safe houses or "stations" on the indirect route. Fugitives evaded capture with the assistance of anti-slavery sympathizers.

received no pay for all her sacrifices before or during the war, and it was not until 1899 that she received a pension. Tubman spent most of the meager sums she earned doing odd jobs to support her elderly parents and the former slaves she boarded at her home. Friends and admirers were outraged at the poverty she endured and periodically raised monies for her support. She also earned royalties from her biographies.

In Tubman's later years, she discovered a new cause: the women's suffrage movement. When asked by a white woman if she thought females should be able to vote, she replied, "I suffered enough to believe it." Advocates of women's suffrage Susan B. Anthony and Emily Howland counted Tubman as a colleague and friend. In 1903, she donated land she owned to create a home for aged and poverty-stricken blacks. The Harriet Tubman Home for the Aged opened on June 23, 1908, and it was there that Tubman died, as a resident, nearly five years later.

**TUBMAN (FAR LEFT) WITH HER FAMILY**

- **1890s** Becomes actively involved in the suffrage movement, attending both black and white suffrage conventions; continues to do this into the early 1900s.
- **1896** Purchases 25 acres (10 hectares) adjoining her property to establish a home for elderly and sick African-Americans.
- **1908** The Harriet Tubman Home for the Aged is opened by the African Methodist Episcopal Zion Church.
- **1913** Dies on March 10 at the age of 91, and is buried at Fort Hill Cemetery in Auburn, New York.

> " This is the **only military command** in American history wherein **a woman, black or white, led the raid** ..."
>
> SECRETARY OF WAR EDWIN M. STANTON ON THE COMBAHEE RIVER RAID

When the war began few whites, in the North as much as in the South, thought it appropriate or even safe to permit African-Americans to enlist as soldiers.

## EMANCIPATION PROCLAMATION

The formation of **black regiments** was sanctioned by the **Emancipation Proclamation** « **160–61**. For Lincoln, enlisting black soldiers was a **practical measure** to assist in preserving the Union, but he feared repercussions from the border states, where the idea of **arming black men was repugnant** to most white citizens.

## STATE-RAISED BLACK REGIMENTS

After the **Confiscation Acts** passed by the U.S. Congress in 1862, Massachusetts, Connecticut, and the military governments of occupied Louisiana and South Carolina began forming black regiments. Response to recruitment drives was mixed—in the states of New England **free blacks had been turned away** when they tried to join up in 1861 and now some thought twice about enlisting. In the occupied South, **freed slaves flocked to join up**, excited by the prospects of steady pay and striking a **blow against their former masters.**

# The Role of Black Troops

**The idea of black soldiers was initially anathema to many in the North, but by mid-1863, state-raised black regiments had begun to see action and regiments of the United States Colored Troops (U.S.C.T) were being formed. By the war's end, African-Americans were a vital component of the Federal armies.**

In addition to the hazards of battle and other dangers of military life, black soldiers faced other difficulties. Confederates reacted strongly to the prospect of black Union soldiers. President Jefferson Davis issued a proclamation in December 1862 that directed all Confederate military officers in the field to turn over captured black Union soldiers and their white officers to state—not Confederate— authorities. In this capacity any prisoners could be indicted for insurrection or inciting insurrection and sentenced to death. On May 1, 1863 the Confederate Congress went one step further and passed a joint

**178,895** The number of men who enlisted in the **U.S.C.T.; at least 94,000 of them came from Southern states and 80,000 from the Northern states and territories; the rest had unknown origins.**

resolution authorizing Davis to allow such captured white officers to be put to death and to sell black enlisted men back into slavery.

Lincoln's response to this was stern: for every captured Federal officer put to death, an imprisoned Confederate officer would be summarily executed in the North. There were no recorded cases of white officers being executed by Rebel authorities but there is strong evidence of seized black soldiers being returned to slavery. Moreover, Southern soldiers finding themselves confronted by black Union soldiers often discarded any semblance of obeying the rules of war.

**Butler Medal, 1864**
Instituted by Major General Benjamin Butler in 1864 to honor the bravery of African-American troops, the Butler Medal was the only one ever struck for black troops. It is inscribed: "Freedom will be theirs by the sword."

**107th Regiment U.S. Colored Infantry**
Although black soldiers fought for their country, they were not U.S. citizens. Frederick Douglass said that by bearing arms "no one can deny that [they have] earned the right to citizenship."

**Battle of Milliken's Bend**
On June 7, 1863 a small Union force was attacked by 1,500 Texans at Milliken's Bend, Louisiana. The bravery of the African-Americans fighting that day earned them new respect, paving the way for black enlistment.

Barbarities were not uncommon; the most notorious were those committed at Fort Pillow, a Union garrison on the Tennessee side of the Mississippi River. On the afternoon of April 12, 1864 Confederate cavalry commanded by Lieutenant General Nathan Bedford Forrest "shot down, bayoneted, and put to the sword in cold blood" hundreds of black soldiers as they tried to surrender. In response to the massacre, black Federal volunteers adopted "Remember Fort Pillow" as their battle cry and thereafter sometimes engaged in their own excesses when dealing with apprehended Confederates.

Whether in a state-raised regiment, such as the famous 54th Massachusetts, or in one of the 166 regiments of the United States Colored Troops (U.S.C.T.), soldiers in a black regiment inverted the two principal Union war goals compared to their white comrades: they fought to free their people first, and preserve the Union second. As Frederick Douglass said, "The iron gate of our prison stands half open. One gallant rush from the North will fling it wide open, while four millions of our brothers and sisters shall march out into liberty."

### White attitudes
The first black volunteers were infused with a profound sense of purpose, which steadied them as a series of challenges were flung their way from within their own army. First, many white soldiers disliked the idea of arming blacks, and some flatly refused to serve near them. Theodore Upson of the 100th Illinois wrote that "none of our soldiers seem to like the idea of arming the Negroes. Our boys say this is a white man's war and the Negro has no business in it." Recent immigrants to the North took a different tack. As one Irish journalist explained: "I'll let Sambo be murthered instead of meself on any day of the year."

### Official discrimination
It took demonstrated bravery on the battlefield for such racial stereotypes and prejudice to subside. By the war's end, most white Federal troops still viewed their black comrades somewhat askance, but few questioned their value and devotion to the Union cause. However, black troops still had to deal with bureaucratized discrimination.

At first, black privates received $12 a month, the same as white soldiers, but in June 1863, the War Department announced that henceforth they would only receive $10, and be required to pay $3 of that toward a clothing allowance. In June 1864, this cruel disparity was remedied, but lasting damage had been done to black morale.

Never redressed was the apparent unfairness of disallowing black officers, with very rare exceptions. In all the black regiments that served in the war, there were only 32 black officers—and most were chaplains and surgeons. A special school to train officer candidates for black regiments opened in Philadelphia in late 1863, but its only graduates were white.

### Routine work
Black regiments were often detailed to mundane second-line duties, such as digging trenches, clearing trees, guarding railroads, and protecting communication lines. Even after black valor was proven by the assault on Port Hudson on May 27, 1863, where the bravery of black regiments first came to the Northern public's attention, troops rarely saw action proportional to their numbers in the Union armies.

When black units were called on to fight in a decisive action, such as at the Battle of the Crater, it was often under adverse conditions that made high casualty rates likely. This fact disgruntled many people in the ranks, leading to recruitment difficulties later. Even so, African-Americans made up 12 percent of Union soldiers by the end of the war.

Despite their impressive combat record, discrimination against black soldiers continued through 1865, and beyond in the postwar U.S. Army.

### FINAL GLORY AND FINAL INSULT
The Union 25th Corps was almost completely composed of **black regiments** and had the honor of being the first to enter Richmond when the **Confederate capital** was captured in April 1865. The next month, as the two Union armies marched in triumph in the **Grand Review** in Washington, **not a single black unit** was among them.

### CONTRIBUTIONS TO VICTORY
By the end of the war, **186,000 black soldiers**—119,000 of them former slaves—had fought for the Union. Black troops earned **21 Medals of Honor** and had suffered over 68,000 casualties, an **astonishing rate of loss**.

**A BLACK WAR VETERAN**

" Whatever **Negroes** can … do **as soldiers**, leaves just so much **less for white soldiers** to do."
ABRAHAM LINCOLN TO ILLINOIS POLITICIAN JAMES C. CONKLING, AUGUST 26, 1863

#### UNION OFFICER (1812–85)
#### MAJOR MARTIN DELANY

The first black field-grade officer in the history of the U.S. Army, Delany had been a prewar abolitionist and was among the first three black men accepted to study medicine at Harvard. During the war he helped recruit thousands for the U.S.C.T. Lincoln was impressed with him when they met in 1865, calling him a "most extraordinary and intelligent man." He was commissioned a major two weeks later, the highest rank attained by an African-American during the war.

# Assault on Fort Wagner

**Strategically located on South Carolina's Morris Island, Fort Wag[ner]
played a crucial role in the protection of Charleston. In July 1863
Union troops unsuccessfully engaged in two battles while
attempting to capture the fort. One of the first African-American
units, Colonel Robert Gould Shaw's 54th Massachusetts Voluntee[r]
Infantry, spearheaded the attack on July 18.**

"The 54th, the past week, has proved itself twice in battle ...
on Saturday afternoon we were marched up past our batteries,
amid the cheers of the officers and soldiers. We wondered what
they were all cheering for, but we soon found out. Gen. Strong r[ode]
up, and we halted. Well, you had better believe there was some
guessing what we were to do. Gen. Strong asked us if we would
follow him into Fort Wagner. Every man said, yes—we were rea[dy]
to follow wherever we were led. You may all know Fort Wagner i[s]
the Sebastopol of the rebels; but we went at it, over the ditch an[d]
on to the parapet through deadly fire; but we could not get into [the]
fort. We met the foe on the parapet of Wagner with the bayonet—
we were exposed to a murderous fire from the batteries of the fo[rt]
from our Monitors and our land batteries, as they did not cease
firing soon enough. Mortal men could not stand such a fire, and
the assault on Wagner was a failure ... at the first charge the 54th
rushed to within twenty yards of the ditches ... the color beare[r]
of the State colors was killed on the parapet. Col. Shaw seized th[e]
staff when the standard bearer fell, and in less than a minute af[ter]
the Colonel fell himself. When the men saw their gallant leader f[all]
they made a desperate effort to get him out, but they were eithe[r]
shot down, or reeled in the ditch below ... I have no more paper
here at present ... so I cannot further particularize in this letter[."]

CORPORAL JAMES HENRY GOODING, 54th MASSACHUSETTS VOLUNTEER INFANTRY,
IN A LETTER OF JULY 20, 1863

**The storming of Fort Wagner**
An 1890 lithograph dramatizes the attack by the 54th
Massachusetts led by Colonel Shaw, who was shot
through the heart. The regiment displayed exceptional
valor in the brutal hand-to-hand combat that ensued.

**EFORE**

st increase in the population of the
States in the years before the war
riven by mass immigration, mainly
inct groups of northern Europeans.

**PEAN IMMIGRATION**

g in the 1830s and increasing steadily
861, **thousands of immigrants** from
, Germany, and Scandinavia set sail
heir native lands in hope of **a new life**
erica. Nearly all of them settled in the
ed ethnic neighborhoods of the great
rn cities or, taking advantage of Federal
ant incentives, **moved to the frontier**
ratched a living from the soil.

**ORTY-EIGHTERS**

al émigrés from the **failed Prussian**
cratic revolutions of 1848–49, were
as the Forty-Eighters. They fled the area
ope that is now Germany after the liberal
se was suppressed by force. In their new
they developed significant **political clout**.
held radical, even socialist views, most
d Lincoln in 1860, and all **hated slavery**.

**NION GENERAL (1824–1902)**

**RANZ SIGEL**

nz Sigel emigrated from Germany after
nting in the unsuccessful revolution
1848. By 1860 he was a prominent
ember of the German community in
Louis, Missouri, working as an educator
d well-known for his anti-slavery views.
om the start of the war he did much to
cruit German-Americans for the Union
ces, but was less successful as a
neral. He did play a major role in the
nion success at Pea Ridge (Elkhorn
vern) in 1861, but later failed as a
rps commander with the Army of the
tomac and when given an independent
mmand in the Shenandoah Valley.

# Immigrants in the Ranks

**Immigrants to the United States came mainly from Ireland and Germany, and since relatively few settled in the South, both groups rallied to the Union side. Many joined "ethnic" regiments, but by 1863 immigrant enthusiasm for the Northern cause had begun to wane.**

The U.S. census of 1860 counted over 13 percent of the population as foreign-born. Most of these people lived in New England and the Mid-Atlantic states, and nearly all the rest in the Old Northwest. Fewer than 10 percent resided in the South, mainly because of their inability to compete with slave labor. New York, Philadelphia, Boston, Pittsburgh, Cincinnati, Chicago, and Milwaukee all boasted German, Irish, and Scandinavian-born populations of over 33 percent.

On the eve of secession, New York City was the third-largest German-speaking city in the world. On many city streets in the North storefronts displayed signs in German, and only the German language—or Irish Gaelic—was spoken. In the Midwest, entire rural communities were composed of just Norwegians or Swedes. In the South,

**5 MILLION** The number of European immigrants who came to the United States between 1815 and 1860. By 1860, three-quarters of the foreign-born population were Irish or Germans.

immigrants rarely ventured beyond the largest towns. New Orleans, Richmond, and Charleston all had sizeable German and Irish communities, but none exceeded 25 percent of the population.

## Proving their worth
When the war came, ethnic Americans rallied behind their respective causes like "native-born" Anglo-Americans. But they did not enlist simply to protect the flag, the Constitution, or hearth and home. Northern Germans and Irish especially wanted to "prove" their worthiness as adopted citizens by volunteering and believed that in doing so, they might eliminate lingering nativistic, anti-immigrant trends in Northern society. In the 1850s the Know-Nothing Party rose briefly to national prominence on a platform devoted to political war on the foreign-born. However, the sentiments they unleashed died hard, and ethnic Americans were eager to do something important in the war to overcome their fellow-citizens' fear of foreigners.

By the end of 1861 an entire division of German-born troops, composed of German-speaking regiments from New

**German soldiers at Second Bull Run**
The German units of Franz Sigel's First Corps were heavily engaged at Stony Ridge and Henry House Hill on August 29 and 30, during the Second Battle of Bull Run, but their badly coordinated attacks were unsuccessful.

York, Ohio, and Pennsylvania, was placed under the command of Brigadier General Ludwig Blenker in the defenses of Washington, D.C. Around the same time, the Irish formed the soon-to-be-famous Irish Brigade, under the command of Irish nationalist Thomas Francis Meagher, and the Irish Legion, led by Michael Corcoran.

The majority of ethnic soldiers—approximately 70 percent—served in "mixed" regiments composed both of immigrants and native-born Americans, but the spotlight quickly fell on the ethnic regiments

as their political leaders boasted of their inherent martial abilities compared to the "American farmboys." It helped that the majority of German recruits had seen military service or even fought as revolutionaries at some point before coming to the United States, as had a fair number of the Irish.

## Ethnic regiments in action
By the end of 1862, the German and Irish regiments had earned different reputations in the Northern public's eye. Valiant assaults on the Sunken Road at Antietam and Marye's Heights at Fredericksburg had earned the Irish Brigade a badge of courage that persists in the public imagination even to this day. But plundering in the Shenandoah Valley Campaign of 1862, caused by inadequate provisioning by the Federal War Department, had given Blenker's Germans a different report. Labeled "Hessians," "Dutchmen," or "Blenkerites," the Germans labored under a false reputation for waging war on civilians while not performing well in battle. At Cross Keys and at Second Bull Run, the German regiments of the East fought well, despite poor generalship; while early Union victories in the West, such as Pea Ridge, where Franz Sigel and many German units fought courageously, were downplayed.

By the summer of 1863, however, Irish and German-American soldiers and civilians had come to share something: a feeling of indignation

**GARIBALDI GUARD!**

PATRIOTI ITALIANI!
HORVEDEK! FRIHEDEN
AMIS DE LA LIBERTÉ!
DEUTSCHE FREIHEITS KÆMPFER!

**APPEAL!**

**Wanted at once,
250 ABLE-BODIED MEN!**
Italians, Hungarians, Germans, and French, Patriots of all Nations.
**AROUSE! AROUSE! AROUSE!**

**Multilingual recruitment poster**
New York's Italian community provided recruits for the Garibaldi Guard, more formally known as the 39th New York Volunteer Infantry Regiment. Raised in June 1861, it served throughout the war.

**Irish regimental flag**
The Union's Irish Brigade was composed initially of New York regiments, later joined by units from Pennsylvania and Massachusetts, including the 28th Massachusetts, a Boston regiment, whose flag is shown here.

and disenchantment with the Union war effort. The Irish Brigade had shrunk to a shell of its former self. Recruitment dropped off due to Irish dissatisfaction with Emancipation, state draft laws, economic hardship at home, and a perception that they had been used as cannon fodder in previous battles.

## Mixed reactions

German-Americans felt the sting of a resurgent nativism after the Battle of Chancellorsville, in which the Northern public placed most of the blame for the Union defeat on the shoulders of the German Eleventh Corps (the successor organization to Blenker's Division). Outraged at what they perceived as unfair aspersions and ugly lampooning,

German-born Northerners questioned their participation in the war and began to turn inward, toward themselves and their ethnic communities, for sympathy and support. The supply of recruits for the German regiments also dried up, although most German units fought on much as before through the end of the war, commanded by German officers but diluted by non-German

## Sunday Mass

Irish-Americans welcomed Catholic chaplains in their units. Here Father Thomas Mooney says Mass for the 69th New York Regiment, with Colonel Michael Corcoran standing on his right.

draftees. For the ethnic communities of the North, nothing was the same after the summer of 1863.

In the end, 25 percent of all Union soldiers were born overseas, most of them in Germany or Ireland. Most of these men served in nonethnic regiments, bolstering the strength of these units as the war dragged on. Without them, the North would have been hard-pressed to secure victory.

## AFTER

The nation's various ethnic communities retained their distinctive identities and political interests, even as they participated fully in war service.

### NEW YORK CITY DRAFT RIOTS
In late July 1863, the Union's largest city **erupted in violence** as primarily Irish-American citizens, angered at the **new draft laws**, went on a rampage of burning, larceny, and lynching that was only quelled by the arrival of **Federal troops fresh from Gettysburg 202–203 »**.

### FRÉMONT MOVEMENT
Displeased with Lincoln's handling of the war, Midwestern **German-American radicals** sponsored John C. Frémont as an **alternative to Lincoln** for the Republican presidential nomination in 1864. **Their attempt to unseat Lincoln failed 236–37 »**.

# The Battle of Chancellorsville

**By early 1863 the Union Army of the Potomac was more than twice as strong as the Confederate Army of Northern Virginia. By boldly dividing his army and maneuvering rapidly against the Union flank, General Robert E. Lee achieved an unlikely victory at Chancellorsville, but lost many men.**

## « BEFORE

The Eastern Theater had seen a series of bloody battles in 1862 in which, largely through poor generalship, the increasing Union strength had gained little advantage.

**HOOKER REFORMS THE FEDERAL ARMY**
Replacing the inept Burnside as commander of the Army of the Potomac after the **defeat at Fredericksburg** « 136–37, Major General Joseph Hooker restored morale by revising uniforms and ensuring rations and pay were distributed on time. He also improved the army's organization, **creating a military intelligence service**, consolidating the cavalry under one command, and **decentralizing the artillery**.

MAJOR GENERAL JOSEPH HOOKER

Major General Joseph Hooker drew up a grand operational plan for the Army of the Potomac in the spring of 1863. He would divide his 134,000-man force and lead three corps around General Lee's western flank, marching through the dense woods of the Virginia wilderness. At the same time, Major General John Sedgwick and the remaining three corps held Lee's attention at Fredericksburg.

Hooker's flanking force began its trek without incident in late April 1863 and succeeded in crossing both the Rapidan and Rappahannock Rivers with minimal resistance. Hooker then turned east, moving his 70,000 men through the wilderness, past a large estate locally known as Chancellorsville, and into the open country five miles to the west of Fredericksburg.

### Battle is joined
Lee and his lieutenant, Stonewall Jackson, reacted quickly to the threat. On May 1, Lee left General Jubal Early and 12,000 men to watch Sedgwick at Fredericksburg, while Jackson and the rest of the army marched down the Orange Plank Road to meet Hooker.

### Battle sketch
Civil War artist Alfred Waud made drawings of the conflict for the American press. Here, an injured soldier is stretchered off the Chancellorsville battlefield. General Howard's headquarters at Dowdall's Tavern is nearby.

**A general's great march**
Stonewall Jackson led 33,000 men on his flank march. The tired men traveled many miles to the strike the enemy. One rebel noted, "I reckon the Devil himself would have run with Jackson in his rear."

Near the Zoan Church, General Lafayette McLaws' Division ran head first into part of George Meade's Union Fifth Corps. For a while the Federals pushed McLaws back, but when the Confederate threw in his reserve, they retreated, calling for reinforcements.

Hooker was shocked at the resistance his advance had met. Losing his nerve, he ordered his two forward corps to withdraw to Chancellorsville. The

mood among the Union commanders on the night of May 1 was incredulous. Lee and Jackson, on the other hand, could hardly believe their good luck.

Later that night, the Southern chieftains conferred. General J.E.B. Stuart's cavalry scouts had discovered the Union right wing was "hanging in the air" so Jackson and 33,000 troops of his corps would march off through the thick woods on the morning of May 2 to attack the unprotected Federal

**134,000** Strength of Hooker's Army of the Potomac at the start of the campaign.

**62,000** Strength of the Confederate Army of North Virginia on the same date.

flank. Lee would keep only 14,000 men to confront all of Hooker's force at Chancellorsville, should he attack.

### The "Flying Dutchmen"
Men of Major General Daniel Sickles' Third Corps, stationed on a cleared hill called Hazel Grove just to the west of Chancellorsville, discovered Jackson's flank march not long after it got started. Hooker and Sickles misinterpreted the movement as a Confederate retreat. Eleventh Corps commander, Oliver Otis Howard, stationed on the extreme right of the Union line—exactly where Jackson was headed—also believed the enemy was retreating. Scouts reported the enemy massing in the forest to the right, but Howard dismissed them.

About 5:30pm, with darkness falling, Jackson unleashed 26,000 Confederates, screaming the rebel yell, into the 8,500

Tavern – Howards Hd-Qtrs.

## Union failure at Chancellorsville

After Jackson's rapid march to outflank the Union right on May 2, the Union army was outfought in the fierce action of the following day. Union commander Joseph Hooker lost his nerve and retreated back across the Rappahannock.

men of the Eleventh Corps. There was no time for the Union regiments to realign and react; the only safety was in flight. But further along the Orange Turnpike, two stubborn holding actions delayed the Southern advance, including a stand made by Brigadier General Carl Schurz's totally German Third Division at the Wilderness Church. Unfairly labeled by nativistic Anglo-Americans as the "flying Dutchmen," these men had in fact bought time for the rest of the Federal Army to react.

### Lee's greatest day

Frustrated by the failing momentum of his attack, and in the pitch black of the woods, Jackson reconnoitered in front of his lines to ascertain the positions of the Union forces and was accidentally shot by his own men. Stuart took over.

May 3 dawned a brilliant, crisp day, and by the time the sun was rising above the trees at Hazel Grove, this key terrain was in Confederate hands. Southern artillery swarmed the open ground, dominating the clearings of Fairview and Chancellorsville, and opened a murderous fire on Union infantry and artillery holding those positions. Waves of Southern infantry assaulted hastily prepared Federal brigades posted in the woods to the

north and south of Fairview. Some of the most vicious fighting of the war occurred before Hooker ordered the abandonment of first Fairview, and then Chancellorsville.

Despite having two corps standing idly by that could have crashed into Stuart's northern flank, Hooker chose

to retreat. Nearly all his subordinates agreed that Chancellorsville was one of the greatest Northern lost opportunities of the war. Against all odds, Lee had scored a tactical victory, inflicting 17,000 casualties on the enemy while suffering 13,000 of his own—though among these was the irreplaceable Jackson.

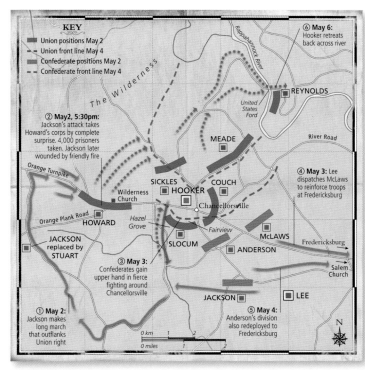

**KEY**
- Union positions May 2
- Union front line May 4
- Confederate positions May 2
- Confederate front line May 4

The Wilderness

⑥ May 6: Hooker retreats back across river

Rappahannock River

REYNOLDS

United States Ford

River Road

② May2, 5:30pm: Jackson's attack takes Howard's corps by complete surprise. 4,000 prisoners taken. Jackson later wounded by friendly fire

MEADE

Orange Turnpike

SICKLES    COUCH

Wilderness Church    HOOKER

Chancellorsville

④ May 3: Lee dispatches McLaws to reinforce troops at Fredericksburg

Orange Plank Road    HOWARD

Hazel Grove

Fairview

McLAWS    Fredericksburg

JACKSON replaced by STUART

SLOCUM    ANDERSON

Salem Church

③ May 3: Confederates gain upper hand in fierce fighting around Chancellorsville

JACKSON    LEE

① May 2: Jackson makes long march that outflanks Union right

⑤ May 4: Anderson's division also redeployed to Fredericksburg

0 km  1  2
0 miles  1  2

N

AFTER

The strategic initiative in the East passed to the Confederates. As the Union army reorganized, Lee's next major move would be the advance to Gettysburg.

### SALEM CHURCH

Union Major General Sedgwick and his Sixth Corps attacked Jubal Early at Fredericksburg on the morning of May 3. They pushed him off Marye's Heights, and proceeded west down the Orange Turnpike toward Lee's rear. A desperate stand by Brigadier General Cadmus Wilcox's Rebel brigade at Salem Church stopped Sedgwick cold. The next day, the Confederates launched a series of uncoordinated assaults on Sedgwick, who beat each of them off in turn and escaped relatively unscathed back across the river. Confronting his tired and unsuccessful division commanders, Robert E. Lee reportedly lost his temper over this lost opportunity.

### "WHAT WILL THE PEOPLE SAY?"

Upon hearing news of Hooker's withdrawal across the Rappahannock River, a horrified President Lincoln turned to a colleague and said, "My God, my God, what will the people say?" Yet another campaign in the East had come to nothing. Northern morale plummeted.

**CASUALTIES AT MARYE'S HEIGHTS**

> "At that moment I believed my **commanding general** a **whipped man**."
>
> DARIUS COUCH, COMMANDING THE UNION SECOND CORPS, ON HOOKER'S LOSS OF NERVE, MAY 1, 1863

# The **Death** of **Jackson**

**At the Battle of Chancellorsville, General Stonewall Jackson was accidentally shot by his own troops while reconnoitering in front of his battle line. His left arm was so badly injured that it had to be amputated, but he was thought to be recovering when he contracted pneumonia. He died eight days later on May 10, much to the grief and dismay of his soldiers and fellow Confederate leaders.**

"His mind now began to fail and wander, and he frequently talked as if in command upon the field, giving orders in his old way; then the scene shifted and he was at the mess-table, in conversation with members of his staff; now with his wife and child; now at prayers with his military family. Occasional intervals of return of his mind would appear, and during one of them I offered him some brandy and water, but he declined it, saying, 'It will only delay my departure, and do no good; I want to preserve my mind, if possible, to the last ...'

   A few moments before he died he cried out in his delirium, 'Order A. P. Hill to prepare for action! Pass the infantry to the front rapidly! Tell Major Hawks,' then stopped, leaving the sentence unfinished. Presently a smile of ineffable sweetness spread itself over his pale face, and he cried quietly and with an expression as if of relief, 'Let us cross over the river and rest under the shade of the trees'; and then, without pain or the least struggle, his spirit passed from earth to the God who gave it. "

DR. HUNTER McGUIRE, MEDICAL DIRECTOR OF JACKSON'S CORPS, FROM THE
SOUTHERN HISTORICAL SOCIETY PAPERS, RICHMOND, 1886

"The intelligence of the death of Gen. Jackson came upon us like a shock. We feel that his death is a national calamity. The poorest soldiers among us appreciated his worth—loved the man, and mourn his loss ... Among the many heroes of this revolution, none have lived so much adored, none have died so much deplored, and none have left a character as spotless as that of Stonewall Jackson. Could his life have been spared till the close of this cruel war, the unanimous voice of a grateful people would have proclaimed him chief ruler of the nation. "

COLONEL ABRAM FULKERSON, A FORMER STUDENT OF JACKSON'S, IN A LETTER
TO HIS WIFE ON MAY 18, 1863, VIRGINIA MILITARY INSTITUTE ARCHIVES

**Misdirected fire**
After routing the Union Eleventh Corps in a surprise attack, Jackson grew impatient with the assault's progress when darkness fell. On reconnaissance near his own front line, he was mortally wounded by Confederate fire.

# Lee Advances North

**The Confederate high command approved Lee's strategy of invading the North for a second time. In mid-June 1863, the Army of Northern Virginia began its advance toward Pennsylvania. The Union army was initially wrong-footed, engaging the Rebels unsuccessfully at Brandy Station and Winchester.**

After the Battle of Chancellorsville, the South had the advantage. Now it was the turn of the Confederacy to decide where it would strike the Union army next rather than simply reacting to Northern advances. For the next few weeks, debates raged in the capital, Richmond, over what to do. On his way to rejoin General Robert E. Lee at Fredericksburg, General James Longstreet proposed to President Davis that he and two divisions travel by rail to Tennessee to assault Major General William Rosecrans. Longstreet would thereby relieve pressure on Vicksburg. Secretary of War James Seddon then

### Confederate general Ewell
Despite losing a leg at Second Bull Run, Ewell justified Lee's confidence in him at this point in the war by raiding the Union garrison at Winchester.

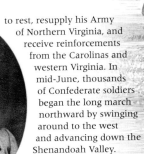

countered with a wild proposal to send Longstreet directly to Mississippi to attack General Ulysses S. Grant's rear at Vicksburg, but Lee stepped in at this point, arguing convincingly for another thrust north. Lee proposed that now was the time to deal the Union a strategic death blow before conditions in the West deteriorated to a point of no return. He was also keen to advance while both the Northern peace movement and the Army of Northern Virginia were still strong.

### Commander's strategy
Lee was certain that a Confederate victory or series of victories in Pennsylvania or northern Maryland at this juncture would strengthen the Copperheads— Northern Democrats opposed to the Civil War who favored a peace agreement with the South. Thus, he reasoned, Lincoln would become a president without a party in the next election. Furthermore, farmers in Virginia would be relieved of the burdens of conflict for at least a season, and the Confederate army could live off the Northerners' land for a change. The chance of recognition by foreign powers might again come back on the table, not to mention an outright peace with the North should Lee and his forces destroy the Army of the Potomac and capture Washington or Baltimore.

The possibility of achieving Southern independence was finally within sight, and when the Confederate cabinet voted on Lee's proposal, only one member, Postmaster General John Reagan, a Texan, disagreed. Longstreet also retained some doubts about the wisdom of the decision, but loyally followed his commander's directives. Lee took off the earlier part of June

### Cavalry charge near Brandy Station
On June 9, 1863 more than 19,000 cavalry clashed for 12 hours along the Rappahannock River in a surprise encounter. It resulted in a Southern victory, but alerted the Union to Lee's unexpected advance northward.

to rest, resupply his Army of Northern Virginia, and receive reinforcements from the Carolinas and western Virginia. In mid-June, thousands of Confederate soldiers began the long march northward by swinging around to the west and advancing down the Shenandoah Valley.

### Shock for Stuart
Just as the Army of Northern Virginia was beginning its final preparations for the movement North, the flamboyant Major General Jeb Stuart and his Confederate cavalry received a nasty shock from their Union counterparts. On June 9, at Brandy Station in Culpeper County, Virginia, a large Union cavalry force under the command of General Alfred Pleasonton surprised Stuart's troopers in their encampment. Following a hard day's fighting in which both sides gained the upper hand at different times, the Union cavalry finally yielded the battlefield to the Southerners and withdrew. Tactically, the engagement was the largest horse-mounted combat of the Civil War and a Confederate triumph—strategically, it assumed far greater proportions.

Union horsemen had gained confidence from it, believing that they could now stand toe-to-toe against the Southern cavaliers. Henceforth they would be more aggressive. Stuart emerged from the battle physically unscathed but with a bruised ego. He asked Lee for permission to ride around Major General Joseph Hooker's corps slowly advancing to the east—Stuart's goal was to gain better intelligence on Union movements, but in the process he hoped to salvage his reputation.

### Testing times for Lee
Having extracted a promise from Stuart that he would quickly rejoin the main Confederate force, Lee agreed, and on June 25 he suddenly found himself without Stuart and his three best cavalry brigades. The cavalry chief had left Lee

## BEFORE

**In the wake of Stonewall Jackson's death, Lee reorganized his army to prepare for an offensive thrust. The Union, meanwhile, was disheartened after repeated failures.**

### CONFEDERATE PROMOTIONS
Eager to reorganize the Army of Northern Virginia, **Lee abandoned the old system** of two wings led by two corps commanders. He recommended the **promotion of generals Richard Ewell and A. P. Hill** to corps command, with Ewell taking over most of Jackson's old force. Hill was to retain the rest, along with new troops gathered from other parts of Virginia and the Carolinas. Longstreet kept command of his corps, and became Lee's chief lieutenant.

### NORTHERN DESPONDENCY
The North had little to celebrate in May and June of 1863. **Grant had yet to take Vicksburg**, and the first attempt to attack Charleston, South Carolina, ended in failure on April 7, when eight monitors were repulsed by Rebel guns at Fort Sumter. **Northern Copperheads 201 ≫ lamented that Confederate independence was near** and the time had come for negotiations with the South.

**DAMAGED MONITOR TURRET**

> "I shall **throw an overwhelming force** on their advance, crush it, follow up the success . . . and **virtually destroy** the [Army of the Potomac]."
>
> GENERAL LEE IN A LETTER TO MAJOR GENERAL ISAAC TRIMBLE, 1863

**Lee crosses the Potomac**
In mid-June, Lee and his 75,000-strong army crossed the Potomac River into Maryland. This contemporary illustration shows Lee in three-quarter view in the foreground conferring with an officer.

with just enough horsemen to screen the Southern army from Union cavalry probes, but not enough to provide him with a rapid scouting force for his infantry. The timing could not have been worse—the Confederate infantry had just begun crossing the Pennsylvania state line as his cavalry commander departed. Lee would be operationally blinded until Stuart returned from reconnaissance. For his part, Joseph Hooker refused to believe that Lee's initial movements represented another great raid. Rather, he rationalized that the enemy was simply trying to get on his operational flank by moving to the west. To foil him, Hooker proposed to Lincoln a rapid descent on Richmond. The Confederates, he considered, would be forced to retreat to protect their capital.

"I think Lee's army, and not Richmond, is your true objective point," Lincoln responded curtly. He added that the Confederates had to be spread out as they headed west and north, and urged Hooker to attack and defeat the enemy posthaste, declaring: "The animal must be very slim somewhere. Could you not break him?"

The general chose to disobey Lincoln, however, and instead of attacking, he trailed Lee's advance cautiously, while keeping between the Confederates and Washington. As he did so, Confederate general Richard Stoddert Ewell's corps successfully attacked and destroyed the Union garrison at Winchester on June 13–15. During this raid, Ewell was able to capture many thousands of prisoners, artillery, horses, and supplies in a masterly manner, reminiscent of Stonewall Jackson's seizure of Harpers Ferry the year before. Hooker resigned on June 28, 1863, following continued arguments with Lincoln.

### The road to Gettysburg
Union attempts to determine the whereabouts of the Confederate army met with repeated failure. The president despaired as the telegraph wires grew increasingly hot with frantic appeals from Pennsylvania governor, Andrew Curtin, who reported that the Confederates had entered his state and were threatening the Pennsylvania capital, Harrisburg. Where was the Army of the Potomac?

Lincoln's patience was wearing thin, citizens in Pennsylvania's border counties girded themselves for occupation by the Confederates, and the North held its collective breath as all eyes turned to south-central Pennsylvania.

**907** The number of Union casualties during the cavalry battle at Brandy Station in Virginia, on June 9, 1863. Confederate casualties numbered 523, and it was the first time Jeb Stuart's leadership was criticized.

**Stars and Bars**
This example of the 11-starred version of the first Confederate national flag was said to have been captured by the 93rd Ohio Volunteers in Tennessee in 1863.

**AFTER** »

Despite the approaching enemy, morale among the soldiers in the Northern encampments remained strong. But Lee's Confederates were also bolstered.

**RENEWED NORTHERN MORALE**
Within the Union army itself, most soldiers were regaining their morale as **reports of the enemy** in their "home" territory reached their encampments. Fighting and losing in Virginia because of inept commanders was one thing, but **engaging the Confederates on Northern soil** was another. Under a new commander—General George Meade—the Army of the Potomac was ready for the chance to defeat the Confederates. As one officer reported: "The **men are more determined** than I have ever before seen them."

**INVINCIBLE SOUTHERNERS**
As the Confederates moved northward, **optimism among the men in the ranks soared**. Southerners were eager to crush the Yankees once and for all. **An aura of invincibility** ran throughout the Rebel camps, a confidence bred of repeated battlefield success and **unwavering trust in their leader, Robert E. Lee**.

« BEFORE

Robert E. Lee's invasion of the North began with an advance into Pennsylvania, which initially met little Union resistance.

### ORDERS AND COUNTER-ORDERS

As advance elements of General Richard Ewell's Confederate corps **crossed the Mason-Dixon Line**, local residents either fled or tried to hide their possessions from **Southern foraging parties**. Lee now ordered Ewell to divide his corps. One division marched toward York, capturing that city in late June, but **could not cross the Susquehanna River** because Union militia burned the only bridge. Another column headed up the **Cumberland Valley toward Carlisle**, to strike Harrisburg from that direction. But before they could cross the river, Lee recalled his scattered army to **concentrate near Cashtown**. The Federal army was drawing near and Lee wanted to be ready.

### LINCOLN RELIEVES HOOKER

Slow to react to Lee's initial movements north in June, **Union general Joseph Hooker**, in command of the Army of the Potomac, **lost his remaining credibility** with Abraham Lincoln. On June 28, Lincoln replaced him with **Major General George G. Meade**.

# The Battle of Gettysburg

**Neither side intended to fight a major battle at Gettysburg but both poured troops into the area after their initial clashes. In the first two days the Southern forces failed to capitalize on their initial numerical superiority. The ferocious combat of the third day would result in a disastrous defeat for the South.**

A decision by Union cavalry commander Brigadier General John Buford precipitated the battle. At the end of June 1863, his division of the Army of the Potomac was near the town of Gettysburg, Pennsylvania, when he learned that the Confederates were coming quickly in his direction. At the same time, Union infantry corps were moving up from Maryland. Realizing the danger of the Confederates reaching Gettysburg first, Buford made a stand on the ridges west of Gettysburg in a bid to hold them off until the Federals could mass and hold the high ground (Cemetery Hill, Culp's Hill, and Cemetery Ridge) south of town. Lee had no intention of fighting at Gettysburg, but Buford's stand forced him to engage before he was ready.

### Death of General Reynolds

Reynolds commanded the Army of the Potomac's left wing. The circumstances of his death are disputed: he may have been killed by a Southern sharpshooter or by "friendly fire" from his own side.

Early on July 1, Southern troops under Brigadier General Henry Heth blundered into Buford's men along the Chambersburg Pike and were forced to deploy. Although Buford's troopers had the edge in firepower with their breech-loading carbines, Heth's men

began to push them back—but not fast enough. By mid-morning, Buford's tired command had received support from the First Corps under Major General John Reynolds. Intense fighting erupted between Reynolds's veteran troops and Confederate divisions under Heth and Major General Dorsey Pender. Reynolds was shot from his horse as he led his Iron Brigade into position. Yet despite

### The retaking of East Cemetery Hill

On July 2, the "Louisiana Tigers" Brigade overran the Union position on East Cemetery Hill. Peter F. Rothermel's *The Repulse of the Louisiana Tigers* (1866) shows Union troops rushing the hill and driving the Tigers off again.

his death and savage casualties in the Iron Brigade, the Union forces pushed the Southerners back through McPherson's Woods and were poised to hold the ridges west of town.

## Corps against corps

Word now arrived that gray-clad troops were moving down from the North. These were General Ewell's Second Corps, and they were headed precisely for the flank of the Union First Corps. Before they could get there, however, the Union Eleventh Corps, under Oliver O. Howard, had arrived dusty and thirsty after a rapid march from Emmitsburg and positioned itself to support the First Corps' right. Howard deployed his brigades too far forward and dangerously stretched an already tenuous defensive line. When Ewell's divisions came on the field, General Lee, riding forward from the west, grasped the opportunity presented to

him. He ordered Ewell and General A. P. Hill, in command of Third Corps, to attack in force.

Four Confederate divisions swept forward in a semicircle from the west and north, driving in the Eleventh Corps, then the First Corps. By late afternoon, both corps were in retreat through the

**Union drum**
Drums were used for communication on the battlefield. Each regiment had several drummers who would beat out signals to the troops on the commanding officer's order.

streets of Gettysburg, the victorious Confederates hot on their heels. Safety for the bluecoats beckoned on the high ground of Cemetery Hill, which was occupied by reserves that Howard had wisely left there.

Now those forces would serve as protection against the expected Confederate assault as the sun began to sink lower in the sky. But that assault never came. Lee knew that the rest of the Union army was on its way and that now was the time to strike the final blow. He turned to Ewell and ordered him to attack the heights "if practicable." Ewell, aware of his troops' exhaustion and worried by reports of Federals to his left, did not find an attack practicable. Most of the defeated Union Eleventh and First Corps escaped to Cemetery Hill where, shaken and hurt, they regrouped.

## The second day begins

General George G. Meade, commander of the Army of the Potomac, rode up before midnight. Conferring with Second Corps commander, Lieutenant General Winfield S. Hancock, he inspected the positions, and deemed them secure. By the early morning of July 2, three more Union corps had joined their comrades on Cemetery Hill.

Frustrated by the hollow victory of the previous day, Lee met his generals to consider options. Rejecting a proposal from Lieutenant General James Longstreet to move around the enemy and reposition between them and

Washington, Lee decided on a double envelopment. Longstreet's First Corps would attack the Union southern (left) flank with two divisions and a third from Hill's corps, while Ewell would try to deceive the enemy with a show of force against Cemetery and Culp's hills.

Longstreet was slow in sending forward his two divisions, commanded by generals Lafayette McLaws and John Bell Hood, both tired from a forced march the night before. Federal signalers on Little Round Top at the end of the Northern line spotted their initial movements. Longstreet's infantry lost valuable time as it doubled back to take an unobserved route. By the time McLaws and Hood charged forward about 4 p.m., General Daniel Sickles' Union Third Corps had advanced to the Emmitsburg Road Ridge and blocked their way. Had Sickles not been there, Lee's plan to roll up Meade's left flank might well have worked.

## Fighting withdrawal

Through the rest of the afternoon and into early evening, Longstreet's troops attacked Sickles' corps. At the Peach Orchard, Devil's Den, and Wheatfield, Sickles' men, reinforced by brigades from the Fifth and Sixth Corps, retreated and counterattacked until finally forced to yield their positions. The climax on the southern end of the field occurred at Little Round Top, as Hood's tired and thirsty Alabamans and Texans assaulted—and almost captured—the anchor to Meade's position. Colonel Joshua L. Chamberlain and his 20th Maine would become famous for their defense of the hill's southern slope. Moreover, it is likely that Meade would have sent in the bulk of Sixth Corps to retake it. Union numbers and interior lines were starting to make a difference.

»

# "I think this the **strongest position** by nature upon which to **fight a battle** that I ever saw."

LIEUTENANT GENERAL WINFIELD S. HANCOCK, UNION ARMY, JULY 1, 1863

---

**UNION GENERAL (1815–72)**

## GEORGE GORDON MEADE

Born in Spain of American parents, Meade was a career army officer who had worked as an engineer and seen action against the Seminole Indians and in the War with Mexico of 1846–48. He served in the Army of the Potomac from the start of the Civil War. With the temper and appearance of an "old googly-eyed snapping turtle," he had the character and tactical skill to beat Lee at Gettysburg, but he was criticized for failing to follow up Lee's retreating army in the aftermath. Meade stayed in command of the Army of the Potomac until the end of the war, although in the final campaigns he fought under the close supervision of Ulysses S. Grant, the Union general-in-chief.

CONFEDERATE GENERAL (1825–75)

## GEORGE EDWARD PICKETT

After graduating last in his West Point class, Pickett, a native Virginian, saw service on the Western frontier and in the War with Mexico. As a Confederate, he fought at Gaines' Mill and commanded a division at Fredericksburg. He led his Virginia troops in the fateful Pickett's Charge at Gettysburg on July 3, though he did not originate the plan. Pickett served until the end of the war with limited success. What he lacked in tactical knowledge he made up for with a dashing personality that made him a favorite with subordinates and superiors alike.

Robert E. Lee was discouraged by the events of July 2. When cavalry under General Jeb Stuart rejoined the Confederate army that evening, Stuart got only the tersest of greetings. He boasted he had brought 100 captured Union wagons. "What good are they to me now?" Lee replied.

### A fatal mistake

Lee's decision to attack the Union center on the third day of Gettysburg has been long debated. His judgment may have been impaired—he was tired and suffering from diarrhea and a heart

### Napoleon gun-howitzer

U.S.-made versions of the French-designed 12-pounder (5.5kg) Model 1857 Napoleon gun-howitzer were the war's most widely used field artillery weapon, seeing service with both North and South.

condition. He thought he had thinned Meade's line by obliging him to reinforce his flanks the previous day. He also believed his men could do anything he asked of them and was determined to win the decisive victory that had seemed so close the last two days. Longstreet again urged Lee to disengage and go around the Federal flank. Lee refused.

Meanwhile, General Meade held a council of war around midnight on July 2. He listened to his generals' opinions, and resolved to stay and fight it out. Both armies had suffered badly in the previous two days, but the Union army still held the high ground. Meade was determined to keep it.

At 1 p.m. on July 3, 150 Confederate cannons opened fire from Seminary Ridge in the greatest Southern artillery

barrage of the war. Federal guns answered, and for two hours the ground shook with the impact of exploding shells. The noise could be heard as far away as Pittsburgh. Meant to smash Union positions on Cemetery Ridge, the bulk of the Confederate shells fell on the rearward slope, disrupting only hospitals and reserve artillery. Then suddenly the

### The third day at Gettysburg

The outcome of the battle was decided by Lee's decision to launch an all-out attack on the Union center in the afternoon. The assault on Cemetery Ridge resulted in unsustainable Confederate casualties.

Federal counter-battery fire fell silent as Union artillerists cooled their overheated guns. Thinking he had suppressed them, Longstreet's artillery chief recommended that the infantry attack should begin, following Lee's plan of battle.

### Pickett's Charge

Longstreet could only nod dourly when General George Pickett, commanding a fresh division of Virginians, asked permission to advance. Two depleted divisions of A. P. Hill's corps, under General Johnston Pettigrew and General Isaac R. Trimble, also stepped

**160,000** The number of men fielded by the two armies at Gettysburg, roughly 70,000 Confederate and 90,000 Union troops. About 51,000 became casualties —killed, wounded, or captured.

out of the protection of the wood line and began a march of 1 mile (1.6km) to the Union center. With bands playing and banners snapping in the breeze, the Southern line moved forward. Union defenders in Winfield S. Hancock's Second Corps felt a sense of awe at the approach of this grand assault.

When their enemies were about a third of the way across the field, Union artillery opened up with a vengeance,

---

**Map legend:**

① Jul 3, 11 a.m.: Confederate attack on Culp's Hill is driven back

② 1 p.m.: Start of intense Confederate barrage

③ 1:15 p.m.: Union forces reply with bombardment of Confederate positions

④ 3 p.m.: Over 13,000 men mount charge against the Union center

⑤ 4 p.m.: Small group of men led by General Lewis A. Armistead briefly penetrates Union line, but the breach is soon filled

⑥ 5 p.m.: Only half the men make it back to Confederate lines

**KEY**
- Union forces July 3
- Confederate forces July 3

---

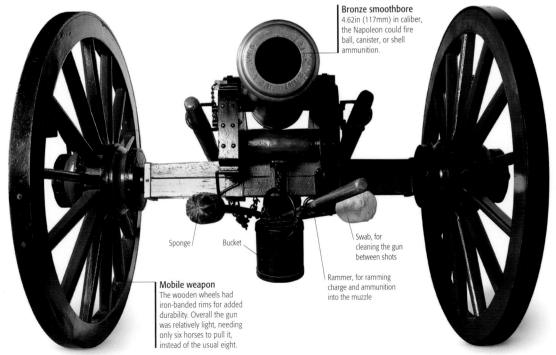

**Bronze smoothbore**
4.62in (117mm) in caliber, the Napoleon could fire ball, canister, or shell ammunition.

**Sponge**

**Bucket**

**Swab,** for cleaning the gun between shots

**Rammer,** for ramming charge and ammunition into the muzzle

**Mobile weapon**
The wooden wheels had iron-banded rims for added durability. Overall the gun was relatively light, needing only six horses to pull it, instead of the usual eight.

ripping great holes in the advancing gray ranks. The gaps filled, and the Confederates kept coming. As they crossed the Emmitsburg Road, Union infantry joined in with devastating volleys. Some of the men in blue chanted "Fredericksburg, Fredericksburg!" in reference to the recent Union defeat in December the previous year. Now it was their turn to be victorious.

## Repelled and defeated

Most of Pettigrew's and Trimble's shredded commands disintegrated before they reached Cemetery Ridge, but a few joined the remnants of Pickett's division as about 200 Southerners jumped over the stone wall, planted their flags on the Union position, and fought hand-to-hand using clubbed muskets and bayonets. A few of Hancock's regiments were overrun and started to turn for the rear, but timely reinforcements bolstered the Union line and prevented the breakthrough.

Brigadier General Lewis Armistead, one of Pickett's commanders, fell while leading his men with his hat on the tip of his sword, minutes after his old

**Visual record**
Photographers visited the Gettysburg battlefield in the aftermath of the battle, documenting scenes like this of a dead Confederate sharpshooter. His body has been moved and posed among the rocks of Devil's Den.

friend Hancock had been wounded. The men who followed him were killed, wounded, or captured. Pickett's charge had failed. Through the smoke, survivors trudged back to Seminary Ridge. Lee greeted some of them, and lamented, "All this has been my fault."

In the evening of July 4, the Army of Northern Virginia began its long retreat back to the safety of

Virginia. Leaving in a downpour, it wound its way west across the South Mountain to Chambersburg, then turned south toward Hagerstown and the Shenandoah Valley, from which it had come. The line of ambulances filled with wounded stretched back for 17 miles (27km) along the road.

Meade's army had also suffered badly, and he followed too cautiously, much to the exasperation of Lincoln, who saw another opportunity to crush Lee north of the Potomac River lost.

## The human cost

Union losses at Gettysburg came to just over 23,000 men, the costliest battle yet for the North. Confederate losses were estimated at between 23,000 and 28,000. Such destruction of manpower meant that Lee could never again take the strategic offensive. The loss of experienced officers was especially devastating. Lee's gamble to crush the Army of the Potomac had only weakened the Confederacy.

### AFTER

After Gettysburg, Confederate fortunes began an almost uninterrupted decline in all theaters of the war. Only minor inconclusive actions were fought in the East for the rest of 1863.

**VICTORIES AND REVERSES**
On July 4, the day Lee began his retreat from Gettysburg, Confederate forces **surrendered at Vicksburg 190–95 »**. Union **prospects in the West** were matching the success in the East.
In Tennessee, Union armies **launched an offensive** in late June 1863. The Confederates, under General Braxton Bragg, **abandoned Chattanooga** in early September, but fought back with a **victory at Chickamauga 210–13 »**. In the aftermath, the Union army was **besieged in Chattanooga 214–15 »**.

**GRANT PROMOTED**
On October 17, 1863, in response to the reverses in Tennessee, Lincoln appointed Grant, hero of the capture of Vicksburg, to **overall command of the Western theater 196–97 »**.

**Ambulance at Gettysburg**
The Army of the Potomac's Ambulance Corps was the first medical organization on either side specifically established to ensure that wounded men were evacuated from the battlefield as soon as possible.

# Little Round Top

**On the second day of the Battle of Gettysburg, the Union defense extended from Culp's Hill, around Cemetery Hill, and along Cemetery Ridge. The stone-strewn hillside of Little Round Top served as the Union's left flank and the 20th Maine was its last line of defense. After battling repeated Confederate assaults, the regiment, low on ammunition, men, and energy, leveled their bayonets in a desperate counterattack.**

"When 130 of our brave officers and men had been shot down where they stood, and only 178 remained—hardly more than a strong skirmish line—and each man had fired the 60 rounds of cartridges he carried into the fight, and the survivors were using from the cartridge-boxes of their fallen comrades, the time had come when it must be decided whether we should fall back and give up this key to the whole field of Gettysburg, or charge and try and throw off this foe. Colonel Chamberlain gave the order to 'fix bayonets,' and almost before he could say 'charge' the regiment leaped down the hill and closed in with the foe, whom we found behind every rock and tree. Surprised and overwhelmed, most of them threw down their arms and surrendered.

Some fought till they were slain; the others ran 'like a herd of wild cattle,' as Colonel Oates himself expressed it."

H. S. MELCHER, 20TH MAINE INFANTRY, FROM *BATTLES AND LEADERS OF THE CIVIL WAR*, 1888

"I ordered my regiment to change direction to the left, swing around, and drive the Federals from the ledge of rocks, for the purpose of enfilading their line … gain the enemy's rear, and drive him from the hill. My men obeyed and advanced about half way to the enemy's position, but the fire was so destructive that my line wavered like a man trying to walk against a strong wind, and then slowly, doggedly, gave back a little … We drove the Federals from their strong defensive position; five times they rallied and charged us, twice coming so near that some of my men had to use the bayonet, but in vain was their effort … The Maine regiment charged my line, coming right up in a hand-to-hand encounter … There never were harder fighters than the Twentieth Maine men and their gallant Colonel. His skill and persistency and the great bravery of his men saved Little Round Top and the Army of the Potomac from defeat."

CONFEDERATE COLONEL WILLIAM C. OATES, 15TH ALABAMA INFANTRY, FROM *THE WAR BETWEEN THE UNION AND THE CONFEDERACY*, 1905

**Valor in defense**
At 650ft (198m) high, Little Round Top had great tactical significance during the Battle of Gettysburg. Hazlett's New York battery—shown here—defended the summit; the 20th Maine defended its southern slope.

CONFEDERATE LIEUTENANT GENERAL Born 1821 Died 1904

# James **Longstreet**

## "I hope … to see my … **comrades march** side by side **with Union** veterans."

LONGSTREET AT A MEMORIAL DAY PARADE, 1902

D ubbed an "old war horse" by General Robert E. Lee, James Longstreet was one of the most accomplished corps commanders of the Civil War. Serving under Lee in the east and, later, under General Braxton Bragg in the war's Western Theater, he was instrumental in several significant Confederate victories.

**Storming Chapultepec**
Among the victories of the War with Mexico was the Battle of Chapultepec, in which Longstreet saw action and which culminated in the storming of the hilltop castle, shown in this lithograph after a painting by James Walker.

### A likeable character
James Longstreet was born in 1821 to a cotton planter in Edgefield District, South Carolina. He spent the first nine years of his life on his father's plantation and earned the nickname "Pete" after the apostle Peter, for his apparent steadfast behavior. His father died in 1833 and his mother moved to Alabama. It was through her connections in that state that he obtained his appointment to West Point in 1838. Only through grit and good fortune did he graduate (54th out of 56 cadets) in 1842. Despite his academic difficulties, he was well-liked by his classmates, who included George Pickett and especially Ulysses S. Grant, who graduated a year later. His first posting was to Jefferson Barracks, Missouri, with the 4th U.S. Infantry. During this period, Longstreet

courted Maria Louisa Garland, the daughter of his regimental commander. The couple were to enjoy a 40-year marriage and have 10 children.

In the War with Mexico in 1846–48, Longstreet was twice brevetted (given acting promotions). At Chapultepec in 1847, he was shot in the thigh while carrying the regimental standard and handed it to Lt. George Pickett, who planted the colors on the summit of Chapultepec Hill. After the war, Longstreet served at various Texas frontier posts, where he consolidated more friendships that would prove beneficial in the Civil War.

When secession came, he was not ardently supportive of the Southern cause but, believing in the states' rights doctrine, felt compelled to offer his services to Alabama, where his mother still lived and where he knew he would receive a high-ranking appointment as the senior West Point graduate. In 1861, he resigned his U.S. commission.

### Rapid promotion
Longstreet, here photographed by Mathew Brady during the war, was promoted from lieutenant colonel to major general within four months of accepting his commission. Lee trusted him implicitly, affectionately calling him "my old warhorse."

### A man of military promise
Called to Richmond, the new Confederate capital, Longstreet was commissioned as a lieutenant colonel in

## The Chickamauga Campaign

A weary Longstreet arrives at Braxton Bragg's headquarters, Chickamauga Creek, Georgia, on September 18, 1863. He receives his orders to prepare for battle the next day.

the Confederate States Army and took command of a Virginia brigade. At the First Battle of Bull Run in July 1861, he saw little action but recommended an immediate thrust toward Washington in the aftermath, before the enemy could regroup. Here was a glimpse of the future corps commander: an operational-level leader with the vision and foresight to predict second and third-order effects of tactical decisions. Promoted to major general in October, he took command of a division, which saw action during the 1862 Peninsula Campaign.

## Winning Lee's trust

General Lee realized what an excellent lieutenant he possessed in "Old Pete" by the time of the Second Bull Run Campaign, where Longstreet commanded half the Army of Northern Virginia. But Longstreet's delays in launching an attack against an unprepared General John Pope and the Federal Army of Virginia frustrated Lee, who ordered him forward three times on August 29.

When Longstreet finally attacked, at 6:30p.m., the best chance to destroy Pope had slipped away. He redeemed himself the next day by throwing every brigade at his disposal against Pope's left flank. The massive assault overwhelmed Pope and earned Longstreet a reputation for slow but relentless attacks that started late but ended up in decisive victory. Such a characterization may

have surprised Longstreet, who felt most at home repulsing ill-conceived enemy attacks. In September 1862, he did just that at Antietam, utilizing the terrain to protect his troops. Yet, at the end of the day, he felt that more time would have allowed the construction of fieldworks and artillery "killing zones." At Fredericksburg in December, he set up overlapping fields of fire for his artillery and infantry and prepared safe positions behind which his men easily repelled Union assaults.

After Fredericksburg, Longstreet consistently urged Lee to seek an "offensive-defensive" battle, in which the Confederates took the war to the enemy operationally, but then assumed

move around the flank of the Federal Army and reposition between it and Washington. He was convinced that the attack on the Union center, sometimes called Longstreet's Assault, but better known as Pickett's Charge, was doomed to failure.

## Later war years

After Gettysburg, Longstreet transferred with most of his corps to Bragg's Army of Tennessee. After a 775-mile (1,240km) ride on ramshackle railroads, he and his men arrived at a timely moment at Chickamauga. His wing poured through a gap in the Federal lines, routed half the Union army, and created the greatest Southern victory in the Western Theater. In November 1863, Longstreet independently led his command in the ill-fated Knoxville Campaign, which had little effect on the war except to diminish his corps, predispose some of his subordinates against him, and deprive Bragg of much-needed troops at Chattanooga.

In the spring of 1864, Longstreet and his two divisions returned to the Army of Northern Virginia. At the Battle of the Wilderness, Longstreet launched a vicious counterattack against the Union Second Corps, nearly driving it from the field using skirmish-order tactics that compensated for his inferior numbers. Badly wounded, Longstreet was forced to sit out the rest of the Overland

> " ... a **rock of steadiness** when sometimes in battle the world seemed **flying to pieces**."
> G. MOXLEY SORREL, CONFEDERATE STAFF OFFICER, ON LONGSTREET

Campaign but rejoined Lee in October for the Siege of Petersburg, where he performed ably, and surrendered with Lee at Appomattox in April 1865.

After the war, pro-Lee partisans and neo-Confederates blamed Longstreet for insubordinate lethargy at Gettysburg, which cost the South a victory that could have won the war. Longstreet kept quiet in the face of these accusations until the publication of his book, *From Manassas to Appomattox* (1896), in which he ably defended his actions but criticized the revered Lee. Such criticism, his enduring friendship with Ulysses S. Grant, and conversion to the Republican Party made Old Pete a pariah long after the guns had fallen silent. After serving in various public appointments, he moved to Gainesville, Georgia, where he met his second wife. Longstreet died in Gainesville, and was buried there, at Alta Vista Cemetery.

**LONGSTREET'S MONUMENT AT GETTYSBURG**

### Missed opportunities

Now in formal command of Lee's First Corps, Longstreet missed the campaign at Chancellorsville while on detached duty with two of his divisions near Suffolk, Virginia. He gathered much-needed supplies and contained the Federal threat to southside Virginia, but lamented a lost opportunity to shift his divisions either to Lee's army or to Bragg's in Tennessee, where they might have had a decisive bearing on the war.

At Gettysburg in July 1863, Longstreet was wary and delayed his assaults on July 2 and July 3, quite possibly because he felt Lee had unreasonably rejected his proposal to

a tactically defensive role on ground of their choosing. Longstreet reasoned that this would weaken the Union armies to the point of war-weariness but preserve precious Southern manpower.

**Longstreet's autobiography**
Toward the end of his life, Longstreet wrote *From Manassas to Appomattox*, in which he refuted the popular opinion that he had been key to the Confederate defeat at Gettysburg.

**PICKETT'S CHARGE, GETTYSBURG**
On the third day of battle at Gettysburg, the heroic but catastrophic charge by George Pickett's infantry division on the Union center clinched the Confederate defeat. Almost 15,000 men advanced over open fields and encountered relentless Federal artillery and infantry fire that caused severe casualties. The event is depicted in this famous cyclorama—a huge circular painting—of 1883 by the French artist Paul Philippoteaux.

# The Vicksburg Campaign

**By late 1862, Vicksburg was the last significant Confederate bastion along the entire length of the Mississippi River. General Ulysses S. Grant resolved to capture the city, but faced a long initial struggle to get his army into position to attack. With control of the Mississippi at stake, this was a vital battle.**

After consolidating his army at Memphis, Tennessee, in the fall of 1862, Grant decided on a two-pronged offensive downriver against the Confederate Mississippi bastion at Vicksburg.

A swift descent by 40,000 men of General William Tecumseh Sherman's wing of the army along the Mississippi would be followed by Grant himself taking an overland route. But Confederate cavalry raids by Earl Van Dorn and Nathan Bedford Forrest so badly disrupted Grant's logistical and supply lines, that the Union commander was compelled to call off his advance.

The telegram informing Sherman of this change never reached him, and so the Confederates at Vicksburg, under the command of General John C. Pemberton, mobilized to meet Sherman head-on. At Chickasaw Bayou on December 29, Sherman launched 20,000 of his troops against the steep

### The port of Vicksburg
Steamboats had made Vicksburg a major trading center. A Confederate stronghold controlling traffic on the Mississippi River, the city was an essential strategic target of Union campaigns in the Western Theater.

bluffs and suffered 1,800 casualties to the Confederates' 200. Grant would never again attack from the north. He now considered the problem.

The terrain north and west of the city presented numerous obstacles to an army on the march. It was swampy, forested, streaked by bayous and streams, and offered very few usable roads. Vicksburg itself was defended by well-placed heavy cannon that could devastate any Union fleet floating downstream. Four times Grant tried to bypass the city to the west by cutting canals and using the bayous to get his army below, but torrential rains aggravated the already formidable logistical challenges, and he failed.

Grant now resolved to march his army down the western bank of the river. David Porter's fleet would run past the Vicksburg batteries, rendezvous with the troops downstream, and ferry them to the eastern bank just south of the city.

It was a bold plan, and Sherman and James Birdseye McPherson, Grant's chief lieutenants, both balked at it. They urged him instead to reconsolidate at Memphis, but Grant knew that both the Union and Lincoln needed a military success. It was now or never—so on March 31, the long march began.

## Preliminary moves
On the night of April 16, 1863, Porter's gunboats made their bold dash past Vicksburg. One transport was sunk and the enemy scored 68 hits on the fleet overall, but the fast current and the element of surprise worked to Porter's favor. A few nights later, Porter got

> To effect his assault on Vicksburg, Grant had 70 miles (113km) of corduroy road (made from tree trunks laid across the route) built between his base and the river crossing-point at Hard Times.

most of the rest of his fleet past. Meanwhile, Grant moved his army overland to the crossing point of Hard Times, and stood ready to transport his men across the river.

Theoretically, Pemberton could still contest the crossing, so Grant ordered a diversion. Brigadier General Benjamin Grierson, in command of a Union

### Grant's routes to Vicksburg
The Vicksburg campaign was not straightforward. Grant had to march his men through the swampland west of the Mississippi River, then drive off Confederate forces east of the city before digging in for a long siege.

## BEFORE
«

During 1862, a series of Union successes on land in Tennessee and by river flotillas on the Mississippi cleared most of the Confederate positions along the river.

### NORTH AND SOUTH
The **capture of New Orleans ‹‹ 96–97 opened the Mississippi** to Union warships coming up from the south. **Union river forces** also gained the upper hand in actions **on the Ohio** and attacked south from Missouri on the Mississippi itself. After defeating Southern vessels near **Memphis in June 1862**, they reached the Yazoo River above Vicksburg and were **joined there** by some of **Farragut's force** from New Orleans **‹‹ 100–101**.

### GRANT'S FIRST VICTORIES
In the spring of 1862, General Grant fought the successful **Henry and Donelson campaign** in northern Tennessee **‹‹ 104–105**, then narrowly avoided defeat at **Shiloh ‹‹ 106–107**. By fall 1862, further victories had confirmed the **Union hold on Memphis** and Corinth.

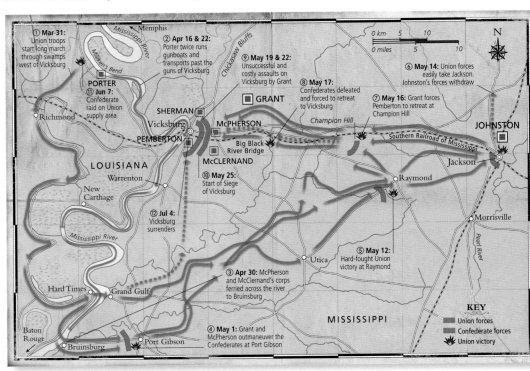

① **Mar 31:** Union troops start long march through swamps west of Vicksburg

② **Apr 16 & 22:** Porter twice runs gunboats and transports past the guns of Vicksburg

⑨ **May 19 & 22:** Unsuccessful and costly assaults on Vicksburg by Grant

⑥ **May 14:** Union forces easily take Jackson. Johnston's forces withdraw

⑧ **May 17:** Confederates defeated and forced to retreat to Vicksburg

⑦ **May 16:** Grant forces Pemberton to retreat at Champion Hill

⑪ **Jun 7:** Confederate raid on Union supply area

⑩ **May 25:** Start of Siege of Vicksburg

⑫ **Jul 4:** Vicksburg surrenders

⑤ **May 12:** Hard-fought Union victory at Raymond

③ **Apr 30:** McPherson and McClernand's corps ferried across the river to Bruinsburg

④ **May 1:** Grant and McPherson outmaneuver the Confederates at Port Gibson

**KEY**
Union forces
Confederate forces
Union victory

Memphis • Mississippi River • Chickasaw Bluffs • 0 km 5 10 • 0 miles 5 10 • N
PORTER • Millien's Bend • GRANT • SHERMAN • McPHERSON • Champion Hill • Southern Railroad of Mississippi • JOHNSTON
Richmond • Vicksburg • PEMBERTON • Big Black River Bridge • McCLERNAND • Jackson
LOUISIANA • Warrenton • New Carthage • Raymond • Morrisville • Pearl River
Mississippi River • Utica
Hard Times • Grand Gulf • MISSISSIPPI
Baton Rouge • Bruinsburg • Port Gibson

cavalry brigade, was sent south, deep into Mississippi, to destroy the railroads supplying Vicksburg, confuse Pemberton, and keep the Confederates off balance. The raiders rode southward to the east of Jackson, eventually swinging west to join up with Union troops at Baton Rouge, Louisiana. The ruse worked.

Pemberton sent most of his cavalry and an entire division on a wild goose chase after the elusive Grierson, while

**General John C. Pemberton**
Pemberton was a Northerner but chose to fight for the South in 1861—he believed in states' rights, and his wife was from Virginia. His unsuccessful defense of Vicksburg was his only significant part in the war.

Grant ferried his army to the Mississippi shore of the river. Sherman's corps also covered this operation, threatening a new advance on Chickasaw Bluffs. Grant's force moved swiftly inland, cut off from their supply lines, and lived off the enemy's land. He defeated a small Confederate garrison at Port Gibson on May 1, then marched northeast toward the state capital at Jackson.

### Confederate confusion
In a matter of days, Grant's boldness had shattered Pemberton's confidence. His titular theater commander, Joseph E. Johnston, was also surprised. Both had supposed that Johnston would have several months to assemble an army, which, combined with Pemberton's 35,000 men, would allow them to attack on numerically equal terms at a time and point of their choosing. Grant had deprived them of that opportunity and was moving to strike them in detail (systematically). Pemberton thought he was the likely first target, as Grant's easy option would have been to march him due north, up the river, with his flank guarded by Porter's fleet. Instead, Grant moved to the east away from Vicksburg.

### Union victories
The War Department in Richmond finally ordered Johnston to concentrate his growing command at Jackson, but Sherman's and McPherson's fast-moving

corps beat him to the city. Defeating about 6,000 graycoats entrenched outside the city on May 14, the Union soldiers went to work burning railroad yards, factories, and arsenals. Civilian homes close to the fires also went up in flames. Looking on Jackson's smoking ruins, Union soldiers derisively dubbed them "Chimneyville." This destruction of the enemy's infrastructure and civilian property set a precedent for future Union operations in the Western Theater.

Undeterred, Johnston urged Pemberton to move quickly to join his own remaining 6,000 men. On May 16, Grant struck hard at Pemberton's

**Steaming past Vicksburg**
On the night of April 16–17, Admiral Porter led 12 Union gunboats and transports south past Vicksburg, to carry supplies to the position where Grant planned to cross the river. Only one Union vessel was lost.

advance force at Champion Hill, between Jackson and Vicksburg. The Confederates occupied high ground, but McPherson's corps relentlessly struck their left flank, stunning the defenders. Pemberton's poor tactical leadership made matters worse, and by the end of the day the Confederates were in full retreat. It was a superb tactical victory for Grant's army. »

---

**UNION ADMIRAL (1813–91)**

## DAVID DIXON PORTER

Born into a distinguished naval family, Porter served in the U.S. Navy from 1829. In the Civil War his first notable tasks were, as Farragut's subordinate, in helping plan and carry out the capture of New Orleans and the later Mississippi operations. His achievements in these brought him command of the Mississippi River Squadron in October 1862. In this post he made a major contribution to Grant's capture of Vicksburg. He later commanded Union naval forces in the Red River expedition of 1864, organizing the retreat successfully after the land campaign went awry. Finally, in 1865, he led the successful assault on Fort Fisher, North Carolina.

The Big Black River was the last natural barrier before the eastern approaches to Vicksburg. If Grant's army could breach this obstacle, only the formidable Confederate entrenchments around the city would stand between Grant and victory.

On May 17, troops of John A. McClernand's corps, eager to prove their mettle, attacked a strong Confederate position along this last line of defense before the Vicksburg entrenchments. The assault might have failed, but John C. Pemberton left a bridge standing that should have been burned. The Confederates were routed, losing another 1,750 men. In the aftermath of the Battle of Big Black River, the Confederate army could only withdraw to Vicksburg. Civilians in the Southern stronghold were

### "Whistling Dick"
This 18-pounder (8kg) gun in the Vicksburg defenses gained its nickname from the unusual noise its shells made. The barrel could be aimed to fire downward at targets on the river from its position on the Vicksburg bluffs.

appalled at the condition of Pemberton's men as they dejectedly filed into their positions. One eyewitness summed up their condition as "humanity in the last throes of existence."

### The start of the siege
Believing correctly that his enemy was demoralized, Grant immediately ordered an attack in force on May 19. Union soldiers confidently charged forward but were greeted with walls of musketry fire from the well-protected Rebels. Nonplussed, Grant tried again on May 22, preceding the infantry assault with a massive artillery bombardment.

The result: far worse Union casualties when lodgments initially secured by McClernand's corps went unexploited. Morale in Pemberton's army soared, but he failed to take the opportunity to evacuate the city before the Union encirclement was complete.

Although these failures were disheartening, Grant realized that if he had not allowed his men to try a direct assault against Vicksburg, they might not have accepted the drudgery of the ensuing siege. He and his bluecoats, now reinforced to 70,000 strong, settled into a five-week siege. For their adversaries,

### The siege of Vicksburg
Union troops man their siege lines around impregnable Vicksburg. More than 200 Union guns pounded the city every day, while Porter's gunboats kept up a barrage from the river, until the inhabitants could take no more.

trapped within Vicksburg's defensive works, the constant artillery barrage strained their nerves, and the scarcity of food tested their physical stamina.

Pemberton's soldiers went on half and then quarter-rations as the balmy weeks of June progressed. Skinned rats and mulemeat became food. Civilians abandoned their homes and sought safety in dugouts excavated from the hillsides.

Despite these harsh conditions, Vicksburg's denizens remained defiant, confident that Joseph E. Johnston's relief army would soon lift the siege and attack Grant from the rear. "We may look at any hour for his approach," wrote the editor of the Vicksburg newspaper, now printed on the back of old wallpaper. "Hold out a few days longer, and our lines will be opened, the enemy driven away, the siege raised." Johnston's army, hovering to

## Union dugouts

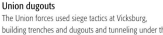

The Union forces used siege tactics at Vicksburg, building trenches and dugouts and tunneling under the Southern lines. Here troops of Logan's Union division are seen near the "White House," northeast of the town.

the east of the city but blocked by seven Federal divisions under Sherman, had grown to 30,000 men in a matter of weeks, but many were inexperienced troops or untested conscripts. Worse, their commander was hesitant to attack the numerically superior Yankees.

### The Confederates try to fight back

At the end of June, under immense pressure from a frantic Jefferson Davis, Johnston feebly probed with his five divisions against Sherman, but with no result. A more serious attempt had been made in early June by General Richard Taylor, in command of Louisiana's Confederate forces. However, Taylor had even fewer troops than Johnston and was stopped cold at Milliken's Bend, a fortified Federal supply depot north of Vicksburg.

Among the defenders at Milliken's Bend were several regiments of freshly trained black troops, who fought desperately against their attackers. Taylor's infuriated men shouted, "No quarter!" as they stormed forward. They succeeded in capturing several dozen of their enemy (some of whom were later sold into slavery), before being driven off.

### Tightening the noose

Within Vicksburg, as the realization set in that Johnston and Taylor were not coming to their relief, the city's defenders lost the high morale they had in May, along with their physical strength. Grant wired Washington: "The fall of Vicksburg and the capture of most of the garrison can only be a question of time." Every day

## "Grant is my man and I am his for the rest of the war."

ABRAHAM LINCOLN, AFTER THE FALL OF VICKSBURG

Pemberton's soldiers grew weaker; by the end of June, almost half were on regimental sick lists.

Consulting with his generals, the Confederate commander confirmed his suspicions that a breakout attack would certainly fail. He was determined to hold out, however, despite the long odds, confident that some event outside his entrenchments would either draw Grant away or force him to lift the siege. On June 28, Pemberton received a letter signed by a group of enlisted men declaring that, "If you can't feed us, you had better surrender us,

horrible as the idea is …" He knew the game was up. The letter threatened mutiny and mass desertion if he failed to see General Grant to discuss terms.

On July 3, the same day that Pickett's Charge was repulsed at Gettysburg, John C. Pemberton, the Pennsylvania-born Southern general, met with Ulysses S. Grant, the former Illinois leather tanner, and agreed to surrender his army. Grant wanted to make the terms "unconditional surrender" as before, but soon realized that 30,000 Rebel prisoners headed north would swamp Union logistical capacity in the area. He therefore paroled every one of Pemberton's men, fully expecting to fight some of them again. Indeed, well over half of Vicksburg's captured defenders broke their parole. In fact, some were in action again with the Confederate army later in 1863.

### Federal jubilation

On July 4, 1863, Union troops marched into the city. One soldier wrote, "This was the most glorious Fourth I ever spent." Despite the feelings of pride in their hearts, Grant's victors displayed compassion and restraint to their erstwhile foes, sharing provisions with

#### Refuge from the siege

Many of the civilian population of Vicksburg abandoned their homes because of the incessant bombardments from Union river gunboats, and took refuge in caves dug into the hillsides. Only a handful of Vicksburg civilians died from enemy action.

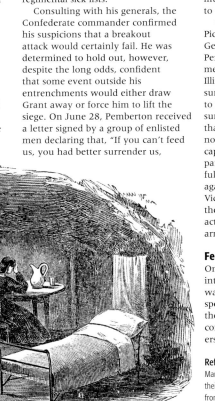

The loss of Vicksburg and the simultaneous defeat at Gettysburg made the South's demise almost inevitable, but the rest of 1863 did not see constant Union success.

#### CLEAR PASSAGE

Port Hudson, the last Confederate outpost on the Mississippi, fell on July 9. Unarmed Union ships could now sail from St. Louis to the sea.

#### JOHNSTON SLIPS AWAY

Johnston hoped to lure Union forces into a frontal assault against his prepared positions at Jackson. Instead, Sherman began encircling Johnston's army. On July 16, Johnston made a masterly withdrawal and escaped.

#### CHICKAMAUGA AND CHATTANOOGA

Union forces next went on the offensive in eastern Tennessee. Though they captured Chattanooga, they were defeated at Chickamauga in September 1863 and then besieged 210–13 ». They were relieved only after Grant was appointed to command.

#### ENDURING CONFEDERATE SYMPATHIES

So humiliating was the capture of Vicksburg that it was not until the 1930s that its citizens again formally celebrated the 4th of July.

**29,495** The number of Confederate troops who surrendered at Vicksburg. The two sides each lost about 10,000 killed and wounded in the campaign.

starving soldiers and civilians alike. One woman, watching the victorious Union troops, observed these "stalwart, well-fed men" and contrasted them with the city's emaciated former defenders, who had been "blindly dashed" against them.

### Confederate loss, Union gain

In Richmond, Jefferson Davis blamed the loss on Pemberton, and to a slightly lesser extent, Johnston. In Washington, a grateful Abraham Lincoln waxed, "The Father of Waters [the Mississippi] again goes unvexed to the sea."

The fall of Vicksburg split the Confederacy irrevocably into two and ensured that cattle, metals, and grains from the Trans-Mississippi region would rarely again find their way to the Rebel states east of the river. Grant captured precious heavy cannon that the Confederacy could no longer replace, and the surrender of almost 30,000 men was a heavy blow to a South running out of manpower. Most significantly, the Union forces could now concentrate their efforts, and their growing numerical strength, against the remaining Confederate strongholds farther east.

# Surrender at Vicksburg

**After two attacks on Vicksburg failed, General Grant used siege warfare to compel the city to surrender. From May 25, the inhabitants endured constant bombardment from Union positions around the city and from gun boats on the Mississippi. With supplies cut off and rations reduced, starvation began to take its toll until, on July 4, Confederate commander John Pemberton surrendered.**

"Every day further progress was made in digging and mining, and at length a point was reached where the batteries could send their screaming shells directly to the heart of the city. A reign of terror took possession of the town, and its inhabitants dug themselves caves in the earth, seeking protection against the missiles of destruction which daily and nightly dropped in their midst. Such cannonading and shelling has perhaps scarcely been equaled. It was not safe from behind or before, and every part of the city was alike within range of the Federal guns ... For six weeks our batteries never ceased dropping their shot and shell on the doomed city. Food became scarce, and the inhabitants grew wan and thin in their narrow dens. At last, despairing of Johnston's aid in raising the siege, and believing that Grant was ready for another assault on his works, they hung out the white flag in front of Gen. A. J. Smith's Division."

FROM THE *HISTORY OF THE 48TH OHIO VETERAN VOLUNTEER INFANTRY* BY MAJOR JOHN A. BERING AND CAPTAIN THOMAS MONTGOMERY, PUBLISHED 1880

"How sad was the spectacle that met our gaze: arms stacked in the center of the streets, men with tearful eyes and downcast faces walking here and there; men sitting in groups feeling that they would gladly have given their life-blood on the battlefield rather than hand over the guns and sabers so dear to them! ... Men looked so forlorn, some without shoes, some with tattered garments, yet they would have fought on.
    While this gloom hung over the Confederate forces a glance over the hills to the north and east of the city brought into view the bright shining bayonets and sabers of a mighty host approaching the city ..."

LUCY McRAE, AN INHABITANT OF VICKSBURG, FROM HER DIARY ENTRY FOR THE DAY OF THE SURRENDER, JULY 4, 1863

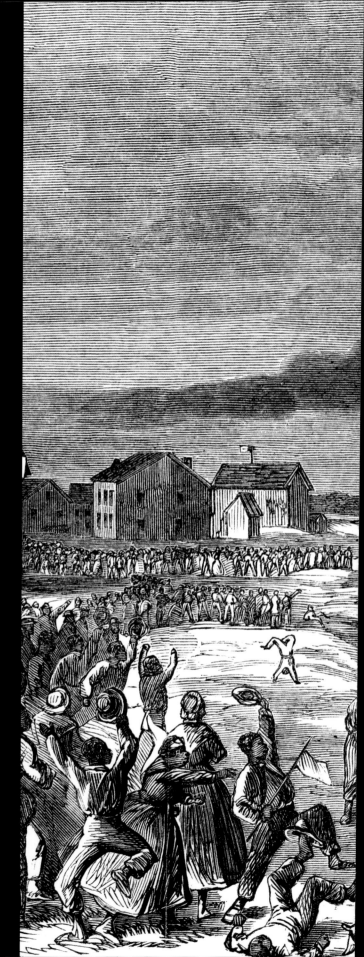

**Arrival of the Union fleet**
With the Confederate shore batteries along the Mississippi River silenced, Admiral David Dixon Porter's fleet steamed into Vicksburg on the day of the surrender. The flag-bedecked steamers are greeted by a crowd of jubilant slaves on the quayside.

UNION GENERAL-IN-CHIEF Born 1822 Died 1885

# Ulysses S. Grant

## "I have never **advocated war** except as a **means of peace**."

ULYSSES S. GRANT, FROM HIS *PERSONAL MEMOIRS*, 1886

Ulysses S. Grant was the top commander of the Union Army for much of the Civil War, leading it to victory in the most bitter conflict in American history. After the war, in 1868, he became the 18th president of the United States, but his administration was blighted by reports of corruption, scandal, and impropriety.

### Humble beginnings

Born Hiram Ulysses Grant on April 27, 1822, in a two-room log cabin in Point Pleasant, Ohio, the future general grew up working on his father's farm—though even as a young man he had ambitions for greater things. He attended West Point, where his name was mistakenly recorded as Ulysses Simpson Grant, and he kept the erroneous middle initial for life.

At West Point he excelled in horsemanship but was not the best scholar, nor was he considered an exceptional military mind. He eventually graduated 21st out of a class of 39. Grant's early military experiences echoed his relationship with his former instructors: He did not take orders well and he often clashed with his superiors. He also had a tendency to drink to excess when feeling "blue and depressed."

### An "unjust" war

While serving in the War with Mexico (1846–48), Grant was outspoken in his criticism of the conflict. Feeling it to be unjust, he stated publicly that he was "bitterly opposed" to it. Yet he showed great bravery and cunning when, during the Battle of Chapultepec, he climbed

### Dogged fighter

Grant is pictured outside his headquarters after the Union defeat at Cold Harbor in June 1864. With his qualities of aggression, determination, coolness under fire, and clarity of purpose, he finally achieved his goal to "get possession of Lee's army."

to the top of a church bell tower with a howitzer and brought devastating fire down on an enemy battalion, which resulted in its surrender.

Grant married Julia Dent, the sister of a fellow West Pointer, in 1848, but after the War with Mexico was posted to California. He was so lonely that he resigned his commission in 1854 and

**At Chapultepec**
A woodcut by Thure de Thulstrup shows Lieutenant Grant directing howitzer fire from the bell tower of San Cosme church toward Mexican defenders during fighting for La Verónica and San Cosme causeways, outside Mexico City.

returned east to join his family. His various business ventures did not prosper, and when Civil War broke out, Grant was working as a clerk in the family leather store in Illinois. He immediately re-enlisted, but was unable to get a commission again in the U.S. Army, and was appointed to command the 21st Illinois Infantry, a volunteer regiment.

He soon rose to the rank of brigadier general due to his previous military experience. Based in Tennessee, he led

**Grant on horseback**
A natural horseman, Grant is portrayed leading his men into battle in this lithograph published in 1864, the year he became general-in-chief of the Union army and thus took command of 533,000 men.

Richmond followed, which resulted in Lee's surrender at Appomattox Court House on April 9, 1865. Grant's generous terms allowed Confederate officers and soldiers to return to their homes.

### Warrior to statesman
After the formal Confederate surrender, Grant disagreed with President Andrew Johnson on his lenient stance toward the South. Grant thought the South should be treated like a conquered nation—a position that won him favor among the more radical Northern citizenship.

Grant won a bid for the presidency in 1868 (and would be re-elected in 1872). However, he did not always conduct himself in the statesmanlike manner that the people expected. He took personal gifts (unaware that it was thought improper), appointed friends to Cabinet positions (which he saw as a form of loyalty), and made sincere—but ultimately disastrous—policy decisions that led the country into a depression. In the "Whiskey Ring," one of a series of scandals that blighted his administration, corrupt officials stole more than $3 million in taxes from the Federal government. It is thought that Grant was not personally involved in any of this, but his reputation was tarnished.

Grant's post-presidency career fared little better. Bad investments, swindles, and mismanagement left him bankrupt, and in an effort to pay off his debts he wrote his memoirs. Published by Mark Twain, they earned the Grant family more than half a million dollars following his death on July 23, 1885.

Despite the war and the controversy surrounding his presidency, Grant is today considered a great American because of his wartime achievements, his loyalty, and his resolve. His legacy is celebrated every day by the many people who visit Grant's Tomb on the Upper West Side of Manhattan in New York City.

**TIMELINE**

**ULYSSES S. GRANT IN 1843**

**April 27, 1822** Born in Point Pleasant Ohio, the son of a tanner and merchant.

**1839–43** Studies at West Point, emerging 21st in a class of 39. He is assigned to the infantry.

**1846–47** Fighting in the War with Mexico, he performs with bravery and initiative under fire at Monterrey and in the attack on Chapultepec.

**1848** Marries Julia Dent, the sister of a friend from West Point; they will have four children.

**April 1854** Resigns from the U.S. Army while serving as a captain in California.

**April 1861** At the outbreak of the Civil War, raises a volunteer company and is swiftly promoted to colonel and then brigadier general.

**February 1862** His successful attacks on Fort Henry and Fort Donelson in Tennessee, with the capture of over 12,000 Confederate soldiers, win him praise and promotion to major general.

**April 6–7, 1862** Almost routed at Shiloh, but retrieves the situation. His reputation is harmed by the high casualties suffered.

**May–July 1863** Traps 30,000 Confederate soldiers at Vicksburg and forces them to surrender after a six-week siege.

**October–November 1863** Taking command of the besieged Army of the Cumberland at Chattanooga, he wins a notable victory at Missionary Ridge (November 25).

**March 1864** Promoted to general-in-chief of all Union armies with the rank of lieutenant general, Grant moves to the Eastern Theater to lead the fight against the main Confederate force, Lee's Army of Northern Virginia.

**May–June 1864** Leads a Union advance through Virginia in the Overland Campaign, fighting Lee at the Wilderness, Spotsylvania, and Cold Harbor.

**June 1864–March 1865** Fights trench warfare around Petersburg and Richmond, Virginia, wearing down the Confederate defense.

**April 9, 1865** Accepts General Lee's surrender at Appomattox Court House, effectively bringing the war to an end; the terms allow Confederate soldiers and officers to return to their homes.

**1869–1877** Serves two terms as president.

**July 23, 1885** Dies at Mount McGregor, New York, of throat cancer.

---

his men to an early victory at Belmont, and then took Forts Donelson and Henry, demanding unconditional surrender. At the time, other Union generals were suffering heavy defeats. Grant's successes led to his promotion to major general.

On April 6, 1862, when Grant and his forces were encamped at Shiloh on the Tennessee River, Confederate troops launched a surprise attack. The first day ended in near defeat for Grant, but the next day he launched a counterattack, and his troops prevailed, in the face of fierce Southern attacks, thanks to his determination and the sheer force of

at Chattanooga later in the year, confirmed his abilities as a commander and his status as a national hero. Lincoln summoned him to Washington and on March 9, 1864, Grant was appointed general-in-chief of the Union armies. He was also made lieutenant general, a rank that had previously been held only by George Washington.

### Bludgeoning tactics
Finally, Grant directed the converging Union drives that brought about the defeat of the Confederacy. He had a simple strategy for fighting the Confederate Army. He knew the North

## "The war is over—the **rebels** are **our countrymen again**."

GRANT AFTER LEE'S SURRENDER AT APPOMATTOX COURT HOUSE, APRIL 9, 1865

numbers. His troops suffered devastating losses in what was one of the bloodiest confrontations of the war to that point. This sparked demands for Grant's removal, but President Lincoln famously responded by saying,"I can't spare this man—he fights."

Grant's next major objective was Vicksburg, Mississippi. After a brilliant campaign, he took this Confederate stronghold in July 1863, freeing the Mississippi River to Union traffic and in effect dividing the Confederacy. Further successes in Tennessee, in particular the defeat of Braxton Bragg

had greater industrial resources, manpower, and money, and he was willing to use them all in order to win. "Strike at the enemy as hard as you can" and "Wear them out," he said.

Leaving Sherman in charge in the west, Grant personally led the relentless Union attacks by the Army of the Potomac in Virginia, the war's principal battlefront. He gradually wore down General Robert E. Lee's forces during the Overland Campaign. The siege of Petersburg and the fall of

**Grant's field glasses**
Faded and frayed, these field glasses were used by Grant to follow troop movements on the battlefield.

Prewar partisanship carried over into the war years, especially in the North. Republicans were much more likely to support the Lincoln administration's war measures than Democrats.

**PARTY LINES**

Both parties were in turn divided into factions that waxed and waned as wartime events inspired or deflated political aspirations. The Northern Democrats were divided between **War Democrats**, who generally supported the war against the Confederacy, and the **Peace Democrats, also known as Copperheads,** who steadfastly resisted Republican war measures to the point of being declared traitorous. The **Republicans had "radicals" and "moderates,"** who frequently disagreed about how best to reconstruct occupied areas of the South, deal with the freedmen, and treat captured enemies. Prewar political affiliations thus dictated home-front support of the war, especially at the local level.

# The Home Front

**The Civil War was fought on two fronts: the battlefield and the home front. Although civilians far away from the fighting were not directly in harm's way, they were profoundly affected by the war, and in turn influenced the course of campaigns by giving or withholding their political, social, or economic support.**

In the South, the demands of war exacerbated prewar class differences. It was in areas of the Confederacy where stratification among whites was most evident, such as in upcountry Alabama and western Virginia, that support for the war effort was most divided. Initially, nearly all classes were enthusiastic about fighting for independence, but as the Union army advanced deeper into the South and Confederate war measures became more demanding, prewar class distinctions became harmful to Southern national unity. The draft and tax-in-kind—tax paid in the form of goods, crops, or even impressed slaves taken into Confederate service—both struck the lower and middle classes the worst, leading to cries among yeoman and hardscrabble farmers that this was a "rich man's war and a poor man's fight."

## Northern growth

Because of sound financial policies shepherded by Secretary of the Treasury Salmon P. Chase and his Wall Street mogul Jay Cooke, the Union's economic health began in critical condition and ended in robust prosperity. In 1862, the treasury was empty, and a solution had to be found—fast. Chase hired Cooke to market Federal war bonds, which were eagerly scooped up by investors. This was followed by the introduction of "greenbacks" (Federally issued paper money backed by gold), so pressure on the Northern economy lessened. Import duties, the traditional source of Federal income, continued to bring in revenue, but so did a graduated national income tax, the first in American history.

These financial measures, overseen by men who understood money, ensured that the capital existed not only to fund the war effort, but also to fuel a boom that assured American prosperity for the rest of the 19th century. Overall,

> **WAR BONDS** Government-issued bonds (securities) used to finance a war. Members of the public are encouraged to buy them as a gesture of support.

The Civil War was one of the most significant events in the movement toward female equality in the United States. As men marched off to war, women took their places in factories, fields, and stores.

### WOMEN'S ROLES EXPAND

In North and South alike, women's activities in ladies' aid societies, and as nurses in national organizations, gained them recognition as integral contributors to the war effort. In so doing, they **expanded what was regarded as "respectable" women's work**.

Spared invasion and occupation, Northern women benefited the most from the war and **reignited the women's rights movement in the postwar decades**. Southern women, often devastated by the loss of property and deaths of family members, were less likely to profit socially but **became hardened to privations**. One woman in Warrenton, Virginia, wrote: "We keep true to the South amid all our sore trials—and at times are to be pitied." Despite this, their experiences operating farms and plantations in their husbands' absence and witnessing war firsthand helped to **crack the gender barriers of the old South**.

the Northern economy grew in all areas as a result of the war—agriculture, mining, transportation networks, the service sector, and manufacturing.

### Southern inflation

The situation in the Confederacy was starkly different. Because the nation was starting from scratch, there was no initial balance of credit and few gold reserves with which to fund the war effort. Hence, in March 1861, Secretary of the Treasury Christopher Memminger asked the Confederate Congress to authorize the printing of a million dollars in paper notes. These bills were backed by nothing more than the population's faith in the government and almost immediately began to devalue. In late 1861, a Confederate dollar was worth 80 cents in gold; by 1865 it was worth 1.5 cents. Inflation plagued rebel currency all through the war, simultaneously strangling private and public trade, the collection of taxes, and the payment of debts.

**Five dollars' worth**
Confederate banknotes were often beautifully designed, but inflation ate away constantly at their monetary value. This one shows Secretary of the Treasury, German-born Christopher Memminger, in the bottom right corner.

sank into a barter system reminiscent of the European Middle Ages as officials and private citizens haggled over what constituted payment of taxes.

### Volunteer aid societies

Within months of the firing on Fort Sumter, almost 20,000 local aid societies organized in both the Union and the Confederacy. Many, especially in the South, withered and died as wartime hardships disrupted their activities, but thousands persisted. The societies and their national counterparts supplied soldiers in the field with homeknit clothing, jams and preserves, writing supplies, newspapers, Bibles, and books.

Most of these organizations were run locally by wives and daughters of soldiers, and aimed at the physical and

**Farewell to home and family**
William D. T. Travis, staff artist with the Union Army of the Potomac, painted this glamorized depiction of an officer outside his mansion bidding farewell to his family as he leaves to fight for the North.

## "I sell my eggs and butter from home for $200 a month. Does it not sound well … But in what? In Confederate money. *Hélas!*"

MARY CHESNUT, *A DIARY FROM DIXIE*, SEPTEMBER 19, 1864

To help offset inflation, Memminger resorted to selling bonds as Chase did, but he had no financier to assist him and fewer investors willing to wager their funds. More paper money was printed, and direct taxation forced on an unwilling populace. But only seven percent of the Confederacy's income was generated in this way. Instead, the hated tax-in-kind, or "impressment," initiated in March 1863, provided the bulk of the government's revenue. In many parts of the South, the economy

### Ammunition workers

Engravings from *Harper's Weekly* show workers, including many women, filling cartridges at Watertown Arsenal, Massachusetts. The artist was the young Winslow Homer, later known for his landscape paintings.

emotional comfort of their menfolk. Often they raised money through fairs and bazaars to purchase items to be sent to the soldiers. These philanthropic events were highlights on the social calendars of Northern and Southern communities, and in the larger cities thousands turned out to buy homemade goods produced by the societies' members. Raffles, benefit balls, and musical entertainment also were popular fundraising methods. Infused with patriotism, good will, and religious fervor, these activities kept the war at the forefront of peoples' minds, especially in the North, where the physical effects of the conflict were minimal and only the absence of military-age males showed that life had changed.

**Patched up**
With the Union blockade biting ever deeper, the South, which produced most of the world's raw cotton, found itself starved of the finished fabric. Clothes, like this dress, had to be endlessly patched and repatched.

# War-weary People

**The Civil War was a "people's war" fought between two democratic republics. This meant that public morale was as important to the war efforts of both sides as the successes or failures of their armies. As the long, bloody conflict dragged on into its third year, war weariness was taking a heavy toll.**

Conscription, also known as the draft, was a key factor in making the Civil War a people's war, but this did not make it any the less resented on either side. In the South, growing anger at the draft was compounded by the hated "Twenty-Negro Law," which exempted owners and overseers of 20 or more slaves. The right of large slave-owners to opt out of military service infuriated many poorer whites, who started to question their sacrifices on behalf of rich men and their property.

## BEFORE

**In March 1862, the Confederacy introduced compulsory military service for all men between the ages of 18 and 35. It was a response to waning numbers of volunteers and the impending disintegration of rebel armies as the 1861 enlistment terms expired.**

**CONSCRIPTION AND RIOTS**
In September 1862, the Southern draft was further expanded to include **men up to age 45**, and subsequent amendments **allowed even 16-year-olds to be drafted**. The measure was hated by most Confederate citizens and viewed as an **unnecessary intrusion by the national government** on the rights of both states and individuals.

The Union government also passed a draft law in late 1862—the so-called **"militia draft."** This obliged states to formally register **all white men between 18 and 45** as liable for military service in state regiments and for up to nine months' service in the Federal armed forces. The law was **wildly unpopular and incited rioting and resistance** across the North, prompting President Abraham Lincoln to temporarily suspend habeas corpus in certain areas of the Union.

President Jefferson Davis, General Robert E. Lee, and others in the Southern high command believed not only that the draft was an unfortunate necessity, but also that the exemption clause was vital to maintain the Confederate economy. Southern women, often driven to the poverty line by the absence of their men, disagreed and rioted in several towns and cities throughout 1862 and 1863. The most famous of these disturbances was the Richmond Bread Riot of March 1863, during which Jefferson Davis somewhat ineffectually attempted to mollify the mob by throwing money to it from his coat pockets. Only the arrival of troops stopped the mayhem.

## Northern draft
In the North, the "militia draft" of 1862 was followed in March 1863 by the Enrollment Act. Unlike the earlier piece of legislation, this new measure was formally organized at the national rather than the state level. It mandated

> Northerners who hired substitutes to fight for them included many luminaries of America's postwar Gilded Age: John D. Rockefeller, Andrew Carnegie, J. P. Morgan, and Theodore Roosevelt Sr., father of future President "Teddy" Roosevelt.

that all Northern males between ages 20 and 45 were eligible for conscription. People could, however, hire a substitute by paying a $300 commutation fee and so escape the current draft round. The $300 exemption clause, like the Confederate equivalent for large slave-owners, created immense dissatisfaction among the North's urban poor and led to rioting, notably the infamous New York City Draft Riots, which rocked the city for four

**"Sowing and Reaping"**
In May 1863, *Frank Leslie's Illustrated Newspaper*, a Northern publication, included these two scathing cartoons, showing Southern women "hounding their men on to rebellion" (on the left) and then "feeling the effects of rebellion and creating bread riots" (right).

days in July 1863. Parts of the city were burned to the ground, hundreds of free blacks were killed, an orphanage for black children was destroyed, and Republican and abolitionist property was looted and damaged before Federal troops arrived fresh from the Battle of Gettysburg. They imposed order at the point of the bayonet.

## Deserters and "bounty-jumpers"
As the war extended into its third year, the Northern and Southern home fronts grew ever more resistant to the draft. Men conscripted into the army or navy frequently deserted at the first possible moment, especially toward the end of the war. Worse, a black-market enterprise, called "bounty-jumping,"

developed in the North that took advantage of state and Federal incentives to encourage volunteers, rather than draftees, to sign up. According to the Enrollment Act, if a particular district or city was able to supply a certain number of volunteers, it no longer had to enact the draft.

A number of communities offered generous "bounties"—monetary incentives—to entice volunteers and thus, they hoped, to avoid the need for conscription. A lively criminal practice started, in which men signed up for a particular district or regiment, received the bounty, then "jumped" to another geographic area, where they repeated the process. Small fortunes were illicitly amassed in this way, and many bounty-jumpers were never caught.

### Execution parade
Desperate to stem the tide of desertion, in August 1863 the Union high command ordered the public execution by firing squad of five deserters from the Army of the Potomac. Artist Edwin Forbes captured the scene.

**After the battle**
Events like the Union bombardment of Fredericksburg in 1862 inevitably took their toll on morale. A painting by David E. Henderson shows a family amid the devastation.

In a letter of January 1863, Major Charles Fessenden Morse of the 2nd Massachusetts Infantry wrote of the apathy in the North in the war's middle period: "What we need is to feel that we are fighting for our lives and liberties; that is the way the Rebels feel … Our people seem to be in an indifferent state." Civilian war weariness and lack of interest were increasingly among President Lincoln's greatest enemies.

### "Copperhead" Democrats
Some states of the Union, such as Minnesota and Iowa, were more concerned about Indian uprisings than the Southern rebellion. Others were so remote from the effects of the war and its sacrifices that Confederate independence did not seem like a terrible prospect. Still other sections, such as southern Ohio, Pennsylvania, Indiana, and Illinois, at times outrightly resisted the Federal war effort, not only by protesting the draft laws, but also by electing antiwar or "Copperhead" Democrats to the state and national legislatures.

The Copperheads earned their nickname from the copper pennies they supposedly wore on their coat lapels as identification. They controlled a strong minority in the national Democratic Party, and enjoyed a majority, for brief periods, in certain statehouses. The draft laws and the Emancipation Proclamation threw fuel on their fire, attracting thousands of followers to their cause.

Clement L. Vallandigham of Ohio, one of the most outspoken Copperheads, claimed the war was being fought "for the purpose of crushing our liberty and erecting a despotism … a war for the freedom of the blacks and enslavement of the whites." Arrested for treason, Vallandigham reveled in the attention he received. Had it not been for the Union victories in summer 1863, he might have created serious political trouble for Lincoln. As it was, after a brief incarceration, he was banished to the Confederacy in the fall of 1863.

#### Democratic Party candidate
A Republican cartoon from the 1864 presidential campaign portrays Democrat candidate George McClellan as a Peace Democrat or "Copperhead"—also a venomous snake.

HEADS OF THE DEMOCRACY.

By the summer of 1864, Gettysburg and the other Union victories of the previous July had faded in the Northern public's memory and were replaced by stalemate, immense bloodshed, and defeat.

### MORALE EBBS AND FLOWS
President **Lincoln needed victories** as much as, if not more than, his Confederate counterpart, Jefferson Davis. Lincoln's reelection in November 1864 depended on Northern civilian perceptions of the war. General William T. **Sherman's capture of Atlanta 292–93 ≫** in September helped turn the tide of Northern feeling. By year's end, Sherman had reached Savannah—the March to the Sea **296–97 ≫**—while in Virginia Confederate General Robert E. Lee was **stuck in a siege at Petersburg 274–75 ≫**. Now Southern morale plummeted, encouraging desertion from already depleted armies.

# Riots in New York

**Civil War battlefields were not the only places where violence and death occurred in the 1860s. From July 13–16, 1863, rioters stormed the streets of New York City when a shortage in military recruits led Congress to pass the North's first conscription act. Violence erupted over a clause that allowed wealthy men to pay a $300.00 commutation fee to avoid military service.**

"The draft began on Saturday, the twelfth, very foolishly ordered by the government, who supposed that these Union victories would make the people willing to submit ... by Monday morning there were large crowds assembled to resist the draft. All day yesterday there were dreadful scenes enacted in the city. The police were successfully opposed; many were killed, many houses gutted and burned: the colored asylum was burned and all the furniture carried off by women: Negroes were hung in the streets! All last night the fire-bells rang, but at last, in God's good mercy, the rain came down in torrents and scattered the crowds, giving the city authorities time to organize ... I did not wonder at the spirit in which the poor resented the three-hundred-dollar clause."

DIARY OF MARIA LYDIG, A "UNION LADY" MARRIED TO A NEW YORK JUDGE

"I stepped to the window and saw a light in the sky ... others joined me in viewing the wanton destruction of property by the infuriated mob ... while I was wondering at the doings of the infuriated people, a drunken man passed along the street and what he might say in such a condition would speak the sentiments of the mob. He said that 'a poor man had to be drafted and go to the war, but a rich man could pay his money and stay at home. Thats whats the matter.' This is the sentiment that lies at the foundation of the whole trouble as far as the rioters are concerned ... more than thirty have been brot in injured by clubs and fire arms. Men, women, and children have been wounded by gun shots, so eager have they been to see the fray ... some will get well and others will die. They all say they were not participants but merely lookers on. For such I have some pity but I don't believe all they say about their innocence."

JOURNAL OF JOHN VANCE LAUDERDALE, NEWLY QUALIFIED AS A DOCTOR IN NEW YORK CITY WHEN HE SIGNED ON AS A CONTRACT SURGEON FOR THE UNION ARMY

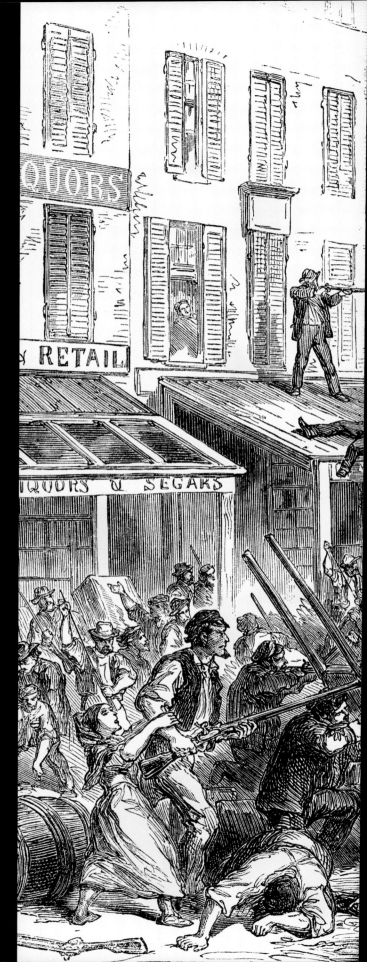

**Mayhem in New York**
Enraged by the unfair Enrollment Act, angry mobs, many of whom were Irish immigrants, went on the rampage. They looted buildings and attacked civilians, especially African-Americans, with whom they competed for jobs.

**BEFORE**

By 1861, the medical profession was transforming itself from one rooted in guesswork, gut instinct, and folklore, into a more scientific vocation.

**MODERN MEDICINE**
The old 18th-century ideas of **"miasmic vapors"** and imbalances in bodily **"humors"** were giving way to **modern medical practices and theories**. Education of doctors and nurses still varied widely. Some people were required to graduate from university programs and **others simply learned by experience**. Diagnosis, prescription, therapy, and even surgery often took place at the patient's home, sometimes literally on the kitchen table. **Formal hospitals were rare**, and existed only in the big cities.

**WARTIME TREATMENT**
At the time of the war, **surgical techniques were crude**, often involving rough amputations and painful probing of wounds to **extract foreign objects**. Luckily for most injured soldiers, anesthesia—in the form of ether and chloroform—was routinely given prior to surgery.

# Medicine and Medical Services

**At the time of the war, medical care for wounded or sick soldiers was primitive. Bacteriology and sepsis theory were still in their infancy, and modern weapons could inflict grievous wounds. This imbalance, combined with the high risk of infection in the camps, created unprecedented numbers of casualties.**

When the war began, the U.S. Army's medical corps was comprised of one surgeon general, 30 surgeons, and 83 assistant surgeons; 24 resigned to serve the Confederacy. These men became the core of the Union and Confederate medical departments; by the war's end, almost 12,000 doctors had been employed by the North and 3,237 by the South.

This massive wartime expansion was necessitated by the unprecedented scale of the conflict and the high number of injured troops. Not everyone was qualified for their duties; many had been medical students before the war or learned on the job as surgeon's assistants, but both sides lowered standards in order to fill the need for doctors. Civilian contractors and volunteers helped plug the gaps that the uniformed medical services could not fill, especially in the first two years. Volunteer nurses and relief organizations—such as the U.S. Sanitary Commission in the North and the Association for the Relief of Maimed Soldiers in the South—proved crucial in saving lives after major battles. In the South, private homes often served as makeshift hospitals, their female occupants providing Confederates with more personalized care than they might otherwise have received.

### Recruiting staff

After July 1862, each Union regiment was required to have a surgeon and two assistant surgeons who were, in turn, overseen by brigade and divisional surgeons. Stretcher-bearers and field hospital orderlies—at first, drawn from regimental and brigade musicians— were ill-trained, but later made up a special branch within the Union medical department. Confederate regiments were supposed to have one surgeon and one assistant surgeon, and followed a similar hierarchy up the

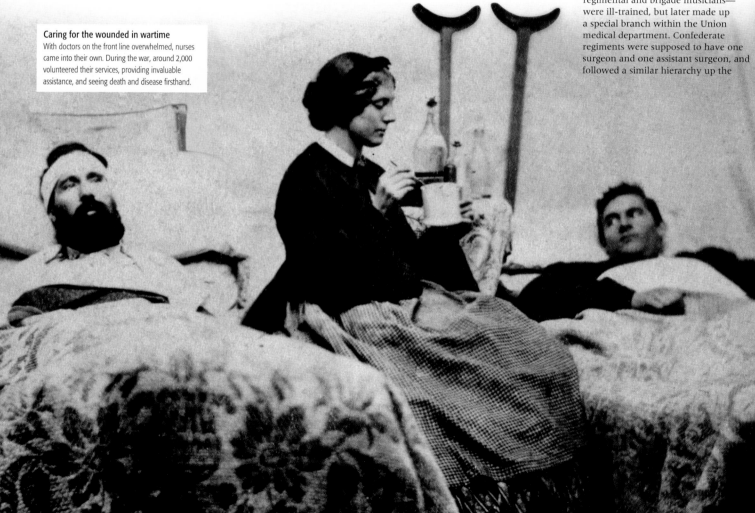

**Caring for the wounded in wartime**
With doctors on the front line overwhelmed, nurses came into their own. During the war, around 2,000 volunteered their services, providing invaluable assistance, and seeing death and disease firsthand.

Union hospital in Washington, D.C.
Field hospitals were hastily put together and inadequate. As the poet Walt Whitman wrote: "I suppose you know that what we call hospital here in the field, is nothing but a collection of tents, on the bare ground for a floor, rather hard accommodations for a sick man."

## "[The war] was fought at the end of the **medical Middle Ages**."
UNION SURGEON GENERAL WILLIAM A. HAMMOND

REFORMER AND NURSE 1802–87

### DOROTHEA DIX

Born in Hampden, Maine, Dorothea Dix was a reformer on behalf of the mentally ill prior to the Civil War, but immediately volunteered her services after the bombardment of Fort Sumter. In June 1861, Dix was made superintendent of female nurses for the Union Army, a position she held until the end of the war. Under her firm and judicious leadership, a team of 3,000 nurses treated thousands of wounded soldiers in army hospitals. Neither friend nor enemy were neglected. When Lee withdrew from Gettysburg, he abandoned his Confederate wounded—these men were cared for by Dix's nurses.

chain of command. All their doctors had to pass a special examination administered by a military medical board, except when civilian doctors were recruited after large battles. The United States Colored Troops had a separate medical department that mirrored the overall Union model, but with less stringent requirements for doctors and nurses. Consequently, death rates for wounded or ill African-American soldiers were much higher than for their white counterparts.

### Infectious diseases
Disease killed twice as many troops as battlefield injuries. Sometimes entire campaigns were called off because of sickness. In May 1862, Confederate general P. G. T. Beauregard abandoned Corinth, Mississippi, to advancing Federals under General Henry Halleck because one-third of his force was incapacitated. When the Union Army took the city in June, Halleck called off his invasion for the same reason.

Dysentery, diarrhea, typhoid, and malaria—all caused by poor sanitation—were rampant in the camps. Measles, smallpox, and common colds were passed around by the men, and pneumonia developed quickly among green troops exposed to the elements. Quinine was available to treat malaria and most armies routinely inoculated against smallpox, but outbreaks of both diseases occurred regularly. Opium, castor oil, and Epsom salts were prescribed to combat diarrhea and dysentery.

In most cases, the cure was bed rest, but rest was difficult for campaigning soldiers or those in the rigors of initial

training. Many came to call the first few months of service "the hardening," as they struggled to condition themselves and their immune systems to army life. Thousands could not and died before they ever left camp.

Union surgeon W. W. Keen described caring for the wounded: "We operated in old blood-stained and often pus-stained coats [with] disinfected hands … We used undisinfected instruments from undisinfected plush-lined cases … and used marine sponges which had been used in prior pus cases and had been only washed in tap water."

### Staying alive
Although chloroform or whiskey deadened the pain of major surgery, secondary infections caused by ignorance often killed those who had initially lived through the trauma of an operation. Almost one in four amputations resulted in death. Much depended on how quickly the wounded could be evacuated from the field. Soldiers' immune systems and physical strength could better handle the shock of surgery if rapidly treated. After some battles, such as Second Bull Run and Chancellorsville, the injured lay in agony on the field for days, or in some cases, more than a week, and thus were far less likely to survive. Jonathan W. Letterman, medical director of the Army

### Prosthetic limb
Nearly two-thirds of battlefield wounds occurred in the extremities, and amputation under anesthesia was the typical remedy. Lucky amputees were given prosthetic devices—this one replaced a severed foot.

of the Potomac, recognized the need for speedy evacuation of the wounded, and to that end created a Federal Ambulance Corps composed of specially selected and trained litter bearers, ambulance drivers and horses, and specifically constructed ambulances. These reforms succeeded in

### Life for a veteran
Congress granted pensions to those soldiers wounded on the battlefield—but first they had to prove their claim. Veterans without obvious injuries had to track down their comrades to write a statement on their behalf.

saving thousands of Union soldiers' lives. The Confederates experimented with similar ideas, but failed to create an efficient, army-wide field evacuation apparatus. Both armies utilized a tripartite system: regimental dressing stations directly behind the front lines, divisional field hospitals (often set up in local barns, houses, or churches), and formal military hospitals in the cities (such as Richmond's famous Chimborazo) for those wounded who required long convalescences.

**AFTER**

After the war, the combination of scientific discoveries and practical battlefield experience set the stage for greater survival rates in future wars.

#### PIONEERS OF MEDICINE
Medical practitioners during the Civil War could only do so much. Bad sanitation often got the better of them, and infections were difficult to combat. **But the world of medicine was changing**. In France during the 1860s, the chemist and microbiologist **Louis Pasteur** proved his **germ theory**—that bacteria from the environment caused disease—and discovered vaccines against rabies and anthrax. In 1865, Englishman **Joseph Lister used carbolic acid** to prevent infection in the wound of an 11-year-old boy with a compound fracture of his tibia.

#### ANTIBIOTICS DISCOVERED
Alexander Fleming's accidental **discovery of the antibiotic penicillin** in 1928 changed the course of medical practice forever. In **World War II, thousands of soldiers were saved** from disease and postoperative complications.

# Medical Equipment

...Civil War was fought as medicine was on the brink of the modern scientific era. ...thetic compounds were increasingly available to reduce some of the horrors of ...efield surgery, but antiseptic procedures and medication were not yet in use.

...dicine chest Surgeons carried a range of anesthetics ...nkillers, such as chloroform, ether, and morphine. ...Union blockade of the South tightened, surgeons in ...th found themselves increasingly short of medical ...s. **2 Tool tray** Contains a range of probes used to ...ny bullets or fragments in the wound. **3 Surgeon's ...ng case** Such kits were often elaborate sets of ...ents fitted in fabric-lined wooden cases. **4 Tool tray** ...ntains a chain saw, used for cutting through bone ...he location of the injury was inaccessible to a bone ...**Bone saw** Used for cutting through the larger bones ...nd arms during amputations. **6 Trephine** ...lly used to drill holes in the skull to relieve pressure ...by a fracture. **7 Grips** These removable handles ...ached to the chain saw to allow the surgeon to operate the saw. **8 Hey's saw** Used to cut the cranium around a fracture. **9 Bone crimper** Used to remove rough bony edges on the stump after an amputation. **10 Bullet extractor** These forceps were specially designed to remove a bullet, fragments, or other material from a wound. **11 Bone cutter** Designed to remove ragged bits of fractured bone. **12 Amputation knives** Used for cutting soft tissue during an amputation. They came in a variety of sizes. **13 Scalpels and lancets** These were important tools for incising and dissecting smaller tissue. **14 Surgical saw** Injuries from artillery fire often left soldiers with smashed arms or legs which required amputation. **15 Pocket surgery kit** Belonging to the first female Union Army surgeon, Mary Walker, this kit contains a range of scissors, forceps, and probes.

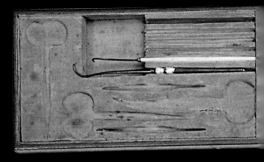

**2 TOOL TRAY**

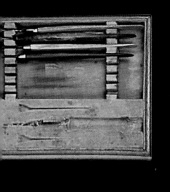

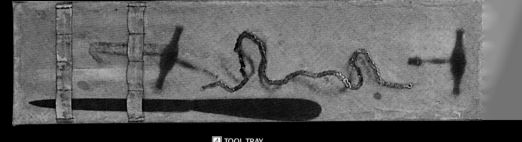

4 TOOL TRAY

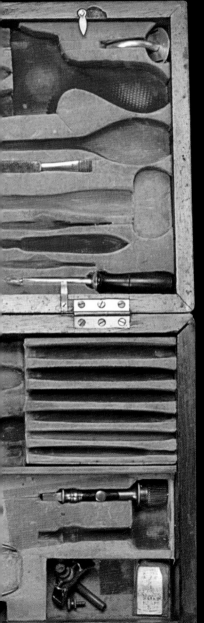

5 BONE SAW

6 TREPHINE          7 GRIPS          8 HEY'S SAW

9 BONE CRIMPER                    10 BULLET EXTRACTOR

12 AMPUTATION
KNIVES

11 BONE CUTTER

13 SCALPELS AND LANCETS

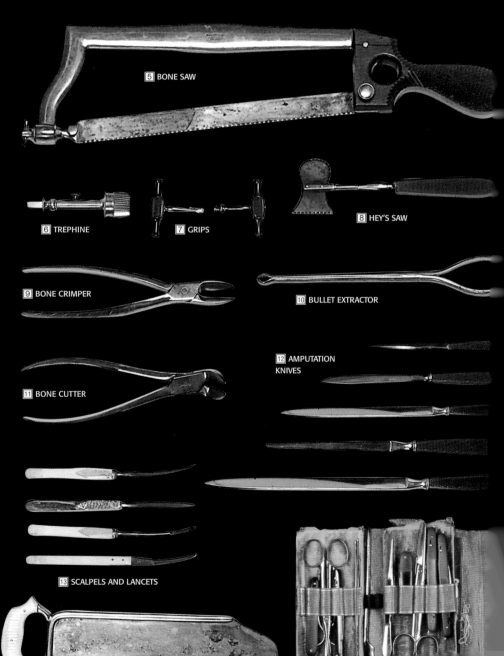

NURSE AND HUMANITARIAN Born 1821 Died 1912

# Clara Barton

## "The patriot blood of my father was warm in my veins."

CLARA BARTON, WRITING OF HER DECISION TO WORK ON THE BATTLEFIELD

Clarissa Harlowe Barton, known as "The Angel of the Battlefield," was one of the best-known women of the Civil War era, eclipsing other nurses and female wartime reformers through her role as founder and first director of the American Red Cross in the postwar period. Her efforts during the war saved countless lives, and her work on behalf of missing soldiers eased the grief of thousands of loved ones after the war was over.

### "What could I do but go with them?"

Having worked for several years as a teacher, Barton was working at the Patent Office in Washington at the outbreak of the war in 1861. She quickly recognized that the disorganized and understaffed Federal Medical Department was woefully unprepared for the scale of casualties that the conflict would produce. When Washington was deluged with wounded following the First Battle of Bull Run in late July, she created a civilian agency devoted to gathering and distributing items of comfort for the wounded, and worked with other relief organizations to the same end.

These efforts alone were not enough for her. For a year she lobbied the Medical Department and other governmental organizations for permission to accompany the Union Army of the Potomac and administer to the wounded on site. Finally, with the powerful political patronage of Massachusetts Senator Henry Wilson, Barton was granted leave to pursue practical nursing duties.

It was not a moment too soon. Delayed by the mud and slow-moving wagons at the rear of the Federal columns, Barton and her small entourage arrived in the middle of the Battle of Antietam. The bloodiest day of the war was Barton's first experience of treating wounded soldiers on the battlefield, coming under fire in the process. Setting up camp next to the Union field hospital at the Poffenberger Farm just north of the infamous Cornfield, she witnessed harried surgeons attempting to dress soldiers' wounds with cornhusks as the medical supplies were held up behind the lines. Instantly, Barton donated all of her carefully gathered supplies, and when

### Tireless humanitarian

Reportedly a shy child, Clara Barton grew to be a confident, determined woman, as this 1862 photograph suggests. Besides her achievements as a nurse and first president of the American Red Cross, she organized relief work for natural disasters and espoused African-American and women's rights.

night fell, she gave the surgeons her lanterns as well. Steadfastly she worked alongside them, bringing water to the wounded, preparing food in the nearby farmhouse, and assisting the surgeons. At one point she was kneeling next to a wounded soldier, giving him water, when she felt her sleeve quiver—and discovered a bullet hole. The bullet had pierced her sleeve and killed the man to whom she was ministering.

After the battle she kept on working, refusing sleep and taking little time to eat. A few days later she collapsed from exhaustion and typhoid and was taken back to Washington, delirious. Barton recovered quickly and returned to the front. She accompanied the Army of the Potomac on many

permission to accompany her brother David, who was quartermaster of the Eighteenth Corps, to South Carolina.

In the summer of 1864, Barton headed to Bermuda Hundred, below Richmond, where Benjamin Butler's Army of the James lay bottled up in

### Tending the wounded
Clara Barton worked days and nights on end to help wounded soldiers on the battlefield, especially after the bloody clash at Antietam in 1862. Her selfless work was the subject of many popular engravings and lithographs.

information comforted countless loved ones in the North who yearned for news that could confirm the fate of a husband, brother, or son who had not returned. Under the auspices of her new position, Barton was instrumental in identifying nearly 13,000 dead Union prisoners of war at Andersonville, Georgia, and placing headstones over their graves.

### American Red Cross
In 1870, at the outbreak of the Franco-Prussian War, Barton was in Europe and offered her assistance to the sick and wounded of both sides. Working mainly in Strasbourg and Paris, she learned much about the International Red Cross and became an enthusiastic supporter of the organization. Returning home, she led a crusade to found an American branch of the society, meeting strong institutional and governmental resistance. Finally, in 1881, Barton's persistence bore fruit as she was sworn in as the first president of the American Red Cross.

She remained at the head of the organization until 1904, when she resigned over criticism of her management—some of which may have stemmed from her work on behalf of the women's suffrage movement, in which she was also active until her death. Living another eight years in retirement, Barton died aged 90 at her home in Glen Echo, Maryland.

### Andersonville graves
Barton was involved in the monumental task of tracing all the men who had gone missing in the war. Many had died—of malnutrition and disease—in the hellish prison camp at Andersonville, Georgia, where she played a major part in organizing their grave markers.

> " … General McClellan … sinks into insignificance beside the **true heroine** of the age, the **angel of the battlefield**."
>
> DR. JAMES DUNN, A SURGEON AT ANTIETAM, ON CLARA BARTON, SEPTEMBER 1862

major campaigns, but the Army Medical Department had been fully mobilized since 1863 and civilian volunteers such as Barton, though still welcome, could do little to augment the army's medical systems. In April 1863, she was given

entrenchments. Butler was so taken by her character and efficiency that he appointed her "lady in charge" of all the nurses in his hospitals at the front.

### Missing Soldiers Office
As the war drew to a close, President Lincoln, aware of her selfless efforts on behalf of the sick and wounded, made her the supervisor of the Missing Soldiers Office. Most of the missing men were never found, but Barton's office succeeded in locating hundreds of soldiers' remains, their graves, and, occasionally, a live soldier. This

## TIMELINE

- **December 25, 1821** Born Clarissa Harlowe Barton, the youngest of five children, in Oxford, Massachusetts.
- **1832** Aged 11, she nurses her brother David for three years after he is injured in a farm accident.
- **1838** Starts a teaching job in Massachusetts.
- **1854** She establishes the first free school in New Jersey, at Bordentown, but is overlooked as principal in favor of a man.
- **1854** Moves to Washington, D. C., where she becomes the first woman to work as a clerk at the Patent Office.
- **July 1861** Leaves the Patent Office and sets up an agency to help wounded Union soldiers in Washington. Receives clothing and other donations from all over the country.
- **August 13, 1862** Arrives in Virginia a few days after the Battle of Cedar Mountain, having obtained permission to take medical supplies to the front.
- **September 17, 1862** Nurses the wounded on the battlefield of Antietam. Returns to Washington to recover from exhaustion and typhoid, but soon rejoins the Army of the Potomac on campaign.
- **April 1863** Travels to South Carolina. She is present at the siege of Fort Wagner in July.
- **Spring 1864** Tends the wounded at Fredericksburg, and works in a mobile field hospital with General Butler's Army of the James.
- **1865** Put in charge of finding missing Union soldiers by President Lincoln. Does valuable work identifying those who died at the notorious Confederate prison at Andersonville.
- **November 1866** Embarks on a lecture tour of the United States entitled, "Work and Incidents of Army Life," recounting her war experiences.
- **1869** Travels to Europe. While in Switzerland, she learns about the Geneva Convention and International Red Cross.
- **1870–71** In the Franco-Prussian War, Barton helps injured soldiers and organizes relief work.
- **1873** Returns to the United States in poor health.
- **1877** Travels to Washington to campaign for the United States to sign the Geneva Convention and recognize the International Red Cross.
- **1881** The American Red Cross is formed with Barton as its first president.
- **1898** In the Spanish-American War, Barton works in hospitals in Cuba at the age of 77.

**AMBULANCE FROM SPANISH-AMERICAN WAR**

- **1904** Resigns as president of the American Red Cross amid criticism of her leadership.
- **April 12, 1912** Dies at Glen Echo, Maryland.

**Crossing the Tennessee**
Rosecrans's troops cross the Tennessee River west of Chattanooga, in early September 1863, as depicted in William Travis's epic panorama on the exploits of the Army of the Cumberland.

# The Chickamauga Campaign

**Spurred by Washington to duplicate the successes of Gettysburg and Vicksburg, Major General William S. Rosecrans and the Army of the Cumberland moved to drive the Rebels out of Tennessee and further divide the Confederacy.**

Reactivated to command the Army of the Ohio, General Ambrose Burnside marched on Knoxville, the "capital" of East Tennessee. On September 3, 1863, he was greeted with joy by most of its citizens, who were Union sympathizers. Meanwhile, Rosecrans had been on the move since mid-August, advancing virtually unopposed the last few miles to Chattanooga, thanks to various feints and deceptions that fooled General Braxton Bragg about his final objective.

On September 8, the Confederates evacuated Chattanooga, to the great dismay of Jefferson Davis, who wrote, "We are now in the darkest hour of our political existence." But Davis had weathered similar military disappointments before and was determined to turn this one around. Bragg withdrew to northern Georgia, where he received two divisions from Joseph E. Johnston's inactive army, bringing the strength of the Army of Tennessee almost on par with Rosecrans's force. To provide Bragg with the numerical superiority that might bring victory, Davis also sent him the bulk of Longstreet's corps from the Army of Northern Virginia.

Lee protested, claiming that he needed Longstreet and his divisions for a new offensive against General Meade, but Davis rightly understood that the decisive theater of war was, for now, in the West.

### Tension mounts
On September 9, the first of Longstreet's seasoned troops boarded trains for a 550-mile (885-km) journey through Virginia, Carolina, and Georgia. The direct route from Virginia to Tennessee no longer existed because of the fall of Chattanooga to the Union. It would take nine days for these reinforcements—12,000 strong—to reach Bragg from the East, but they would arrive just in time.

In early September, Bragg made a series of attempts to bait Rosecrans into advancing his army corps. On three occasions the Union commander took the bait, and could have been badly mauled. But in each instance one or other of Bragg's subordinates failed to follow his orders sufficiently.

### The Confederate advance
In Alfred Waud's drawing, the Confederate line is shown advancing uphill through forest toward the Union line on the second day of the Battle of Chickamauga. British-born Waud worked as an artist-correspondent for *Harper's Weekly* magazine.

« BEFORE

**After the near defeat at Stones River « 146–47**, Rosecrans spent the spring and early summer of 1863 rebuilding his strength, much to Lincoln's exasperation.

**THE TULLAHOMA CAMPAIGN**
When Rosecrans finally moved in late June and early July, he succeeded in **driving Bragg out of south-central Tennessee**, leaving the major railroad junction of Chattanooga **vulnerable to capture**.

In one week, Union troops **pushed their foes back almost 80 miles** (129km) at the cost of only 570 casualties—an advance known as the Tullahoma Campaign. But then **Rosecrans stalled**, waiting for repairs to railroads and more supplies, before he moved forward again.

**34,000** The estimated total number of casualties resulting from the Battle of Chickamauga. Bragg lost around 18,000 men to Rosecrans's 16,000—more than one-quarter of their combined forces.

Rosecrans grew cautious, consolidating his army along the West Chickamauga Creek. Bragg was determined to flank him and to get between him and his base at Chattanooga. On September 18, the first of Longstreet's troops arrived, and after a day of desultory skirmishing, Bragg decided to wait to the morrow to hit the Union army in full force.

## The Battle of Chickamauga

As the sun rose on September 19, the pickets of each side, after lying close to each other the night before, opened fire with a sharp exchange. The fire grew in intensity, especially on the Union left, where, despite the thick woods, Bragg attempted to outflank General George Thomas's corps. Brigade after brigade was sent in by both sides in an attempt to win the field, but by the end of the day neither side had gained the advantage.

That night Thomas ordered his men to dig entrenchments, while Rosecrans reinforced him. Meanwhile, the majority of Longstreet's two

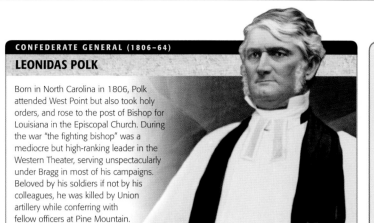

### CONFEDERATE GENERAL (1806–64)
### LEONIDAS POLK

Born in North Carolina in 1806, Polk attended West Point but also took holy orders, and rose to the post of Bishop for Louisiana in the Episcopal Church. During the war "the fighting bishop" was a mediocre but high-ranking leader in the Western Theater, serving unspectacularly under Bragg in most of his campaigns. Beloved by his soldiers if not by his colleagues, he was killed by Union artillery while conferring with fellow officers at Pine Mountain.

" There is **not a man in the right wing** who has any **fight in him**."

BRAGG'S COMMENT TO LONGSTREET ON THE ECHELON ATTACK, SEPTEMBER 20, 1863

failed to pierce the enemy line, he had arranged his brigades in columns.

When Longstreet ordered the attack at about 11:30 a.m., it hit the enemy with tremendous power and, unfortunately for Rosecrans, precisely in a location that one of his divisions

Thomas held firm, his valor and steadfast conduct later earning him the nickname "The Rock of Chickamauga."

As the sun set on the bloodsoaked field, Thomas finally withdrew his weary command and joined the rest of the Union army at Chattanooga.

The Battle of Chickamauga proved to be a bloody Confederate tactical victory that temporarily shifted the course of the Civil War in the Western Theater.

### BRAGG AND ROSECRANS STUNNED
Rosecrans **had escaped destruction** and now lay behind Chattanooga's fortifications. Both Longstreet and Nathan Bedford Forrest urged Bragg to move at once against the Union forces before they could recover, but the Confederate commander was **as stunned in victory as Rosecrans was in defeat**. Incredulous about his superior's inertia, Forrest asked, "What does he fight battles for?" In the weeks to come the **strategic fruits of Chickamauga** slipped away into an exhausting **siege of Chattanooga 214–15 »**, which the Confederates were ill-equipped to undertake. As for Rosecrans, Lincoln wrote that he behaved "**confused and stunned** like a duck hit on the head."

### CHATTANOOGA UNDER SIEGE
Rosecrans found himself and his army in an unusual situation after Chickamauga: a Union army occupying a Southern city **besieged by a Confederate army**. By October, food was running out for the Union troops, and Bragg had cut off all but one **fragile supply line** across the Cumberland Mountains. If Rosecrans were to surrender, **Union momentum would have stalled considerably**.

Revolving cylinder

**Colt 1853 revolving rifle**
Developed by Samuel Colt, this rifle had a revolving cylinder that increased its rate of fire. It was used by the 21st Ohio Volunteers at Chickamauga.

divisions joined Bragg's army. Bragg decided to renew the fight the next day with an army-wide attack *en echelon*, in a slightly staggered right-to-left sequence. Leonidas Polk's wing was to start the action on the right, which would progress to Longstreet, who controlled the left.

On the morning of September 20, Polk's divisions—which had started late—battered against Thomas's entrenched defenders to no avail. Bragg became frustrated with Polk and canceled the echelon attack, and ordered Longstreet to assault with everything he had. Unbeknownst to either Bragg or Rosecrans, Longstreet had prepared his troops for such an event. Perhaps remembering Pickett's Charge, where linear formations had

had just mistakenly vacated. Poor staff work was responsible for an error that now left a quarter-mile (402-m) gap in the Union lines, and as Longstreet's veterans poured through, they demolished the Federal right and sent one-third of Rosecrans's army running for their lives to Chattanooga. The Union commander joined the flight, abandoning his army to its fate.

Longstreet now smelled a victory of strategic proportions and ordered in his last reserves, at the same time begging Bragg to send him reinforcements. When none materialized, a nonplussed Longstreet pressed forward nonetheless, only to come up against Thomas's corps. The Union general had ordered them to make a rearguard stand on Horseshoe Ridge, in a bid to protect the retreat of the rest of the army. Longstreet responded by throwing assault after assault, but each time

### The second day at Chickamauga
The course of the battle changed on September 20, when Longstreet's men broke through and routed the Union right. But George Thomas's men on Horseshoe Ridge held out bravely until dusk, when the battle ended.

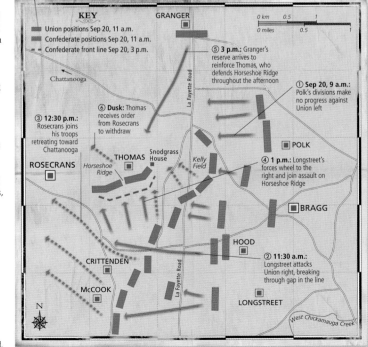

KEY
- Union positions Sep 20, 11 a.m.
- Confederate positions Sep 20, 11 a.m.
- Confederate front line Sep 20, 3 p.m.

GRANGER

0 km    0.5    1
0 miles    0.5    1

Chattanooga

⑤ **3 p.m.:** Granger's reserve arrives to reinforce Thomas, who defends Horseshoe Ridge throughout the afternoon

① **Sep 20, 9 a.m.:** Polk's divisions make no progress against Union left

③ **12:30 p.m.:** Rosecrans joins his troops retreating toward Chattanooga

⑥ **Dusk:** Thomas receives order from Rosecrans to withdraw

ROSECRANS    Horseshoe Ridge    THOMAS    Snodgrass House    Kelly Field    POLK

④ **1 p.m.:** Longstreet's forces wheel to the right and join assault on Horseshoe Ridge

BRAGG

HOOD

CRITTENDEN

② **11:30 a.m.:** Longstreet attacks Union right, breaking through gap in the line

La Fayette Road

McCOOK

LONGSTREET

N

West Chickamauga Creek

**THE ROCK OF CHICKAMAUGA**
After the Union army's defeat at Chickamauga, General George Thomas and his men covered the retreat of the rest of the army into Chattanooga. They held fast on high ground until sunset, earning Thomas his nickname. Although he lost the battle, his desperate stand saved the Army of the Cumberland from destruction. This scene is from a 33-panel panorama, painted by William D. T. Travis after the war, which tells the story of the Army of the Cumberland.

**The summit of Lookout Mountain**
Capturing Lookout Mountain from the Confederates was no mean feat for General Hooker's troops. Much of the ground that they covered was rough, steep, and rocky, while some areas were deeply wooded.

# The Chattanooga Campaign

AFTER ≫

Union general William Rosecrans's army, besieged in the Southern town of Chattanooga, had to be relieved or the momentum gained earlier in the summer of 1863 was in danger of being lost. Ulysses S. Grant—in command of the new Division of the Mississippi—was sent to take care of the situation.

In mid-October, Lincoln reorganized the Union's Western geographic command structure. The new Division of the Mississippi, which included all of the territory between the Appalachians and the river, fell under the command of Ulysses S. Grant. With his new authority, Grant headed for Chattanooga, where he relieved Rosecrans and installed George Thomas as commander of the Army of the Cumberland.

One Federal officer wrote about Grant's arrival, "We began to see things move. We felt that everything came from a plan." By the end of October the crisis in the city had ended. New supply lines were in place, and 17,000 fresh troops had arrived under Sherman. Union morale was restored. Conversely, their Confederate foes, though still occupying the high ground that dominated the Federal positions, were again outnumbered and racked with command and morale problems.

## The Battle of Lookout Mountain

Grant's plan to push the Rebels off their positions overlooking the town and return to a war of maneuver was simple: attack both flanks and fix the enemy in the center. Major General Joseph

## BEFORE

Despite their victory, the Confederates were in disarray after Chickamauga ≪ 210–11. Meanwhile, the Union leadership rallied to redeem what it could from defeat.

### SITUATION AT CHATTANOOGA
Bragg's lethargy after **Chickamauga** caused his principal generals to turn against him, claiming he was **unfit for command**. But Longstreet did not wish to take command of the army himself, so Bragg was retained, **leaving morale low**.

Bragg's forces **controlled the high ground to the east of Chattanooga** and prevented supplies from reaching the town except by one circuitous route. This did not allow enough food to reach the besieged Union army. Lincoln knew something must be done. The man he chose to resolve the crisis was **Ulysses S. Grant**, fresh from **his triumph at Vicksburg** ≪ 190–93.

**Union camp in Chattanooga**
Once inside the city, soldiers hastily knocked down many houses for firewood and shelters while making their camp. In the foreground, planks still covered in wallpaper form part of the fencing.

Hooker, now reinstated to command the Eleventh and Twelfth Corps, would attack Bragg's southern flank, anchored on Lookout Mountain; Thomas and his Army of the Cumberland would keep Bragg's attention in front of Missionary Ridge; and Sherman would attack the northern flank at Tunnel Hill.

On November 24 Hooker and Sherman moved out. Hooker sent three divisions against Lookout Mountain, and with the help of some fog, drove off its Southern defenders at the cost of only 500 casualties. Next morning a huge Union flag could be

**CRACKER LINE** The new supply line to Chattanooga established at the end of October, so called for the hardtack that was the staple of army rations.

seen waving from the summit, inspiring Federal troops in the valley below. Sherman's men initially made good progress toward their objective, but poor reconnaissance led them to the wrong position. Undeterred, on November 25 they fiercely attacked General Patrick C. Cleburne's Confederate division, but were repeatedly repulsed. Cleburne commanded the best division in Bragg's army, and his men had not been infected with low morale. They resolutely held their ground, inflicting heavy casualties on Sherman's troops. Meanwhile, Grant became increasingly frustrated. After storming Lookout Mountain, Hooker had been held up by poor roads and a destroyed bridge, and now Sherman was stalled.

## Missionary Ridge
At 2 p.m., Grant ordered Thomas to probe the Confederate center at Missionary Ridge, to relieve some of the pressure on Sherman. Though Grant had intended a limited assault, Thomas sent four divisions—23,000 men—headlong against the heavily defended ridge. It could have been a repeat of Pickett's Charge, the ill-fated Confederate attack at Gettysburg, but instead, eager to redeem themselves from the stain of Chickamauga, the soldiers of the Army of the Cumberland surged over three Confederate trench lines, up the rugged slope of the imposing ridge, and over its

The Union victory at Chattanooga reinforced Northern resolve after the defeat at Chickamauga had tarnished the jubilation of Gettysburg and Vicksburg.

### REACTIONS NORTH AND SOUTH
**Copperhead politicians** who appeared poised to win control of **key districts** in the lower North now doubted their chances. In the South the **optimism of September** was destroyed.

### CONFEDERATE MORALE EBBS
The Confederates now faced the possibility of an **invasion into northern Georgia**, while Joseph E. Johnston replaced Bragg in command.

summit. They captured much of Bragg's artillery and sent his defenders fleeing to northern Georgia. Watching the assault go forward from their command post, Grant and Thomas were astonished. An angry Grant asked who had ordered the

**Establishing the "Cracker Line"**
Union troops floated downstream from Chattanooga in flatboats under cover of darkness to drive off Confederates guarding Brown's Ferry. They then built a pontoon bridge that became a crucial link in the new supply line.

men up the ridge, and Thomas denied that he had done so. Had the men failed, Thomas's career would have ended right there. His troops had prevailed, however, partly because of confusion among Southern soldiers in trenches at the base of the ridge about how many volleys to fire before retreating, and partly because of the poor placement of the Rebel artillery.

Low morale in Bragg's army also had much to do with their defeat. Bragg wrote to Davis after the battle, "The disaster admits of no palliation. I fear we both erred in the conclusion for me to retain command here." Casualties were relatively light for both armies at this point, but the results were clear: Grant had won the battle and opened a path to Atlanta and the Southern heartland.

### Watching the action
Grant, Thomas, and their staffs watch the fighting on Missionary Ridge, as depicted in this lithograph from a painting by Swedish-born Thure de Thulstrup.

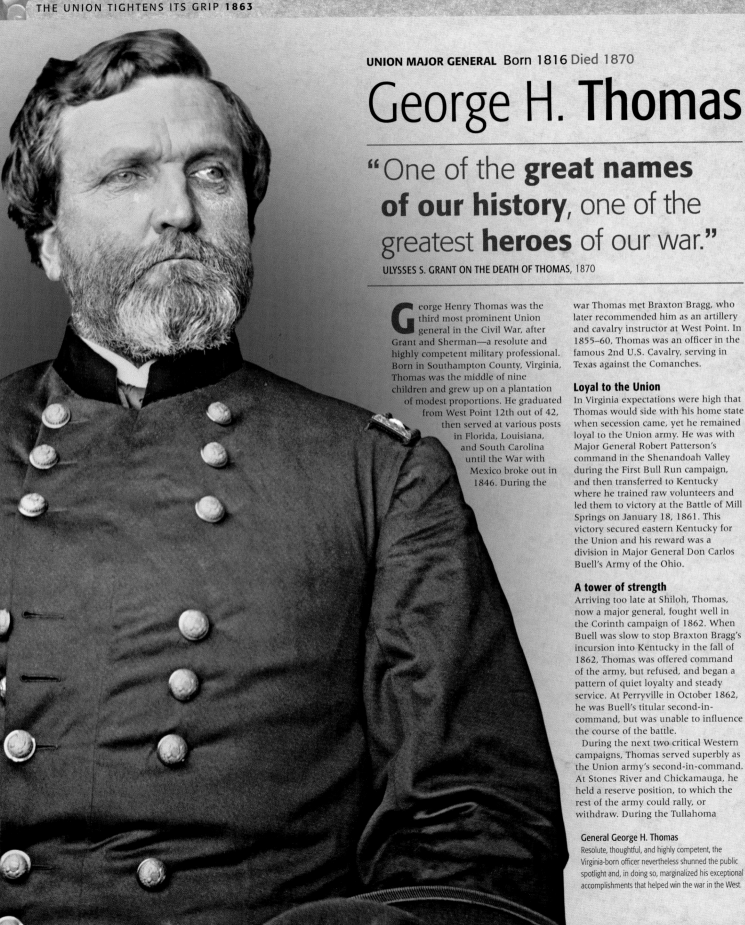

UNION MAJOR GENERAL Born 1816 Died 1870

# George H. Thomas

## "One of the **great names of our history**, one of the greatest **heroes** of our war."

ULYSSES S. GRANT ON THE DEATH OF THOMAS, 1870

George Henry Thomas was the third most prominent Union general in the Civil War, after Grant and Sherman—a resolute and highly competent military professional. Born in Southampton County, Virginia, Thomas was the middle of nine children and grew up on a plantation of modest proportions. He graduated from West Point 12th out of 42, then served at various posts in Florida, Louisiana, and South Carolina until the War with Mexico broke out in 1846. During the war Thomas met Braxton Bragg, who later recommended him as an artillery and cavalry instructor at West Point. In 1855–60, Thomas was an officer in the famous 2nd U.S. Cavalry, serving in Texas against the Comanches.

### Loyal to the Union
In Virginia expectations were high that Thomas would side with his home state when secession came, yet he remained loyal to the Union army. He was with Major General Robert Patterson's command in the Shenandoah Valley during the First Bull Run campaign, and then transferred to Kentucky where he trained raw volunteers and led them to victory at the Battle of Mill Springs on January 18, 1861. This victory secured eastern Kentucky for the Union and his reward was a division in Major General Don Carlos Buell's Army of the Ohio.

### A tower of strength
Arriving too late at Shiloh, Thomas, now a major general, fought well in the Corinth campaign of 1862. When Buell was slow to stop Braxton Bragg's incursion into Kentucky in the fall of 1862, Thomas was offered command of the army, but refused, and began a pattern of quiet loyalty and steady service. At Perryville in October 1862, he was Buell's titular second-in-command, but was unable to influence the course of the battle.

During the next two critical Western campaigns, Thomas served superbly as the Union army's second-in-command. At Stones River and Chickamauga, he held a reserve position, to which the rest of the army could rally, or withdraw. During the Tullahoma

#### General George H. Thomas
Resolute, thoughtful, and highly competent, the Virginia-born officer nevertheless shunned the public spotlight and, in doing so, marginalized his exceptional accomplishments that helped win the war in the West.

**Thomas's military headquarters**
This small cabin on Snodgrass Hill served as Thomas's headquarters during the final phases of the Battle of Chickamauga, in which the general and his men resolutely repulsed repeated Confederate assaults.

## TIMELINE

- **July 31, 1816** Born, one of nine children, on a small plantation in Southampton County, Virginia.
- **1836** Enters West Point. Befriends William Tecumseh Sherman while at the Academy.
- **1840** Graduates from West Point. Commissioned Second Lieutenant in the 3rd Artillery.
- **1841–1842** Serves with distinction in the Seminole Wars.
- **1843–1847** Posted to forts and installations including Fort McHenry and New Orleans.
- **1847** Serves at Monterrey and Buena Vista during the War with Mexico. Brevetted to major.

**BATTLE OF BUENA VISTA**

- **1851–1853** Instructor of Cavalry and Artillery at West Point. Marries Frances Lucretia Kellogg.
- **1855** Serves at Fort Yuma and is promoted to major in the Regulars, then posted to the 2nd Cavalry in Texas where he serves under both Col. Albert S. Johnston and Lt. Col. Robert E. Lee.
- **1861** Remains loyal to the Union when Virginia secedes. Promoted to colonel and then brigadier general. Serves in the Shenandoah Valley and then transfers west to Kentucky.
- **January 1862** Promoted to major general following the Battle of Mill Springs—the first decisive Union victory in the West.
- **January–October 1863** Takes command of Fourteenth Corps after the Battle of Stones River. Leads Tullahoma Campaign. Succeeds Rosecrans as commander of the Army of the Cumberland.
- **1864** Leads Army of the Cumberland as part of Sherman's advance on Atlanta. Blocks Hood's advance into Tennessee after the fall of Atlanta, and decisively defeats him at Nashville.
- **1865** Remains in Tennessee as commander of occupation forces at war's end.
- **March 28, 1870** Dies in San Francisco, after serving his last years as commander of the Military Division of the Pacific.

> "[He] looked upon the **lives of his soldiers** as **a sacred trust**, not to be carelessly **imperiled**."
>
> LT. COL. HENRY VAN NESS BOYNTON, WHO FOUGHT UNDER THOMAS IN 1863

Campaign that preceded Chickamauga, it was Thomas who led the Union advance, and at Chattanooga in November 1863, it was the Army of the Cumberland, now under his direct command, that stormed the Rebel works on Missionary Ridge, winning the battle for Ulysses S. Grant.

Thomas's Army of the Cumberland was also central to General Sherman's Atlanta Campaign in 1864. The logistical, intelligence, and staff work of Thomas's command were integral to the advance against Joseph E. Johnston, and later it was Thomas who stopped the Confederates under John Bell Hood at Peachtree Creek on July 20, in their first attempt to end the siege of Atlanta.

When Hood moved north to sever Sherman's supply and communication lines in Tennessee, Thomas was sent to stop him. At Franklin on November 30, John M. Schofield, under Thomas's command, repulsed Hood's assaults and bought time for Thomas to concentrate all available forces at Nashville. Thomas waited almost too long to assemble his troops, so Grant became impatient and actually began the journey west to intervene personally. But Thomas had the situation under control, and as soon as the wet ground had dried sufficiently for a successful assault, he attacked Hood in a vicious two-day battle that all but destroyed the Confederate Army of Tennessee. For this victory Thomas now became known as "The Sledge of Nashville."

### Shunning politics

Thomas was a key general in the Reconstruction period. He earned a reputation as a friend to freed slaves and refused promotion to lieutenant general, knowing the Senate had to confirm the appointment and would necessarily politicize it. To that end he burned his private papers before his death in 1870, from a stroke.

### Roll of honor

A certificate presented to the next of kin acknowledged the services of those who died serving the Army of the Cumberland. Six scenes from the Civil War depict the call to arms, fields of combat, and grieving relatives.

**THOMAS'S MEMORIAL IN WASHINGTON**

# The Railroad in War

**The introduction of railroads revolutionized how future wars would be fought. The vast geographic scope of the Civil War meant that they were the only realistic way to move troops with any measure of speed. Never again would army logistics rely solely on wagons and roads.**

## BEFORE

By 1860, America had some 30,000 miles (48,280km) of railroad tracks, mostly owned by a dozen prominent companies.

**NORTHERN DEVELOPMENTS**

Every year, **new engine designs increased the power of locomotives** and also their load capacity. In the North, where **industry and population centers demanded rapid transit** and banks wanted to invest in the infrastructure, **railroads flourished** and expanded.

**SOUTHERN RAILROADS**

The railroads of the South were chiefly built **to transport cash crops**, such as cotton, from plantations to riverfront depots or seaports. **Track gauges were often incompatible** between lines, and there was a shortage of locomotives. Few railroads crossed state borders or rivers.

### TECHNOLOGY

### RAIL POWER

Union victory clearly "rode the rails." Not only were Northern commanders able to use the railroads to transport heavy artillery to and from the battle zone, they also created mobile "railroad batteries" (above)—heavy guns mounted on flatcars, often protected by armor. Unlike horse-drawn artillery, railroad batteries could be fired on the move.

The North's technological and strategic advantage in using the railroads was vital to its victory. In 1864, rail capacity was the sole reason that General William T. Sherman could contemplate his advance on Atlanta, despite Rebel cavalry raids that targeted Federal railroads. General Ulysses S. Grant's siege of Petersburg relied heavily upon the efficient operation of the U.S.M.R.R.

In the first year of the war, the Lincoln administration recognized the need for an overarching authority to harness the power of the Northern railroads. The Railroad and Telegraph Act, passed on January 31, 1862, gave President Lincoln full authority to nationalize any railroad and impress its equipment or employees into federal service. The War Department wasted no time in creating the United States Military Railroads (U.S.M.R.R.) in February, and Lincoln placed Daniel C. McCallum, an experienced railroad administrator, at its head. McCallum and the U.S.M.R.R coordinated all rail supply of the federal armies with the private companies. They also repaired and made use of damaged Southern railways, as well as building and operating military lines.

Assisting McCallum in his task was a retinue of officers and directors, of whom the most prominent was the German-born Herman Haupt, the U.S.M.R.R's chief of construction and maintenance in Virginia. Through most of 1862 and 1863, Haupt supplied several Union armies by railroads. In the Second Bull Run campaign, General Stonewall Jackson destroyed a critical bridge in northern Virginia, which temporarily crippled Union resupply efforts. Haupt and his motley crew of railroad workers, engineers, and contraband slaves repaired the bridge in two weeks using only green lumber and saplings. This feat prompted Lincoln to say, "I have seen the most remarkable structure that human eyes ever rested upon. That man, Haupt, has built a bridge … over which loaded trains are running every hour, and upon my word, gentlemen, there is nothing in it but beanpoles and cornstalks."

### Against the odds

For the South, the history of railroad construction and operation during the Confederacy's brief lifespan was one of initial success followed by steady deterioration. President Jefferson Davis, like Lincoln, realized the significance that railroads would have and, in December 1862, the Confederate War Department appointed Colonel William M. Wadley as supervisor "of all railroads in the Confederate States."

Until late 1863, Wadley and his successor Frederick W. Sims managed impressively, despite a chronic lack of raw materials or factories, to repair lines and equipment. In July 1861, General Joseph E. Johnston moved an army in the Shenandoah Valley by rail to arrive just in time for the First Battle of Bull Run. In the spring of 1862, railroads in Mississippi, Louisiana, and Alabama allowed General Albert S. Johnston to assemble his army before the Battle of Shiloh. In July 1862, more than 30,000 men under General Braxton Bragg were dispatched by rail from Mississippi to Chattanooga in under two weeks. This speedy transfer allowed Bragg to launch his invasion of Kentucky in the fall that year.

A year later, many key railheads had fallen to the Union. In 1864, even more were seized, including the critical junction at Atlanta. This effectively crippled the South's ability to use its railroads and gave the Union armies more opportunities to redeploy troops for decisive victories.

> **21,276** The miles of railroad track (34,240km) in the Union states at the start of the war in 1861, compared with the Confederate states' 9,000 miles (14,500km).

**Mobile mortar**
In 1864–65, Union forces used this railcar-mounted 13-in (330-mm) mortar—nicknamed the "Dictator" or "Petersburg Express"—to pound the Confederate-held town of Petersburg from a distance of 2.5 miles (4km).

**Line repairs**
Union laborers work on track near Murfreesboro, Tennessee, after the Battle of Stones River in late January 1863. A new railroad had to be built from Nashville to enable the Union army to continue its advance.

## AFTER

By the end of the Civil War, the North had built an additional 4,000 miles (6,440km) of railroad, while the South had built only 400 miles (644km).

**WEB OF IRON**

The massive reach of the U.S.M.R.R. network covered **16 Eastern and 19 Western railroads**. Along these ran **419 locomotives** pulling **6,330 cars**.

The growth of the railroad industry during the war created investment opportunites for postwar entrepreneurs willing to bet their livelihoods on the iron horse. Such celebrated figures as **Cornelius Vanderbilt, Andrew Carnegie, and Andrew Mellon all invested heavily in railroad lines**. One such, the **Transcontinental Railroad**, completed in 1869, **connected the Pacific Coast states** with the rest of the nation.

**Over the bridge**
The locomotive "Fire Fly," built for the U.S.M.R.R. in 1862 by the Philadelphia-based Norris Locomotive Works, crosses a bridge on the Orange and Alexandria Railroad in Virginia.

**BEFORE**

In previous wars, commanders had relied on messages being hand-delivered. By the outbreak of the Civil War, civilian telegraph services could send messages by wire.

**THE PONY EXPRESS**

**PREWAR TELEGRAPHY**

Using special codes to send messages over long distances, the telegraph was not a new technology in 1861, having existed since the 1840s. More than 50,000 miles (80,467km) of wire were already in place when war broke out, with 1,400 stations employing 10,000 people. The famous **Pony Express**, which was set up in April 1860 to provide a fast mail service between the East and West coasts, **was put out of business** by a transcontinental telegraph line that was completed in fall 1861.

Like the railroad, **nearly all telegraph infrastructure and investment was located in the Northern states**, with only about 10 percent delegated to the South. However, what did exist there was immediately put to use.

# Communications

**The telegraph system revolutionized command and control procedures during the Civil War. Both the Union and the Confederacy made increasing use of this new technology, but the North was able to harness it most effectively. A signaling system using flags and lamps was also used on the battlefield.**

Following in the wake of the Union and Confederate armies were the telegraph services, putting up poles and wires needed for sending messages to and from the front. The telegraph system allowed commanders-in-chief based far from the battlefield to exercise direct control over operational and even tactical events, and to keep abreast of important developments as they arose. Presidents Abraham Lincoln and Jefferson Davis both used the telegraph extensively to keep in close communication with the commanders of their principal field armies, and their commanders, in turn, developed ciphers and codes to transmit and receive messages in secret. Both sides developed wiretapping and code-cracking capabilities during the war, but the information gleaned from these methods rarely created decisive military results.

In October 1861, the Lincoln administration established the U.S. Military Telegraph Service (U.S.M.T.S.).

**The federal telegraph service**

The U.S.M.T.S. was initially reliant on civilian companies, with the government placing it under the control of the Quartermaster Corps. The service was operated by civilian personnel, most of whom were employees of the major

**Telegraph operator**
Both sides in the war used telegraphy to send or "wire" messages over long distances. Most operators were civilians, and the messages relayed everything from train dispatches to battle plans.

**Repairs to the line**
A telegraph company employee carries out the vital task of repairing the lines. This was dangerous work, often performed under fire from the enemy or in areas where enemy guerrilla fighters operated.

> **Future conflicts came to rely on the instantaneous communications provided by the telegraph.**
>
> **POPULARITY OF THE TELEGRAPH**
> The telegraph continued to be the **preferred method of fast communication** over long distances in the postwar United States. Its successful use by both sides during the war also impressed European military observers, who **believed it would become indispensable**. Helmut von Moltke, future Chief of the Prussian General Staff, viewed the telegraph and railroad as linchpins for success in modern war, and used both to strategic effect in the **Austro-Prussian (1866) and Franco-Prussian (1870–71) wars.**

**Night lantern**
A member of the Signal Corps uses a kerosene lantern on a long handle for wigwag signaling at night, moving the lantern back and forth to send messages. Beside him a man watches for the replies.

telegraph companies before the war, and included a significant percentage of women. Military supervision of an essentially civilian organization caused friction. Major General George Meade frequently complained about the cavalier attitude of telegraphers in the U.S.M.T.S., who occasionally left for home during critical moments of campaigns. By 1864, however, enough trained personnel were employed to maintain a continuous service. During the siege of Petersburg, General Ulysses S. Grant enjoyed almost uninterrupted telegraph communication with both Washington, D.C., and his subcommanders operating throughout the South.

## Confederate telegraph services

Two civilian companies operated in the South prior to the war, one of which was the American Telegraph Company. The director of its southern branch was Dr. William S. Morris. In 1862, Postmaster General John H. Reagan made Morris "agent of the Confederate States," responsible for managing all military telegraph lines in the South. Morris and Reagan shared the duties.

For the first three years of the war, the telegraph allowed Jefferson Davis to keep in close touch with his primary generals, although some of them disliked communicating under the

watchful eye of Morris and Reagan. General P. G. T. Beauregard, for example, created his own telegraph system around the Charleston defenses. Rebel snags with the telegraph were primarily caused by supply shortages and raiders.

As Confederate fortunes waned, Southern telegraph operators rose to the challenge and kept the lines humming. During General Sherman's March to the Sea, Georgia's agent advised: "Keep your offices open night and day. If you have to fall back, take it coolly and gather up the operators, instruments, and material as you retire."

**15,000** The number of miles (24,140km) of new telegraph lines that were constructed in the North during the Civil War, in addition to existing commercial systems.

## Signaling on the battlefield

In 1856, Lieutenant Albert J. Myer had created a system of "wigwag" signaling, which was used before the introduction of the telegraph. Standing on a platform, the signaler waved a single flag (or a lantern at night) back and forth to represent different letters of the alphabet. By 1861, the system had been accepted by the U.S. Army and Myer had been made founding officer of the U.S. Signal Corps. On both sides, officers were assigned at various levels of army command to facilitate communication primarily on

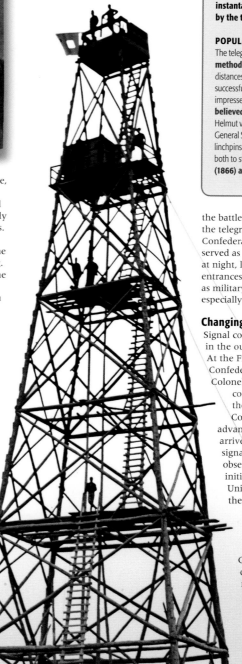

**Telegraph tower**
Signalers man a tall telegraph tower at the Bermuda Hundred, on the left of the Union line near the Appomattox River, Virginia. These tall towers were used to send telegraphs over short distances.

the battlefield and on the march, where the telegraph was less useful. In the Confederacy, signal corpsmen also served as guides for blockade runners at night, lighting lanterns along entrances to the major ports, and as military intelligence gatherers, especially in Virginia.

## Changing the course of battle

Signal corpsmen proved decisive in the outcome of some key battles. At the First Battle of Bull Run, a Confederate wigwag team warned Colonel Nathan Evans that his command had been turned by the Union army, allowing the Confederates to delay the Union advance until reinforcements arrived. At Gettysburg, Union signalers on Little Round Top observed General Longstreet's initial movements toward the Union left on July 2, whereupon the Confederate general redirected his troops—using up most of the day and losing the element of surprise, which allowed General George Meade to deploy enough soldiers to meet the Southern attack. Often targeted by enemy snipers, signal corpsmen on both sides suffered disproportionately high losses but provided invaluable services throughout the Civil War.

C. Schussele
Philada. 1862

**GREAT INVENTORS OF THE AGE**
This pantheon of American inventors was painted by Christian Schussele in 1862 under the title *Men of Progress*. Several were responsible for technological advances that changed the nature of warfare. Samuel Colt, the gun manufacturer, stands third from the left, John Ericsson, designer of the ironclad *Monitor*, is to the right of the pillar in the center, while the dominant figure, seated with a mane of white hair, is Samuel Morse, inventor of the electric telegraph.

**Recapturing a wagon train**
Union cavalry recapture a wagon train seized by a Mosby raiding party. Guerrillas and partisan rangers operated behind enemy lines, using their intimate knowledge of the terrain to great effect.

« **BEFORE**

American history offered many examples of successful insurgency and counter-insurgency that both sides in the Civil War could draw on for guidance and inspiration.

**THE REVOLUTIONARY WAR**
During the American Revolution, **irregular fighters** such as Francis Marion (famous as the "Swamp Fox"), Thomas Sumter, and Daniel Morgan led their men on repeated and successful **hit-and-run raids** against British supply columns and isolated outposts.

A precedent had therefore been established, especially in the South, for guerrilla-type warfare. The memory of Kings Mountain and Cowpens, where regular British and Loyalist units were decimated by **effective guerrilla tactics**, lived long in the Southern mind, as did the exploits of those who led these and other operations.

**MEXICAN WAR COUNTERINSURGENCY**
The regular U.S. Army undertook numerous antiguerrilla and stability operations during the War with Mexico (1846–48) that, if not codified, still **created procedures** for combating an irregular threat. General Winfield Scott issued a series of directives on **how to deal with enemy insurgents** and the civilians who harbored them that **effectively eliminated** most irregular Mexican resistance.

# Guerrillas and Partisans

**The formal battles of the Civil War were accompanied by many smaller-scale raiding operations against military and civilian targets. These were often little different from banditry and, with the escalating reprisals that they provoked, left a legacy of bitterness in many areas long after the war.**

As soon as the Union armies occupied parts of the South, Southern irregulars rose up to oppose them. Drawing on memories of earlier conflicts, intimate knowledge of local conditions, and aware of every ambush site and hiding place, these fighters focused on lightning-fast raids against isolated garrisons and supply areas. They rarely wore uniforms and easily blended back into the civilian population.

Lincoln's administration at first advised restraint and kindness toward both captured irregulars and the civilian populations that harbored them. The idea was to restore good faith and belief in the Federal government.

Before he rose to lead the Army of the Potomac, Major General George B. McClellan exhorted his

command in Western Virginia to "use every effort to conciliate the people and strengthen Union feeling." He continued, "You are here to protect, not destroy. Take nothing, destroy nothing … respect the right of private opinion."

Unfortunately for the Union, such policies, along with Lincoln's propensity to pardon captured guerrillas who had been sentenced to death, generally emboldened local irregulars instead of pacifying them. Even when Union garrisons rebuilt shattered Southern infrastructure, fed the destitute, and regulated otherwise broken-down municipal authorities, any goodwill this generated among the local population was often dissipated by vicious guerrilla

**Face of a guerrilla**
Alfred Waud's contemporary drawing of a hard-featured guerrilla with slouch hat and unkempt appearance gives a hint of the life he led, driven by a zeal to damage the Union cause and protect Southern autonomy.

reprisals against civilians who had cooperated with Union forces. Union officers in parts of Virginia, Tennessee, and Mississippi especially struggled as they occupied, evacuated, and then reoccupied locales after major Confederate incursions. As General Benjamin Butler said in 1862, "It is cruel to take possession of any point unless we continue to hold it with an armed force, because when we take possession of any place those well disposed will show us kindness and good wishes; the moment we leave, a few ruffians come in and maltreat every person who has not scowled at the Yankees."

## Bloody Missouri

This problem was most manifest in the border state of Missouri, which had a mix of extreme secessionist enclaves and pro-Union communities supported by loyal Kansas militias and occupying Federal troops. A miniature civil war broke out in the absence of formal military operations, and the barbarities committed by both sides were extreme.

**1,200** The number of Union troops said to have been captured, killed, or wounded by John Mosby's partisan rangers by late 1864, although there were never more than 400 men in his command.

When some sisters and wives of men in the band of notorious guerrilla leader William C. Quantrill died while incarcerated by Union authorities, the enraged Quantrill brought together every Confederate guerrilla group in Missouri he could find and led 450 men on a raid of revenge against the Free-Soil town of Lawrence, Kansas. On August 21, 1863, Quantrill and his men reached the unprotected hamlet, deep in Union territory. He ordered, "Kill every male and burn every house." Three

### The Sack of Lawrence

In the raid on Lawrence of 1863, Quantrill's men not only burned most of the town and killed the men, they also robbed the bank. Among the raiders were future outlaws Cole Younger and Frank James.

hours later, 182 men and boys lay dead and 185 buildings had burned to the ground. Union reprisals failed to track down many of those responsible, but succeeded in killing and burning out even more civilians. In Missouri, the Civil War was also a war on civilians.

Because of the escalating difficulties in dealing with Confederate guerrillas, Union officers began to take matters more and more into their own hands. Guerrillas caught destroying Federal property were frequently shot on sight, and captured irregulars were often killed "while trying to escape." Disloyal civilians were blacklisted and had their freedoms curtailed.

Increasingly, the treatment of Southern civilians and irregular fighters depended on the judgment of the local Union commander. The War Department began to follow their lead in late 1862, calling all Southern guerrillas "the common enemies of mankind [to be] hunted and shot without challenge wherever found."

### The Lieber Code

Two consequences emanated from the hardening Northern measures: a Federal code of conduct and a new, hybrid Confederate formation. The first, entitled the Lieber Code after its author, legal expert Francis Lieber, was transformed into Union army doctrine as General Orders 100. It classified Southern irregulars into four distinct

categories—partisan rangers, guerrillas, "war rebels," and bushwhackers—and suggested courses of action on how to deal with each. Lieber advised that rangers and guerrillas should generally be treated as prisoners of war, but for the other two groups, which, he said, ignored the rules of war and failed to wear uniforms, harsh treatment was permitted. These official guidelines sanctioned local Union officers' counterinsurgency efforts, and marked the first time that a government had issued a document that regulated military conduct toward irregulars and enemy civilians.

The second consequence was the formal creation, in the spring of 1862, of Confederate partisan ranger units. Jefferson Davis and Robert E. Lee recognized the value of quasi-military units working independently behind enemy lines and answering to formal military authority. The most famous of these units was Colonel John S. Mosby's battalion of Virginia Partisan Rangers, which so terrorized Union authorities in northern Virginia that the area was referred to as "Mosby's Confederacy." Mosby repeatedly raided the B&O Railroad, attacked Union wagon trains, and tied down thousands of Union troops in garrison duty. Ulysses S. Grant was so bothered by Mosby's activities that in 1864, he ordered all captured Mosby partisans to "hang without trial," thereby violating the spirit of the Lieber Code.

> ## "**Irrepressible Mosby** is again in the saddle carrying **destruction** and **consternation** in his path."
> *RICHMOND WHIG*, OCTOBER 18, 1864

**AFTER**

Tough Union antiguerrilla actions mirrored Grant's and Sherman's ruthless operations. In some areas, these combined to leave a legacy of hatred and lawlessness.

NOTICE!
$5,000 REWARD
will be paid for the capture of

COLE YOUNGER
MEMBER OF THE NOTORIOUS JAMES BAND!
WANTED FOR TRAIN ROBBERY
SIGNED
ST. LOUIS MIDLAND RAILROAD

**COLE YOUNGER, TRAIN ROBBER**

### GUERRILLAS INTO OUTLAWS
When the Confederate armies surrendered, many guerrilla fighters, such as the James brothers and Cole Younger, **turned to crime**; others joined the **Ku Klux Klan 340–41 ≫**.

### LONG-LIVED ANIMOSITIES
Long after the Civil War, many Southern communities harbored a **bitter animosity against Yankees**. Wherever the irregular war had been most intense, this animosity persisted the longest and **hampered reconciliation**.

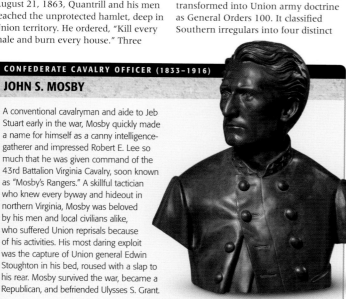

**CONFEDERATE CAVALRY OFFICER (1833–1916)**

## JOHN S. MOSBY

A conventional cavalryman and aide to Jeb Stuart early in the war, Mosby quickly made a name for himself as a canny intelligence-gatherer and impressed Robert E. Lee so much that he was given command of the 43rd Battalion Virginia Cavalry, soon known as "Mosby's Rangers." A skillful tactician who knew every byway and hideout in northern Virginia, Mosby was beloved by his men and local civilians alike, who suffered Union reprisals because of his activities. His most daring exploit was the capture of Union general Edwin Stoughton in his bed, roused with a slap to his rear. Mosby survived the war, became a Republican, and befriended Ulysses S. Grant.

# Operations in the Indian Territory and Texas

**Although they were fought with great intensity, the battles in the Western states and territories took place on a much smaller scale than those in the East. Neither did they conclude with such overwhelming Union success as eventually resulted in other areas.**

**Native American fighter**
Units of Native Americans from the Indian Territory fought on both sides in the Civil War, which divided tribes and pitted them against each other. The units were known for their fearless mounted rifle attacks.

## BEFORE

Texas and Arkansas both declared for the South and Missouri was the focus of much prewar conflict. Other territories had divided loyalties.

### THE INDIAN TERRITORY
The Indian Territory (modern-day Oklahoma), was occupied primarily by **eastern Native American tribes** that had been **forcibly relocated** there in the 1830s. When the war broke out, most of these tribes **sided with the Confederacy** in the belief that Southern independence represented their **best chance for greater autonomy**.

### THE BATTLE OF PEA RIDGE
On March 7, 1862 a Union army routed a numerically superior Confederate force at Pea Ridge, the battle in northern Arkansas often termed **the Gettysburg of the West**.

**THE BATTLE OF PEA RIDGE**

The Trans-Mississippi area—Texas, Arkansas, the Indian Territory, Missouri, and Kansas—did not see as much conventional fighting as the Western and Eastern Theaters. But military events in this region affected Northern and Southern morale, and thus the political arena. Confederate domination of this region would spell political disaster for Abraham Lincoln, whereas Union control could hamper, but not cripple, the Rebel struggle for independence.

| 28,700 | The approximate number of Native Americans who served either in the Union army or the Confederacy. |

### Pea Ridge and Prairie Grove
The Union victory at Pea Ridge opened up much of Arkansas to Union conquest and wrecked Confederate strategic aspirations in the Trans-Mississippi. General Earl Van Dorn and his routed army transferred to the eastern side of the Mississippi in the late spring of 1862. Arkansas now lay open to Federal invasion, and after some initial skirmishes in the north of the state, Union general James G. Blunt pushed south. At Prairie Grove on December 7, 1862, he and his small army defeated a hastily created Confederate force led by General Thomas C. Hindman.

### The Confederates react
Despairing over the series of defeats in Missouri and Arkansas, Jefferson Davis reorganized the command structure of the Trans-Mississippi Department in the spring of 1863, giving overall command to General Edmund Kirby Smith. But before Smith could gather sufficient forces to challenge the Federals, they had marched quickly toward Little Rock, the Arkansas capital.

General Blunt, with a small Union army of 3,000, had entered the Indian Territory in April 1863 and reestablished a post at Fort Gibson, briefly held by the Union in 1861. After reoutfitting his men, he planned to march on Little Rock as part of a pincer strategy focused on the Arkansas capital. The Confederates, however, were not going to give him that opportunity. Brigadier General Douglas Cooper collected about 6,000 troops at Honey Springs, a Rebel outpost some 20 miles (32km) southwest of Fort Gibson, and awaited only the arrival of another 3,000 to launch an attack on Blunt. Cooper's men were badly armed—only 75 percent of them had serviceable firearms, many of these being old smoothbore guns. They also had only four artillery pieces. But the Texas cavalry and Cooper's Choctaw and Chickasaw regiments had high morale and were aching for a fight. Blunt, now well aware of the danger if the two Confederate commands united, launched a preemptive attack on Cooper on July 17. Outnumbered two to one, Blunt's multiracial command was composed of a black regiment, some Unionist Native American units, and white regiments from the Midwest. As one historian put it, it was "the first rainbow coalition." Blunt's men were almost all armed with the rifled Springfield musket and had good artillery. For the first half of the battle, which lasted four hours,

**General James G. Blunt**
A prominent abolitionist before the war, Blunt helped raise Native American regiments for the Union in 1861 and led them to victory at Maysville in October 1862.

their technological advantage was nullified by the Rebel numbers and terrain. A determined midday assault by the 1st Kansas Colored Infantry against the center of the Confederate line, however, forced the outgunned Southern artillery to withdraw, and with it the rest of Cooper's force.

Though Honey Springs would be the largest battle ever fought in the Indian Territory, in terms of casualties the engagement was insignificant— Union losses were fewer than 200 and Confederate casualties no more than 600. But the Union victory all but assured the conquest of Little Rock. About seven weeks later, on September 10, the Arkansas capital fell to the other half of the Union pincer movement, placing three-quarters of Arkansas firmly under Northern control.

Honey Springs also demonstrated, at a sensitive point in the war, the fighting prowess of black Northern troops. Blunt lavished praise on the 1st Kansas in his report but unfortunately the deeds of the regiment were destined to pass almost unnoticed by the Northern public, because the 54th Massachusetts' assault on Fort Wagner, South Carolina, occurred one day later.

### The Battle of Sabine Pass
The Union went on the offensive in Texas as well, occupying the major port of Galveston in October 1862. Having then lost the port to a miraculous Confederate counterattack on January 1, 1863, Major General Benjamin Butler, commanding Union forces in New Orleans, decided to retake it.

On September 7, four gunboats, 19 transports, and 5,000 bluecoats arrived offshore from Sabine Pass, which commanded a seaborne approach toward Galveston. There were only 47 Southern gunners in the main fort commanding the pass, but they had relieved their boredom over the previous months with target practice. Each of the guns was accurately registered to hit a designated target in the Texas Channel. The practice paid off when, waiting patiently until the Union gunboats passed directly by those

### Delaware scouts
The Delaware overwhelmingly backed the Union during the war, and acted as scouts for the army. Although originally from the East, by 1860 most of the Delaware people had been moved to the Indian Territory. .

targets, the Confederate commander suddenly ordered his six guns to open fire. The Union ships were pummeled with direct hits that put the first two gunboats out of action and blocked the channel.

Instead of landing the infantry at an alternate location, the Yankees were overawed by the fierce defense, and turned their remaining boats around, sailing back to New Orleans. Jefferson Davis and the Confederate Congress acclaimed Sabine Pass as a glorious victory and pumped up its significance to help restore lagging Southern morale. Special medals for each of the 47 gunners were struck to commemorate the heroic defense, and Galveston eventually remained the only major Southern port still under Confederate control at the end of the war.

## AFTER

**Most of Texas remained in Confederate hands to the end of the war. The valuable eastern districts produced cotton and grains and maintained slavery well into 1865.**

### RED RIVER CAMPAIGN
Frustrated by the failure at Sabine Pass and determined to win east Texas and subdue the rest of Louisiana, the Lincoln administration authorized an incursion into **northwestern Louisiana** in the spring of 1864. Two Union armies **converged on Shreveport** from Arkansas and New Orleans. Both were plagued by **poor leadership** and, meeting determined Confederate resistance, were **forced to retreat**.

### MISSOURI AND THE INDIAN TERRITORY
Both regions were, in effect, occupied by Union forces until the end of the war, though General **Sterling Price's 1864 raid** into Missouri briefly drove Union forces out. In both places, however, a **vicious guerrilla war** erupted that pitted neighbors and relatives against each other.

# "They **fought like veterans** … their **line unbroken** … Their **coolness and bravery** I have never seen surpassed."
MAJOR GENERAL JAMES G. BLUNT, ON THE 1ST KANSAS COLORED INFANTRY

### The Second Battle of Galveston
During the battle, the USS *Westfield* ran aground and was blown up to prevent its capture. The charge detonated too soon, and Captain Renshaw and his crew, escaping in lifeboats, were killed in the blast.

# The Gettysburg Address

**On November 19, 1863, President Abraham Lincoln delivered a brief speech that would soon become one of the most famous in American history. Delivered at the dedication of the Soldiers' National Cemetery in Gettysburg, Pennsylvania, this two-minute discourse came to be known as the Gettysburg Address.**

**"**Four score and seven years ago our fathers brought forth on this continent a new nation, conceived in liberty, and dedicated to the proposition that all men are created equal. Now we are engaged in a great civil war, testing whether that nation, or any nation, so conceived and so dedicated, can long endure. We are met on a great battle-field of that war. We have come to dedicate a portion of that field, as a final resting place for those who here gave their lives that that nation might live. It is altogether fitting and proper that we should do this.

But, in a larger sense, we can not dedicate, we can not consecrate, we can not hallow this ground. The brave men, living and dead, who struggled here, have consecrated it, far above our poor power to add or detract. The world will little note, nor long remember what we say here, but it can never forget what they did here. It is for us the living, rather, to be dedicated here to the unfinished work which they who fought here have thus far so nobly advanced. It is rather for us to be here dedicated to the great task remaining before us—that from these honored dead we take increased devotion to that cause for which they gave the last full measure of devotion—that we here highly resolve that these dead shall not have died in vain—that this nation, under God, shall have a new birth of freedom—and that government of the people, by the people, for the people, shall not perish from the earth.**"**

ABRAHAM LINCOLN, AT THE DEDICATION OF THE SOLDIERS' CEMETERY, GETTYSBURG, NOVEMBER 19, 1863

**"**Abraham Lincoln is the idol of the American people at this moment. Anyone who saw and heard as I did, the hurricane of applause that met his every movement at Gettysburg would know that he lived in every heart. It was no cold, faint, shadow of a kind reception—it was a tumultuous outpouring of exultation ... at the sight of a man whom everyone knew to be honest and true and sincere in every act of his life, and every pulsation of his heart.**"**

FROM THE JOURNAL OF BENJAMIN BROWN FRENCH, COMMISSIONER OF PUBLIC BUILDINGS FOR THE NORTH

**Immortal words**
Lincoln's address followed a two-hour speech by the orator Edward Everett, the main speaker of the day. The eloquent words of the president (hatless at center, looking down) acquired yet more significance as time went on.

# 5

# GRANT, SHERMAN, AND TOTAL WAR

## 1864

A cohesive strategy in place at last, the Union pressed the Confederacy so hard that by year's end great stretches of Virginia and Georgia lay in ruins, one major Confederate army was destroyed at Nashville, and the other caught in a death grip in the Petersburg trenches.

**« A decisive battle**
At the end of 1864, George H. Thomas's Union forces held Nashville while John Bell Hood's Army of Tennessee dug in on the heights to the south. Waiting for the right moment to attack, Thomas burst from the city's fortifications and in two days of battle—December 15–16—routed the Confederates, effectively ending the war in the Western Theater.

# GRANT, SHERMAN, AND TOTAL WAR

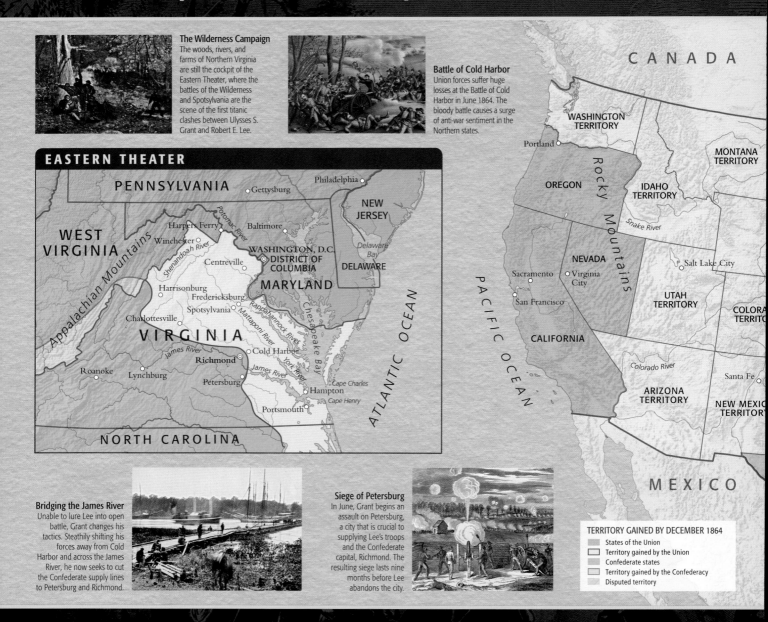

**The Wilderness Campaign**
The woods, rivers, and farms of Northern Virginia are still the cockpit of the Eastern Theater, where the battles of the Wilderness and Spotsylvania are the scene of the first titanic clashes between Ulysses S. Grant and Robert E. Lee.

**Battle of Cold Harbor**
Union forces suffer huge losses at the Battle of Cold Harbor in June 1864. The bloody battle causes a surge of anti-war sentiment in the Northern states.

## EASTERN THEATER

PENNSYLVANIA
Gettysburg
Philadelphia
NEW JERSEY
WEST VIRGINIA
Harpers Ferry
Potomac River
Baltimore
Winchester
Shenandoah River
Delaware Bay
WASHINGTON, D.C.
DISTRICT OF COLUMBIA
DELAWARE
Centreville
MARYLAND
Harrisonburg
Fredericksburg
Spotsylvania
Rappahannock River
Mattaponi River
Charlottesville
Chesapeake Bay
VIRGINIA
Appalachian Mountains
James River
Cold Harbor
York River
Roanoke
Richmond
Lynchburg
James River
Petersburg
Cape Charles
Hampton
Cape Henry
Portsmouth
ATLANTIC OCEAN
NORTH CAROLINA

CANADA
WASHINGTON TERRITORY
Portland
MONTANA TERRITORY
Rocky Mountains
OREGON
IDAHO TERRITORY
Snake River
NEVADA
Sacramento
Virginia City
Salt Lake City
San Francisco
UTAH TERRITORY
COLORADO TERRITORY
PACIFIC OCEAN
CALIFORNIA
Colorado River
Santa Fe
ARIZONA TERRITORY
NEW MEXICO TERRITORY
MEXICO

**Bridging the James River**
Unable to lure Lee into open battle, Grant changes his tactics. Stealthily shifting his forces away from Cold Harbor and across the James River, he now seeks to cut the Confederate supply lines to Petersburg and Richmond.

**Siege of Petersburg**
In June, Grant begins an assault on Petersburg, a city that is crucial to supplying Lee's troops and the Confederate capital, Richmond. The resulting siege lasts nine months before Lee abandons the city.

**TERRITORY GAINED BY DECEMBER 1864**
- States of the Union
- Territory gained by the Union
- Confederate states
- Territory gained by the Confederacy
- Disputed territory

**B**y 1864, the war had become a grinding, exhausting struggle, but once Ulysses S. Grant was elevated to overall command of the Union's field armies in March, a coordinated strategy to defeat the Confederacy was finally at hand. In early May, over a front extending from Virginia to Georgia, Union armies marched off nearly in unison to begin the spring campaign. The major effort was in Virginia, where Grant made his headquarters and came to grips with Robert E. Lee's Army of Northern Virginia. For six weeks a series of terrible but inconclusive battles—the Wilderness, Spotsylvania, Cold Harbor—raged across the woods and fields north of Richmond. At the same time, General William T. Sherman grappled with the Confederacy's other great army, General Joseph E. Johnston's Army of Tennessee. After three months of battle and maneuver, Sherman had the Rebels backed up against the gates of Atlanta. Though

# 1864

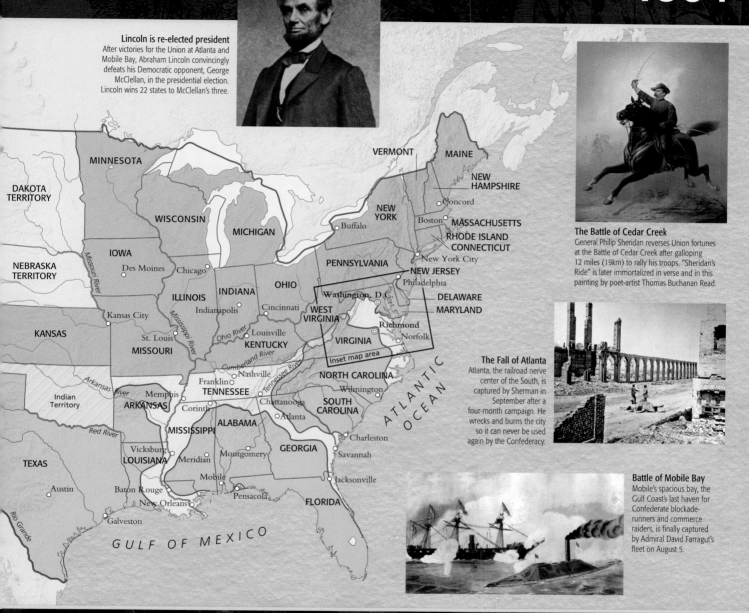

**Lincoln is re-elected president**
After victories for the Union at Atlanta and Mobile Bay, Abraham Lincoln convincingly defeats his Democratic opponent, George McClellan, in the presidential election. Lincoln wins 22 states to McClellan's three.

**The Battle of Cedar Creek**
General Philip Sheridan reverses Union fortunes at the Battle of Cedar Creek after galloping 12 miles (19km) to rally his troops. "Sheridan's Ride" is later immortalized in verse and in this painting by poet-artist Thomas Buchanan Read.

**The Fall of Atlanta**
Atlanta, the railroad nerve center of the South, is captured by Sherman in September after a four-month campaign. He wrecks and burns the city so it can never be used again by the Confederacy.

**Battle of Mobile Bay**
Mobile's spacious bay, the Gulf Coast's last haven for Confederate blockade-runners and commerce raiders, is finally captured by Admiral David Farragut's fleet on August 5.

Johnston was soon replaced by the aggressive General John Bell Hood, Confederate attacks around the city's perimeter were repulsed, and Atlanta fell to Sherman on September 1. Before the year ended, Hood would bleed the remnants of the Army of Tennessee dry on the battlefields of Franklin and Nashville. As summer turned to fall, while Grant slowly crushed Lee's army in the trenches at Petersburg, he other components of his grand strategy were also falling into

place. Admiral David Farragut had won the contest for Mobile Bay. General Philip Sheridan had cleared Rebel forces from the Shenandoah Valley, torching the "Breadbasket of the Confederacy" along the way. Sherman would soon undertake a scorched earth campaign across Georgia, intended to break the Southern will. When Lincoln won re-election in November it was due in no small part to these victories on the battlefield. The end of the war was in sight.

# TIMELINE 1864

The Wilderness Campaign ▪ **Battle of Cold Harbor** ▪ The Valley Campaign ▪ **Siege of Petersburg** ▪ Battle of the Crater ▪ Sinking of the CSS *Alabama* ▪ Battle of Mobile Bay ▪ The Atlanta Campaign ▪ Franklin and Nashville ▪ **March to the Sea**

| JANUARY | FEBRUARY | MARCH | APRIL | MAY | JUNE |
|---|---|---|---|---|---|
| **JANUARY** Though little large-scale fighting takes place, there is much skirmishing from Virginia to Tennessee and Mississippi. | **FEBRUARY 14–20** A raiding column from Vicksburg, led by General William T. Sherman, arrives at Meridian, Mississippi. For five days it destroys Confederate railroads, depots, storehouses, arsenals, and hospitals. | **MARCH 1–2** General Judson Kilpatrick leads a Union cavalry raid on Richmond, Virginia, hoping to free its prisoners of war; instead his forces are turned aside and scattered by local militiamen. | **APRIL 8–9** Confederates at Mansfield and Pleasant Hill decisively halt Banks's advance up the Red River toward Shreveport, Louisiana. | **MAY** Grant's coordinated offensives against the various Confederate armies get underway. **MAY 5–6** In Virginia, Grant and Lee first clash in the fiery Battle of the Wilderness. | **JUNE 3** At Cold Harbor, Lee repulses Grant with heavy losses. **JUNE 8** In Baltimore, Lincoln is nominated for a second term by the National Union Party. |
| **JANUARY 20** Confederate worries that Union naval vessels might try to capture Mobile Bay in Alabama are justified when Admiral David Farragut makes a reconnaissance in force. | | | | **MAY 7** In Georgia, Sherman confronts General Joseph E. Johnston's Army of Tennessee. **MAY 8–21** In Virginia, the "Bloody Angle" struggle on May 12 marks the fiercest fighting in the Battle of Spotsylvania. | **JUNE 10** In Mississippi, Forrest wins a brilliant victory over superior numbers at Brice's Crossroads. |
| **JANUARY 29–31** The Union bombardment of Charleston, South Carolina, begun five months earlier, intensifies with 583 rounds being fired in three days. | **FEBRUARY 17** For the first time in history a submarine, the CSS *Hunley*, sinks a warship, the USS *Housatonic*, outside Charleston Harbor. | ⌃ Grant appointed commander-in-chief **MARCH 9** General Ulysses S. Grant is appointed commander-in-chief of all Union armies. | | **MAY 11** A major Union cavalry raid on Richmond, led by General Philip Sheridan, encounters General Jeb Stuart's Confederate horsemen at Yellow Tavern, only 6 miles (9.5km) north of the city. Stuart is mortally wounded. May 13-15 | **JUNE 18** After unsuccessful Union attempts to capture the rail junction of Petersburg, Virginia, Grant and Lee settle down to a nine-month siege. |
| ANDERSONVILLE PRISON | **FEBRUARY 20** The Battle of Olustee, the major engagement of the war in Florida, results in a Union defeat. | **MARCH 10** General Nathaniel Banks undertakes a two-month, joint army-navy expedition up Louisiana's Red River to thwart Confederate forces in the Trans-Mississippi western United States. | ⌃ Nathan Bedford Forrest **APRIL 12** Confederate forces commanded by Forrest capture Fort Pillow on the Mississippi River, massacring many of the black soldiers in the garrison. | **MAY 16** At the Battle of Drewry's Bluff south of Richmond, General P. G. T. Beauregard compels Union General Benjamin Butler to retreat to the Bermuda Hundred peninsula. ⌄ Benjamin Butler | ⌃ Union sailor's cap **JUNE 19** Off the coast of France, USS *Kearsarge* sinks the commerce raider CSS *Alabama*. |
| | **FEBRUARY 27** The first Union prisoners arrive at Andersonville, or Camp Sumter, in Georgia. | **MARCH 16** Confederate General Nathan Bedford Forrest mounts a month-long raid into Union-held Tennessee and Kentucky. | **APRIL 20** Confederate forces and the ironclad ram CSS *Albemarle* recapture the port of Plymouth, North Carolina. | | **JUNE 27** In Georgia, Johnston checks Sherman at Kennesaw Mountain. |

⌃ Plan of Andersonville prison

> "Not expecting to see you again before the Spring campaign opens, **I wish to express** ... my **entire satisfaction** with what you have done up to this time."

LINCOLN'S FINAL DIRECTIVE TO GRANT ON THE EVE OF THE 1864 CAMPAIGN

| JULY | AUGUST | SEPTEMBER | OCTOBER | NOVEMBER | DECEMBER |
|---|---|---|---|---|---|

**JULY 11**
Confederate General Jubal Early leads his small Army of the Valley to the outskirts of Washington, D.C., creating consternation in the capital.

**AUGUST 5**
Admiral David Farragut finally leads a fleet of 18 Union warships past forts and through minefields to win the Battle of Mobile Bay.

**SEPTEMBER 1**
Having been defeated at Jonesboro, Hood evacuates Atlanta and Union troops soon capture the city.

**SEPTEMBER 17**
Frémont drops out of the presidential race, leaving the contest to Lincoln and McClellan.

**OCTOBER**
Sheridan burns barns and mills in Virginia's fertile Shenandoah Valley, destroying the "Breadbasket of the Confederacy."

**DECEMBER 15–16**
In a series of assaults on Hood's positions before Nashville, General George Thomas's Union forces overwhelm and nearly destroy the Confederate Army of Tennessee.

≫ Sheridan's sword

**AUGUST 18–19**
Union forces capture the Weldon Railroad leading south from besieged Petersburg, Virginia.

**SEPTEMBER 19**
General Philip Sheridan's Army of the Shenandoah smashes Jubal Early's Confederates at the Third Battle of Winchester.

**OCTOBER 19**
After Confederates launch a surprise attack, Sheridan rallies his demoralized troops and decisively wins the Battle of Cedar Creek.

**DECEMBER 21**
Sherman's "March to the Sea" reaches its end with the capture of Savannah, Georgia.

≪ William T. Sherman

**JULY 20–28**
Replacing Johnston as commander of the Army of Tennessee, General John Bell Hood launches a series of bloody battles—Peachtree Creek, Decatur, and Ezra Church—that fail to destroy Sherman's forces.

According to the Law of Ohio you must write the name of your County on your ticket.

UNION

THE UNION MUST BE PRESERVED AT ALL HAZARDS
[Extract from McClellan's Letter of Acceptance.]

**Democratic Ticket**
Election Tuesday, Nov. 8, 1864.
FOR PRESIDENT,
GEO. B. M'CLELLAN,
OF NEW JERSEY.
FOR VICE PRESIDENT,
GEO. H. PENDLETON,
OF OHIO.
FOR ELECTORS
Of President and Vice President of the United States
CHARLES REEMELIN

**OCTOBER 23**
General Sterling Price, leading a massive Confederate raid into Missouri, is defeated at Westport, near Kansas City.

≫ Price's Raid

**NOVEMBER 8**
Abraham Lincoln is reelected president of the United States.

**NOVEMBER 16**
After burning much of Atlanta, Sherman embarks on his "March to the Sea," cutting a swath of destruction through Georgia.

**DECEMBER 24–25**
Nearly 60 Federal warships bombard Fort Fisher outside Wilmington, North Carolina, but General Butler's assault force is repulsed by Confederates. The fiasco will lead to Butler's being removed from command.

**JULY 30**
Union forces explode an enormous mine beneath Confederate lines at Petersburg, but their subsequent attacks are decisively defeated at the Battle of the Crater.

≫ Laying powder kegs at Petersburg

**SEPTEMBER 29–30**
Grant launches coordinated attacks at each end of the Richmond-Petersburg line—at Fort Harrison to the north and at Peebles' Farm to the southwest.

≫ McClellan's presidential campaign ticket

**AUGUST 31**
General George McClellan is nominated for president by the peace-leaning Democratic Party.

**OCTOBER 27**
Union attempts to cut the Boydton Plank Road, a vital supply route for Lee's beleaguered army at Petersburg, are frustrated by Confederate troops.

**NOVEMBER 30**
Hood, embarking on an ambitious scheme to drive north through Tennessee to the Ohio River, attacks strong Union positions at Franklin and loses nearly a third of his infantry.

John Bell Hood ≫

# Lincoln Prevails

**Since 1864 was an election year, President Abraham Lincoln needed to swing the balance of the war permanently in the Union's favor or face defeat at the polls. With the political parties splintering over the war, Lincoln sought salvation in a new general, Ulysses S. Grant.**

On the evening of March 8, 1864, at a glittering White House reception, Abraham Lincoln had his first good look at its guest of honor, General Ulysses S. Grant. The short, slightly stooping figure was disappointing in appearance, except for his blue eyes, which to one army officer always suggested a man determined to drive his head through a brick wall. It was an expression that Lincoln welcomed.

Grant won battles. That was why Lincoln had now appointed him general-in-chief of all Union armies. Together they planned how to win the war that year. Grant advocated coordinated advances: south to Mobile; southeast to Atlanta, to cut off General Robert E. Lee's supplies; and a three-pronged advance on Lee himself—in his front, up through the Shenandoah Valley, and to his rear via a landing south of Richmond.

### Lincoln's future in the balance
Much depended on the success of Grant's plans. Lincoln was facing a re-election battle, and his party had split over his policies. Hard-line Radical

> **COPPERHEADS** Those Northerners opposed to war with the Confederacy, named for a poisonous snake. They were most numerous in the Ohio River states, with traditional ties to the South.

Republicans, convinced Lincoln had mismanaged the war and could not be re-elected, were decamping to the Radical Democracy Party or "Copperheads." This new party convened in late May in Cleveland, Ohio, and nominated the ever-popular soldier politician, John C. Frémont, for president. Republicans still loyal to Lincoln felt they could not win unless they joined with "War Democrats," who were crossing the party line to disassociate themselves from the Copperheads. The result was called the National Union Party, and it convened in Baltimore during early June. Lincoln was renominated, but Vice President Hannibal Hamlin, a Radical Republican,

was dropped from the ticket. He was replaced by Andrew Johnson, military governor of Tennessee and a leading War Democrat. The National Unionists hoped the new ticket would underscore the national character of the war.

### Esteem for McClellan
Meanwhile, Lincoln sensed that defeat was imminent. Grant's strategy was failing. The death toll at the Wilderness, Spotsylvania, and Cold Harbor had staggered the nation—and still Lee held Grant at bay at Petersburg. General Jubal Early, with but 10,000 Rebels, had threatened to walk into the White House. Widespread discouragement was starting to swell the ranks of the Copperheads. General George B. McClellan, fired by Lincoln in 1862, was riding high in public estimation; as the fatalities mounted he looked ever

**Lincoln campaign button**
Due to the constraints of war, the 1864 electoral campaign produced fewer embossed copper tokens, framed *cartes de visite* (card portraits), and brass pins than did the 1860 race.

## ≪ BEFORE

Abraham Lincoln was elected the 16th U.S. President in November 1860. He won his votes entirely in the North, not being on the ballot in ten Southern states.

### FINDING A GENERAL
On November 5, 1862, Lincoln **dismissed General George McClellan ≪ 64–67** as commander of the **Army of the Potomac**. Dissatisfied with many of his replacements, Lincoln's eye had finally fallen on **Ulysses S. Grant ≪ 196–97** of Vicksburg fame.

### THE GREAT TASK REMAINING
On January 1, 1863, Lincoln issued the **Emancipation Proclamation ≪ 160–61**, freeing slaves in **ten Confederate states**. Despite growing casualty lists and **rising antiwar sentiment** in the North, he was steadfastly dedicated to the war, which he declared in his **Gettysburg Address ≪ 228–29** as "the great task remaining before us."

more attractive as the man to bring the fighting to an end in a manner that would satisfy both South and North.

In August, the Democrats held a convention in Chicago. They, too, were divided over the war. The more moderate Peace Democrats advocated a negotiated peace on terms favorable to the Union, while the Copperheads declared the war a fiasco that should be immediately terminated. The convention sought to bridge the divide by nominating McClellan, a pro-war moderate, while adopting a sweeping peace platform—which McClellan deplored.

## A two-horse race

Frémont saw the Democratic platform as tantamount to "Union with Slavery," and withdrew his candidacy. Winning the war was, to him, more important

An anti-McClellan broadside
To the left, Lincoln stands for "Union and Liberty," shaking hands with free labor. To the right, McClellan, personifies "Union and Slavery," shaking hands with Jefferson Davis, a slave auction in the background.

than winning the presidency. That left Lincoln and McClellan to battle it out. Across the North, campaign ribbons and bunting vied with fall leaves for color. People sported their candidates' badges; broadsides (newspaper bulletins) and cartoons endorsed one nominee and decried the other. In camps and trenches, troops of both North and South huddled around grimy newspapers. Depending

on the camp or trench, the news of General William T. Sherman's taking of Atlanta or General Philip Sheridan's clearing of the Shenandoah Valley was met with either cheers or curses. As the tide of Union victories planned by Grant finally rolled in, it began crushing the hopes of the Confederacy. November 8 was Election Day. After the ballots were counted, Lincoln had won by over 400,000 votes, securing an overwhelming majority in the Electoral College. His soldiers had given him over 70 percent of their support. For the president and his commanding general, the scent of victory was in the fall air.

### Grant at the White House
Peter Rothermel's 1867 painting *The Republican Court in the Days of Lincoln* depicts the reception at which Lincoln welcomed Grant to Washington as the army's new general-in-chief. It still hangs in the White House.

**AFTER**

Lincoln's second inaugural address, on **March 4, 1865**, stressed that Reconstruction of the defeated Confederacy should be undertaken with national healing in mind.

**LINCOLN'S ASSASSINATION**
President Lincoln **served only four months** of his second term. On April 14, just days after **Robert E. Lee's surrender to Grant at Appomattox 316–17 ≫**, Lincoln was **assassinated 320–21 ≫**. Eight months later, on December 18, 1865, the **13th Amendment to the Constitution 308–309 ≫**, abolishing slavery in the United States, was officially enacted.

**LINCOLN'S SECOND INAUGURATION**

## "God gave us Lincoln and Liberty, let us fight for both."
ULYSSES S. GRANT, IN A TOAST DURING THE VICKSBURG CAMPAIGN, FEBRUARY 22, 1863

**Fighting in the Wilderness**
Winslow Homer's *Skirmish in the Wilderness* (1864) shows scattered fighting among the trees—what one soldier called "bushwhacking on a grand scale."

# The Wilderness Campaign

**The duel between generals Robert E. Lee and Ulysses S. Grant commenced with a battle in a tangled woodland called the Wilderness. Fighting resumed in the fields around Spotsylvania Court House, where deadly assaults reached a pitch of sustained ferocity seldom equaled in the war.**

«

## BEFORE

In March 1864, Lincoln put Ulysses S. Grant in charge of all Union armies in the field. Grant's plan called for simultaneous Union advances against Atlanta in the West and against Lee in the East.

### LEE VERSUS GRANT

Grant changed the Union objective from the capture of Richmond to the **destruction of Lee's Army of Northern Virginia**, and established his headquarters with the **Army of the Potomac**, which, in early 1864, was encamped on the Rapidan River. Grant decided to **outflank the Confederate positions** across the river by slipping through the Wilderness on the Confederate right, where a year earlier, at the **Battle of Chancellorsville ‹‹ 174–75**, Lee had **nearly destroyed the Army of the Potomac**.

Before dawn on May 4, 1864, Ulysses S. Grant opened his advance against Robert E. Lee. The first of nearly 120,000 men, 4,300 supply wagons, and 850 ambulances making up the Army of the Potomac crossed the Rapidan River well downstream of Lee's Army of Northern Virginia, nestling behind formidable defenses on the other side.

If Grant could get through the Wilderness, on the Confederate right, before Lee could react, he might lure the Southern general into the open and destroy him. So all day long the blue-clad divisions tramped down the road between walls of somber pines and oak thickets, dense with thorny, foot-entangling vines. It was a "region of gloom and the shadow of death," as one officer put it, and many veterans felt an ominous dread as they went into bivouac that night. Dismayed scouts had reported that Lee, who had been watching the Union army, was on the move, heading swiftly up the Orange Turnpike and Orange Plank Road, parallel tracks that led east into the Wilderness.

## The Battle of the Wilderness

Until James Longstreet's First Corps, marching from a different direction, could join him, Lee would be attacking Grant with only one-third of his opponent's strength. Nevertheless, on the morning of May 5 he slammed into a Federal army that was still deploying to meet him. Union troops in Gouverneur Warren's Fifth Corps tried to stem Richard Ewell's Second Corps' onslaught on the Turnpike; 3 miles (4.8km) away, a single Union division held the Brock Road, running across Orange Plank Road, as A. P. Hill's

### Micah Jenkins's sword

In the din and confusion of Longstreet's May 6 flank attack, South Carolina's General Micah Jenkins was mistakenly but mortally wounded by fellow Confederates.

# "The **incessant roar** of the rifles … men **cheering, groaning,** yelling, swearing, and **praying**!"

PRIVATE THEODORE GERRISH, 20TH MAINE INFANTRY, IN *ARMY LIFE*, 1882

Third Corps bore down on them. Thousands of men on both sides were soon clawing their way through briars and stumbling across ravines, trying to form orderly battle lines. Formations and directions of advance rapidly went astray in the tangled maze of undergrowth.

The confused fighting continued all day. At Grant's headquarters, the general ceaselessly whittled sticks and chain-smoked cigars as he waited for reports. In the woods, the volume of musketry was rapidly becoming a deafening cacophony as yelling men, groping blindly, shot point-blank at muzzle flashes in the gloom—"firing by earsight." Storms of bullets tore through the woods and cut men down in droves. Brush fires

**3,750** The approximate number of men in the two armies who were killed in action in the Battle of the Wilderness. Hundreds of others, recorded as "missing," probably died in the brush fires ignited by the fighting.

W. S. Hancock's Second Corps, at the Brock Road, smashed through the underbrush into A. P. Hill's ragged lines, which broke and fled.

Lee himself rode into the bedlam, trying desperately to rally his troops before all was lost. With only his staff and a single artillery battery standing between his army and disaster, Lee saw that Longstreet's divisions were finally arriving down the Plank Road. "Who are you, my boys?" Lee cried above the uproar. "Texas boys," came the reply. "Texans always move them!" the general shouted, waving his hat, and with a strange light in his eyes began to lead them into battle. Grimy hands tugged at his bridle, as men yelled, "Go back, General Lee! Lee to the rear!"

**Escaping the flames**
As flames swept the thickets, many wounded men, left behind by the ebb and flow of battle, were carried or crawled to safety. But many of those who were unable to move were burned to death.

became runaway infernos, burning to death many of the helpless wounded, whose hideous screams could be heard above the din. Smoke had turned the sun a lurid bloodred long before twilight finally descended and the battle subsided. Weary survivors literally fell to sleep, rifles in hand.

Early on May 6, the fighting resumed as Grant went on the attack. The Union right wing kept up the pressure, then

Brigadier General John Gregg's 800 Texans surged forward and stopped the onslaught, although at a fearful price. Fewer than 250 of the men who charged emerged unscathed.

## Confederate riposte
By mid-morning, some of Longstreet's men had discovered an unfinished railroad cut to the south and, concealed from view, turned Hancock's flank, rolling it up brigade by brigade until the Union troops were in mass retreat. In the din and confusion, some Confederates saw horses galloping toward them through the smoke and

leveled a volley. Among the men and animals left sprawled on the ground were South Carolina's General Micah Jenkins, shot in the head, and Lee's "Old War Horse," Longstreet himself, severely wounded in the neck.

With that the Southern attack faltered; when it was renewed in late afternoon it was decisively repulsed by Federal troops deployed behind breastworks along Brock Road. A roar of musketry to the north was that of John B. Gordon's Georgians trying to outflank the Union right, but the shooting slackened with darkness, with neither side able to break through. A second horrid night descended on the burning, bullet-shredded Wilderness. Grant called off his attacks; Lee dug in.

By dawn on May 7, with both armies well entrenched and the fighting ended for the moment, Grant had made the decision not to retreat, as his predecessors had too often done when faced with a setback. Rather, he planned to slide left and south, ordering the Army of the Potomac's high command to strike that evening for Spotsylvania

### Skeletal remains
Alongside fragments of clothing, cartridge boxes, perforated canteens, rotting shoes, ruined breastworks, and shattered trees, the bones of hastily buried men littered the Wilderness for years.

### Wilderness and Spotsylvania Court House
The two armies first clashed on May 5 in the thickly wooded Wilderness area. Then, on the night of May 7, Grant ordered his army to march southeast to Spotsylvania Court House. The Confederates, however, managed to get there before him. They dug in and repelled a series of desperate Union attacks.

Court House, a hamlet located some 10 miles (16km) to the southeast of the Wilderness battlefield. It stood at a crossroads that controlled the routes to Richmond.

Grant was determined to position his forces between Lee and the Confederate capital. He knew this was the only way he could compel the enemy to fight in the open, and he did not want to see Lee's outnumbered veterans get behind breastworks. The task of prying them out would lead to further grueling and costly fighting. »

**Felled oak**
Now in the American History Museum of the Smithsonian, this 22-in (56-cm) oak tree stump was felled by bullets—testimony to the fierceness of the fighting at the Bloody Angle, a once-peaceful meadow in Virginia.

Grant hoped to begin his maneuver around Lee's right flank without being detected by his adversary. He slipped most of the army behind Hancock's Second Corps, still manning the Brock Road and thus masking the movement. The press of wagons and exhausted men made for slow going. As Grant and his staff rode through the logjams, thousands of begrimed soldiers, seeing his horse was trotting south, raised cheer after lusty cheer. Finally, they were not retreating before the Army of Northern Virginia.

Lee had not failed to spot the clouds of dust from Grant's wagons and felt certain they were heading toward the key point of Spotsylvania He

ordered Richard Anderson, who had replaced Longstreet, to move the First Corps out at dawn. The fires that night, however, still lit up the Wilderness in a terrifying display few of the veterans ever forgot; so Anderson, unable to bivouac his soldiers there, got an early and, in the event, lucky start.

### Lee's response
Throughout the day on May 8, Confederate cavalrymen fought fierce delaying actions, slowed the Union advance, and allowed Anderson's soldiers, hastening down a parallel route, to choose their ground. They arrived at the village minutes ahead of the Union vanguard, and General Jeb Stuart deployed them across the high ground to the west, where they were soon repulsing one piecemeal attack after another. As darkness fell, more and more units were fed into the ensuing fight, each stumbling into position along a lengthening front. As Grant had feared, Lee had his troops dig in.

By morning, a forbidding arc of Confederate earthworks, fronted by abatis (felled treetops) and sharpened

**Confederate fieldworks**
Abatis—obstructions made of felled treetops—and rows of sharpened stakes were erected by Lee's soldiers in front of their earth-and-log breastworks.

**30,000** The casualty total of the two armies at Spotsylvania Court House. Although the Union losses (18,000 killed and wounded) were larger, Lee's much smaller force suffered more heavily in proportion.

stakes, was snaking through the woods and fields. At a 1-mile (1.6-km) bulge in the line, known as the Mule Shoe Salient by the Confederates, these works were dauntingly impressive—packed-earth breastworks framed by log revetments (retaining walls), rifle ports topped by shielding head logs, and stout traverses (intercepting embankments) jutting rearward to protect the defenders against flanking fire or crossfire. However, because the position had been hastily sited in the dark, for all its defenses it had a weakness: a breach by Grant could divide Lee's army.

### Attempted breakthroughs
Having failed to outmaneuver his opponent, Grant hammered away at Lee's defenses. Numerous attacks against the Rebels entrenched on Laurel Hill and the Spindle Farm were ill-coordinated and bloodily repulsed. Then, on the evening of May 10, in the woods across from the Mule Shoe Salient, Colonel Emory Upton quietly packed 12 Union regiments into one dense wedge. Bursting out of the woods, the column charged with such

momentum that it actually breached the salient. Despite its eventual repulse (although the attackers carried with them a number of prisoners), this fleeting success convinced Grant, as a steady rain began falling, to plan a similar, only much bigger, assault, spearheaded by Hancock's Second Corps. The target would be the apex of the salient.

### The Union assault
Dawn on May 12 brought more rain, along with a mist so thick that the Confederates manning the apex defenses barely heard the tramp and splash of innumerable feet until some 20,000 Union soldiers were upon them. If faulty intelligence had not persuaded Lee to remove 22 cannon from the salient, and if many of its defenders had not let their powder get dampened by the rain, the onslaught might have been repulsed.

The Northern attackers easily surmounted the works and were seemingly everywhere, killing or

**General John Sedgwick**
Union Sixth Corps commander General John Sedgwick famously chided troops scurrying for cover from snipers with the words: "They can't hit an elephant at this range." Moments later he was fatally wounded.

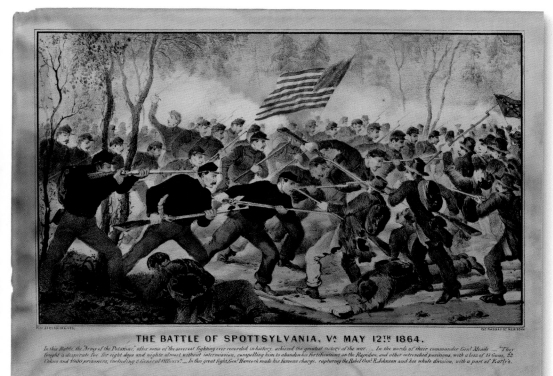

THE BATTLE OF SPOTTSYLVANIA, VA MAY 12TH 1864.

PUB. BY CURRIER & IVES.

62 NASSAU ST. NEW YORK.

In this Battle, the "Army of the Potomac," after some of the severest fighting ever recorded in history, achieved the greatest victory of the war. ... In the words of their commander Genl Meade .... "They fought a desperate foe for eight days and nights almost without intermission, compelling him to abandon his fortifications on the Rapidan, and other intrenched positions, with a loss of 18 Guns, 22 Colors and 8000 prisoners, including 2 General Officers." ... In this great fight, Genl Hancock made his famous charge, capturing the Rebel Genl E. Johnson and his whole division, with a part of Early's.

While Grant struggled ferociously with Lee at Spotsylvania, subsidiary operations were unfolding elsewhere in Virginia.

**DEATH OF STUART**
On the evening of May 12, 1864, Lee's cavalry chief, Jeb Stuart, died in Richmond of a wound received **fighting Sheridan's troopers at Yellow Tavern 248–49 >>**.

**DEFEAT IN THE VALLEY**
Four days later, on May 15, Franz Sigel's Union army was defeated by John C. Breckinridge's Confederates at the **Battle of New Market 254–55 >>**, delaying Grant's hopes for a successful **Shenandoah Valley offensive**.

**BUTLER BOTTLED UP**
On May 5, 1864, General Benjamin Butler landed his **Army of the James** at Bermuda Hundred, but P. G. T. Beauregard's forces were soon able to confine him there **254–55 >>**.

**Battle trophies**
Hancock's May 12 assault on the Mule Shoe Salient was lauded in this 1864 portrayal as the "greatest victory of the war." The fighting was brutal, but Hancock's Second Corps succeeded in capturing thousands of prisoners, including two generals.

# "Nothing in history equals this contest. Desperate, long, and deadly it still goes on …"

CORPORAL WELLES TAYLOR, 110TH PENNSYLVANIA REGIMENT, TO HIS WIFE, MAY 17, 1864

capturing thousands of Rebels. At this desperate hour, it was Lee himself who once more rode into the maelstrom. His hat swept from his head, his silver hair shining, he again tried rallying his broken soldiers. Again the cry rose, "Lee to the rear! Lee to the rear!" but their commander, his blood up, would have none of it until a sergeant firmly took his bridle, leaving General John B. Gordon to coordinate a series of ferocious counterattacks.

Yard by costly yard, the Confederates reclaimed every part of the salient, but the bluecoats only regrouped along the outside face of the breastworks, ready to renew their assault. Lee needed his weary veterans to hold the Northerners while a new defensive line was hastily constructed.

## The "Bloody Angle"
The Confederates held their line, as the musketry roared for most of the day. Nowhere did the fighting rage as violently as it did along the 600-ft (183-m) stretch of works known as the West Angle. There the deafening roar reached a level of sustained frenzy seldom equaled in any conflict. The air,

heavy with rain, exploded with shot and shell. Thousands of soldiers wallowed in the mud and blood, screaming and firing point-blank. A battle mania took hold. Fierce hand-to-hand struggles surged back and forth across the parapet.

The incessant shooting continued for 20 hours and more, each sputtering lull followed by a renewed brutal crescendo. Darkness brought no respite from the slaughter, the muzzle flashes becoming just a continuous sheet of flame. By midnight, nearby trees were crashing to the ground, chipped and sheared in half by the volume of flying lead.

By 4 a.m., the firing had eased. It soon ceased altogether, as the surviving Southerners escaped to Lee's newly completed defensive line, abandoning the salient. Dawn revealed a hideous scene. Before the splintered works the Union dead lay in heaps, so chewed and lacerated by bullets as to be unrecognizable. Among the traverses,

### Coehorn mortars
Some weighing only 296lb (134kg) apiece, these portable artillery pieces were ideally suited for trench warfare. Some Confederates called their arcing, unpredictably falling shells "demoralizers."

Confederate bodies were churned many layers deep and in the mud writhed the wounded. Soon the West Angle would understandably be nicknamed the "Bloody Angle."

## Exhausted stalemate
After the horrific events of May 12, the rain continued to fall while both exhausted armies marked time in the mud. Attempts at maneuver were completely bogged down until a fitful sun at last reappeared. Grant then launched another attack. At daybreak on May 18, after a thundering barrage, 12 Union brigades swept over the wrecked and abandoned salient, still littered with corpses, toward Lee's final

defensive line, which was bristling with cannon. But the Confederate artillery alone was enough to shatter the onslaught, their infantry never even raising a rifle.

Failing to pry Lee out of his works, Grant began shifting his forces eastward, sidling them past Lee's entrenched right flank. On May 19, a large Rebel force did emerge to investigate what the Union Army was doing. The bloody but inconclusive fight at the Alsop and Harris farms was the final clash in the battles around Spotsylvania Court House. By May 21, Grant had his men hurrying south for the North Anna River, still aiming to get between Lee and Richmond.

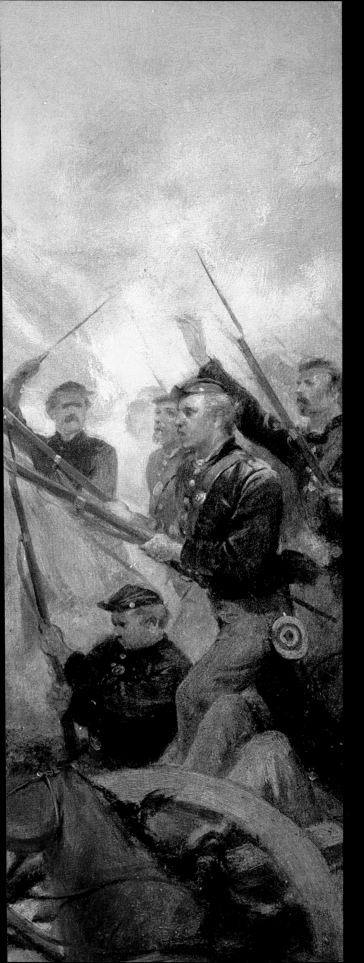

# In the **Trenches** at Spotsylvania

**During the Battle of Spotsylvania—May 8–12, 1864—Union General Winfield S. Hancock seized Confederate entrenchments known as the Mule Shoe Salient. The Confederates fought back, however, and an encounter on the northwest face of the salient on May 12 created the "Bloody Angle." Here, in the most brutal, close-quarter fighting, blood tinged red the soil of Virginia as thousands of soldiers died.**

**"**Infantrymen, from opposite sides of the works, climbed up and fired into the faces of their opponents; they grappled one another and attempted to drag each other across the breastworks; bayonet thrusts were made through crevices; the continuous musketry fire cut off large trees standing in the line of the works, the dead and the dying had to be flung to the rear to give room for the living, fighting ones, in the trenches and, to add to the horrors of combat, a cold, heavy rain set in and partly filled the trench, where the combatants stood, until they seemed to fairly run with blood … the writer, who was on this field of awful combats, does not believe that human ear ever listened to a more steady and continuous roar of musketry and artillery than that which rose from the field of fierce contention, from the dawning to the day until late in the afternoon.**"**

JEDEDIAH HOTCHKISS, CONFEDERATE TOPOGRAPHER, ON THE "BLOODY ANGLE," FROM *CONFEDERATE MILITARY HISTORY*, 1899

**"**No tongue can describe the horrors of the scene around me. Dead and dying men by scores and hundreds lie piled upon each other in promiscuous disorder. God has seen fit so far to spare me, for which I truly feel thankful. I cannot even attempt to give you a slight idea of this field of death. All around you lie the unmistakable evidences that death is doing its most frightful work. Do not worry about me. We have driven the enemy at every point, but Oh! at what a sacrifice of life … I am more dead than alive. We have no regiment. It is so scattered that hardly a dozen can be got together. So fearful has been our loss, that it now seems we have no place here: but we shall all find enough to do … the rebels fight like devils! We have to fairly club them out of their rifle pits. We have taken thousands of prisoners and killed an army; still they fight as hard as ever.**"**

DANIEL HOLT, ASSISTANT SURGEON WITH THE 121st NEW YORK VOLUNTEER INFANTRY, IN A LETTER TO HIS WIFE, FROM *A SURGEON'S CIVIL WAR*, 1994

**Fleeting victory**
General Hancock (mounted) led the overwhelming attack on the Mule Shoe Salient on the Confederate line. But his unexpected success led to disorganization among his forces, and days of bitter fighting followed.

# Photography in the War

**The American Civil War was the first conflict to be thoroughly documented by the camera.**
**Thanks to such photographers as Mathew Brady and Alexander Gardner, many of its images**
**are among the world's most moving and memorable views of war in the 19th century.**

*Carte de visite*
This photographic card depicts a Union soldier. Such inexpensive portrait cards were extremely popular with soldiers, and could be sent through the mail in an ordinary envelope.

**« BEFORE**

Only two decades old, photography on the eve of the Civil War had attracted a mass following.

**WET-PLATE PHOTOGRAPHY**
Wet-plate photography **took hold in the 1850s**. A glass plate coated in collodion (a mixture of bromide and iodides) was dipped in a photosensitive silver nitrate solution and exposed in the camera. Some versions produced single positive images, others negatives from which prints could be made.

**WAR PHOTOGRAPHY**
Although a few photographs were made during the **War with Mexico** (1847–48), it was in the **Crimean War** (1853–56) that British photographer Roger Fenton, with **more than 350 negatives**, pioneered war photography.

**ILLUSTRATED JOURNALS**
There were no means of reproducing photographs in journals—the scenes had first to be **engraved on wood**. The mainstays of such popular magazines as *Harper's Weekly* were talented sketch artists, such as Alfred Waud, and the engravers who brought their work to the public.

I n January 1858, Mathew Brady opened a photographic studio in Washington, D. C., hiring a young Scotsman named Alexander Gardner to run it. The most famous photographer in America, New York-based Brady had made his name with his portraits of the illustrious men and women of the era.

**From portraits to battlegrounds**
People saw their likenesses in delicate ambrotypes, each a unique image on glass produced by the wet-plate collodion process and enclosed in a small case, or on popular *cartes de visite*, photographic visiting cards consisting of prints made from negatives and often collected in leather albums.

The business of portraiture was booming by the time the Civil War began. Photographers set up makeshift studios wherever the soldiers pitched their tents. Many portraits taken of soldiers were tintypes. A less expensive alternative to ambrotypes, tintypes were also produced using the wet-plate collodion process, but a thin sheet of blackened iron replaced glass as the image substrate, making them more robust than ambrotypes. They could be mailed safely to sweethearts and loved ones. But whatever the format, hundreds of thousands of small portraits were made during the Civil War. Many survive, and though their subjects' identities may have long

faded away, their images remain, some elegant and refined, others tremulously hopeful, still others swaggering, brandishing swords or pistols—all insisting, in the words of one historian: "I was here. Remember me when I'm gone."

As well as being the first conflict to have its participants thus immortalized, the Civil War was also the first to have its field operations

**1,000,000** The estimated number of **photographs made during the war, over 90 percent of which were portraits.**

Plate holder

Camera back

Camera case

Lens

Focusing lever

Shutter

Bellows for focusing

**Wet-plate camera**
A mahogany-encased wet-plate camera of Civil War vintage. After a sensitized glass plate was inserted into the plate holder, the holder would be slotted into the back of the camera and the lens focused with the focusing lever.

**A photographic record**
Published in 1866 and accompanied by explanatory text, the 100 mounted photographs in Alexander Gardner's *Photographic Sketchbook of the War* came to define how Americans envisioned the conflict.

documented. In 1861, Brady was determined to photograph every facet of the war, dispatching teams of photographers to cover as many armies as he could get permits for. Most of the leading cameramen of the day, including Gardner, Timothy O'Sullivan, George Barnard, and James Reekie, worked for Brady at one time or another. But every image produced by a photographer on his payroll was nevertheless credited "Photo by Brady," perhaps because he bore the considerable expense of putting them in the field. Gardner eventually left to set up his own shop, enticing O'Sullivan and others to join him.

### Field activity

Brady's access to the war was not exclusive. Other photographers were active, some under contract to the government. Captain Andrew Russell shot the railroads, trestle bridges, and supply depots of the Railroad Construction Corps, as well as military burials, gun emplacements, and the burned ruins of Richmond. Still others were employed at Union headquarters, photographing maps and plans for distribution to staff officers.

## "I had to go. A **spirit in my feet** said 'Go,' and I went."
MATHEW BRADY

In the South, A. D. Lytle of Louisiana worked for the Confederate Secret Service, slyly documenting Union activities in occupied Baton Rouge. He was among those Southern photographers—including George Smith Cook, called the "Photographer of the Confederacy" for the range of his coverage—who had to smuggle their chemicals from New York, the iodides and bromides labeled "quinine."

Those not employed by the government had commercial contracts and passes permitting them access in military areas. Brady's teams were preeminent among them, frequently seen bumping around in horse-drawn portable darkrooms the soldiers dubbed "what-is-it?" wagons. The men worked in pairs, one setting up the tripod and camera, while the other, working in the por-table darkroom, mixed the chemicals and spread them over the glass or metal plate, sensitizing it to light. They had but a few short minutes in which to prepare the plate, take the picture, get the exposed plate to the darkroom, and develop it before the fast-drying collodion solution lost its sensitivity. A single exposure might entail a half-hour's work. The collodion was also limited in its photosensitivity; 20 or 30 seconds might be needed to make a good exposure on overcast days. Photographers either settled for static landscape shots or posed their pictures.

Though the U.S. Army Medical Department compiled seven volumes of photographs of grotesquely disfiguring battlefield injuries, no Civil War images have proved so haunting as the several dozen exposures made

**Mathew Brady**
The most famous figure associated with Civil War photography, Brady rarely operated a camera himself. Instead he employed many of the conflict's most talented photographers.

**"What-is-it?" wagon**
Mathew Brady is credited with introducing the horse-drawn darkrooms that Union soldiers dubbed "what-is-it?" wagons. According to one veteran, the "novelty of its awkward mystery never quite wore off."

of the battlefield dead. Gardner's depictions of mangled, bloated Confederate bodies at Antietam, when displayed in Brady's New York gallery, stunned the public. "Let him who wishes to know what war is look at this series of illustrations," urged Oliver Wendell Holmes. And the *New York Times* noted, "If he has not brought bodies and laid them in our dooryards and along streets, he has done something very like it."

### Bringing the war home

Gardner and O'Sullivan, who together made the "harvest of death" pictures on the sodden, corpse-strewn fields of Gettysburg, and Thomas Roche, who photographed the Rebel dead littering the Petersburg trenches, fed the public's increasing demand for realistic images of the war. While photographs printed as wood engravings were appearing more often in the popular magazines, stereo cards were also being eagerly snapped up.

With one eye on their commercial potential, photographers in the field used stereoscopic cameras that produced parallel negatives. Mounted on cardboard, the resulting albumen prints could be viewed through a stereoscope, providing a good simulation of three-dimensional reality. Marketed through the E. & H. T. Anthony Co. of New York, these stereo cards were the principal means by which the visual horrors of the war were seen in American parlors. Though the images offered only the briefest glimpses of the carnage, this did not lessen their impact on people

who had never seen anything like it before—the dead on the fields of Antietam and Gettysburg and the corpses in the muddy trenches at Spotsylvania and Petersburg.

And no one was the wiser if photographers occasionally manipulated a battlefield scene by laying a rifle across a dead soldier for added drama. The images would have a lasting impact on the history of photography. Alongside the portraits of Abraham Lincoln, Robert E. Lee, and other prominent figures in the struggle, the images of the slain would achieve a hallowed status in American memory.

### AFTER »

Though many Civil War negatives were lost, the surviving images have succeeded in becoming part of the world's photographic inheritance.

**THE PHOTOGRAPHERS**
After the war, Mathew Brady, who had invested $100,000 in cameras, wagons, and equipment, **went bankrupt**, selling many of his priceless negatives. Fortunately, the Federal government purchased a set in 1875. Alexander Gardner documented the **trials and executions** of the Lincoln assassination conspirators. Timothy O'Sullivan became a noted photographer of the **American West**.

**HALFTONE PHOTOENGRAVING**
The invention of halftone photoengraving in the 1880s finally made it possible to **reproduce photographs** in the pages of books and periodicals. That made available to people around the world the **most significant Civil War photographs**.

**MATHEW BRADY AT GETTYSBURG**
The photographer Mathew Brady and his team reached Gettysburg some days after the end of the fighting, by which time the dead had been buried. Brady chose to produce a series of evocative shots of sites that had witnessed significant or tragic episodes in the battle. In this photograph Brady himself is gazing across a field to the woods where, early on the first day of the battle, General John F. Reynolds had been killed by a Confederate sniper.

# Maneuvering toward Richmond

**In May 1864, on the muddy roads to Richmond, a massive Union cavalry raid was repulsed at the gates of the city, while General Robert E. Lee, matching General Ulysses S. Grant's offensive maneuvers, nearly managed to trap a divided Union army on the south bank of the North Anna River.**

On May 8, 1864, as the opening battles at Spotsylvania were beginning, the 10,000 troopers of General Philip Sheridan's cavalry corps swung into their saddles and set off on a massive raid on Richmond, 50 miles (80km) to the south. Three days later they were nearly at the city's outer defenses when they learned that Confederate cavalry blocked their way.

General Jeb Stuart, with a third of Sheridan's numbers, had hastily deployed across a ridge just north of a tumbledown inn called Yellow Tavern. Stuart's men and mounts were

### BEFORE

**While the armies of Grant and Lee lurched from the ferocious Battle of the Wilderness to the grim struggle at Spotsylvania, concurrent offensives started elsewhere.**

**SHERIDAN'S PLANS**
On **April 5**, General **Philip Sheridan**, one of Grant's protégés from the Western Theater, arrived in Virginia to take command of the **Army of the Potomac**'s newly established cavalry corps, whereupon he devised a plan to **defeat Confederate cavalry chief Jeb Stuart**.

**SHERMAN MOVES OUT**
On **May 7**, General **William T. Sherman**, leading the **Union's second major strategic offensive**, commenced operations against General Joseph E. Johnston in northwestern Georgia. Within a week, Sherman's forces would **outmaneuver Johnston's army** at Rocky Face Ridge and force a retreat to Resaca.

exhausted, but they put up a spirited resistance for three hours. Then, just as a late afternoon thunderstorm broke, Sheridan's troopers charged up the ridge. Galloping along his lines, Stuart shouted encouragement. He had just reached the First Virginia Cavalry, when he was shot and seriously wounded. "Go back! Go back!" he yelled to his men, who were about to break under the force of the assault, "I had rather die than be whipped!" Still they could not hold their line, and were driven off the ridge a few minutes later.

The road to Richmond was open, but Sheridan shied away from the city's defenses and headed east. Rebel cavalry harried his flanks and rear, but eventually he made his way to the Army of the James at Bermuda Hundred. He had fulfilled his vow to "whip Jeb Stuart out of his boots." The seriously wounded Stuart was taken to Richmond, where he died of his wound on the evening of May 12, as fighting raged at Spotsylvania's "Bloody Angle."

### Meeting at the North Anna River
Ten days later, Grant left Spotsylvania and sent his advance units once more on the roads toward Richmond.

#### Pontoons on the North Anna River
On May 24, 1864, Union engineers constructed pontoon bridges across a fordable section in the North Anna River, where the banks were less steep, as depicted in this pencil drawing by Alfred Waud.

**Campaign chair**
Complete with a velvet seat, this sturdy piece of portable furniture—a typical 19th-century camp chair—was used by Grant during the Civil War.

The cat-and-mouse game began again, with Lee matching Grant's progress mile for mile, as rain lashed the slogging troops. Before darkness descended on May 22, Lee had concentrated his army behind the south bank of the North Anna River, 21 miles (34km) from the Confederate capital. Grant arrived on the opposite bank the next day. General Gouverneur K. Warren's Fifth Corps splashed across a shallow ford at Jericho Mill and was attacked that evening by a division from General A. P. Hill's corps. Warren drove Hill's troops off after a sharp and bloody fight.

### Union failure
The following morning, General Winfield S. Hancock's Second Corps crossed the North Anna 5 miles (8km) downstream, meeting little resistance. Hopeful rumors began to circulate that Lee had retreated again. In mid-afternoon, however, one Union division encountered Confederates near Hanover Junction, dug in behind entrenchments. An hour later, General Ambrose

Burnside's Ninth Corps tried crossing at Ox Ford, only to be stopped by the strong Rebel defenses.

By evening it was apparent that the Army of Northern Virginia had been lurking in the midst of Union forces and was shielded behind a formidable set of fortifications shaped like an inverted "V." The apex was on Ox Ford and the rear was protected by steep-banked streams.

In a masterstroke, Lee had divided the Union army, but was himself too ill to organize an attack. Grant could not unite the two wings of his army, which were already on the south bank. He therefore retreated from this most ingenious of defensive arrangements, withdrawing across the river. A day passed. Then, on the evening of May 26, Grant feinted to the west, and again pivoted his army to the southeast.

**4,500** The approximate number of Union and Confederate casualties at the North Anna River—where there was no major battle.

### AFTER

**While Grant and Sherman attacked Rebel breastworks in Virginia and Georgia, Lee chose a new leader to be the "eyes and ears" of his army.**

**NEW COMMANDER**
To replace Jeb Stuart, Lee chose General **Wade Hampton**, who would soon fight Sheridan to a draw at the June 11–12 Battle of **Trevilian Station**.

WADE HAMPTON

**IN GEORGIA**
Johnston was **repulsing Sherman's assaults** in the battles of New Hope Church and Pickett's Mill **292–93 ≫**, while Grant faced Lee at the North Anna.

**LEE'S DEFENSES**
Grant concluded that **without ground protection**, Lee's army would **totter and fall** if given a strong push, which he now tried doing near a crossroads called Cold Harbor **260–61 ≫**.

**Grant's council of war**
Wreathed in cigar smoke, Grant holds a council of war on the pews from Massaponax Church near Spotsylvania, May 21, 1864, as he and his generals plan their next move against Lee.

CONFEDERATE MAJOR GENERAL Born 1833 Died 1864

# Jeb **Stuart**

## "**All I ask of fate** is that I may be killed **leading a cavalry charge**."

JEB STUART, ON BECOMING COLONEL OF 1st VIRGINIA CAVALRY, 1861

**Jeb Stuart**
Photographed probably in the winter of 1863–64, Stuart had a cinnamon-colored beard and blue-gray eyes that in battle were said to "flash fire."

With his plumed hat and golden spurs, his setters, and tame raccoon, James Ewell Brown Stuart seemed more the leader of a hunting party than a cavalry chief. His retinue included a banjo player, a band, and a Prussian giant, Major Heros von Borcke. The flamboyant Jeb—as he was known from the initials of his name—loved merriment and pranks, and styled himself a Virginia cavalier.

In battle, though, Stuart pushed his men hard and himself harder. And he routinely gleaned such valuable intelligence about enemy dispositions that General Robert E. Lee dubbed him the "eyes and ears" of his army.

### Serving under Lee

Stuart was one of 11 children born to the politician Archibald Stuart and Elizabeth Pannill. He was initially educated at home, then attended college before enrolling at West Point. There, as a cadet, he met Robert E. Lee, the military academy's superintendent, who noticed that the young horseman from Virginia had acquired many demerits before he graduated in 1854.

In 1859, after five years fighting Indians on the frontier, Stuart, by now a lieutenant, was ordered to join Lee in putting down John Brown's raid on Harpers Ferry. In June 1862, Lee, now in command of the battered Confederate army during the Peninsula Campaign, turned to Stuart to gather intelligence.

As a cavalry officer, Stuart had already distinguished himself during First Bull Run: he screened General Joseph E. Johnston's movement from the Shenandoah Valley to reinforce P. G. T. Beauregard's troops. But it was Stuart's "Ride around McClellan" that not only gave Lee the vital intelligence he needed to drive the Union army away from Richmond, but also won Stuart early fame. Stuart lost only one man on that ride—Captain William Latané, the depiction of whose burial

became a popular print in Confederate parlors. But he quipped that he had also left a "general" behind—"General Consternation."

### An exemplary cavalryman

Stuart flourished under Lee, eventually becoming chief of the Army of Northern Virginia's cavalry corps. At Second Bull Run, he toyed with Union commander, John Pope, when his men raided Pope's headquarters, ransacking his tent and escaping with $350,000. A month later Stuart made a second ride around McClellan's newly restored troops.

Stuart's finest moment came at Chancellorsville, when command of the army's Second Corps devolved

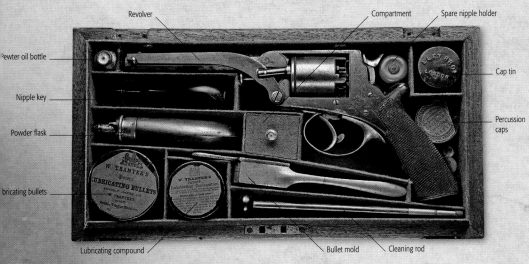

Revolver | Compartment | Spare nipple holder

Pewter oil bottle

Nipple key

Powder flask

Cap tin

Percussion caps

Lubricating bullets

Lubricating compound | Bullet mold | Cleaning rod

TIMELINE

**February 6, 1833** Born at the Stuart family home of Laurel Hill in Patrick County, Virginia.

**July 1854** Graduates from West Point and soon departs for the Western frontier to fight Apaches and Cheyenne.

**November 14, 1855** Marries Flora Cooke, the daughter of Colonel Philip St. George Cooke, at Fort Riley, Kansas, and is soon promoted to first lieutenant.

**October 18, 1859** Negotiates the surrender of abolitionist John Brown and his insurrectionists in the arsenal at Harpers Ferry.

**May 14, 1861** Following Virginia's secession, Stuart resigns his commission as captain in the U.S. Army and becomes colonel of the 1st Virginia Cavalry.

**July 21, 1861** Leads a key charge in the First Battle of Bull Run; promoted to brigadier general.

## "He **never** brought me a piece of false information … I can scarcely think of him **without weeping**."

CONFEDERATE GENERAL ROBERT E. LEE, ON STUART'S DEATH, 1864

upon him after Stonewall Jackson's mortal wounding. The cavalryman handled the infantry brilliantly, leading thousands of foot soldiers through thick brush and heading several of the charges that broke the Union back. On June 9, 1863, Stuart was hit by a surprise Union attack at Brandy Station, Virginia. In the largest cavalry clash of the war, Stuart's men just managed to fend off the Union horsemen, but it

was a bloody affair. Annoyed, Stuart mounted an audacious cavalry raid across the Potomac; he captured numerous supply wagons, but lost touch with Lee, then on his second invasion of the North. Temporarily deprived of his "eyes and ears," Lee stumbled into a battle not of his choosing at Gettysburg.

At Spotsylvania Court House, Stuart practically saved Lee's army, when his troopers held up General Grant's oncoming Union juggernaut long enough for Stuart to herd the arriving

### The four-day ride
This lithograph depicts Jeb Stuart in his plumed hat as he leads his cavalry on the reconnaissance trip that became known as his first "Ride around McClellan" on June 12–15, 1862.

### Cased revolver
Stuart's chief of staff and closest friend, the Prussian officer, Major Heros von Borcke, presented him with this English-made Tranter revolver in June 1863.

Confederate soldiers into battle lines west of the village. He might indeed have made a superb corps commander of infantry, but never got the chance.

Only days after the outbreak of fighting at Spotsylvania, Stuart and his outnumbered horsemen were battling Sheridan's troopers at Yellow Tavern outside Richmond. As Stuart galloped into the thick of the fight, his bugler remarked, "General, I believe you love bullets." Stuart merely replied, "I don't reckon there is any danger." Moments later, a retreating Michigan private took a parting shot at a figure in gray who had been emptying his pistol at them. Stuart spun in his saddle.

He was removed to his brother-in-law's house in Richmond, where he died 24 hours later. As his funeral cortege wound through the city's streets, there was no music and no pageantry, only the muffled roar of cannons as the fighting raged on outside the capital.

**JEB STUART'S JACKET**

**June 12–15, 1862** Undertakes his first "Ride around McClellan," circling the Army of the Potomac in three days with 1,200 troopers, cutting Union supply lines, burning wagon trains, and losing only one man. Soon promoted to major general.

**October 10–12, 1862** With 1,800 troopers undertakes his second ride around McClellan, raiding as far north as Chambersburg, Pennsylvania.

**May 3–6, 1863** During the Battle of Chancellorsville, takes command of the wounded Stonewall Jackson's Second Corps and helps drive Hooker back across the Rappahannock River.

**June 9, 1863** Leads his troopers at Brandy Station, the largest cavalry battle of the war.

**June 28–July 3, 1863** Captures 125 Union supply wagons near Rockville on a raid north of the Potomac; swings over to join Lee and leads the cavalry fight at the Battle of Gettysburg.

**May 7–8, 1864** His cavalry holds the approaches to Spotsylvania Court House long enough for Lee's infantry to move into position to thwart Grant's battle plan.

**May 11, 1864** Stuart intercepts Sheridan's raid on Richmond at Yellow Tavern, only 6 miles (9.5km) north of the capital, but is fatally wounded by a pistol ball and dies the next day, only 31 years old.

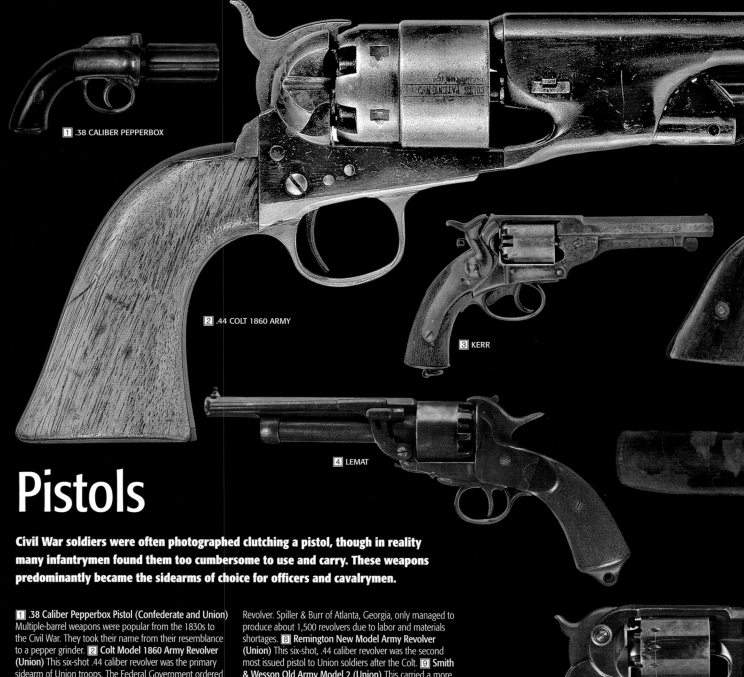

**1** .38 CALIBER PEPPERBOX

**2** .44 COLT 1860 ARMY

**3** KERR

**4** LEMAT

# Pistols

**Civil War soldiers were often photographed clutching a pistol, though in reality many infantrymen found them too cumbersome to use and carry. These weapons predominantly became the sidearms of choice for officers and cavalrymen.**

**1** **.38 Caliber Pepperbox Pistol (Confederate and Union)** Multiple-barrel weapons were popular from the 1830s to the Civil War. They took their name from their resemblance to a pepper grinder. **2** **Colt Model 1860 Army Revolver (Union)** This six-shot .44 caliber revolver was the primary sidearm of Union troops. The Federal Government ordered more than 127,000. **3** **Kerr Revolver (Confederate)** manufactured in Great Britain by the London Armoury Company, the Kerr was used by the Confederate cavalry. **4** **LeMat Revolver (Confederate)** The unique feature was the second smoothbore barrel designed to fire buckshot. LeMats were popular among high-ranking Confederate officers, such as Jeb Stuart. **5** **Dance Brothers Revolver (Confederate)** The Union blockade forced the Confederacy to increase arms production. J. H. Dance and Brothers of Columbia, Texas, manufactured between 325 and 500 revolvers modeled on the Colt Dragoon. **6** **Smith & Wesson Model 1 Revolver (Union)** was the first firearm produced by the company, commencing in 1857. It held seven .22 short rimfire cartridges. **7** **Spiller & Burr Revolver (Confederate)**, a design based on the Whitney

Revolver. Spiller & Burr of Atlanta, Georgia, only managed to produce about 1,500 revolvers due to labor and materials shortages. **8** **Remington New Model Army Revolver (Union)** This six-shot, .44 caliber revolver was the second most issued pistol to Union soldiers after the Colt. **9** **Smith & Wesson Old Army Model 2 (Union)** This carried a more powerful .32 cartridge than the Model 1. It was a popular private purchase for soldiers. **10** **.44 Colt Army Revolver** in a typical contemporary holster. **11** **Deringer Pistol (Confederate and Union)** Known as a "Pocket Pistol" (and often misspelled as Derringer), this readily concealed but effective weapon was sometimes carried for use in emergencies. **12** **Lefaucheux Pinfire Revolver (Confederate and Union)**, imported from France and used low-power cartridges. The Union replaced them later in the war as more Colts and Remingtons became available. **13** **.36 Colt Model 1861 Navy Revolver (Union)** Manufactured from 1861 to 1873, it was designed much like the Colt Army Model 1860 but had a barrel one half-inch (12.7mm) shorter. **14** **.36 Caliber Ball Mold** This brass mold was used to produce lead slugs for pistols and could make nine at a time.

**5** DANCE BROTHERS

6 .22 CALIBER SMITH & WESSON OLD ARMY MODEL 1

7 SPILLER & BURR

8 .44 REMINGTON ARMY

9 .32 CALIBER SMITH & WESSON OLD ARMY MODEL 2

10 ARMY COLT HOLSTERED

11 DERINGER

12 LEFAUCHEUX PINFIRE

13 .36 COLT NAVY 1861

14 .36 BALL MOLD

## « BEFORE

In May 1864, as Ulysses S. Grant began operations against Robert E. Lee, other Virginia campaigns were getting underway.

**BUTLER'S ARMY OF THE JAMES**
In April, a new army of over 30,000 soldiers was formed under Benjamin Butler. Its task was to sail up the James River, land south of Richmond, and **cut the Richmond–Petersburg railroad.**

**SIGEL'S FORCES IN THE VALLEY**
On May 2, General Franz Sigel began advancing up the **Shenandoah Valley**, where Stonewall Jackson had defeated him **« 110–11** two years earlier. Sigel was to cut the railroad leading to Richmond, while also preventing **Confederate reinforcements from reaching Lee.**

**CONFEDERATE OPPONENTS**
In April, General **P .G. T. Beauregard** became commander of forces in **North Carolina and Virginia south of the James River.** Lee selected General **John C. Breckinridge** to confront Sigel in the **Shenandoah Valley.**

# Rebel Victories

While Grant battled Lee in eastern Virginia, his strategy elsewhere broke down. The Confederates penned in General Butler on the Bermuda Hundred peninsula and sent General Sigel reeling at the Battle of New Market, a Rebel victory capped by the charge of the Virginia Military Institute cadets.

On the morning of May 5, when Union general Benjamin Butler landed on the Bermuda Hundred peninsula between the Appomattox and James rivers, he had a chance few generals are ever offered. His Army of the James was halfway between two key Confederate cities—15 miles (24km) from Richmond and 8 miles (13km) from Petersburg—which between them could muster a garrison of only 5,000 militiamen. What was more, the new commander of the garrison, General P. G. T. Beauregard, had still to arrive from Charleston.

Yet Butler missed his opportunity. Although he did send tentative probes out to the Richmond–Petersburg Railroad, he spent too much time and energy making sure that he was thoroughly entrenched at his new base. The Confederates, meanwhile, were using the time to pull in reinforcements from everywhere they could, and General Beauregard arrived to organize them.

When Butler did move ponderously against a target, Beauregard took him by surprise. On May 16, Butler attacked batteries at Drewry's Bluff, which commanded a bend in the James River and had long been the bane of Union gunboats. In a vicious battle in a tangled, swampy, foggy pinewood—a battle that saw bodies piled high outside makeshift breastworks—Beauregard nearly succeeded in cutting Butler off from his base. He further pummeled Butler near Ware Bottom Church on May 20. After that, the Union general was happy to regain the safety of his camp at Bermuda Hundred. With barely half Butler's numbers, Beauregard simply walled him in there, building a line of fortifications across the base of the peninsula. Beauregard had "corked" Butler up, Grant ruefully acknowledged, as if in a bottle.

### First Battle of Petersburg
In June, Butler blundered again. Having heard that Petersburg might be very lightly defended, because most of Beauregard's forces were in the Bermuda Hundred lines, Butler sought to win some long-overdue military laurels by raiding the city. On June 9, 3,400 infantrymen and 1,300 cavalrymen crossed the Appomattox River and approached the Dimmock Line, as Petersburg's encircling fortifications were called. While the tocsins (alarm bells) rang in the city,

**Confederate General Breckinridge**
Former U.S. vice president and the presidential candidate who in 1860 finished second only to Abraham Lincoln, John C. Breckinridge was a Kentuckian whose efforts to avert the war continued until September 1861, when he finally joined the South.

calling the militia to arms, the assaulting infantrymen were too intimidated by the frowning parapets and redoubts to mount an attack. Instead they pulled back to the safety of Bermuda Hundred.

A few miles away Butler's cavalry was in a severe fight. Storming the southern part of the Dimmock Line along the Jerusalem Plank Road, they came up against the Battalion of Virginia Reserves—125 "gray-haired sires and beardless youths," including city councilmen, shopkeepers, and teenagers—led by the retired Colonel Fletcher H. Archer, a veteran of the War with Mexico. In what became famous as the "Battle of Old Men and Young Boys," this scratch force, many armed only with ancient muskets, repulsed repeated assaults for nearly two hours. Even hospital patients helped fight the Union horsemen who finally also retreated to Bermuda Hundred.

**60** The percentage of Fletcher H. Archer's Battalion of Virginia Reserves killed, wounded, or taken prisoner in the "Battle of Old Men and Young Boys," June 9, 1864.

### Valley defeats
Grant's plans for a Shenandoah Valley offensive had been thwarted, too. In May, General Franz Sigel's army was first bogged down by rain, then saw action at New Market. This was one of the handsome towns through which the Valley Turnpike rolled, as did the road leading east across the Blue Ridge Mountains and down into the cockpit where Lee and Grant were slugging it out. Lee believed Sigel would use that route to attack his flank, and on Sunday, May 15, General John C. Breckinridge was trying to prevent that.

Cannonfire had driven many of New Market's residents into the cellars, but the noise was even more terrifying because thunderstorms continually vied with the artillery. To counter Sigel's 6,000 soldiers, Breckinridge had mustered a force of 4,000,

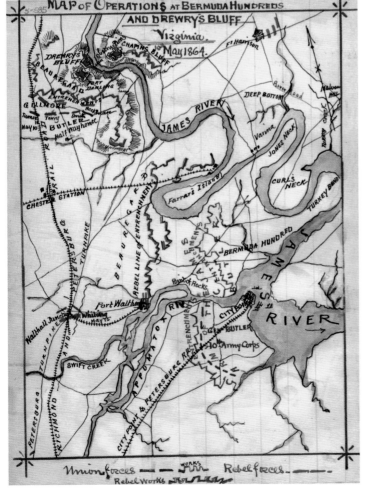

**Bermuda Hundred operations**
A hand-drawn map depicts the Bermuda Hundred peninsula, where Butler was confined by Beauregard. Petersburg is just off the map in the bottom left-hand corner, Richmond off the top left-hand corner.

# "A **blanket would have covered the three**. They were awfully **mangled** by the **canister**."

CADET JOHN S. WISE, DESCRIBING HIS COMRADES KILLED AT NEW MARKET

including a reserve of 247 soaked and shivering cadets from the Virginia Military Institute, the "West Point of the South," who had arrived after marching 70 miles (112km) in four days from their Lexington school. Lee, accustomed to worse odds, had merely wished Breckinridge luck: "I trust you will drive the enemy back."

### Sigel's failure

In the event, many of Sigel's men were still far down the Valley Turnpike, the only macadamized road in a sea of rain-churned muddy lanes. As the fighting surged back and forth over the pastures and knolls outside the town, the Union commander could only place what troops he did have along a ridge overlooking the fields and orchards of a farm belonging to the local Bushong family. There he also positioned 18 of his guns.

Breckinridge, who at Shiloh and Chickamauga had proved a remarkably fine soldier, led a Confederate assault that advanced up those boggy slopes. But as rain lashed the fields and the Union guns raked the attacking troops, a dangerous gap appeared in the Southern ranks. Before the Northern soldiers could seize the opportunity, Breckinridge called reluctantly for the cadets—"Put the boys in, and may God forgive me for the order"—to move up and plug the hole.

Dressed as if on parade, the lines of cadets crossed a plowed field that rain had made such a quagmire they lost their shoes in the mud. Passing through a field of green wheat, some of the youths were torn to pieces by canister (artillery shot used at close quarters). Continuing onward, their comrades wavered only when Union riflemen began piling volleys into them; many

**Cadet's medal**
After the war, Virginia presented bronze medals to each of the cadets who fought at New Market—or if killed or mortally wounded in action, to the cadet's next of kin.

of them fell, but the remainder pressed forward and, sinking to their knees, reached their assigned place.

After a weak Union counterattack turned into a shambles, Sigel's artillerymen began limbering up their guns. The cadets then sprang to their feet and swept up the hill. A Union officer remembered it as the most "sublime" sight he ever witnessed in the war. The rest of the Confederate line rose in response and stormed the ridge, routing Sigel's men, who retreated pell-mell down the Valley Turnpike, not stopping for a day and a night. With them went Grant's hopes for a Shenandoah Valley offensive. Lee's flank was secured, and Breckinridge was able to march his small force east to reinforce the Army of Northern Virginia.

Nearly a quarter of the Southern cadets had been killed or wounded. The rest returned to Lexington as conquering heroes. "We were still young in the ghastly game," one would recall, "but we proved apt scholars."

## AFTER

**The failures of Sigel and Butler not only allowed Breckinridge and Beauregard to reinforce Lee, they also gave the Confederates another military advantage.**

### PETERSBURG DEFENSES
As a result of Butler's abortive raid on Petersburg, Beauregard began strengthening that **city's defenses**, just in time to **parry General Grant's initial assaults** on it the following week **260–63 »**.

### A NEW VALLEY CAMPAIGN
Another Shenandoah Valley campaign began in June after a raid by Union General **David Hunter**, in which he burned the Virginia Military Institute, the "hornet's nest," in retaliation for New Market. Lee sent General **Jubal Early** to confront Hunter, leading to a **summer of battles** culminating in **Sheridan's victory** over Early **268–69 »**.

### Virginia Military Institute cadet
Benjamin A. Colonna was one of the cadets who fought at New Market. He is depicted on the field over which the cadets charged. Colonna survived the war as a captain in the Confederate Army.

# Prisoners of War

**Neither side was prepared to handle the large numbers of prisoners that, by 1864, were being marched into makeshift stockades. Overcrowding, starvation, lack of sanitation, and occasional cruelty stalked Northern prisons as much as they did those in the South.**

When captured in battle in 1862, a Civil War soldier on either side might expect some rough handling, sometimes within sound and sight of the fighting, perhaps in a holding area in the rear. If he was lucky, he might quickly be paroled in exchange for an enemy soldier of the same rank or expect to be exchanged in the near future. By 1864, capture meant only one thing: a prison camp.

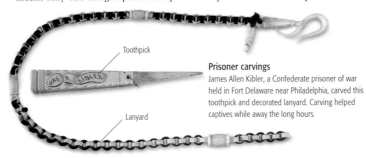

Toothpick

Lanyard

**Prisoner carvings**
James Allen Kibler, a Confederate prisoner of war held in Fort Delaware near Philadelphia, carved this toothpick and decorated lanyard. Carving helped captives while away the long hours.

## BEFORE

At the outbreak of war, neither side had the facilities or infrastructure to handle large numbers of prisoners.

**INFORMAL ARRANGEMENTS**
Lincoln opposed prisoner-of-war exchange agreements, feeling they lent **legitimacy to the Confederacy**. However, field commanders worked out informal exchanges, based on the **parole-and-exchange** system, to keep the numbers of prisoners at **manageable levels**.

**DIX-HILL EXCHANGE CARTEL**
In July 1862, both sides agreed to an official exchange system, called the **Dix-Hill Cartel** after the Union and Confederate officers who negotiated it. For prisoners who agreed to **refrain from military service when released**, this system allowed for the **exchange of prisoners of equal rank**. This worked well, and prisoner-of-war camps soon **began to empty**.

**COLLAPSE OF THE CARTEL**
The system began collapsing once the Union army began **recruiting black soldiers**. The Confederacy refused to exchange them, instead threatening to treat them as **runaway slaves**. In May 1863, the Federal government **suspended the cartel**. Soon the numbers of prisoners began swelling to **unmanageable levels**.

The parole-and-exchange cartel that had existed in the early part of the war collapsed in 1863, and in April 1864, General Grant refused to exchange any more prisoners.

What awaited the captive now would be a fearsome ordeal at best. He might have had an equal, or better, chance of survival had he remained on the battlefield. There were more than 150 prisoner-of-war camps across the United States during the conflict. Every conceivable kind of facility had to be pressed into service. They included existing prisons and jails, converted warehouses, disused barracks, old fortifications, and stockades that were no better than cattle pens. What they all had in common, both in the North and the South, was not a policy of deliberate mistreatment, but rather bureaucratic fecklessness and a dire lack of resources: poor food, shelter, hygiene, and medical attention. Thousands of men died.

### Mixed fortunes
Early in the war the best-known Confederate prisoner-of-war camp was Richmond's Libby Prison. Some 125,000 Union prisoners may have passed through this grim, three-story brick warehouse and former ship's chandlery, for Libby was a prisoner processing station, from which captives were sent on to other camps across the South. Within its dank, fetid walls it had room for about 1,000 inmates, but upwards of five times that number congregated in the rat-infested corridors. Almost all were officers, educated men who subsequently wrote many accounts of their experiences as prisoners of war. They were the lucky ones; they had only to look out their barred windows to see how the other

half lived. Out there, Belle Isle "prison" could be glimpsed, a rocky outcropping in the midst of the James River rapids. This was the other extreme, a natural prison with few or no facilities on which congregated perhaps 8,000 enlisted men, scrambling for the shelter of only 3,000 tents and a handful of shacks. Conditions at Illinois' Rock Island, in the middle of the Mississippi River, were not much better. Although they had some shelter, its Confederate prisoners were too often exposed to the burning summer sun and harsh winters. In 1864, a fast-spreading smallpox epidemic virtually emptied the prison.

Point Lookout in Maryland was the Belle Isle of the North. Once a resort jutting out into the Chesapeake Bay, it provided only enough tents for 10,000 men, but the actual number of Southern captives rose much higher than that. As many as 3,500 of them may have died there, many of exposure, during the two years the prison was in operation.

### High mortality rates
Some 26,000 captured Confederates were held at one time or another in Camp Douglas, built originally as a training barracks. The camp was sited on a damp, low-lying bit of prairie

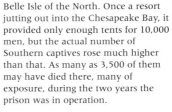

**Record death toll**
Of the 150 prison camps operating during the Civil War, Camp Douglas in Chicago had the highest death rate for any one-month period, with some ten percent of its captives perishing in February 1863.

outside Chicago. It earned the grim reputation of having a higher percentage of deaths in a single month than any other prison camp in the war—387 out of 3,884 men in February 1863. Altogether more than 4,000 of its captives never saw their homes in the South again; many of them lie buried in one mass grave in Chicago's Oak Woods Cemetery.

By far the highest overall mortality rate of any Union prisoner-of-war camp—reaching a staggering 24 percent—was recorded at Elmira. Located in western New York State, Elmira (or "Hellmira," as it was known to its inmates) first opened on July 6, 1864, when 400 Southern prisoners were marched into a former barracks that might have held 5,000. Although it was a large camp, Elmira was nowhere near big enough for the 9,500 men it held when the population was at its peak. Many of them had to sleep outdoors in New York's freezing winter, without blankets or any other provision for shelter.

### Plan of Andersonville Prison

Memories of Andersonville lingered long, and after the war veterans groups were prominent in efforts to preserve the site. Today it is a National Historic Site, with a National Cemetery and the National Prisoner of War Museum.

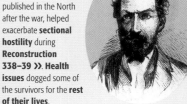

Libby Prison mess kit
Although Libby Prison was severely overcrowded, Union captives held there were comparatively well treated. These items were issued to Colonel John S. Crocker of the 93rd New York Volunteers upon his arrival.

Nearly 3,000 men died there—the majority from exposure, disease, and malnutrition—in the 12 months that Elmira operated.

### A living hell

Andersonville, or Camp Sumter, was all these camps writ large. Carved out of the pinewoods of southwestern Georgia in early 1864, it was a stockade built for 10,000 Union prisoners that soon held three times that number. It offered no shelter. The sweltering inmates stretched rags on sticks and burrowed into the ground to escape the relentless sun. Its one creek was both water source and camp sewer. Dysentery was rampant, medical attention nonexistent, and rations sparse. Nearly 13,000 men died there—30 percent of the prison's population. Andersonville became the most infamous of Civil War prison camps, but all of them shared, to an extent, its sins.

Over 400,000 men were at some point held as prisoners of war during the conflict, and more than 56,000 of them died in captivity. Ultimately the death rate for both North and South together was approximately 13 percent—more than twice the death rate on the battlefield.

Mass grave at Andersonville
Prisoners lay one of their fellow inmates in one of the mass graves outside the stockade. This was a daily duty for the men held at Andersonville.

> " The sight is **worse** than **any sight of battlefields** or any collections of the wounded, **even the bloodiest**. "
>
> WALT WHITMAN, ON RELEASED UNION PRISONERS OF WAR, *SPECIMEN DAYS,* 1882

AFTER »

In 1865, the Confederacy changed its policy on captured black soldiers and prisoner exchanges were resumed, but these never reached their earlier rates.

#### GOING HOME

After the war ended—sometimes months after—**Confederate prisoners** in northern camps took a **loyalty oath** and were given train passes to go back home.

#### LEGACY OF BITTERNESS

Images of **emaciated** Andersonville survivors, published in the North after the war, helped exacerbate **sectional hostility** during **Reconstruction 338–39 »**. **Health issues** dogged some of the survivors for the **rest of their lives**.

HENRY WIRZ

#### CRIMINAL OR SCAPEGOAT

Henry Wirz, **commander at Andersonville**, was tried by a U.S. military court and convicted of **"impairing the health and destroying the lives of prisoners."** He was hanged in November 1865, the **only prison official** on either side to be **executed for war crimes**.

# Andersonville Prison Camp

**In February 1864, Andersonville—also known as Camp Sumter—in Georgia, received its first Union prisoners. Throughout the remaining months of the war, over 45,000 Union soldiers would languish in this overcrowded prison. A lack of shelter, food, medicine, and sanitation led not only to rampant disease, but also to the death of approximately 13,000 Union prisoners of war.**

Friday, May 27, 1864

**"**Inside the camp death stalked on every hand ... one third of the original enclosure was swampy—a mud of liquid filth, voidings from the thousands, seething with maggots in full activity. This daily increased by the necessities of the inmates, the only place being accessible for the purpose. Through this mass pollution, passed the only water that found its way through the Bull Pen ... I have known 3,000 men to wait in line to get water, and the line was added to as fast as reduced, from daylight to dark, yes, even into the night ... the heat of the sun, blistering him, or the drenching rains soaking him, not a breath of fresh air, and we had no covering but Heaven's canopy. Air-loaded with unbearable, fever-laden stench from the poison sink of putrid mud and water, continually in motion by the activity of the germs of death. We could not get away from it—we ate it, drank it and slept in it. What a wonder that men died, or were so miserable as to prefer instant death to that which they had seen hourly taking place.**"**

Tuesday, July 19, 1864

**"**The cases of insanity were numerous. Men, strong in mentality, heart and hope were in a few short months, yes, often in a few weeks, reduced to imbeciles and maniacs. Today they know you and look upon you as friends and comrades; tomorrow they are peevish, whining, childish creatures, or raving maniacs. Some would beg for something to eat; others asked for wife, mother, children, or other relatives ... the mental anguish of those days and months was the slowest torture to him who still had a clear brain.**"**

DIARY OF CORPORAL CHARLES HOPKINS OF THE 1st NEW JERSEY INFANTRY; IMPRISONED IN ANDERSONVILLE FOR ALMOST TEN MONTHS, HE TOOK NEARLY A YEAR TO RECOVER

**Intolerable conditions**
The starving inmates of Andersonville were held in an exposed, makeshift facility that grew daily more overcrowded. By August 1864, 33,000 prisoners were living in an area originally intended to hold 10,000.

# The Battle of Cold Harbor

**Grant's maneuvers were blocked once more by Lee's army, which constructed a 7-mile (11-km) line of fieldworks—the most daunting yet seen in the Overland Campaign—near the junction at Cold Harbor. The only way to break through that line—so Grant thought—was to launch one massive assault.**

## BEFORE

In the wake of Ulysses S. Grant's masterly disengagement from the North Anna River **《 248–49**, both armies continued their running battle, sparring southeastward.

### HAW'S SHOP

General Robert E. Lee took up a strong position on the south bank of **Totopotomoy Creek**, with Pamunkey River to the north and Chickahominy River to the south. On May 28 he sent a cavalry **reconnaissance eastward** to test Grant's position. His men met Union horsemen near **Haw's Shop**, a local forge, and the resulting five-hour battle became one of the **bloodiest cavalry engagements** of the entire war.

### BETHESDA CHURCH

On May 30 Grant pushed across Totopotomoy Creek, seeking Lee's right flank. The infantry of both armies **clashed at Bethesda Church**. Farther east, cavalry units fought at Old Church, but the Confederate horsemen fell back on a crossroads called **Cold Harbor**. Grant, believing Lee's lines unbreakable, was also casting an eye on Cold Harbor. A **major battle** was shaping up.

### TECHNOLOGY

#### TRENCH WARFARE

Spending nearly two weeks—from June 1 to June 12, 1864—in flat open fields, swept by artillery and sniper fire, soldiers of both armies dug a complex maze of trenches around the road junction at Cold Harbor. Behind their parapets, troops constructed bombproof shelters to sleep in and excavated holes to build fires. They filled gabions (open-ended wickerwork cages) with dirt for shock absorption—a technique they would use again at Petersburg (pictured). Rain turned the trenches into rivers, and in the sun, blankets stretched between bayoneted rifles screened the men.

The dusty little hamlet of Cold Harbor sat in country so flat that only ravines cut by sluggish streams provided relief. Five roads radiated from the settlement like wheel spokes, including two to the southwest, which led over bridges across the Chickahominy River to Richmond, 8 miles (13km) away.

On June 1, 1864, this hamlet saw cavalry units fighting for its possession. As the afternoon wore on, infantry began arriving. Troopers in blue held

#### The Battle of Cold Harbor

This postwar chromolithograph, issued by the firm Kurz and Allison, depicts the gruesome battle in the stylized, romantic vein popular in the 1880s.

the crossroads as Lee's divisions began approaching from the north. Grant's soldiers were marching along a parallel track, but some of them had become lost and were slow coming up. Although Lee's line stretched nearly 7 miles (11km), from Totopotomoy Creek in the north to the banks of the Chickahominy, the leading elements managed to block the road to Richmond. Lee's veterans dug in where they halted. Grant's men aligned opposite, and as evening fell the Union commander hurled them at

> **6,500** The estimated number of Union soldiers who fell within the first hour of the charge at Cold Harbor on June 3, 1864—over one-quarter of the 25,000 men sent to attack the Confederate fieldworks that morning.

the Southern line. "Aim low and aim well," one Confederate general advised his troops. For a few minutes, the Confederate lines blazed with rifle fire. Everywhere the Yankees fell back, except where one division nearly opened a breach, using a ravine for cover. This near-breakthrough impressed Grant, who thought one big push might divide the Army of Northern Virginia. He therefore ordered a huge attack for June 2, but not all the Union troops were in place, so he reluctantly postponed to the following morning.

That night Lee's engineers strengthened their lines, shoring up weak spots and designing a broad zigzag pattern that created converging

**Union battery at Cold Harbor**
During the battle of June 1, these Union Sixth Corps gunners fought so close to the Confederate line that they were nicknamed "Battery Insult."

fields of fire, staked out with measured distances so that the artillery could better estimate range. The art of field fortification that the Confederates had been working on since Spotsylvania was now perfected in the flat fields around Cold Harbor. Though there was a steady patter of falling rain, the ominous noise of the Confederate soldiers strengthening their breastworks carried hundreds of yards to the ears of waiting Union soldiers. Grim premonitions swept through the ranks; many men pinned their names to their tunics so that burial parties would be better able to identify them.

## Battle resumes

At 4:30 a.m. on June 3, the signal gun fired and some 25,000 Union soldiers emerged from their works and crossed the muddy fields. Few of them had time to study the Rebel breastworks.

Across the nearly 7-mile (11-km) line, a mighty crash of Confederate cannon and rifle fire erupted that lit up the dawn sky and rattled the windows in Richmond.

Volley after murderous volley tore through the blue-clad ranks. Entire lines were cut down, and whole regiments disintegrated. In the midst of the pandemonium, General Francis Barlow's brigade briefly took a section of the Confederate earthworks, amidst a scene of sheer slaughter. In some places only minutes passed before survivors were pinned down by rifle fire as their officers urged them forward in vain.

Yet Grant and his staff remained unaware of the situation on the ground. Barlow's fleeting success only prompted more orders to attack. The result was near mutiny among the generals, and it was midday before Grant finally halted the debacle. By then the full extent of casualties was becoming known. While some Confederate divisions reported no casualties, the Union troops had been decimated. Of the 6,500 to 7,000 men felled during the first hour of battle that morning, most had been hit during the first fatal ten minutes.

## The wounded abandoned

Among the casualties were masses of wounded men strewn across the ravaged fields. Still the Confederate gunners kept firing. Survivors could only dig in where they lay, using bayonets and tin cups as entrenching

> **BREASTWORK** A rapidly constructed, temporary fortification, erected as a defense in battle. The name comes from its walls being breast height.

tools. The following day, Grant conferred with Lee about collecting the wounded, who had lain exposed for over 24 hours. Grant refused to ask for a formal truce, and Lee distrusted Grant's motives. For three days, dead bodies lay on the fields. Under cover of darkness some soldiers tried slipping out to recover their moaning comrades. But with the battle lines sometimes only 150ft (45m) apart, sharpshooters dared any man who raised his head. Some tried digging trenches to reach the wounded instead. Finally, on the evening of June 7, Grant asked for a formal truce and Lee agreed. By that time there were few wounded still alive in the fields of festering corpses. Burial parties were given tots of whiskey to help brace them for their task.

News of the repulse at Cold Harbor came as a shattering blow to the North. After a month of bloody assaults, some of Grant's commanders were growing restive; far and wide he was being decried as a "butcher." Grant never responded to the criticism. Two decades later, however, when he was writing his memoirs, Grant, dying of throat cancer, revealed his true feelings: "I have always regretted that the last assault at Cold Harbor was ever made."

**Berdan sharpshooter frock coat**
Named for their commanding officer, Colonel Hiram Berdan, the 2nd U.S. Volunteer Sharpshooters were a crack Union regiment. They fought at Cold Harbor, but with less success than their Confederate counterparts.

Continued bad news from the battlefields kept support for the war discouragingly low in the Northern states.

**LINCOLN'S REELECTION IMPERILED**
News of the **carnage at Cold Harbor** sapped spirits at the **Republican national convention**, meeting on June 7–8 in Baltimore to **nominate President Lincoln for a second term**.

**SHERMAN IMPEDED**
In Georgia, Joseph E. Johnston, withdrawing from one line of **forbidding entrenchments** to another, eluded Sherman's traps, stalling **Union progress toward Atlanta 292–93 ≫**.

**SHATTERED CONFIDENCE**
Soldiers in the Army of the Potomac were so **unnerved by the slaughter** that, days later, they balked at attacking the thinly defended trenches outside **Petersburg 262–63 ≫**.

DIGGING UP THE REMAINS OF THE FALLEN AT COLD HARBOR, ONE YEAR AFTER THE BATTLE

**" I had seen nothing to exceed this. It was not war; it was murder."**
CONFEDERATE GENERAL EVANDER McIVOR LAW

**Bridging the James River**
Between June 14 and June 17, 1864, Union engineers laid a pontoon bridge, employing 101 pontoons, to span a nearly half-mile (800-m) wide stretch of the James River.

**‹‹ BEFORE**

The stalemate at Cold Harbor as the two armies faced each other from their trenches grew intolerable for both Grant and Lee.

**GRANT LOOKS SOUTH**
After **Cold Harbor ‹‹ 260–61**, Grant continued to refine his strategy. He ordered a detachment of Sheridan's cavalry to **destroy the railroads west and southwest of Richmond**, knowing that Lee's cavalry would **set off in pursuit**, leaving him temporarily blind. Grant was **planning an intricate move**, with an eye on the **railroad junction at Petersburg**, 20 miles (32km) south of Richmond and beyond the James River.

**PETERSBURG'S DEFENSES**
The city was partially protected by formidable fortifications, called the **Dimmock Line**, after military engineer Charles Dimmock, who had directed their construction in 1862. In May, General **P. G. T. Beauregard**, in charge of the city's defenses, had bottled up Butler's Army of the James at **Bermuda Hundred ‹‹ 254–55**. That allowed him to send many of his troops to reinforce Lee, but left him with **scant forces to defend Petersburg** against a surprise attack.

# Grant Advances to Petersburg

**Having brilliantly extricated his Union army from Cold Harbor, Grant soon had many of his troops and supplies crossing the James River over a 2,100-ft (640-m) pontoon bridge. But his field commanders failed to capture the key railroad junction of Petersburg before Lee and his army caught up with them.**

**First attack at Petersburg**
On June 15, 1864 the Union Eighteenth Corps carried a significant portion of the Dimmock Line, as depicted in this illustration from Frank Leslie's *Illustrated Newspaper*. This initial success was not followed up.

A s the night of June 12, 1864 fell on the ravaged fields around Cold Harbor, Union soldiers were quietly on the move. Once well to the rear, they assembled into regiments and then into corps. At dawn, Lee received the astonishing news that the Army of the Potomac had vanished with the night. Grant decided to move against the Confederate supply lines, especially the five railroads intersecting in Petersburg. To do this, however, he needed to steal a march south and cross the James River, which in places was several miles wide.

**Feats of transportation**
While Grant was "all-observant, silent, inscrutable," as one subordinate put it, the Eighteenth Corps under General William F. Smith marched northeast to board troop transports waiting on the York River. Most of the infantry marched south to the north shore of the James River, and were ferried to the opposite bank. The remainder—

nervously. The assault was launched that evening, and it was so overwhelming that the triumphant Union troops captured great stretches of the Dimmock Line, forcing Beauregard back to find another defensible position. For a moment, Smith held the key to Petersburg, but he let it slip from his grasp. Convinced that more Confederates opposed him than was actually the case, he failed to follow up his success. Beauregard

**2,500** The approximate number of troops at Beauregard's disposal to man the defenses of Petersburg on June 15, 1864. Many of them were old men and young boys of the militia.

hastily dug a second line of defense, his men frantically scraping the earth with bayonets and tin cups, while Grant pushed his generals to "carry Petersburg before the enemy could reinforce its garrison."

Lee was temporarily confused. "I do not know the position of Grant's army," he wrote to his superiors in Richmond the next day. But Beauregard, now fending off more than 40,000 enemy troops, identified the blue-clad soldiers confronting him as belonging to the Army of the Potomac. On receiving that news, Lee sent his veterans hastening down the road to Petersburg.

### Beauregard's finest hour
Meanwhile, Grant had arrived in front of the beleaguered city and ordered another assault for that very evening. Beauregard still held out. It had not been much of an attack: "Our men are tired," General Meade admitted.

The following day, June 17, brought heavy fighting, but the attacks were fitful. Beauregard kept the Union assaults at bay, shifting his few troops from pressure point to pressure point as needed. By daybreak on June 18, the riflemen were firing with deadly accuracy, for they repulsed yet another dawn attack. That afternoon the lead elements of the Army of Northern

Virginia began to arrive. Holding out for four days, Beauregard had inflicted as many casualties as he had men to command. The Union soldiers were stymied, and so they dug in. "Grant has pushed his Army to the extreme limit of human endurance," one staff officer complained privately.

### An opportunity missed
Grant had maneuvered to Petersburg with great skill. But his exhausted troops and subordinate commanders had missed a great opportunity. Seemingly Grant had exchanged one labyrinth of trenches at Cold Harbor for another at Petersburg.

#### Petersburg from Lee's headquarters
An artist for the *Illustrated London News* sketched a panorama of Petersburg and environs as seen by General Lee and his staff, while they were "watching the enemy's movements through a field-glass."

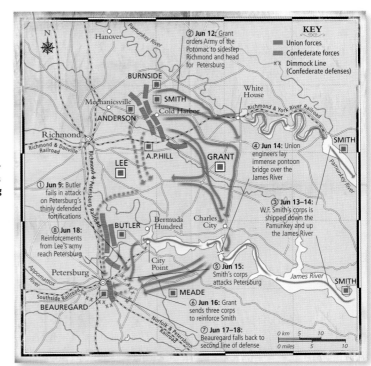

**KEY**
- Union forces
- Confederate forces
- Dimmock Line (Confederate defenses)

① Jun 9: Butler fails in attack on Petersburg's thinly defended fortifications

② Jun 12: Grant orders Army of the Potomac to sidestep Richmond and head for Petersburg

③ Jun 13–14: W.F. Smith's corps is shipped down the Pamunkey and up the James River

④ Jun 14: Union engineers lay immense pontoon bridge over the James River

⑤ Jun 15: Smith's corps attacks Petersburg

⑥ Jun 16: Grant sends three corps to reinforce Smith

⑦ Jun 17–18: Beauregard falls back to second line of defense

⑧ Jun 18: Reinforcements from Lee's army reach Petersburg

#### From Cold Harbor to Petersburg
Grant's advance to Petersburg was a triumph of logistics, but the men of the Army of the Potomac were too tired after the rigors of weeks of fighting and marching to break through the city's weak defenses.

one corps and one division, plus all the artillery—crossed the river on a pontoon bridge that had been erected in only seven hours. The troops were followed by 5,000 wagons, 56,000 horses and mules, and 2,800 head of cattle. For three days an unbroken cavalcade plodded over the bridge.

### Initial attacks
Smith's Eighteenth Corps was the first to arrive, disembarking at City Point on June 15 and marching 10 miles (16km) toward Petersburg. Behind the Dimmock Line, General Beauregard's Confederate defenders waited

**AFTER**

Grant had wanted to avoid a protracted siege at Petersburg, but his failure to take the city when the chance arose would prolong the war into another year.

**NORTHERN DISILLUSION**
Lee's war of attrition was wearing down the North's will to fight. **Copperheads, Peace Democrats, and other defeatist elements** were gaining support. If Lee could hold out long enough, the issue might be decided by the **presidential election ❮❮ 236–37** in November. Meanwhile, Grant kept **extending his Petersburg lines 274–75 ❯❯** to the south and west, hoping to weaken Lee's own lines and capture his remaining railroads.

**SOUTHERN VICTORIES**
On June 10, **Nathan Bedford Forrest** routed a force twice the size of his own at **Brice's Crossroads, Mississippi 288–89 ❯❯**, while on June 11–12, Wade Hampton stopped Sheridan's troopers at **Trevilian Station, Virginia**. On June 27, **Sherman was defeated at Kennesaw Mountain outside Atlanta 292–93 ❯❯**, while Jubal Early was preparing to **march on Washington 268–69 ❯❯**. All in all, it was a summer of doubt for the Union.

**Army supply base**
Soldiers sit on a bank above the Union supply depot at Cumberland Landing on the Pamunkey River during the 1862 Peninsula Campaign. Virginia's tidal rivers eased logistics for generals McClellan and Grant.

# Supply, Transportation, and Logistics

**During the Civil War, the armies' constant need for food, clothing, ammunition, and medical supplies determined the nature and outcome of some of the conflict's most significant campaigns. Logistics dominated everything from grand strategy to battlefield tactics.**

**Ammunition packages**

Cartridges usually came in packages of ten—such as these for the British-made Enfield rifle—or in wooden cases of a thousand. Where wagons could not go, pack mules might carry the ammunition cases forward.

## BEFORE

**The Civil War was the first major war in which railroads played a crucial role. At sea, the Union naval blockade posed a special problem for the South.**

### RAILROAD ADVANTAGE

The **North, with many more miles of track** « 218–19, held the advantage with their railroads. But the **South's interior lines of transportation made it easier** to transfer troops and material from place to place.

### ANACONDA PLAN

General Winfield Scott's "Anaconda Plan" « 64–65 and the Union blockade « 72–73 were intended to **cut off the South from overseas trade and supplies**. In response, **Southern blockade-runners delivered cargoes** containing everything from Enfield rifles and German sabers to cognac and medicine.

---

### UNION GENERAL (1815–72)

#### HENRY HALLECK

"Old Brains," as Henry Halleck was often called, was author of *Elements of the Military Art*, one of the West Point Military Academy's most venerated textbooks in the 1850s. Although a theoretician of the first rank and the Union's general-in-chief from July 1862, Halleck proved not to be a field commander. His talents lay more in administration, planning, and logistics. In 1864, when President Lincoln replaced him as general-in-chief with Ulysses S. Grant, he made Halleck the army chief of staff. In that position Old Brains found his niche, ensuring that Union forces had everything necessary to guarantee victory.

---

In the spring of 1863, if a Union army—such as Major General William S. Rosecrans's Army of the Cumberland—came marching down a dusty highway, its thousands of tramping infantrymen, its horse-drawn artillery and caissons (ammunition wagons), and its ambulance train all would constitute just part of the spectacle of an army in motion.

### Wagon trains

Marching armies would be followed by a seemingly interminable procession of white-topped wagons, a hundred of them for each mile of road. If the wagons rolled along in single file, they might reach back for 20 or even 30 miles (32–48km), since up to 3,000 wagons could accompany an army. While the army's infantrymen each carried three days' rations and 40 cartridges, the wagons carried the tons of extra food, ammunition, medical supplies, and baggage that would be needed. They also carried forage for the animals pulling the wagons, which might amount to thousands of sacks of grain.

Pulled by a six-mule team, the canvas-covered army wagon rolled along at less than 3 miles (4.8km) an hour. But slow though it was, the wagon was the vital link between the individual soldier's haversack and cartridge box, and the huge depots well to the rear that stockpiled essential supplies—coffee, sugar, hardtack, salt

> **16,000** The number of officers and men in the U.S. Army in 1860, before the war. A year later it had swollen to 186,000, and by the end of the war the Union army totaled more than a million men.

pork, dried peas, tents, blankets, overcoats, lumber, axes, shovels, saddles, bridles, harnesses, bullets, bandages, and coffins.

### Policies and problems

Supply depots were established near railroads and steamship wharves. The North had little trouble gathering up supplies from its farmlands and industries and depositing them in the depots. In contrast, the South had been trammeled by the North's naval blockade, shortcomings in its infrastructure, and bureaucratic inefficiencies, and so faced greater difficulties in amassing supplies and transporting them to where they were needed. In the middle of the war, the Confederate Army of Tennessee found itself particularly short of supplies. The logistics policy meant that it was deprived of its natural resource base in Tennessee. Local foodstuffs were gathered and diverted instead to the Confederate depot in Atlanta, from where they were shipped by train to Petersburg to feed Lee's Army of Northern Virginia.

By 1864, the Union campaigns against the railroad hubs at Petersburg and Atlanta faced contrasting logistical issues. At Petersburg, where General Ulysses S. Grant had the James River at his back, his supply base was close to his headquarters. He had established a depot at City Point, where mountains of war material was piled amidst railroads, wharves, hospitals, repair shops, blacksmith forges, and even bakeries making 100,000 loaves daily.

### Food foraging

A contemporary illustration shows Union troops foraging near Wacsaw Sound, Georgia, during General Sherman's 1864 March to the Sea. Sherman's 62,000 soldiers appropriated almost all of the local agricultural resources.

Ten miles (16km) away, General Robert E. Lee fought to protect the last of the Petersburg railroads still bringing in supplies from the Confederacy's rapidly shrinking resource base in southern Virginia and North Carolina.

### Railroad to Atlanta

At Atlanta, Union general William T. Sherman was also dependent on a single lifeline. Supplies had to be brought over a single-track railroad that snaked back hundreds of miles through the hills of Georgia to supply bases in Tennessee. To protect the route from Confederate raiders, he garrisoned every mile of it and then stockpiled depots along the route. Without the railroad, he asserted, his four-month campaign would have required "36,800 wagons."

## AFTER »

**By the war's end, the Union army had embraced a scorched earth policy to disrupt Confederate supply networks.**

### SCORCHED EARTH

In the fall of 1864, General **Sheridan burned the Shenandoah Valley 268–69 »**. Shortly after, General Sherman embarked on the **march through Georgia and the Carolinas 296–97 »** that devastated the heart of the Confederacy and caused perhaps $100 million in damage.

### NEW DEVELOPMENTS

**Mechanized transportation**, along with **advances in military telegraphy, signaling, and airborne observation**, ushered in a revolution in military logistics and communication.

**UNION WAGON TRAIN**

Any large-scale invasion of enemy territory during the Civil War presented formidable problems of logistics. General George McClellan did an excellent job of organizing, equipping, and supplying the Army of the Potomac for the Peninsula Campaign of 1862. A vast wagon train is seen here crossing a stream on the Virginia Peninsula. The artist John B. Bachelder made numerous sketches of this campaign, and Union officers vouched for the accuracy of his lithographs.

# The Valley Campaign

**In the war's final duel for control of the strategic Shenandoah Valley in Virginia, Confederate General Jubal Early, whose soldiers briefly menaced Washington, D.C., was soundly defeated by General Philip Sheridan, who darkened the Valley's skies in what would become known as "The Burning."**

Jubal Early was nothing if not audacious. In June 1864, having won control of the Shenandoah Valley, he planned to take his Army of the Valley—Stonewall Jackson's old Second Corps—on an invasion of the North.

Having scattered his enemies—some into the mountains of West Virginia—Early seized the opportunity to relieve pressure on Robert E. Lee, struggling with Ulysses S. Grant at Petersburg, Virginia. Early planned to threaten Washington, D.C., and perhaps draw off some of Grant's soldiers. Crossing the Potomac River, Early brushed aside Union forces on July 9 at the Battle of Monocacy. Three days later, his men marched down Rockville Pike toward Washington's defenses. Though the fortifications were manned by a force of militiamen twice the size of Early's

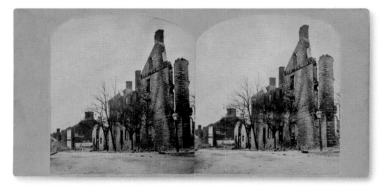

**Chambersburg in ruins**
Hundreds of buildings were destroyed when, on July 30, 1864, much of Chambersburg, Pennsylvania, was torched by Confederate cavalry in retaliation for Union depredations in Virginia and failure to pay a ransom.

## ❮❮ BEFORE

**Once famous far and wide for its beauty, the Shenandoah Valley had been ravaged by two years of war.**

### A STRATEGIC PAWN
For the Union, the Valley had been a potential backdoor route to Richmond; to the South, it was the **"breadbasket of the Confederacy"** and the **natural invasion route to the North.**

### CONFEDERATE CONTROL
In June, Union general David Hunter, who replaced Franz Sigel after the **Battle of New Market ❮❮ 254–55**, advanced back up the Shenandoah Valley and **put many buildings and homes to the torch,** outraging Virginians. Approaching the Confederate supply depot at Lynchburg, he was defeated on June 17–18 by General Jubal Early, commander of the new Army of the Valley. Hunter retreated into West Virginia, **leaving the Valley to Early**.

army, the city itself was on the verge of hysteria. The Confederates were so close that they could see the Capitol dome from their bivouac. But with thousands of Union reinforcements arriving from Petersburg, Early turned and soon recrossed the Potomac. He had sown panic and depleted Grant's Petersburg lines, and had also destroyed railroads and telegraph stations.

Back in the Shenandoah Valley, Early continued defeating scattered Union incursions. On July 24, over the same fields and fences where Stonewall Jackson once fought, he vanquished Federal forces at the Second Battle of Kernstown. He then sent his cavalry, commanded by John A. McCausland, across the Potomac again. On the morning of July 30, the troopers rode into Chambersburg, Pennsylvania, demanding $100,000 in gold as compensation for General David Hunter's burning of Virginia homes the previous month. When the ransom could not be produced, McCausland torched the town.

### The Union response
The North was incensed, as was General Grant, who summoned his pugnacious cavalry chief, Philip Sheridan. "I want Sheridan to be put

in command of all the troops in the field," Grant declared, "with instructions to follow the enemy to the death."

It proved to be a pivotal decision. "Little Phil"—as the diminutive Sheridan was affectionately known—entered the Valley near Harpers Ferry in August at the head of the Army of the Shenandoah, nearly 40,000 soldiers strong. Encamped outside Winchester, Early marched and countermarched his heavily outnumbered troops, hoping the resulting dust clouds would create the impression of a much larger force. Sheridan bided his time, and struck on September 19.

The Third Battle of Winchester was a bloody, daylong fight that surged back and forth across rolling fields. Though they repulsed a number of Union assaults, the Confederates finally broke when cavalry attacked their flanks. Having suffered nearly 40 percent casualties, Early's troops streamed back through the streets of Winchester and entrenched on Fisher's Hill, 15 miles (24km) to the south.

Three days later, at sunset on September 22, Sheridan attacked at Fisher's Hill. The Union soldiers scrambled over rocks, walls, and felled trees with their commander urging them on: "Forward! Forward everything! Go on, don't stop, go on!" Outflanked again, Early's men abandoned their positions, losing more than 1,000, and were chased deep into the night by their relentless foe.

### Utter devastation
Sheridan next turned his attention to the surrounding landscape, whose crops had been supplying the Confederate army. Grant had ordered him to "turn the valley into such a barren waste that even a crow flying over it would have to carry his own rations." As the torches were handed out, his soldiers began igniting the many fires that, taken together, would always be remembered

by residents as "The Burning." Far and wide, immense pillars of smoke arose as every barn, stable, mill, haystack, and supply of forage went up in flames. Some 2,000 barns and 120 mills with their stocks of grain and flour were consumed by fire. Countless fences, wagons, and farming implements were destroyed. Livestock was run off. Hundreds of square miles of once-beautiful farmland were wrecked and scorched. There was little that the Confederacy could do about it. Partisan activities by cavalry commander John Mosby's group and others only brought reprisals. When Early's cavalry pressed too close, it was driven off at the Battle of Tom's Brook on October 9. George

> ## "He just **moved around our flank**, **swept down** upon it, and **whipped us out of existence**."
> CONFEDERATE GENERAL JOHN B. GORDON, ON SHERIDAN'S VICTORY AT CEDAR CREEK

**Custer torching the Valley**
War artist Alfred Waud sketched General George Custer's division retiring from the Mount Jackson area on October 7, 1864, burning agricultural resources along the way.

With Sheridan's triumph at Cedar Creek, the guns began to fall silent on one of the most significant battlegrounds of the war.

**THE VALLEY REDEEMED**
Having been disputed for nearly three years, the Shenandoah Valley, cleared of Confederate armies and ravaged agriculturally, **ceased to be of strategic importance**. Union military activity was largely relegated to chasing partisans and the ever-elusive Confederate guerilla leader, John Singleton Mosby, and his men.

**CAMPAIGNS MILITARY AND POLITICAL**
Sheridan's victories at Winchester, Fisher's Hill, and Cedar Creek, coming on the heels of Farragut's triumph at **Mobile Bay 286–87** » and Sherman's capture of Atlanta **292–93** », bolstered President Lincoln's chances for re-election **236–37** ».

**TWILIGHT OF AN ARMY**
After Cedar Creek, Early's demoralized divisions regrouped and lingered through the winter of 1864–65 near Staunton, at the headwaters of the Shenandoah River. On March 2, 1865, at the Battle of Waynesboro, **Sheridan defeated "Old Jube" for the last time**, capturing 1,600 men and 11 guns, almost all that was left of the Confederate Army of the Valley.

mountain trail as they rounded the lightly picketed Union left flank. Dawn on the 19th opened with a Rebel yell and a thunder of guns. The Union soldiers were caught literally in their beds. Thousands fled to the rear in panic. Wagons, supplies, some 24 cannons, and 20 battle flags fell to Early's men; but barefoot, famished, and in rags, most of them turned aside to plunder, and Early called off the pursuit. "This is glory enough for one day!" he exulted.

Increasingly alarmed, Sheridan arrived at the scene to see the shambles of his army pouring rearward. Ordering up fresh troops from Winchester, Sheridan rode along the wagon-thronged Valley Pike, cursing, cajoling, coaxing, and cheering; waving his hat forward. "Come on back, boys! Give 'em hell, God damn 'em! We'll make coffee out of Cedar Creek tonight!" Increasing his pace almost to a gallop, he kept it up for nearly 12 miles (19km), roaring encouragements and waving his hat, until by some miracle of inspiration the army began to steady, then to reform its lines. By 4:30 p.m., the tide was turning. An overwhelming wave of bluecoats then rolled back into its former camps. In the chaos, the Confederates turned in flight. As Union cavalry slashed at their flanks, fleeing soldiers clogged the Valley Pike so

**435,802** The number of bushels of wheat that were destroyed or seized by Sheridan's troops in the valley, along with 77,176 bushels of corn, and 874 barrels of flour.

thickly that at one place a small bridge collapsed. Everything the Confederates had captured, and more, they now lost, to the point where Early's army nearly ceased to exist. "When we left the field that evening," General John B. Gordon acknowledged, "the Confederacy had retired from the Shenandoah."

### The Battle of Fisher's Hill
A period Currier & Ives lithograph depicts the moment when Federal cavalry drove Confederates from their entrenchments during the Battle of Fisher's Hill, September 22, 1864.

Armstrong Custer's jeering horsemen nicknamed the galloping stampede the "Woodstock Races" as the Confederates retreated for more than 20 miles (32km).

### The Battle of Cedar Creek
Secure in his control of the lower valley, and believing Early's divisions to have withdrawn, Sheridan departed for Washington. But Early was closer than

Sheridan realized, and had lost none of his audacity. Though outnumbered four to one, he still hoped to prevent Sheridan from reinforcing Grant, and planned a surprise attack on the Union army encamped behind Cedar Creek, 12 miles (19km) south of Winchester.

On the night of October 18, as Sheridan arrived back in Winchester, Early's men were hugging a precipitous

**CONFEDERATE GENERAL 1816-94**

## JUBAL ANDERSON EARLY

Arrogant and acerbic, rumpled and careless of appearance, Early was a graduate of West Point who had quit the Army to become a country lawyer. With the outbreak of the Civil War, the native Virginian returned to uniform as an outstanding Confederate brigade and divisional commander, seeing action at First and Second Bull Run, Antietam, Fredericksburg, Gettysburg, and other major battles. Lee called him "my bad old man" for his profanity, but prized his craftiness, resolve, and fearlessness.

UNION MAJOR GENERAL Born 1831 Died 1888

# Philip Sheridan

## "He felt **no doubt**, he would submit to **no defeat**, and he **took his army with him** as on a **whirlwind**."

A. F. WALKER, 11TH VERMONT VOLUNTEERS, ON SHERIDAN IN THE VALLEY CAMPAIGN

Scarcely bigger than a drummer boy, "Little Phil" Sheridan must have looked an improbable candidate to become, one day, general of the army. Of his contemporaries, the only others to attain this elevated rank were Ulysses S. Grant and William T. Sherman. But Sheridan was as combative as a gamecock in his love of a fight. He also possessed what Grant himself most admired, "that magnetic quality of swaying men which I wish I had—a rare quality in a general." Soldiers responded to his presence and rallied at his command.

### Pugnacious youth
Philip Henry Sheridan grew up in Somerset, Ohio, where town legend had it that he won every boyhood fight that came his way and even once chased his schoolmaster up a tree. But he was nearly rejected by the examining board at West Point because of his peculiar build. He was broadchested but tiny—his height was later generously estimated at 5ft 5in (1.65m). And the lanky Abraham Lincoln famously described Sheridan as a "brown, chunky little chap, with a long body, short legs, not enough neck to hang him, and such long arms that if his ankles itch he can scratch them without stooping." West Point

**Grand Victory March**
This sheet music for a march by Edward Mack is "respectfully dedicated to Major General P. Sheridan." After the Valley Campaign in 1864, Sheridan became one of the most widely admired Union generals.

cadets, however, had to beware— Sheridan did not take kindly to teasing. Long arms made for a fine swordsman; and he was suspended once for waving a bayonet at a cadet for some perceived parade-ground slight.

### Meteoric career
As the son of Irish immigrant parents, Sheridan had an astonishing rise in the Civil War that could not be ascribed to family or political connections, which was the case with a number of officers. The young lieutenant on the Western frontier was also distant from influential contacts and had very few friends. When war did come, he earned his promotions through performance. Though his first postings were as a quartermaster and commissary officer in St. Louis, his efficiency and naturally bellicose streak soon won him the

**Dauntless Sheridan**
Mathew Brady's portrait of Sheridan captures a hint of the general's combative personality. The distinctive, flat-crowned hat was a style he particularly favored.

colonelcy of the 2nd Michigan Cavalry. Sheridan then saw combat in most of the major encounters in the West: Perryville, Stones River, Chickamauga, Chattanooga. Grant was so impressed by his dash at Missionary Ridge in the victory at Chattanooga that he invited him east for the coming campaign against General Lee, appointing him the Army of the Potomac's chief of cavalry.

## Praise and controversy

To his admirers, Sheridan was "Grant's flail," smashing the Confederates from Yellow Tavern to the Shenandoah Valley, which he thoroughly scourged. The valley was also the scene of his greatest triumph: his 10-mile (16-km) ride from Winchester to Cedar Creek, during which he rallied his demoralized troops, reeling from a surprise attack, and turned the tide of battle. On arrival, he was surrounded by thousands of cheering men. George Armstrong Custer raced up, threw his arms around Sheridan's neck and, as Frank Burr of the 2nd Michigan Cavalry put it, "kissed him in the face of the army. 'Little Phil' was the supreme incarnation of war." Sheridan's Ride was commemorated in a poem of that name, which so delighted Sheridan that he changed the name of his black charger, Rienzi, to Winchester.

In April 1865, it was Sheridan who cut Lee's final avenue of escape at Appomattox. "Sheridan's pursuit of Lee," in Grant's opinion, "was perfect in its generalship and energy." Some officers still resented his success, and

Sheridan, moreover, had his problems with military authority. In 1862, he had been arrested on a charge of insubordination, and three years later on the battlefield at Five Forks, he summarily stripped General Gouverneur K. Warren of his corps command for reasons later deemed untenable. Yet Theodore Lyman of George Meade's staff spoke for most officers when he grudgingly admitted, "Sherman is our first military genius, while Sheridan is most remarkable as a 'field fighter,' when the battle is actually engaged."

Grant was chief of the many who envied the field fighter's battlefield magnetism. "Gallant Phil" himself,

### Sheridan's saber

The sword Sheridan carried was an ornate version of the 1840 model cavalry saber, nicknamed the "wristbreaker" because it was so heavy. The gilded scabbard is engraved with the names of the battles in which he fought.

Sheridan was unsparing of himself and never spared others. He was curt, sarcastic, and combative even with his staff, and his picturesque profanity was legendary. In a rout of Confederate cavalry at the Battle of Five Forks, he galloped all over the field, urging his men on to greater efforts: "Come on; go at 'em! They're all getting ready to run now!" Even when one soldier collapsed before him, blood spurting

## "He belongs to the very **first rank of soldiers**, not only **of our country** but **of the world**."

ULYSSES S. GRANT ON PHILIP SHERIDAN

however, merely ascribed it to his penchant for fighting alongside his men. At the Battle of Stones River, where he pulled his division out of the shattered grove of cedars that they had defended against repeated Confederate attacks, while losing a third of their comrades, Sheridan was bareheaded, having lost his hat in the melee. After the battle, his soldiers honored him by providing him with one of their own.

from his neck, Sheridan, declaring he was not a bit hurt, ordered him to pick up his gun and get moving.

After the war Sheridan, headstrong and undiplomatic as ever, continued to flourish in army life. For years he was effectively in charge of the Indian wars in the West, where his opponents included Sitting Bull and Crazy Horse. Even after his marriage at the age of 44, he remained in active service.

From 1871, Sheridan involved himself in the preservation of the Yellowstone area. He opposed any development of the region and to ensure this, ordered it to be protected by the 1st U.S. Cavalry, an arrangement that continued until it was taken over by the National Park Service in 1916.

### The highest rank

In 1883, Sheridan was made general-in-chief of the army. After suffering one of a series of heart attacks in 1888, he was promoted to the highest rank—General of the Army of the United States—equivalent to a modern four-star general. He died soon afterward, and was buried in Arlington National Cemetery.

### The Valley Campaign of 1864

This sketch of Sheridan outside his tent shows him listening intently to a report of the day's fighting despite the late hour. As a general, he liked close contact with his troops and a "headquarters in the saddle."

### TIMELINE

- **March 6, 1831** Born in Albany, New York, the third of six children, to Irish immigrants John and Mary Sheridan; grows up in Somerset, Ohio.
- **June 1853** Graduates from West Point, 34th in a class of 52, and is commissioned a second lieutenant in the infantry.
- **March–May 1861** With the advent of war, is promoted to first lieutenant, then captain. Holds various staff positions, including quartermaster general of the Army of Southwest Missouri.
- **May 27, 1862** Arrested for insubordination—refusing to "steal" horses for the army. Appointed colonel of the 2nd Michigan Cavalry.
- **July 1, 1862** After the Battle of Booneville, is promoted to brigadier general.
- **December 31, 1862** Promoted to major general after the Battle of Stones River.
- **November 25, 1863** Impresses Grant with his assault on Missionary Ridge.
- **April 5, 1864** Takes command of the Army of the Potomac's cavalry corps.
- **May 9–23, 1864** Leads a massive cavalry raid, battling Jeb Stuart's troopers at Yellow Tavern, where Stuart is fatally wounded.
- **June 12, 1864** On a raid to disrupt Confederate supply lines in western Virginia, is defeated by General Wade Hampton at Trevilian Station.
- **August 7, 1864** Takes command of the Army of Shenandoah, charged by Grant with destroying the Valley's usefulness as a Confederate granary.
- **October 19, 1864** Gallops from Winchester, Virginia, to Cedar Creek, to rally his troops—an episode known as "Sheridan's Ride."
- **April 9, 1865** Cuts off Lee's escape at Appomattox, forcing the Confederate surrender.
- **March 1867** Appointed governor of the Fifth Military District, covering Louisiana and Texas, but is soon removed by President Andrew Johnson after a clash over Reconstruction policy.
- **August 1867** Appointed chief of the Military Department of Missouri, responsible for operations against the Lakota and Cheyenne.
- **March 4, 1869** Promoted to lieutenant general on Grant's accession to the presidency.
- **June 3, 1875** Marries Irene Rucker, 22 years his junior. They have four children.
- **November 1, 1883** Succeeds Sherman as general of the Army.
- **August 5, 1888** Dies of a heart attack in Nonquitt, Massachusetts, at the age of 57.

**SHERIDAN WITH HIS FAMILY, 1888**

# Sheridan's ride

**Also known as the Battle of Belle Grove, the Battle of Cedar Creek erupted on October 19, 1864, in Virginia's Shenandoah Valley. General Philip Sheridan's ride to the battle from Winchester revived Union morale, and fighting barely lasted a day before Union troops emerged victorious. The loss was devastating for the Confederates.**

"About 9 o'clock, everything looked very gloomy. General Sheridan was absent, a portion of the army much demoralized, the whole of it driven back from its chosen and fortified position on the bank of Cedar Creek. About 10 o'clock, General Sheridan arrived on the field of disaster, amid the cheers of his army, cheers more deafening than the artillery which was then engaged. The tide of battle immediately turned. Stragglers began to organize and to return to the battle. The line of battle was at once strengthened with new spirit and numbers … the musketry was fearful and terrific, exceeding anything at the Winchester fight and reminding our veterans of Gettysburg … the Rebel rear made but one effort to resistance, giving our heroes one volley and then fled in perfect confusion. It was now dark. Unknown, our boys entered amid the enemy and mingled in their perfectly demoralized columns … We routed them as never a large army was routed."

LOUIS N. BEAUDRY, 5TH NEW YORK CAVALRY, FROM *THE DIARY OF A UNION CHAPLAIN COMMENCING FEBRUARY 16, 1863*

"My Dear Allie,
Oh what a victory we had yesterday morning—What a defeat yesterday evening! I hardly know how to write about it to you. I am nearly dying for sleep. Just think I have slept but one hour in over sixty hours, besides undergoing the most constant & arduous labor … oh how distressed I am. Thank the Good Being for my safety. I have another bullet as a keepsake. It struck me & lodged in my clothes … this is my first defeat on a battlefield. I did all I could. I hurled the brigade alone against the charging Yankee line, in the evening drove them back, but they came back again, lapped me on all sides, when I retired with the balance—poor me—poor me—what I did gain in the morning—and lost all in the evenings."

CONFEDERATE GENERAL CLEMENT ANSELM EVANS IN A LETTER TO HIS WIFE, OCTOBER 20, 1864

**Rallying Union troops**
As Sheridan rode along rallying his men, he waved his hat and was said to shout: "Retreat—Hell! We'll be back in our camps tonight." Artists such as Thure de Thulstrup, shown here, later depicted him carrying a pennant.

# The Siege of Petersburg

**The battle for Petersburg was fought over months of siege warfare. Union general Ulysses S. Grant and Confederate general Robert E. Lee matched each other earthwork for earthwork—over 100 miles (160km) altogether—though Grant continually tried to break the stalemate by stretching Lee's lines to breaking point.**

## BEFORE

Since May 1864 the Union Army of the Potomac and the Confederate Army of Northern Virginia had been fighting each other north of the James River.

### TRENCH WARFARE

Union troops assaulted Confederate forces that were firmly planted behind **cunningly contrived earthworks**. But as the soldiers settled into the Richmond-Petersburg lines, the Confederate **mastery of field fortifications was soon matched** by that of the Union armies. **Stalemate loomed**.

**88,000** The estimated number of total casualties—killed, wounded, captured, and missing—incurred by both armies during the six weeks' fighting from the Battle of the Wilderness to Cold Harbor.

### SUPPLY LINES

After failing to defeat Lee in open battle, Grant shifted his strategy, hoping to **sever the Confederate supply lines**—the railroads running to the south and west that kept the Army of Northern Virginia in the field.

During the siege of Vicksburg ❮❮ 190–93, Grant had tightened a ring around the defending army so no supplies could get in and starved it into submission—a tactic that he would pursue again.

In June 1864, Lee remarked to his staff that if Grant managed to cross the James River and arrive before Petersburg, "it will become a siege, and then it will be a mere question of time." By July the military situation had indeed taken on all the appearance of a siege. For 35 miles (56km), a curving line of entrenchments stretched from north of Richmond to west of Petersburg— a labyrinth of front lines, secondary lines, bombproof shelters, rifle pits, and small forts, or redoubts, scarred the flat landscape. Sharpshooters ruled this denuded world, picking off the unwary. Artillery always thundered somewhere. It was a life lived almost entirely underground. Dirt, mud, sun, rain, wind, and sky—and the occasional whizzing bullet— marked its boundaries.

## Mining the line

As the standoff settled into a lethal stalemate, members of the 48th Pennsylvania Volunteers, who had been coal miners in civilian life, persuaded their commander, Lieutenant Colonel Henry Pleasants, a mining engineer, that it was possible to dig a mine beneath a Confederate redoubt called Elliott's Salient, pack it with explosives, and blow a hole in the enemy lines. Though doubting its usefulness, Grant eventually approved the scheme.

Digging began on June 25 and by July 17 the miners had excavated a 510-ft (155-m) shaft, ending directly beneath Elliott's Salient, only 20ft (6m) above them. They had cleverly concealed their work, devising ingenious ways to provide ventilation. But the inevitable noise had alerted the Confederates who sank countermines in response. Those went wide of the mark, so the Pennsylvanians dug lateral tunnels—like the crossbar on a "T"— which they packed with 230 kegs of

gunpowder, totaling four tons of charge, sandbagged to direct the force upward. The miners retraced their steps, unwinding a 98-ft (30-m) fuse. The plan was to break the enemy line in an instant, then exploit the breach with waves of assault troops who would pour through the punctured works and roll up the Confederate army.

At 4:45 a.m., on July 30, Elliott's Salient erupted in an earthshaking roar, a blast that carried skyward men, cannons, gun carriages, and tons of earth. When the dust had cleared, the Salient was gone, replaced by a 170-ft (52-m) long crater, nearly 80ft (24m) wide and 30ft (9m) deep. The assault troops clambered out of their trenches, reached the edge of the crater, then halted, stupefied at the sight of shattered men and guns strewn across its bottom. Other troops managed to get around it, but since their leaders had

### Inside the mine
War artist Alfred Waud made this sketch with accompanying notes. It shows Lieutenant Colonel Henry Pleasants as he supervised the laying of powder kegs in the mine shaft that later became the Crater.

*Carrying powder into the mine. The soldiers detailed for this duty carried the powder - a keg in either end of a grain bag thrown acros the shoulder. A portion of the covered way "along which they had to pass, was exposed to the enemies fire. At the dangerous points they would watch their opportunitys and dash over the exposed ground into comparative safety.*

remained behind, they quickly became disorganized. In the ensuing chaos, the Confederates recovered enough to mount counterattacks, and the Battle of the Crater, as it would be called, degenerated into a savage struggle. Screaming men pounded each other, amid cries of "No quarter!" Black Union troops, trapped in the crater, were shot down even after surrendering. One Southerner later recalled with horror: "My heart sickened at the deeds I saw done." Those Union survivors who had not been captured fled back to their own lines. Grant admitted that it was "the saddest affair I witnessed in the war."

## Railroads and a cattle raid

Grant redoubled his efforts around the armies' edges, seeking to thin the Confederate lines until they broke. On August 18–21, Major General Gouverneur K. Warren's Fifth Corps

**38** The number of black regiments at the siege of Petersburg. Secretary of War Edwin Stanton stated, "The hardest fighting was done by the black troops."

seized another of Lee's arteries to the south. In the Battle of the Weldon Railroad, troops of General A. P. Hill's Third Corps slammed into Warren's, forcing them back into open fields. There the Union infantry held, despite Hill's repeated assaults—and held the railroad too.

Loss of the Weldon Railroad raised the specter of starvation for Lee's soldiers. In mid-September, General Wade Hampton and 4,000 troopers rode around the Army of the Potomac, almost as far as Grant's massive supply depot at City Point. They raided the Union cattle corral, rustling some 2,000 head and, driving the herd back the way they had come, managed to lose only 60 men.

## CONFEDERATE GENERAL 1825–65

### AMBROSE POWELL HILL

Hill's name was on both Robert E. Lee's and Stonewall Jackson's dying lips, such was the impression the slight, red-bearded "Little Powell" made as a fighter. The Virginian Hill and his Light Division saved the day in numerous closely fought battles, including the Seven Days Battles. As commander of the Third Corps, Hill was one of Lee's most trusted lieutenants before being killed in action outside Petersburg—barely a week before the Confederate surrender at Appomattox.

> "Hold on with a **bulldog grip**, and **chew and choke** as much as possible."
>
> ABRAHAM LINCOLN IN A TELEGRAM TO ULYSSES S. GRANT, AUGUST 17, 1864

## Taunting the enemy

Winslow Homer's *Defiance: Inviting a Shot Before Petersburg* (1864) shows a Confederate soldier standing on the earthworks taunting Union sharpshooters. On one such occasion the man was instantly shot.

That fall, Grant continued his war of maneuver. On September 29–30, Union forces took Fort Harrison, a key bastion in the Richmond defenses. At the same time, on the other end of the line, a Union reconnaissance force pushed 3 miles (5km) west of the Weldon Railroad, only to be beaten back by A. P. Hill and Wade Hampton in a brutal two-day fight at Peebles' Farm.

On October 27, Grant's Second Corps and part of his Fifth Corps, with a cavalry screen, reached out even farther west in an attempt to cut the Boydton Plank Road, an important link to the southwest. By exploiting a gap between the two corps, the Confederates succeeded in turning their enemies back, though several thousand more names were added to the casualty rolls. Lee desperately struggled to keep his remaining supply line, the South Side Railroad, from being severed.

### Dark winter days

As winter set in, Lee faced another worry: desertion. Union pickets knew that "Johnnie Reb" (the archetypal Southerner) was waiting for the results of the presidential election in the North. After Lincoln prevailed, hope went out of the Army of Northern Virginia. Each day for months on end, the incessant shelling continued. Nerves were breaking. Self-inflicted gunshot wounds, and occasional suicides, were reported. At night, scores of men disappeared, some coming into the Union lines to surrender. A truce was called at Christmas, and soldiers emerged from the trenches without fear of snipers. Robert E. Lee's winter of discontent was upon him, and the prospects for spring looked bleak.

### Union artillery shelling

The near-daily bombardment of Petersburg made most of its citizens refugees. More than 800 buildings were struck by shells, while many others were hit by fragments. In spite of this, probably fewer than half a dozen residents were killed.

### AFTER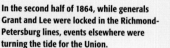

In the second half of 1864, while generals Grant and Lee were locked in the Richmond-Petersburg lines, events elsewhere were turning the tide for the Union.

#### A ROUND OF UNION VICTORIES

Union successes continued until late in the year. In December 1864, General George H. Thomas destroyed the remnants of the Confederate Army of Tennessee at **Franklin and Nashville 300–301 ≫**. General William T. Sherman captured not just Atlanta, but Savannah as well, at Christmas. This set the stage for him to **lead his victorious troops to the state where the war had started: South Carolina 310–11 ≫**. The destruction of the capital, Columbia, was another example of total war.

#### THE ROAD TO APPOMATTOX

The Petersburg stalemate continued until April 1865, when Grant, having outdug and outgunned Lee, **finally shattered the Confederate right flank 314–15 ≫**. This forced the beleaguered Army of Northern Virginia out of its entrenchments and onto **the road to Appomattox 316–17 ≫**.

# Siege Artillery and Siege Warfare

**Throughout history, armies have laid siege to cities and citadels. The Civil War sieges combined established techniques of siegecraft, including the choking off of supply routes and the undermining of fortifications, with the deployment of more modern and powerful heavy artillery.**

### « BEFORE

After the War of 1812, the United States began constructing a series of masonry forts to protect its harbors and coastal cities from invasion.

#### AMERICAN COASTAL ARTILLERY

Because they constituted the nation's **first line of defense**, the heavy guns in the forts had received most of government spending on ordnance (weapons and ammunition), **much more than had the field artillery « 128–29**. Most of the guns were 8- and 10-in (200- and 250-mm) smoothbore Columbiads, **muzzle-loading cannons invented in 1811.**

#### CONFEDERATE COASTAL ARTILLERY

By 1861, **more than 60 forts and batteries** ringed the U.S. coast. Some were so lightly manned, however, that the **Confederate states were able to seize them** and their guns intact, thus gaining a **wide range of heavy artillery** at the start of the war. Augmented by **imports from Britain** and guns made by **the few cannon foundries in the South**, this artillery would defend not only the forts of the Confederacy, but also such besieged cities as Vicksburg **« 190–95** and Petersburg **« 274–75.**

Vicksburg remains the classic example of a Civil War siege. On May 25, 1863, General Ulysses S. Grant, looking up the bluff at fortified Vicksburg, released his Special Order 140: "Corps Commanders will immediately commence the work of reducing the enemy by regular approaches." Every officer knew what "regular approaches" entailed: It meant digging their way up the hill. Its aim was a kind of slow, subterranean strangulation, the attacker taking every advantage of terrain to move his forces, with small loss of life, close enough to smash a defender's fortifications with artillery.

### Improvised attack

When Grant attacked Vicksburg, his army had just fought its way through the Mississippi swamps. He had no siege equipment, no engineering troops, and no siege train. As his soldiers dug their way up the bluff, they improvised building materials and made serviceable mortars from wooden cylinders wrapped in iron bands. A 12-mile (19-km) coil of

### Deceptive defenses

Short of real guns, the Confederacy turned to "Quaker guns," logs set in embrasures and painted to look like cannon barrels, to intimidate the enemy. Here a "gunner" pretends to fire the weapon.

#### Wooden quadrant

This simple quadrant was used by gunners to check the elevation of a cannon in order to give the shell the correct angle of trajectory to hit its target.

Rule

Quadrant, marked in degrees

Plumb bob

siege works tightened around Vicksburg. A second line of works was built around the first but facing outward to repel any Confederate attempt to lift the siege.

At Vicksburg, Grant also used mining techniques. He laid several kinds of mine, including one resembling a smaller version of the densely packed mine that triggered the Battle of the Crater at Petersburg. Finally, Grant won the artillery duel with only his field artillery and some heavy ordnance loaned to him by Union gunboats.

### Heavy artillery old and new

Siege artillery was often dwarfed by coastal artillery: large-caliber Columbiads and similar monsters fired from fixed platforms. By the time of the Civil War, however, these great smoothbores and their enclosing forts were becoming obsolete, as new artillery with rifled—or grooved—barrels came into use. These weapons were faster to fire, more accurate, and had a greater range. The thick masonry walls of Fort Pulaski outside Savannah were reduced to rubble in two days in April 1862 by the new rifled ordnance of the Union fleet. Earth forts fared better, however, as they absorbed the blow and shock of an exploding shell. Battery Wagner outside Charleston, made of packed dirt, sand, and palmetto logs, withstood weeks of bombardment before the Confederates abandoned it and its 14 coast guns. These included a 10-in (250-mm) Columbiad that fired a 128-lb (58-kg) shell.

Many of these huge guns eventually blew up, because of flaws in casting technology. On average the South's ordnance and munitions proved the more unstable, but Union guns often exploded, too. During the 1863–64 siege of Charleston, the "Swamp Angel," a 24,000-lb (10,890 kg), 8-in (200-mm) Parrott gun, had the dubious distinction of shooting the first incendiary shells into the city; but it blew up after only 36 rounds.

### Civil War sieges

In the 1862 Peninsula Campaign, General George B. McClellan dragged a massive siege train through the Virginia swamps. No fewer than 101 guns—with 20-, 30-, and even 100-pounder (9-, 14-, and 45-kg) Parrott guns and huge mortars—were erected on platforms before Yorktown, itself "protected" by a few fake cannons, or "Quaker guns," named for the pacifist Quakers.

In the Civil War, the term "siege" was often applied to any grinding struggle involving fortified positions—Atlanta and Petersburg among them. These battles borrowed many elements of traditional sieges, including mining, countermining, labyrinths of enclosed entrenchments, and the often commanding use of heavy artillery.

Sherman had been at Vicksburg, but he once declared, "I'm too impatient for a siege." In 1864, when he attacked Atlanta, the city was ringed with fortifications, but most of the fighting took the form of battles of maneuver

**80,000** Estimated number of mortar shells fired during the ten-month siege of Petersburg.

> "The sky was lit up by the **broad flame** of **mortars** and by the twinkling and shooting stars ..."
>
> A. S. TWITCHELL, 7TH MAINE LIGHT BATTERY, AT PETERSBURG, MARCH 29, 1865

## The "Dictator"
Weighing 17,000lb (7,711kg) and known as the "Dictator," this 13-in (330-mm) siege mortar could fire 200-lb (90-kg) shells more than two miles (3.2 km). It was used at Petersburg for two months.

around its outskirts. Regular approaches were never attempted, although Sherman did bring up four 4.5-in (114-mm) rifled guns that lobbed 30-lb (13.6-kg) shells into the city to supplement his field artillery.

## Petersburg
At Petersburg, Grant's officers urged him to consider regular approaches, but he preferred maneuver to engineering. First, he ordered that the redoubts on the main line be enclosed as forts to deter Confederate attacks. He then embarked on offensives to cut Rebel communications and stretch their lines to breaking point. After each gain, Grant consolidated and then pushed out a few miles farther, overstraining Lee's engineering resources. Strong forts were interspersed along Grant's ever-creeping lines; even the defensive line running along his rear was studded with forts.

Instead of coiling ever tighter around the city, the honeycomb of trenches, forts, rifle pits, bombproofs, and wire entanglements snaked outward, with artillery emplacements everywhere. No siege guns were more effective than mortars, mostly 8- and 10-in (200- and 250-mm) giants, which could lob shells behind enemy parapets.

Siege artillery made for spectacular nocturnal fireworks. In some Union forts at Petersburg, watching the display

became an evening ritual. "Sometimes more than twenty shells would be in the air at the same time, looking like twinkling stars shooting and plunging madly," recalled one observer at Fort Haskell. "Then a wide, sudden sheet of flame would terminate its flight, and woe to him or them who came within its deadly circle."

### TECHNOLOGY
## KETCHUM GRENADE

Detonated by a percussion cap in its nose, the Ketchum grenade used cardboard stabilizing fins to help direct its flight. Thousands were used by the Union army and navy during the Civil War, in various sizes ranging between 1-5lb (0.5-2.2kg), often being tossed into enemy trenches during siege operations. They were not always reliable, and might be thrown back at the attacker. Another grenade was the Adams, a small, handheld weapon that resembled a tiny cannonball. In the heat of battle, instead of using a grenade, soldiers sometimes simply lit the fuses on artillery shells and heaved or rolled them over a defensive parapet into an attacking infantry force.

**AFTER** »

The Civil War would have a large impact on the art of fortification, but there were many lessons still to be learned about siege warfare.

### A NEW ERA IN FORTIFICATION
The **range, power, and accuracy** of rifled artillery had **ended the era** of stone and masonry forts, often pulverizing them while strongholds of packed earth and sand withstood bombardment much better. Still, coastal forts were **rarely taken by naval guns** alone; joint operations between land and sea forces would in the future become the norm.

### REPERCUSSIONS
European observers, impressed by the **deadly accuracy** of rifled guns and their increased rates of fire, returned home with new ideas on how better to construct fortifications that might **withstand modern sieges**. The maze of **muddy trenches**, forts, and bombproofs at Petersburg proved to be an omen of the appalling conditions on the **Western Front (1914–18)**.

Scene of the Explosion ~ Saturday

# The **Battle** of the **Crater**

**During the siege of Petersburg, Colonel Henry Pleasants and his coal-mining troops (the 48th Pennsylvania) laid a mine beneath the Confederate lines. The explosion produced an enormous crater, burying hundreds of Rebel troops in debris. But the Union advantage turned into catastrophe as Confederates had time to counterattack, and many Union soldiers became fatally trapped in the crater.**

**"**I was lying on the ground resting my head on my hand and thinking of the probable result, when the denouement came. I shall never forget the terrible and magnificent sight. The earth around us trembled and heaved so violently that I was lifted to my feet. Then the earth along the enemy's lines opened, and fire and smoke shot upward seventy-five or one hundred feet. The air was filled with earth, cannon, caissons, sand-bags and living men, and with everything else within the exploded fort ... Our orders were to charge immediately after the explosion, but the effect produced by the falling of earth and the fragments sent heavenward that appeared to be coming right down upon us, caused the first line to waver and fall back, and the situation was one to demoralize most troops.**"**

BREVET MAJOR CHARLES H. HOUGHTON, 14TH NEW YORK HEAVY ARTILLERY, FROM *BATTLES AND LEADERS OF THE CIVIL WAR*, 1888

**"**Little did these men anticipate what they would see upon arriving there: an enormous hole in the ground about 30 feet deep, 60 feet wide, and 170 feet long, filled with dust, great blocks of clay, guns, broken carriages, projecting timbers, and men buried in various ways—some up to their necks, others to their waists, and some with only their feet and legs protruding from the earth ...

The whole scene of the explosion struck every one dumb with astonishment as we arrived at the crest of the debris. It was impossible for the troops of the Second Brigade to move forward in line ... Before the brigade commanders could realize the situation, the two brigades became inextricably mixed ... Up on the other side of the crater they climbed ... In doing so members of these regiments were killed by musket-shots from the rear, fired by the Confederates who were still occupying the traverses and intrenchments to the right and left of the crater ... This coming so unexpectedly caused the forming line to fall back into the crater.**"**

UNION MAJOR WILLIAM H. POWELL, FROM *BATTLES AND LEADERS OF THE CIVIL WAR*, 1888

**After the explosion**
War artist Alfred R. Waud drew the scene after the mine exploded. In the foreground Union soldiers head from their entrenchments toward the Confederate line, beyond the mounds of earth thrown up by the explosion.

« BEFORE

**By 1850, the age of sail was waning as steam engines increasingly replaced ships using wind and canvas.**

### FIRST IRONCLADS

The Crimean War (1853–56) augured **the end of the wooden hull** for warships, as powerful new rifled artillery and explosive shells encouraged navies to protect their vessels with iron armor. By 1861, the **first steam-powered ironclad warships**, the French *Gloire* and British *Warrior*, were roving the seas. The **first combat between ironclads** was the engagement, on March 9, 1862, between the Union's *Monitor* and the Confederacy's *Virginia* (or *Merrimack*) « **94–95**.

### MINES AND SUBMARINES

**Torpedoes**—floating kegs of gunpowder also known as mines—**first appeared** during the American Revolution. They were deployed in large numbers during the Crimean War.

Since the end of the 18th century, many navies had shown a passing interest in **building submersible warships**, but most experiments were not promising. With the outbreak of the Civil War, efforts were quickly renewed as both **Union and Confederate engineers raced** to overcome design challenges and develop the **first dependable and operationally effective submarine**.

# Naval Developments

**Occurring on the cusp of a revolution in naval warfare, the American Civil War spurred a great wave of innovation and experimentation in the design of ships and weapons, which included the use of mines, the first torpedo boats, and even submarines.**

When war broke out, the U.S. Navy had fewer than 70 serviceable ships, while the Confederates counted less than a dozen. Yet "inequality of numbers," the Southern Secretary of the Navy, Stephen Mallory, asserted, "may be compensated by invulnerability." He was referring to the ironclads. He hoped that they would prove so impervious to enemy guns that a single one might breach the Union blockade to attack and burn New York City.

## Ironclads and mines

In the event, the South's lack of industrial resources forced Mallory to choose the simplest ironclad designs. In contrast, Lincoln's stern-faced navy secretary, Gideon Welles, harnessed factories, foundries, and shipyards to build technologically sophisticated ironclads, 65 in all. Most ships were refinements on the first Union ironclad, the *Monitor*, launched in 1862, but were

**Underwater mine**
A typical stationary "torpedo" was held in place a few feet beneath the surface of the water, by cables weighted to the bottom. Many torpedoes became waterlogged, rendering them harmless.

longer, mounted with heavier guns, and even had more than one turret. Low-slung and formidable, they were more versatile than any of their Confederate counterparts. Mallory had

another card to play: "torpedoes." The Confederacy's secretive Torpedo Corps and Submarine Battery Service experimented with all kinds of these "infernal machines." Most exploded on contact with a ship, but some were detonated via insulated wires controlled by agents hidden onshore. Torpedoes sank or damaged 43 Union vessels in all, making them the Confederacy's most effective defense against Union naval superiority. Torpedoes were also used in direct attacks. Fixed to the end of a long underwater spar that protruded forward from the bows of specially designed boats, the torpedo was rammed into the enemy ship. In 1863, General P. G. T. Beauregard, commander of Charleston's defenses,

NAVY SECRETARY 1812–73

### STEPHEN RUSSELL MALLORY

When Mallory, a Florida senator, became secretary of the Confederate navy, he had to start from scratch. He assembled a small armored fleet, hoping it might offset the advantages of the U.S. Navy's larger wooden ships. He gambled on winning the war at sea through a combination of raids on Union commerce and the use of ironclads and ingeniously contrived torpedoes.

**Confederate torpedo boat**
The sleek torpedo boat CSS *David* was depicted by an anonymous artist moored to a Charleston wharf. At least half a dozen similar craft, called "Davids," were built in Charleston.

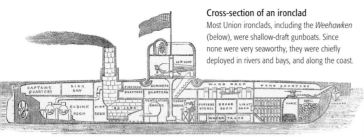

**Cross-section of an ironclad**
Most Union ironclads, including the *Weehawken* (below), were shallow-draft gunboats. Since none were very seaworthy, they were chiefly deployed in rivers and bays, and along the coast.

## TECHNOLOGY
### SUBMARINES

The *Hunley* was not the Confederates' first attempt at submarine warfare. In October 1861 they used an unnamed underwater craft, designed by engineer William Cheeney, to try to sink USS *Minnesota* off the Florida coast. The attack failed after the craft became entangled in protective netting around the warship. The Confederates also tested the 30-ft (9-m) *Pioneer*, but scuttled her as Union forces approached New Orleans. On the Union side, the 47-ft (14-m) USS *Alligator* sank in a storm while being towed to her first deployment. Major Edward Hunt designed a one-man "submarine battery," but died of carbon monoxide poisoning while putting her through trials at Brooklyn Navy Yard.

hoped to use a semi-submersible torpedo boat, CSS *David*, to break the Union stranglehold on the harbor. On the night of October 5, the *David* attacked the Goliath of the blockading squadrons, USS *New Ironsides*, exploding 100lbs (45kg) of gunpowder against her starboard side. The damage was minor, but more *David*-style craft, forerunners of modern torpedo boats, followed.

Spar torpedoes were used by both sides. On the night of October 27, 1864, Lieutenant William B. Cushing and 14 volunteers from the U.S. Navy entered the Roanoke River on a boat fitted with a spar torpedo. Their target was the CSS *Albemarle*, a Confederate ironclad that had started driving off the Union naval forces on the North Carolina shore. With only a 6-ft (1.8-m) draft, the *Albemarle* was able to navigate rivers where no Union warship could follow. At 3 a.m., braving small-arms fire and the ironclad's roaring cannon, Cushing sank the monster with his well-placed torpedo.

### Underwater attack
The use of spar torpedoes dramatically changed naval warfare, because they gave small ships the ability to damage or sink larger ones. Lookouts posted in the tops of Union vessels blockading Charleston harbor were always on the alert for wakes on the surface of the water from semi-submersibles.

In August 1863, a train pulled into Charleston carrying, at General Beauregard's request, a flatcar with a very special freight. Unveiled was a 40-ft (12-m) submersible made from an old locomotive boiler with a tapered bow and stern added. Only 4ft (1.2m) in diameter, she was a tight fit for her crew of nine, one to steer and eight to crank her propeller. Though several practice dives proved fatal—one of them taking the life of its inventor, Horace L. Hunley—another crew volunteered, commanded by Lieutenant George Dixon. Christened CSS *Hunley*, her craft had a spar torpedo attached to her snout. When attacking, *Hunley* would stay just above the surface of the water until she closed in on her target. Then she would use her rudders to submerge.

On the night of February 17, 1864, lookouts on the screw sloop USS *Housatonic* reported a slight wake approaching. Their ship already had a head of steam up and was just getting underway to avoid the assailant, when the barbed head of a 130-lb (59-kg) spar torpedo lodged in her timbers. The torpedo exploded, and in a few minutes the *Housatonic* settled to the bottom in shallow water. Only five of her crew had been killed; most of the rest climbed into the rigging to await rescue. From there they spied lantern signals from a nearby vessel, but these vanished. The *Hunley*, the world's first submarine to sink an enemy ship, had foundered for some unknown reason and gone down with all hands.

# "... these **cheap, convenient, and formidable** devices ..."
UNION ADMIRAL JOHN A. DAHLGREN, AFTER THE *HUNLEY* SANK THE *HOUSATONIC*

> **TORPEDO** From the Latin word *torpere*, meaning to stupefy, the term once applied to all military and naval mines, presumably because of their sudden shocks.

## AFTER

In the years following the war, the U.S. Navy was cut from 626 to 60 vessels, and most of the 65 ironclads were scrapped or sold. But the surge of innovation driven by the war spread to navies all over the world.

### IRON AND STEEL
By the 1890s, the **revolution in naval design** had reconfigured warships aross the globe. Gone were masts and sails; vessels were now **built entirely of steel**, strong as iron but lighter, and powered by steam. Guns were housed in armored turrets or protected by armored shields called "barbettes."

### TORPEDOES
Speedy torpedo boats, designed to attack the lumbering new battleships, launched **self-propelled torpedoes**, refined in Europe while the Civil War was still being fought. **Improved naval mines** became ubiquitous in blockade operations and harbor defense, particularly after the 1904–05 Russo-Japanese War.

### SUBMARINES
Engineers continued to design new and improved submarines throughout the rest of the 19th century. But it was only in 1900 that a submersible was deemed **reliable enough to be put into service by the U.S. Navy**.

The first cruise of the *Sumter*
This 19th-century lithograph shows the commerce raider CSS *Sumter* eluding USS *Brooklyn* to break through the Federal blockade at the mouth of the Mississippi River, on June 30, 1861.

Confederate secretary of the Navy, Stephen Mallory, believed that raids on U.S. maritime commerce might hurt Northern business interests, deprive the North of war material, and weaken the blockade.

## THE PRIVATEERING TRADITION

**Privateering** was a time-honored if not-quite-honorable practice in use since at least the 16th century. With a **Letter of Marque and Reprisal** issued by a belligerent government, a privately owned ship could **raid enemy commercial shipping**. Captured ships became prizes, subject to adjudication by a recognized court.

In 1861, the Confederate government issued Letters of Marque to privateers daring enough to elude the **Federal blockade « 72–73**. Most neutral nations, however, refused to allow prizes to be brought into their ports. The Lincoln administration, moreover, **did not recognize the Confederacy as a legitimate nation** and threatened to **hang its privateers as pirates**. Those willing to run the risk soon discovered that more money was to be made in **blockade-running**, than in privateering.

## COMMERCE RAIDERS

Confederate navy secretary Mallory had little confidence in privateers. The alternative was to entrust the task to fast naval **ships**. With no cruisers, Mallory **converted steamships**, like CSS *Sumter*, and **sent agents abroad to procure**, clandestinely, well-designed and **well-armed commerce raiders**.

# Confederate Raiders

**It was not enough for Southern blockade-runners to elude the U.S. Navy squadrons patrolling inshore waters around the ports of the Confederacy. Fast and graceful Confederate blockade-runners and raiders also took to the high seas to circumvent U.S. maritime commerce around the world.**

When, in June 1861, Captain Raphael Semmes and CSS *Sumter* left the Mississippi River for the Gulf of Mexico, outrunning the ships of the Union blockade, he was following Stephen Mallory's instructions to "do the enemy's commerce the greatest injury in the shortest time."

Across the Atlantic in England, James D. Bulloch, a Confederate agent, had a similar brief: "Get cruising ships afloat," Mallory had told him, "with the quickest possible dispatch." While Semmes made his name in the *Sumter*, Bulloch managed to circumvent both British neutrality laws and U.S. diplomatic protests to procure 18 ships. Eleven became blockade-runners, seven commerce raiders. Three ships became legends.

## The *Florida*

The first of the legends was built in Liverpool, England, as the *Oreto*, but off a deserted cay in the Bahamas the ship took on arms and, in August 1862, became CSS *Florida*. During the next 14 months, cruising mostly in the West Indies, *Florida* took 38 prizes. Her career ended one October night in 1864 when, anchored in the neutral port of Bahia, Brazil, she was commandeered by daring Union sailors—while most of her crew was ashore—and sailed to the United States.

## Unrivaled success

Another legend began life in a Liverpool shipyard as *Hull 290* before sailing for the Azores in July 1864 as the *Enrica*. On August 24, her new captain, the redeployed Raphael Semmes, hoisted the Confederate ensign and commissioned her as CSS *Alabama*.

The *Alabama* was the epitome of the Confederate commerce raider—a three-masted, bark-rigged sloop-of-war, long, sleek, and very fast. She carried eight guns, and, while capable of 13 knots under both steam and sail, made most of her captures under sail alone. In the sea lanes between Newfoundland and Bermuda and through the West Indies into the Gulf of Mexico, the *Alabama* ravaged U.S. merchant shipping. She also hunted along the coasts of Brazil and Africa, and even sailed across the Indian Ocean to Java and Singapore.

A raider usually approached her target flying a British or Dutch ensign, or flag. Only at close range was the Confederate ensign run up. Semmes boarded nearly 450 ships in *Alabama*'s two years at sea, 65 of them U.S. merchantmen or whalers. He burned most of the ships, but not before removing their crews, whom he placed aboard neutral ships or ashore in neutral ports. At any given time, up to a dozen Union

### Sailor's flat cap
The Civil War brought standardization to naval uniforms. Clothes became practical; fabrics repelled dirt and provided protection against the elements.

ships were hunting the *Alabama*. Huge crowds came to see the famous ship when she anchored in Cape Town in August 1863. But the days of this raider were doomed to be short. On June 11, 1864, the *Alabama* sought haven in Cherbourg, France. After 22 months, mostly spent at sea, both crew and ship were in need of rest and repair. Three days later, the sloop-of-war USS *Kearsarge* appeared outside the harbor. Her commander, Captain John Winslow, had been a shipmate of Semmes when they were both young.

### The sinking of the Alabama

"My intention is to fight the *Kearsarge* as soon as I can make the necessary arrangements," Semmes wrote to a U.S. diplomat through an intermediary. "I beg she will not depart until I am ready to go out." On June 19, dressed in his finest uniform, Semmes sailed the *Alabama* out into the English Channel, where the *Kearsarge* was waiting just beyond the 3-mile (4.8-km) territorial limit. Thousands thronged the Normandy cliffs to watch the duel, which lasted little more than an hour. Maneuvering slowly around each other, the combatants were soon engulfed in smoke. The *Alabama* fired 370 rounds, but many were too high or failed to explode. The *Kearsarge* fired only 173 shots, but with her superior gunnery they had telling effect, first disabling the raider's steering mechanism and then tearing a gash in her side at the waterline.

Water poured into the *Alabama*, and the ship struck her colors (lowered her flag as a sign of surrender) before sinking stern first. The *Kearsarge* recovered most of the survivors, but a number of the *Alabama*'s officers, including Semmes, were rescued by a British yacht and escaped to England.

> Not a single U.S. merchant sailor lost his life as a result of the *Alabama*'s raids on commercial shipping.

### Last of the raiders

James Bulloch, the Confederate agent, put one more famous raider to sea. Since tightened neutrality laws made it impossible to build another vessel in Britain, he converted one instead. The *Sea King* departed London in October 1864—ostensibly for Bombay and points east. Fitted with guns and munitions, she became CSS *Shenandoah*. Captained by James Waddell, the ship spent the next year cruising seas unexplored by former commerce raiders. Sailing south, she crossed from the Cape of Good Hope to Australia and then sailed far into the Pacific, where she preyed upon Yankee whalers venturing north to the Aleutian Islands and the Arctic Ocean. In June 1865, still taking prizes (some 37 in all), Waddell read in a newspaper about General Lee's surrender. On August 2, off the coast of California, he confirmed that the Confederacy had indeed collapsed. Disarming his ship, he avoided U.S. ports, where piracy charges awaited. Instead, he steered for Cape Horn, and on to Britain, a voyage of nearly 19,000 miles (30,000km).

On November 5, 1865, the battered *Shenandoah* steamed up the Mersey River into the English port of Liverpool. At 10 a.m. the following day, the ship's ensign was hauled down—the last Confederate flag to be struck, and only one to have circumnavigated the globe. Waddell then surrendered his ship to British authorities.

After the war, the U.S. government took stock of the damage to its maritime commerce. Confederate raiders had taken 257 merchant ships and whalers, about five percent of the nation's merchant marine. Though the raiders did not wreak the havoc that Stephen Mallory had hoped for, they had driven insurance rates sky high and forced many vessels to adopt foreign registry. Nor did their activity draw many Union ships away from blockading the Southern waterways, much affect the blockade. At any one time, only a few score Union warships out of the hundreds on blockade duty were hunting for the raiders—barely a dozen—that embarked on the high seas.

**Confederate navy frock coat**
This typical Confederate officer's frock coat belonged to Lieutenant William F. Robinson of the Confederate States Navy, who served on various ships in the waters around New Orleans and Mobile.

---

**CONFEDERATE SEA CAPTAIN 1809–77**

## RAPHAEL SEMMES

"Old Beeswax," as his sailors called Semmes after his waxed mustaches, was a native of the state of Maryland and a U.S. naval officer. At the outbreak of war, he followed his adopted state of Alabama into the Confederacy. He first won fame by taking 18 prizes as captain of CSS *Sumter*. After that ship was trapped in Gibraltar, the dashing Semmes escaped to England, where he took command of the fabled *Alabama*, the most successful commerce raider of the war. In 1865, back in Virginia, Semmes was given command of the James River Squadron; but its sailors were soon turned into makeshift infantry, and when he surrendered them in April, he was holding the rank of brigadier general.

**Boarding ax**
Boarders used this multipurpose ax to help them climb onto enemy vessels when dueling ships lay alongside each other. It was also a handy weapon and a tool for clearing decks of torn rigging and broken timbers.

---

## AFTER »

> Most Confederate commerce raiders were lost during or soon after the war, but their legacy still lingers.

### THE ALABAMA CLAIMS

After the war, the U.S. government claimed **war damages from Britain** for compromising her neutrality by knowingly permitting the *Alabama* and the *Florida* to be built in England. **The dispute escalated** to a dangerous level, with some senators demanding that Britain relinquish Canada as payment, before the **1871 Treaty of Washington** established an international tribunal to arbitrate the "*Alabama* Claims." In the end, the U.S. was **awarded $15.5 million**, and the case helped introduce **the principle of arbitration** in matters of international law.

### FINAL RESTING PLACES

The *Florida* **sank** in 1864, after a collision off Newport News, Virginia—**possibly a deliberate act** to keep the ship from being returned to Brazil and re-entering Confederate service. The *Shenandoah* **was sold** by the U.S. government to the Sultan of Zanzibar, renamed *El Majidi*, and sank in the 1870s after a typhoon drove it onto an East African reef. And **in 1984, the French navy discovered the *Alabama*** lying beneath 200ft (60m) of water off Cherbourg.

# The **Duel** of the *Alabama* and the *Kearsarge*

**Captained by Raphael Semmes, the CSS *Alabama* proved to be the Confederacy's most formidable commerce raider. After capturing 64 U.S. merchant vessels—many in international waters—the *Alabama*'s successful career as a raider came to an end when she was sunk during a duel with the USS *Kearsarge* off the coast of Cherbourg, France, in June 1864.**

"By this time, we were distant about one mile from each other, when I opened on him with solid shot, to which he replied ... It became necessary to fight in a circle; the two ships steaming around a common center, and preserving a distance from each other ... When we got within good shell range, we opened upon him with shell ... The firing now became very hot, and the enemy's shot, and shell soon began to tell upon our hull, knocking down, killing, and disabling a number of men, at the same time, in different parts of the ship. Perceiving that our shell, though apparently exploding against the enemy's sides, were doing him but little damage, I returned to solid-shot firing ...

After the lapse of about one hour and ten minutes, our ship was ascertained to be in a sinking condition, the enemy's shell having exploded in our sides, and between decks, opening large apertures through which the water rushed with great rapidity."

CAPTAIN RAPHAEL SEMMES OF THE CSS *ALABAMA*, FROM HIS OFFICIAL REPORT OF THE ENGAGEMENT TO FLAG OFFICER SAMUEL BARRON, JUNE 21, 1864

"The action was now fairly begun ... A shot from an early broadside carried away the spanker-gaff of the enemy, and caused his ensign to come down by the run. This incident was regarded as a favorable omen by the men who cheered ... The Alabama returned to solid shot, and soon after fired both shot and shell to the end. The firing of the Alabama was rapid and wild, getting better near the close; that of the Kearsarge was deliberate, accurate, and almost from the beginning productive of dismay, destruction, and death ...

The effect upon the enemy was readily perceived, and nothing could restrain the enthusiasm of our men. Cheer succeeded cheer; caps were thrown in the air or overboard; jackets were discarded; sanguine of victory, the men were shouting, as each projectile took effect ..."

SURGEON JOHN M. BROWNE OF THE USS *KEARSARGE*, FROM *THE DUEL BETWEEN THE "ALABAMA" AND THE "KEARSARGE," THE CENTURY MAGAZINE*, APRIL 1886

**To the rescue**
The great French artist Édouard Manet may have witnessed the battle between the *Alabama* and the *Kearsarge*. His painting of the episode shows a small French craft racing to pick up survivors of the *Alabama*.

## BEFORE

Early on in the war, the Confederate government decided not to defend the entire coast but instead to concentrate its efforts on holding the major harbors.

### VITAL PORT

After the **loss of New Orleans in April 1862 ❮❮ 96–97**, Mobile became the principal Confederate port on the Gulf Coast and the base for the **blockade-runners operating the important link with Cuba** that brought in much-needed supplies.

### IRONCLAD BATTLE

The first clash between armored ships, or "ironclads," was the inconclusive **Battle of Hampton Roads in March 1862 ❮❮ 94–95**. In this famous engagement CSS *Virginia*, an iron-plated warship commanded by Admiral Franklin Buchanan, took on the newly designed, shallow-draft USS *Monitor*, but neither could inflict significant damage on the other. **Buchanan led the Southern force** at Mobile Bay.

# The **Battle** of **Mobile Bay**

**Union Admiral David Farragut's advance into Mobile Bay resulted in the destruction of a Confederate naval squadron and, more importantly, closed one of the last ports available to blockade-runners. Mobile itself remained in Confederate hands but it could no longer be used as a supply center.**

The Battle of Mobile Bay was a significant defeat for the Confederacy. It was fought principally on August 5, 1864, though follow-up actions continued later into the month.

Mobile Bay is located where the Mobile and Tensaw rivers meet before they enter the Gulf of Mexico. Before the Civil War, as part of a plan to strengthen its coastal defenses, the United States government had erected

#### Union Navy telescope

Alongside the compass and sextant, the portable folding telescope was an essential naval accoutrement. Most officers had two telescopes, a day and a night model.

three forts to shield Mobile from possible enemy fleets. Standing at the mouth of Mobile Bay was the massive Fort Morgan, a brick edifice completed in 1834 and defended by 46 guns and a garrison of 600. Pentagonal-shaped Fort Gaines was situated on Dauphin Island, directly opposite Fort Morgan. Fort Gaines mounted 26 guns and could also accommodate 600 troops. The smallest of the three was Fort Powell, with 18 guns and space for 140

troops. Although the forts were well positioned to repel any seaborne invasion, they were vulnerable to an assault from their rear.

Farragut's mission in 1864 was to destroy the Confederate fleet in Alabama, commanded by Admiral Franklin Buchanan. His small fleet included the formidable ironclad CSS *Tennessee*, with its heavy armor plating, and three smaller ships; Farragut commanded four monitors

**Steaming into Mobile Bay**
Julian Oliver Davidson's *Battle of Mobile Bay* (1886) shows Farragut's warships and ironclads exchanging fire with Fort Morgan on the left. The Union monitor *Tecumseh*, on the right, has hit a mine and is sinking.

KEY MOMENT

## SURRENDER OF THE *TENNESSEE*

The CSS *Tennessee* was the pride of the Confederate fleet stationed at Mobile Bay. In the final conflict she went head to head with Admiral Farragut's flagship, USS *Hartford*, and came close to ramming her, but could only manage a glancing blow. Pounded from all sides by the *Hartford* and the other wooden Union ships, the *Tennessee* (in the foreground) had her funnel shot away, reducing engine power, and her rudder mechanism destroyed. Then the Union monitor *Chickasaw* began a relentless close-range fire. The *Tennessee*'s armor held but the crew was powerless to fight back. Admiral Buchanan himself was wounded and had no option but to surrender.

and 14 wooden vessels. In the light of dawn on August 5, Farragut concluded that conditions were ideal to attack.

The Confederates had deployed mines at the entrance to the bay. If an invading fleet were to avoid these "torpedoes," it would have to steer dangerously close to the forts. Though one of his monitors, the *Tecumseh*, struck a mine and quickly sank, Farragut ordered the rest of his ships to steam straight through the minefield at full speed. No other vessels were damaged, since many of the mines had corroded. As the ships passed the guns of Fort Morgan, they came under heavy fire. Admiral Buchanan, hoping to intercept the Union fleet, then steamed out in his flagship, CSS *Tennessee*. Believed to be

**Farragut's service dress**
This wool jacket and cap with a leather brim were worn by Farragut while directing the fire of the *Hartford* at Mobile Bay.

unsinkable due to her heavy armor, the *Tennessee* was too slow to ram any invading ships. As the fleets battled in the waters of Mobile Bay, most of the Union vessels concentrated on disabling the *Tennessee*, pummeling it with heavy guns and making repeated attempts to ram her.

The *Tennessee* gave as good as she got. While Union cannonballs bounced off the iron plating, the *Tennessee*'s broadsides ravaged the wooden hulls of her adversaries. But the sheer volume of Union firepower soon began to tell. Buchanan's three other ships had either sunk, surrendered, or escaped to Mobile. Soon the *Tennessee*, rammed repeatedly and facing 157 Union guns, was too damaged to continue resisting. With her surrender, the fighting came to a halt. It was an overwhelming Union victory, but not without cost.

### Final toll
By the end of the battle, 150 Union sailors were killed, many of them in the sinking of the *Tecumseh*, and 170 were wounded. Only 12 Confederate sailors were killed and 19 wounded.

## "Damn the torpedoes! Full speed ahead."

ATTRIBUTED TO DAVID FARRAGUT, ON BEING TOLD THAT MOBILE BAY CONTAINED HIDDEN MINES ("TORPEDOES"), AUGUST 5, 1854

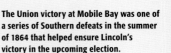

**AFTER**

**The Union victory at Mobile Bay was one of a series of Southern defeats in the summer of 1864 that helped ensure Lincoln's victory in the upcoming election.**

**FORTS CAPTURED**
Victorious at sea, the Union forces completed the **capture of Forts Morgan, Gaines, and Powell by the end of the month**. Together with Sherman's capture of Atlanta in late August and Union advances on other fronts, Farragut's success maintained the **crushing Union pressure on the South**.

**SEALING THE BLOCKADE**
The **last port on the Atlantic seaboard was Wilmington**, North Carolina, through which some supplies could reach Lee's embattled Army of Northern Virginia. After the powerful Confederate ship CSS *Albemarle* was sunk in October, **Union forces were able to close in** on Wilmington's outpost Fort Fisher. The first attacks in December were unsuccessful, but a **renewed assault in January 1865 brought Fort Fisher's surrender 310–11 ≫**.

**PETERSBURG CAMPAIGN**
On the war's main land battlefront around Petersburg, Virginia, **Grant's relentless siege was supplemented by a series of attacks** around the perimeter of the Petersburg position. These failed to encircle Petersburg itself and were halted in late October as winter set in. Full-scale fighting was resumed in late March 1865, when the **Confederate forces were quickly defeated 314–15 ≫**.

# Mississippi Operations

**Union control of the Mississippi River had split the South in half. But large Confederate forces under generals Richard Taylor and Sterling Price guarded the lands to the west of the river, while to the east cavalry leader Nathan Bedford Forrest posed a constant threat to Northern troops.**

**William T. "Bloody Bill" Anderson**
The most notorious of the Missouri "bushwhackers" (Confederate guerrillas), Anderson led a gang that included Frank and Jesse James. His atrocities ranged from murder to scalping and even disemboweling his victims.

## « BEFORE

After the Union captures of New Orleans **« 96–97**, Memphis **« 100–101**, and Vicksburg **« 190–93**, the North controlled the Mississippi River, but the Confederates were still active in the river's hinterland.

### CONFEDERATE COMMANDS
Southern forces held **most of Mississippi**—the state's black prairie region was an important granary, and **General Nathan Bedford Forrest's feared horsemen** roamed the pinewoods. West of the Mississippi River, Confederate General Kirby Smith was based in Shreveport, Louisiana. **General Sterling Price**, the victor at Wilson's Creek in 1861 **« 70–71**, faced Union forces in southern Arkansas.

### UNION STRATEGY
In his grand strategy for 1864, General Ulysses S. Grant planned for **General Sherman to advance on Atlanta**, leaving detachments in Tennessee to patrol his long supply lines against Forrest's raiders. Grant hoped that **General Nathaniel Banks** in New Orleans might advance on Mobile, Alabama. But President Lincoln wanted Banks, in conjunction with Admiral David D. Porter's river fleet, to attack **Shreveport via Louisiana's Red River**. He hoped to isolate Texas and thwart any Confederate alliance with the French in Mexico.

For Union general William T. Sherman, the Red River Campaign of March–May 1864 was one "damn blunder from beginning to end." General Nathaniel Banks's target was Shreveport, Louisiana, the Confederate headquarters of the Trans-Mississippi West, standing on the Red River, a tributary of the Mississippi. But he was routed by Richard Taylor at the Battle of Mansfield on April 8. Although Banks rallied the next day to fend off Taylor at Pleasant Hill, Union reinforcements from Arkansas were also defeated, spelling doom for the expedition. On the campaign's naval front, Admiral David D. Porter's gunboats were stranded upriver by low water. They only escaped after the herculean efforts of the 10,000 men who built wing dams, which stemmed the current enough to refloat the ships.

### The "Wizard of the Saddle"
In Mississippi, meanwhile, the Union's woes could be summed up in three words: Nathan Bedford Forrest. The fearsome Confederate cavalryman—nicknamed the "Wizard of the Saddle"—had for years been wreaking havoc in Union-held Kentucky and Tennessee. He also triggered outrage across the North when, on April 12, 1864, while sacking

### Battle of Pleasant Hill
Readers of the May 14, 1864 edition of Frank Leslie's *Illustrated Newspaper* could study this depiction of General Nathaniel Banks's repulse of Confederate forces during his ill-starred Red River expedition.

Fort Pillow to the north of Memphis, he appeared to condone the massacre of many of its black soldiers.

As spring turned to summer, the Confederate forces in Mississippi, guarding the western approaches to the South's vital Selma Arsenal in Alabama, were increasingly needed in the campaign against Sherman, who had begun to move on Atlanta. Forrest spurred northward to raid Sherman's long supply line, which snaked back through the hills of Tennessee. Sherman dispatched General Samuel Sturgis from Union-held Memphis to stop Forrest.

With only 4,800 troopers in his command, Forrest lured Sturgis and his 8,500 men ever deeper down the rutted Mississippi lanes. Then, on June 10, at Brice's Crossroads, Forrest sprang his trap. Sturgis's long columns, nearly prostrated by unseasonable heat, were bogged in mud and enclosed by thickets. In a series of masterful frontal and flank attacks, Forrest pushed the Union soldiers back against the rain-swollen Tishomingo Creek, rolled his artillery forward, and broke their line. His troopers chased the Northerners nearly back to Memphis. Having destroyed a

## "There will never be **peace in Tennessee** until **Forrest is dead**!"

**GENERAL SHERMAN IN A LETTER TO WAR SECRETARY EDWIN STANTON**, JUNE 15, 1864

force twice his size, Forrest captured wagons, cannons, ammunition cases, provisions, and prisoners.

Sherman then dispatched an entire corps under General Andrew J. Smith, who reached as far south as Tupelo, Mississippi, before deciding to dig in. On July 14–15, Forrest, reinforced with infantry, threw charge after charge against Smith's earthworks, but each was repulsed, and Smith managed to withdraw in good order. Forrest had been kept from attacking Sherman's supply line, and the Union commanders in Memphis, protected by 6,000 troops, could congratulate themselves on a victory. Yet on August 21, the "Wizard" materialized in their midst, with 1,500 troopers galloping through the Memphis streets seeking prisoners, supplies, and horses, and chasing the Union district commander, General Cadwallader Washburn, out of his bed clad only in a nightshirt. After that, more Union troops, who would have been better employed elsewhere, had to be pulled back into the city.

### Raiding Missouri
A week later, in Arkansas, Confederate General Sterling Price and 12,000 ragtag cavalrymen trotted north on a raid into Missouri, where Price had once been governor. They hoped to take that state for the Confederacy, or at least cause a defeat that would harm Lincoln's

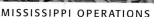

East.

"CLOSE UP" "DOUBLE QUICK!"

By Samuel J. Reader Indiana Ks.

Members of the 2d Reg't Kans. State Militia, prisoners of war.

"PRICE RAID," October, A.D. 1864. An eye-witness.

On the way to "Camp Ford" prison pen, near Tyler, Texas.

1865.

FEB. 13. 65.

**Prisoners of war illustration**
Kansas militiaman Samuel J. Reader was among the prisoners taken by General Price's Confederate troops in their raid on Missouri. He kept a diary of the war, later publishing it with his own illustrations.

chances for re-election. Since St. Louis was too well garrisoned to chance an assault, they veered west along the Missouri River's south bank, and Price swept up whatever horses, mules, cattle, and supplies he could find. Price was, however, no Forrest. No doubt alarmed by the fresh scalps he saw hanging from the bridle of the bushwhacker leader "Bloody Bill" Anderson, he failed to deploy Missouri's hordes of Confederate bushwhackers in the Union rear. Above all, Price moved too slowly—after looting the state he was encumbered by a long train of cattle and wagons.

Inevitably, Union troops closed in— 35,000 of them. In October, Price made a run west for Kansas and then south for Indian Territory (today's Oklahoma). Pitched battles occurred as he tried to ford swollen rivers. On October 23, at Westport near Kansas City, he repeatedly charged a Union line but failed to break it before enemy cavalry was at his rear.

Over the next few days, a running fight developed until Price abandoned his booty and fled south. The very day that he crossed the Arkansas River to safety—November 8—was Election Day in the North. Not only had Price's raid failed to capture Missouri for the South, but his ignominious retreat had actually helped Lincoln's victory—an ironic end to the Confederacy's final campaign west of the Mississippi.

## AFTER

**By the end of 1864, the war in the states that bordered the Mississippi River had mostly ended.**

### FINAL ENCOUNTERS
In August 1864, Admiral David G. **Farragut overcame Mobile's seaward defenses** << **286–87**, while the city itself held out until war's end. In November, after continued raiding in Tennessee, Forrest and his command joined the Army of Tennessee on its fateful march to Franklin and Nashville **300–301** >>. **Forrest's glory days**

were over, however. In early 1865, a massive Union cavalry raid through Alabama and Georgia **310–11** >>, led by **General James H. Wilson**, defeated Forrest at each encounter.

### PRICE'S EXILE
Rather than surrender in 1865, General **Price led many of his men into Mexico**, where they hoped to serve the Emperor Maximilian. They established a Confederate exile colony in Veracruz.

**GENERAL JAMES H. WILSON**

**CONFEDERATE GENERAL** Born 1821 Died 1877

# Nathan Bedford Forrest

> "Any man in favor of a **further prosecution** of this war is a fit subject for a **lunatic asylum**."
>
> NATHAN BEDFORD FORREST, SHORTLY BEFORE SURRENDERING HIS COMMAND, MAY 1865

It was said that General Robert E. Lee called Forrest the greatest soldier produced by the Civil War. To Union general Grant, he was "that devil," while General Sherman thought he deserved killing even "if it costs 10,000 lives and breaks the Treasury."

### Devil on horseback

Wounded four times and having had 29 horses shot beneath him, Forrest was not easy to kill. One characteristic episode occurred in the aftermath of the Battle of Shiloh in April 1862. Encountering a force led by Sherman, Forrest galloped forward so recklessly that he left his escort behind and leaped unaccompanied into Sherman's lines. Saber flashing, he tried cutting his way out, but was shot in the back. Apparently untroubled by the bullet lodged against his spine, Forrest swept up a Union soldier with one arm and planted him on his saddle to act as a shield. Then he rode back to safety. For Bedford Forrest life had been, in his own words, "a battle from the start." Son of a backwoods blacksmith who died when Forrest was 16, he grew up with barely six months of formal schooling. Nevertheless, he went on to achieve success. Working to support his family from an early age, he proved a shrewd businessman, his fortune based on the slave trade. He attained the pinnacle of prewar Southern society—life as a wealthy cotton planter—but never forgot his frontier origins. This was a world where honor often demanded the use of knife or gun, and Forrest remained skilled with both.

He was as single-minded in the pursuit of love as of success. At age 24, he gallantly rescued a mother and daughter after their buggy broke down while crossing a river. The girl's name was Mary Ann Montgomery. Forrest asked permission to visit. On his first call, he proposed to Mary Ann. She accepted on the third visit.

### Captured in oils

German-American painter Nicola Marschall persuaded the notoriously impatient Forrest to sit for this portrait in 1867. When parting from his troops, Forrest had urged them: "Obey the laws, preserve your honor, and the Government to which you have surrendered can afford to be, and will be, magnanimous."

---

CITY DIRECTORY. 251

**FORREST & MAPLES,**
**SLAVE DEALERS,**
87 Adams Street,
Between Second and Third,
**MEMPHIS, TENNESSEE,**
Have constantly on hand the best selected as-
sortment of
**FIELD HANDS, HOUSE SERVANTS & MECHANICS,**
at their Negro Mart, to be found in the city.
They are daily receiving from Virginia, Ken-
tucky and Missouri, fresh supplies of likely
Young Negroes.

**Negroes Sold on Commission,**
and the highest market price always paid for
good stock. Their Jail is capable of containing Three Hundred, and for comfort, neatness
and safety, is the best arranged of any in the
Union. Persons wishing to purchase, are invited to examine their stock before purchasing
elsewhere.
They have on hand at present, Fifty likely
young Negroes, comprising Field hands, Mechanics, House and Body Servants, &c.

### Forrest & Maples

This advertisement for Forrest's prewar firm appeared in the *Memphis City Directory*, 1855–56. The lucrative business of slave trading made Forrest, born in rural poverty, one of the wealthiest men in the South.

### The Fort Pillow massacre

This grim depiction of the massacre at Fort Pillow was published in the April 30, 1864, edition of *Harper's Weekly*, two weeks after the events took place.

However, her uncle and guardian, a Presbyterian minister, knew the young man by reputation, and when Forrest asked his consent, the uncle protested, "Why, Bedford, I couldn't consent. You cuss and gamble, and Mary Ann is a Christian girl." Forrest replied, "I know it, and that's just why I want her." Weeks later, the uncle himself married them. The marriage was lasting and devoted.

## Tactical genius

When the Civil War broke out, the tough 40-year-old Memphis slave-trader and planter had no military experience. Of all the war's famous generals, he was the only one who was neither a professional soldier nor a graduate of West Point. Yet his tactical victories, especially at Brice's Crossroads in June 1864, were so brilliantly executed that they are still studied. His cavalry fought as mounted infantry, the horses being used for speed of movement. When battle loomed, his men tethered their horses, then advanced in loose formation as infantry skirmishers. Never having read an artillery manual, Forrest ran his guns up to the very front of his line, often with devastating effect.

Even military superiors quailed before his hair-trigger temper. "If you ever again try to interfere with me," he threatened General Braxton Bragg, "or cross my path it will be at the peril of your life." In battle such fury might be targeted at the enemy. However, his temper does not seem to have been the issue when his forces attacked the Union position at Fort Pillow, Tennessee, in April 1864. An indiscriminate butchery that began in the furor of combat ultimately took the lives of nearly two-thirds of the Union garrison, including nearly 200 black troops, many slain while surrendering. The question remains open whether Forrest did or did not order, or condone, a deliberate massacre. At the very least, he bears the responsibility for his men's actions.

myth, had indeed been an imposing figure, broad shouldered and 6ft 2in (1.88m) tall. Shortly before he died, Forrest's former troopers found him a haggard, white-haired shadow of his former self. Though he had always been abstemious, neither drinking nor smoking, under Mary Ann's influence he had also become devout. "I am not the man you were with so long and knew so well," he told one old comrade in his inimitable Tennessee drawl. "I hope I am a better man."

# "Get there first with the most men."

### FORREST'S MOTTO FOR WINNING MILITARY VICTORIES

At the war's end, Lieutenant General Forrest surrendered his command and urged his men to become good citizens. In 1866, however, ex-Confederate veterans, who feared that Radical Reconstruction would eradicate cherished Southern traditions, founded a secret paramilitary organization, the Ku Klux Klan. They recruited Forrest, who is thought to have become the organization's first grand wizard. Not explicitly racist, the original Klan was nevertheless defending a way of life whose bedrock had been slavery and white supremacy. Its vigilante bands began terrorizing freedmen across the South, and this brought a crackdown by the Federal government. In 1869, Forrest issued a disbanding order; by 1872, the Ku Klux Klan had largely disappeared, only to be revived in later years.

### Hero or villain?

Forrest has remained one of the Civil War's most polarizing figures. In the South, he became a storybook hero—the rough-hewn frontier counterpoint to the chivalric Lee. In the North, "Fort Pillow" Forrest was seen as a violent guerrilla and racist. The man, as opposed to the

### Klansmen in disguise

Two Alabama members of the original Ku Klux Klan pose for a photograph in 1868, two years after the organization was founded and a year before Forrest disbanded it. The Klan was re-founded in the wake of World War I.

DEFENDER OF SELMA
WIZARD OF THE SADDLE
UNTUTORED GENIUS
THE FIRST WITH THE MOST

**FORREST MONUMENT, SELMA**

« BEFORE

**No part of Grant's 1864 grand strategy « 238–39, besides the struggle against Lee in Virginia, was more important than that entrusted to General William T. Sherman.**

**JOHNSTON OR ATLANTA**

Just as Grant would seek to **destroy Lee's Army of Northern Virginia**, or failing that, **take Richmond**, Sherman was to destroy **Joseph E. Johnston's Army of Tennessee**, or failing that, **take the railroad junction of Atlanta**. As the campaign unfolded, the capture of Atlanta became Sherman's principal aim.

**A SYMBOLIC PRIZE**

Carved out of a pine forest in 1840, **Atlanta** was **a child of the railroads**, four of them intersecting in the city. In the two decades leading up to the war, it had grown into a small bustling city, **second only to Richmond** as a **Southern industrial base**. As Sherman prepared to fight his way there across the intervening **mountains and ridges of northwestern Georgia**, it gained symbolic value, as both North and South pinned their hopes on the **capture or defense of Atlanta**.

---

**CONFEDERATE GENERAL (1831–79)**

## JOHN BELL HOOD

"All lion, none of the fox," tawny-maned John Bell Hood was a soldier of unbridled aggressive instincts. Though born in Kentucky, he was a Texan by choice, and "Hood's Texas Brigade" became Robert E. Lee's favorite shock troops. Hood also made a superb divisional commander, despite losing a leg at Chickamauga and the use of an arm at Gettysburg. When he succeeded Joe Johnston in July 1864, he became, at 33, the youngest man in the war to lead a major army—perhaps a factor in the rash way he bled the army to death at the battles of Atlanta and Franklin.

# Sherman's Advance to Atlanta

**In the summer of 1864, William Tecumseh Sherman maneuvered his army to the outskirts of Atlanta, outfought several Confederate commanders, and after four months and 50,000 casualties, conquered the "Gate City of the South."**

From the outset, it was a campaign of maneuver. When Sherman and his 110,000 soldiers marched out of Ringgold, Georgia, on May 7, 1864, he faced a wily adversary in Joseph E. Johnston. With only half Sherman's troop strength, Johnston was a master of the military delaying game. He continually blocked the 80-mile (129-km) road to Atlanta with strong defensive works, inviting Sherman to attack. Sherman preferred to pin Johnston behind those breastworks with his Army of the Cumberland, and outflank him—first in one direction, then in another—with his more nimble Armies of the Tennessee and Ohio.

**Confederate defenses**
Fortifications, fronted by *chevaux-de-frise* (rows of wooden spikes) ringed Atlanta. Almost a ton of shot and shell tore through the white house in the background in the course of the siege.

### Defensive strategy

Johnston always anticipated Sherman, withdrawing just far enough to settle into another defensive line. Sherman would again advance, and the deadly game would begin anew. There was, of course, plenty of fighting. Names like Resaca, Cassville, New Hope Church—the bloodiest battle in the region known as the "hell hole"—Pickett's Mill, Dallas, and Kennesaw Mountain, where the impatient Sherman tried a direct assault against Johnston's formidable earthworks, only to be thrown back with heavy losses, would be added to both armies' regimental standards.

Nevertheless, Sherman was making a steady advance, and when he reached the northern edge of Atlanta's fortifications two months later, he was facing a new opponent. On July 17, Johnston was relieved of command and replaced by the more aggressive John Bell Hood.

### New leader, new tactics

Hood struck immediately. On July 20, he surged out from behind his defenses and hit a part of the Union army that was separated from the rest by steep-banked Peachtree Creek, 10 miles (16km) to the north. But the attacks were piecemeal, the onslaught costly. Union commanders reported hundreds of Confederate dead piled up before their defenses.

Undaunted, Hood wheeled to the east and two days later attacked the other half of Sherman's forces outside Decatur. Throughout the long evening of July 22, the Confederates again hurled a series of ferocious but disjointed assaults against the Union lines, and were repulsed with twice as many losses as their opponents. By the end of the night, at the Battle of

Atlanta, as this engagement came to be called, a procession of wagons was rumbling into the city, carrying thousands of wounded men. On July 28, Sherman moved west around Atlanta's defenses, trying to reach the Macon & Western Railroad, the city's southern lifeline. Hood attacked at Ezra Church. One terrific charge followed another, all repulsed with fearful casualties.

Unable to reach around Atlanta to cut its southern lifeline, Sherman settled for a round-the-clock bombardment of the city. Houses were damaged and scores of citizens were injured or killed. Meanwhile, the entrenched armies

## The Atlanta Campaign

It took the Union armies nearly three months to fight their way through northern Georgia to the heavily fortified city of Atlanta, where Sherman's advance was temporarily halted. The Union victory at Jonesboro sealed the city's fate as its rail links were severed.

engaged in a war of skirmishing. "The picket firing never ceased, day nor night," recalled one soldier.

## The final act

In late August, the Union army slipped out of its trenches at night and seemingly disappeared. At first baffled, Hood then discovered that his enemy had marched around the city and was approaching the Macon & Western Railroad at Jonesboro, 15 miles (24km) to the south. Desperately, Hood sought to counter the movement, but two days of fruitless assaults only resulted in thousands more Confederates being killed or maimed. The railroad was cut, and Atlanta was doomed.

Throughout the night of September 1, 1864, as Hood's army evacuated the city, the sky glowed red as flames devoured the supplies and depots they left behind. Nearly 80 freight cars of ammunition were burned; the din of their detonation continued for five hours. Ashes still drifted over the city when Sherman, on September 3, wired the president, "Atlanta is ours, and fairly won!"

## The Battle of Atlanta

Also called the Battle of Decatur, the pivotal July 22, 1864, engagement outside Atlanta was depicted in the 1880s, on one of the largest painted cycloramas in the world.

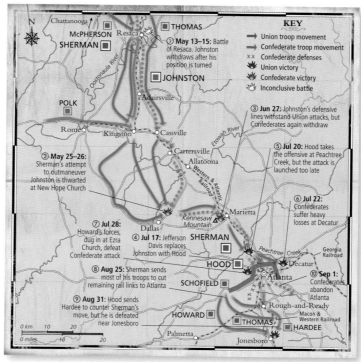

**KEY**
→ Union troop movement
→ Confederate troop movement
×× Confederate defenses
✹ Union victory
✹ Confederate victory
✹ Inconclusive battle

① May 13–15: Battle of Resaca. Johnston withdraws after his position is turned

② May 25–26: Sherman's attempt to outmaneuver Johnston is thwarted at New Hope Church

③ Jun 27: Johnston's defensive lines withstand Union attacks, but Confederates again withdraw

⑤ Jul 20: Hood takes the offensive at Peachtree Creek, but the attack is launched too late

⑥ Jul 22: Confederates suffer heavy losses at Decatur

④ Jul 17: Jefferson Davis replaces Johnston with Hood

⑦ Jul 28: Howard's forces, dug in at Ezra Church, defeat Confederate attack

⑧ Aug 25: Sherman sends most of his troops to cut remaining rail links to Atlanta

⑨ Aug 31: Hood sends Hardee to counter Sherman's move, but he is defeated near Jonesboro

⑩ Sep 1: Confederates abandon Atlanta

## " … all the **thunders of the universe** seemed to be blazing and **roaring over Atlanta**."

WALLACE PUTNAM REED, NEWSPAPERMAN AND HISTORIAN, 1886

**AFTER**

While the fall of Atlanta led to despair in the South, it sparked elation in the North. But Sherman's campaign in Georgia was not over. His next goal was the port of Savannah on the Atlantic coast.

## LINCOLN'S RE-ELECTION

Not the news of **Farragut's** sealing of Mobile Bay **≪ 286–87**, nor that of **Sheridan's** conquest of the Shenandoah Valley **≪ 268–69**, indeed none of the good tidings for the North from 1864's fall of Union victories eclipsed the news of Sherman's capture of Atlanta. It had an electrifying effect on the North, and though Grant and Lee were still **entrenched before Petersburg ≪ 274–75**, Lincoln's chances for re-election **≪ 236–37** soared.

## MARCH TO THE SEA

When Sherman occupied Atlanta, he continued the devastation begun by the Confederates themselves. Throughout October he built up supplies, and when he rode out of the city in November he embarked on a **trail of destruction across Georgia 296–97 ≫**, to prove to the Southerners the **futility of further resistance**.

## GRAND CONFEDERATE PLANS

After evacuating Atlanta, Hood planned to take the Army of Tennessee **north into Tennessee**, **cut Sherman's communications**, and either **invade the North** or cross the mountains to **reinforce Lee at Petersburg**. But his grandiose plans foundered at the **disastrous battles of Franklin and Nashville 300–301 ≫**.

**DESTRUCTION OUTSIDE ATLANTA**
Despite assuming the offensive on four separate occasions, John Bell Hood could not stall William T. Sherman's four-month Atlanta campaign. On September 2, 1864, Hood evacuated the city, his troops destroying anything that might aid the Union war effort. Military installations and supplies were burned, and nearby railroad tracks torn up. Hood and his men retreated deeper into Georgia, leaving Sherman to wreak yet more havoc on the beleaguered city.

# Sherman's March to the Sea

**Leaving Atlanta in flames and a trail of destruction in their wake, General William T. Sherman and his 62,000 veterans marched 300 miles (480km) in less than a month to the coastal city of Savannah. Outraged at his devastation of Georgia, Southerners named Sherman the "Attila of the West."**

On November 15, 1864, General Sherman's 62,000 soldiers filed out of their camps around Atlanta, many marching over the battlefields of the previous summer. From their high vantage point, they could look back over the debris of empty cartridge boxes and shredded breastworks, and observe a terrible sight—Atlanta, in the distance, engulfed in a vast sheet of flame and smoke. Sherman, having declared it a Union fortress and deported its citizens, was burning the city in the process of abandoning it. Atlanta would never be useful to another Confederate army.

Before them more destruction awaited. Sherman's rule of never returning by the road he had come meant his veterans were leaving behind their old lifeline—the single-track railroad around which they had maneuvered their way to Atlanta. Having dispatched adequate forces to shadow General John Bell Hood's wounded Army of Tennessee in Alabama, Sherman was heading for the sea. He had persuaded Lincoln and Grant that a march to the Georgia coast was a good idea—putting his chosen 62,000 within easy reach of troop transports that could ferry them to Petersburg. The general had convinced himself that by cutting a path of destruction through the heart of the Confederacy, he might "make Georgia howl."

## Sherman's orders

Heading generally southeast toward Savannah, the army advanced in two columns, staying 20–40 miles (32–64km) apart. They carried supplies with them but intended to live off the land. Each brigade was allotted its share of the army's 2,500 supply wagons along with its own party of foragers, or "bummers." Sherman had given his forces strict instructions in the form of his "Special Field Orders, No. 120." The order gave broad freedom in the requisitioning of horses, mules, forage, and provisions, but expressly forbade entering civilians' property or using "abusive or threatening language" to householders. If, passing through any given district, the army was unopposed, mills, cotton gins, and homesteads were not to be destroyed. If opposed, however, commanders should impose "a devastation more or less relentless." But the rules were not enforced. In fact, the two columns gauged each other's position by the pillars of smoke on the horizon: burnings marked their progress.

It might have been the war's most roguish march were it not for its punitive intent. In Milledgeville, Georgia's capital, the invading army held a mock session of the legislature in the abandoned chambers, repealing the ordinance of secession. Sherman slept that night in the Governor's pillared mansion, but in his own camp bed

**Sherman's "bummers"**
A name that once designated stragglers, "bummers" eventually included foragers as well. They roamed at some distance away from the main army, often plundering and ransacking at will.

**Campaign wagon**
Wagons such as this one used on Sherman's march were essential pieces of equipment, with bummers "aiming at all times to keep in the wagons at least ten day's provisions for the command and three day's forage."

## « BEFORE

**After the fall of Atlanta « 294–95, Sherman weighed up his next move, even as Confederate General John Bell Hood intended to maneuver him into battle.**

### A STRATEGIC SHIFT

Having left Atlanta, John Bell Hood and his Army of Tennessee still hoped to bring Sherman to battle. But after pushing Hood into northern Alabama, Sherman left him there, assigning George Thomas's **Army of the Cumberland** to protect the Union rear. He turned his back on Hood, having persuaded a reluctant Lincoln and Grant to approve instead a **march through Georgia** to the sea.

### SHERMAN'S PLAN

Sheridan, in devastating the Shenandoah Valley, had **demonstrated the effectiveness of a scorched-earth policy « 268–69**. Sherman planned a similar campaign on a larger scale, torching everything that his army could not consume and **waging total war** on the South.

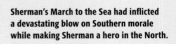

**View from the press**
"General Sherman's Grand March through Central Georgia," complete with plantation houses and distant pillars of smoke, was depicted in the December 10, 1864 issue of *Harper's Weekly*.

**AFTER** »

Sherman's March to the Sea had inflicted a devastating blow on Southern morale while making Sherman a hero in the North.

**INTO THE CAROLINAS**
Sherman did not burn Savannah like he did Atlanta and Columbia, South Carolina. Instead, he spent the winter there, putting his veterans on the road again a few weeks later—**this time headed north**. And rather than dispatching his men to Petersburg to reinforce Grant, he **plundered his way through the Carolinas** in the same way he had done through Georgia. General Joseph E. Johnston, brought back from retirement, would try to stop him with an **army of barely 30,000 men 310–11 »**.

**DESTROYING HOOD'S ARMY**
Before Sherman departed Atlanta, he had quipped that if Hood would go "to the Ohio River, I'll give him rations ... **my business is down south**." Hood had tried doing just that, but he and his Army of Tennessee were virtually **destroyed by George Thomas at the Battle of Nashville 300–301 »**.

because all the furniture had been hidden. The soldiers destroyed railroads, ripping up tracks and twisting them into "Sherman neckties." They devoured all livestock in their path. They stripped farms of all their forage and root crops. They burned barns, corncribs, cotton gins, houses, and once an entire town. Coming across Camp Lawton, a prisoner-of-war stockade, the veterans were so enraged by the brutalities they

found that Sherman ordered nearby Millen to be destroyed with "ten-fold" times the usual measure. As the Union army advanced over a front nearly 60 miles (97km) wide, all the South could do was narrow the zone of destruction.

**Rebel resistance**
The only formal resistance was met near Griswoldville, where Georgia militia tried to stem Sherman's advance. The militia were slaughtered—650 killed or injured, with only 62 Union casualties. Most of the fighting took the form of skirmishing against scattered militia and the few thousand Confederate cavalrymen led by General Joseph Wheeler, whose men took horses and valuables well before the army arrived. They even applied the torch themselves, using scorched-earth tactics to foil the bummers.
The devastation inevitably got out of control, and was further aggravated by marauding groups of deserters and renegades. Even the Confederate cavalry—now branded "Wheeler's robbers"—let discipline slip. And, to complicate matters, thousands of jubilant ex-slaves were swept up in the wake of the march.

**Savannah in sight**
By early December, as the army skirted the low country swamps and marched beneath trees festooned with Spanish moss, Sherman's increasingly scruffy soldiers were being called the "Lost Army" by the North. The men emerged

## $100 MILLION
**Sherman's estimate of damages inflicted during the march. A fifth of this was militarily justified, the "remainder ... simple waste and destruction."**

into view by December 11, "within sight of the spires of Savannah," one of them wrote, "if there were not so many trees in the way."
Savannah was garrisoned by 10,000 soldiers and was protected by a ring of defenses mounting over 100 siege guns. But the packed-earth Fort McAllister, 12 miles (19km) below the city, was Sherman's main concern. It had long defied Union warships; but on December 13, in an all-out assault, his infantrymen stormed through the circle of sharpened stakes and mounted the parapets. Its 230 defenders resisted bravely but futilely. Four days later, Sherman formally demanded the city's surrender. The garrison commander, General Hardee, chose to evacuate instead. After dark on December 20, lit only by distant fires as the navy yard was set alight, a line of men and wagons moved across the Savannah River to South Carolina on a vast pontoon bridge. The next night the ironclad CSS *Savannah* exploded, lighting up the sky for miles. "The concussion was fearful," one witness reported, "rocking the city."

**Sherman's gift to Lincoln**
When nervous city fathers gathered to surrender the city to the Union, they had to scramble to find carriages, most having been stolen by Wheeler's vacating cavalry. Many citizens were frantic that

their city would go the same way as Atlanta. But when Sherman rode in on December 22, he found the same town of handsome squares and shade trees that he remembered so fondly. As his tattered legions marched down the grand avenues, he sent a telegram to President Lincoln: "Dear Sir," he began, "I beg to present you as a Christmas Gift, the City of Savannah ..."

**Haul of ammunition**
The capture of Fort McCallister outside Savannah, which had long been a menace to Union warships, brought with it a sizable haul of guns, shells, and cannonballs.

**"Oh, just burn a barn or something. Make a smoke like the Indians do."**
GENERAL WILLIAM T. SHERMAN, ON HIS METHOD FOR LOCATING HIS CAVALRY

UNION GENERAL Born 1820 Died 1891

# William Tecumseh Sherman

## "Those who brought war ... **deserve all the curses** ... a people can pour out."

WILLIAM T. SHERMAN, ATLANTA, 1864

Having just met the redoubtable William Tecumseh Sherman in March, 1865, Colonel Theodore Lyman of Massachusetts wrote to his wife, "All his features express determination, particularly the mouth, which is wide and straight, with lips that shut tightly together. He is a very homely man, with a regular nest of wrinkles in his face, which play and twist as he eagerly talks on each subject; but his expression is pleasant and kindly. But he believes in hard war."

Perhaps that was deliberately understated. "War is cruelty and you cannot refine it," Sherman himself had once stated. He had addressed those scathing words to Confederate general, John

### Sherman's campaign hat

This battered hat was worn by General Sherman while on campaign. Of military life he remarked, "In our Country ... one class of men makes war and leaves another to fight it out."

Bell Hood, who had protested against Sherman's treatment of Atlanta's civilians. "You might as well appeal against a thunderstorm as against these terrible hardships of war," he went on. "They are inevitable, and the only way that the people of Atlanta can hope once more to live in peace and quiet at home is to stop the war, which can alone be done by admitting that it began in error and is perpetuated in pride."

The man who could declare, "Let us destroy Atlanta and make it a desolation," might have been born a warrior. Perhaps that's what his father had hoped for when he named his third son after the famous Shawnee chief, Tecumseh. "William" was added at his baptism, and for most of his life he was affectionately known as "Cump." But if

### Yankee warrior

In Colonel Theodore Lyman's words, Sherman was the "concentrated quintessence of Yankeedom." He is shown here in May 1865 wearing a black ribbon of mourning for the recently assassinated President Lincoln.

he was a born a warrior, it was of the most unusual kind. The tall, lanky youth, who graduated from West Point widely respected for his brilliance, proved to be restless in the army. So much so that he soon resigned in hope of becoming a successful businessman. The bank he ran in California, however, failed during a depression; so he moved to Louisiana and became the superintendent of a small military academy.

## Southern admirer

Sherman was, perhaps surprisingly, an emotionally complex man. For one thing, he loved the South. He loved its easy grace and charm, its refined society. He might have been content to live there the rest of his life had not the storm clouds of secession gathered. He was no abolitionist, but he could not abide the idea of secession. The breaking of that storm is what drove him back into the U.S. Army; but after resigning his superintendency of the academy when Louisiana seceded, he wept at his leave-taking.

Although the new Union colonel withstood his baptism of fire admirably at the Battle of Bull Run in July 1861, only a few months later he asked to be relieved as commander of the Department of the Cumberland in Kentucky, which at the time was threatened with imminent Confederate invasion. Sherman may have had a nervous breakdown, a form of anxiety, or bipolar disorder brought on by stress, overwork, and lack of sleep.

His detractors thought he was insane and for several months, he remained depressed, even suicidal. Soon, however, he began working his way back into active service.

The rest of Sherman's military career was a tale of redemption. Each step up that ladder—the fighting and campaigning, as colonel and then general, alongside General Ulysses S. Grant at Shiloh and Vicksburg; his mastery of maneuver, in command of three armies, down that deadly railroad to Atlanta; and the unparalleled March to the Sea through Georgia and the Carolinas—saw tactical blunders but revealed a strategic prowess. He grew used to the carnage. "I begin to regard the death and mangling of a couple of thousand as a small affair, a kind of morning dash," he wrote to his wife. "It may be well that we become hardened."

## Redoubtable general

Perhaps most disturbingly, Sherman's appetite for war was growing with each step up the career ladder; "a manic elation," as critic Edmund Wilson observed, "that compensated for the earlier demoralization." The wake of burning wreckage that marked his passage from Atlanta, Georgia, to Columbia, South Carolina, over a period of three months had proved Sherman to be a formidable foe.

## Sherman and his generals

In May 1865, Sherman and his staff officers—Howard, Logan, Hazen, Davis, Slocum, and Mower—were photographed together in Washington, D.C. on the occasion of the Grand Review of the Armies.

Then, in an about-face, he was all conciliation. In April 1865, Sherman offered Joseph E. Johnston, who was negotiating the surrender of the Confederacy's remaining armies, terms so generous that an enraged secretary of war, Edwin M. Stanton, tried relieving him of command.

Sherman remained in uniform after the Civil War, but opposed the Republicans' harsh measures under Reconstruction. That didn't stop him from succeeding Grant—elected the Republican president in 1869—as the Commanding General of the Army. He held the post for the next 15 years, when the Indian Wars in the West approached their tragic culmination. Despite being named for an Native-American warrior, both Sherman and his successor, Philip Sheridan, shared the hostility toward Native Americans felt by the majority of Regular Army officers during the 19th century.

## Society figure

Sherman seemed to settle more comfortably into old age. In 1875, he was among the first of the Civil War's leading generals to publish his memoirs. He resolutely declined any invitation to enter politics. When in Washington, St. Louis, or New York City, he was instead a sociable, witty figure at parties and the theater. Former adversaries Joseph Johnston and Joe Wheeler dined in his home; and Sherman's son recalled that one day a sad-eyed, one-legged man came calling. His father was helping former Confederate general John Bell Hood, who had fallen on hard times, to sell his military papers to the government.

Sherman's long run as the nation's preeminent soldier ended when he died of pneumonia on February 14, 1891. The sound of muffled drums and mournful bells accompanied his funeral procession down New York's Fifth Avenue. In the Midwest, crowds gathered to see the funeral train pass on its way to Calvary Cemetery in St. Louis. Tributes were published and statues erected to the celebrated general. But despite Northern plaudits, Sherman's name remained anathema across the South.

### Sherman's sword

General William Tecumseh Sherman wore this Model 1850 staff and field officer's sword, made by the Ames Manufacturing Company of Chicopee, Massachusetts, during the Battle of Shiloh in Tennessee on April 6–8, 1862.

## TIMELINE

- **February 8, 1820** Born William Tecumseh Sherman in Lancaster, Ohio, the third son of Charles and Mary. After the death of his father he is reared by Senator Thomas Ewing, a family friend.
- **Summer 1840** Sherman graduates from West Point. As a second lieutenant in the artillery, he is soon battling the Seminole Indians in Florida during the Second Seminole War (1835–42).
- **May 1, 1850** Marries his stepsister, Eleanor Boyle Ewing. President Zachary Taylor is a guest.
- **September 6, 1853** Resigns from the army but remains restless and unhappy in various jobs.
- **May 1861** Sherman rejoins the U.S. Army.
- **July 5, 1861** His daughter Rachel, the first of eight children, is born.
- **July 21, 1861** As colonel in charge of a brigade, he distinguishes himself at the First Battle of Bull Run (Manassas) and is promoted to brigadier general.
- **November 1861** After two months in charge of the Department of the Cumberland, covering most of Kentucky, Sherman asks to be relieved following a nervous breakdown.
- **April 7, 1862** After being reinstated and assigned to Grant's Army of West Tennessee, he helps lead the successful Union counterattack at Shiloh. As a result, he is promoted to major general.
- **October 16, 1863** After serving at Vicksburg he succeeds Grant as commander of the Army of the Tennessee, leading it throughout the Chattanooga campaign.
- **March 18, 1864** When Grant takes control of all Union forces, Sherman is given command of the Military District of the Mississippi, effectively in charge of all the Union's Western armies.
- **May 5, 1864** Leaving Ringgold, Georgia, he sets his three armies—the Tennessee, the Ohio, and the Cumberland—on the road to Atlanta.
- **September 1, 1864** Sherman captures Atlanta.
- **November 15, 1864** Embarks on the "March to the Sea," arriving less than a month later in Savannah, which on December 22 he presents to President Lincoln as a Christmas gift.
- **February 17, 1865** He captures Columbia, South Carolina.
- **March 21, 1865** Defeats General Joseph E. Johnston's makeshift Confederate army at the Battle of Bentonville.
- **April 26, 1865** At Durham, North Carolina, he accepts Johnston's surrender of all Rebel forces remaining in the Carolinas, Georgia, and Florida.
- **January 1869** As General of the Army, he directs wars against the Native Americans, including the Cheyenne, Sioux, and Apache.
- **February 1884** Retires from the U.S. Army.
- **February 1891** Dies in New York City on the 14th.

**SHERMAN AND HIS DAUGHTER RACHEL**

> "There is many a boy here today who looks on war as **all glory**, but boys it is **all hell**."
>
> SHERMAN, AT THE GRAND REUNION OF THE FEDERAL ARMY, COLUMBUS, 1880

« BEFORE

After Atlanta's fall General John Bell Hood embarked on an invasion of Union-held Tennessee, but Union generals George H. Thomas and John M. Schofield were waiting.

### THE ROAD TO FRANKLIN
Hood hoped he might cut Union supply lines or maybe **join General Lee at Petersburg** **« 274-75**, but General Thomas, in the city of Nashville with 40,000 men, lay in his path. General Schofield and his army of 30,000 were near Pulaski. Hood hoped to defeat them before they could join Thomas, setting a trap for them on November 29, some 15 miles (24km) south of Franklin.

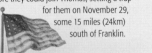

# Franklin and Nashville

**General John Bell Hood's daring but ultimately doomed Tennessee campaign in the fall of 1864, culminated in two battles, one at the town of Franklin and the other before the city of Nashville, which spelled the end for the once-proud Confederate Army of Tennessee.**

On the afternoon of November 30, 1864 General Hood was still angry that the night before, through a series of blunders, his Army of Tennessee had somehow allowed 30,000 Union troops to slip past it. The Federals had dug in near the town of Franklin, Tennessee, which Hood's commanders could see 2 miles (3.2km) away from their temporary headquarters on the hilltop.

Although most of Hood's artillery and an infantry corps had still not arrived, the impetuous general had decided to attack the positions at Franklin anyway; his commanders were filled with foreboding.

At 4 p.m., 18 brigades—nearly 20,000 men—moved out, lines dressed, flags flying, drums beating, and bands playing. Before them stretched those 2 miles (3.2km) of open, undulating fields browned by recent frosts. Rabbits bounded away as the tramping feet of this last great Confederate charge of the war approached.

### Southern slaughter
General John Schofield's Union men watched spellbound as the Rebels approached. Crouched behind strong fieldworks fronted by felled trees, they shouldered impressive firepower; and massed artillery, some of it positioned to fire into the attacking columns from the flanks, backed them up. When the onslaught was within a hundred paces of the main

line every Union trigger was squeezed. With a deafening roar a deadly hail of shot, shell, and canister tore through the Confederate ranks, shredding all formation and turning the regiments into blood-spattered mobs. Many troops, trapped in the tangle of felled trees, were caught in a murderous crossfire of small arms and artillery. Others could be glimpsed, through the pall of smoke that soon descended, regrouping and charging again and again—several Federals counted up to 13 charges.

But in some places, the Confederates poured across the Union line, the battle surging back and forth around a barn, outbuildings, and brick farmhouse that

### Combat at Franklin
The Battle of Franklin was sometimes called the "Pickett's Charge of the West," so quickly did the Rebels advance. Though moving "with the speed of an avalanche," the Army of Tennessee was all but devastated in five hours.

# "The **death-angel was there** to gather its last harvest. It was the **grand coronation** of death."

PRIVATE SAM WATKINS, 1ST TENNESSEE INFANTRY, ON THE BATTLE OF FRANKLIN

belonged to the Carter family. Desperate hand-to-hand fighting spilled over fences into the gardens. Nightfall brought no letup in the frenzy; it only raged the more spectacularly along the main line of breastworks, where for hundreds of yards men standing three or four deep in the bloody ditches fired at each other over the parapet as quickly as they could be handed loaded rifles. One man described the muzzle flashes in the dark as "but one line of streaming fire." The inconclusive battle sputtered to a halt by 9 p.m. At midnight a whispered order was passed down the Union line: "Fall in." The Federals slipped away before dawn, heading north for Nashville, carrying at least 13 Confederate battle flags but leaving behind 2,500 casualties, including most of their seriously wounded.

## Confederate losses

Daylight revealed a scene of appalling carnage. One man recalled how the dead were piled "one on the other all over the ground" and especially how numerous horses "had died game on the gory breastworks." The Confederates buried 1,750 of their mangled comrades on the field that day. Around 3,800 wounded crowded the makeshift hospitals. Hood had lost nearly a third of his available infantry; some

## Union defense

Nashville was occupied by Union forces in 1862, and the city's defensive centerpiece was the star-shaped Fort Negley. Two years later, Nashville was among the most impressively fortified cities in the United States.

regiments counted upward of 64 percent casualties. No less than 12 generals and 54 regimental commanders had been killed or wounded—a captain becoming the most senior ranked officer in some brigades.

Nevertheless, Hood soon had the survivors marching north on Nashville too. General George H. Thomas had assembled at least 55,000 Union troops, including Schofield's battered army, behind the city's daunting fortifications. The Confederate Army of Tennessee entrenched itself in a range of low hills 4 miles (6.4km) to the south, inviting Thomas to attack. For two weeks, when not shivering through ice storms, the opposing sides glared at each other.

## Thomas attacks

General Ulysses S. Grant was on the point of relieving Thomas for inactivity when the weather improved. On December 15 Thomas struck. As the fog lifted that morning, the Confederates saw the long blue lines, flags flying, moving toward them. Union artillery fired a barrage so deafening that individual guns could not be distinguished. Hood's men repulsed the assaults on their front; but that was only a diversion. The Federals turning their left flank were the real striking force. They swarmed over fields and stone walls taking one Rebel position after another, capturing 16 guns and a thousand prisoners before winter darkness halted their momentum. That night Hood withdrew to another set of bluffs, where his weary soldiers cut trees and entrenched in the dark. Dawn revealed an imposing new line of Confederate works curving over a steep 3-mile (4.8-km) front.

### Union surge

Gray clouds and cold rain had arrived by the time Thomas's attack again got underway. On the Confederate right, the Federals struggling upward were slaughtered in terrible profusion. But to his left, Hood's line had been sited too far up the slope; the defenders could

### General George H. Thomas

Born in Virginia, the stalwart Thomas remained loyal to the Union during the Civil War, for which he was permanently ostracized by members of his family.

AFTER

**The collapse of Hood's Tennessee Campaign spelled the end of major fighting in that state—and very different ends for the two commanding generals.**

### TENNESSEE CONCLUSION

In early January 1865, General Hood would tender his resignation, his **career now in ruins**. In March, General Thomas would receive the **"Thanks of Congress"** for his victory at Nashville.

### END OF AN ARMY

The Army of Tennessee's demoralized survivors —those who didn't head for home after the **disaster at Nashville**—were continually harried by Union forces as they retreated south. They might have been completely destroyed were it not for Major General Nathan Bedford Forrest and his cavalry who kept much of the pursuit at bay. Many **soldiers limped barefoot** through the ice until they reached Tupelo, Mississippi. In March 1865, when they joined General Johnston for the **last campaign in the Carolinas 310–11 »**, they mustered only 4,500—ten percent of the force that Hood had commanded.

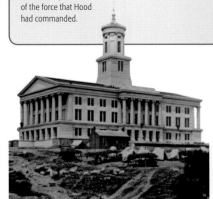

**Tennessee State Capitol**
Modeled after a Greek Ionic temple, the Tennessee State Capitol building in Nashville was completed in 1859 and was one of the tallest structures in the United States at the time of the Civil War.

not train their guns on the enemy until it was too late. Hood's left began giving way, and when the Union cavalry got into its rear, it broke. Panic spread like wildfire. Down the line exultant Federals seized guns, ammunition, flags, and thousands of dazed Confederates. Entire divisions melted away, soldiers fleeing to the rear ignoring their officers' cries to rally. It was as decisive a victory as any in the war. The Army of Tennessee, once among the proudest in the Confederacy, had reached the limit of its endurance. Its men fled down the Franklin Pike in the rain. Later that night, Hood was observed "much agitated and affected, pulling his hair with his one hand and crying like his heart would break."

# 6

# COLLAPSE OF THE CONFEDERACY

## 1865

Military reverses in the last months of 1864 had left the Confederacy reeling, but the Union armies still had much to do before they could claim victory. In 1865, they took the struggle to the Southern heartland and finally found the decisive breakthrough they sought in Virginia.

**« Fall of Petersburg**
Less than 30 miles (48km) from the Confederate capital of Richmond, Petersburg had become the central focus of the conflict. When General Robert E. Lee's Army of Northern Virginia was eventually forced to abandon the town in April 1865, the end

# COLLAPSE OF THE CONFEDERACY

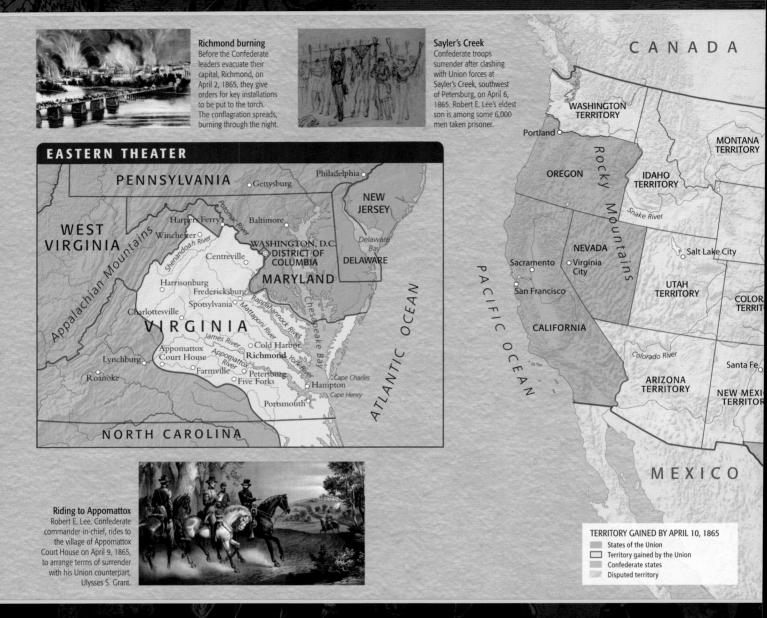

**Richmond burning**
Before the Confederate leaders evacuate their capital, Richmond, on April 2, 1865, they give orders for key installations to be put to the torch. The conflagration spreads, burning through the night.

**Sayler's Creek**
Confederate troops surrender after clashing with Union forces at Sayler's Creek, southwest of Petersburg, on April 6, 1865. Robert E. Lee's eldest son is among some 6,000 men taken prisoner.

## EASTERN THEATER

PENNSYLVANIA
Gettysburg
Philadelphia
NEW JERSEY
WEST VIRGINIA
Harpers Ferry
Potomac River
Baltimore
Winchester
Shenandoah River
Centreville
WASHINGTON, D.C.
DISTRICT OF COLUMBIA
Delaware Bay
DELAWARE
Harrisonburg
Fredericksburg
MARYLAND
Charlottesville
Spotsylvania
Mattaponi River
Rappahannock River
Chesapeake Bay
Appalachian Mountains
VIRGINIA
James River
Cold Harbor
Appomattox Court House
Appomattox River
Richmond
York River
Lynchburg
Farmville
Petersburg
Cape Charles
Roanoke
Five Forks
Hampton
Cape Henry
Portsmouth
ATLANTIC OCEAN
NORTH CAROLINA

CANADA
WASHINGTON TERRITORY
Portland
MONTANA TERRITORY
OREGON
Rocky Mountains
IDAHO TERRITORY
Snake River
NEVADA
Salt Lake City
Sacramento
Virginia City
San Francisco
UTAH TERRITORY
COLOR TERRIT
PACIFIC OCEAN
CALIFORNIA
Colorado River
Santa Fe
ARIZONA TERRITORY
NEW MEXI TERRITOR
MEXICO

**Riding to Appomattox**
Robert E. Lee, Confederate commander-in-chief, rides to the village of Appomattox Court House on April 9, 1865, to arrange terms of surrender with his Union counterpart, Ulysses S. Grant.

**TERRITORY GAINED BY APRIL 10, 1865**
- States of the Union
- Territory gained by the Union
- Confederate states
- Disputed territory

O n the eve of Robert E. Lee's surrender of his army on April 9, 1865, large areas of the southeastern United States were still nominally in Confederate hands. In reality, the situation was in flux, and none of the developments favored the Southern cause.

With the fall of Richmond six days before Lee's surrender, the Confederate government had lost its capital, and President Jefferson Davis had become a fugitive, dependent on those railroads still operated by the Confederacy to stay out of Federal hands. Eleven days before that, Union general William T. Sherman, advancing northward from Savannah through the Carolinas, had successfully rendezvoused at Goldsboro with another Federal force, under John M. Schofield, which was moving inland from the port of Wilmington. The remaining Confederate forces in the area were no match for the combined strength of Sherman and Schofield.

# 1865

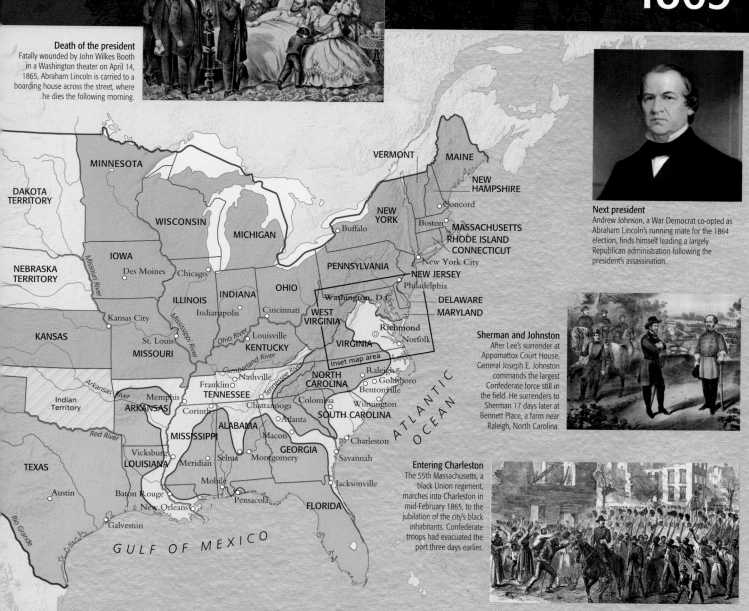

**Death of the president**
Fatally wounded by John Wilkes Booth in a Washington theater on April 14, 1865, Abraham Lincoln is carried to a boarding house across the street, where he dies the following morning.

**Next president**
Andrew Johnson, a War Democrat co-opted as Abraham Lincoln's running mate for the 1864 election, finds himself leading a largely Republican administration following the president's assassination.

**Sherman and Johnston**
After Lee's surrender at Appomattox Court House, General Joseph E. Johnston commands the largest Confederate force still in the field. He surrenders to Sherman 17 days later at Bennett Place, a farm near Raleigh, North Carolina.

**Entering Charleston**
The 55th Massachusetts, a black Union regiment, marches into Charleston in mid-February 1865, to the jubilation of the city's black inhabitants. Confederate troops had evacuated the port three days earlier.

MINNESOTA
DAKOTA TERRITORY
WISCONSIN
MICHIGAN
IOWA
Des Moines
NEBRASKA TERRITORY
Chicago
ILLINOIS
INDIANA
OHIO
Indianapolis
Cincinnati
Kansas City
KANSAS
St. Louis
MISSOURI
Louisville
KENTUCKY
Nashville
Franklin
TENNESSEE
Memphis
ARKANSAS
Corinth
Chattanooga
Indian Territory
ALABAMA
MISSISSIPPI
Atlanta
Macon
Vicksburg
Selma
Montgomery
GEORGIA
TEXAS
LOUISIANA
Meridian
Mobile
Austin
Baton Rouge
Pensacola
New Orleans
FLORIDA
Galveston
Rio Grande
Red River
Arkansas River
Missouri River
Mississippi River
Ohio River
Cumberland River
Tennessee River

VERMONT
MAINE
NEW HAMPSHIRE
Concord
NEW YORK
Boston
MASSACHUSETTS
RHODE ISLAND
CONNECTICUT
Buffalo
PENNSYLVANIA
New York City
NEW JERSEY
Philadelphia
Washington, D.C.
WEST VIRGINIA
DELAWARE
MARYLAND
Richmond
Norfolk
VIRGINIA
Inset map area
Raleigh
NORTH CAROLINA
Goldsboro
Bentonville
Colombia
Wilmington
SOUTH CAROLINA
Charleston
Savannah
Jacksonville

ATLANTIC OCEAN

GULF OF MEXICO

Meanwhile, Union armies were also making progress in Alabama. A cavalry force under James H. Wilson was striking south from the Tennessee border at the same time that troops under Edward Canby were besieging the port of Mobile at the southern end of the state. Mobile finally fell on April 12, just three days after Lee's capitulation; on the same day, Wilson's raiders entered the state capital of Montgomery. For a time, Jefferson Davis refused to

accept the reality of the situation, but his remaining commanders soon convinced him that their troops were no longer in a condition to fight. Joseph E. Johnston, leading Confederate forces in the Carolinas, entered negotiations with his adversary, Sherman, on April 17, formally surrendering nine days later. Confederate commanders in Alabama and the Trans-Mississippi Department followed suit shortly after, bringing the war to an end by early June

# TIMELINE 1865

The Thirteenth Amendment ▪ **Lincoln's second term as president** ▪ Battle of Bentonville ▪ **Siege of Petersburg** ▪ Fall of Richmond ▪ Surrender at Appomattox Court House ▪ **Assassination of Lincoln** ▪ Last battle at Palmito Ranch

## JANUARY

**JANUARY 15**
Union forces under General Alfred H. Terry storm Fort Fisher on the North Carolina coast, cutting off the Confederate-held port of Wilmington from the sea.

❯ Storming Fort Fisher

**JANUARY 19**
Northern troops under General William T. Sherman move north out of Savannah, Georgia, launching the Union invasion of South Carolina.

**JANUARY 31**
Congress passes the Thirteenth Amendment to the Constitution, abolishing slavery in U.S. territory.

❯ Detail from the Thirteenth Amendment

*Thirty-Eighth* Congress of the United States of America;

*At the Second Session,*

*Begun and held at the City of Washington, on Monday, the fifth day of December, one thousand eight hundred and sixty-four.*

**A RESOLUTION**

*Submitting to the legislatures of the several States a proposition to amend the Constitution of the United States.*

*Resolved by the Senate and House of Representatives of the United States of America in Congress assembled,*
*(two-thirds of both Houses concurring,) that the following article be proposed to the legislatures of the several States as an amendment to the Constitution of the United States, which, when ratified by three-fourths of said*

## FEBRUARY

**FEBRUARY 3**
President Lincoln and Secretary of War Edwin M. Stanton meet Confederate commissioners aboard the steamboat *River Queen* for abortive peace talks.

**FEBRUARY 5–6**
The rival forces entrenched outside Petersburg fight an inconclusive engagement at Hatcher's Run to the south of the city.

❮ Robert E. Lee

**FEBRUARY 6**
President Jefferson Davis names Robert E. Lee general-in-chief of all Confederate armed forces.

**FEBRUARY 17**
Sherman's troops take Columbia, capital of South Carolina. That night, much of the city goes up in flames. In North Carolina, Confederate forces evacuate the port of Charleston.

**FEBRUARY 22**
A Union force under General John M. Schofield occupies Wilmington, North Carolina.

**FEBRUARY 23**
At Lee's insistence, General Joseph E. Johnston takes command of the Confederate forces facing Sherman's Union army in the Carolinas.

**FEBRUARY 27**
General Philip H. Sheridan's Army of the Shenandoah moves out of winter quarters, under instruction from Union commander-in-chief Ulysses S. Grant to head east.

## MARCH

**MARCH 2**
In the Shenandoah Valley, Sheridan defeats Jubal Early's Confederate force at Waynesboro.

**MARCH 4**
Lincoln begins his second term as U.S. president.

**MARCH 7**
At the Second Battle of Kinston, Confederate forces under General Braxton Bragg fail to halt the progress of Union troops advancing from Wilmington to join Sherman.

**MARCH 13**
In a last-ditch attempt to counter manpower shortages, the Confederate Congress authorizes the conscription of black troops.

**MARCH 16**
Confederate forces led by William J. Hardee vainly try to delay the left wing of the Union advance in North Carolina at Averasboro.

**MARCH 19–21**
General Joseph E. Johnston's Confederate army makes a final, unsuccessful attempt to halt Sherman's advance through North Carolina at the Battle of Bentonville.

**MARCH 22**
A Union cavalry force under General James H. Wilson launches a raid southward through Alabama, intended to destroy Confederate resistance in the state.

❯ Lincoln's gold mounted, engraved Henry rifle

**MARCH 23**
Sherman's Union army, driving northward through North Carolina, succeeds in rendezvousing at Goldsboro with Schofield's force, marching inland from Wilmington.

**MARCH 25**
A Confederate assault on Fort Stedman in the Union lines outside Petersburg initially succeeds, but is soon beaten back at a heavy cost in men.

❮ Sherman's sword

**MARCH 28**
Grant and Sherman meet with President Lincoln and Admiral David D. Porter on the *River Queen* to discuss Union strategy for ending the war.

**MARCH 29**
General Grant launches the final operation of the Petersburg campaign, designed to prevent a Confederate breakout to the southwest of the city.

> "Thank God I have lived to see this. It seems to me that I have been **dreaming a horrid dream** for four years, and **now the nightmare is gone**."
>
> PRESIDENT ABRAHAM LINCOLN ON HEARING THAT THE CONFEDERATE CAPITAL OF RICHMOND HAD FINALLY FALLEN, APRIL 3, 1865

## APRIL

## MAY

## JUNE

**APRIL 1**
Union forces break through the right wing of the Confederate lines outside Petersburg at Five Forks, threatening Lee's last supply line and making his position untenable.

**APRIL 9**
Generals Grant and Lee meet at the village of Appomattox Court House in south central Virginia. Lee accepts the terms of surrender offered by the Union commander, bringing the war in Virginia to an end.

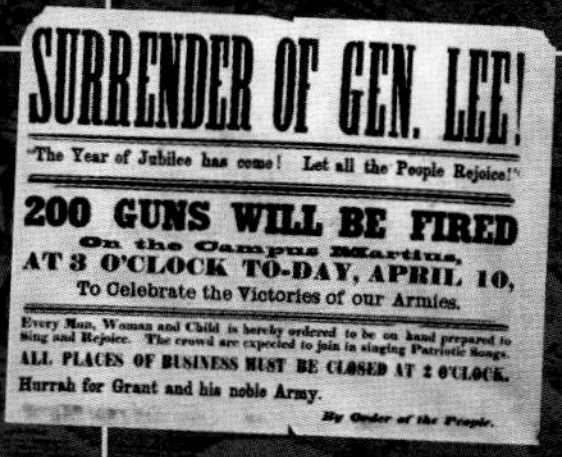

**JUNE 2**
Edmund Kirby Smith, commander of Confederate forces in the Trans-Mississippi Department, surrenders.

⌃ Lincoln's funeral procession

**APRIL 2**
In face of a Union assault, Confederate forces withdraw from Petersburg after an eight-month siege. In Alabama, James H. Wilson's Union cavalry breaks through Confederate lines to capture Selma.

**SURRENDER OF GEN. LEE!**
"The Year of Jubilee has come! Let all the People Rejoice!"
**200 GUNS WILL BE FIRED**
On the Campus Martius, AT 3 O'CLOCK TO-DAY, APRIL 10,
To Celebrate the Victories of our Armies.
Every Man, Woman and Child is hereby ordered to be on hand prepared to Sing and Rejoice. The crowd are expected to join in singing Patriotic Songs.
ALL PLACES OF BUSINESS MUST BE CLOSED AT 2 O'CLOCK.
Hurrah for Grant and his noble Army.
By Order of the People.
⌃ News of Lee's surrender

**MAY 4**
Abraham Lincoln's body is laid to rest in Oak Ridge Cemetery, outside his hometown of Springfield, Illinois.

**MAY 12–13**
The final battle of the Civil War is fought at Palmito Ranch on the Rio Grande in Texas. Ironically, it ends in a Union retreat.

**JUNE 2**
The Confederate cruiser *Shenandoah* ceases operations against Union shipping in the Bering Sea.

**APRIL 2**
The first Union troops arrive in Richmond, the day after the Confederate government has evacuated the city.

**APRIL 12**
Union forces under Edward Canby take the city of Mobile, Alabama. Wilson's Union forces occupy Montgomery, Alabama's capital, before swinging eastward into Georgia.

**MAY 8**
General Richard Taylor, the Confederate commander in Alabama, agrees to terms of surrender, ending the war in the south.

**MAY 23**
The Army of the Potomac parades through Washington, D.C., in a gigantic victory celebration. Sherman's Army of Georgia repeats the performance on the following day.

⌄ Victory parade

**JUNE 23**
Stand Watie, the Cherokee commander of Kirby Smith's cavalry division, finally agrees to a ceasefire.

Stand Watie ≫

**APRIL 6**
Union forces pursuing Lee's retreating army cut off almost a quarter of the Confederate force at Sayler's Creek, capturing some 7,700 men.

⌃ President Lincoln's top hat

**MAY 10**
The fugitive Confederate president, Jefferson Davis, is captured by Union troops in Georgia.

**APRIL 7**
Union commander-in-chief Ulysses S. Grant sends a note to Lee inviting him to surrender. Lee temporizes, asking for details of the terms.

**APRIL 14**
President Lincoln is shot by the actor and Confederate supporter John Wilkes Booth.

**APRIL 26**
In the Carolinas, Union general William T. Sherman accepts the surrender of General Joseph E. Johnson.

# The Thirteenth Amendment

**Lincoln's Emancipation Proclamation of 1863 established the abolition of slavery as a Federal war aim, but abolitionists feared that it might be set aside as a temporary measure once the conflict ended. The passing of the Thirteenth Amendment to the Constitution ensured that slavery was banned in the United States.**

## « BEFORE

The Thirteenth Amendment outlawing slavery throughout the United States came to be seen as a summary of the war's moral purpose. Yet four years earlier, the situation had looked very different.

### THE 1861 AMENDMENT

Ironically, the Thirteenth Amendment in 1865, **to address the instution of slavery**, was not the first adopted by Congress. In 1861, when a final attempt was made to conciliate the South, an amendment that guaranteed the rights of slaveholding states had **passed the House and Senate**. Although it had been signed by President Buchanan on his last day in office, it had **never been ratified by the individual states**. The difference between it and its successor marked **the distance the U.S. had traversed politically** in the intervening four years.

### THE EMANCIPATION PROCLAMATION

President Abraham Lincoln's **Emancipation Proclamation of 1863 « 160–61** changed fundamentally the character of the Civil War. By embracing the **abolition of slavery** as the backbone of Union policy, it gave the conflict a fresh **moral dimension**. However, the form it took was dictated by expediency. If slavery was to be abolished once and for all, **more permanent measures** were called for.

President Lincoln's Emancipation Proclamation of 1863 left unfinished business. It gave freedom to slaves only in the ten named Confederate states that had failed to rejoin the Union by January 1st, the date on which the proclamation came into force. Some territories were specifically exempted from its provisions, among them the city of New Orleans and the 48 Virginia counties then in the process of forming the state of West Virginia. Other slaveholding border states, where the president still hoped to court moderate opinion in favor of rejoining the Union, were simply not mentioned at all. It was clear, then, that some further measure would be required if slavery was to be banned forever across the United States.

## Passing the amendment

Lincoln himself believed that the only suitable vehicle would be a constitutional amendment. Yet there were formidable obstacles in the way of such a move. No new amendment had been passed in 60 years, and successful passage would require the support of two-thirds of the members of both Houses of Congress, and then ratification by three-quarters of the individual states. To make the measure truly binding, Lincoln took this to mean three-quarters of all states, including those in the South that had taken up arms to defend slavery.

The easy part proved to be getting the amendment through the Senate, whose Republican majority ensured its smooth passage on April 8, 1864. The House of Representatives proved more recalcitrant, however, and the measure failed to get the necessary two-thirds majority by 13 votes.

Its fate then became a leading issue in the 1864 presidential election campaign, with the Republicans eagerly adopting the cause as a central plank of their platform. The Democrats denounced the amendment as "unwise, impolitic, cruel, and unworthy of the support of a civilized people." Lincoln's re-election in November 1864 effectively

### Jubilant scenes

In his diary, Republican congressman George W. Julian wrote of the reaction in the House: "Members joined in the shouting and kept it up for some minutes. Some embraced one another, others wept like children."

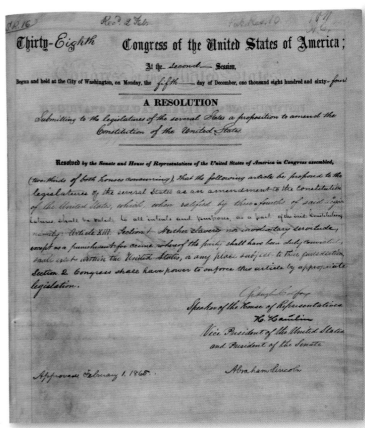

settled the debate between the two parties. But instead of choosing to wait for the sitting of the Republican-dominated 39th Congress in March 1865, the president used his annual message to Congress on December 6, 1864, to introduce the measure.

### Cheers in the House

Lincoln preferred to solicit the support of dissenting Democrats in the lame-duck 38th Congress, wanting to make its passage a bipartisan measure. With some arm-twisting, the necessary backing was obtained; on January 31, 1865, the

### The Thirteenth Amendment

Section 1 of the Thirteenth Amendment declared that "Neither slavery nor involuntary servitude, except as a punishment for crime ... shall exist within the United States, or any place subject to their jurisdiction."

amendment passed the House with two votes to spare. The news was greeted with wild rejoicing in Congress itself and by a 100-gun salute in Washington, D.C. It was fitting that among those celebrating inside the House were African-Americans, who had been admitted to the public galleries for the first time the previous

> "there is only a **question of time** ... may we not agree that **the sooner the better?**"
>
> PRESIDENT LINCOLN, IN HIS MESSAGE TO CONGRESS, DECEMBER 6, 1864

### A celebration of emancipation

In this Thomas Nast print of 1865, African-Americans are shown in the center enjoying a comfortable home life. On the left are scenes of their former slavery; the right shows a future with equality in the workplace and education for all.

year. George W. Julian, a Republican congressman, noted, "I have felt, ever since the vote, as if I were in a new country."

Unlike the struggle in the House of Representatives, ratification itself proved relatively straightforward. Most Northern states quickly fell into line, and as the Civil War came to an end it was made known to former

## 27
**The number of states that had voted to ratify the amendment by December 6, 1865.**

Confederate states that acceptance was a precondition for full re-admission into the Union. The necessary quorum was achieved on December 6, 1865, and 12 days later Secretary of State William H. Seward proclaimed the amendment adopted. For abolitionists, the passing

of the Thirteenth Amendment served as moral justification for the war. The fact that slavery was no longer legal anywhere in U.S. territory was befitting considering all the deaths and suffering that the nation had endured.

### The implications

In practical terms, the implementation of the measure still had to play out. Emancipated, or freed, slaves were no longer in legal bondage, but most of them still had to earn a living tilling the lands on which they had formerly worked, and their rights had to be won and protected. Full civil rights for blacks would be a long time coming and the fight would span far into the next century.

In the meantime, the thousands of former slaves who poured onto the nation's streets to celebrate the passing of the amendment experienced personally an important milestone. The United States had changed decisively and they were no longer regarded as property. Still they looked forward to the day when they could vote and live among whites with true equality.

### A new life

For most former slaves the amendment's passing was a joyful time. Celebrations took place on plantations throughout the South. Couples were finally allowed to marry, and many people dropped their slave names.

**AFTER** »

Ratification of the amendment was the final measure in ending slavery in the United States. The way was legally open for the integration of former slaves into society.

**DEFINING FREEDOM**
The amendment guaranteed that **slaves would be free**, but the exact nature of that freedom remained to be defined. Other measures were needed. The Fourteenth Amendment, ratified in 1868, **gave former slaves U.S. citizenship**, and the Fifteenth, passed into law the following year, guaranteed their **right to vote**.

**THE ONGOING DIVIDE**
White opposition in the South later rolled back integration by making voter registration harder. In practice, the South's black population would have to wait almost another century, until the **Civil Rights Act of 1964** and the **Voting Rights Act of 1965**, to win effective enfranchisement.

# The **Carolinas** and **Alabama**

**In the wake of General Sherman's march through Georgia to the sea, the year 1865 saw further Union incursions bringing total war to the Southern heartland. South Carolina, where the war had begun four years earlier, was a particular target.**

## « BEFORE

Sherman's march through Georgia had badly damaged Confederate morale. Union leaders now sought to reap the benefits.

**BRINGING THE WAR HOME**
Earlier in the war, the **deep Southern states had escaped much of the fighting**, which was concentrated in border areas to the north and west. That **situation changed** dramatically with Sherman's invasion of Georgia and the evaporation of large-scale armed resistance after the fall of Atlanta. The question now was how best to **press home the advantage**.

**REVIVING THE ANACONDA PLAN**
With General Sherman in Savannah, Federal strategists saw a chance at last to **implement fully the Anaconda Plan**, originally proposed by General Winfield Scott in 1861 **« 64–65**. The project involved enveloping and **finally suffocating the remaining Confederate command centers** in Virginia.

Initially, General Grant—fearing the hazardous state of South Carolina's roads in the winter—wanted to ship General William T. Sherman's victorious troops from Savannah to support his own forces in Virginia. Sherman, however, insisted that his men were up to the task of overcoming any difficulties confronting them. Given that it would have taken two months to arrange the shipping option, Grant let himself be persuaded.

Although Sherman was to encounter formidable obstacles in his path, the opposition forces were the least of his worries. General P. G. T. Beauregard, commanding Confederate troops in South Carolina, had only about 17,500 men scattered across the state to combat Sherman's 60,000 battle-hardened veterans. In addition, morale in the Union ranks was extremely high. Most of the men were champing at the bit at the prospect of carrying the war to the state where the fighting had started. In the minds of many Northerners, South Carolina was more responsible than any other state for the suffering the nation had endured for nearly four years.

## Natural obstacles
The logistical problems of marching an army through the swamps and rain-swollen rivers that lay between Savannah, Georgia, and South Carolina's state capital, Columbia, presented a greater challenge than did the Confederate troops. In many places the roads were impassable, and Sherman's men had to create causeways by the slow process of "corduroying." This entailed cutting down trees, stripping off the bark, and flattening them on one side, then laying them crosswise, interspersed

burned. By the following morning, two-thirds of it lay in ashes.

The fate of Columbia was only part of the trail of destruction Sherman's forces blazed across the state. In their path they looted farms and torched villages to the ground. The Confederate forces opposing them felt the pinch because they were forced to live off the land as best they could.

On February 23, at Robert E. Lee's insistence, Joseph Johnston took command of all Southern forces in

**458** **The number of buildings estimated to have been burned in South Carolina's capital Columbia, including six churches, eleven banks, and a printing plant where Confederate currency was minted.**

the Carolinas. Under the circumstances, the best that he could manage was a holding action designed to delay Sherman's progress.

From Columbia, the Union commander headed north toward Goldsboro, North Carolina, where he

> "The **truth** is, the whole army is burning with an insatiable desire to **wreak vengeance** upon **South Carolina**. I ... feel that **she deserves all** that seems in store for her."
>
> GENERAL WILLIAM T. SHERMAN IN A LETTER TO MAJOR GENERAL HENRY W. HALLECK, UNION ARMY CHIEF-OF-STAFF, DECEMBER 24, 1864

## KEY MOMENT
### THE FALL OF FORT FISHER

By late 1864, Wilmington, North Carolina, was the only major port through which overseas supplies were still reaching the Confederate armies. It was protected from attack by Fort Fisher, a massive log-and-earth bastion at the mouth of the Cape Fear River, defended by 47 guns, 22 facing the ocean and 25 facing the land.

On January 15, 1865, a fleet under Admiral David D. Porter bombarded the fort from the sea, while the troops of General Alfred H. Terry attacked from the land. Under these two men, a combined force of 6,500 Union soldiers and sailors took the fort in a single day, with battle raging into the night. At 10 p.m. the Confederates under General W. H. C. Whiting surrendered to General Terry.

The Union forces had taken the garrison with 2,000 men inside. Wilmington itself fell soon after, leaving the Southern heartland cut off from trade with foreign countries.

with saplings, to form a usable surface for the men and the supply wagons. In spite of the difficulties, Sherman's bummers made extraordinarily fast progress, covering almost 10 miles (16km) a day. By February 17, barely a month after leaving Savannah, they reached Columbia. That night, the city

**Defending Charleston**
Soldier and painter Conrad Wise Chapman was stationed in Charleston in 1864 and often sketched while under fire. After the war, he made a series of paintings from his sketches.

expected to rendezvous with 20,000 additional Federal troops under General John M. Schofield, marching from the Confederate port of Wilmington, recently captured after the Battle of Fort Fisher.

## Confederate strategy

General Sherman had split his troops into two columns, and Johnston's only realistic hope lay in attacking the splintered Union forces. The Confederates attempted to delay one of the two columns outside the village of Averasboro before launching a fully fledged attack on the Federal left wing at Bentonville, barely a day's march south of Goldsboro.

The initial Confederate successes were soon countered by the arrival of Union reinforcements, and Sherman was able to rendezvous successfully with Schofield on March 23.

## The Alabama campaign

Meanwhile, Union leaders had devised a two-pronged strategy to carry the war into Alabama. One force under General E. R. S. Canby was sent to invade the state from the south through lower Mobile Bay, which had been occupied by Union forces after a naval battle the previous August. Canby succeeded in taking the city of Mobile itself in April 1865. In the meantime, a 27-year-old

cavalry commander, James H. Wilson, led a mounted troop of 13,000 men south from Tennessee into northern Alabama. There, he was confronted by Confederate cavalry under General Nathan Bedford Forrest.

The youthful Wilson managed the capture of northern Alabama brilliantly. He outmaneuvered and outnumbered Forrest and destroyed the Confederate munitions complex at Selma. Wilson then moved east to capture the state capital of Montgomery before heading into southern Georgia.

### Entering Charleston
As the 55th Massachusetts Colored Regiment entered the city on February 21, they sang "John Brown's Body." The line "John Brown died that the slave might be free" caused rejoicing among former slaves.

By the time Wilson's force took Macon, Georgia, on April 20, the war was effectively over. Although less decisive than the confrontation between Grant and Lee in Virginia, the Carolina and Alabama campaigns had between them put several more nails in the coffin of the Confederate cause.

**AFTER**

The success of Federal forces in the Carolinas and Alabama effectively thwarted Confederate hopes of a second line of defense if Richmond fell.

**THE TIGHTENING NOOSE**
The setbacks in the South increased the **pressure on Robert E. Lee's army** defending Petersburg, which increasingly came to be seen as the **last point of resistance** to a Union victory. The Union advance in the Carolinas had cut Lee off from the sea, leaving him increasingly reliant on a handful of westbound roads and railroad lines for all his supplies.

**EBBING HOPES**
News of Union incursions also had **a devastating effect on the morale** of Confederate soldiers. Many came from areas affected by the fighting, leading to an **upsurge in desertions** among men desperate to return home to check on their families' fate.

**JOHNSTON'S SURRENDER**
Confederate general **Joseph Johnston finally surrendered** to William T. Sherman on April 26 **324–25 》**, 17 days after General Lee's **surrender at Appomattox Court House 316–17 》**. The Battle of Palmito Ranch, Texas, on May 19, was the war's last battle.

**PLANNING THE END OF THE WAR**
On March 28, 1865, President Lincoln met with his generals (from left) William T. Sherman and Ulysses S. Grant, and Rear Admiral David D. Porter on the *River Queen*, Grant's floating headquarters at City Point, Virginia. The talks covered the strategy for ending the war, as well as the terms of surrender. The artist George P. A. Healy immortalized the occasion in his painting, *The Peacemakers*, and was indebted to his friend Sherman for its authenticity of detail.

# The **Fall** of **Petersburg** and **Richmond**

**The war's central conflict between the armies of Grant and Lee had become bogged down in a bloody stalemate in the trenches outside Petersburg, Virginia. When Union troops finally broke through in April 1865, the Confederate capital of Richmond was doomed, falling barely 24 hours later.**

**Major General John B. Gordon**
Gordon was one of Lee's most trusted lieutenants in the final stages of the war. He fought in many of the most important battles, from First Bull Run through Antietam and Gettysburg, and was wounded numerous times.

« **BEFORE**

**By early 1865, the plight of Robert E. Lee's Army of Northern Virginia was becoming increasingly desperate. If it was defeated, the Confederate capital would fall.**

**OTHER CONFEDERATE ARMIES**
Late 1864 saw a **succession of Southern defeats** throughout Georgia and Tennessee. General William T. Sherman concluded his devastating **March to the Sea « 296–97** with the **capture of Savannah**. Meanwhile, General John Bell Hood's **invasion of Tennessee** was smashed at **Nashville « 300–301**.

**LENGTHENING ODDS**
**Immobilized in the trenches outside Petersburg « 274–75** since June 1864, the Confederate force confronted a **numerically stronger, better-supplied enemy**. With the odds lengthening week by week, Lee's only recourse lay in bold action. But the chances of success were never good.

As 1865 dawned, the opposing armies dug in outside Petersburg were stymied. In a campaign that foreshadowed the trench warfare of World War I, both sides had made repeated attempts to achieve a breakthrough without gaining any decisive advantage.

### Union superiority
Yet the situation was much more serious for Robert E. Lee's army than it was for Ulysses S. Grant's. The Southern army was outnumbered by more than two to one, and the odds were worsening week by week as a steady stream of desertions further sapped its manpower. Grant had been able to use his numerical advantage gradually to extend his lines, which stretched Lee's resources to the limits. Moreover, the Confederate supply routes had been cut one by one, with the loss of

> **Major General George E. Pickett and Fitzhugh Lee, the senior officers of the Southern forces in the decisive encounter at Five Forks, were absent for much of the fighting, having been invited to a shad (fish) bake nearby by a fellow general.**

Wilmington, the only surviving link to the sea, delivering a particularly devastating blow.

With only bad news coming from the Carolinas, Lee knew that it could only be a matter of time before General Sherman's forces would be able to link up with the Army of the Potomac and complete his encirclement. To avoid that scenario, Lee had to extricate his army as soon as possible.

Lee turned to Major General John B. Gordon, commander of the Second Corps, who devised a strategy that involved sending armed troops masquerading as deserters to launch

a surprise assault on Fort Stedman, a strongpoint at the eastern end of the Federal lines. At first the ploy succeeded, but after four hours' fighting, Union forces staged a successful counterattack and Gordon's men were driven back with heavy losses.

### Decisive clash at Five Forks
Grant at once determined to take advantage of this reverse. On March 29, he sent an infantry corps accompanied by General Philip Sheridan's cavalry, newly arrived from the victorious Union campaign in the Shenandoah Valley, to probe the western end of Lee's lines. Lee took vigorous measures to counter the move, and there was hard fighting on March 30, with neither side managing to achieve an advantage. The next

### The Battle of Five Forks
Union cavalry break the Confederate line, as depicted by French artist Paul Philippoteaux. General Sheridan personally led the decisive charge that broke Pickett's division. About 3,000 Confederate troops were captured.

**Evacuation order**
Jefferson Davis's order to evacuate the Confederate capital was issued on April 2. He and various members of his cabinet abandoned the city that night, heading by train for Danville, Virginia.

The defeat at Five Forks, sometimes called the "Waterloo of the Confederacy," threatened Lee's last remaining lines of communication to the west and south and his position was untenable. The next morning, April 2, he sent word to Jefferson Davis that Petersburg would fall and that when it did, Richmond itself would have to be abandoned.

As it happened, the message had barely reached the Southern president, who was attending a Sunday-morning church service at the time, when Grant's men launched an all-out attack along Lee's lines at Petersburg. The Confederates resisted, but only as a holding action designed to give the army time to withdraw in some semblance of order from the beleaguered city. By the following morning, Petersburg was in Union hands.

day, Philip Sheridan's horsemen confronted General George E. Pickett's division at a crossroads known as Five Forks, 20 miles (32km) southwest of Petersburg.

Sheridan dispatched the Fifth Corps of the Army of the Potomac under Major General Gouverneur K. Warren with orders to attack the Confederate left flank. Despite confusion in the plan's execution, the pincer attack worked. By 7 p.m., Pickett's force had collapsed, with half the men surrendering and the rest taking flight. The Union breakthrough had finally been achieved.

### The fall of Richmond

With Petersburg fallen, Richmond could not be defended. As soon as Lee had telegraphed Jefferson Davis that

**Richmond in flames**
Confederate troops destroyed the city's arsenals and factories before they fled. The explosions started fires in residential areas, and all night long the citizens rushed away in "every description of cart, carriage, and vehicle."

April 2 morning to abandon the city, the evacuation had commenced. Orders were given to torch everything of military or strategic value.

After the civil authorities had departed, the city was unpoliced and the conflagrations spread uncontrolled until the first Union detachments arrived next morning to accept the city's formal surrender and to begin dousing the flames. By then, much of the Southern capital was in ruins; an estimated 25 percent of its buildings had burned down, and remaining hopes for the Confederacy lay smoldering.

## "We took Richmond at 8:15 this morning … The enemy left in great haste … "

UNION GENERAL GODFREY WEITZEL, IN A TELEGRAM TO GRANT, APRIL 3, 1865

**AFTER**

Following the fall of Richmond, the Confederacy became a country and a cause without a capital. Lee's retreating army was its only remaining bulwark.

**EVACUATING RICHMOND**
Jefferson Davis used the city's **last rail link** to **escape to Danville**, 130 miles (210km) to the southwest, where he issued a **defiant promise** to continue the struggle.

**LINCOLN'S TRIUMPH**
In contrast, **Abraham Lincoln** who happened to be visiting the Army of the Potomac when Richmond fell, **traveled into the city** barely a day after Davis had left it. He was **welcomed as a liberator** by the city's black population. "You are free, free as air," the President told them. But **Lincoln would die** within two weeks **320–21 »**.

**LAST BATTLES**
Lee **hoped to escape** with his army to the Danville area and **fight on**, but the **move was blocked by Grant 316–17 »**. With this, Lee had no option left but to surrender.

**LINCOLN IN RICHMOND**

# The Appomattox Campaign

**Following the abandonment of Petersburg and Richmond, General Robert E. Lee's army found itself on the run, retreating westward to railroad lines that would permit an orderly escape from the pursuing Union forces. The road led to the village of Appomattox Court House.**

The single greatest imperative facing General Robert E. Lee after the loss of Petersburg was the need to reestablish supply lines to feed his hungry men. His immediate target was the village of Amelia Court House, which lay on the Richmond and Danville railroad line. There he hoped to find not just ample supplies of food but also a base from which he could evacuate his army by rail south to Danville, Virginia, where Confederate President Jefferson Davis was waiting. From Danville he hoped to effect a rendezvous with General Joseph E. Johnston's Army of North Carolina, which was the only other substantial Confederate army in the field.

« BEFORE

**On April 3, the Southern capital Richmond fell to Union troops ❮❮ 314–15.** Confederate hopes now lay in tatters, yet General Robert E. Lee's army still had not yet been defeated.

**SHRINKING OPTIONS**
The **Army of Northern Virginia's only remaining hope** lay in evading its Union pursuers until it could **join up with General Joseph Johnston's Army of North Carolina**. But Lee's men were outnumbered—25,000 against 125,000 Union troops under General Ulysses S. Grant. They were also exhausted, while the Union forces were buoyed by the prospect of final victory.

**RACING TO RAILROADS**
To have any chance of making contact with Johnston, Lee would have to **evacuate his troops by rail**. The retreat westward thus became **a desperate race to reach railheads**—a race in which the Union troops had the advantage from the start.

The opening battle of the war, First Bull Run, was fought on land belonging to Wilmer McLean, a sugar broker, who also owned the house in which Lee and Grant signed the surrender.

Yet his hopes would be sorely dashed. In the confusion of the flight from Petersburg the wrong orders were dispatched, and what the Confederate troops found on arriving at Amelia station was a huge stash of ammunition—worse than useless to the army, as their supply wagons could barely carry the ordnance they already had.

## Lost time
Lee knew that his exhaused men could not continue without sustenance, and valuable time was lost while foraging parties hunted for provisions. By the time the army lurched forward again, it had lost any lead it had hoped to gain. Anticipating Lee's movements, General Ulysses S. Grant had dispatched General Philip Sheridan's cavalry to cut off the rail links west of Amelia Court House. In particular, Sheridan's force was told to seize the important rail junction at Burkeville, where the Southside

### Flag of truce
This linen dish towel was pressed into service as a flag of truce, when Lee sent General James Longstreet to deliver his reply to Grant's invitation to surrender.

### A time to rejoice
A Detroit broadside announces General Lee's surrender and—"By Order of the People"—calls on all citizens to come to a victory celebration in the city's central park, the Campus Martius.

railroad crossed the Danville and Richmond line. The Union infantry followed close behind them.

## The pursuit westward
For almost a week, the two armies marched on parallel courses westward, as Union scouting parties clashed with outlying Confederate detachments. The most serious of the engagements came at Saylers Creek on April 6, when three Union corps cut off a quarter of Lee's army, capturing some 6,000 men.

Their strength sapped by overnight marches in heavy rain on minimal rations, many soldiers simply gave up the march, lying by the roadside until picked up by pursuing forces. For two more days, Lee's army trudged on until it approached the village of Appomattox Court House, 90 miles (145km) west of Richmond. Lee rallied his troops for a final effort, seeking to break through the Union forces in order to reach the Virginia and Tennessee railroad at Lynchburg. The Confederates cleared a screen of Union horsemen, only to confront two infantry corps falling into line. Other Northern troops were approaching from the rear. Lee's redoubtable Army of Northern Virginia—what was left of it—was finally trapped.

Faced with the situation he had sought to avoid, Lee called a meeting of his commanders. Fighting on, it was agreed, would be a useless sacrifice. Someone suggested letting the men slip away into the countryside to fight as guerrillas, but Lee rejected the proposal. To do so, he said, would inflict destruction on regions that might otherwise have escaped it.

### Surrender house
A family sits on the front steps of the McLean House, made famous a few days previously, wherein General Lee signed his army's surrender.

"We would bring on a state of affairs it would take the country years to recover from," he concluded.

That left only one course of action. Grant had already put out peace feelers a couple of days earlier, but Lee had sent a temporizing response. Now with a heavy heart, he dispatched a message to his opponent; he was ready to discuss "the surrender of this army."

### Lee surrenders
It took some hours to arrange a meeting and find a suitable venue. The McLean House, the best-appointed residence in the village, was chosen. When the two generals met face to face, they formed a study in contrasts.

# "There is **nothing left** for me to do but **go and see General Grant**, and **I would rather die** a thousand deaths."

**ROBERT E. LEE SPEAKING TO HIS STAFF**, APRIL 8, 1865

Lee was every inch the Southern aristocrat, in full-dress uniform with sash and jeweled sword; Grant, the shorter of the two, wore a private's blouse and mud-spattered trousers and boots, his best outfit in the circumstances.

The oddly matched pair exchanged cordialities, but when they turned to business, the terms that Grant offered proved more generous than Lee had expected. Confederate officers and men must give their word not to take up arms again against the U.S. government and deliver up their weapons and other supplies as captured property. Officers would be permitted to keep their sidearms, horses, and personal baggage. All men would be free to return to their homes, "not to be disturbed by United States authority so long as they observe their paroles and the laws in force where they may reside." This last phrase meant that the defeated soldiers were freed from the threat of further punishment or of prosecution for treason. In addition, Grant agreed to Lee's request that common soldiers, too, should be allowed to keep their horses or mules for use as farm animals.

The formal act of surrender took place three days later. A line of Confederate soldiers tramped between columns of Union troops commanded by Major

General Chamberlain to lay down their arms and battle standards. In exchange, they received written passes assuring them of a safe passage homeward. Lee himself headed back to Richmond, a commander without an army; as a mark of respect, a troupe of Union cavalry accompanied him for part of the way.

## AFTER

The surrender at Appomattox removed the last Confederate hopes of a negotiated peace, but it did not in fact end the war.

### THE SOUTH BEHEADED

General Lee's surrender **did not apply to all Confederate forces** in the field. In theory, other troops in other theaters were free to fight on. In practice, though, none stood a realistic chance of long-term military success. April 1865 had seen the **South lose both its capital and its principal fighting force**. With Lee defeated and Confederate President Jefferson Davis in flight 324–25 ❯❯, the South had no leader. General **Joseph E. Johnston** surrendered in North Carolina on **April 26**, General **Richard Taylor** in Alabama on **May 4**, and General **Kirby Smith** in the Trans-Mississippi region on **May 26, 324–25 ❯❯**.

---

## UNION GENERAL 1828–1914

### JOSHUA LAWRENCE CHAMBERLAIN

Nobody's idea of a typical military commander, Chamberlain was an academic by profession, who was teaching modern languages at Bowdoin College, Maine when the Civil War broke out. He quickly rose to the rank of colonel in the Union army, commanding a detachment of New Englanders at the Battle of Gettysburg, where in a crucial defensive action his men held the Little Round Top hill against repeated assaults. At Petersburg, he was a brigade commander and twice wounded, once so seriously that he was initially given up for dead. Yet he recovered and was given the honor of presiding offfficer at the ceremonial laying down of arms by Confederate forces following Lee's surrender.

**Souvenirs of surrender**
Now on display at the Smithsonian Institution, these are the chairs used by Lee and Grant and the table upon which they signed the surrender document.

LEE'S CHAIR    SPOOL TABLE    GRANT'S CHAIR

# Surrender at Appomattox

**After General Robert E. Lee's Army of Northern Virginia made a final stand at Appomattox Court House, he found his Confederate army to be both surrounded and exhausted. Lee exchanged a series of letters with General Ulysses S. Grant on April 9, 1865. Later that afternoon, the two men met to draw up the formal terms of surrender.**

"At a little before 4 o'clock General Lee shook hands with General Grant, bowed to the other officers, and with Colonel Marshall left the room. One after another we followed, and passed out to the porch. Lee signaled to his orderly to bring up his horse, and while the animal was being bridled the general stood on the lowest step and gazed sadly in the direction of the valley beyond where his army lay—now an army of prisoners. He smote his hands together a number of times in an absent sort of a way; seemed not to see the group of Union officers in the yard who rose respectfully at his approach, and appeared unconscious of everything about him. All appreciated the sadness that overwhelmed him, and he had the personal sympathy of every one who beheld him at this supreme moment of trial. The approach of his horse seemed to recall him from his reverie, and he at once mounted. General Grant now stepped down from the porch, and, moving toward him, saluted him by raising his hat. He was followed in this act of courtesy by all our officers present; Lee raised his hat respectfully, and rode off to break the sad news to the brave fellows who he had so long commanded ..."

GENERAL HORACE PORTER, WHO SERVED ON GRANT'S STAFF, FROM AN ARTICLE IN *THE CENTURY* MAGAZINE, NOVEMBER 1887

"For us they were fellow soldiers as well, suffering the fate of arms. We could not look into those brave, bronzed faces, and those battered flags we had met on so many fields where glorious manhood lent a glory to the earth that bore it, and think of personal hate and mean revenge. Whoever had misled these men, we had not. We had led them back, home. Whoever had made that quarrel, we had not. It was a remnant of the inherited curse for sin. We had purged it away, with blood offerings."

GENERAL JOSHUA L. CHAMBERLAIN, WHO OVERSAW THE OFFICIAL LAYING DOWN OF ARMS BY THE CONFEDERATE ARMY OF NORTHERN VIRGINIA AT APPOMATTOX, IN HIS MEMOIRS *THE PASSING OF THE ARMIES*, 1915

**Signing the terms of surrender**
An hour and a half's discussion was enough to end four years of war. This 1867 painting of *Lee's Surrender to Grant at Appomattox* by Louis Guillaume now hangs at the Appomattox Court House National Historical Park.

# The Assassination of Lincoln

**With the war effectively won and the Union virtually restored, the nation needed a leader of vision to heal the wounds of four years in which brother had fought brother. John Wilkes Booth's murderous action on Good Friday of 1865 removed the man best fitted for the task.**

## « BEFORE

President Lincoln had every reason to be optimistic in the wake of Robert E. Lee's surrender at Appomattox Court House. But within six days, fate cruelly intervened.

### THE FIRST CONSPIRACY
Although the president had no way of knowing, **John Wilkes Booth and a band of Southern sympathizers** had made plans to **kidnap Lincoln** the previous year. Their hopes had been to hold the president as a bargaining tool in order to gain the release of **Confederate prisoners of war « 256–57**. At the time the plot was aborted, but the conspirators **remained in contact**.

### PUNCTURED HOPES
The dawning **prospect of peace « 312–13** brought great relief to Lincoln, who was intent on **promoting reconciliation with the Rebel states**. Yet the very news that cheered the president only **reignited the anger of his enemies**. A speech in which Lincoln lent his support to the cause of black enfranchisement unwittingly **sealed his fate**. Booth was now determined to **silence him forever**.

Lincoln was in an upbeat mood on the morning of Good Friday, April 14, 1865; a political colleague remarked that he had never seen the president looking so happy. Although he was very aware of the challenges that lay ahead, the knowledge that the war was almost over gave him good reason to celebrate. Yet he was not free of personal anxieties.

### A portentous dream
Just three days before, Lincoln had described to his wife and friends a dream in which he had wandered through the rooms of a deserted White House only to find a body laid out in state. When he asked an attendant who it was that had died, he was told it was the president, killed by an assassin. "I slept no more that night," Lincoln told his audience, "and although it was only a dream, I have been strangely annoyed by it ever since."

### The assassination
A print captures the moment that John Wilkes Booth fired the fatal shot. Taking no chances, the assassin holds a knife as he takes aim at President Lincoln's head.

Lincoln had good reason to be disturbed. From the beginning of his presidency, he had received hate mail, some of which contained threats on his life. Now lurked John Wilkes Booth. The 26-year-old, a member of a celebrated American acting

Bird's head grip

**Booth's derringer pistol**
Ideal because of its size, Booth's weapon was this single-shot, muzzle-loading pocket pistol. It was recovered from the presidential box after Booth had fled Ford's Theatre.

Trigger guard

dynasty, was one of the nation's leading players and a familiar face around Washington, D.C., where he often performed. A passionate supporter of the Confederate cause, the Maryland-born actor was eager to leave his mark on history through some great, dramatic act. He had gathered around him a group of followers who shared his hatred of the president, and over a period of months they had discussed various ways of doing him harm.

### The plot takes shape
News of Lee's surrender at Appomattox brought matters to a head. The day before, Booth had heard Lincoln give an impromptu speech from a window of the White House, in which the president gave his support to the enfranchisement of black voters. For Booth, who was an ardent advocate of slavery, this was the final straw and it was time to act.

The plot that he and his co-conspirators hatched was multi-pronged. Booth took it upon himself to assassinate Lincoln. A 20-year-old Confederate veteran named Lewis Powell was assigned the task of killing Secretary of State William Seward, while 29-year-old George Atzerodt, the German-born owner of a Maryland carriage-repair business, was instructed to murder Vice President Andrew

Johnson. The warped goal was to remove the Union's top leadership in one bloody night, thereby avenging the Confederate defeat and giving the South a chance to rally and gather new forces to continue the struggle.

The timing of the attack was settled when Booth heard that Lincoln was to attend a performance of a comedy, *Our American Cousin*, at Ford's Theatre in Washington on the Good Friday evening. Initially, the President's intention had been to take along General Ulysses S. Grant and his wife as guests of himself and the First Lady, but the general—no great lover of social occasions—had made an excuse and left town to visit relatives. In their place, Mary Todd Lincoln invited a friend of the family, Major Henry Rathbone, and his fiancée, Clara Harris.

### The events of the evening
Booth knew the theater well, having performed there on many occasions. A familiar figure backstage, he had no trouble in gaining access to the building and wandering around its corridors at will. In the course of the day he took the precaution of drilling a small spy hole in the door of the presidential box, to provide him with a view of what was happening inside. That evening, he waited until the play was well underway before taking action. He knew the script himself, and had settled on one line as a cue for his deed—it always got a good reaction from the audience, and Booth hoped he could count on the laughter in the theater to help conceal the sound of the shot. Stealing into the presidential box with his pistol, he shot Lincoln in the head at the chosen moment, and then leaped down onto the stage, shouting, "*Sic semper tyrannis*" ("Thus always to tyrants"), to the astonishment of the theatergoers. Upon landing, he broke his leg, but managed to limp to a horse he had waiting

> Owner of the boarding house where the conspirators met, Mary Surratt, hanged for her alleged part in the plot, was the first woman executed by the U.S. government.

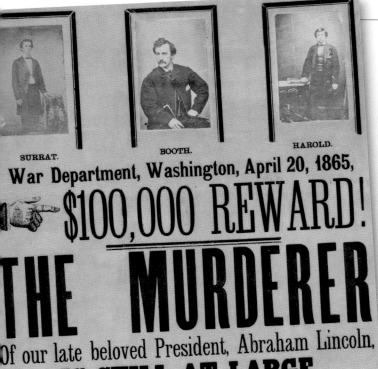

**Reward poster**
A massive $100,000 was offered as a reward for the capture of Booth and his coconspirators. Pictured among them is Mary Surratt's son, John, who escaped conviction by fleeing the country.

outside. He then fled the city. Booth's two accomplices were less successful. Powell entered William Seward's house and managed to make his way to the bedroom where the statesman was lying injured, having broken his arm and jaw in a carriage accident nine days earlier. When his gun jammed, Powell pulled a knife and stabbed his victim repeatedly, but not fatally. The brace supporting Seward's broken arm diverted the worst of the blows, When help arrived, Powell broke off the attack, exited the house, and, like Booth, escaped on a waiting horse. Seward subsequently made a full recovery. As for Atzerodt, his courage simply failed him. He spent the evening drinking in the bar of the hotel where the vice president was staying, then wandered off into the night without having even approached his target.

### Lincoln fights for survival
Meanwhile, desperate attempts were being made to save Lincoln's life. Too badly injured to be taken back to the White House, he was carried instead to a boarding house across the street from the theater. But there was little the doctors could do. Fatally wounded by a single bullet to the brain, the president died early the following morning without having regained consciousness. The hunt for the conspirators now began to intensify.

### Capturing the culprits
Powell was the first to be apprehended, three days after the attack, when he returned to the boarding house where the plot had been hatched. Powell found federal agents sent to arrest the owner, a Confederate sympathizer named Mary Surratt, waiting for him there. Atzerodt was tracked down three days later on a Maryland farm some 25 miles (40km) from the capital. John Wilkes Booth managed to evade capture until April 26, when he was traced to a barn in Virginia and shot dead. Others who were party to the plot were also arrested, including David Herold. He had accompanied Booth on his flight,

but chose to surrender to the pursuing troops rather than die trapped in the Virginia barn as it burned around him.

### Toward a united country
Lincoln's murder was unprecedented at the time—no previous president had ever been assassinated. His death deprived the nation of sound leadership, while his successor, Andrew Johnson, was generally considered lacking in wise counsel. Some Unreconciled Confederates applauded Booth's deed; however, the bulk of the nation was united in grief. Although federal authorities were at first suspicious of a Confederate conspiracy, Lincoln's death helped bind the nation in common sympathy.

**Lincoln's hat**
Despite his impressive height of 6ft 4in (1.9m), Lincoln was renowned for wearing tall or high hats. On the night of his assassination, he wore this one, now in the Museum of American History, Smithsonian Institution.

### AFTER

Lincoln's death plunged the nation into mourning and opened new wounds at a time when old ones had not yet started to heal.

#### POLITICAL AFTERSHOCKS
**Vice President Andrew Johnson** became president. Thus a **Southern Democrat**, drafted to attract swing voters in 1864, now headed a **Republican administration**. Lacking Lincoln's political and moral authority, he was ill-equipped for **the task of Reconstruction 340–41 ≫**.

#### THE FATE OF THE CONSPIRATORS
**Eight suspects went on trial.** Held in isolation, their heads were covered in cotton-lined canvas hoods with **a slit for eating but no ear or eyeholes**. Powell, Herold, Atzerodt, and Mary Surratt were condemned to death and **hanged on July 7, 1865**. Three others received sentences of **life imprisonment**, while another, a carpenter at Ford's Theatre accused of **assisting in Booth's escape**, got six years.

" But **O heart! heart! heart!** **O the bleeding** drops of red, Where on the deck my **Captain lies**, / Fallen **cold and dead**. "
WALT WHITMAN, FROM HIS POEM, *O CAPTAIN! MY CAPTAIN!*, 1865

# The Last Hours of Lincoln

**At approximately 10 p.m. on April 14, 1865, John Wilkes Booth shot President Abraham Lincoln at Ford's Theatre in Washington, D.C. The bullet pierced Lincoln's skull above his left ear, causing a wound that was immediately recognized as fatal. Carried to a nearby boarding house, Lincoln would utter his last breath at 7:22 a.m. the next morning.**

"The giant sufferer lay extended diagonally across the bed, which was not long enough for him … A double guard was stationed at the door and on the sidewalk to repress the crowd, which was of course highly excited and anxious. The room was small and overcrowded … I remained in the room until then without sitting or leaving it, when, there being a vacant chair which some one left at the foot of the bed, I occupied it for nearly two hours, listening to the heavy groans and witnessing the wasting life of the good and great man who was expiring before me. About 6 a.m. I experienced a feeling of faintness, and for the first time after entering the room a little past eleven I left it and the house and took a short walk in the open air. It was a dark and gloomy morning, and rain set in before I returned to the house some fifteen minutes later. Large groups of people were gathered every few rods [several yards], all anxious and solicitous. Some one or more from each group stepped forward as I passed to inquire into the condition of the President and to ask if there was no hope. Intense grief was on every countenance when I replied that the President could survive but a short time. The colored people especially—and there were at this time more of them, perhaps, than of whites—were overwhelmed with grief. A little before seven I went into the room where the dying President was rapidly drawing near the closing moments. His wife soon after made her last visit to him. The death struggle had begun … The respiration of the President became suspended at intervals and at last entirely ceased at twenty-two minutes past seven."

GIDEON WELLES, U.S. SECRETARY OF THE NAVY 1861–69, FROM THE *DIARY OF GIDEON WELLES: SECRETARY OF THE NAVY UNDER LINCOLN AND JOHNSON*, 1911

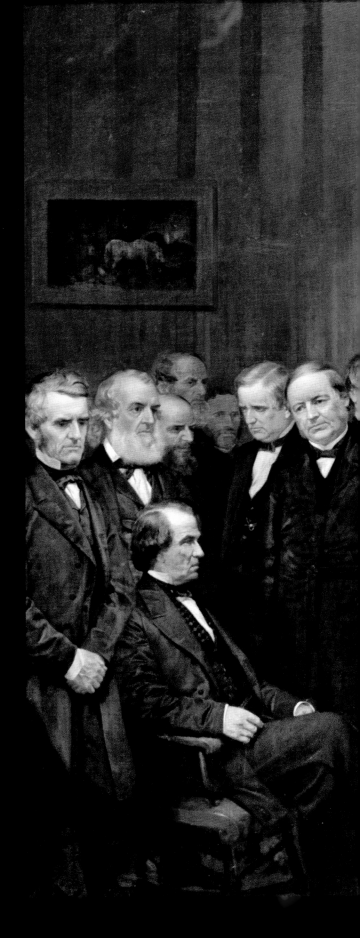

**The death of a president**
*The Last Hours of Lincoln* (a detail is shown here), a fictional scene painted by Alonzo Chappel in 1868, depicts all the people who visited the dying President—including his wife Mary, his son Robert, and members of the Cabinet.

# Last Terms of Surrender

**General Robert E. Lee's surrender at Appomattox Court House left some 175,000 Confederate soldiers still in arms in three armies and numerous garrisons scattered across the South. The war's final acts were played out in North Carolina, Georgia, Alabama, Texas, and even Liverpool, England.**

**The surrender of Johnston**
Confederate General Johnston (on the right) surrenders to General Sherman on April 26, 1865. The two men became firm friends, and a quarter of a century later Johnston was a pallbearer at Sherman's funeral.

## « BEFORE

**After April 9, 1865, when General Lee's Army of Northern Virginia laid down its arms « 316–19,** most of the South's generals accepted that the cause was lost.

**DIEHARD RESISTANCE**
Some Southern leaders, however, **wanted to fight on.** The most prominent of these diehards, **Confederate President Jefferson Davis « 48–49 was still urging resistance** three weeks after Lee's surrender. By then, he and his cabinet had abandoned the Confederate capital, Richmond, and **fled south to Greensboro, North Carolina.** The cabinet met for the last time on May 5, 1865, in Washington, Georgia, after which Davis went into hiding.

**A NEW PRESIDENT**
Meanwhile, events in Washington, D.C. had taken a dramatic turn with the **assassination of President Lincoln « 320–21,** fatally shot on April 14. Lincoln was succeeded by his vice president, the Southern War Democrat **Andrew Johnson 326–27 »,** who was swiftly sworn in as 17th President of the United States on the morning after the shooting.

By far the largest and best organized of the Confederate armies remaining in the field after Lee's surrender was the one confronting General William T. Sherman in North Carolina under the command of General Joseph E. Johnston. Here, the balance of power had altered in late March 1865, when Sherman made a successful rendezvous with reinforcements from Wilmington. Confronted with the Union's overwhelming superiority in numbers, Johnston retreated westward to the North Carolina state capital, Raleigh.

### Meeting with Davis
Johnston was preparing to abandon Raleigh to Sherman's advancing Union forces when word came of events at Appomattox. While still digesting the news, Johnston was summoned to a meeting with Confederate President Jefferson Davis in Greensboro, about 80 miles (130km) away. When the two men met on April 12, Davis— without even requesting Johnston's opinion of the military situation— talked ramblingly of gathering up deserters to fight on. Once Johnston was eventually given a chance to speak, he was blunt: "My views are, sir, that our people are tired of war, feel themselves whipped and will not fight." Shocked into silence, Davis unwillingly gave Johnston permission to put out peace feelers to Sherman.

In the meeting that followed—held on April 17, in a log cabin near Durham Station—Sherman initially went beyond his remit from Washington. He held out to Johnston the prospect of the readmission of Southern states to the Union on terms of full citizenship with no threat of persecution for treason or war crimes. In doing so, he strayed into political rather than purely military territory. He was subsequently reprimanded by the authorities in Washington and General Ulysses S. Grant was sent to take over the negotiations. Grant made it clear that while the military terms offered at Appomattox still stood and applied to Johnston's army as well as Lee's, there could be no bargaining on the larger postwar settlement.

### Johnston surrenders
When Davis was informed of Grant's conditions, he was eager to fight on. Johnston's reply was scathing. "We have to save the people, spare the blood of the army, and save the high civic functionaries," he told the Confederate president. He added that "your plan, I think, can do only the last." The next day, April 26, Johnston agreed to surrender the forces under his command, including Confederate troops in Georgia, Florida, and the Carolinas, a total of almost 90,000 men.

In Alabama, the Confederate commander, General Richard Taylor, watched developments to the north with fatalistic gloom. Like Johnston, he had

been fighting a losing battle, in his case against two separate Union forces in the north and south of the state. As soon as he heard of Johnston's negotiations with Sherman, he too sued for peace. On May 8 at Citronelle, Alabama, he

> A three-man detachment posted to Virginia's Great Dismal Swamp are thought to have been the last Confederate soldiers to lay down their arms. They finally emerged in July 1866, 15 months after Lee's surrender.

agreed with General Edward Canby, the Union commander-in-chief in the state, to accept terms similar to those that had been offered to Lee and Johnston.

> **"My small force is melting away like snow before the sun ..."**
> JOSEPH E. JOHNSTON, APRIL 13, 1865

By that time only one Confederate army was still officially at war with the Union: that of the vast Trans-Mississippi Department, under the command of General Edmund Kirby Smith. Not having suffered the reverses that Johnston and Taylor had known, Kirby Smith proved less willing to come to terms. On the day after Taylor's capitulation, he flatly refused a Union invitation to lay down his arms. On May 12 and 13, a final engagement was fought at Palmito Ranch, a Confederate outpost on the Rio Grande. Twice the position fell to attacking Union regiments, and twice the defenders reclaimed it. Ironically, it was the Confederates who thus won the last battle of the Civil War, at a cost of four men killed and a dozen or more wounded—the Union force suffered 30 casualties.

### Imprisoned president
A contemporary sketch shows the captured Jefferson Davis at Fort Monroe on the Virginia coast. He was held a prisoner there for two years until released on bail paid by wealthy citizens from both North and South.

## Jefferson Davis captured

Meanwhile in Georgia, Jefferson Davis had been captured near Irwinville. At dawn on May 10, Union cavalrymen surrounded the Confederate leader, his wife, their four children, and a small group of loyal officials, all of whom had been camping out in a pine forest. The Union troops consisted of two separate units, neither of which was aware of the other at first. In the ensuing confusion, two of the cavalrymen were killed as a result of "friendly fire."

The South's fate was now firmly in the hands of the U.S. Government, headed by Lincoln's successor, President Andrew Johnson. The first indication of Johnson's intentions came in two proclamations issued on May 29. One granted pardons and restored property to almost all Southerners who were willing to take an oath of allegiance. The other, directed at North Carolina, set a pattern for states wishing to rejoin the Union. Delegates were to be elected to draft a new state constitution, with the power to determine the qualifications required of voters in future state elections.

In the Trans-Mississippi region, Kirby Smith was starting to feel the pressure of changed circumstances. As news of Jefferson Davis's arrest spread, many of his men laid down their arms and set off for home. With his army dissolving around him, the general also learned that Grant was sending the redoubtable General Philip Sheridan to enforce peace. Recognizing the inevitable,

Kirby Smith sent word to General Canby, now in New Orleans, that he too was prepared to negotiate a surrender. The document was signed on June 2.

### Final surrenders

Even then, some groups held out. Brigadier General Stand Watie, a Cherokee in command of the Native American cavalry in Kirby Smith's army, only accepted a ceasefire on June 23. On August 2, the Confederate cruiser *Shenandoah*, which had been raiding Union ships in international waters, was in the Pacific when its crew learned of the capitulations. They continued to England, rather than a U.S. port, where they risked being tried for piracy. They surrendered in Liverpool on November 6. The crew dispersed, and the British later turned the ship over to the U.S. government.

**Victory parade**
Mounted Union officers ride down Pennsylvania Avenue in Washington, D.C. during a Grand Review held on May 23–24, 1865. Soldiers from both Meade's and Sherman's armies marched on consecutive days.

**Stand Watie**
Principal chief of the Cherokee Nation since 1862, Brigadier General Stand Watie commanded the First Indian Brigade under General Kirby Smith. Before the war, he had been a successful plantation- and slave-owner.

### AFTER

The restoration of peace left huge questions about the direction the reunited nation would take. First and foremost, former Confederate soldiers had to be resettled.

**LIVES TO REBUILD**
By the **terms offered to Robert E. Lee and his army at Appomattox Court House** ❮❮ **316–19**, soldiers who surrendered were **free to return home** with their horses or mules and, in the case of officers, with their sidearms as well. They carried with them **signed parole passes** that guaranteed them the right to remain undisturbed as long as they kept their paroles and "the laws in force where they reside."

Yet many soldiers returned to find their homesteads ravaged. In addition, the former Confederacy's **transport infrastructure had been badly damaged**, with much of the region's rail network destroyed. A huge task of **national reconstruction** lay ahead **340–41 ❯❯**.

PRESIDENT OF THE UNITED STATES Born 1808 Died 1875

# Andrew **Johnson**

## " The goal to strive for is a **poor government** but a **rich people**."

ANDREW JOHNSON, QUOTED IN *ANDREW JOHNSON, PLEBEIAN AND PATRIOT* BY ROBERT WATSON WINSTON (1928)

The assassination of Abraham Lincoln thrust Andrew Johnson into the spotlight, conferring on him a role that he had never been expected to play. Born into poverty in North Carolina, he had no formal schooling. Instead, he was apprenticed to a tailor at an age when most children would still have been attending lessons.

In his teens, Johnson abandoned the apprenticeship and ran away with his brother to Tennessee, where he found work as a tailor in the town of Greeneville in the east of the state. This was a land of smallholders, who had little in common with the slaveholding estate owners of the deep South. It was these people, the smallholders, whose views Johnson would represent over the course of his political career. In contrast, he always maintained a deep-seated resentment against the great estate owners.

In Greeneville, the young Johnson met and married a shoemaker's daughter, Eliza McCardle, who is said to have taught him writing and arithmetic, and encouraged him in his political ambitions. In 1829, at just 20, he became a municipal alderman, and four years later he was elected town mayor. A talent for oratory took him to the Tennessee House of Representatives two years after that. Over the next three decades his political career went from strength to strength. He was elected to the lower house of Congress in 1843, then became Governor

**Campaign flag**
The Republican Party chose War Democrat Johnson to run with Abraham Lincoln in the 1864 presidential election in the hope of uniting pro-war opinion. They easily beat George McClellan, the Democratic candidate.

of Tennessee. In 1857, he entered the Senate as a Democrat, and was serving in that capacity at the outbreak of the Civil War. Although a Southerner, Johnson was fiercely opposed to secession, a cause he identified with the planters he had always stood against. When fighting broke out, he was the only U.S. senator from a Southern state to remain loyal to the Union.

As a War Democrat—having split from those among the Democratic Party who opposed the war—Johnson attracted the attention of Republican strategists seeking a vice-presidential candidate for the 1864 election. The party needed to reach out to Democrats willing to back the war effort. Their choice of Johnson as Lincoln's running mate, both on a National Union ticket, served to show that the Union represented something more than just the Republicans under another name.

**Unpopular president**
Photographer Mathew Brady took this portrait of Andrew Johnson around 1865. A Unionist, he was against civil rights for blacks and lacked the ability to reunite the nation after the war.

**Taking office**
Johnson's first public appearance in his role as vice president did not inspire confidence. Suffering the after-effects of typhoid fever, he prepared for his swearing in with several shots of

**Johnson pardons Rebels**
An contemporary illustration shows Johnson pardoning Rebels at the White House. All Rebels except the Confederate leaders were pardoned, and all property was returned except slaves.

## "Now that we have **peace**, let us **enforce the Constitution**."

ANDREW JOHNSON SPEAKING TO CITIZENS OF WASHINGTON, FEBRUARY 22, 1866

whiskey. He gave a rambling, incoherent inauguration speech and was generally held to have disgraced himself. Six weeks later, following the seismic shock of Lincoln's death, there was further consternation at the thought of Johnson as the new president.

His position was politically awkward. A lifetime Democrat, he found himself at the head of a Republican administration, and it soon became apparent that his political agenda was very different from that of much of the party.

### Controversy brews
The falling out began barely six weeks into Johnson's presidency, when he issued two key proclamations. One granted amnesty and restored property to almost all Southerners prepared to swear allegiance to the Union. The other set in motion a process by which former Confederate states could be readmitted to the Union. Although intended specifically for North Carolina, it came to be seen as a model for other states as well. The process provided for the election of a representative body to frame a new state constitution. Crucially, the electorate involved would be exclusively white.

Johnson's proposals brought into focus the clash between two very different views of the future of the nation. On one side, the radical wing of the Republican Party imagined a transformed South in which emancipated blacks would have the same citizenship rights as their white neighbors, including the right to vote. On the other, Democrats

and moderate Republicans, as well as the vast body of white opinion in the South itself, visualized a situation in which little would have changed in the postwar states except for the abolition of slavery as an institution.

### Support for the South
Great tact and political sure-footedness were required to keep the two sides from each other's throats, and Johnson failed to show either. Through the summer of 1866, the situation became inflamed, as the new administrations of the former Confederate states passed a series of Black Codes severely restricting the rights of black people. There were reports, too, of attacks on black citizens by white mobs: In Memphis 46 people were killed, in New Orleans 40. Opinion among hardline anti-Southern Republicans, known as Republican Radicals, was outraged, and much of the ire was directed at Johnson, who had

**The parrot**
Johnson parrots the word "Constitution," referring to his support for the South during Reconstruction.

vetoed a bill to extend the life of the Freedmen's Bureau, a federal agency set up under Lincoln to protect black rights in the South. Worse still, he went on to veto a Civil Rights Bill that would have given citizenship to blacks on the same terms as the rest of the population. Infuriated radicals and moderates came together to override both vetoes and push the measures through.

> Johnson was the only former U.S. president to serve in the Senate after leaving the White House. He was re-elected as a senator for Tennessee, a post he had previously held from 1857 to 1862.

The conflict simmered for the next two years, eventually polarizing into a struggle between Johnson and his secretary of war, Edwin M. Stanton, a champion of the Republican Radical cause. To prevent Johnson from purging his cabinet of radicals, Congress took the unprecedented step of passing a Tenure of Office Act, forbidding the president from removing high-ranking officials without the Senate's approval.

When Johnson flouted the act by seeking to replace Stanton, the power struggle between legislature and executive came to a head. The House voted to impeach the president—the first time that it had done so in its 80-year history—and Johnson was duly forced to stand trial. In the event, enough moderate Republican senators rallied to the president's cause to deny the impeachers the two-thirds majority they needed by just one vote. Johnson had been saved by the skin of his teeth, and served out the remaining eight months of his term. He was succeeded in office by the Union war hero Ulysses S. Grant.

Johnson retained support in the South, and in time was re-elected to the Senate, serving for five months before his death from a stroke. Since then, his reputation has risen and fallen in line with attitudes to Reconstruction as a whole. Generally, historians have placed Johnson in the category of presidents found wanting.

**Impeachment ticket**
This is a facsimile of a ticket that admitted the bearer to the gallery to watch the Senate proceedings against President Johnson. Only a limited number were available each day.

U.S. SENATE
Impeachment President
ADMIT THE BEARER
APRIL 6TH 1868.
GALLERY
Geo. T. Brown
Sergeant-at-Arms.

To be taken up at MAIN ENTRANCE
U.S. SENATE
No. 6

---

TIMELINE

**JOHNSON'S TAILOR SHOP IN GREENEVILLE**

- **December 29, 1808** Born in Raleigh, North Carolina, the third child of stableman Jacob Johnson and his wife Mary, a weaver.
- **1812** His father dies, leaving the family in poverty. Johnson has no formal education.
- **1822** Apprenticed to a tailor.
- **1825** Runs away with his brother, William, to Greeneville, Tennessee, where Andrew finds work as a tailor.
- **1827** Marries Eliza McArdle, with whom he will have five children over the next 25 years.
- **March 4, 1843** Enters the U.S. House of Representatives as a Democrat. Over the next ten years he will serve five consecutive terms in the House.
- **October 17, 1853** Takes office as Governor of Tennessee.
- **October 8, 1857** Enters the U.S. Senate as junior senator for Tennessee. As such he argues passionately against secession.
- **March 12, 1862** President Lincoln appoints him military governor of Tennessee following Union gains there. His area of authority grows as Union armies expand their grip on the state.
- **June 1864** Selected as Abraham Lincoln's running mate for the presidential election of that year. The two men stand in the name of the newly created National Union Party.
- **March 4, 1865** Takes office as vice president of the United States. He is widely criticized for being drunk when giving his inauguration speech to the Senate.
- **April 15, 1865** On the morning after Lincoln's assassination, Johnson is sworn in as 17th president of the United States.
- **March 27, 1866** Breaks with the Republicans in Congress by vetoing the Civil Rights Bill, which would confer citizenship on freed slaves.
- **March 5, 1868** Impeachment proceedings get underway in the Senate, with Johnson accused of intentional violation of the Tenure of Office Act.
- **May 26, 1868** The Senate proceedings are adjourned, his accusers having failed by one vote to secure the two-thirds majority needed to impeach the president.
- **March 4, 1869** Leaves office at the end of his four-year term after announcing a controversial amnesty for all Confederates not covered by previous pardons.
- **March 4, 1875** Re-enters the Senate, voted in by the Tennessee legislature.
- **July 31, 1875** Dies of a stroke at age 66, at his daughter's house near Elizabethton, Tennessee.

# 7

# LEGACIES OF THE WAR 1865–1877

Confederate surrender ensured the survival of the Union and the freedom of slaves. The costly peace, however, did not end conflict. Sharply divisive questions remained about the role that Southerners and freed African-Americans would play in the postwar nation

**« Grand review of the armies**
A victory parade to mark the end of the war took place in Washington, D.C., on May 23 and 24, 1865. George Meade's 80,000-strong Army of the Potomac marched down Pennsylvania Avenue on the first day. The next day, William T. Sherman's Army of Georgia, 65,000 strong, took six hours to pass the reviewing stand. Two weeks later, both armies were disbanded.

# LEGACIES OF THE WAR

**The impeachment of Johnson**
Andrew Johnson, Lincoln's vice president, is thrust into office after Lincoln's assassination. A Southern Democrat, he continually clashes with the Republicans in Congress. In 1868, he is even impeached, but is found not guilty. Here he receives the impeachment papers.

**Grant's presidency**
War hero Ulysses S. Grant has a troubled presidency in 1869–77. He is the obvious candidate to replace Johnson but, once elected, shows little aptitude for Washington politics and is mired in scandals created by corrupt members of his administration.

## VIRGINIA AND SURROUNDING AREA

PENNSYLVANIA
Philadelphia
NEW JERSEY
WEST VIRGINIA 1863
Harpers Ferry
Winchester
Baltimore
Potomac River
Shenandoah River
Centreville
WASHINGTON, D.C.
DISTRICT OF COLUMBIA
Delaware Bay
DELAWARE
Harrisonburg
MARYLAND
Charlottesville
Fredericksburg
Rappahannock River
Mattaponi River
Chesapeake Bay
VIRGINIA 1870
James River
Richmond
York River
ATLANTIC OCEAN
Roanoke
Lynchburg
Petersburg
James River
Cape Charles
Hampton
Cape Henry
Portsmouth
Appalachian Mountains
NORTH CAROLINA 1868

CANADA

WASHINGTON TERRITORY
Portland
MONTANA TERRITORY
OREGON
IDAHO TERRITORY
Rocky Mountains
Snake River
WYOMING TERRITORY
NEVADA
Sacramento
Virginia City
Salt Lake City
San Francisco
UTAH TERRITORY
COLORADO TERRITO[RY]
CALIFORNIA
Colorado River
Santa Fe
ARIZONA TERRITORY
NEW MEXICO TERRITORY
PACIFIC OCEAN
MEXICO

**Richmond in ruins**
The Confederate capital is reduced to ruins by fires that burn even as the city is being evacuated by Lee's forces in 1865. With so much of its wealth destroyed, the South's rebuilding becomes a protracted process.

**Remembering the war**
The Gettysburg anniversary commemoration in 1913 sees some 50,000 veterans from both sides attend in a spirit of reconciliation. They are addressed by President Woodrow Wilson, the first Southern-born president to hold the office since the end of the Civil War.

THE UNITED STATES OF AMERICA 1877
- States of the Union
- Year of readmission of Confederate states to the Union
- U.S. Territories

The Civil War was by far the bloodiest in American history, with most families, North and South, suffering some form of loss. This had lasting effects—disabled veterans were a common sight into the 20th century, and pension payments to veterans long remained a major cost. Wars often produce unexpected consequences, too—few in the North had sought the abolition of slavery when the war began, but it had come to pass. The struggle had been asymmetrical at its start, and its consequences were equally so. The war had inspired industrial and economic growth in the North; conversely some 60 percent of Southern wealth was destroyed or, in the case of the capital value of slaves, abolished in the war.

The other of the war's great issues, the doctrine of states' rights, met a decisive setback. The Federal government had taken and used powers that would have seemed excessive in 1860, setting about the

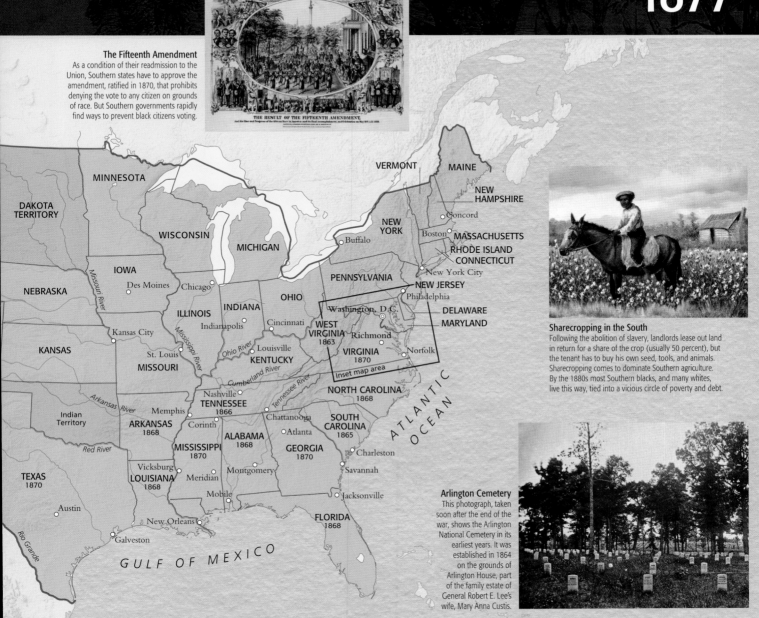

### The Fifteenth Amendment
As a condition of their readmission to the Union, Southern states have to approve the amendment, ratified in 1870, that prohibits denying the vote to any citizen on grounds of race. But Southern governments rapidly find ways to prevent black citizens voting.

THE RESULT OF THE FIFTEENTH AMENDMENT.
And the Rise and Progress of the African Race in America and its final Accomplishment, and Celebration on May 19th A.D. 1870.

MINNESOTA

DAKOTA TERRITORY

WISCONSIN

MICHIGAN

VERMONT

MAINE

NEW HAMPSHIRE

Concord

IOWA

Des Moines

Chicago

NEBRASKA

NEW YORK

Buffalo

Boston

MASSACHUSETTS

RHODE ISLAND

CONNECTICUT

New York City

ILLINOIS

INDIANA

OHIO

PENNSYLVANIA

NEW JERSEY

Philadelphia

Indianapolis

Cincinnati

Washington, D.C.

DELAWARE

MARYLAND

KANSAS

Kansas City

St. Louis

MISSOURI

Ohio River

Louisville

KENTUCKY

WEST VIRGINIA 1863

Richmond

VIRGINIA 1870

Norfolk

Missouri River

Mississippi River

Cumberland River

Inset map area

Nashville

NORTH CAROLINA 1868

Indian Territory

Arkansas River

Memphis

TENNESSEE 1866

Chattanooga

SOUTH CAROLINA 1865

ATLANTIC OCEAN

Tennessee River

ARKANSAS 1868

Corinth

ALABAMA 1868

Atlanta

GEORGIA 1870

Charleston

Red River

MISSISSIPPI 1870

TEXAS 1870

Vicksburg

LOUISIANA 1868

Meridian

Montgomery

Savannah

Austin

Mobile

Jacksonville

Rio Grande

New Orleans

FLORIDA 1868

Galveston

GULF OF MEXICO

### Sharecropping in the South
Following the abolition of slavery, landlords lease out land in return for a share of the crop (usually 50 percent), but the tenant has to buy his own seed, tools, and animals. Sharecropping comes to dominate Southern agriculture. By the 1880s most Southern blacks, and many whites, live this way, tied into a vicious circle of poverty and debt.

### Arlington Cemetery
This photograph, taken soon after the end of the war, shows the Arlington National Cemetery in its earliest years. It was established in 1864 on the grounds of Arlington House, part of the family estate of General Robert E. Lee's wife, Mary Anna Custis.

establishment of a national banking system, imposing an income tax, creating a huge railroad corporation, and much else. Much of this came about through the impetus of war and the same enthusiasm for radical change persisted to some extent into the postwar years. But the far-reaching Reconstruction measures attempted by Congress into the early 1870s soon met intransigent opposition in the South and became mired in political squabbles in Washington, D.C. By the 1870s, the North no longer had much interest in sorting out Southern problems, and white veterans on both sides spoke increasingly of reconciliation. Whites soon regained most of their former economic and political dominance in the South. Former slaves made undoubted gains, being able to lead real family lives and have some control over their futures, but the political changes hinted at in the postwar constitutional amendments and civil rights laws still lay far ahead.

# TIMELINE 1865–1877

**Reconstruction** · First "black codes" · **Thirteenth Amendment** · Civil Rights Act ·
Formation of Ku Klux Klan · **Fourteenth Amendment** · Impeachment of President
Johnson · **Fifteenth Amendment** · Grant administration · End of Reconstruction

## 1865

⌃ Swearing oath of loyalty

**MAY**
With most Confederate forces having surrendered, President Andrew Johnson issues a general amnesty to all "rebels," other than senior Confederate officers and officials.

**JUNE**
President Johnson appoints governors for six former Confederate states and restores Tennessee to the Union.

**NOVEMBER**
Mississippi enacts laws to establish the first "black codes." These deal with labor law, vagrancy, and similar issues, and are designed to restrict the rights of former slaves.

**DECEMBER**
The Thirteenth Amendment to the U.S. Constitution, abolishing slavery, comes into effect, having been ratified by 27 states.

## 1866

**FEBRUARY**
Congress passes a law extending the powers of the Freedmen's Bureau to ensure that former slaves are treated fairly. President Johnson later vetoes the measure, but Congress overrides his veto.

≪ Black veteran

**APRIL**
Congress passes a Civil Rights Act, over another presidential veto, declaring blacks to be citizens entitled to equal protection under the laws.

Union veteran's medal ≫

**MAY**
Six Confederate veterans form an organization called the Ku Klux Klan in Pulaski, Tennessee. Initially a social club, it will become the largest of various vigilante groups using terrorist methods to limit black rights.

**JUNE**
Congress adopts the Fourteenth Amendment to the U.S. Constitution. It extends citizenship to blacks and limits the Congressional representation of any state that does not allow blacks to vote.

**NOVEMBER**
Republican supporters of the Fourteenth Amendment win a landslide victory in Congressional elections. They have radical Reconstruction plans despite the president's opposition.

**NOVEMBER**
Former Union soldiers establish the Grand Army of the Republic. This veterans' organization will develop considerable political influence.

## 1867

**MARCH**
Nebraska is admitted to the Union, becoming the 37th state.

≪ The First Vote

**MARCH**
Congress passes a Reconstruction Act, dividing the South into military districts and providing for new elections. The latter will establish state constitutions giving the vote to blacks.

**MARCH**
Congress also passes the Tenure of Office Act. This limits the president's ability to obstruct Reconstruction measures by changing officials whose appointment originally required approval by the Senate.

**APRIL**
The Senate approves the treaty for the purchase of Alaska from Russia, but the process will not be completed until 1868 when the House of Representatives approves the necessary payment.

**JULY**
Congress passes new Reconstruction laws increasing the powers of the military governors in the South. They are answerable to General Ulysses S. Grant as commander of the Army, and not to the president.

**AUGUST**
With Congress out of session, President Johnson suspends Secretary of War Edwin Stanton, a Radical Republican, from office. This is contrary to the Tenure of Office Act, which Johnson believes to be unconstitutional.

⌄ Edwin Stanton

## 1868

**FEBRUARY**
President Johnson dismisses Secretary of War Stanton. In response, Congress votes to impeach the President.

**MARCH**
President Johnson's trial in the Senate begins. Johnson is narrowly acquitted in May, but will be a lame duck for the remainder of his term.

**MAY**
General Ulysses S. Grant is nominated as the Republican candidate in the upcoming presidential election.

**JUNE**
Seven former Confederate states are readmitted to the Union, having accepted the provisions of the Reconstruction Acts to enfranchise blacks and disqualify former Confederate office-holders.

**SEPTEMBER**
The Georgia state legislature expels its black members. Military government is reimposed.

**NOVEMBER**
General Grant wins the presidential election.

> "The question now is, do you mean to **make good to us** the promises in your Constitution?"

FREDERICK DOUGLASS ADDRESSING THE 1876 REPUBLICAN CONVENTION

| 1869 | 1870 | 1871 | 1872-73 | 1874-75 | 1876-77 | » |
|------|------|------|---------|---------|---------|---|

**1869**

**FEBRUARY**
Congress proposes a Fifteenth Amendment to guarantee the right of all citizens to vote, regardless of "race, color, or previous condition of servitude." At this date only a minority of states, North or South, allow blacks to vote.

**MARCH**
Ulysses S. Grant is inaugurated as president. He will be a rather passive president and, though personally honest, will be badly let down by the corruption of many of his appointees.

**MAY**
North America's first transcontinental railroad is completed in a ceremony held at Promontory Point, Utah.

**OCTOBER**
Democrats regain control of the state legislatures in Virginia and Tennessee, largely halting the Reconstruction process in these states.

**DECEMBER**
Women are granted the right to vote in the Wyoming Territory, the first area of the United States to make this change.

**1870**

**FEBRUARY**
The Fifteenth Amendment is ratified, but blacks are still widely denied the right to vote by such means as tax, property, or literacy tests. Mississippi is readmitted to the Union.

**MAY**
Congress passes a "Ku Klux Klan" or Enforcement Act in an attempt to limit intimidation of prospective black voters.

**JULY**
Georgia is readmitted to the Union. All former Rebel states have now been readmitted.

**DECEMBER**
Congress convenes with representatives from all states present for the first time since 1860.

**1871**

**FEBRUARY**
Congress passes a second Ku Klux Klan Act.

≫ Ku Klux Klan targets a black family at home

**APRIL**
Congress passes a third Ku Klux Klan Act. President Grant initially takes effective steps to enforce it, but by the time it is struck down by the Supreme Court in 1883, it has long since become a dead letter.

**MAY**
A dispute with Britain over the operations of British-built Confederate commerce-raiding warships is resolved, with compensation to be settled by an arbitration tribunal.

**1872-73**

**MAY 1872**
The Republican Party splits. A new Liberal Republican group nominates Horace Greeley as its presidential candidate. They call for honest government and an end to military intervention in the South.

**MAY 1872**
Congress passes an Amnesty Act, allowing most former Confederates to seek public office.

**NOVEMBER 1872**
President Grant is reelected.

**SEPTEMBER 1873**
The Panic of 1873 is triggered by the failure of a major bank, Jay Cooke & Co., because of problems with its railroad investments. The banking crisis and a major economic depression last for the next five years.

≫ Panic of 1873: start of five-year depression

**1874-75**

**NOVEMBER 1874**
Democrats win a majority in the House of Representatives in the national elections. They also control state legislatures in seven former Confederate states.

**MARCH 1875**
Congress passes a Civil Rights Act giving all citizens equal access to public facilities, such as hotels and transportation. The Supreme Court will declare this unconstitutional in 1883.

**NOVEMBER 1875**
The Democrats win a majority in Mississippi state elections after much intimidation of prospective black and Republican voters. President Grant's administration refuses to help the Republican governor to ensure a free election.

« Ulysses S. Grant

**1876-77**

**JUNE 1876**
Presidential nominations are Rutherford Hayes, Republican, and Samuel Tilden, Democrat.

≫ Republican candidates, 1876 election

**NOVEMBER 1876**
In the presidential election Tilden wins a small majority in the popular vote, but the Republicans challenge the validity of the returns in three Southern states on the grounds of intimidation.

**MARCH 1877**
A Congressional commission awards the disputed presidential election to Hayes, who is inaugurated later in the month.

**APRIL 1877**
Hayes begins to fulfil the political bargain that has won him the presidency by awarding the governorship of South Carolina to a "redeemer." Federal support for Reconstruction is now effectively abandoned.

**The Union dead**
During the assault on Charleston, South Carolina, the 3rd New Hampshire Infantry was based at Hilton Head Island. Many fell victim to disease and were buried in primitive graves in the Union cemetery.

# The **Cost** of the **War**

**The Civil War resulted in a toll of death and injury unparalleled on American soil. The price for the Confederacy was much the greater, with long-lasting social and economic consequences for the South. Despite its heavy sacrifices, the Union went forward stronger with a new sense of American nationalism.**

« **BEFORE**

**The institution of slavery was a primary influence on the society and economy of the prewar South.**

**THE OLD SOUTH**
While the South was not a uniform region, slavery united its people. On this captive labor force rested the cash-crop plantation system. Slaves grew a variety of staples including cotton—and "King Cotton" gave the South **great political power**. But its "slave society" meant more than the racial and economic domination of 4 million slaves « **64–65**. It **maintained white privilege** and Southerners argued that the North had lost values of honor and community in the pursuit of materialistic gain.

**A SLAVE BEING AUCTIONED**

The Civil War took its horrifying toll on American society, with both the North and the South suffering terrible losses. The total number of military deaths in the war exceeded 620,000—two percent of the entire population in 1860. The military death toll for the Civil War was the same as that for all other American wars from the Revolution through the Korean War combined. A higher proportion of men entered military service during the Civil War than in World War II, and the death rate was six times higher.

During the 19th century, in an era of imperfect medicine and unskilled practitioners, disease was the greater scourge—accounting for roughly two-thirds of those who perished. Though hundreds of thousands of soldiers survived their injuries, untold numbers suffered throughout the rest of their lives. Amputation was a common surgical remedy for seriously wounded limbs. The Union's multivolume *Medical and Surgical History of the War of the Rebellion* tabulated 30,000 reported amputations on Union soldiers alone, giving details of thousands of surgical cases. However, despite recording all this data, medical services on both sides did not understand the connection between combat and mental trauma. Large numbers of veterans were haunted for years by the horrific memories of war—afflicted by what is today known as post-traumatic stress disorder.

**The Confederate war**
In many ways Confederate sufferings were greater than those of the Union. An estimated 80 percent of military-aged men entered service and nearly one-third of those who fought were killed. Most of the fighting took place

"Next year their **lands will be taken**, for in war we can take them, **and rightfully**, too."
WILLIAM T. SHERMAN IN A LETTER TO MAJOR R. M. SAWYER, JANUARY 31, 1864

### Mosby's crutches
Confederate Commander John S. Mosby found the war brutal, as his repeated need for crutches attested: "They were first used in August 1863 ... I again used them in September 1864 and December 1864."

in the South with dramatic impact. Armies swept over the countryside, consuming food and wood at the expense of local inhabitants, with perhaps 40 percent of Southern livestock taken for military purposes. An unknown number of civilians died and hundreds of thousands of whites and blacks became refugees. Confederates returned to a devastated South.

War destroyed two-thirds of the wealth of the South, most in the value of slaves. The Southern economy became a shambles. Reliance on printed currency led to astronomical inflation (over 9,000 percent) and worthless Confederate money. Southern banks held insufficient capital for rebuilding. And the Confederate government had increasingly seized much-needed supplies from its people in exchange for worthless currency.

### The ravaged South
Half of the South's farm machinery had been destroyed along with hundreds of miles of railroad track. Additionally, large portions of Richmond, Mobile, Columbia, and Atlanta were damaged by fire. The "hard hand of war" fell unevenly on the Confederacy and those hardest hit were in the path of Sherman's March or Sheridan's raid in the Shenandoah Valley. Republican politician and German émigré Carl Schurz saw the devastation of the march and wrote that South Carolina "looked

for many miles like a broad black streak of ruin and desolation—the fences all gone; lonesome smoke stacks, surrounded by dark heaps of ashes and cinders, marking the spots where human habitations had stood; the fields along the road wildly overgrown by weeds." This was not the norm, however, and in other parts of the South, the Union army acted with more restraint.

The economic impact of the conflict was felt long after the fighting ended. Manufacturing and transportation had largely recovered by the 1870s, but agriculturally the South would remain a stagnant region of relative poverty for decades to come.

### The effects in the North
While Union forces suffered up to a third more casualties than the Confederates, the war had a less damaging effect on the North. Only half of the military-aged men had enlisted in the army or navy, one-quarter of them immigrants. In contrast to the Confederates, a lower proportion died in actual service—roughly one-sixth. The North had far greater financial, agricultural, and industrial resources. A better managed economy, including increased taxes, national currency, and successful bonds drives, contained wartime inflation to 80 percent. Suffering was largely offset by high employment and a rise in wages. Food production rose to meet military demand and voluntary efforts by civilians supplemented war needs for rations, clothing, and medical supplies. The remaining war debts

were a fraction of those incurred by the Confederacy and no large impediment to the postwar economy. The war slowed immigration and industrial growth but only temporarily, as the Union economy emerged stronger from the conflict. The greatest lingering costs were the pensions to hundreds of thousands of veterans, totaling 40 percent of the Federal budget in the 1890s.

### The new nation
A key legacy was a new American nationalism in which the Union was deemed perpetual. Symbolically, the name "The United States" became a singular noun and a stronger national government came forth. In wartime, the nation had instituted compulsory national conscription, direct federal income tax, greenback (paper) currency, and a suspension of civil liberties. In support of these powers, Republicans had worked to fashion a new sense of patriotism emphasizing unconditional loyalty to the government.

Though many expanded authorities faded during peacetime, the precedent of national administration remained. To ease reconciliation, the Union government conducted no treason trials. In May 1865, Jefferson Davis was imprisoned for two years in Fort Monroe, Virginia, but released without trial. General Robert E. Lee was never arrested. The only high-profile case was that of Captain Henry Wirz. The commander of Andersonville Prison, Wirz was hanged on November 10, 1865, for crimes of mismanagement. Union soldiers at his execution chanted, "Wirz, remember Andersonville."

> **850,000** The estimated number of soldiers who entered the Confederate military. The First Conscription Act was passed in 1862.

### Locomotive in ruins
At the Richmond and Petersburg Railroad depot a wrecked engine is surveyed. Damage both by the Confederates in retreat and the advancing Union army added to the heavy postwar cost borne by the South.

Most Confederates were ultimately restored to rights by the end of Reconstruction. However, postwar Republican dominance did have other consequences. One was Southern political and economic marginalization. Another was the United States' entry into an expansive era of industrial growth with little government oversight, famously described by Mark Twain as the "Gilded Age."

**AFTER** »

The Civil War transformed fundamental aspects of the postwar South, leaving the region impoverished and politically weak compared to the rest of the country.

#### THE NEW SOUTH
The Civil War brought an end to slavery and Reconstruction would give **further rights and freedoms to former slaves 338–39 »**. Free-labor relations replaced slavery, and blacks received a share of the returns for their work. "Sharecropping" allowed laborers to work the lands of others for a share of the crop. **The South would remain mainly agricultural** but railroad development, manufacturing, and urbanization would increase dramatically 340-41 ».

The wealth of this "New South" went largely to Northern investors or white Southern merchants and businessmen. For whites and blacks at the bottom of society, the **postwar years were marked by poverty**. Beset by crop failures, white owners of small farms found themselves **increasingly reliant on cotton to pay debts**. But overproduction lowered prices and indebted the farmers. The main consequence was the **loss of political influence**—not to return until the 20th century.

### A home destroyed
Henry Mosler's painting, *The Lost Cause*, portrays a war-weary soldier returning home to find a devastated homestead and his family gone. Mosler sketched the conflict regularly for the magazine, *Harper's Weekly*.

## THE FALL OF RICHMOND

On April 2, 1865, General Lee sent word to Jefferson Davis that Richmond should be abandoned because Confederate lines were irretrievably broken. That night the exodus from the capital began, and chaos quickly ensued. Confederate troops torched hundreds of buildings, the arsenal exploded, warships on the James were blown up, and starving mobs looted shops and houses. The following day the Union Army was greeted by smoldering, eerily silent ruins.

# The Politics of Reconstruction

**In the debate on how to rebuild the Union, Northern politicians disagreed over what cost the South should pay for disunion and how much Southern society should change as a result. The Democrat President Johnson clashed with Radical Republicans, who envisioned a new era of African-American freedoms.**

## « BEFORE

Northern victory had determined that the Union was indivisible and that slavery was abandoned forever. But crucial issues of reconciliation, retribution, and black civil rights remained to be addressed.

### LINCOLN AND RECONSTRUCTION

The **Emancipation Proclamation «< 160–61** of 1863 granted freedom to slaves, but only in those states in rebellion against the Union. Lincoln's **"Proclamation of Amnesty and Reconstruction"** of December 1863 pardoned Rebels who swore loyalty oaths and readmitted states when **ten percent of adult men** did so. However, the proclamation made no demands for black rights beyond freedom, and would quickly restore former Confederates to political power.

With the **Thirteenth Amendment «< 308–309**, the issue of slavery was finally resolved, but the conditions under which Rebel states could be readmitted to the Union was still to be decided. That task would fall to **Andrew Johnson** who had succeeded to the presidency after **Lincoln's assassination «< 320–21**.

The so-called Radical Republicans were members of Lincoln's party who thought that his attitude toward the reconquered South had been far too lenient. Before Andrew Johnson became president, his fierce condemnation of rebellion encouraged Radical Republicans to think he would help them punish the South and remake it in the way they wanted. When Johnson announced his program for Reconstruction on May 29, 1865, it was not what they had hoped for.

### The Reconstruction plan

Most of the presidential proclamation followed the policies advocated by Lincoln. An oath of loyalty to the Union and the promise to support the Constitution and obey Federal laws were required from all. Property rights—with the obvious exception of slaves—were restored and a framework was set up for working toward reestablishing state governments with new constitutions incorporating the Thirteenth Amendment.

**7,000** The number of pardons granting amnesty to wealthy Southern landowners signed by President Johnson by 1866.

Johnson was a complicated character. As a Southern Democrat he supported unquestioningly the rights of slaveholders. He was a Unionist, however, who saw secession as treason and blamed disunion on the plantation owners. Johnson's modest origins alienated him from the aristocratic elite who dominated Southern politics. This helps explain a unique provision of his Reconstruction policy: Southerners who owned more than $20,000 in personal property would not be pardoned except by special application to the president.

As it turned out, Johnson's actions showed no vindictive desire to punish rich planters. He appointed governors from their class who in turn readmitted many members of the Southern elite, including former Confederates, to state offices. On the issue of land confiscation, Johnson ordered militarily seized lands to be returned to their previous owners. He also pardoned large numbers of individuals excluded under his Reconstruction plan.

Johnson's racism would not allow him to elevate blacks to social and political equality. He imagined wrongly that freed slaves would remain under the influence of former masters, voting as directed and giving more political power to Southern leaders. He argued that suffrage was a matter of states' rights, not to be interfered with by the Federal government.

### Johnson's obstructionism

The desire to enact black suffrage was the most crucial goal that bound Radical Republicans together. The two leading figures in the movement were the Massachusetts Senator Charles Sumner and Pennsylvania Congressman Thaddeus Stevens. After the 1866 elections, the Radical Republican majority was so unassailable that Congress could override the President's veto. He even tried to veto the landmark 1866 Civil Rights Bill that granted citizenship and all its civil rights and protections to black Americans, rights that were subsequently enshrined in the Fourteenth Amendment. Johnson also opposed any expansion of Federal assistance to Southern blacks.

In March 1865, Congress created an organization known as the Bureau of Refugees, Freedmen, and Abandoned Lands—the "Freedmen's Bureau." Employing fewer than 900 agents, the Bureau dispensed food, medicine, and supplies to former slaves. It also helped to establish schools for them and to mediate labor disputes. President Johnson opposed continued funding for the agency, claiming: "A system for the support of indigent persons in the United States was never contemplated by the authors of the Constitution," but he failed to stop the agency's work.

The political feud between the Radical Republicans and Johnson culminated in an attempt to impeach

**Thaddeus Stevens**
A leading figure of the Radical Republicans during the Reconstruction era, Stevens was one of the seven committee members who sought to impeach Johnson.

**President Johnson's impeachment summons**
In spring 1868 Johnson became the subject of the first-ever impeachment proceedings against a U.S. President. Here he is served with the summons by George T. Brown, the Sergeant-at-Arms of the Senate.

> **KEY MOMENT**
>
> ### THE 1866 CIVIL RIGHTS ACT
>
> The act was guaranteed to widen the rift between the Radical Republicans in Congress and President Johnson. "In every State and Territory in the United States" it granted the same rights enjoyed by white citizens to all males, "without distinction of race or color, or previous condition of slavery or involuntary servitude." In March 1866, Johnson vetoed the bill, declaring that "the distinction of race and color is by this bill made to operate in favor of the colored and against the white race." The veto was overturned by a two-thirds majority in Congress, and passed into law in April.

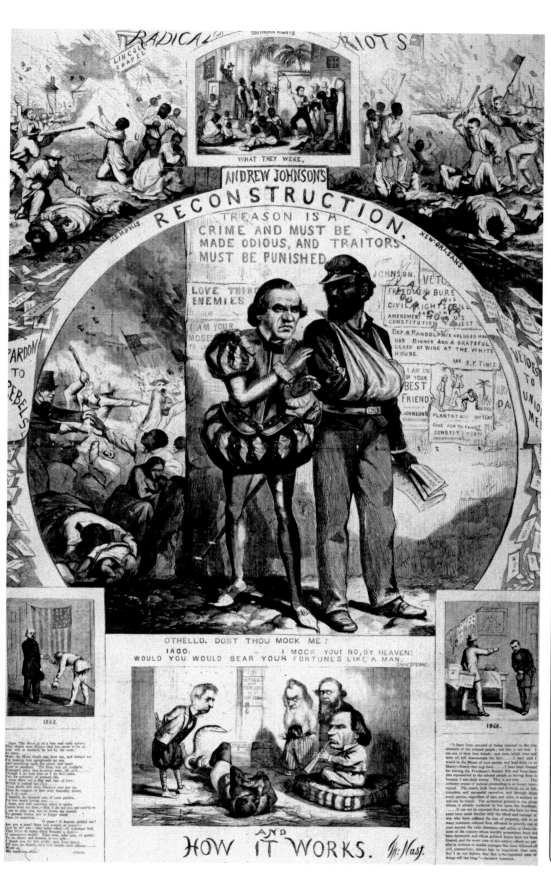

**Johnson's Reconstruction in practice**
Published on September 1, 1866, in *Harper's Weekly*, this cartoon by Thomas Nast fiercely attacks Johnson's pro-Southern policies. In the center, he is portrayed as Shakespeare's Iago deceiving Othello (a black veteran).

the president in 1868. The Republicans used the Tenure of Office Act, which they had passed the year before. This prevented the president from removing from office anyone who had been appointed by a past president unless the Senate ratified his decision. Johnson had suspended his secretary of war, Edwin Stanton, and when the Senate failed to ratify his decision, he was impeached. He survived Senate conviction by a single vote, but was now virtually powerless.

## Military districts
On March 2, 1867, Congress passed the First Reconstruction Act. This divided the South into five military districts, each under the command of a U.S. general. One of the tasks of the governors was to ensure voting rights for blacks in the former Confederate states. To guarantee black voting rights, Congress also authored the Fifteenth Amendment, which stated that the right to vote could not be denied on account of race. Congress also outlined its terms for readmitting Southern states. New state constitutions were required that affirmed black voting rights and ratified the Fourteenth Amendment. Until this was done, the Southern states would stay under occupation and Southern legislators would not be allowed entry to Congress.

### AFTER

Johnson was succeeded as president in 1869 by Ulysses S. Grant, whose well-intentioned Reconstruction policies were blocked by Southern Democrats as they won back control of the former Confederate states.

**READMISSION TO THE UNION**
By 1870, **all the Southern states had ratified the Fourteenth Amendment** and were readmitted to the Union. At first they were under Republican rule, but elections were accompanied by mounting **violence in the South**, first from the **Ku Klux Klan**, then by groups such as the **White League 342–43 »**. Freedmen were supposed to enjoy the same rights as whites, but **voting discrimination**, in the form of poll taxes and literacy tests, became widespread.

**THE REDEEMER MOVEMENT**
In Grant's second term, Southern Democrats, or **"Redeemers,"** gradually won **control of the state legislatures 342–43 »** and by 1877 all were in Democrat hands 344–45 ».

# The Reality of Black Freedom

**For former slaves, Reconstruction changed everyday life considerably. African-Americans shaped their own communities and achieved long-sought rights and freedoms. Yet Reconstruction remained an "unfinished revolution" while African-Americans faced continuing racism and economic inequality.**

Former slaves greeted freedom as the coming of "Jubilee," an ancient Hebrew principle that had promised emancipation after a period of enslavement to a landowner. But they understood that freedom alone was not enough to overcome racism and poverty and, like many white Americans, they regarded land ownership as the very foundation of true freedom.

### Forty acres and a mule

Some Northerners agreed that without land and education Southern blacks would not advance in society. During the war, the Union army had begun temporary experiments to give plantation lands to refugee slaves. In early 1865, Union general William T. Sherman's Special Field Order No. 15 distributed abandoned or confiscated land along the South Carolina and Georgia coast to more than 10,000 families in parcels of 40 acres. Some were also given an army mule. But when the matter of land redistribution came before Congress

**Freedmen's school**

A teacher and her pupils are pictured outside a Freedmen's school in North Carolina. In the 1860s, the Freedmen's Bureau established thousands of such schools for black children.

later in the year, it lacked the necessary support, and President Andrew Johnson ordered the return of confiscated properties. As a result, former slaves felt deeply betrayed. On Edisto Island, South Carolina, petitioners wrote angrily to Johnson, declaring that the rights of traitorous former masters outweighed those who had "made these lands what they are." They urged plaintively, "We wish to have a home if it be but a few acres. Without some provision ... our situation is dangerous."

### Sharecropping

Former slaves saw freedom in the same terms as Lincoln had done—"the God-given right to enjoy the fruits of their own labor"—yet they achieved minimal economic gains in the years after the war. The failure to obtain land or compensation left people few options. Without savings or influence, they were at the mercy of white landowners and politicians. A labor system known as "sharecropping" spread throughout the South, offering the illusion of upward mobility. This system bound tenant farmers to the land through an annual contract under which the tenant's crop was "shared," typically fifty-fifty, with the landowner. Several factors worked against the success of the system, including low crop prices, accumulated debts on the

**"The First Vote"**

A contemporary magazine cover illustrates black voters in the South casting their votes for the first time, in state elections in 1867.

part of the sharecroppers to local merchants, and periods of crop failure. After harvest, many sharecroppers found themselves mired deep in debt. While a minority of them began to rise in life, many remained trapped in a poverty that affected them and the region for decades.

### Building black communities

Although racism and discrimination remained, Reconstruction brought many changes to everyday life. The significant social transformations that took place appear all the greater when compared with the hardships of slavery. Slave marriages were not legally binding, and families could be separated through sale. In freedom, former slaves married and labored to reunite lost family members. Black families tried to turn the ideal of the bread-winning father, home-making wife, and properly schooled children into reality.

Newly founded churches played crucial roles in the community. Formal black churches had been uncommon under slavery, while in the master's church, sermons described slavery as worthwhile and godly. During Reconstruction, the flourishing black churches became community centers. Black ministers prophesied a new age of freedom, comparing emancipated slaves to the Israelites released from

**Marriage of a black soldier**

A black couple is married by Chaplain Warren of the Freedmen's Bureau. On being freed, many black couples married, knowing they could not be lawfully separated.

## BEFORE

**As slaves, African-Americans were considered property by law and had no basic human rights.**

**MALTREATMENT**

**If a master killed his slave** by abuse, it was **not considered a felony**. Slaves could also be whipped, branded, or bound in painful collars and cuffs. Masters could **take sexual advantage of female slaves** with impunity.

**EDUCATION OUTLAWED**

In most slave states it was **against the law to teach a slave to read and write** out of the fear that knowledge would lead to rebellion.

**NO RIGHTS**

Supreme Court Chief Justice Roger Taney wrote in 1857 that African-Americans "had **no rights which the white man was bound to respect**" **<< 26–27**. Among other restrictions, slaves could not sue in court, testify against whites, or protect their families from separation.

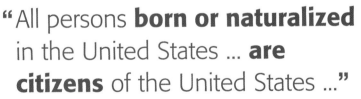

> "All persons **born or naturalized** in the United States ... **are citizens** of the United States ..."
>
> SECTION 1 OF THE 14TH AMENDMENT TO THE U.S. CONSTITUTION, RATIFIED IN 1868

bondage. Churches hosted local events, offered help writing letters and reading newspapers, and nurtured political participation.

Education mattered greatly to freedmen. Most states had banned slave education, and literacy rates were low. With help from the Federal government and Northern missionaries, black communities established schools that attracted people of all ages. In time, Reconstruction schools multiplied along with the number of influential black teachers.

## African-American citizenship
Northerners might agree that slavery should end, but they debated sharply among themselves what that freedom

### A Southern sharecropper
A sharecropper surveys a field of cotton, the most common crop to be grown under the sharecropping system. When cotton prices dropped, sharecroppers' incomes were meager.

"The first colored senator and representatives"
In 1870, Republican Hiram Rhodes Revels (far left) was elected a senator for the state of Mississippi. He is shown here with some of the first black members of the House of Representatives.

should mean in regard to former slaves. On the other hand, blacks saw clearly that, along with ownership of land as the basis for economic independence, freedom should include citizenship and the right to vote. The Reconstruction Amendments (Thirteenth, Fourteenth, and Fifteenth) and civil rights legislation effected radical change. Slavery had denied African-Americans their humanity, treating them as a form of property. The Fourteenth and Fifteenth Amendments went far beyond mere emancipation. They defined freedmen as

citizens, guaranteed "equal protection of the law," and outlawed voting discrimination based on color. In addition, state and local laws acknowledged that blacks must be able to exercise basic rights, such as property ownership and use of the courts, though not without limitations.

Many Southern blacks became politically active on behalf of the Republican Party. Notable among them were former Union soldiers, prominent ministers, and teachers. They helped maintain Republican Party dominance in the South during the early Reconstruction period, and many were elected to public office, including, in 1870, Hiram Rhodes Revels from Mississippi, the first black member of the Senate, and Joseph Rainey of South Carolina, the first black member of the House of Representatives.

**AFTER**

The expansion of rights and freedoms was limited by the resistance of Southern whites and by growing Northern apathy. With the end of Reconstruction, many hard-fought gains were lost.

**LOSING HARD-WON RIGHTS**
In the late 1880s, Southern states began introducing **Jim Crow laws**, which challenged the Fourteenth Amendment. These laws **legalized segregation between whites and blacks** in areas such as public transportation, waiting rooms, theaters, schools, hospitals, and other public institutions. **Facilities for blacks** were usually **of inferior quality**. In many states, marriage between whites and African-Americans was banned.

**EDUCATIONAL GAINS**
After the war, **black colleges** (Howard University, Fisk University, and Hampton University) were established with the aim of training teachers. By 1869, in the 3,000 Freedmen's schools, more than half the teachers were black. However, in the next decade, few children received any formal education. **Literacy among African-Americans increased** in the postwar period from one in ten in 1865 to one in two by 1900.

# "Redeeming" the South

**For many white Southerners, Reconstruction was a period of political uncertainty, poverty, and momentous social change. Although they had lost the war, they attempted to maintain traditions of white control, using desperate means to "redeem" the South from Northern domination.**

**BEFORE**

At the height of their power in the South, Republicans politically dominated the former Confederate states.

**REPUBLICAN VOTERS**
The **First Reconstruction Act of 1867** **‹‹ 338–39** authorized the military to enroll eligible black voters in the South. They registered 735,000 African-Americans, giving them a **majority over white voters** in five Southern states. The Republican Party was also supported by a minority of Southern whites who were "**Unionist**" in perspective, and was strongest in up-country areas where there were few large plantations.

**REPUBLICAN ACHIEVEMENTS**
Beyond granting **black suffrage**, Republicans used their power to create new progressive state constitutions **‹‹ 338–39**. These documents legislated **universal voting rights** for men, expanded social services, and established public schools for whites and blacks, at the cost of higher property taxes. In 1868 seven former Confederate states were **restored to the Union**, with the remainder brought back by 1870.

**THE DEFEATED SOUTH**
Southerners were **devastated by defeat** and unwilling to have further changes to their traditions imposed on them by the victorious North. They did not want to see former slaves, whom they considered socially inferior, as political equals. They also needed blacks to remain a **dependent workforce** in order to grow the cash crops on which the South depended: **cotton, tobacco, sugar, and rice**.

**The new rules**
Under the black codes, a freedman who has been charged with a crime is sold at public auction in payment of his fine.

Life for many whites in the South was difficult during Reconstruction because the region was plagued by crop failures and poor market conditions. Even wealthy planters faced ruin and had trouble finding enough workers. Many Southerners also resented the meddling of Northern capitalists, occupying soldiers, and "carpetbaggers"—men who migrated South looking for economic opportunity or in support of social reform. In addition, many white Southerners regarded the imposition of Federal control under the rule of Radical Republicans as corruption, and vowed to "redeem," or recover, the governments of their states.

## The black codes
Southern governments were required by the Federal government to grant rights to former slaves, but they wanted to direct the extent of change. Between 1865 and 1867 both state and local governments enacted laws, known as black codes, to keep African-Americans in a subordinate position. The laws, which were not uniform throughout the South, came in many guises.

On the one hand, these statutes granted African-Americans the rights to own property, marry, and use the courts, but the majority of the black codes were discriminatory laws that denied rights. For example, there were codes that required blacks to sign yearly labor contracts, restricted freedoms of travel and speech, or outlawed such practices as the purchase of non-agricultural land and the ownership of guns. Heavy penalties were instituted for people deemed "vagrants," including the sale of their labor at public auction to repay fines. Such laws were designed to bind workers to Southern farms.

The flourishing of black codes was a major cause of anger among even moderate Northerners and it

> Carpetbagger was a belittling term used by Southerners to describe Northerners who came South, carrying their belongings in just one bag made of carpet material, implying their thrifty opportunism.

contributed to the passage of the Reconstruction Amendments that granted African-Americans citizenship and the right to vote.

## The Ku Klux Klan
In 1866 the goal of white supremacy and the limiting of black political rights led to the foundation of the Klu Klux Klan in Tennessee by Confederate veterans. By 1868 it had spread throughout the South. The Klan was composed of white Southerners of all classes who wanted to limit the changes introduced by Reconstruction and the power of the Republicans controlling it.

**"In the North I was a nobody"**
A songsheet of around 1869 mocks the carpetbagger, showing him in front of a Southern plantation house, his bag brimming with booty from Reconstruction.

To accomplish their aims, Klan members used violence, intimidation, and murder, and were noted for their all-covering white robe and hood, although their identities were often known. Their main targets were politically active blacks, white people who helped them, and institutions whose aim was to aid blacks, including schools and churches.

Some Southern states tried to curb Klan activities, but the laws were often weak or not enforced. Republicans appealed to Congress, which passed the Ku Klux Act in 1871. This act was enforced by Federal troops, not state militia, and cases were tried in Federal court where juries had many black members. Hundreds of Klan members were convicted and by 1872 the Klan had been suppressed. However, much damage had already been done. Klan terrorism had stopped blacks from voting and severely weakened the leadership and organization of the Republican Party in the South.

## Politics and the White League
Following the suppression of the Klan, white Southerners turned to the Democratic Party to achieve "home rule." In 1867, Democratic leaders encouraged voters to shun elections for the state constitutional conventions, where new constitutions enshrining universal manhood suffrage, or the

**Klan violence**
His face concealed in a hood, a Klu Klux Klan member takes aim at a black family at home in their cabin, with his accomplices looking on. A wave of violence against blacks swept through the Southern states after the war.

# "... these **infamous associations** ... rob, they murder, they whip ..."

FROM AN ARTICLE ENTITLED "WORSE THAN SLAVERY," *HARPER'S WEEKLY*, 1874

right of black men to vote, were to be written. They also boycotted the elections to ratify these new progressive constitutions. But resistance failed to stop the constitutions from being ratified, and most Southern states were readmitted to the Union by 1868.

Other organizations appeared, including the White League, which started in Louisiana in 1874 and expanded across the South. It disavowed secrecy in favor of open political activity supplemented by armed intimidation, election fraud, and unapologetic violence, maintaining pressure on Republican organizers in the South. Through legal and illegal efforts, Southern whites continued to work to end Reconstruction.

### "Hang, curs, hang!"
This cartoon in the *Independent Monitor* of Tuscaloosa, Alabama, warned carpetbaggers and scalawags (Southern whites who supported Reconstruction) that they might be lynched by the Klu Klux Klan.

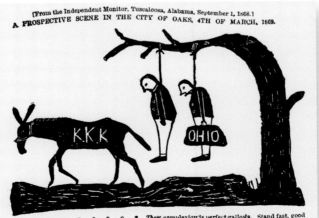

[From the Independent Monitor, Tuscaloosa, Alabama, September 1, 1868.]
A PROSPECTIVE SCENE IN THE CITY OF OAKS, 4TH OF MARCH, 1869.

K.K.K  OHIO

"Hang, curs, hang! * * * * *  *Their* complexion is perfect gallows. Stand fast, good fate, to *their* hanging! If they be not born to be hanged, our case is miserable."
  The above cut represents the fate in store for those great pests of Southern society—the carpet-bagger and scalawag—if found in Dixie's land after the break of day on the 4th of March next.

A Facsimile put in Evidence before the Congressional Committee.

**AFTER** »

Largely due to the resistance of Southern whites, Republican control of the South began to wane in the mid-1870s.

**DISPUTED RULE**
Elections in the South were noted for **violence and accusations of fraud**. Many elections were contested, with Louisiana being one of the most troublesome states. In 1872 Democratic and Republican leaders claimed victory and established **rival governments in New Orleans**. Bloody battles between armed militias failed to resolve the crisis. The **Republicans were forced to compromise**, granting Democrats control of the lower house so that the Republican Governor could stay in office.

**RETURN OF DEMOCRATIC CONTROL**
States with **white voting majorities** were the first to elect Democrats. By 1875 Virginia, Georgia, Texas, Alabama, Mississippi, Tennessee, and Arkansas were **led by Democrats**. The rest of the South was "redeemed" in the **election of 1876** and its eventual compromise **344–45** »

# The End of Reconstruction

**The Northern "retreat from Reconstruction" brought the era to a conclusion in 1877. The causes ranged broadly and included Republican political corruption in the Grant years, an economic depression that crippled the nation, the rise of virulent racism, and the hotly contested presidential election of 1876.**

Disillusionment with the Republican Party was a major factor in the failure of Reconstruction. In 1869, General Ulysses S. Grant succeeded Andrew Johnson as president, but during the course of his two terms in the White House, a scandal-racked administration made the word "Grantism" a synonym for political corruption. Grant himself was honest, but he was inexperienced—at age 46 when first inaugurated, he was the youngest U.S. president until that time—and politically inept. Loyalty to old comrades made him appoint men who proved to be all too fallible. In addition, the very nature of the political "spoils system"—by which elected politicians were able to obtain government jobs for party supporters—encouraged dishonesty. Men close to

### Fraud and corruption
Entitled "It makes him sick," a cartoon from *Puck* magazine shows Ulysses S. Grant, a heavy smoker, sickening from revelations of corruption. These included the Crédit Mobilier scandal involving fraud by the Union Pacific Railroad.

« BEFORE

The Republican Party chose Union war hero Ulysses S. Grant as its presidential candidate in 1868 because he was popular and a firm supporter of Reconstruction.

#### TWO TERMS
In the 1868 election, **Grant won 52.7 percent of the popular vote and 214 votes in the Electoral College** against 80 for his Democratic rival, Horatio Seymour. Despite a deluge of scandals, Grant himself remained popular and won a second term in 1872, when his rival was the veteran *New York Tribune* editor, Horace Greeley « 20–21, leading an uneasy coalition of breakaway Liberal Republicans and Democrats. This time, **Grant won 55.8 percent of the popular vote** and 286 electoral college votes.

#### THE FIFTEENTH AMENDMENT
First proposed in Congress a few weeks before Grant's inauguration, the Fifteenth Amendment « 338–39 states: "The **right of citizens of the United States to vote shall not be denied or abridged** … on account of race, color, or previous condition of servitude." The ratification process was completed on February 3, 1870.

Grant, some of whom were his relatives, were exposed. Cabinet ministers, such as interior secretary Columbus Delano, were found guilty of accepting bribes.

### Election violence
Outside political circles, hardening racial attitudes took their toll on Northern willingness to enforce Reconstruction. Even in the North, the implementation of the Fifteenth Amendment—affirming the right of all citizens to vote, regardless of color—proved divisive. In Philadelphia, for example, there was violence during elections for local government offices in October 1871 as new, mostly Republican-supporting black voters upset the balance of power in traditional Democratic bastions. One victim was a prominent black teacher

and civil rights campaigner, Octavius Catto. He was shot on election day by a Democratic Party worker and died as a result of the wounds. The onset of economic depression further hardened Northern attitudes. Although the depression's causes were complex and international, in the United States the root was a frenzy of government-sponsored railroad development following the Civil War. Massive investment in unneeded railroad schemes created a speculative bubble that burst in 1873 as railroad stocks lost value. This led to widespread bank and business failure—notably the collapse of Jay Cooke & Co., the very bank that had raised hundreds of millions of dollars for the Union war effort by masterminding the

In 1870, James Webster Smith from South Carolina became West Point's first black cadet. He was severely harassed by fellow cadets, including President Grant's son, Fred.

selling of government bonds. This financial turmoil led to unemployment and wage cuts. Prosperity would not return until the 1880s.

Northerners suffering their own economic misfortunes were less likely to sympathize with the plight of blacks and the costs associated with Reconstruction programs. The Democratic Party capitalized on voter frustration and won enough seats in the 1874 election to gain control of the House of Representatives. From now on, Reconstruction policies would require accommodation to Democratic wishes.

### The "Southern question"
With the war a decade past, the "Southern question" grew tiresome for many Northerners. In the immediate postwar period, most had been willing to support dramatic transformations in black civil rights in the South. Yet many, even former abolitionists, held racist

**OCTAVIUS V. CATTO,**
Assassinated in Philadelphia, Oct. 10th, 1871.
One more Martyr to the cause of Constitutional Liberty.

**Civil rights martyr**
Just 32 when he died, Catto was born in Charleston, South Carolina, but grew up mainly in Philadelphia. He was an enthusiastic baseball player and one of the founders of the successful black Pythian Base Ball Club of Philadelphia.

> " The **whole public are tired out** with these **annual, autumnal outbreaks** [of election violence] in the South."

PRESIDENT GRANT TO ATTORNEY GENERAL EDWARD PIERREPONT, SEPTEMBER 1875

was both parties' central message. Both candidates had genuine reform credentials, but it was unclear what Hayes intended to do about the South, since his platform called for conflicting notions of "permanent pacification" and protection of equal rights.

By this time, the Democratic Party once more controlled most Southern states, the exceptions being South Carolina, Florida, and Louisiana. There were widespread outbreaks of violence in the South during the election, and these stifled Republican voters, although to an unknown degree. Tilden had a

**264,292** Democratic candidate Samuel J. Tilden's lead in the popular vote over his Republican rival Rutherford B. Hayes in the presidential election of 1876. A total of 8.4 million votes were cast.

small lead in the popular national vote, but the votes were contested, and accusations of fraud were aimed at both sides. The result was uncertainty about who the next president would be, which threatened to continue well into 1877.

In the end, an Electoral Commission set up to resolve the issue declared the Republican Hayes the winner, but the result was unsatisfactory since Republicans narrowly dominated the commission. Democratic opposition only ended with a backroom deal between Southern Democrats and representatives of Hayes. The Democrats agreed to recognize Hayes as president. In exchange, the Republicans promised to pull Federal troops out of the South—where the soldiers' duties had included protecting the rights of black and Republican voters. They would also relinquish control of South Carolina, Florida, and Louisiana to the Democrats. For their part, Southern Democrats were to respect the civil rights of African-Americans—a promise that they failed to keep. The year 1877, therefore, saw the end of Reconstruction of the South. Black voting and office holding continued in some places into the 1890s, but for the most part the United States entered a dark chapter of segregation that lasted for a century.

**Republican candidates**
A chart issued by the Republicans in the 1876 campaign shows their candidate, Rutherford B. Hayes (above, left), with his vice-presidential running mate, William A. Wheeler.

assumptions about supposed black inferiority. The same people who were committed to notions of equality before the law often did not believe in true social equality. Public newspaper reports increasingly highlighted corruption and chaos in Southern governments, depicting black voters and politicians in unfavorable terms. The perennial Southern violence at election time seemed insurmountable. Judging the mood of the North, President Grant was hesitant to extend further federal power to keep the peace and enforce black rights.

In 1875, came the largest blot on the President's scandal-prone record: the exposure of the "Whiskey Ring." Liquor taxes had been raised in the postwar years to help the government pay off the costs of the conflict. In response, a group, or "ring," of Midwestern distilleries bribed Federal agents to allow them to keep back most of the tax revenue. As a result, the Treasury was being defrauded of millions of dollars. Grant's own private secretary, Orville E. Babcock, a former Union general, was implicated, but the President shielded him by praising his character.

**Contested election**
The hinge point in bringing Reconstruction to a close was the presidential election of 1876. The two candidates were Governor Rutherford B. Hayes of Ohio for the Republicans and New York Governor Samuel J. Tilden for the Democrats. With little public interest any longer in the old war issues, the need for government reform

**Panic on Wall Street**
An illustration from *Scribner's Magazine* shows the chaos outside the New York Stock Exchange on September 18, 1873, the day that the bank Jay Cooke & Co. declared bankruptcy.

## AFTER

Although lackluster in the defense of Reconstruction, President Hayes took important steps to reform the "spoils system," which had been a significant source of political corruption.

### CIVIL SERVICE REFORM
In June 1877, Hayes issued an **executive order forbidding Federal employees from being involved in party politics**. The next year he put this into effect when he **fired the Republican Chester A. Arthur as collector of customs at the Port of New York**. New York Senator Roscoe Conkling had obtained the lucrative job for Arthur, who was in turn accused of employing staff for party allegiance rather than competence. Ironically, **Arthur, when he became president,** was responsible for key civil service reforms.

### THE GREAT RAILROAD STRIKE
Violence returned to the nation in July 1877, when a strike by railroad workers led to widespread riots in several cities. Controversially, Hayes sent in **Federal troops to restore order and protect the railroads**. The strike and its repression left **more than 100 people dead**.

**1** FAREWELL TO HOME AND FAMILY

**2** THE ARMY OF THE CUMBERLAND

**3** THE BATTLE OF PERRYVILLE

**4** THE CONFEDERATES RETREAT TO TENNESSEE

**9** EMANCIPATING THE SLAVES

**10** THE BATTLE OF STONES RIVER

**11** THE FIGHT FOR MIDDLE TENNESSEE

**12** HARD-EARNED VICTORY

**17** CROSSING THE TENNESSEE RIVER

**18** SURRENDERING CHATTANOOGA

**19** BENEATH LOOKOUT MOUNTAIN

**20** DIVISION OF THE UNION ARMY

**25** A VIRTUAL STATE OF SIEGE

**26** ESTABLISHING THE "CRACKER" SUPPLY LINE

**27** THE BLUE ARMY STANDS ITS GROUND

**28** "THE BATTLE ABOVE THE CLOUDS"

**30** STORMING MISSIONARY RIDGE

**31** ROSECRANS AND HIS VICTORIOUS OFFICERS

**32** ROSECRANS AND OTHER OFFICERS

**33** TRAVIS'S PARTING

5 BURNING THEIR BRIDGES    6 PLANNING FOR THE NEXT BATTLE    7 ATTACKS ON UNION SUPPLY LINES    8 THE BLUE (UNION) CAVALRY ADVANCES

13 FORAGING FOR FOOD    14 RECOVERY FOR THE ARMY OF THE CUMBERLAND    15 ONWARD TO CHATTANOOGA    16 BRAGG'S RETREAT

21 THE GRAY (CONFEDERATE) ARMY STRIKES    22 HOLDING ON TO CHATTANOOGA    23 DEFENDING BOTH FRONTS    24 THE ROCK OF CHICKAMAUGA

29 LAST LINK OF THE SUPPLY LINE

# The **Travis Panorama**

**As the Civil War drew to its close, Union veterans of Major General William S. Rosecrans's Army of the Cumberland commissioned artist William (Bill) D. T. Travis to commemorate their campaigns in a massive painted "panorama," 528ft (161m) long.**

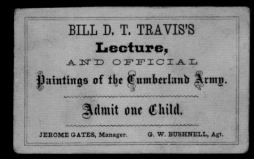

Attached to the Union army as a staff artist working for two illustrated news weeklies, Travis had already observed and sketched the scenes he would now be painting. In all, his creation consisted of **33 panels, each measuring 16x8ft (4.9x2.4m)** and telling a different part of the story of the Army of the Cumberland. The panels were painted onto coarse cotton for flexibility and then **stitched together in chronological order to form a single, vast canvas**—an example of the "moving panoramas" that were a popular entertainment at the time. For public viewing, the panorama was set up on a stage between two spools, then hand-cranked slowly from one side of the stage to the other. The series of sequential images memorialized the **army's progress from October 1862 to the end of 1863.** The

had witnessed, from the **Battle of Perryville in Kentucky** through the **defeat at Chickamauga**, and ending with the **breaking of Braxton Bragg's Confederate army at Missionary Ridge**. Travis also chronicled some of the finer details of army life, including soldiers leaving home and loved ones to go to war, foraging for food, and establishing supply lines. From 1865 to 1871 Travis, with his brother James, took the panorama on a **tour of the Midwest**, where many Army of the Cumberland veterans were now living. Handling the equipment themselves in churches and lecture halls, one brother would crank the images across the stage while the other narrated the events of the campaigns to the audience. General Rosecrans was well satisfied with the result. He stated that Bill Travis had created one of the "great

# The War Remembered

**The Civil War remains central in the national memory, though how the war is remembered has changed over time. The initial guardians of that memory were the veterans themselves, who formed organizations to address their needs, commemorate their sacrifices, and instill the past in the nation's children.**

**Gray and blue united**
In 1913, veterans from both sides came together at the Great Reunion on the Gettysburg battlefield. During the week-long encampment, former enemies put aside their differences and united on soil once stained with blood.

**« BEFORE**

**In November 1863, President Abraham Lincoln delivered his immortal address on the battlefield of Gettysburg, foretelling the "new birth of freedom."**

**UNION TROOPS AT THE BATTLE OF GETTYSBURG**

**THE NEW CHAPTER**
By late May 1865, when Union veterans of the great eastern and western armies marched through the streets of Washington, D. C., in a **final Grand Review**, Lincoln was dead. After the fiery trial of war, a new chapter was opening in the nation's history. It would be written by the hundreds of thousands of **Northern and Southern veterans** now returning home.

Unsurprisingly, Northerners and Southerners held different perspectives on the origins and meaning of the Civil War. The vanquished Confederates fashioned a set of ideas that became known as the "Lost Cause." The term itself emerged shortly after the conclusion of the war. It was coined by Richmond journalist Edward Pollard in his 1866 history of the war by the same name.

The "Lost Cause" was the Southern attempt to explain and soothe defeat, while at the same time protecting honor. It promoted the view that the South was defeated by overwhelming Northern resources of men, industry, technology, and money. It romanticized the struggle by emphasizing the inevitability of Confederate defeat. The view denied that slavery was the primary sectional tension, stressing instead an unbridgeable constitutional divide over states' rights. Its authors further idealized what they saw as Southern "civilization," while demonizing Northern developments of industry and urbanization. While the "Lost Cause" began largely as a Southern view, elements were absorbed into the national way of thinking over the course of time. The most corrosive aspect, however, was that many U.S. citizens lost sight of the importance of slavery in the conflict's beginnings. Furthermore, they disavowed the significance of emancipation as one of the war's great legacies. This sorry historical amnesia lasted well into the 20th century.

**400,000** The number of Union Army veterans in the G.A.R. during the 1890s.

### Veterans' organizations
While former soldiers found it difficult to discuss their time on the battlefield, they saw the value in creating veterans' organizations. These groups enabled them to remain in contact with their comrades and provided a platform in which to share their experiences. Former Union Army surgeon Benjamin Franklin Stephenson set up the Grand Army of the Republic (G.A.R.) in Decatur, Illinois, on April 6, 1866.

The organization was built on the tenets of "Fraternity, Charity, and Loyalty," and soon expanded across the North and South, as regional posts were established. The G.A.R. held conventions nationally and played prominent roles in local civic rituals. Its members, who were restricted to the "veterans of the late unpleasantness," numbered more than 400,000 in the 1890s, and the organization wielded significant political influence. It lobbied on behalf of its members on issues that included pensions and the care of veterans and their families. The G.A.R. was instrumental in establishing May's Decoration Day—which became Memorial Day—as a national holiday, and was also an important constituency of the Republican Party. The organization was finally disbanded in 1956, following the death of its last member, Albert Woolson.

### Voice of the Confederacy
Confederate veterans risked Northern charges of disloyalty in organizing their own groups, but, in 1889, they created the United Confederate Veterans (U.C.V.). Without the benefaction of the Federal government, local U.C.V. "camps" established their own veterans' relief associations, providing for widows and orphans, and pressuring state governments for pensions. By the first decade of the 20th century, the U.C.V. had more than 160,000 members.

To an important degree, veteran groups from the North and the South were also guardians of the memory of the war. They tenaciously promoted their own perspective on the conflict, especially through the education of children. The G.A.R. considered a pledge of allegiance as a valuable tool in instilling a sense of nationalism.

### Remembering the fallen
Civil War battle reenactments have grown in popularity over the years. Serving as a memorial to the fallen, they are also an important educational resource. Reenactments take place all over the United States—here, the Battle of Cedar Creek in the Shenandoah Valley is re-created.

> "The Civil War is our **felt history**—history lived in the **national imagination**."
>
> SOUTHERN AUTHOR ROBERT PENN WARREN, *THE LEGACY OF THE CIVIL WAR*, 1961

**CONFEDERATE**  **UNION**

**Veterans' memorial medals**
Medals were struck to commemorate reunions. Left: A badge from the Army of Northen Virginia veterans group. Right: A Pennsylvania G.A.R. badge from the encampment on the 25th anniversary of the Battle of Gettysburg.

Its members also defended the legacy of emancipation. A large number of posts were integrated and its speeches and writings recalled the valor of black soldiers and the nobility of their work as liberators. Likewise, the U.C.V. maintained a Historical Committee to review textbooks, and from 1893 to 1932 published *Confederate Veteran* as its soldiers' voice. With articles about the war, the magazine also allowed its readers to maintain connections with their peers.

### Reconciliation and healing
At the end of the 19th century, as the Civil War receded into memory, Northern and Southern sections of the United States entered a period of reconciliation. The Spanish-

American War of 1898 was an important milestone, creating a shared sense of American nationalism. With both sides facing a common enemy, the war brought the North and the South together once and for all. Veterans from the Union and Confederate armies began appearing together in joint reunions, highlighting their shared sacrifices and bravery.

The 50th anniversary of the Battle of Gettysburg in 1913 was the apex of veterans' memorialization, with more than 50,000 former soldiers attending the Great Reunion. At the "Peace Jubilee," President Woodrow Wilson declared, "We have found one another again as brothers and comrades in arms, enemies no longer, generous friends rather, our battles long past, the quarrel forgotten."

Civil War battlefields became sacred sites, places of national healing for veterans and tourists alike. In the 1890s, Congress established the beginning of the National

Military Park system at Chickamauga, Gettysburg, Shiloh, and Vicksburg. These sites preserved the memory and heroism of soldiers from both sides for many future generations.

The building of monuments was another form of public memory in the final decades of the 19th century. Communities erected simple memorials to their honored sons, just as ambitious larger works and equestrian statues paid national homage to the heroes of the battlefields. Washington and Richmond became the focal points of monuments immortalizing President Lincoln, General Robert E. Lee, and a pantheon of others. Richmond's equestrian statue of Lee, by French sculptor Antonin Mercié, was unveiled in 1890. The long-delayed Lincoln Memorial, which takes the form of a Classical Greek temple in the Doric style, was finally dedicated in 1922.

**AFTER**

Segregation swept away many of the civil rights established by Reconstruction. It was not until the 20th-century civil rights movement that the Federal Government redressed the shame of discrimination.

**BROWN V. BOARD OF EDUCATION**
In 1954, the U.S. Supreme Court struck a blow against the segregation of public schools when it ruled in favor of **Oliver L. Brown and other African-American parents** against the Board of Education of Topeka, Kansas. The court ordered "prompt and reasonable" **desegregation**.

**CIVIL AND VOTING RIGHTS**
President **Lyndon Johnson**'s **Great Society** program included the **Civil Rights Act** of 1964, which banned discrimination in voter registration, federally assisted programs, employment hiring, schools, and public accommodations. In 1965, the **Voting Rights Act** removed the obstacles that had disenfranchised African-Americans, outlawing any "voting qualification or prerequisite" that denied voting rights on racial grounds.

# In their Footsteps

Testimony to the many men who fought during the Civil War are the numerous places throughout the country that commemorate the war. Visitors have an opportunity to see the homes and headquarters of the military leaders, to witness the sites of historic battles, and to pay their respects to those who lost their lives. From imposing forts to solemn monuments, these memorial sites bring the Civil War to life for all who visit.

## ALABAMA

### First White House of the Confederacy
Home to President Jefferson Davis while the capitol of the Confederacy was in Montgomery, Alabama, from February 1861 until late May 1861. This 1835 Italianate-style house is furnished with original period pieces from the 1850s and 1860s and is open to the public.
http://www.firstwhitehouse.org

## ARKANSAS

### Pea Ridge National Military Park
Preserves the site of the March 7–8, 1862, Civil War battle that led to the Union's total control of Missouri.
http://www.nps.gov/peri

## DELAWARE

### Fort Delaware
A Union fortress located on Pea Patch Island. The fort was built to protect the ports of Wilmington and Philadelphia but became home to hundreds of Confederate prisoners of war. Accessible via a ½-mile (0.8-km) ferry ride from Delaware City.
http://www.destateparks.com/park/fort-delaware

## FLORIDA

### Camp Milton Historic Preserve
Home to more than 8,000 Confederates in 1864, Camp Milton was the largest encampment of Confederate forces in Florida. The park has an interpretive/educational center, a farmhouse, a large historical reenactment field, and access to a historic railroad line.
http://www.preserveflorida.org/parks/camp-milton-historic-preserve.html

### Fort Pickens
The largest fort to defend Pensacola Bay and its navy yard, Fort Pickens was one of four Southern forts never to fall to Confederate forces during the Civil War.
http://www.nps.gov/guis/planyourvisit/fort-pickens.htm

### Olustee Battlefield State Historic Site
Commemorates the largest Civil War battle in Florida, which took place on February 20, 1864. In proportion to the number of troops involved, it was one of the bloodiest battles of the war.
http://www.floridastateparks.org/olusteebattlefield

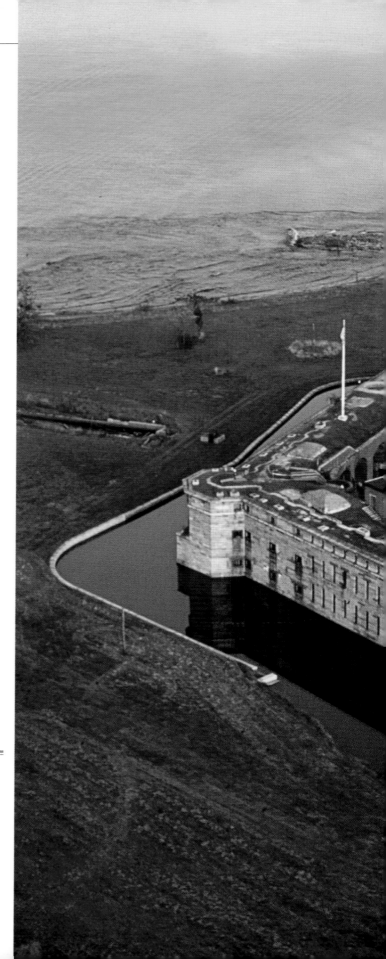

Fort Delaware
This granite and brick fortress was used throughout the Civil War as a prison for Confederate soldiers. By the end of the war, Fort Delaware had held almost 30,000 men.

## GEORGIA

### Andersonville National Historic Site

Camp Sumter, commonly called Andersonville, was one of the largest military prisons established by the Confederacy during the Civil War. More than 45,000 Union soldiers were imprisoned in Camp Sumter during its 14 months of existence. Almost 13,000 inmates died in the camp, and were buried in the cemetery outside the prison walls. Today, visitors can see the former site of Camp Sumter military prison, the Andersonville National Cemetery, and the National Prisoner of War Museum, which honors US prisoners of war in all wars. http://www.nps.gov/ande

#### Andersonville National Cemetery

The gravestones of Union soldiers in the Andersonville National Cemetery are decorated with Memorial Day flags. The cemetery was established in 1865, and it is the burial place of Union soldiers who died in battles, hospitals, or prison camps throughout the region.

#### Georgia Monument

Located in the Andersonville National Cemetery, the Georgia Monument is a memorial to all US prisoners of war. The three bronze figures do not have any insignia or uniforms, to ensure that they are universal in their representation.

# GEORGIA

## Chickamauga and Chattanooga National Military Park

This, the first national military park, honors Civil War soldiers who fought for control of Chattanooga—the Gateway to the Deep South—in the fall of 1863. The battlefield includes sections on both sides of the Georgia/Tennessee border.
http://www.nps.gov/chch

## Fort Pulaski National Monument

It was here, on April 11, 1862, that defense strategy changed worldwide, when Union rifled cannon first overcame a masonry fortification after only 30 hours of bombardment.
http://www.nps.gov/fopu

## Kennesaw Mountain National Battlefield Park

This park preserves the start of the Atlanta campaign, including the Civil War battles of Kolb's Farm, June 22, 1864, and Kennesaw Mountain, June 27, 1864.
http://www.nps.gov/kemo

## National Civil War Naval Museum

Dedicated to the naval story of the Civil War, the museum contains CSS *Albemarle*, CSS *Chattahoochee*, the raised CSS *Jackson*, and a replica of CSS *Water Witch*.
http://www.portcolumbus.org

# ILLINOIS

## Lincoln Home National Historic Site

Home to Abraham Lincoln until he assumed the presidency. This 12-room Greek Revival house has been restored to its 1860 appearance.
http://www.nps.gov/liho

# INDIANA

## Lincoln Boyhood National Memorial

Childhood home of the 16th president who lived here from 1816 to 1830.
http://www.nps.gov/libo

Chickamauga and Chattanooga National Military Park

This monument honors the 15th US Infantry, who fought for the Union in the Battle of Chickamauga. It was the first major battle to be fought in Georgia, and the combined losses were second only to Gettysburg.

## KANSAS

### Fort Scott National Historic Site

This fort, including regimental camps, a supply depot, a military prison, and 40 miles (64km) of fortification, became the largest and strongest Union point south of Fort Leavenworth. http://www.nps.gov/fosc

## KENTUCKY

### Abraham Lincoln Birthplace National Historic Site

Site of the birthplace of Abraham Lincoln, the 16th president of the United States and commander-in-chief of the Union during the Civil War. http://www.nps.gov/abli

### Jefferson Davis State Historic Site

The president of the Confederate States was born here on June 3, 1808. The visitor's center includes exhibits on Davis's political life, Kentucky handicrafts, and Civil War memorabilia. http://parks.ky.gov/parks/historicsites/jefferson-davis

## MARYLAND

### Antietam National Battlefield

General Robert E. Lee's first invasion of the North ended here on September 17, 1862, in a battle that resulted in more than 23,000 men killed, wounded, and missing. Lasting 12 hours, the Battle at Antietam was the bloodiest of the war and led Abraham Lincoln to issue the preliminary Emancipation Proclamation. http://www.nps.gov/anti

### Monocacy National Battlefield

Known as the "Battle That Saved Washington," the Battle of Monocacy on July 9, 1864, marked the last attempt of the Confederacy to launch a campaign into the North. http://www.nps.gov/mono

Antietam National Battlefield
The Bloody Lane was the site of intense fighting on September 17, 1862, during the Battle of Antietam in Maryland. In just three hours of combat, 5,500 soldiers were killed or wounded on the sunken farm road, and neither side gained a key advantage.

## MISSISSIPPI

### Brices Cross Roads National Battlefield Site

The Confederate cavalry, led by Major General Nathan Bedford Forrest, was employed with extraordinary skill here during the battle of June 10, 1864.
http://www.nps.gov/brcr

### Rosemont Plantation

Childhood home of Jefferson Davis, President of the Confederate States of America, and his family. An example of Federal architecture adapted to the Mississippi frontier, the plantation house with its original furnishings and Davis family memorabilia is open to the public.
http://www.rosemontplantation1810.com

### Tupelo National Battlefield

Lieutenant General Nathan Bedford Forrest tried to cut the railroad supplying the Union's march on Atlanta here on July 13–14, 1864.
http://www.nps.gov/tupe

### Vicksburg National Military Park

Commemorates one of the most decisive battles of the Civil War—the campaign, siege, and defense of Vicksburg—which took place from March 29 to July 4, 1863.
http://www.nps.gov/vick

## MISSOURI

### Wilson's Creek National Battlefield

The Battle of Wilson's Creek (August 10, 1861) was the first major Civil War battle fought west of the Mississippi River.
http://www.nps.gov/wicr

**Vicksburg National Military Park**
The Illinois Monument was modeled on the Roman Pantheon. The monument has 47 steps, one for each day of the Siege of Vicksburg, and there are 60 unique bronze tablets inside, naming all 36,325 Illinois soldiers who fought in the Vicksburg campaign.

## NEW MEXICO

### Fort Craig National Historic Site

Established in 1854, this fort situated in the Rio Grande Valley played a critical role in Indian campaigns during the Civil War. On February 21, Confederate General H. H. Sibley engaged Union troops led by Colonel E. R. S. Canby at Valverde Crossing—the largest Civil War battle in the Southwest. http://www.blm.gov/nm/st/en/prog/ recreation/socorro/fort_craig.html

### Pecos National Historical Park

On March 26–28, 1862, the Battle of Glorieta Pass, known as "the Gettysburg of the West," was fought within what is now Pecos National Historic Park. This was the decisive battle in New Mexico, and it was here that Union forces were able to turn back the Southern troops. http://www.nps.gov/peco

## NEW YORK

### General Grant National Memorial

Overlooking the Hudson River is the final resting place of Ulysses S. Grant and his wife. It is the largest tomb in North America. The site, generally known as Grant's Tomb, also serves as a memorial to Grant's life and accomplishments. http://www.nps.gov/gegr

## NORTH CAROLINA

### Confederate States Military Prison Site and Salisbury National Cemetery

A 16-acre (6.5ha) prison compound with wooden stockades and a nearby burial site. After prisoner exchanges stopped in August of 1864, the facility swelled, housing over 10,000 troops and necessitating a mass grave system which included 18 trenches spanning 240ft (73m) each. Union general George Stoneman set fire to the prison in April, 1865. http://www.salisburyprison.org

## OHIO

### Johnson's Island Prisoner of War Depot

Built in 1861–62, this depot housed over 9,000 prisoners in a 40-month period. http://www.johnsonsisland.org

### Sherman House Museum

The birthplace of General William Tecumseh Sherman has been restored to its 19th-century appearance. The museum includes family memorabilia, a re-creation of General Sherman's Civil War field tent, a sound and light presentation, and other Civil War artifacts. http://www.shermanhouse.org

**Johnson's Island Prisoner of War Depot**
A memorial for those who were buried on Johnson's Island, the Confederate Soldier Statue was dedicated on June 8, 1910. It is the largest monument in the island's cemetery.

**General Grant National Memorial**
The interior of Grant's tomb is constructed of marble, with reliefs and mosaics depicting Grant's victory. The red granite sarcophagi of Grant and his wife are located in the crypt.

# PENNSYLVANIA

## Gettysburg National Military Park

The largest battle ever waged in the Western Hemisphere was fought here on July 1–3, 1863. The Union victory was a major turning point in the war, ending General Lee's invasion of the North. The battle inspired President Abraham Lincoln's famous Gettysburg Address, which he delivered at the dedication of the Soldiers' National Cemetery.
http://www.nps.gov/gett

### Virginia Monument

The largest of the Confederate monuments in Gettysburg National Military Park is the Virginia Monument. It commemorates the 19,000 Virginians who joined the Army of Northern Virginia at Gettysburg. Virginia contributed the largest contingent from the twelve Confederate states.

### Gettysburg Illumination

Each November, candles are lit on the soldiers' graves in the Gettysburg National Cemetery to commemorate the anniversary of Lincoln's Gettysburg Address.

## SOUTH CAROLINA

### Fort Sumter National Monument

The first engagement of the Civil War took place here on April 12–13, 1861, when the Confederates opened fire on this federal fort. Fort Sumter surrendered after 34 hours. Union forces eventually reclaimed the fort four years later, in 1865. The park also includes Fort Moultrie on Sullivan's Island, scene of the patriot victory of June 28, 1776.
http://www.nps.gov/fosu

**Fort Sumter cannons**
Although only 2.4 acres (1 hectare), Fort Sumter was built to accommodate 135 artillery pieces. The fort was well armed, but the Confederates bombarded it with an estimated 3,000 shots in 34 hours. With their ammunition stores depleted, the Union troops were forced to surrender.

**Aerial view**
Fort Sumter's coastal placement allowed it to control Charleston Harbor. The five-sided, three-tiered fort was built with a foundation of more than 70,000 tons (63,503 metric tons) of granite and other rock.

365

# TENNESSEE

### Fort Donelson National Battlefield
On February 14–16, 1862, Confederate and Union soldiers fought furiously before the Southern troops surrendered "unconditionally" to Grant's troops to prevent civilian starvation. The fall of the fort (along with its sister, Fort Henry) opened up the Tennessee and Cumberland Rivers, giving the Union a first big victory and access to the Confederacy.
http://www.nps.gov/fodo

### Fort Pillow State Historic Site
Confederates under Major General Nathan Bedford Forrest attacked the fort, including 265 U.S. Colored Troops on April 12, 1864. The resulting fight ended in the massacre of all but 62 of the colored troops.
http://tn.gov/environment/parks/FortPillow/

### Shiloh National Military Park
Celebrates the largest engagements of the Mississippi Valley campaign at Shiloh Church and Pittsburg Landing (August 6–7, 1862). The park also includes the Corinth Interpretative Center, which commemorates the Siege and Battle of Corinth (April 28–May 30, 1862).
http://www.nps.gov/shil

### Stones River National Battlefield
Honors the battle that took place at Stones River between December 31, 1862, and January 2, 1863. It allowed the Union Army to control middle Tennessee.
http://www.nps.gov/stri

**Shiloh National Military Park**
Built in 1917, the Confederate Monument honors all Confederate troops who fought in the Battle of Shiloh. The central figure represents the Confederacy, surrendering the laurel wreath of victory to Death and Night, who stand beside her.

# VIRGINIA

### Appomattox Court House National Historical Park

Here, on April 9, 1865, General Lee surrendered his Army of Northern Virginia to General Ulysses S. Grant. http://www.nps.gov/apco

### Arlington House, The Robert E. Lee Memorial

Showcases biographical highlights of General Lee, who lived here for more than 30 years. The imposing home of the Custis and Lee families overlooks the Potomac River and Washington, D. C. http://www.nps.gov/arho

### Cedar Creek and Belle Grove National Historical Park

On October 19, 1864, the Confederates under Lieutenant General Jubal A. Early routed the Federal army here. http://www.nps.gov/cebe

### Danville Museum of Fine Arts and History

Built for William T. Sutherlin in 1859, Sutherlin Mansion became the "Last Capitol of the Confederacy" during the final week of the Civil War. In 1974, the house opened as the Danville Museum of Fine Arts and History. http://www.danvillemuseum.org

### Fredericksburg and Spotsylvania County Battlefields Memorial

This, the largest military park in the world, features portions of four Civil War Battlefields: Fredericksburg, Chancellorsville, the Wilderness, and Spotsylvania Court House. http://www.nps.gov/frsp

### Hampton Roads Naval Museum

Celebrates more than 200 years of U.S. naval history. Houses a large gallery dedicated to the Civil War that contains artifacts from USS *Cumberland*, CSS *Virginia*, USS *New Ironsides*, and CSS *Florida*. http://www.hrnm.navy.mil

Appomattox Court House National Historical Park
The McLean house was the site of General Lee's surrender in 1865. The three-story house has been reconstructed, complete with mid-nineteenth century furnishings. Various outbuildings are also open to the public.

**Fredericksburg and Spotsylvania County Battlefields Memorial**
Hazel Grove was captured by the Confederates and used as a key artillery position during the Battle of Chancellorsville in Spotsylvania County.

**Manassas National Battlefield**
Confederate troops destroyed the Stone Bridge over Bull Run stream in March 1862, during the First Battle of Bull Run. The current bridge was rebuilt on the same site in the 1880s.

# VIRGINIA

### Manassas National Battlefield

The Battles of First and Second Bull Run were fought here July 21, 1861, and August 28–30, 1862.
http://www.nps.gov/mana

### Museum of the Confederacy

Home to the most comprehensive collection of Confederate States' artifacts, including photographs, manuscripts, and soldiers' uniforms. Adjacent to the museum is the White House of the Confederacy where President Jefferson Davis lived from 1861–1865.
http://www.moc.org

### National Civil War Chaplains Research Center and Museum

Houses images, Bibles, religious tracts, and personal effects of Union and Confederate chaplains, priests, and soldiers.
http://chaplainsmuseum.org

### Petersburg National Battlefield

Setting for the longest siege in American history (9½ months) after General Grant failed to capture Richmond in the spring of 1864.
http://www.nps.gov/pete

### Richmond National Battlefield Park

Commemorates 11 sites associated with the Union campaigns to capture Richmond, including the battlefields at Gaines' Mill, Malvern Hill, and Cold Harbor.
http://www.nps.gov/rich

### Stonewall Jackson House

Preserves Thomas J. "Stonewall" Jackson's former home, and presents him as a professor, church leader, businessman, husband, soldier, and community leader.
http://www.stonewalljackson.org

**Richmond National Battlefield Park**
President Abraham Lincoln and his son Tad visited Richmond for peace talks on April 4, 1865. In 2003, Lincoln's visit was commemorated with a life-size statue at the historic Tredegar Iron Works, now the Richmond Civil War Visitor Center.

# WASHINGTON, D.C.

### African American Civil War Memorial and Museum

The African American Civil War Museum helps visitors understand the African-Americans' brave, yet often unknown, struggle for freedom. There are many photographs and documents. The museum is located two blocks west of the memorial in the historic U Street neighborhood. http://www.afroamcivilwar.org

### Civil War Defenses of Washington

Also known as Fort Circle Parks, this forested area outside the nation's capital includes the remnants of a complex system of Civil War fortifications built by Union forces. Includes Fort Dupont, named for Flag Officer Samuel F. Du Pont. http://www.nps.gov/cwdw http://www.nps.gov/fodu

### Ford's Theatre National Historic Site

The site of President Abraham Lincoln's assassination on April 14, 1865, at the hands of actor John Wilkes Booth. Lincoln was carried to Petersen's Boarding House across the street, where he died on April 15, 1865. The museum contains portions of the Oldroyd Collection of Lincolniana. http://www.nps.gov/foth

### Lincoln Memorial

National monument devoted to the 16th President honoring his role as the Great Emancipator, and preserver of the nation. Located on the National Mall, the Lincoln Memorial has been the location of subsequent rallies and events dedicated to liberty and civil rights. http://www.nps.gov/linc

### President Lincoln's Cottage and the Soldier's Home

Newly opened to the public, this site marks where President Lincoln and his family spent the summer months from 1862 to 1864. http://www.lincolncottage.org

### Smithsonian Institution

Established in 1846, the Smithsonian Institution comprises 19 museums and 9 research centers, the majority of which are situated in Washington near the National Mall. The National Museum of American History displays Civil War artifacts from its extensive collections in permanent and special exhibitions. The National Portrait Gallery is a center for American portraiture and is housed in the historic Patent Office Building, once used as a Civil War barracks and hospital. The Smithsonian American Art Museum shares this building and occupies the nearby Renwick Gallery, once the office of the Union army's quartermaster general. A National Museum of African-American History and Culture is scheduled to open in 2016. http://americanhistory.si.edu

# WEST VIRGINIA

### Harpers Ferry National Historical Park

Changing hands eight times during the Civil War, Harpers Ferry was the site of several historical events, the best known being the famous John Brown raid in October 1859. http://www.nps.gov/hafe

HEAVY ARTILLERY, YORKTOWN

GEN. JOHN HOOD'S D

Smithsonian Institution
The Price of Freedom exhibition at the National Museum of American History includes a section on the Civil War. Images from photographer Alexander Gardner are projected above a case of materials related to the battles of Antietam, Vicksburg, and Gettysburg.

DESTROYED RAILROAD BRIDGE, HARPERS

ASHVILLE

RALLY! RALLY! RALLY!
TO MEN OF COLOR!
A REGIMENT
MEN OF COLOR
FOR 100 DAYS

COL. TAGGART
$50 CITY BOUNTY

Early Southern Victories

**Civil War reenactment**
Participants take the role of Union soldiers in the Thunder on the Roanoke Civil War reenactment in Plymouth, North Carolina. Taking place around the US, such events recreate historical battles in detail.

# Index

Page numbers in **bold** refer to main subject entries; page numbers in *italics* refer to illustrations.

# Acknowledgments


The publisher would like to thank the following for their kind permission to reproduce their photographs:

**Key:** a-above; b-below/bottom; c-center; f-far; l-left; r-right; t-top.

**Smithsonian sources:** National Museum of American History (**NMAH**), National Portrait Gallery (**NPG**), Cooper-Hewitt National Design Museum, National Museum of African American History and Culture, Smithsonian American Art Museum, National Postal Museum

**1 The Bridgeman Art Library:** Confederate Memorial Hall, New Orleans, Louisiana, USA/Photo © Civil War Archive (r); Gettysburg National Military Park Museum, Pennsylvania, USA/Photo © Civil War Archive (l). **2-3 Library Of Congress, Washington, D.C.:** LC-DIG-ppmsca-20753. **4 Corbis:** Bettmann (l/background); Junior Gonzalez/fstop (cr); Owaki/Kulla (tc). **Smithsonian Institution, NPG, Washington, D.C.:** (br). **5 Corbis:** Ethel Davies/Robert Harding World Imagery (t). **Smithsonian Institution, NMAH, Washington, D.C.:** (bl) (br). **6 Dorling Kindersley:** Courtesy of the Southern Skirmish Association (t). **Smithsonian Institution, Washington, D.C.: NPG** (bl) **NMAH** (br). **7 Corbis:** Kevin Fleming (cr); Frans Lanting (cl). **Smithsonian Institution, Washington, D.C.: NMAH** (bl) **NPG** (br). **8 Smithsonian American Art Museum, Washington, D.C. 10-11 Corbis:** Bettmann (background). **TopFoto.co.uk:** The Granger Collection. **12 The Bridgeman Art Library:** Private Collection (br). **Corbis:** Bettmann (tl). **Library Of Congress, Washington, D.C.:** LC-DIG-ppmsca-09398 (tr). **Photo Scala, Florence:** © 2010. Image copyright The Metropolitan Museum of Art/Art Resource (bl). **12-13 Corbis:** Bettmann (background). **13 The Bridgeman Art Library:** © Massachusetts Historical Society, Boston, MA, USA (cr); St. Louis Art Museum, Missouri, USA (br). **Corbis:** Bettmann (t). **14 The Bridgeman Art Library:** Private Collection/© Michael Graham-Stewart and Art Galleries, UK (bc). **Corbis:** David J. & Janice L. Frent Collection (br). **Getty Images:** The Bridgeman Art Library (tl). **Smithsonian Institution, NMAH, Washington, D.C.:** (bl). **TopFoto.co.uk:** The Granger Collection (tr). **14-15 Corbis:** Bettmann (background). **15 Smithsonian Institution, Washington, D.C.:** (tl) **NPG** (br) (clb) (tr) **NMAH** (ca). **TopFoto.co.uk:** The Granger Collection (bl). **16 The Bridgeman Art Library:** St. Louis Art Museum, Missouri, USA (tr). **Smithsonian Institution, NMAH, Washington, D.C.:** (cl) (bl). **16-39 Corbis:** Owaki/Kulla (t). **17 The Bridgeman Art Library:** Private Collection/Peter Newark American Pictures (c). **Getty Images:** The Bridgeman Art Library (br). **18-19 Smithsonian American Art Museum, Washington, D.C. 20 Corbis:** Bettmann (bl). **Library Of Congress, Washington, D.C.:** LC-DIG-pga-00800 (tr). **20-21 TopFoto.co.uk:** The Granger Collection (b). **21 Corbis:** David J. & Janice L. Frent Collection (t). **Smithsonian Institution, NMAH, Washington, D.C.:** (br). **22 Corbis:** Bettmann (t). **Getty Images:** FPG (cl). **Smithsonian Institution, NMAH, Washington, D.C.:** (b). **23 Library Of Congress, Washington, D.C.:** LC-DIG-ppmsca-09398 (b). **Smithsonian Institution, NPG, Washington, D.C.:** (tr). **24 Smithsonian Institution, NPG, Washington, D.C.:** (l). **25 Alamy Images:** Aurora Photos (c). **The Art Archive:** (t). **Corbis:** Kelly-Mooney Photography (br). **26 The Bridgeman Art Library:** Private Collection/© Michael Graham-Stewart and Art Galleries, UK (t). **Smithsonian Institution, NPG, Washington, D.C.:** (b). **27 The Bridgeman Art Library:** © Massachusetts Historical Society, Boston, MA, USA (l). **Library Of Congress, Washington, D.C.:** (r). **TopFoto.co.uk:** The Granger Collection (b). **28-29 The Bridgeman Art Library:** © Chicago History Museum, USA. **30 Smithsonian Institution, NPG, Washington, D.C.:** (tl). **NMAH** (tr). **31 Corbis:** (t); Bettmann (b). **32 Library Of Congress, Washington, D.C.:** LC-USZ62-92043 (t). **TopFoto.co.uk:** The Granger Collection (bl). **33 Getty Images:** (l). **Smithsonian Institution, NMAH, Washington, D.C.:** (r). **34 Corbis:** (b). **Library Of Congress, Washington, D.C.:** (t). **35 Photo Scala, Florence:** © 2010. Image copyright The Metropolitan Museum of Art/Art Resource (tr). **Smithsonian Institution, Washington, D.C., NMAH:** (t) **NPG:** (bl). **36 Corbis:** Bettmann (cl); David J. & Janice L. Frent Collection (t). **TopFoto.co.uk:** The Granger Collection (b). **37 Corbis:** Bettmann (tr). **Library Of Congress, Washington, D.C.:** LC-USZ62-48564 (br). **Smithsonian Institution, NMAH, Washington, D.C.:** (c). **38 Smithsonian Institution, NPG, Washington, D.C.:** (l) (r). **39 Corbis:** Walter Bibikow (tl); David J. & Janice L. Frent Collection (br). **Smithsonian Institution, NPG, Washington, D.C.:** (tr) (bl). **40-41 Getty Images. 42 Corbis:** (br). **Getty Images:** The Bridgeman Art Library (tl). **Library Of Congress, Washington, D.C.:** LC-DIG-pga-00335 (bl). **42-43 Corbis:** Bettmann (background). **43 Corbis:** Bettmann (cr). **Getty Images:** (br). **Library Of Congress, Washington, D.C.:** LC-DIG-pga-02051 (t). **New York State Military Museum & Veterans Research Center, Division of Military and Naval Affairs:** (tr). **44 Corbis:** Bettmann (bl) (cb). **Dorling Kindersley:** Confederate Memorial Hall, New Orleans (tc); LC-USZ62-42025 (cr). **Library Of Congress, Washington, D.C.:** LC-DIG-pga-02817 (tl). **U.S. Naval Academy Museum:** (br). **44-45 Corbis:** Bettmann (background). **45 Alamy Images:** Mary Evans Picture Library (cr). **The Bridgeman Art Library:** © Collection of the New-York Historical Society, USA (tl). **Corbis:** (tr); Museum of the City of New York (bl). **Smithsonian Institution, Washington, D.C.:** (bc) **NMAH** (c). **46 Library Of Congress, Washington, D.C.:** LC-USZC4-4584 (b). **Smithsonian Institution, NPG, Washington, D.C.:** (tl). **46-77 Corbis:** Junior Gonzalez/fstop (t). **47 Corbis:** (tr). **Dorling Kindersley:** Confederate Memorial Hall, New Orleans (br). **Library Of Congress, Washington, D.C.:** LC-DIG-pga-02817 (l). **48 Corbis:** Bettmann (r) (l). **49 Library Of Congress, Washington, D.C.:** LC-DIG-ppmsca-23869 (br). **Smithsonian Institution, NPG, Washington, D.C.:** (t) (cb). **50 The Bridgeman Art Library:** © Collection of the New-York Historical Society, USA. **51 Corbis:** (bl); Bettmann (tr). **Getty Images:** The Bridgeman Art Library (br). **52-53 Corbis:** Bettmann. **54 Smithsonian Institution, NPG, Washington, D.C.:** (t). **54-55 The Bridgeman Art Library:** Virginia Historical Society, Richmond, Virginia, US (b). **55 Corbis:** Bettmann (t). **56 The Bridgeman Art Library:** Private Collection/Photo © Civil War Archive (br). **Dorling Kindersley:** Peter Keim (bl). **New York State Military Museum & Veterans Research Center, Division of Military and Naval Affairs:** (cr). **Smithsonian Institution, NMAH, Washington, D.C.:** (tr) (bc) (cl). **57 Dorling Kindersley:** Confederate Memorial Hall, New Orleans (cra) (bl) (cl) (crb) (tc) (tr). **Smithsonian Institution, NMAH, Washington, D.C.:** (tl) (br). **58 The Art Archive:** Culver Pictures (l). **The Bridgeman Art Library:** © Chicago History Museum, USA (br). **59 The Bridgeman Art Library:** © Collection of the New-York Historical Society, USA (b). **New York State Military Museum & Veterans Research Center, Division of Military and Naval Affairs:** (t). **60 Library Of Congress, Washington, D.C.:** LC-DIG-pga-00335 (t). **61 Corbis:** Bettmann (br). **Dorling Kindersley:** Confederate Memorial Hall, New Orleans (t); LC-USZ62-103202 (cr). **Library Of Congress, Washington, D.C.:** LC-DIG-cwpbh-01095 (l). **62-63 Corbis:** Museum of the City of New York. **64 Corbis:** Bettmann (b). **65 Corbis:** Tria Giovan (bl). **Getty Images:** (t). **Library Of Congress, Washington, D.C.:** LC-DIG-pga-00385 (br); LC-USZC4-1739 (bl). **66 Library Of Congress, Washington, D.C.:** LC-DIG-ppmsca-19389 (r). **67 Corbis:** (c). **Library Of Congress, Washington, D.C.:** LC-DIG-ppmsca-17561 (br). **Smithsonian Institution, NMAH, Washington, D.C.:** (t) (bl). **68 Corbis:** Bettmann (b). **Dorling Kindersley:** Confederate Memorial Hall, New Orleans (tr). **Library Of Congress, Washington, D.C.:** LC-DIG-ppmsca-07785 (tl). **69 Courtesy of the Putnam County Historical Society & Foundry School Museum, Cold Spring, New York:** John Ferguson Weir (1841-1926) , The Gun Foundry, 1866 (t). **Getty Images:** (b). **70 Kansas State Historical Society:** (tl). **Smithsonian Institution, NPG, Washington, D.C.:** (tr). **The State Historical Society of Missouri:** (b). **71 Corbis:** Bettmann (t). **Library Of Congress, Washington, D.C.:** LC-DIG-pga-02051 (b). **72 Library Of Congress, Washington, D.C.:** LC-USZ61-146 (t). **72-73 Corbis:** Francis G Mayer. **73 Library Of Congress, Washington, D.C.:** LC-DIG-npcc-19646 (r). **Smithsonian Institution, NPG, Washington, D.C.:** (t). **74-75 U.S. Naval Academy Museum. 76 Alamy Images:** Mary Evans Picture Library (b). **Corbis:** (r). **Library Of Congress, Washington, D.C.:** LC-USZ62-42025 (tl). **77 Alamy Images:** Mary Evans Picture Library (tr). **The Bridgeman Art Library:** Chateau de Versailles, France/Giraudon (l). **78-79 Library Of Congress, Washington, D.C.:** LC-DIG-pga-01860. **80 Corbis:** Bettmann (tr); David Muench (tl). **Getty Images:** Time & Life Pictures (br). **Smithsonian Institution, NMAH, Washington, D.C.:** (bl). **80-81 Corbis:** Bettmann (background). **81 Getty Images:** (br); LC-DIG-pga-00540 (cr). **Library Of Congress, Washington, D.C.:** LC-DIG-pga-03975 (tr). **Smithsonian Institution, Washington, D.C.:** (tc). **82 The Bridgeman Art Library:** Private Collection/Photo © Civil War Archive (clb). **Corbis:** (c); The Corcoran Gallery of Art (cr); LC-DIG-cwpb-01693 (tr). **Library Of Congress, Washington, D.C.:** LC-DIG-ppmsca-20506 (br). **Smithsonian Institution, Washington, D.C.:** (bl). **82-83 Corbis:** Bettmann (background). **83 Alamy Images:** Witold Skrypczak (br). **The Bridgeman Art Library:** American Antiquarian Society, Worcester, Massachusetts, USA (tl). **Corbis:** Bettmann (c). **Library Of Congress, Washington, D.C.:** LC-DIG-cwpb-03791 (tr). **Smithsonian Institution, Washington, D.C.:** (tc). **84 The Bridgeman Art Library:** Museum of the Confederacy, Richmond, Virginia, USA/Photo © Civil War Archive (b) (tr); Private Collection/Peter Newark American Pictures (tl). **84-153 Corbis:** Ethel Davies/Robert Harding World Imagery (t). **85 Corbis:** Tria Giovan (t). **Library Of Congress, Washington, D.C.:** LC-USZC4-13352 (b). **86 The Bridgeman Art Library:** Confederate Memorial Hall, New Orleans, Louisiana, USA/Photo © Civil War Archive (tr); Museum of the Confederacy, Richmond, Virginia, USA/Photo © Civil War Archive (c); Private Collection/Photo © Civil War Archive (clb) (bl) (r). **Dorling Kindersley:** Confederate Memorial Hall, New Orleans (bc); Southern Skirmish Association (cl). **87 The Bridgeman Art Library:** Confederate Memorial Hall, New Orleans, Louisiana, USA/Photo © Civil War Archive (ftl) (bc) (br) (cl) (tl); Museum of the Confederacy, Richmond, Virginia, USA/Photo © Civil War Archive (ftr) (cr); Private Collection/Photo © Civil War Archive (tr) (c). **Corbis:** Tria Giovan (bl). **88 The Bridgeman Art Library:** Gettysburg National Military Park Museum, Pennsylvania, USA/Photo © Civil War Archive (tr). **Corbis:** Tria Giovan (bl). **89 The Bridgeman Art Library:** Indianapolis Museum of Art, USA/James E. Roberts and Martha Delzell Memorial Funds (l); Private Collection/Photo © Civil War Archive (tr). **90 The Bridgeman Art Library:** Gettysburg National Military Park Museum, Pennsylvania, USA/Photo © Civil War Archive (cla) (tr/hardee); Private Collection/Photo © Civil War Archive (ftl) (c) (ftr) (tl). **Corbis:** Tria Giovan (b) (clb) (cr). **Dorling Kindersley:** US Army Heritage and Education Center - Military History Institute (br). **91 The Bridgeman Art Library:** Museum of the Confederacy, Richmond, Virginia, USA/Photo © Civil War Archive (ftr); National Museum of American History, Smithsonian Inst., USA/Photo © Civil War Archive (bl) (cl); Private Collection/Photo © Civil War Archive (cra) (br). **92 The Bridgeman Art Library:** Private Collection/Photo © Civil War Archive (bc). **Library Of Congress, Washington, D.C.:** LC-USZC4-6128 (cl). **Smithsonian Institution, Cooper-Hewitt National Design Museum, Washington, D.C.:** (tr). **93 Corbis:** Bettmann (br). **Smithsonian Institution, NMAH, Washington, D.C.:** (c). **94 The Bridgeman Art Library:** Private Collection/Peter Newark American Pictures (bl). **Naval Historical Foundation, Washington, D.C.:** (br). **94-95 Corbis. 95 Dorling Kindersley:** US Army Heritage and Education Center - Military History Institute (bl). **Library Of Congress, Washington, D.C.:** LC-DIG-cwpbh-04058 (br). **96 Corbis:** Medford Historical Society Collection. **97 The Bridgeman Art Library:** Private Collection/Peter Newark American Pictures (t). **Corbis:** Bettmann (r). **Getty Images:** (br). **Smithsonian Institution, NMAH, Washington, D.C.:** (cb). **98 Corbis:** Bettmann (r) (l). **99 Corbis:** Bettmann (r); Burstein Collection (b). **Smithsonian Institution, NMAH, Washington, D.C.:** (t). **100 Corbis:** Bettmann (l). **100-101 The Bridgeman Art Library:** © Chicago History Museum, USA. **101 Corbis:** Bettmann (tl). **Library Of Congress, Washington, D.C.:** LC-USZC4-1737 (r). **102-103 Naval Historical Foundation, Washington, D.C.. 104 The Bridgeman Art Library:** © Chicago History Museum, USA (b). **104-105 Library Of Congress, Washington, D.C.:** LC-DIG-pga-03975 (t). **105 Corbis:** (br). **Library Of Congress, Washington, D.C.:** LC-DIG-cwpb-07216 (c). **106 Corbis:** Bettmann (bl). **107 Library Of Congress, Washington, D.C.:** LC-DIG-pga-00540. **108-109 Library Of Congress, Washington, D.C.:** LC-DIG-pga-04037. **110 Corbis:** Tria Giovan (tr). **110-111 Getty Images:** James Green/Robert Harding. **111 Library Of Congress, Washington, D.C.:** LC-DIG-ppmsca-20506 (tl). **112 Corbis:** Tria Giovan (bl). **Smithsonian Institution, NPG, Washington, D.C.:** (r). **113 Corbis:** Bettmann (r). **Getty Images:** (bl). **Library Of Congress, Washington, D.C.:** LC-USZ62-116988 (t). **114 The Bridgeman Art Library:** Private Collection/Photo © Civil War Archive (t) (c). **Dorling Kindersley:** Confederate Memorial Hall, New Orleans (b). **Rock Island Auction Company:** (ca/Mississippi). **Smithsonian Institution, NMAH, Washington, D.C.:** (ca/Enfield). **115 The Bridgeman Art Library:** Gettysburg National Military Park Museum, Pennsylvania, USA/Photo © Civil War Archive (c) (bl) (cb); Museum of the Confederacy, Richmond, Virginia, USA/Photo © Civil War Archive (br). **Dorling Kindersley:** Gettysburg National Military Park, PA (crb/sword bayonet). **Smithsonian Institution, NMAH, Washington, D.C.:** (cb/Barnett Enfield) (t) (tr/Richmond). **116 Library Of Congress, Washington, D.C.:** LC-DIG-cwpb-01693 (bl). **Smithsonian Institution, NPG, Washington, D.C.:** (br). **116-117 Photograph © 2010 Museum of Fine Arts, Boston:** Gift of Maxim Karolik for the M and M Karolik Collection of American Paintings, 1815-1865, 45.890 (t). **118 The Bridgeman Art Library:** American Antiquarian Society, Worcester, Massachusetts, USA (t). **Corbis:** Bettmann (br). **119 Getty Images:** Time & Life Pictures (b). **Library Of Congress, Washington, D.C.:** LC-USZ62-90541 (cr). **Smithsonian Institution, NMAH, Washington, D.C.:** (t). **120 Library Of Congress, Washington, D.C.:** LC-DIG-ppmsca-22377 (t). **121 Corbis:** Bettmann (tl); David Muench (bl). **Library Of Congress, Washington, D.C.:** LC-DIG-ppmsca-20512 (br). **122-123 Corbis:** Bettmann. **124 The Bridgeman Art Library:** Private Collection/Peter Newark American Pictures (r). **Corbis:** The Corcoran Gallery of Art (l). **125 The Bridgeman Art Library:** Private Collection (br). **Corbis:** Bettmann (t); Tria Giovan (bl). **126 Corbis:** Bettmann (tl); LC-DIG-ppmsca-20602 (tr). **Library Of Congress, Washington, D.C.:** LC-DIG-pga-01231 (bl). **127 Library Of Congress, Washington, D.C.:** LC-DIG-cwpb-04106 (b). **Smithsonian Institution, NPG, Washington, D.C.:** (tr). **128 Dorling Kindersley:** Confederate Memorial Hall, New Orleans (br) (ca/case shot); Gettysburg National Military Park, PA (ca) (bl) (cb); US Army Heritage and Education Center - Military History Institute (t). **129 The Bridgeman Art Library:** Private Collection/Photo © Civil War Archive (ca/quadrant); Confederate Memorial Hall, New Orleans (fcl). **Dorling Kindersley:** Confederate Memorial Hall, New Orleans - Collection of Mike Cherry (cl); Gettysburg National Military Park, PA (b) (ftr) (tc) (tr). **130 Corbis:** Tria Giovan. **131 The Bridgeman Art Library:** Museum of the Confederacy, Richmond, Virginia, USA/Photo © Civil War Archive (cr). **Library Of Congress, Washington, D.C.:** G1291.S5 H6 1865 Vault : Hotch 2 (t); LC-DIG-cwpbh-04849 (bl). **Smithsonian Institution, NPG, Washington, D.C.:** (br). **132 Getty Images:** Hulton Archive (br). **132-133 The Bridgeman Art Library:** Antietam Battlefield Park, Maryland, USA/Photo © Civil War Archive (t). **133 Corbis:** Bettmann (br) (bl). **134-135 Getty Images. 136 Library Of Congress, Washington, D.C.:** LC-DIG-cwpb-03791 (t). **137 Alamy Images:** Witold Skrypczak (br). **Corbis:** Medford Historical Society Collection (tr). **Library Of Congress, Washington, D.C.:** LC-USZ62-134479 (bl). **138-139 The Bridgeman Art Library:** Private **Corbis:** Bettmann (tl). **Library Of Congress, Washington, D.C.:** LC-DIG-cwpb-05992 (tr). **140-141 Corbis:** George H.H. Huey (b). **141 The Art Archive:** National Archives Washington D.C. (tr). **Smithsonian Institution, NMAH, Washington, D.C.:** (tl). **142 Library Of Congress, Washington, D.C.:** LC-DIG-ppmsca-22939 (bl). **Smithsonian Institution, NMAH, Washington, D.C.:** (t). **143 Alamy Images:** offiwent.com (bl). **Library Of Congress, Washington, D.C.:** LC-DIG-cwpb-06052 (br). **144 Corbis:** Bettmann (l). **145 Corbis:** Tria Giovan (bl). **Smithsonian Institution, NPG, Washington, D.C.:** (t). **Mark Yearian:** (br). **146-147 Corbis. 148 The Bridgeman Art Library:** Vermont Historical Society, VT, USA (tr). **Dorling Kindersley:** Musée de l'Emperi, Salon-de-Provence (tl). **Getty Images:** (b). **149 The Bridgeman Art Library:** Private Collection/Photo © Civil War Archive (br). **150-151 Library Of Congress, Washington, D.C.:** LC-DIG-pga-01855. **152 The Bridgeman Art Library:** Private Collection/Photo © Civil War Archive (ca) (cb). **Dorling Kindersley:** Confederate Memorial Hall, New Orleans (b); Gettysburg National Military Park, PA (cb/saber). **Smithsonian Institution, NMAH, Washington, D.C.:** (ca/Spencer) (c/Spencer). **153 The Bridgeman Art Library:** Gettysburg National Military Park Museum, Pennsylvania, USA/Photo © Civil War Archive (t); Museum of the Confederacy, Richmond, Virginia, USA/Photo © Civil War Archive (br); Private Collection/Photo © Civil War Archive (cl) (bc). **Dorling Kindersley:** Confederate Memorial Hall, New Orleans (c) (cb) (cr); Gettysburg National Military Park, PA (ca); US Army Heritage and Education Center - Military History Institute (fcr). **154-155 TopFoto.co.uk:** The Granger Collection. **156 Corbis:** Bettmann (tl) (br). **Smithsonian Institution, NPG, Washington, D.C.:** (tr) (bl). **156-157 Corbis:** Bettmann (background). **157 Corbis:** Bettmann (tc) (tr). **Getty Images:** (br). **Library Of Congress, Washington, D.C.:** LC-DIG-pga-01846 (cr). **158 Dorling Kindersley:** Confederate Memorial Hall, New Orleans (cb). **Getty Images:** (tr) (cr); LC-DIG-ppmsca-22467 (br). **Library Of Congress, Washington, D.C.:** LC-DIG-ppmsca-19395 (bl). **Smithsonian Institution, NMAH, Washington, D.C.:** (tl). **158-159 Corbis:** Bettmann (background). **159 Dorling Kindersley:** Gettysburg National Military Park, PA (cra). **Library Of Congress, Washington, D.C.:** LC-DIG-cwpb-03431 (tr). **Smithsonian Institution, Washington, D.C.: NPG** (crb) **NMAH** (bl). **State Museum of PA, PA Historical and Museum Commission:** (cl). **160 Corbis:** Bettmann (t). **160-229 Dorling Kindersley:** Courtesy of the Southern Skirmish Association (t). **161 The Bridgeman Art Library:** © Collection of the New-York Historical Society, USA (cr). **Corbis:** Tim

Shaffer/Reuters (bl). **Getty Images:** Hulton Archive (br). **Smithsonian Institution, NMAH, Washington, D.C.:** (t). **162 Library Of Congress, Washington, D.C.:** LC-USZC4-4609 (l). **Smithsonian Institution, NPG, Washington, D.C.:** LC-DIG-ppmsca-20701 (br). **Photo Scala, Florence:** © 2010. Photo The Newark Museum/Art Resource (l). **164–165 Corbis:** Bettmann. **166 Getty Images: Smithsonian Institution, National Museum of African American History and Culture, Washington, D.C.:** (bl). **167 The Bridgeman Art Library:** Private Collection/Peter Newark American Pictures (br). **168 Corbis:** Bettmann (b). **Smithsonian Institution, NMAH, Washington, D.C.:** (t). **169 Corbis:** Bettmann (br). **Photo Scala, Florence:** © 2010. Image copyright The Metropolitan Museum of Art/Art Resource(cr). **170–171 Getty Images. 172 The Bridgeman Art Library:** © Collection of the New-York Historical Society, USA (br). **Corbis:** Bettmann (t). **Library Of Congress, Washington, D.C.:** LC-DIG-cwpb-05088 (tl). **173 Corbis:** Medford Historical Society Collection (b). **State House Flag Collection, Massachusetts Art Commission:** Second Irish color 28th Massachusetts Volunteers (1987.304) (t). **174 Alamy Images:** North Wind Picture Archives (tr). **Library Of Congress, Washington, D.C.:** LC-DIG-ppmsca-19395 (l). **174–175 Library Of Congress, Washington, D.C.:** LC-DIG-ppmsca-22467 (b). **175 Corbis:** Bettmann (cr). **176–177 Getty Images. 178 Corbis:** Bettmann (bl); Medford Historical Society Collection (t). **Library Of Congress, Washington, D.C.:** LC-DIG-ppmsca-22378 (b). **179 Corbis:** Bettmann (t). **The Museum of the Confederacy, Richmond, Virginia:** Photography by Katherine Wetzel (b). **180 Library Of Congress, Washington, D.C.:** LC-DIG-ppmsca-20161 (t). **State Museum of PA, PA Historical and Museum Commission:** (l). **181 Corbis:** Bettmann (br). **Smithsonian Institution, NMAH, Washington, D.C.:** (t). **182 Dorling Kindersley:** Gettysburg National Military Park, PA (b). **Library Of Congress, Washington, D.C.:** LC-USZ6-284 (t). **183 Alamy Images:** Ivy Close Images (b). **Library Of Congress, Washington, D.C.:** LC-USZC4-1825 (t). **184–185 Getty Images:** LC-DIG-pga-02604 (t). **186 Library Of Congress, Washington, D.C.:** LC-DIG-cwpb-06085 (t). **187 Alamy Images:** John Van Decker (b). **Getty Images:** Brian Parkhill Rare Books, Philadelphia: (bl). **188–189 The Gettysburg Foundation:** photo © Bill Dowling. **190 Getty Images:** (t). **191 Getty Images. Library Of Congress, Washington, D.C.:** LC-USZ62-90939 (bl). **Smithsonian Institution, NPG, Washington, D.C.:** (br). **192 Corbis:** Bettmann. **Library Of Congress, Washington, D.C.:** LC-DIG-pga-01871 (t). **193 Florida Center for Instructional Technology:** (bl). **Getty Images:** (t). **194–195 TopFoto.co.uk:** The Granger Collection. **196 Alamy Images:** North Wind Picture Archives (r). **Smithsonian Institution, Washington, D.C.:** (l). **197 Smithsonian Institution, Washington, D.C.:** NPG (tl) (tr) NMAH (b). **198 Smithsonian Institution, NMAH, Washington, D.C.:** (t). **199 Smithsonian Institution, Washington, D.C.:** NMAH (b). **Library Of Congress, Washington, D.C.:** (bl). **200 Getty Images:** (t). **Library Of Congress, Washington, D.C.:** LC-DIG-ppmsca-22558 (b). **201 The Bridgeman Art Library:** American Antiquarian Society, Worcester, Massachusetts, USA (b); Gettysburg National Military Park Museum, Pennsylvania, USA/Photo © Civil War Archive (t). **202–203 Getty Images:** Time & Life Pictures. **204 Corbis:** Bettmann (b). **205 Library Of Congress, Washington, D.C.:** LC-USZC4-13346 (t). **Smithsonian Institution, Washington, D.C.:** NMAH (bl) Cooper-Hewitt National Design Museum (cb) NPG (t) **206 The Bridgeman Art Library:** Museum of the Confederacy, Richmond, Virginia, USA/Photo © Civil War Archive (l). **206–207 Dorling Kindersley:** Gettysburg National Military Park, PA. **207 National Museum of Health and Medicine:** (r). **208 Corbis:** Bettmann. **209 The Bridgeman Art Library:** Private Collection/Peter Newark American Pictures (l). **Library Of Congress, Washington, D.C.:** LC-DIG-ppmsca-05602 (br). **210 Library Of Congress, Washington, D.C.:** LC-DIG-ppmsca-21066 (b). **Smithsonian Institution, NMAH, Washington, D.C.:** (t). **211 Corbis:** Tria Giovan (t). **Library Of Congress, Washington, D.C.:** LC-DIG-cwpb-06714 (b). **212–213 Smithsonian Institution, NMAH, Washington, D.C. 214 Library Of Congress, Washington, D.C.:** LC-DIG-cwpb-03431. **215 Corbis:** Medford Historical Society Collection. **Library Of Congress, Washington, D.C.:** LC-DIG-pga-04032 (t). **Smithsonian Institution, NMAH, Washington, D.C.:** LC-DIG-cwpb-07196; LC-USZ62-22955 (tr). **217 Library Of Congress, Washington, D.C.:** LC-USZC4-5152 (bl). **Photolibrary:** Barry Winiker (br). **TopFoto.co.uk:** Ullsteinbild (t). **218 The Bridgeman Art Library:** Private Collection/Peter Newark American Pictures (bl); LC-DIG-ppmsca-08270 (r). **Library Of Congress, Washington, D.C.:** LC-DIG-cwpb-02135 (b). **219 Corbis:** Medford Historical Society Collection; LC-DIG-ppmsca-10408 (bl). **220 Library Of Congress, Washington, D.C.:** LC-DIG-

ppmsca-21043 (br). **Smithsonian Institution, National Postal Museum, Washington, D.C.:** LC-DIG-cwpb-01958 (r). **221 Library Of Congress, Washington, D.C.:** LC-DIG-ppmsca-23180 (tl). **222–223 Smithsonian Institution, NPG, Washington, D.C. 224 Corbis:** Bettmann (t). **Library Of Congress, Washington, D.C.:** LC-DIG-ppmsca-20034 (b). **225 The Bridgeman Art Library:** Private Collection/Peter Newark American Pictures (cr). **Smithsonian Institution, NPG, Washington, D.C.:** (bl); LC-DIG-cwpb-06818 (br); LC-DIG-pga-01888 (t). **226 Library Of Congress, Washington, D.C.:** LC-DIG-ppmsca-21155 (t). **227 Corbis:** Bettmann. **TopFoto.co.uk:** The Granger Collection. **228–229 Corbis:** Bettmann. **230–231 The Bridgeman Art Library:** Private Collection/Peter Newark American Pictures. **232 Corbis:** Bettmann (br); LC-DIG-cwpb-03994 (bl). **Library Of Congress, Washington, D.C.:** LC-DIG-pga-01881 (tr). **New Britain Museum of American Art:** Skirmish in the Wilderness, 1864, Oil on canvas, mounted on masonite, 18 x 26 ? in., New Britain Museum of American Art, Harriet Russell Stanley Fund, 1944.05. Photo Alex Morganti (tl). **232–233 Corbis:** Bettmann (background). **233 Getty Images:** Time & Life Pictures (crb). **Smithsonian Institution, NPG, Washington, D.C.:** (t) (tr). **TopFoto.co.uk:** (br). **234 Alabama Department of Archives and History, Montgomery, Alabama:** (c). **Getty Images:** (bl). **Smithsonian Institution, NPG, Washington, D.C.:** (t) (br) (crb). **234–235 Corbis:** Bettmann (background). **235 Corbis:** Bettmann (br). **Kansas State Historical Society:** (cr). **Library Of Congress, Washington, D.C.:** LC-DIG-ppmsca-21357 (tl). **Smithsonian Institution, Washington, D.C.:** NMAH (cl) NPG (tr). **236 Library Of Congress, Washington, D.C.:** LC-DIG-ppmsca-19442 (tr). **236–237 White House Historical Association:** (t). **237 Library Of Congress, Washington, D.C.:** LC-USZ6-201 (cr). **TopFoto.co.uk:** The Granger Collection (t). **238 The Bridgeman Art Library:** Private Collection/Photo © Civil War Archive (b). **New Britain Museum of American Art:** Skirmish in the Wilderness, 1864, Oil on canvas, mounted on masonite, 18 x 26.25 in., New Britain Museum of American Art, Harriet Russell Stanley Fund, 1944.05. Photo Alex Morganti (t); LC-DIG-ppmsca-23676 (tr). **239 Library Of Congress, Washington, D.C.:** LC-DIG-ppmsca-21457 (cl). **240 Corbis:** Bettmann (br). **Library Of Congress, Washington, D.C.:** LC-USZ62-53692 (tr). **Smithsonian Institution, NMAH, Washington, D.C.:** (l). **241 The Bridgeman Art Library:** American Antiquarian Society, Worcester, Massachusetts, USA (r). **Library Of Congress, Washington, D.C.:** LC-DIG-cwpb-00698 (b). **242–243 The Bridgeman Art Library:** © Chicago History Museum, USA. **244 Alamy Images:** The Art Archive. **Smithsonian Institution, NMAH, Washington, D.C.:** (tl). **245 Corbis:** Hulton-Deutsch Collection (bl). **Getty Images:** Hulton Archive (t). **Smithsonian Institution, NMAH, Washington, D.C.:** (t). **246–247 Corbis:** Hulton-Deutsch Collection; LC-DIG-cwpb-07539 (br). **248 Library Of Congress, Washington, D.C.:** LC-DIG-ppmsca-21161 (r). **Smithsonian Institution, NMAH, Washington, D.C.:** (t). **249 Library Of Congress, Washington, D.C.:** LC-DIG-pga-01674. **250 Library Of Congress, Washington, D.C.:** LC-DIG-cwpb-07546. **251 Getty Images:** Hulton Archive (br). **Smithsonian Institution, NMAH, Washington, D.C.:** (t). **Virginia Historical Society:** (r). **252 Dorling Kindersley:** Gettysburg National Military Park, PA (tl). **Rock Island Auction Company:** (r) (br). **Smithsonian Institution, NMAH, Washington, D.C.:** (tr) (ca). **253 Dorling Kindersley:** Confederate Memorial Hall, New Orleans (tr) (cr); Gettysburg National Military Park, PA (bl); US Army Heritage and Education Center - Military History Institute (cl). **Rock Island Auction Company:** (crb). **Smithsonian Institution, NMAH, Washington, D.C.:** (tl) (bc) (cra). **254 Alamy Images:** Classic Image (t). **Getty Images:** (b). **255 VMI Museum, Lexington, VA:** (r) (t). **256 Getty Images:** (b). **Smithsonian Institution, NMAH, Washington, D.C.:** (tl). **257 Corbis:** Bettmann (b) (bc). **Getty Images:** (br). **Smithsonian Institution, NMAH, Washington, D.C.:** (cl). **258–259 Corbis:** Bettmann; LC-DIG-pga-01881 (r). **260 Library Of Congress, Washington, D.C.:** LC-DIG-cwpb-02570 (bl); LC-DIG-ppmsca-12615 (cr). **261 Library Of Congress, Washington, D.C.:** LC-USZ62-115849 (t). **Smithsonian Institution, NMAH, Washington, D.C.:** (br); LC-USZ62-111179 (b). **262 Library Of Congress, Washington, D.C.:** LC-DIG-cwpb-03994 (t). **263 Virginia Historical Society:** (b). **264 Library Of Congress, Washington, D.C.:** LC-DIG-cwpb-01402. **265 The Bridgeman Art Library:** Atlanta Historical Society. Georgia, USA/Photo © Civil War Archive (r); Private Collection/Peter Newark American Pictures (bc). **Library Of Congress, Washington, D.C.:** LC-DIG-ppmsca-06956 (bl). **266–267 The Bridgeman Art Library:** Virginia Historical Society, Richmond, Virginia, US. **268 Library Of Congress, Washington, D.C.:** LC-DIG-stereo-1s01824 (l). **269 The Bridgeman Art Library:** American Antiquarian Society, Worcester, Massachusetts, USA (br). **Getty Images:** (br); LC-DIG-ppmsca-21134 (r). **270 Duke University:** Historic American Sheet Music," Major General

Sheridan's Grand Victory March", Music #1444, Duke University Rare Book, Manuscript, and Special Collections Library. **Library Of Congress, Washington, D.C.:** LC-DIG-cwpb-01010 (r). **271 Library Of Congress, Washington, D.C.:** LC-DIG-ppmsca-21296 (b). **Smithsonian Institution, NMAH, Washington, D.C.:** (t). **TopFoto.co.uk:** Curt Teich Postcard Archives/HIP (br). **272–273 The Bridgeman Art Library:** Private Collection/Peter Newark American Pictures; LC-DIG-cwpbh-00463 (bl). **274 Library Of Congress, Washington, D.C.:** LC-DIG-ppmsca-21357 (t). **275 The Bridgeman Art Library:** Detroit Institute of Arts, USA/Founders Society purchase and Dexter M. Ferry Jr. fund (t). **Corbis:** Bettmann (bl). **276 Library Of Congress, Washington, D.C.:** LC-DIG-cwpb-00942 (b). **Smithsonian Institution, NMAH, Washington, D.C.:** (t). **277 The Bridgeman Art Library:** Private Collection/Photo © Civil War Archive (fbr). **Library Of Congress, Washington, D.C.:** LC-DIG-cwpb-03851 (t). **278–279 Library Of Congress, Washington, D.C.:** LC-DIG-ppmsca-20996. **280 akg-images:** (l). **Alamy Images:** INTERFOTO. **280–281 Corbis:** Bettmann (b). **281 The Granger Collection (tr);** The Granger Collection (tc). **282 Corbis:** Bettmann (t). **Smithsonian Institution, NMAH, Washington, D.C.:** (b). **283 The Bridgeman Art Library:** Museum of the Confederacy, Richmond, Virginia, USA/Photo © Civil War Archive (c); Private Collection/Photo © Civil War Archive (bl). **Getty Images:** (tl). **284–285 Corbis:** © Philadelphia Museum of Art. **286 Dorling Kindersley:** Confederate Memorial Hall, New Orleans (b). **Smithsonian Institution, NMAH, Washington, D.C.:** (t). **287 Smithsonian Institution, NMAH, Washington, D.C.:** (b). **TopFoto.co.uk:** (t). **288 Corbis:** Bettmann (b). **The State Historical Society of Missouri:** (t). **289 Kansas State Historical Society:** (b). **Library Of Congress, Washington, D.C.:** LC-DIG-cwpb-06208 (br). **290 Alabama Department of Archives and History, Montgomery, Alabama:** (cr). **291 Alamy Images:** Philip Scalia (b). **The Bridgeman Art Library:** Dallas Historical Society, Texas, USA (bl). **Corbis:** Bettmann (t). **292 Corbis:** Bettmann (b). **Library Of Congress, Washington, D.C.:** LC-DIG-cwpb-03415 (t). **293 Atlanta Cyclorama and Civil War Museum:** (t). **294–295 Corbis:** Bettmann. **296 The Bridgeman Art Library:** Siege Museum, Petersburg, Virginia, USA/Photo © Civil War Archive (r). **Library Of Congress, Washington, D.C.:** LC-DIG-ppmsca-20772 (t). **297 Corbis:** Bettmann (t). **Library Of Congress, Washington, D.C.:** LC-DIG-cwpb-03159 (b). **298 Corbis:** Bettmann (l). **Smithsonian Institution, NMAH, Washington, D.C.:** (r). **299 Getty Images:** Time & Life Pictures (br). **Smithsonian Institution, NMAH, Washington, D.C.:** (t) (b). **300 Library Of Congress, Washington, D.C.:** LC-DIG-pga-01852. **301 Getty Images:** Science and Society Picture Library (t); LC-USZ62-4697 (cr). **Library Of Congress, Washington, D.C.:** LC-DIG-cwpbh-00679 (bc). **302–303 Getty Images. 304 Corbis:** Bettmann (tl). **Library Of Congress, Washington, D.C.:** LC-DIG-ppmsca-21458 (tr). **Smithsonian Institution, NPG, Washington, D.C.:** (b). **304–305 Corbis:** Bettmann (background). **305 Library Of Congress, Washington, D.C.:** LC-USZ62-105560 (b). **Smithsonian Institution, NPG, Washington, D.C.:** (t) (cr) (cra). **306 Alamy Images:** Historical Art Collection (HAC) (t). **Smithsonian Institution, NMAH, Washington, D.C.:** (tr). **The US National Archives and Records Administration:** (bl). **Smithsonian Institution, NPG, Washington, D.C.:** (bc) (br). **306–307 Corbis:** Bettmann (background). **307 The Bridgeman Art Library:** Private Collection/Peter Newark American Pictures (tr). **Smithsonian Institution, NPG, Washington, D.C.:** (bl) (br). **TopFoto.co.uk:** The Granger Collection (cr) (tl). **308 Library Of Congress, Washington, D.C.:** LC-USZ62-127599 (b). **The US National Archives and Records Administration:** (b). **308–327 Corbis:** Frans Lanting; LC-DIG-pga-03898 (t). **309 Library Of Congress, Washington, D.C.:** LC-DIG-ppmsca-10978 (ba). **310 Alamy Images:** Historical Art Collection (HAC) (bl). **Smithsonian Institution, NPG, Washington, D.C.:** (cl). **311 The Bridgeman Art Library:** Museum of the Confederacy, Richmond, Virginia, USA/Photo © Civil War Archive (b). **Library Of Congress, Washington, D.C.:** LC-USZ62-105560 (t). **312–313 Corbis. 314 Library Of Congress, Washington, D.C.:** LC-DIG-cwpb-06014 (t). **314–315 The Bridgeman Art Library:** (b). **315 Corbis:** Bettmann (tr). **Smithsonian Institution, NMAH, Washington, D.C.:** National Postal Museum (t) NPG (br). **316 Smithsonian Institution, NMAH, Washington, D.C.:** (t). **TopFoto.co.uk:** The Granger Collection (b). **317 Library Of Congress, Washington, D.C.:** LC-DIG-cwpbh-03163 (bl). **Smithsonian Institution, Washington, D.C.: National Archives and Records Administration** (t) NMAH (b). **318–319 Appomattox Court House National Historical Park. 320 Corbis:** Bettmann (l). **Library Of Congress, Washington, D.C.:** LC-DIG-highsm-04710 (t). **321 Smithsonian Institution, Washington, D.C.:** NPG (l) NMAH (r). **322–323 The Bridgeman Art Library:** © Chicago History Museum, USA. **324 Library Of Congress, Washington, D.C.:** LC-DIG-ppmsca-21144 (b). **Smithsonian Institution, NPG, Washington, D.C.:** (t). **325 Library o f Congress,**

**Washington, D.C.:** (l). **TopFoto.co.uk:** The Granger Collection (r). **326 Corbis:** David J. & Janice L. Frent Collection (r). **Getty Images:** (l). **327 Corbis:** Bettmann (tl) (r); David J. & Janice L. Frent Collection (r). **328–329 Alamy Images:** North Wind Picture Archives. **330 Corbis:** Smithsonian Institution, NPG, Washington, D.C.:** (br); Bettmann (tl). **Getty Images:** Smithsonian Institution, NPG, Washington, D.C.:** (bl); Bettmann (background). **331 The Bridgeman Art Library:** The Historic New Orleans Collection/The Monroe-Green Collection (b). **Corbis:** Bettmann (br). **Smithsonian Institution, NPG, Washington, D.C.:** (t). **332 Photo Scala, Florence:** © 2010. Image copyright The Metropolitan Museum of Art/Art Resource (cr). **Smithsonian Institution, Washington, D.C.: American Art Museum** (tl) NMAH (bl) NPG (br) (tr). **332–333 Corbis:** Bettmann (background). **333 The Art Archive:** Culver Pictures (c). **The Bridgeman Art Library:** Delaware Art Museum, Wilmington, USA (bl). **Corbis:** Bettmann (tl). **Library Of Congress, Washington, D.C.:** LC-DIG-pga-03113 (tr). **334 Corbis:** Bettmann (t). **Library Of Congress, Washington, D.C.:** LC-DIG-ppmsca-05453 (bl). **334–349 Corbis:** Kevin Fleming (l). **335 Library Of Congress, Washington, D.C.:** LC-DIG-cwpb-02704 (tr). **Morris Museum of Art:** (t). **Smithsonian Institution, NMAH, Washington, D.C.:** (b). **336–337 Corbis:** Bettmann. **338 Corbis:** Bettmann (b). **Library Of Congress, Washington, D.C.:** LC-USZC4-63460 (t). **339 Smithsonian Institution, NPG, Washington, D.C.:** (b). **340 Corbis:** Bettmann (b). **Smithsonian Institution Libraries, Washington, D.C.:** (t). **TopFoto.co.uk:** The Granger Collection (b). **341 The Bridgeman Art Library:** The Historic New Orleans Collection/The Monroe-Green Collection (b). **Library Of Congress, Washington, D.C.:** LC-DIG-ppmsca-17564 (t). **342 TopFoto.co.uk:** The Granger Collection (cr) (bl). **343 Corbis:** Bettmann (b). **344 The Art Archive:** Culver Pictures. **345 The Bridgeman Art Library:** Delaware Art Museum, Wilmington, USA (b). **Library Of Congress, Washington, D.C.:** LC-DIG-pga-03113 (r). **346–347 Smithsonian Institution, NMAH, Washington, D.C. 347 Smithsonian Institution, NMAH, Washington, D.C.:** (bl). **348 Corbis:** Smithsonian Institution, NMAH, Washington, D.C.:** (bl). **349 Corbis:** Richard T Nowitz (t). **Smithsonian Institution, NMAH, Washington, D.C.:** (b). **350–384 Library Of Congress, Washington, D.C.:** (t). **350–351 Corbis:** Kevin Fleming. **352–353 Corbis:** Kevin Fleming (br). **353 Getty Images:** Universal Images Group (br). **354–355 Getty Images:** Stephen Saks / Lonely Planet Images. **356–357 Alamy Images:** Kevin Shields. **358–359 Alamy Images:** Ian Dagnall (b). **360 Alamy Images:** Steve Paddon (bl). **360–361 Getty Images:** Ryan D. Budhu / Moment. **362 Getty Images:** Michael Melford / National Geographic (bl). **362–363 Getty Images:** Greg Dale / National Geographic. **364–365 Getty Images:** Richard Cummins / Lonely Planet Images. **366–367 Alamy Images:** North Wind Picture Archives. **368 Getty Images:** VisionsofAmerica / Joe Sohm / Photodisc (bl). **368–369 Alamy Images:** Kevin Shields. **370–371 Alamy Images:** Pat & Chuck Blackley. **371 Alamy Images:** Jeremy Graham / dbimages (br). **372–373 Smithsonian Institution, NMAH, Washington, D.C. 374–375 Corbis:** Michael DeFreitas / Robert Harding World Imagery

All other images © Dorling Kindersley
For further information see: **www.dkimages.com**

The publisher would also like to thank the following people at the Smithsonian Institution for their kind assistance:

Smithsonian Project Coordinator: Ellen Nanney

National Museum of American History: Jennifer Jones, Kathleen Golden, David Miller, Barton Hacker, Lisa Kathleen Graddy, Barbara Clark Smith, Debbie Hashim, Harry Rubenstein, Kay Peterson, Marisa Kritikson, Stacey Kluck, Shannon Perich

National Portrait Gallery: James G. Barber, Beverly Cox, Lizanne Reger, Mark Gulezian

National Museum of African American History and Culture: Lonnie Bunch

Smithsonian American Art Museum: Richard Sorenson

Jacket designer: Mark Cavanagh